JUNGLE LIFE IN INDIA

JUNGLE LIFE IN INDIA;

OR THE

JOURNEYS AND JOURNALS

OF AN

INDIAN GEOLOGIST.

V. BALL, M. A.

GYAN

Published by

Gyan Publishing House
5, Ansari Road
Daryaganj, New Delhi-110002
Phone: 011-47034999, 9811692060
E-mail: books@gyanbooks.com

Distribution Network
gyanbooks.com
India, USA, Canada, UK, Australia, France

ISBN: 978-81-212-8746-3 (PB)
First Published, 1880

2nd Impression 2023

Printed at: Gyan Press, Delhi.

JUNGLE LIFE IN INDIA
Author: V. Ball

JUNGLE LIFE IN INDIA.

Frontispiece.]

TEMPLE ON MAHENDRAGIRI, GANJAM.

(From a Photograph by Capt. W. G. Murray.)

JUNGLE LIFE IN INDIA;

OR THE

JOURNEYS AND JOURNALS

OF AN

INDIAN GEOLOGIST.

BY

V. BALL, M.A.,

GEOLOGICAL SURVEY OF INDIA,

Fellow of the Calcutta University, and of the Geological Societies of London and Ireland; Member of the Asiatic Society of Bengal, the Zoological and Botanical Society of Vienna, and the British Ornithologists' Union.

"*Cœlum non animum mutant qui trans mare currunt.*"
HORACE.

LONDON:
THOS. DE LA RUE & Co., BUNHILL ROW

1880

INTRODUCTION

AND

PREFACE.

IMPERIAL INDIA, India of the Great Cities, Great Rajas and Princes, is not described in these pages. It has been my object to lead my readers away from those scenes of display and splendour to which so much prominence has been given in various works published of late years, and to attempt to present before them pictures of the lives of men, wild beasts and plants, in regions many of which have been seldom visited or described before. In order to do so, two courses were open to me: either to prepare a series of essays on the several regions which I have explored, or to make use of the material ready to hand in the diaries which I have kept with tolerable regularity since I first landed in India. Acting under experienced advice I have adopted the latter alternative, and accordingly the information I have to convey is presented in the form of a personal narrative of my journeys. This has been the cause of a certain amount of repetition in succeeding chapters, which, however, under the circumstances, could not easily have been avoided. It may be thought, perhaps, by some readers, that there is, in places, too much of trivial detail; but to have strung together merely the discoveries and sensational incidents would have given a very incorrect impression of the phase of Indian Official life which I describe; for, if the truth must be told, it is at times a very dull, lonely, and monotonous one.

Although I endeavour to describe briefly the geological structure of the several regions which I have explored, greater prominence is given in these pages to other aspects of nature, as I feel doubtful of my power to interest the majority of readers in a subject like Indian Geology. The few for whom it has an attraction will, of their own accord, naturally refer to the regular sources for information regarding it.

It was a part of my original scheme to have given fuller accounts of the various races and tribes with which I have come in contact, but to have done so would have very much increased the size of the volume. I have, therefore, to a great extent limited my references under these headings to facts which have come under my own personal observation. Similarly, I had intended giving more comprehensive sketches of the Zoology and Botany of the several areas; but, as regards the latter subject, I have not been able to give much time to it of late years, and full and authentic material for such a purpose is not yet available. In two of the Appendices will be found sketches of the Zoology of the principal areas described, but for further details I must refer the reader elsewhere.

Although accounts of shooting and sport frequently occur in these pages, I wish it to be understood that I do not profess to write as a sportsman. Such sport as I have had, though it has been of a most varied kind, has been rather incidental to my every-day life than pursued merely for its own sake. The successful pursuit of sport requires, as a general rule, one's undivided attention, and the claims of my work in the wildest and most likely places—where, camp supplies being scarce, frequent moving had to be the order of the day—often prevented me from availing myself of opportunities for making large bags. For those sportsmen who care for something more than numbering the head of game killed—and they constitute, I believe, the majority in India—these pages will not, I trust, prove devoid of interest.

There are several works which describe portions of country bordering on the region which constitutes the principal area described by me in the following pages. These are "Rural Bengal," "Past Days in India," "Seonee, or Camp Life in the Satpuras," and the "Highlands of Central India." To many of my readers these works, by different authors, are doubtless known. Their respective merits have been duly acknowledged as they appeared, and it is perhaps unnecessary to enlarge here upon the accuracy and value of the information which they contain. They serve, together with many other works, to rebut the sweeping charge as to a deadness in powers of observation, which a few years ago was brought against Anglo-Indians by a distinguished visitor to India. Such a deadness may exist in certain quarters, but it is also none the less the fact that, though the real workers in the scientific exploration of the Ethnology, Zoology, Botany, and Geology of India may be few, the work which is being accomplished by them is great. The appearance of manuals on these subjects, in addition to the publication of papers through the medium of various scientific journals, may be cited as affording the most conclusive proof that these subjects are not being neglected, and that the Geologists and Biologists of the present day in India are accumulating an amount of information from which a most important array of conclusions, as to the past and present history of that portion of the earth, are gradually being evolved.

I need hardly point out to those who read the following pages, that the life of an Indian Geologist is not one of ease; nor is it necessary to indicate the many disadvantages of a social and domestic character which such a life involves. Each season's work is accomplished as the result of arduous labour, for more than half the time in a most trying climate, and in spite of manifold obstructions, discomforts, and, too often, also of sickness.

But the life affords various compensations, without which it would be unbearable. To the lover of nature there are many attractions in it. There is a great, an indescribable pleasure in being the first to take up the geological exploration of a hitherto quite unknown tract—in being the first to interpret the past history of a portion of the earth's crust which no geologist has ever seen before. To each, according to his taste, the incidentals—if I may so call them—the adventures, the sport, the zoology, &c., afford compensations, and serve to keep off the feeling of depression which so lonely a life is otherwise calculated to engender.

It now remains for me to make my acknowledgments, and record my thanks, to those who have aided me in the preparation of this volume. To Dr. E. P. Wright and Dr. J. Todhunter I am especially grateful for their advice and aid in the correction of the sheets as they passed through the press. To them the gratitude of the English readers is due for their excision of Indian terms and Anglo-Indian slang, which, in spite of my utmost care, crept into the manuscript.

For photographs, from which several of the illustrations have been drawn, I am indebted to the kindness of Captains W. J. Murray and J. Waterhouse of the Topographical Survey, and to Mr. T. F. Peppé of the Opium Department.

To the publishers my thanks are also due for the liberal manner in which my views have been carried out and the work produced for presentation before the tribunal of public opinion.

CONTENTS.

PAGE

APPENDICES.

ILLUSTRATIONS.

PLATES.

VIGNETTES.

MAP.

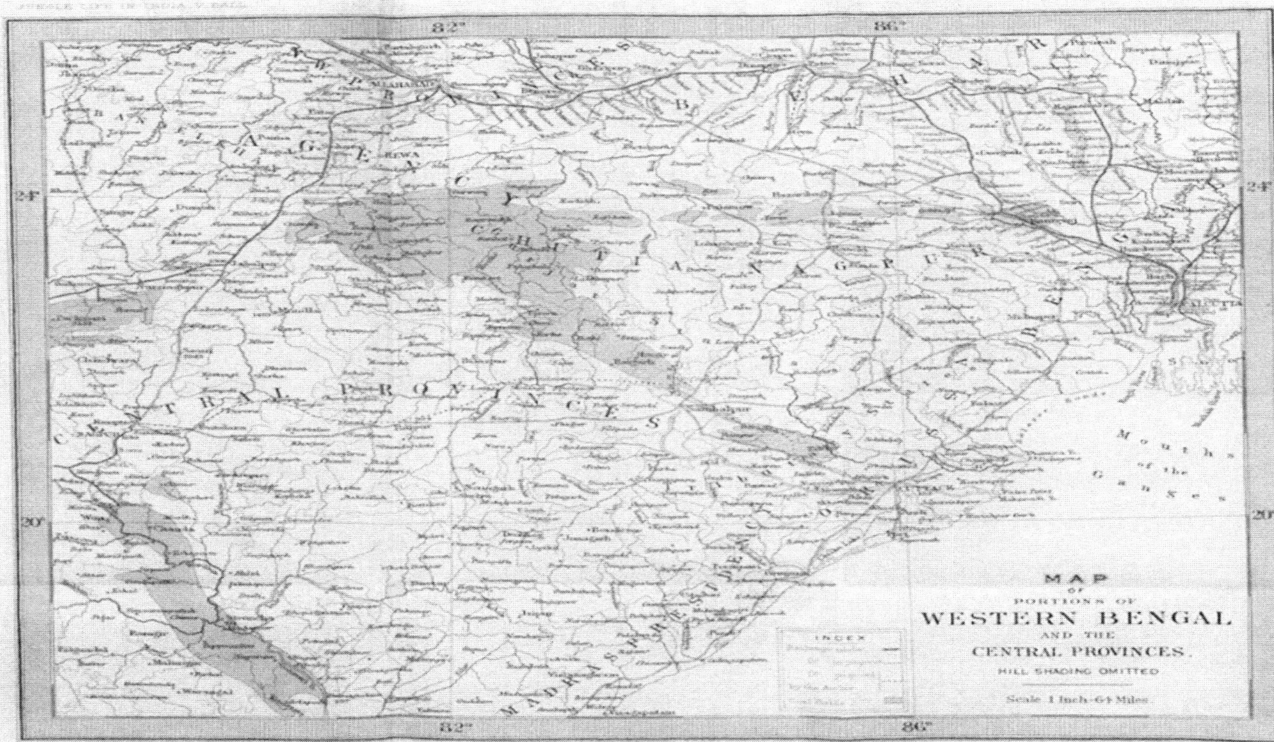
MAP
OF
PORTIONS OF
WESTERN BENGAL
AND THE
CENTRAL PROVINCES.
HILL SHADING OMITTED
Scale 1 Inch-64 Miles
INDEX
82°
86°
24°
20°
Mouths of the Ganges
CENTRAL PROVINCES
CHUTIA NAGPUR
REWA
MADRAS PRESIDENCY

JUNGLE LIFE IN INDIA.

CHAPTER I.

SOUTHAMPTON TO CALCUTTA, MANBHUM, HAZARIBAGH.

1864–65.

VOYAGE TO INDIA—FELLOW PASSENGERS—CYCLONE—START FOR RANIGUNJ—CHARACTER OF COUNTRY AND FLORA BETWEEN CALCUTTA AND RANIGUNJ—RANIGUNJ COAL-FIELD AND MINES—ASSENSOLE—BARAKAR—TRUNK ROAD—TREES—BUTTERFLIES—FIRST ACQUAINTANCE WITH CAMP LIFE—EQUIPMENT AND SERVANTS—GOVINDPUR—TOPECHANCI—PILGRIMS AND OTHER TRAVELLERS ON THE TRUNK ROAD—GOODS AND HORSES—ASCEND PARISNATH—SANITARIUM—FIRST EXPERIENCE OF VILLAGE ROADS—CASTE—THE PASSPORT SYSTEM IN INDIA—SUPPLIES—COAL DISCOVERIES—GUN ACCIDENT—NATIVE MATCHLOCK—ATHLETIC SPORTS—LOG FIRE—THE CHOWKIDAR—BRIGHTNESS OF THE STAR-LIGHT—THE FORCE OF RIDICULE—AN UNCLEAN ABORIGINE—NATIVE POTTERS—BOKARO RIVER—THE SONTALS—LAGU HILL—QUICKSANDS—FIRST CHRISTMAS IN CAMP—TEA PLANTATION—CROCODILE—SICK HINDU—MARCH EAST TO MEET DR. OLDHAM—CHANGE FROM HINDI TO BENGALI—SUPPLIES REFUSED—JERIAH COAL-FIELD—TROUBLES WITH ELEPHANT—SERVANTS *v.* VILLAGERS AND POLICE—SAVE A DROWNING MAN—BENGAL POLICE—SUGAR MANUFACTURE—DISCOVER CELT—HINDU FESTIVAL—WEAVERS—PREPARATION OF EVIDENCE FOR A SHAM CASE—PAY-DAY—NOVEL METHOD OF FISHING—STORMS—BONE SETTING—MAHOMEDANS LONG LIVED—START ON INDEPENDENT WORK—LOSE CAMP—ANTIQUE ORNAMENTS—HESAPURA—DAMUDA RIVER—RAMGURH COAL-FIELD—HYÆNA'S CAVE—FLYING FOXES—ELECTRIC STATE OF ATMOSPHERE—PARASITICAL PLANTS—NIGHT ALARM IN CAMP—HABITS OF ANTS—BEAT FOR LARGE GAME—RAMGURH COAL-FIELD—BURNING JUNGLE—ALBINO—HAZARIBAGH—HINDU FESTIVAL—HINDU WORSHIP—MARCH DOWN GRAND TRUNK ROAD—AN UNGALLANT HORSEMAN—BARAKAR BRIDGE—RANIGUNJ COAL-FIELD—ENGLISH SCHOOL—STORM—DEATH OF HORSE—TENT FLOODED—JEMIDAR'S MISCONDUCT—COAL-MINE—VULTURES—RAIN AND FEVER—PLANTS—PACHETE HILL—FINAL ROW WITH JEMIDAR—FEVER—RETURN TO CALCUTTA—VISIT DACCA.

ON the 20th of September, 1864, I started from Southampton for Calcutta, in the Peninsular and Oriental Company's steamer "Poonah."

As already stated in the introduction, one of the principal

objects of this work is to describe parts of India which are out of the ordinary tracks, so I willingly leave it to others to write about places which are readily accessible to all travellers on their way to Egypt and India.

The voyage was to me very enjoyable, and full of interest. Starting in company with some old friends, who, like myself, were on their first trip to the East, I also made many new acquaintances on board. Among the passengers were two distinguished men who are now dead. These were Sir Henry Holland, who was on one of his annual trips to Egypt, and Dr. Falconer, who, in company with Mr. G. Busk, was on his way to Gibraltar, to visit and explore the bone caves which had been discovered there. This was Dr. Falconer's last journey, as he died some months later from an illness brought on by the exposure and fatigue to which he was subjected on his return through Spain. From him I obtained much useful information and advice about India. His long residence in the country, and his knowledge of its geology, enabled him to speak with especial authority on such subjects.

At Suez we embarked on the "Simla," and on reaching Ceylon received the first tidings of the damage which had been caused by the great cyclone of October, 1864. On our way up the Hugli river to Calcutta, the numerous wrecks, the shattered buildings, and the overthrown trees, afforded abundant evidence of the extreme violence of this storm. In the middle of the botanical gardens lay a large steamer, which had been lifted there by the storm wave, and then left high and dry. The state of many of the houses reminded me of the condition of buildings after the great Neapolitan earthquake; and from the positions of the lines of fracture, I concluded that the storm had caused the houses to rock and oscillate in a manner similar to that produced by earthquakes. On the 28th of October we reached Calcutta.

My preparations for a march up country having been completed, and the requisite number, about a score, of servants having been engaged, I started on the 26th of November, by train to the station of Ranigunj, 120 miles from Calcutta. Soon after leaving Howrah, which is the terminus of the East Indian Railway, and faces Calcutta on the opposite bank of the Hugli, the line of route enables one to form some idea of the general character of the alluvial plains of Bengal. Extensive hedgeless stretches of green paddy (rice) cultivation meet the eye in every direction, with widely scattered clumps and groves of mango and palm trees, in or near which are the hamlets and villages of the cultivators, who may at this season be seen standing up to their knees in the swampy ground, weeding and transplanting the late varieties of rice. Their heads are occasionally protected from the sun by large plaited leaf and bamboo umbrella-like hats; but more commonly these people seem to regard their own natural covering of hair as sufficient protection.

On this, my first trip up country, I was much struck by the number of third class passengers in the train. Only on the occasion of special excursions would a similar number be seen in England. It appeared to me a most marvellous fact that a people, so averse from innovation of any kind, should have taken so universally to train travelling; and to judge from their faces they seemed thoroughly to enjoy it.

The only wild animals which attracted my attention on this occasion were troops of long-tailed monkeys called Langurs,* which were pretty abundant near some of the villages where they live and thieve. They are rarely interfered with by the inhabitants, who regard them with considerable veneration, owing to the part their progenitors are believed to have taken in aiding Rama in his conquest of Ceylon.

From the well-authenticated accounts I had heard of crocodiles, leopards, and even tigers, being occasionally run over by the train, I was rather disappointed at the outset in not meeting with more wild animals; but the mammal fauna of the country between Calcutta and Burdwan is really very small, and as most of the species are nocturnal in their habits, it appears to the traveller to be still smaller than it actually is.

In some few places the scenery is somewhat like that of parts of

---

* *Presbytis entellus*, Dufres.

Europe, but generally the line and the light railings with the level crossings, were the only objects of familiar type to be seen in any direction. The large and important station of Burdwan, the residence of the wealthy and enlightened Maharajah, is reached at a distance of about sixty-eight miles from Calcutta. Thence westwards there is a very notable change in the character of the vegetation, which is determined by the nature of the underlying soil, this changing from a swampy alluvium into a lateritic gravel, which becomes more and more dry and lean till the margin of the rocky portions of Western Bengal is reached, after which the change becomes still more marked. The cocoa-nut groves which support an undergrowth of *Arums*, sedges, and rank grasses, and which with clumps of a remarkably fine species of bamboo, surround Calcutta in every direction, disappear altogether west of Burdwan. Together with the change in the wild and semi-wild vegetation, the cultivation also alters. The rice, instead of being spread over swampy plains, is confined within the limits of terraced fields; and the covered cage-like gardens of plaited wattle, in which the Betel-leaf pepper vine (*Chavica betel*) alone thrives, are seldom seen, and with their disappearance the custom of Betel and Pawn chewing, in a great measure, disappears also, this being most commonly practised by the dwellers in the Ganges Valley and the moist regions of Bengal, Orissa, and Burmah. In other parts of Northern India the practice is chiefly limited to the upper classes and dwellers in cities, and, as is well known, it is connected with public ceremonial. The ordinary constituents of the Pawn which is sold by itinerant vendors in the large cities, are chopped fragments of the nut of the Areca palm, *cutch* or catechu, and lime, which are wrapped up in a leaf of the pepper —each packet forming a mouthful.

The *Kejur* or Toddy Palm (*Phœnix sylvestris*, Roxb.) becomes exceedingly rare in this region; but the *Tal* or Fan Palm (*Borassus flabelliformis*, Linn.) continues for some miles further west, forming at Ranigunj a leading feature in the scenery. The only palm which is really indigenous in the hilly country is a lowly form, the stemless date (*Phœnix acaulis*, Roxb).

On arrival at Ranigunj I was met by the manager of the Bengal Coal Company, who took me off to his hospitable house, which is situated on some high ground in the vicinity of the principal mines, and commands an extensive view of the bed of the Damuda river, and, in the distance, of the bold-outlined hills of Beherinath and Garangi. For several days I remained at Ranigunj in order to familiarise myself with the characters of the typical coal-measure rocks, and to see the methods of mining which were employed. These had many points of novelty about them, and perhaps it may here be useful to make a few remarks on the subject.

The Ranigunj coal-field is the largest and most important of the areas in which coal is worked in India. Its proximity to the main line of railway, and also to the port of Calcutta, tends to give it pre-eminence over other less favourably situated localities. In the year 1774 coal was known to occur there, and so long ago as 1777 was actually worked. In 1830 several collieries of considerable extent had been opened out and were, we have reason to believe, in a flourishing condition.* The total area of coal-bearing rocks which is exposed is about 500 square miles; but it is possible that the real area may be even double that, since on the east the rocks dip under and are completely concealed by alluvium. Throughout this area a central zone includes the principal mines, and the chimneys which dot this tract constitute it the black country of India. At the present time (1879) there are about six principal European companies engaged in the extraction of coal, while many minor firms and native associations contribute to swell the total amount raised.

Formerly a large proportion of the coal was obtained by open workings and quarries: but at the present day most of the seams which were accessible in this way have been exhausted, and regular mining

---

* Before the opening up of the Railway, the coal was conveyed to Calcutta by boats on the Damuda river, which is only navigable during the rainy season. Curious stories are told of the lawlessness of the bodies of retainers which were employed by the several companies to further their own traffic and injure that of opposition firms.

is now carried on with more or less system.* The miners are, however, individually, in some cases, allowed a degree of freedom, or rather licence, which would never be permitted in European mines. They chiefly belong to two races, the Bhowries and the Sontals—the former using the pick, while the latter cannot be induced to work with any other tool than a crowbar, with which they produce an altogether disproportionate amount of small coal and dust. The pillar and stall is generally practised in preference to the long wall system of "getting" the coal. None of the mines are of great depth, and a perfect freedom from fire and choke damp renders it possible to carry on the work without its being necessary to adopt the precautions which in England only too often fail to secure the object aimed at. Many of the seams are of considerable thickness, one which is worked contains nearly 40 feet of coal. As a rule, however, the thick seams, especially those in the lower measures, do not contain the best coal. Compared with ordinary English coal, the Ranigunj coals, and Indian coals generally, are very much inferior in working power, still they are capable of generating steam in both locomotive and other engines, and for this purpose several hundred thousand tons are raised annually from Indian mines.†

I shall not weary the reader with any further details, but must refer those interested to the publications of the Geological Survey of India, in which the principal information on the subject will be found. I have, however, been so frequently asked whether any coal is raised in India that I conclude there is a sufficiently general interest in the subject to secure for me a pardon for this digression from the course of my narrative.

On the 30th of November, my goods and camp equipment were started off in the early morning on four bullock-carts for the next halting place at Assensole, ten miles distant, I following later on

---

* Some of the mines are now admirably managed.

† In 1868 the total amount of coal raised in the Ranigunj mines was 564,933 tons; but in 1872 the total amount was only 322,443 tons. More recent figures are not available to me.

horseback. At Assensole I was the guest of one of the railway engineers, and made the acquaintance of several others, who were about to commence the preliminary surveys for the so-called Chord line, the construction of which has served to materially shorten the route to the North-west Provinces. For the first time since my arrival in India, I was here able to sleep without a mosquito-curtain, and the nights being fairly cool could even enjoy the use of a blanket.

My next day's march was to Barakar, a place of some importance as being the terminus of a branch line then under construction, and at which a large girder bridge over the Barakar river was being built to facilitate the traffic along the Grand Trunk road, which connects Bengal with the North-west Provinces. On the eastern bank of the river there are three highly sculptured Hindu (Sivoid) temples, very similar in character to some which I shall have to describe hereafter in Orissa.

Here I remained for the night, and for the first time in India was able to thoroughly enjoy a fire, as the evenings and mornings were very cold. My host, the engineer of the bridge works, though at that time apparently in good health, died from exposure a few months later, and before my return. On the following day I rode forward and joined the camp of a colleague, the late W. J. Willson, who had halted at a village on the Trunk road, about thirteen miles from Barakar. In the first few miles west of Barakar the road traverses a portion of the coal-field, after which it passes on to metamorphic rocks, when low hills and ranges of gneiss, &c., immediately cause a change in the scenery. I made myself acquainted *en route* with several trees to which frequent allusion will be made in the course of the following pages. Of these the principal were the Sal, Mhowa, Mango, and Palas.* In this region, as has been remarked by Sir J. D. Hooker in his *Flora-Indica*, the scenery is often singularly European and park-like, the trees mentioned, together with some others, doing duty for the familiar forms of temperate climes.

---

* *Shorea robusta, Bassia latifolia, Mangifera indica, and Butea frondosa.*

The butterflies which I saw were neither very beautiful nor numerous in species, but it interested me much to observe how the home species were represented by members of allied, and in some cases perhaps identical genera, wherever the character of their surroundings was similar.

I found my colleague encamped in a picturesque grove near the road, and when my own tent was pitched I had an opportunity of forming some idea of what my future life would be like. And here it will be convenient to enumerate and describe the various items which are found to be requisites in the camp establishment of an Indian geologist. The tent generally used is what is called a single-poled, double-roofed hill-tent, which has an internal superficial area of twelve feet square; and two lateral verandahs which can, if desirable, be enclosed by walls—thus making two side rooms. Small as this area may seem, it is, with a little management, capable of containing all requisite furniture and storage space. The furniture generally consists of a frame bed (or charpoy) with plaited tape; two tables, one for eating purposes, the other for writing materials and for supporting a travelling book-case; these, with a couple of chairs, gun rack, clothes hooks, and sundry portmanteaus and boxes, make up the sum of the internal equipment. Many people who use tents of this size carry a second for their office, and for the purpose of sending on ahead to the new stage; while district officers, except the most junior, generally use several larger and much more commodious tents. However, for a geologist, most of whose time is spent out of doors, and who has no regular office work involving formal intercourse with crowds of natives, such a tent is amply sufficient for all purposes, and is certainly the best in the hilly regions where carriage is difficult. This form of tent, moreover, if properly made of good materials, is wind and weather proof, and will withstand storms which would lay low most others.

A bath tent, and three sleeping *pâls* for the native Doctor, the kitchen, and the Jemidar and Chuprasies respectively, are further requisite; though some people consider the shelter of a tree sufficient for a kitchen, and the huts which the villagers run up with branches as ample protection for the servants. Most Indian servants, if provided with a blanket, think it no great hardship to sleep in the open; but I am fully satisfied that the tale of sickness is much diminished by the provision of proper covering as a protection from the cold by night and the sun by day.

As the geologist requires no clerks or writers, and as until recently there were no native assistants, the list of his followers resolves itself into the following elements:—One native doctor or trained hospital assistant, who is in charge of the health of the men, and is generally competent to deal with the ordinary forms of disease and simple surgical cases. One Jemidar or head man, under whose orders all the rest of the men are supposed to be; his pay is from 10 to 16 rupees per month, and his perquisites, as he keeps accounts of the general expenditure, are no small source of additional income to him. Six Chuprasies, who carry a *chupras* or engraved brass plate on a sash or belt, indicating the service to which they belong. The duties of these men are multifarious: they act as tent pitchers, messengers to post, orderlies and night watchers; they also obtain the supplies from the villages, going on a day in advance in order to make the necessary preparations. The pay of these men is from 6 to 8 rupees per month each.

The bearer, or valet, has charge of the internal arrangements of the tent, and looks after the guns, his pay being from 8 to 10 rupees; while the Barwachi, or cook, receiving 10 or 12 rupees; the Masalchi, or cook's assistant, 4 or 5 rupees; and the Khansamah, or table attendant, receiving also 10 or 12 rupees, are the three functionaries whom custom rigorously prescribes for the due performance of the very simple commissariat arrangements. Next comes the Dhobi, or washerman, on 7 rupees: the Bhisti, or waterman, on 6 or 7 rupees, and the Mathur, or sweeper, who has also charge of the dogs, on 6 rupees. According to the nature of the beasts of burden, and the means of carriage employed, so the numbers of the rest of the establishment will vary. If there are two horses, two sayces or grooms, on 6 to 7 rupees, and two grass-cutters on 4 to 5 rupees, must be employed.

For the first few months I was unprovided with an elephant,

and four bullock-carts, costing 12 rupees a month each, were my only means of carriage; how unsuited they were to the roadless country I had to go through will presently appear. In all then, as I had at first only one horse, my followers were twenty-one in number, and their wages, exclusive of the native doctor's pay, but including the hire of the carts, amounted to between 180 and 190 rupees (£18 to £19) per month. The men were selected for me, or rather I should say obtained for me, by the head native clerk in the Geological Survey Office in Calcutta, and turned out to be, for the most part, useless and incompetent; but before the end of the season I had opportunities for replacing such of the worst of them as I was compelled to dismiss.

Among the whole number, the native doctor, Hosein Ali, alone spoke English, so that I had abundant opportunities for putting in practice the Hindustani I had learnt from books, and in a few months' time found myself able to converse with sufficient fluency for all practical purposes.

On the day following the junction of my camp with Willson's we continued our march westwards to Govindpur, which is a sub-divisional station, and the residence of an Assistant Commissioner, who is subordinate to the Deputy-Commissioner of the district of Manbhum.

We examined a number of river beds near the road, which contained sections admirably illustrative of the characters of the crystalline and metamorphic rocks which stretch over an enormous area in Western Bengal and the adjoining provinces. Hornblendic gneisses, with widely persistent east and west strike of the bedding and foliation, were the most abundant forms of rock met with.

We found our new camp pitched in the compound or garden of a ruined house under the shelter of a grove of mango trees. Here we remained for a second day, and I had a rather narrow escape of never leaving the place. My bearer, to whom I had handed my gun on half-cock, bethought him, like most natives, that the hammer should be down on the cap for safety. Accordingly, he proceeded to let it down when my back was turned, and very nearly lodged the charge in my body. Fortunately no one happened to be exactly in the direction in which the muzzle was pointed.

The habits of Willson's elephant were a source of great interest to me owing to their novelty. The mahout's method of feeding him by placing nests of straw, each containing a few handsful of rice, actually into his mouth, and the quantity of leaves and branches of the banyan *(Ficus Indica)* which the animal managed to dispose of during the night, struck me then as particularly remarkable.

Our next march was to a stage called Rajgunj. On the way I found in some swampy ground a *marsilliaceous* plant, similar apparently to that upon the spore-cases of which some of the Australian tribes are said to subsist, and on which some of the explorers in that country have managed to eke out a miserable existence. While looking for snipe this afternoon I caught sight of a wolf. This was the largest wild animal I had encountered, nothing bigger than a jackal having previously come in my way. From Rajgunj we marched to Topechanci, where there is a rest-house or dak bungalow.

Formerly, before the opening of the railway to the North-west, the Trunk road and its rest-houses were the scenes of much more animation than they are at present. By day and night a constant stream of European travellers in post carriages was to be met with. At the time I write of such travellers were but seldom seen, and the leading features of the traffic were centered in the native pedestrians and the carts laden with produce bound for Bengal. These were, however, by no means deficient in interest for me, for among the pedestrians was to be seen a wonderful variety of ethnological types from the most distant regions of India. The two great lodestones drawing these people so many hundreds of weary miles from their homes were the temple of Jugernath at Puri, for the Hindus, and the sacred hill of Parisnath, for the Jains. Although the stream of pilgrims to Jugernath varies in magnitude according to the time of year, being most considerable before the great car festival, still it is incessant, as many people have no doubt vague ideas as to the distance, and others, becoming footsore and broken-down, spend months longer on the road than they had calculated on when setting forth from their homes.

Some of the better classes were provided with carts, of forms strange to that part of the country, and drawn by cattle of very much finer breeds than those ordinarily seen in lower Bengal. Occasionally glimpses of smiling faces and bright eyes peeping through the chinks of the mat coverings of these carts, indicated the sex of the travellers. Frequently, as a tag to these family parties, might be seen a string of aged and footsore old widows toiling mournfully behind.

Subsequently, on several occasions, when travelling on this same road, I have met solitary individuals progressing by measuring the ground with their full length. Lying down flat on their faces, with an iron spike they draw a line at the point reached by their outstretched hands, then rising they toe this line and repeat the process. Some of these, I believe, spend many months, if not years, on the journey to Jugernath. One of those whom I saw was said to be a Raja: but none, so far as I can remember, wore more than a narrow body cloth, and probably all had to depend, in a great measure, on charity for their subsistence.

Considerable numbers of men carrying *banghys* with baskets covered with brick-red cloth, were also on their road down country. These were professional snake-charmers, who, therefore, in all probability, observe a season for their visits to the lower provinces.

Huge two-wheeled waggons laden with enormous bales of cotton, and drawn by two pair of oxen, with often a miniature bull or ox in front (more for ornament than use) as leader, slowly wended their way down country from far distant cotton-growing regions. At the present day such carts are no longer to be seen, for the railways, since completed, carry all the cotton to the ports of Bombay or Calcutta; the export trade having vastly developed during and since the American war, and the value of time having come to be more appreciated by the merchants.

There were also at this time long strings of horses of the Cabul and other breeds, on their way down from Sonpur near Patna, where an annual fair is held, at which a considerable number of horses and a few elephants are disposed of to private individuals and native dealers. At the present day, owing to the great numbers of Australian horses brought to Calcutta, the trade in the hardy and useful Cabul horses has much decreased.

From Topechanci, I made the ascent of Parisnath, which is the highest peak in Bengal proper, being 4,479 feet above the sea. As has been already stated, it is regarded as a place of sanctity by people professing the Jain religion, which is a modified form of Buddhism.

We first rode to a place called Nimia Ghât, whence we commenced the ascent on foot by a road six miles long which had recently been constructed to afford a means of approach to the buildings then being erected in view of the formation of a sanitarium for sick soldiers. Of the subsequent history of this sanitarium I shall have to speak hereafter. Before its establishment numerous trials were made of the salubrity of the place. Officers were directed to remain up there for the hot months, and report upon their experiences; elaborate minutes were drawn up; the Lieutenant-Governor himself, in 1860, made the summit his official residence; and finally a road up it was made and building operations were commenced.

On either side the road was bounded for the most part with dense and beautiful forests, having here and there an undergrowth of ferns and herbaceous plants, such as are rarely or never seen in the country below. With every new rise in the road the aspect of the lower country varied, till, after toiling for two hours and a-half, we reached the bare culminating ridge which constitutes the top. Thence a grand panorama of the surrounding country, with its winding rivers, its scattered ranges and wooded hills, and its stretches of cultivation, was spread before our eyes; the full effect being, however, somewhat marred by the haze which hung about the lower levels.

On each peak on the hog-backed ridge at the top there are miniature votive temples of white marble, or other material, which have been put up by various wealthy Jain pilgrims, such as the Raja of Jaipur and others. On the western end of the ridge bungalows and other accommodation for the soldiers were being erected, while the principal temples of the place are nearly one and a-half miles distant at the eastern end. In spite of this distance and the fact that the place cleared for the buildings was a portion of unoccupied rocky jungle, the Jains had vigorously protested against any Europeans being permitted to live upon it, and, indeed, claimed the whole hill, on the ground that it was granted to them by a *Sannad* from the Emperor Akbar, which provided that no one should "kill an animal below, or about the mountains and the places of worship and pilgrimage." The *Sannad* concluded with the following:—"May this firman shine like the sun and moon amongst the followers of the Jain Sitambar religion as long as the sun may shine in the day with his resplendent rays and the moon make the night delightful by her light." Experts, however, proved that the *Sannad* was a forgery prepared for the occasion; and, as regards the preservation of life, Government pronounced that it would be inexpedient that the tigers, leopards, and bears should, by a prohibition to sportsmen, be allowed to increase and gain the upper hand. This point being conceded, it was, I suppose, not thought to be of any use to press the question of the killing of animals for food.

The sanitarium failed, as I shall hereafter relate; and I have little doubt that the priests regard its failure as a result of Divine interference and retribution.

On our return to Topechanci, I received a bundle of over-due home letters and papers, which had been wandering about for days. Thus I had early experience of what I have since been only too familiar with—defective postal arrangements.

On the following day I rode on to my colleague's camp for breakfast, and then struck off the Trunk road for the village of Telù, where I expected to find my own camp ready for my reception. Having forded a river called the Jamuna, I found myself on what served the purpose, though it hardly deserved the name, of a road.

Like, as I afterwards found to be the case, all unmade country tracks which are traversed by bullock-carts, there were two ruts, often a foot deep, which had been worn by the wheels of carts and the feet of the oxen, except here and there where a boulder or mass of rock protruded in such a way as to tilt the carts out of the horizontal, often, too, upsetting them. In all my experience I have never known villagers in India—however much they might suffer from injury to their carts or cattle—make the slightest spontaneous effort at repairing their only means of communication.

Having seen this road, I was not much surprised on arrival at the camping-ground, though it was late, to find that the carts had only just arrived before me; and I had to wait some time before the tent was ready for my reception. I was much pleased to observe the vigour with which one of two Brahmins, whom I had engaged in place of two of the weakly and incompetent Calcutta men, did his work. He was a magnificent specimen of a powerfully-built native. Two or three days later, however, he took his discharge, as he found his duties would bring him into contact with fowls, by which his caste would be damaged.

As my next stage, Turrea, was only seven miles distant, I did not make a very early start, thinking my camp would be up at an early hour. Examining the rocks and familiarising myself with the trees, of which I inquired the native names and uses, I made my way leisurely to Turrea, arriving there at two o'clock. The villagers brought out a *charpoy*, or family bedstead, for me to sit upon; but, though pleased with the attention, I did not like the look of it, and took my rest on the ground. Time and custom have rendered me less fastidious. I only mention what is a customary and very ordinary act, as it struck me at the time, just as I mention many other little incidents which then found a place in my diary, but which, having since become matters of ordinary routine, I should not now think worthy of notice. They are such as would attract the notice of a passer-through, but would be deemed too trivial for remark by a resident.

After some time spent in exploration of the river sections in the neighbourhood, I returned to the village; but still there was no sign of the carts. At length, an hour after sunset, my patience being thoroughly worn out, I determined to go to meet them, as I did not wish to be separated from them for the night. About two miles off in the jungle I found them, with men and beasts labouring to the very best of their ability, dragging them over numerous obstructions. With the aid of myself and some men whom I took back with me, the village was at length reached, and at 9 p.m., more than twelve hours after starting, I saw my tent pitched and the men at leisure to cook their first meal. Such an amount of time, labour, and inconvenience spent in the accomplishment of a distance which was only seven miles, measured on the map, made me look forward less cheerfully to my future life than I had been doing before. However, I may at once state that this experience was not again repeated in all my subsequent travels. On the following day (Dec. 10th) I marched to join the camp of another colleague, T. W. H. Hughes, who was engaged upon the survey of the Bokaro coal-field, one of a series of basins of coal-measures in the district of Hazaribagh, of which, at that time, very little was known. It had been arranged that I was to remain with him until I had familiarised myself with camp life, and the characters of the different geological formations with which I should afterwards have to deal alone.

I here first learnt what was meant by a *Parwana.* This is a document drawn up in the vernacular language of a district, signed by the chief civil officer, and addressed to Rajas, heads of villages, the police, or others, as the case may be, intimating that the bearer is a Government officer (supposing such to be the fact) employed on Government service, and that he is to receive all legal assistance in reference to camp supplies and coolies, &c., and that complaints of non-compliance will result in the visitation of extreme displeasure, &c. This is the case, at least, in non-regulation districts. In the regulation districts some officers hold that it is *ultra vires* for them to do more than issue a sort of mild intimation to the rajas and others to the same effect, and such documents are often worse than useless. In fact, as I shall have abundant occasion to shew, the retention of this passport system in British territory, while a relic of barbarism and most objectionable in other respects, is often quite incapable, where the people are ill-disposed, of producing the desired results.

In these wild regions, where fire-wood and straw are of no definite value, they are supposed to be supplied to camps of Government officers free of cost. This, though it seemed to me at first to involve hardship, is seldom regarded as such, and is, at any rate, universally the custom of the country. Less commonly, the earthen pots in which water is carried and rice cooked, are supplied also free of cost, the *kumar*, or potter, being often supported by a piece of land which he holds rent free in requital for his services. However, as he is not always in this position, and as the servants have the greatest objection to paying, injustice in this, and, I regret to say, in many other small matters, is often perpetrated unless the most unremitting supervision is exercised. How the most conscientious may be hoodwinked, and robbery committed under their noses, and, of course, under their protection, will be duly unfolded in the course of these pages. The story of the poor man's ewe lamb is often repeated in India; and, indeed, travellers in Egypt and other Oriental countries bear testimony to the same. For ever it is the same.

> "The good old rule
> Sufficeth them, the simple plan
> That they shall take who have the power,
> And they shall keep who can."

The legitimate prices at that time were, for sheep (very lean, it is true), from one shilling to eighteen-pence each, two shillings being a handsome price; for fowls, from three-halfpence, or less, to three-pence.

With my colleague's aid I was able to remodel my defective establishment; and one of his Chuprasies, an experienced man, but, as he ultimately proved, a rascal, was installed as Jemidar.

The next few days after our junction were spent in the examination and measurement of sections of the coal measures; and one of the first discoveries of economic value was a seam of 90 feet thickness, which was the largest I had ever seen. It appeared to consist, to a considerable extent, of good coal, but had not then, and I believe has not yet, been opened out. This was only one of many which were discovered of smaller, but workable, thickness, as may be seen by reference to the published report on the Bokaro field.*

We used to spend the whole day out, sometimes riding; but, owing to our work being chiefly in the beds of rocky, jungle-bordered streams, usually on foot. For an hour or so we used to rest and refresh ourselves near some village during the hottest part of the day. While doing so, on the 15th of December, the pleasure of an otherwise pleasant and interesting day's exploration was marred by an unfortunate occurrence. One of the Chuprasies, a Brahmin and ex-Sepoy, had gone into a village to procure some milk, shouldering a gun that had been left for a moment resting against a tree. Soon after we heard the report of a gun from the vicinity of the village, and, on going to ascertain the cause, met the Chuprasi coming towards us with the gun over his left shoulder and holding out his right hand, which we at once saw was badly wounded. It appeared that he had passed through a hedge, and that, in drawing the gun after him by the muzzle, it had exploded, and the charge had carried away some of the fleshy part of his hand. We immediately made a tourniquet with our handkerchiefs to stop a copious discharge of blood. Sending a messenger off to camp, which was six miles distant, for the native doctor and bandages, we got together some coolies and had the man carried on a charpoy. On arrival we dressed his hand, and the doctor considered it advisable to administer some laudanum, which it required no little persuasion to induce the man to take. His pride of caste and soldiership enabled him to bear the pain without a murmur, and conduct himself in a most heroic manner; and I am glad to be able to add that he recovered the complete use of his hand, and is still alive and enjoying comparative

* Mem. Geol. Surv. India. Vol. VI.

ease as a guardian of one of the doors in the Geological Museum in Calcutta.

Our guide on the following day possessed a matchlock gun of indigenous manufacture, such as are common enough throughout India; but I had only once seen one like it before in a museum at home, and had then regarded it as an impossible kind of engine of great antiquity, and I was not at all prepared to find that good shots could be made with such a weapon, at short ranges, with any sort of bullet. It required all our care, with an Enfield match rifle, to shoot as well as did the owner of the matchlock with his weapon. As it was heavy he used a rest, and, as is invariably, I believe, done by natives when shooting with these narrow-stocked guns, dropped the stock under his arm as he fired, thus avoiding the recoil. To do this at the proper moment must be an art not easily acquired.

After dinner we used to sit at a large log fire till we found ourselves falling asleep. But let no one suppose that a log fire on a cold night is to be compared with a fire in a cozy room with curtains drawn. The best that can be said for it is that it is nice to look at, and for warming is better than nothing, but the contrast between the scorching of the part of the body presented to it and the coolness of the part most remote produces anything but an agreeable feeling. A log fire has this one advantage, that it is a most convenient place at which to hold converse with natives. When squatted down close to it and able to snuff the smoke well down into their lungs, their tongues are often loosened, and they begin to talk with a freedom that they seldom can be induced to adopt under other less favourable circumstances. On such occasions one may pick up much of interest about manners, customs, and folk-lore, and get information about the animals and sport obtainable in the neighbouring jungles. This often too, perhaps, from individuals who at other times might protest that they knew nothing about the subject, or even affirm more directly, that there were no animals at all.

This is a suitable place to describe that member of the village community known as the *chowkidar*. The chowkidar's functions are to watch all that goes on by day and night in his village. It is his duty to report to the nearest police-station anything that should be made a subject of inquiry. By night he stalks about cudgel in hand, and, like the old English watchman, calls out to evil-doers to make themselves scarce. Frequently his howls and shrieks do not formulate themselves into words, but should be, even from their hideous intonation, still more terrifying than actual threats. Unfortunately for this display, which is particularly vigorous when a Sahib is in camp near the village—there is only too much reason for believing—indeed it is often proved—that the chowkidars are in league with the bad characters, and receive a per-centage of their spoils. Not only, however, are the chowkidars connected with these bands of thieves, but even the zemindars, or landlords, have on frequent occasions been found to be the patrons and chief recipients of the booty of bands of robbers. Hereafter I shall have to give an account of one independent Raja who thus headed the despoilers of his own country; and his was, and perhaps is, only a representative case, by no means without numerous parallels.

As a rule the chowkidars are of the lowest caste of Hindus, or of no caste at all—that is to say they belong to aboriginal tribes; but I have occasionally seen Brahmins occupying these despised posts. The payment of chowkidars is provided for sometimes by land set apart for the purpose, sometimes by a house-tax levied by themselves, and sometimes they are the paid servants of the zemindars, and where these latter happen to be unscrupulous, the results may easily be imagined. However they are paid, their income is but small, and they are generally very poor, and their houses amongst the most tumble-down on the outskirts of the village. Often their sole covering when going their rounds on bitterly cold nights is a thin or ragged cotton cloth.

Of late years I am aware that much has been done in parts of Bengal to reform and systematise the force, if it can be so called; but there are still wide regions in British as well as in semi-independent territory where the chowkidars are at present in the condition I describe. In the first days of my acquaintance with them I was much struck with their alacrity and readiness to act as guides or collect supplies, seldom asking for, or appearing to expect any reward, from a Government servant at least. Had I not recorded this I might now pass it over without notice, as I have come to accept the fact as a matter of course, though not without exceptions where the men have become contaminated by the members of that Augean stable, the Bengal police, or by ill-disposed zemindars.

The nights at this season were magnificent. Going outside the tent one night at one o'clock I was much struck with the brilliancy of the star-decked sky which is often sufficiently luminous to enable one to travel through jungle and over broken roads and stream courses. On the present occasion the moon poured beams of light down on the slumbering camp. On one side, under the shelter of a grove of mangos, the horses were dimly discernible. In front were our two tents with the smouldering embers of the log fire between them. In the rear shone out the five tents of the doctor and the servants, while still further back the outline of the elephant lying on his side could be seen, while his loud snores sufficiently proclaimed that he was taking a short respite from his almost continual munching of branches and leaves. The unceasing hum of crickets and other similar insects is so all-pervading during these tropical nights that one has almost to think of the sound in order to realise its existence. It resembles in a subdued form the hum from a cotton-spinning mill. This noisy silence, if I may so call it, is interrupted from time to time by the cries of jackals and other animals, by the weird notes of various night birds and the gibbering of flying foxes. Together with these natural sounds, the vile notes of the tom-tom, and voices raised in dispute, come wafted on the breeze from some distant hamlet.

On the 21st of December, we moved the camp from Huzari to Dumri, and had a hard day's work. I had been much troubled by my Calcutta sayce having a trick of lagging behind instead of being close at hand to hold my horse when required. Other methods having proved unavailing I thought he would be a good subject upon whom to try the effect of ridicule. To get him carried back to camp suggested itself to me. Four coolies with a *charpoy* were procured from a village we were passing through. The sayce, seeing these preparations and having overheard the order, went down on his knees and implored and entreated to be let off, but he was made to sit on the charpoy, and the coolies entering into the joke of the thing, speedily raised it to their shoulders and carried it a mile to camp. The whole time the sayce remained in a suppliant position, begging to be released. On arrival at the camp he was carried round and was cheered and salaamed to by the men at each of the tents, after which he was allowed to descend. This mode of treatment was found to be very effectual, and I had seldom to find fault with him afterwards.

On the following day we had not got many steps away from camp when we became unpleasantly aware that the aborigine, who was acting as guide, was not remarkable for personal cleanliness; or, to be more accurate, was remarkably unclean. On being asked if he had washed himself for three years, "No," replied the old man, complacently, "it is more than four since I had a wash." Shortly afterwards, on our reaching a village, he was given a public bath, to the great amusement of a crowd of onlookers, and when pronounced deodorized we proceeded and had a long day's work, not returning to camp till late in the evening.

During the day I examined the process employed by the native potters in the manufacture of the rude forms of earthenware which have a widespread distribution in India at the present day. As in so many other arts practised in that country, there is a good deal of ingenuity in some of the details. But a want of mechanical contrivances, and a proper division of labour are causes which serve to render the results very poor when compared with the time and toil expended. The potter's wheel, as I believe is the case in some other Asiatic countries, is not kept in continuous motion by a band, but has to be balanced on an axis and turned by the operator till it attains a momentum which is sufficient to keep it going till the potter has formed the destined vessel in the rough. Before completion fresh impetus has again to be given several times, and at length the vessel appears as a *hundi* or *ghara*, a globular vessel a foot and upwards in diameter, and holding from one to two gallons. This is used for various purposes; for storing or carrying water, and occasionally for cooking rice, though for this latter purpose a similar, but somewhat smaller and more open-mouthed form is preferred. Still smaller vessels of similar form are made for holding milk, and less commonly open basins and water crofts, or *surahis*, in form resembling those seen in Europe; but the last are seldom used by the natives themselves.

These potters in the jungle also roughly mould with their hands grotesque figures of horses, elephants, and various impossible animals, which when baked are used by the aborigines as votive offerings, and are placed close to certain trees or rocks which are spots regarded as sacred to particular sylvan deities, or rather, as I shall have to point out hereafter, to sylvan devils or evil spirits. The baking is effected by building the vessels, when fully sun-dried, in the form of an arched vault over a hollow in the ground, covering the arch with a thick layer of clay and cow-dung, and lighting a fire below.

When the potter is an artist, he sometimes ornaments his vessels with engraved figures, or adds some bands of colour which contrast with the red of the baked product. Finely-powdered mica, also, is sometimes sprinkled on the vessel while still moist, thus producing a sparkling effect. A salt glaze is seldom if ever used, and the vessels are generally highly porous, and consequently they cool water in the most perfect manner.

The scenery of the Bokaro river, which has furnished a name for the coal-field, and in or near which our work lay, appeared to me to be, while very attractive from the boldness of the surrounding hills, still wanting in something which I can only express by the word softness. There is generally a harshness and dryness about the vegetation of these jungles, together with a want of varied colours, which I did not expect to meet with; while I soon found that the tropical luxuriance and density of undergrowth in the forests which I did expect, need not be looked for in these parts of India.

I here made my first acquaintance with the race of aborigines called Sontals. As we were passing a village called Lal Garh, on the banks of the Bokaro we heard a most terrific drumming and flute-playing, and found that the day was one of the very numerous Sontal *Parabs*, or festivals. On going into the village we saw a half-circle of male dancers, all in an advanced state of intoxication, and making the most absurd gestures. Most of the audience were also drunk, the head man or Manji particularly so, and in that stage when the chief characteristics are amiability of an oppressive kind and a great desire to converse.

Having found the village well suited for an encamping place, and thinking that the geniality of the Sontals might help us to spend a merry Christmas, we left one of our men behind us to make the necessary preliminary arrangements; but we had not gone far before he came running after us to say that he had been threatened with a beating by the villagers, and was afraid to remain alone. The Manji, when called up to explain matters, approached us in a most ridiculous manner; stopping at intervals, he would stand on one leg and place his hands in a suppliant position. At last, becoming somewhat sobered, he promised to prepare for our coming.

Christmas Eve.—Starting off our camp to Lal Garh, we ourselves devoted the day to the ascent of Lagú hill, a lofty block formed of the highest and youngest sedimentary rocks of the area, and situated centrically in the Bokaro coal-field. The geological position and age of the Mahadeva or Upper Panchet rocks will be found set forth in the Appendix on the geological formations. It is sufficient here to say that masses similar to that of Lagú, the remnants of denudation, occur in many of the coal-fields of the Damuda Valley and the areas further west. Lithologically they consist of highly ferruginous sandstones, conglomerates, and red clays. They are generally unfossiliferous.

At the eastern end a narrow path led us through heavy forest and over some steep scarps. After a severe climb of about 2,000 feet, we reached the top, which is said to be 3,203 feet above the sea. As is frequently the case in country of this character, we found ourselves, when on the summit, unable to obtain a view of the surrounding country, owing to the vegetation, which completely impeded our vision. However, by climbing trees we were enabled to command a vast extent of country, by far the greatest portion of which was covered by tree jungle—the total area of the patches of cultivation being very insignificant in comparison. On my way to camp I made my first acquaintance with quicksands, and also had an opportunity of admiring the sagacity of my horse. At one spot in the bed of the Bokaro he stopped suddenly, and, on my forcing him a few steps further, he instantly sank to the girths. Later on the same thing happened, but I managed to get him out without damage. Since then I have been many scores of times in similar or worse quicksands; but, as they seem never to be more than about three feet deep, and are generally less, they are not really dangerous, though the sensation of a rapid descent even to that depth is not pleasant.

Christmas Day.—Giving ourselves a holiday, we had athletic sports for the men and Sontal villagers; and after dark an enormous bonfire was lighted, and the Sontals, first the women and then the men, danced and sang. One of the songs struck us much, and especially so as being an improvement on ordinary Hindustani melody. The story of it was, in parts, singularly like the well-known "This is the house that Jack built."

SONTAL SONG.*

* I am indebted to Mr. Hughes for the words: for the music my memory is responsible.

Other songs were apparently impromptus, containing reference to ourselves. Prizes were delivered to the winners in the sports, and so concluded the first of many returns of Christmas which I have spent in the Jungle.

On the 29th of December, being in the neighbourhood of a hill called Jilunga, upon which a tea-garden had been opened out, we ascended it to see what was going on. We found the resident manager at home, and he showed us round. He informed us that there were 300 acres under cultivation, but as since none of the plants were more than two years old and they require five to come to maturity, the garden was still in an experimental stage. One hundred and fifty men were engaged in cutting down jungle and reclamation, and, as there was a rich deposit of soil, great hopes were entertained of the experiment proving successful. These hopes have, I believe, been only in part fulfilled. Owing to the hot winds of summer, it was necessary to protect each plant from direct desiccation by means of a small mat screen. This was found to add considerably to the cost of cultivation, and, coupled with drought, it has rendered tea planting in Western Bengal a somewhat precarious and seldom profitable speculation.

On the 30th of December, shortly after my return to camp, having spent the morning measuring sections in the river bed, some of the servants came to me to say they had just seen a *garial** in a neighbouring tank. It proved, however, to be a *muggur*, or crocodile (*Crocodilus biporcatus*). I was unable to get a shot at it, but just saw its eyes and nose above the surface of the water for a moment when the elephant was walked into the water in order to stir it up. I was then told, what I believe to be the case, that the Hindus sometimes put crocodiles, which are objects of veneration, with some classes at least, into the tanks : an attention which the

---

* In English works on Natural History this is commonly called Gavial (*Gavialis Gangeticus*), a mistake due originally, perhaps, to a clerical error, and not to be compared in enormity with the Anglo-Indian practice of calling crocodiles alligators.

crocodiles reciprocate by preying, when they get the chance, on their benefactor's persons, or on their flocks and herds.

At this time we had one man ill with typhus fever in the camp. He was in a very precarious state. Being a Hindu particular about his caste, he was somewhat difficult to deal with. When sensible, he declared that he would rather die than eat any meat or drink wine. Nor would he take any food willingly that had been cooked by any one of lower caste than himself. The only man of higher caste in the camp was the Brahmin whose hand had been injured, and as his other hand had been burnt, and as moreover he did not care about the job of preparing food for an inferior, the sick man might have died of starvation had he not when insensible been fed by the Mahomedans. Had the Brahmin himself only known that I had dipped my hand into a vessel from which he afterwards drank, I believe he would have almost died of chagrin, or at any rate would have had to spend all his savings in order to regain his caste.

On the last day of the year we got a message from the Superintendent of the Survey, the late Dr. Oldham, requesting us to meet him in the Jeriah coal-field, in the district of Manbhum, which had been surveyed during the previous season.

On the 1st of January, 1865, we made a long march from Leyeo to Hosir, a fine large village with well-to-do and some fair and good looking Hindu inhabitants, who were much better clothed than the Sontal and other aboriginal tribes of the parts we had been in. Shortly after arrival the sick chuprasi breathed his last. He was of the Gwala or cowkeeper caste, and a finer specimen of a Hindu I had not seen. Though of powerful physical proportions he was a strict vegetarian, excepting only that milk formed a part of his diet. He wore a red coral bead suspended from his neck in connection with a vow never to taste flesh or spirits. He was buried, as there was no friend or relative by to see him burnt.

On the following day we crossed the Damuda river to Angwali, and noticed a great improvement in the cultivation, sugar-cane becoming abundant. The people too changed: a strong Bengali element, together with the Bengali language, rapidly replacing the

Hindi-speaking Hindus and the Sontals and other aborigines. There were also water-tanks and reservoirs in much greater abundance than in Hazaribagh, and on them we found great numbers of duck and teal, which afforded capital sport. Other water-birds, such as coots and water-hens, were also abundant.

At our next camping-ground, Ranipokar, supplies of all kinds were point-blank refused. This was the beginning of our troubles in this region. At a village called Telmuchio we joined Dr. Oldham's camp, and on the following day marched to Domra, where we found, already encamped, the Assistant Magistrate and Assistant Superintendent of Police of the sub-division. For several days we were occupied examining sections of the coal-measures. In some places the coal-seams were traversed by trap dykes, which had induced a beautiful columnar structure in the coal, and occasionally a metamorphism of the mineral into impure graphite.

At Kheryo we suffered inconvenience from a block-out by the people. The zemindar was a widow bearing the complimentary title of Rani, who lived in one of a group of houses surrounded by a wall. Her people refused to hold any communication with our servants, and were strengthened in their opposition by a constable of the Bengal Police, who told them, and repeated the same to our faces, that our *Parwana* was of no value, as we, not being magistrates, could not enforce compliance. Instead of taking the law into our own hands, as we were sorely tempted to do, we determined to report him on the first opportunity.

January 7th.—Dr. Oldham left us to march northwards, making over to me an elephant for the carriage of my tent, &c. But the acquisition was not an unmixed good, for *Mowlah*, so he was called, was a very unmanageable animal. His name will again appear in these pages. The first intimation of his character which I received was from the Mahout, who came to me for his dismissal on the ground that the elephant would not obey him, and that he was afraid of it. Such being the case I allowed him to go, and handed over the beast to the assistant or mate, who, at the prospect of becoming Mahout, rose to the occasion and undertook the sole charge till a second man could be obtained. Almost immediately there was a severe trial of his skill and pluck. The elephant being loosed tried to bolt off, but the man drove it back with a spear, and having cowed it by a severe thrashing was enabled to chain it up, when he gave it a further chastisement, after which it acknowledged his mastership. For some minutes before it was caught I was expecting to see it knock over and kill the man. Several times it charged as though it were fully intent upon demolishing him.

January 11th.—On our return to camp we found that our two chuprasies who had been sent on the previous day, had got into trouble in a village they had entered, having missed their way. The villagers, who were Sontals, as was stated, refused a guide, a dispute arose, and one of the latter was either thrown down or his head was cut open with a stick, a slight scalp wound being the result. The chuprasies were detained in the village for the night, and were only released when our elephants with the rest of the servants hove in sight in the morning.

The Sontals were then brought or came down to camp, and we found them and a constable awaiting our arrival.

We could not get at the truth of the matter as both sides were obviously lying to their very utmost, and so dismissed all parties. Ordinarily speaking, the Sontals are quiet and tractable, but when drunk, or, as in this case, when under the influence of Bengalis, they are often troublesome and unmanageable. Whatever our men had done, it was clear that they had been refused a guide and had received other provocation. So good an opportunity for the police to cause us annoyance was not to be lost, so we were not surprised when the next morning, while waiting for guides who refused to come, the Jemidar, or local inspector of the police, made his appearance, to take down statements, as he said, but also to see if he could not arrange with the chuprasies a little bribery and corruption on his own account. To us personally he was civil in his manner. He intimated that a formal complaint had been made against our men, but gave us as his opinion that there was no case. He then remained about the tents for some time, hoping apparently that we would "square" him, which we in spite of the native doctor commending it to us as a politic move, declined to do. He then went away alone, as he had come, without a witness, but returned in the evening to arrest the two chuprasies and one of our jemidars who had detained the men. The Raja of Jeriah was, we learnt, giving material aid to the opposition; indeed much of the annoyance and insolence we received in the district was due to him and his creatures, despite the fact that the demarcation and exploration of the coal-field was calculated to increase the value of his property one hundred-fold, should it be opened up as was at that time probable. But whether his behaviour was due to ignorance of this, or simply to the satisfaction which many Indian zemindars, and more particularly Bengalis, have in being insolent to Europeans who are not magistrates, and vested with direct authority over them, I cannot say.

January 14th.—We encamped to-day at Jeriah Town. After repeated applications, some supplies were sent to our camp from the Raja's house, the bearers in an insolent way demanding absurdly high prices, which we refused to pay.

During the day our men were brought up from the police-office, where they had been at first taken, and, with handcuffs on their hands, were marched triumphantly in front of our tents. The police were apparently most anxious to induce us to break the peace. At the same time, the native doctor told us that it might still be of use to try a bribe, though he lamented that the great opportunity had been lost when we refused to square the Inspector of Nowagurh, who had drawn up the case, and who in a meaning manner had assured us that nothing would come of it. The following day, while we were away at work, the trial commenced before the Assistant Commissioner, but was not concluded till the next, when the decision was arrived at that the Jemidar was to pay ten rupees or eight days' imprisonment, and each of the chuprasies twenty-five rupees or fifteen days' imprisonment. These fines, considering the position of the men, were extravagant in amount and out of all proportion to the alternative imprisonment.

We paid the fines, and did not take the trouble to ascertain whether an appeal lay, as we had no more time to waste over what had been a very annoying piece of business. What had been actually proved against our men we never learnt; but it could not have been anything really serious, and a fine of reasonable amount which the men would have had to pay themselves, would have acted more effectually than one which was so obviously levelled at our pockets, since it was out of the question that we could submit to the personal inconvenience of having our men imprisoned, with the consequent degradation, even for so short a period. This is the only case of the kind in which any of my servants have ever got into trouble during my travels.

January 18th.—Jeriah.—On the following day, in the course of our work, we came to a large tank where there was a considerable number of ducks. Hughes went round to the north side, while I remained upon the south. The second bird I shot fell into the water near my side; but there being no coolies with me, one from the opposite bank jumped in to bring it out. Since we had come into the duck country of Manbhum it had been an almost daily occurrence to send in a man thus to retrieve birds; and, as the men are generally good swimmers, and, indeed, refuse to enter the water if they are not, it did not seem to us that there was any danger.

The man having got the duck, reached a bordering zone of weeds, about forty yards wide. From the bank where I stood I soon observed that he appeared to be struggling a good deal, but fancied it was only because the weeds were retarding him. Hughes then called to me that the man was drowning, and then, seeing his head go under, I thought that a crocodile had caught him. However, as he appeared again at the surface, it seemed most probable that he had been attacked by cramp. Although a crowd of his fellow villagers had assembled, attracted by the shots, no one volunteered to go in to his aid. So, flinging off my clothes, I made my way through the weeds to the unfortunate man, whose struggles had almost ceased when I reached him. Fearing that he might catch me in such a way as to impede my return to the shore, I swam round him, and caught him by the hair; but soon found that he was too far gone to do anything of the kind, though he still convulsively clutched the duck. With some difficulty I got the apparently inanimate body to the shore; and it was not until I had carried out the directions of the Humane Society that his appearance fully satisfied me that his respiration had been restored. One of my chuprasies had followed me into the water, and helped to lift the man; but among the villagers who came trooping up not one would touch him or even fetch a charpoy to carry him on. It appeared that he was a man of low caste, and these gentry contented themselves with squatting down all round and gazing at him as he lay on the ground. After a long wait, his own family having been called to aid, we were enabled to move him up to the village, where they poured oil into his ears and rubbed his body all over with the same, and then shampooed him with hot cloths. His wife testified her sorrow by tumbling about on the ground in a most extraordinary manner, while his mother, a wizened creature of about four feet high, began to keen in a peculiarly shrill and disagreeable key; but whether her declamations were abusive or merely sorrowful, we could not determine. They refused to take the charpoy into his own house, fearing he might die there, an event they seemed to regard for some reason with very much more horror than the mere fact of his dying.

His pulse indicating a speedy recovery, we proceeded on our way; but not before some of the villagers, who had only acted as spectators throughout, intimated that the occasion was, in their opinion, a suitable one for a general distribution of *backshish* all round. It is but just, however, to the Tikidar, or head man of the village, to say that, on our telling him to send the man when recovered to the tents for a present, he replied, "His life has been saved, what else can he wish for?"

However, the old crone, with some others, visited us in the evening, hoping at once to realise their expectations by saying that he was still very bad; but this statement broke down under cross-examination, and the native doctor, whom we sent to report on his state and carry him a present on the following day, found him walking about and completely recovered. The Tikidar informed the doctor that his brother had pulled *me* out of the weeds on my getting stuck in my efforts to save the man, a statement which, to the best of my belief, had not the faintest foundation, as, besides the chuprasi, I saw no one else in the water. This early mythical addition to the story promised well for the embellishment which the adventure would receive by the time it had become one of the traditions of the village.

The Superintendent of Police arrived at Jeriah during the following day. We at once made a formal complaint regarding the constable at Kheryo, who had obstructed and been insolent to us. We were subsequently informed by the Superintendent that, like many others in the force, the man was an old mutineer and a great scoundrel. He was dismissed from the service, an example which was of no little benefit to us afterwards.

The Superintendent was fully aware of the character of the police in the district, but had some hope of reforming them. He told us that when on his way to join his appointment, he stopped at a police-station and asked for some water. The constables and inspector, who were lolling about, told him to go and look for water for himself, that they were not going to provide him with any. They little knew to whom they were speaking, and did not find out till some days afterwards, when he summoned them up to head-quarters to give an account of themselves.

January 20th.—Jeriah to Rangani.—A short distance from Jeriah we came upon a colony of Mahomedans, of all ages, who were busily engaged in expressing juice from sugar canes.

The process employed was simple and apparently effectual, though, I believe, a considerable per-centage of saccharine matter remains in the refuse, even in the most perfect native mills. The crushing mill used consisted of two horizontal rollers, about six inches in diameter, placed in an upright frame, and revolving with an interval of about one inch. At the alternate ends of these two rollers, on the right of the upper and the left of the lower, there are placed a pair of diagonal spokes, by means of which two men, seated on mounds, and using both hands and feet, produce the revolution. The canes are passed and repassed till reduced to fibre, and the expressed juice is run into a trough, and thence into a vessel placed to receive it. It is then evaporated down in flat iron pans, four to five feet in diameter, into a condition resembling molasses, called *goor*, and from which sugar is prepared. This is sold on the spot at a price higher than that paid for properly refined sugar, made in factories on the European system near Calcutta. I was much struck with the beautiful features of the intelligent-looking and bright-eyed Mussulman children who were busily engaged in munching stray pieces of cane. The civility of the men was pleasant after the surliness of the Hindus.

January 23rd.—Rungani to Nagari.—For some time back I had been picking up naturally-fractured quartz pebbles, with a view to seeing how near they approached the well-known forms of artificially-chipped axes. To-day I came across a stone which was perfectly symmetrical in form, and which I could not but accept as the work of man. This was the first specimen of this form (the so-called palæolithic) which had been found in Bengal. Together with subsequent discoveries of other implements, it will be found alluded to in an Appendix.

January 24th.—Nagari.—At a Hindu temple in the village of Kutras which we passed, a festival was going on which attracted our notice for a few moments. The bodies of three sacrificed kids lay on the ground, and the priests, in return for copper coins, were distributing turmeric to a number of women, who, receiving it in their hands, immediately transferred it to their faces, arms, and legs, and then finished their toilets with a daub of blood on their foreheads. To the children cooked rice was distributed.

In most of these villages there are one or more families of weavers, whose business it is to clothe the inhabitants. The loom is in most respects similiar to the old English hand-looms of a bygone age, all the fittings being of the rudest possible description. The cloth, which is about two feet wide and ten long, is sold for one rupee. It is very much stronger and more durable than

Manchester long-cloth, as ordinarily sent to these parts of India, and is accordingly preferred.

January 25th.—Nagari to Milekerra.—One of the coolies who accompanied us to-day rather astonished us by saying "Yes, sir," in reply to a question. He proved to be a returned cooly from Demerara where, as he expressed it, he had learnt to "Some talk English."

January 26th.—Milekerra.—The customs in vogue in this part of the country, in connection with the getting-up of sham cases, were to-day illustrated by the Doctor's bringing up a man for our inspection, whose back was marked with long black stripes, which had evidently been produced by a hot iron; but, when toned down a little, they were intended to be used as evidence that the man had been beaten by some of the Raja's servants. It is possible, nay, very probable, that the man had actually been beaten; but, as the marks had disappeared, recourse was had to this stratagem in order to influence the magistrate's mind.*

January 29th.—Singra.—Pay-day: I settled with the men their rather complicated accounts, each having received different advances. In doing so I observed, what I have since invariably noticed, that, on the monthly day, when wages are being distributed, the men assume an appearance of woeful dejection and misery which I was never able to account for. The fact of backshish being added to the legitimate wage rarely seems even to dispel the cloud. The commencement of the Mahomedan's fast of Ramzan was, with permission, inaugurated by the discharge of all our fire-arms.

January 30th.—Singra to Tetongabad.—Being close to the banks of the Damuda we went to see some men fishing, whom Hughes had seen last year dive down into a deep hole and bring up fish in their hands. Owing to the river having silted up the hole, I was unable to witness this performance; but I did see a man dive down and drive a number of fish into a small net held

* A work recently published, entitled the "Civilian in Lower Bengal," shows to what lengths Bengalis will go in the concoction of false cases.

by another man. The fishermen brought a number of *Thelphusidæ*, or fresh-water crabs, and some prawn-like crustaceans, which I added to a rapidly-increasing spirit collection. They also brought the larvæ of an enormous cricket-like insect which burrowed to great depths in the sand.

February 1st.—Tetongabad.—About this time we had several days' heavy rain, with violent thunder-storms. The occurrence, in this region, of rain in January, though almost normal, is not without exception in some years. Happening to be passing through Jeriah, when a terrible storm came on, I was compelled to ride to the Raja's house for refuge. Having got to what proved to be the grand entrance, I dismounted and found myself face to face with some of the Raja's horses: for the new entrance chamber, under construction, was in temporary use as a stable. Looking through this apartment, I could see in a court within, the Raja, dressed in a red coat and yellow tights, and playing on a tom-tom; and before I had time to arrange a suitable explanation of the circumstances in my still halting Hindustani, he came out to receive me, but seemed to be in a great fright, thinking apparently that I proposed stopping for the night. He then led the way into a dirty little court where he had been playing the tom-tom. Two chairs were brought out, and we had a rather lame conversation. By way of refreshment some milk and a little sugar on a leaf were brought. He then offered me the use of a Palki, which I accepted, and returned to camp.

February 6th.—Bajourdih.—Just as we were going to bed it was announced to us that one of the Khansamahs having gone in pursuit of a jackal, which had been prowling about the kitchen tent, had fallen and broken his arm. Such we found to be the case; and, as the native doctor was away, we had to extemporise splints out of the top of a packing case. Some days after the man left for his home, and the arm was neglected, and when I saw him a few years later the mend was by no means so clean, nor the arm so straight, as they might have been had he not removed the splints too soon.

February 9th.—In the evening an old man who had been in English service, and to whom a number of the neighbouring villages belonged, paid us a visit. He told us he was 108 years old. I have seen men in India reputed to have attained much greater ages than this, but the difficulty of ascertaining the truth in such cases of longevity renders it impossible to compare them with well authenticated cases in Europe. I do not know it to be a fact, but I should say from my own observation, that Mahomedans more commonly attain to great ages than do Hindus, and that the aborigines rarely reach beyond sixty.

February 10th.—*Belonja to Chas.*—To-day I parted company from my colleague and commenced independent work; my first duty being to map the Ramgurh coal-field, a small area on the Damuda river, detached from the Bokaro field.

February 11th.—*Chas.*—The neighbourhood of Chas has a bad reputation for thieves, and we were advised to keep a sharp look out. I placed a loaded revolver under my pillow at night. I do not remember to have ever done so since. The fact is that revolvers, though considered to be necessary to an Indian outfit, are seldom of much use to their possessors in India, though we are supposed to live there on a dormant volcano, and the time may come when they will be wanted.

February 12th.—*Chas to Araldih.*—After a long morning's walk in the beds of rivers I arrived at my destination, but could hear nothing of my men, nor even of the man who had been sent on the day before. Remembering that I had had in the morning some suspicion that the Jemidar was not quite clear as to the place he was to go to, and hearing from a man that he had been informed that there was a tent at a village to the North bearing a somewhat similar name, I started off for that village, and in order to save time struck straight through the jungle, and so managed unwittingly to pass the elephant on the road. After going seven or eight miles to the village I found that my tent was not there; but, in a neighbouring one, I heard that the elephant had passed by a road a short distance off. At last I found its track, and after a most tedious tramp found my camp at the original village (Araldih) at

8 p.m., and my servants in a state of considerable anxiety for my safety. Had the direct route been taken by the men instead of the circuitous one, the camp would have been up and all ready when I got to the village first, and I should have been saved a fourteen hours' walk without food.

February 14th.—Surjadih to Peturbad.—En route I ascended a hill formed of gneiss, called Durgapur, which is about 1,500 feet high. From the summit there was a magnificent view of the surrounding country, much of it open and park-like, with dark green masses of jungle in the background. One of the guides told me that iron was to be found under a ledge of rock near the top. I fancied that he alluded to the occurence of some form of ironstone, but on going to the spot we found a number of fragments of iron bracelets, much corroded by rust, and evidently of great antiquity. Together with them were some earthen vessels which, for size and shape, might be compared to ordinary porcelain insulators for telegraph wires. At first I thought they might have contained the incinerated remains of bodies, but the contents were not to be distinguished from the clay in which the vessels were embedded. With them I also found a fragment of an earthen lamp of modern shape. When and by whom these objects had been placed in so singular a position I was never able to ascertain, and I am not aware of the existence of any custom or rite at present, among aboriginal or other races, to account for their occurrence.

February 16th.—Peturbad to Hesapura. — Hesapura is a picturesque village belonging to a Brahmin who officiates at a beautifully-situated temple, about a mile off, at the junction of the Bera and Damuda rivers. The view of these rivers and the surrounding jungle from this temple, impressed me as being one of the finest I had yet seen in the country. The cold weather channel of the Damuda is cut to a considerable depth in metamorphic rocks with nearly vertical bedding, and sections shewing considerable varieties of gneiss and schists are exposed. Hard as these rocks are they have numerous pot-holes in them, which have been in some cases excavated to depths of upwards of six feet.

In the bed of the Damuda, after half a mile's scramble over huge masses of the gneiss, the bottom beds of the coal-field, consisting of pebble-conglomerates, and sandstones, were met with. One large mass of the conglomerate measured 16' × 8' × 6' = 768 cubic feet, weighing perhaps about fifty tons, had been carried by the river, when in flood, about 100 yards away from the spot where it had become detached—thus affording a good example of the enormous transporting power of water. This was my first ascertained point on the boundary of the Ramgurh coal-field, the position of which had only been somewhat vaguely known before. My business was to demarcate its limits, ascertain its coal-producing capabilities, and describe its geological features and relations. The coal-field has been described by me in a report published in the Memoirs of the Geological Survey,* from which I shall quote a few general remarks in the next chapter.

February 18th.—After my return from work I had intended to go out with the chowkidar, who was a shikari, to get a shot at some deer, which he declared he could shew me. He came, but had not only loaded his gun but had primed himself with *daru*, or native spirits, to such an extent as to be drunk and incapable. The grinning idiot so exasperated me that I admonished him in a suitable manner.

February 20th.—Hesapura.—A party of Sontals armed with bows and arrows and a few guns, spontaneously offered their services as beaters to-day. About one hundred in all assembled, not a sufficient number for the size of the jungle beaten. This my first beat, like many score I have had since, proved a failure. Though there were indications of there being animals about, none were seen. The Sontals managed to drown their disappointment in the flowing bowls of the villages which we passed through, and came back in the evening in an advanced state of jollity.

February 24th.—Chitturpur.—Some of the villagers suggested

---

* Vol. VI., Art. 4, Calcutta.

that I should visit a cave in a small hill south of Chitturpur, where it was believed wild beasts of some kind dwelt. On going there and seeing the unconcerned manner of the coolies I concluded that they did not believe that there was any animal in the cave. Accordingly, giving my gun to one of the men while I scrambled over the rocks, I was not prepared for a hyæna, which suddenly darted out of the cave close to me and trotted off between the great masses of gneiss. I was the more sorry that I had not been ready for him when I found in the cave, besides other bones, two skulls of human beings. These had possibly been taken from graves of the aborigines, many of whom do not burn their dead; but, as they were of children, it is not improbable that the owners may have been carried off alive.

At this season I found it possible to remain out, on foot if necessary, all day, the interest in the work preventing me from thinking of fatigue; but I was frequently compelled to return to camp, by the fact of those who accompanied me, whether villagers or my own men, becoming quite done up.

My tent at Chitturpur was under a *Pipal* fig tree (*Ficus religiosa*) and was visited during the night by great numbers of the large bats (*Pteropus Edwardsi*), known to Europeans as flying foxes, a very suitable name, as the head is extremely like that of a fox in miniature. By day these animals are to be seen, sometimes to the number of many thousands, suspended by their claws, head downwards, from the tops of tamarinds, mangos, and a few other species of trees which they affect. After sunset they take flight and flap off lazily in the direction of whatever trees happen at that particular season to be in fruit. Two species of *Terminalia*, tamarinds, the poison-nut tree (*Strychnos nux-vomica*), mangos, all the species of figs (*Banyan*, *Pipal*, &c.), the betel nut (*Areca catechu*), a species of *Nauclea*, and some others, afford them a succession of crops of food. On arrival at the tree they flap about and snap and squeal, trying to oust one another from good positions. Among gregarious animals I know of none which are more quarrelsome. Many of them on their return to the roosting place carry with them a fruit in their mouths to eat as a last *bonne bouche.* The rejected stones of such fruits as the betel and the *Strychnos* (from which strychnine is prepared) are in consequence to be found at the foot of trees occupied by bats, and being of value are collected for commercial purposes, so that the possession of a colony of these animals is a source of income; and large ones, in Eastern Bengal, are, I have been informed, rented out at from 20 to 25 rupees per annum; but I am unable personally to vouch for the veracity of this statement.

Some of the lower classes of natives eat these bats and the meat is said to be very good, but they are in many respects very repulsive animals, and I fancy but few Europeans have ever tasted them.

February 25th.—The electrical condition of the atmosphere at this season seemed to me noteworthy, and has been, so far as I can remember, unparalleled in my experience. Long-continued rumblings of thunder were accompanied by lightning of such frequency that at night the total period of illumination seemed more considerable than that of darkness.

The parasitical plants on the jungle trees frequently attracted my notice, and to-day I observed a species of *Viscum*, or mistletoe, parasitical on a *Loranthus*, which was itself parasitical on *Sal* (*Shorea robusta*). A vegetable illustration reminding one of the lines—

> " Big fleas have little fleas upon their backs to bite 'em,
> And little fleas have lesser fleas, and so *ad infinitum.*"

The natives apply the term *banda*, meaning slave, to all parasitical and epiphytical plants, including orchids. As a general rule the *Loranthus* kills all the portion of the branch above its point of attachment.

The effects of the insidious and murderous embrace of the two common species of fig, the banyan and pipal, may frequently be seen. Beginning life often on the branch of a large tree, where a bird has deposited a seed, the young banyan sends down a long root to the earth, and, soon gaining strength, begins to creep round and embrace the trunk of the tree in a manner which cannot fail to suggest a resemblance to the intelligence of animals. Ultimately the tree dies, although for some time it may carry on a joint life with the fig, and so form a compound tree.

March 7th.—Having received news that my colleague was ill with fever, I made a forced march of twenty-six miles to his camp at Jeridih. Owing to floods in the Damuda and several other rivers, this was not accomplished without some difficulty. I found him somewhat recovered. During the night there was a great disturbance in camp, the men saying that two animals—tigers, leopards, or hyænas—had come close to the tents attracted by some goats. On searching for footprints on the following morning we could only find those of a spotted deer, which had evidently stampeded through the camp and been the cause of the alarm. On the following day I returned to my own camp.

March 10th.—The manners and customs of many species of ants had ere this particularly attracted my notice. One species,* which is generally found in the vicinity of mango trees, is of a yellowish-red colour, and has a body about half-an-inch long. Its legs are very long, as also are its jointed antennæ. The jaws are large and powerful, and the black eyes very prominent. It makes its nest in the tops of mango-trees by drawing together the growing leaves and binding them with a kind of silk; the globular masses of leaves so formed being sometimes a foot in diameter.

My tent was pitched to-day under a mango-tree containing some of these nests, and I observed numbers of the ants ascending and descending the trunk. A straw, which happened to be between the tree and one of the pegs of the tent-ropes, served as a bridge, of which both the columns availed themselves. Although individuals occasionally changed from one to the other, still all seemed to have particular objects in view. In both lines ants were seen carrying others as big as themselves,

---

* *Formica smaragdina*, Fabr. So named from the greenish colour of the female. *Vide* Jerdon. "Ann. and Mag. Nat. Hist.," 2nd Series, Vol. XIII. 1854.

which they grasped by their jaws either round the neck or by the interval between the thorax and abdomen. The carried ants packed themselves up into the smallest compass—the legs and antennæ being folded like the legs and wings of a trussed fowl. Whether the bearers were taking out their relatives who were lazy or ill, for an airing, or were holding up prisoners of war to the derision of their kind I could not determine; but I observed that when I released some of the captives, though quite lively, they were generally caught again, and, when caught, made no attempt to escape.

As soon as the column of workers from the tree reached the roof of the tent, they spread themselves about in every direction, but always returned to descend by the same rope. That their object was to procure food was apparent from the fact that in the descending column some, apparently more fortunate in their search than others, were carrying down wings and other fragments of dead insects. One by a little coaxing, I induced to march off with a small fragment of paper. In order to see how they would treat another species, I procured a black soldier ant, with huge head and powerful jaws. As soon as I had placed him on the roof of the tent he seemed to be aware of his danger, and rushing off, fell over the edge into a piece of paper which I held out for the purpose of recapturing him. Again I put him down among the other ants, when, as he was trying to make good his escape, a red fellow rushed at him. Rash individual! A pinch from the big jaws rendered him *hors de combat.* His elevated head and outstretched fore legs indicated as clearly as possible the excruciating pain the bite had caused him. Quick as the movement had been, the black fellow had lost his chance of escape; for four or five red ones caught hold of his legs and pinned him down so that he could not move. Others, seeing there was now no danger, rushed forward valiantly, and soon the prisoner was as tightly fixed as was Gulliver when he awoke in Lilliput. The captors looked like bull terriers as they clung on to the outstretched legs. Shortly afterwards I found that the black soldier was dead; but whether he had died from the violence from stings, or from fright, I could not ascertain. That he was not at once removed to the nest was due to the fact that the numerous claimants were dragging him about in opposite directions.

I afterwards put down some small dead black ants on the roof. One of these was speedily dismembered, and I saw his head, legs, and trunk being carried off in a manner that reminded me of an ancient Dutch picture which represents the cannibals, or reputed cannibals, of the Andaman islands, cutting up and walking off with the limbs of Dutchmen whom they had killed. As the fortunate possessor of the head appeared to experience some difficulty in forcing his way through the crowds between him and the top of the rope, I placed him on it, thus giving him a fair start. By pushing the head right in the faces of the ascending column, he so confused them that they were not able to catch hold of it, though most of them made a passing grab at it. At the same time, he walked so fast that those behind had not a chance of catching hold of it. Another dead black ant which I put upon the roof remained for some time unnoticed. At last he was spied by one of the foragers, who, being alone, approached with all due caution. When about the length of his own body away, he held up one of his fore legs in the uncertain, half-frightened way in which dogs do when they do not know whether to go forward or run away. At last, satisfied that there was no danger, he took possession of the body, which soon afterwards became the centre of a struggling crowd.

On one occasion I observed a number of black ants wending their way through a ploughed field. At a certain point many of them stopped, and it was some little time before I could make out their object in so doing. However, I presently saw that they put their heads down into a hole, and, like terriers with rats, drew forth small termites, or white ants, and having murdered them in cold blood, proceeded on their way.

March 10th.—Milebandi.—My colleague being within reach and having recovered from his illness, we arranged to have a beat together for large game, and for this purpose I joined his camp yesterday, leaving my own at Gopo. At about eight o'clock the beaters and shikaris, with their matchlocks, began dropping in from various quarters, and were soon followed by the Tikidar of Hosir who had made all the arrangements. As the natives, unless driven to it, are generally unwilling to commence anything till they feel perfectly warm, and as it still remains to be discovered by them that there are other ways of making oneself warm, besides sitting down over a pile of embers until the sun has reached a considerable height in the heavens—there is often difficulty in commencing a beat before mid-day. At twelve o'clock then we were told that the beaters were in their places, and we accordingly started for the jungle. We found that a line of *machans* or stands had been erected in trees, the distance between each not being more than thirty yards. In each of these a Shikari was placed, who was prepared to shoot any animal that might appear within range. The place we were to occupy was in the centre of this line. It consisted of a huge and lofty covered cage, made of Sal branches, at an elevation of about ten feet from the ground, and under the shade of a large tree. Its chief quality was that it was a perfectly safe place to occupy; but for quick snap-shooting nothing could be more inconvenient or unsuitable. It had been used by a Raja a short time previously; but his share in the sport had been of a very passive kind, as he spent all his time smoking, leaving it to deputies to do the shooting.

I protested against being penned up in this cage, but was assured that it was directly in the track which the animals would take, and, as the beat was commencing, there was no time for a change. Shortly after we had mounted into the cage the cries of the beaters were wafted to us from a distant point to the south. At length we heard a rustling in the brambles ahead of us, and several spotted deer raced past, one of them falling in response to four or five shots which were fired. The beaters, having come up, then surrounded the jungle to the north, and in a quarter of an hour we heard the tom-toms, followed by shouting, and then several shots were fired, but nothing appeared in front of us. At the close of the beat a leopard and a deer were brought in, which had been shot by two of the matchlock men on foot. The excitement of the man, who was the son of the old Tikidar, at having killed a leopard, was considerable. Over and over again he repeated the particulars to a crowd of admirers, and each time the details received augmentation. A procession being formed, headed by ourselves on an elephant, followed by three natives sitting straddle-wise on a very small elephant belonging to the Tikidar, we made our way back to camp: the carcase of the leopard and two deer slung on poles being borne along in our rear.

March 17th.—Milebandi to Gopo.—To-day I returned to my own camp at Gopo, where I remained for several days in order to trace the geological boundaries in the surrounding country; thence I marched to a village called Punu, where, after a few days more, my examination of the Ramgurh coal-field was completed.

March 28th.—Gumia to Chuti.—To-day I rejoined Hughes. Since I had seen him he had been again very ill with fever and dysentery, and I had been compelled to leave the native doctor Hosein Ali with him altogether, and undertake the treatment of my own invalids myself. The scenery surrounding Chuti is very grand, the Jilunga range being seen to great advantage. And at night the burning grass and undergrowth formed long lines of fire spreading for many miles.

March 29th.—Chuti to Hurolah.—Throughout these pages I shall mention the occasions upon which I have met with examples of albinism among the natives, as the subject may be of interest to some of my readers. The first case I have recorded was that of a man whom I met with to-day. His skin was of a somewhat rusty pink colour, mottled here and there with patches of black. His whole body was covered with a fine down-like, white hair, and the hair of his head was also white. His sight was very defective, and he seemed intellectually to be scarcely removed from an idiot. He was hardly able to comprehend the questions which we put to him.

April 1st.—Silwar to Hazaribagh.—Three marches from

Hurolah brought us into the sudder, or chief station of the district of Hazaribagh, which also bears the same name. From its high elevation above the sea, about 2,000 feet, and from the picturesque nature of its surroundings, Hazaribagh is a popular station, and has become more so since the time of which I write, it having been made on several occasions, during the rainy season, the official residence of the Lieutenant-Governor of Bengal. At this time a whole British regiment was quartered there, so that the houses were all full.

April 2nd.—Hazaribagh.—To-day was a Hindu festival, the precise nature of which I did not ascertain, but it may be worth while to reproduce from my journal what I saw.

At about three a.m. we were disturbed by a tremendous beating of tom-toms, and, as sleep was impossible, we went at about five o'clock to a tank near our camp, which was surrounded on all sides by high embankments—access to the water being effected by wide flights of masonry steps. On each side of these flights one or more men were seated hammering away at tom-toms. The crowd consisted chiefly of women, some of whom were accompanied by their children. They were divided into four tolerably equal divisions, and were, for the most part, attired in bright clothes, scarlet being a prevailing colour. Those who were barren and wished for children had entered the water, and remained standing immersed up to their arm-pits till the sun rose. Many of them brought down baskets containing food, and coloured pieces of cloth, with a small oil lamp burning on the top.

Of the food a small portion was thrown into the tank as an offering; but the bulk of it was carried home again. Some of the worshippers, I noticed, showed their reverence for cows by sprinkling grains of rice on the cow-pads lying on the road. At sun-rise all dispersed to their homes.

In the evening we strolled up to a Hindu temple, and as I had never before closely witnessed any Hindu ceremonial rites, and have never since recorded with equal detail any that I may have subsequently been present at, I shall describe what we observed.

The temple was dedicated to Mahadeva or Shiv the destroyer,

as are most in this part of the country, and indeed throughout Bengal generally, I believe.

As we approached, an assistant priest was engaged in cleaning the interior. In the outer chamber he had prepared a small fire of sticks. In the inner a small lamp was burning, so I entered in order to see what the place was like—my companion, more experienced in such matters, refusing to join me. However, the assistant appeared to have no objection to my entering. The chamber measured about six by eight feet, and was closed in by a dome, or bell-shaped roof. This feature gave a peculiarly rich and sonorous tone to the voices of those who, while praying inside, were listened to by the worshippers outside. Mahadeva was represented by two stone *Lingums*, and also, if I was correctly informed, by a figure in relief on a slab of stone, with the arms akimbo. In the outer chamber was a figure of a bull, Mahadeva's servant, which, however, more nearly resembled a dropsical rhinoceros. In a corner lay a basket containing fragments of flowers, some sugar, three leaf-plates with rice on them, a vessel full of ghi, and leaves wrapping up red and white paint, &c. While I was still inside, the priest arrived, and in a very civil way asked me to come out, as he wanted to make "Puja." Shortly afterwards the individual for whom the preparations were being made, came up. He proved to be the Sheristidar or head clerk of the Deputy-Commissioner's Court. Having divested himself of his coat and placed a chain of beads round his neck, he knelt down in front of the images, and prayed aloud in Sanscrit. The priest, in the meantime, was engaged in washing the images with water from a large brass vessel, and in removing from them the traces of former Pujas. He then adorned them with fresh flowers, and daubed them with the red and white paint, after which leaves full of rice were placed in front of each. All were then fumigated with incense. Up to this time the Sheristidar had been busily engaged in prayer, and the assistant outside in kneading a disgusting-looking compound of ghi, rice, and sugar. The Sheristidar then held a small lamp in front of each of the images successively, and, after sprinkling them with water, gave them some few additional daubs of paint, and proceeded to adorn his own countenance with the same. The priest then emptied the rice from the leaves, and tied it up in a corner of his cloth—I suppose, on the ground that if the images wanted the rice they would have eaten it, but that as they did not, it was as well that he should have the use of it. The Sheristidar now burnt an offering of rice, placing it portion by portion on the fire of sticks. At the same time the priest repeated a prayer, and rubbed his hands together all the while, in a somewhat unconcerned manner. The Sheristidar, as he put the last of the rice on the fire, began shouting out *Bom*, *Bom*, *Bom*, and after he had trotted round the outside of the building, resumed his clothes, and the performance terminated.

We had been standing at the door the whole time, and as the worshippers came out we asked them some questions. The answer to one puzzled me. Having asked what the functions of the bull, or, as I thought it then to be, the rhinoceros, were, the Sheristidar replied, or rather *more Hibernico* asked, "He is made by us, how can he do any work? When he gets eyes and is able to see like us, then he will work." Hearing this, after what we had seen, we might fairly entertain doubts as to whether Hindus do or do not worship graven images. Intellectual and educated Hindus maintain strenuously that they do not, but the lower orders unquestionably, I should say, do worship the thing, *i.e.*, the image, which they regard, *per se*, as holy, and an object of adoration.

April 4th.—Hazaribagh to Holung.—My work for the remainder of the season, was to transfer the geological boundaries of a portion of the Ranigunj coal-field from an old published map to new and recently issued maps, which were topographically correct. To reach this ground I had a journey of about eighty miles. By a cross road from Hazaribagh I marched to Bugodar on the Trunk road. The pilgrims and other passengers on the road again attracted my notice. One of them nearly caused me to commit a breach of the peace. He was seated on a gaily-caparisoned horse, which ambled along, while a pretty-looking girl carrying a bundle on her head, though footsore, had to trot wearily at the horse's heels, I felt very much inclined to make the parties change places. It was probably as well that I did not interfere, as it might have led to unpleasant consequences, and the girl would probably have received chastisement as the result of my knight-errantry.

April 8th.—Topechanci to Pitcadih.—A number of invalid soldiers (Europeans) arrived at the Bungalow just as I was leaving it. They were on their way to the sanitarium at Parisnath. On the road I passed numerous pilgrims, and a European stumping bravely along under an umbrella. The heat was intense during the day.

April 10th.—Pitcadih to Govindpur.—On arrival here I heard of the sudden death, from exposure to the sun, of the engineer who had been my host at Barakar when I was starting on my tour. He was the second or third engineer who had died during the construction of the Barakar bridge, and before it was completed another fell a victim. Owing to difficulties about sinking foundations for the piers and other causes, it was not finished for something like fifteen years after the first stone was laid, and when the traffic, which it was destined to accommodate had, in consequence of the extension of railways, materially diminished.

April 14th.—Sonbad.—I had now commenced work in the portion of the Ranigunj coal-field which lies to the west of the Barakar, and north of the Damuda rivers, where there is a considerable tract occupied by coal-measures.

Two elephants belonging to the Survey, which had been released from other work, joined my camp here, so that I was able to dispense with the carts and carry all my goods on the three elephants.

April 16th.—Pothardih.—At this place, the residence of a Dowager Rani, there was an English school, which I was invited to examine. This I did, but was somewhat disconcerted by the cool and barefaced way in which the master prompted the boys with replies to my questions. One of the boys sent me a petition, the gist of which was that I should pay for all the expenses of his education. I suggested that he should apply to some who knew him, whereupon he replied, in rather high-flown language, that if I, whose fame and greatness had been spread over the country, were to refuse him, it would be useless for him to apply to less important individuals. I was not able to see the force of this argument, and just then had to give my attention to the fact that, in spite of my greatness, supplies were not forthcoming. The rice for the elephants was only obtained by a little fable, which my men have been obliged to have recourse to on many subsequent occasions. It was to the effect that if the elephants did not get their dinners they would die, and that the Government would hold the village responsible for the loss. This way of putting the matter, even when supplies for the men have been altogether refused, has always been effectual in securing the elephants' rations.

April 26th.—Dumurkunda.—To-day was a black day for me, as my horse, which, when I rode him into camp at noon, was apparently quite well, suddenly refused to eat, and by five o'clock was dead. What the cause may have been I could not determine, as the symptoms were not exactly those of colic. Poison suggested itself as a possible explanation, and the fact that I had just dismissed the horse-keeper for incompetence made it not unlikely that some may have been administered. The animal had been a most useful nag, and had never before been out-of-sorts for a day.

April 27th.—Dumurkunda.—The first thing to be done this morning was to remove the carcase of the horse. "A simple matter enough!" the reader may exclaim; but then, perhaps he has not been in India. A number of coolies were brought from the village, not suspecting the nature of the work they were called on to perform. On being requested to catch hold of a rope and help to drag the carcase a few yards off, they flatly refused to do so. Seeing that the arguments of my Jemidar were not prevailing, I had to make use of another argument, which produced the desired effect, and the carcase was thrown into an adjoining field, where a very short time elapsed before it was covered by a struggling crowd of vultures.

During the night, owing to the customary trench having been

imperfectly made round the tent, a heavy shower of rain had flooded the interior, the carpet being two inches under water. Altogether my surroundings were not cheerful, more particularly as I had other troubles, caused by my Jemidar, whom I had detected in various misdemeanours, while he was at the same time systematically robbing me.

During this day I descended some coal-mines at Dumurkunda in which operations were no longer going on. My guides, a number of Bowries, were very anxious to see the works reopened.

April 28th.—Dumurkunda.—This afternoon I watched the antics of the vultures, which still found something to attract them in the remains of my poor horse. Some seventy or eighty occupied a small hill near the carcase, and every now and then they would be joined by others, which, having sated their appetites, would waddle up the incline, and then, with outstretched wings, stand till the process of digestion enabled them to return for another gorge. Their run or waddle has a most ludicrous appearance, resembling that of a gouty old alderman with his hands under his coat tails. Two or three giant storks or adjutants had joined the party to-day; and at night the jackals had their revels. Elsewhere in these pages I shall give my reasons for believing, in opposition to Waterton and some others, that vultures are guided to carcases by sight, and not by smell. I derived a melancholy satisfaction from taking some ball practice at these vultures from my tent-door. The slaughter of some of them did not much disconcert the others.

May 1st.—Nowdiha.—A succession of wet evenings and damp nights, together with exposure to the sun by day, was beginning to tell upon me; and this day I felt certain indications which in later years I should have recognised as the precursors of fever.

As I generally was unable to sleep during the hot afternoons, I used to occupy myself with the identification of plants which I had come across during my morning's work.

May 6th.—Raundi.—To-day I ascended to the summit of Pachete Hill, having failed from weakness to do so on the 4th. Owing to a cap of clouds, which rested on the top, I was unable to get a view, as I had hoped to do. The vegetation on the hill is singularly luxuriant and beautiful, and I found many trees which do not occur in the plains below, and which were quite new to me.

After my return to camp I paid the men their wages, and on the Jemidar presenting his account I had a final row with him. His extortion and lies had gone too far to be borne with any longer, and as he was a bad-tempered man, and was even becoming insolent, I regarded his departure as a riddance. He had taken every advantage of my inexperience, and, even after I had learnt the ways of the country, I found it impossible to control him properly.

May 7th.—To-day the Jemidar left for his home, taking with him, contrary to my wishes, his brother and nephew, who were also in my service. I accordingly refused to pay them the balance of about half a month's pay which remained in my hands, whereupon they used every contrivance to extort it from me; finishing by saying that they owed the Bhisti the amount, and they would leave me to pay the debt to him. To this I simply replied, that if the Bhisti saw fit to pay them their wages he might do so; but that I would not refund him. This checkmated them, for they paid their debt to the Bhisti, and then, after another attempt to make me relent, shouldered their packs and departed; but, while still in hearing, the brother, whom from the loss of one of his eyes we had christened Cyclops, called out, "he is a poor Sahib: I make him a present of seven rupees."

After all this, with the coolest effrontery, the Jemidar presented himself at the commencement of the following season under the impression that I would re-employ him. I need hardly add that I did not do so; but he afterwards found service with a colleague to whom I had related all that had happened, and with him too he turned out very badly. The last I heard of him was that in Bombay, where he had gone for service, he recognised, in the proprietor of a shop in the bazaar, one of the mutineers of 1857, for whose capture a large reward had been offered. Accordingly, he gave evidence against him, with the usual result, that he was regarded with great disfavour in his own country. This confirmed a suspicion, that I had long held, that he himself was an old mutineer.

May 10th.—Barakar.—To-day the fever had fully declared itself, so I went off to the Executive Engineer's house at Barakar for a change; but, after two days' spent there, being no better, I was compelled to determine on an immediate return to Calcutta, and accordingly called in my camp, and broke up my establishment.

Looking back at this, my first experience of Jungle life, it had, on the whole, been far from unpleasant; but, during the last month, the great heat, constant storms, and troubles with the servants, had tended to make me weary of it, and look forward, with some pleasure to a return to Calcutta, for which place, however, I had no great love at that time.

On arrival in Calcutta I was appointed to officiate as curator of the Geological Museum, in addition to my other duties, which chiefly consisted in the preparation of a report and maps on my season's field-work.

I did not succeed in shaking off the fever till October, when I took a trip to Dacca in East Bengal. The voyage by river from Kushtia was very pleasant, and fully re-established my health in time for the next season's field-work.

CHAPTER II.

GENERAL SKETCH OF THE CHUTIA NAGPUR DIVISION. MANBHUM AND HAZARIBAGH.

1865–66.

CHUTIA NAGPUR—HILLS—RIVERS—COMMENCE WORK AT BARAKAR—METAMORPHIC ROCKS—PACHETE HILL—PACHETE RAJA—CHRISTMAS DAY—THORNS AND STINGING PLANTS—CUTCH OR CATECHU—SCARCITY OF HERBACEOUS FLOWERING PLANTS—LITHOLOGICAL STRUCTURE OF ROCKS DETERMINING FORMS OF HILLS—FORMATION OF DOMES AND BOSSES—SCANDENT SHRUB—FEVER—A NOVEL MODE OF FISHING—REVISION OF LAST YEAR'S WORK—HEAVY RAIN—NATIVE ORNAMENTS—HUNDRU GHAG WATERFALL—A GOOD TONIC AFTER FEVER—COMMENCEMENT OF HOT WEATHER—KOL GRAVEYARD—TORCH-WOOD TREE—FALL OF THE LEAVES—NILGAI—MOSQUITOS—THE MHOWA TREE—MEET A BEAR—JUNGLE FIRES—BEAT FOR BEARS—PARIAH DOG—SEPOY OF THE RAMGURH RAJA—BIRD CATCHERS—RAT PURSUED BY SNAKE—LOSE CAMP—SINGHARA NUT—APRIL TEMPERATURE IN TENT—SUFFERINGS OF THE JACKALS—CICADA—WOLVES—MAD HINDU—HAIL STORM—PURULIA—SHOOT A BEAR—GREAT HEAT—TEA AS A PICK-ME-UP—RETURN TO CALCUTTA—RAMGURH COAL-FIELD.

BEFORE commencing the account of this season's work, it will be convenient to give a general physical sketch of that portion of Western Bengal which is included in the Chutia Nagpur Division or Province, since nearly three-fourths of my field seasons have been devoted to the exploration of the different districts into which it is sub-divided. In doing so, I shall quote from what I have already elsewhere published on the subject in connection with a general description of the birds of the Division.*

The total area of Chutia Nagpur is 44,000 square miles, or about the size of England without Wales; or, more nearly, it is 12,000 square miles larger than Ireland. It lies between the 81°.30' and 87°.30' meridians of E. longitude, and the 21°.30' and 25° parallels

---

* "Stray Feathers." Vol. II. Calcutta, 1874.

of N. latitude. It is bounded on the north by the districts of Rewa, Mirzapur, Shahabad, Gya, and Monghyr; on the east by Bardwan, Bankura, and Midnapur; on the south by the following tributary states, belonging to Orissa and the Central Provinces, viz., Mohurbunj, Keonjhar, Bamra, and Raigurh, and the British district of Sambalpur; lastly, on the west it is bounded by Belaspur and Rewa.

Politically, Chutia Nagpur consists of four British districts, namely, Hazaribagh, Lohardugga, Manbhum and Singhbhum, and of seven semi-independent *Gurjat* States, otherwise called tributary *Mehals;* these are Sirguja, Jashpur, Udaipur, Gangpur, Korea, Chang-Bokar and Bonai. In these states the administration of justice is in the hands of the local Rajas, who have magisterial powers conferred on them for the purpose. They report to the Commissioner of the division, who is also Superintendent of the tributary Mehals, and before whom all the more serious cases are tried. The British districts occupy the northern, central, and eastern portion of the division, while the *Gurjat* States are situated in the more inaccessible and hilly country of the west and south.

In this wide tract of country there is naturally a considerable variety of scenery and physical configuration. Even in the flattest portions, it is impossible to find any point from whence hills are not in view: this feature at once strikes the eye of visitors from the dead level plains of lower and Eastern Bengal. The surface in the eastern frontier districts rises somewhat gradually from the level of the alluvium of Burdwan and Midnapur, to a maximum elevation of about 700 feet. Close to the frontier out-crops of rock forming ridges first become apparent; then a few isolated hills dot the plain. A little further west, hills occur in clusters, until at Parisnath we meet the highest peak in the Division. Still further west, spurs which lead up to the high-level plateaus of Lohardugga and Hazaribagh, break up the country into valleys. These plateaus have a general average elevation of about 2,000 feet above the sea. The Lohardugga plateau dies away to the south towards Singhbhum, Gangpur, and Sambalpur, and the Hazaribagh plateau disappears in Palamow and the valley of the Sone river. Towards the west the Lohardugga plateau is separated from central Sirguja by a steppe, or barrier of hills, which rises from 1,000 to 1,600 feet higher; this barrier being connected with a considerable extent of high-level country, which forms remarkable plateaus, locally known as *Pâts.* Of these the Mailan and the Main *Pâts* are the principal. Their general elevation is about 3,600 feet above the sea. Being capped with laterite, and having a very inconsiderable deposit of surface soil, their tops generally present the appearance of open plains with a few scattered bushes, thus contrasting strangely with their densely jungle-clad flanks.

The above enumerated plateaus and hill ranges break the Division up into a number of very distinct rain-basins, or catchment areas, as follows:—In the north-west the tributaries of the Sone, of which the principal are the Koel, Kunhur, Rer and Banas, drain a large area of country. The highlands of Barwa, the Main-Pât and Chang-Bokar, form the water-shed, which separates their sources from those of the rivers which make their way southwards to the Mahanadi and Brahmini rivers.

The next rain-basin to the east of that of the Sone, is one which feeds the Mohur, the Mohani, and other rivers whose waters find their way to the Ganges through the plains of Patna.

On the north-east of this last area, lies the rain-basin of the Damuda, and of its principal tributary, the Barakar. They both take their rise in the highlands of Hazaribagh—in their course traversing that district and a portion of Manbhum. A project was at one time started to store the head waters of these rivers in some enclosed valleys, with the view of checking the inundations which occur from time to time in the Bardwan district, and keeping up a constant supply of water for a canal, which was to connect Ranigunj with the Hugli. These rivers are, however, fed by thousands of torrential streams which, when there is no rain, completely dry up, so that in the hot weather it is no uncommon sight to see the water in the Damuda, just above its junction with the Barakar, reduced to a narrow stream that one can almost jump across without wetting the feet. Supposing then that a sufficient number of these tributaries could be dammed up, so as to produce an appreciable effect in the reduction of the extent of country periodically inundated, it is still very doubtful whether, in seasons of drought or even in ordinary years, such reservoirs could send down over the wide absorbing beds of sand a sufficient supply of water to keep a long canal in constant operation.

The next rain-basin to be enumerated is that of the Dalkissur, which occupies a small area in the central portion of Manbhum. Just outside the limits of the Chutia Nagpur Province the Dalkissur passes the station of Bankura, and in the alluvial plains beyond is joined by the Selye and Rupnarain, ultimately debouching into the Hugli, below Calcutta.

The rain-basin of the Kossai occupies nearly all the southern portion of Manbhum, through which it runs for a distance of about 100 miles. At Midnapur, the Kossai has assumed the proportions of a good-sized river, but even there, I believe, the supply of water falls very short in the hot weather—to such an extent, indeed, as to seriously interfere with the practical usefulness of the irrigation system established in connection with it. The Kossai rises in the Jhulda hills and meets the sea near the mouth of the Hugli.

The Subanrika carries off the waters of the south-east corner of the Division. Rising close to the station of Ranchi in Lohardugga, after some winding about, it settles down to a steady south-east direction, and traverses 150 miles of, for the most part, very picturesque country, much of which I shall have occasion to describe in the course of the following pages. I have followed its bed, step by step, throughout that distance, and would certainly assign to it—the golden-sanded river, as its name imports,—the first rank for beauty among the rivers of Chutia Nagpur. The principal tributaries of the Subanrika are the Korkai, which collects the waters of the Singhbhum basin, and the Karkari.

To the west and south-west of the Subanrika rain-basin lies that of the Brahmini. The principal affluents of the Brahmini are the

Sunk and Koel; its delta coalesces with that of the Mahanadi before reaching the sea. The Koel takes its rise close to the station of Ranchi, and not far from the sources of the Subanrika, while the Sunk rises near the sources of the (Sone) Koel, in Barwa.

The last rain-basin to be mentioned is that of the Mahanadi, some of the tributaries of which drain the south-west corner of the Division. The principal of these tributaries are the Eeb, Mand, and Gej. The Mahanadi, with its gold and diamond-bearing sands, will be described in future pages.

In concluding this brief sketch of the rivers, I would commend what I have said on the subject of the natural deficiencies of the water supply to those who periodically strive to press irrigation schemes on the Indian authorities. The irrigation works in connection with the Kossai, in Midnapur, and the Mahanadi, in Orissa, have, in a great measure, proved failures.

This season's field-work I commenced on the 25th of November, starting from Barakar, the already-mentioned terminus of the branch line. The date was rather later than is usual for the commencement of field operations; but I had been detained in Calcutta, where I had, during the rains, as already mentioned, been officiating as Curator of the Geological Museum. The month of December was spent in the examination of a tract of metamorphic rocks south of the Ranigunj coal-field. During the Christmas week my camp was joined by a visitor from Calcutta, and, together with him, on Christmas Day I explored the ancient temples, ruined fort, and tanks which are found on the southern forest-clad slopes of Pachete. These are the only remains of the town of Pachete, once the abode of Rajas who possessed considerable power, and a wide extent of territory in the district of Purulia or Manbhum. The present descendant of this line of kings lives in a fort in the centre of a small town or village called Kashipur, a few miles further south. He has on various occasions, especially during the Mutiny, shown himself to be a *mauvais sujet*, and not very amenable to the constituted authorities. In recent years his neglect to provide the usual supplies for troops marching through a portion of his district, and his conduct with reference to famine, and other matters, have all shewn the bent of his temperament. Some years ago, when striving for freedom from personal attendance at the magistrate's courts, a privilege granted sometimes by Government to natives of position, and much coveted by them, he for a few months resided in the Sudder station of Purulia, and mixed there with the European officials. But, his point gained, he retired again to his fortress, outside of which he has not, I believe, since been seen.

The scenery surrounding the remains of Pachete, owing to the luxuriance of the forest, is very beautiful, and, though little known, is well worthy of a visit from Calcutta. Mixed up with the general forest there are trees of species which are only found in or near villages, and which, when thus occurring in jungle, infallibly mark the position of former habitations, of which perhaps there may be no other traces. Pachete Hill is to the Ranigunj coal-field what Lagú, described on a previous page, is to the Bokaro coal-field, a remnant of the youngest sedimentary rocks which formerly covered the area. At a distance, the stratification, in spite of the thick covering of jungle, is clearly apparent from the lines which mark the junctions of successive beds. Owing to the large block shape of the hill, it is not well suited for purposes of sport, as it is not within the limits of an ordinary beat; but the Sontals, in their annual chases sometimes manage to kill a few Sambar, pigs, and bear. Ducks and teal are occasionally found on the old tanks, but the amount of game to be obtained is too small to tempt anyone to prolong a stay, the more especially as the locality is feverish.

The only amusement which I could provide for my guest on Christmas Day was a Sontal dance or *nach*, when the women appeared with bunches of white flowers in their raven locks, and otherwise suitably arrayed for the occasion. Like most people of this race, they mustered but little beauty among them.

January 2nd.—Muradih to Satori.—Numerous small hills formed of metamorphic rocks stud the plain in this vicinity. Generally speaking they are thickly covered with thorny jungle, including several species of *Acacia* and *Zizyphus*, which render their ascent a matter of considerable difficulty. To altogether avoid the tearing of hands and clothes by these thorns was quite impossible. Not only, however, did they cause inconvenience, but the barbed seeds of spear-grass, and the hairs on the pods of a species of *Mucuna*, were often the cause of intense and painful irritation.

At this season a particular class of the natives were engaged in preparing the substance called *Koir*, which bears the commercial name of cutch, and is otherwise known as catechu. The chopped heart-wood of *Acacia catechu* Willd. is boiled down in earthen vessels, and the resultant red liquid is subjected to further boiling, and, on arriving at a treacly consistency, is poured into clay moulds or wooden troughs. In some places I have been told that the finer qualities are improved by being buried for some months in the earth. It is an article of great value, and the right to manufacture is farmed out by the Zemindars. It is exported to Europe for dyeing and tanning, and in India it forms, as already stated, one of the constituents of pawn for chewing. It is also employed for various other purposes.

January 6th.—I continued to be disappointed with the scarcity of herbaceous flowering plants; and, few of the trees being at this season in flower, there was little to be done in the botanical line.

January 8th.—*Berú.*—This neighbourhood is remarkable for the singularly picturesque outlines of its hills and for the abundance of bosses and tors of syenitic gneiss. The close connection between the forms of the hills and the lithological characters of the particular rocks composing them is here very remarkably exemplified. The Berú hill abounded in caves, in which there were abundant traces of the presence of porcupines; but I could not get any definite information about bears, though the natives professed themselves to be certain of the existence of four in the neighbourhood. Under the shelter of this hill I was surprised to find a group of cocoa-nut palms, which, though nearly 100 miles inland from the coast, and at an elevation of about 400 feet above the sea, bore fruit, and appeared to be in a thriving condition.

January 12th. — *Notundih.* — In this vicinity I first made acquaintance with a peculiar structure, which I subsequently found to be commonly associated in many far distant parts of the country with a particular variety of coarsely porphyrytic granite,* which includes crystals of orthoclase felspar two inches long, and which, though resembling an igneous rock in many respects, is probably of metamorphic origin. This structure gives rise to the formation of most peculiar-looking flattened bosses and domes, sometimes of circular, but more commonly of elliptical, outlines. The surface of these domes is often perfectly smooth, and, affording no means for the retention of soil, is quite unobscured by vegetation. At first sight a glacialist, on seeing one of these masses of rock, like the upturned hull of a vessel, might be tempted to call them *roches moutonnées*, and to attribute their smooth and often polished surfaces to the well-known action of ice. A close examination, however, reveals the fact that this form is due to a sort of concentric structure, and that the mass consists of a series of shells from four inches to one foot thick. Were the rock really of igneous origin, these systems of spherical jointing might be attributed to shrinkage following on cooling; but since they are sometimes seen where the rock shews a foliation indicative of a metamorphic origin, the explanation is not so simple. I do not remember to have seen a similar structure described in other countries, though I can hardly suppose it to be peculiar to India.

A very common scandent shrub in this country is a species of *Terminalia* (*Combretum decandum*, Roxb.) I frequently noticed, and have placed on record, the snake-like swaying about of its terminal branches in an apparently still atmosphere. At that time Dr. Darwin's researches on climbing plants had not been made,

---

* An apparently similar rock is used for pillars in the gardens of St. Cloud, near Paris.

or at least published; and the probable interpretation of the causes of this remarkable swaying was not known to me.

January 13th.—Murgulda.—To-day I was struck down by fever. A most inconvenient attack thus early in the season. For a week I remained on the sick-list, and was not able to resume regular work till the 22nd, when I had still far from recovered my strength.

January 19th.—Bhagaband.—Yesterday I joined the Superintendent of the Survey, Dr. Oldham, who had come out on a tour of inspection of my work and that of two of my colleagues, in adjoining areas.

We were witnesses to-day of a novel method of fishing a tank —perhaps I should say novel to us, since it is probably an old enough custom with the natives. At right-angles to the bank, at one spot, were ranged a number of bamboo cages with funnel-shaped entrances, like those of a well-known form of rat-trap. These cages measured about 14 × 10 × 4 inches; others being placed at right-angles to those in the first row. A considerable portion of the tank, included between the bank and these two rows of cages was then closed with a moveable wall of weeds. Two men then gradually contracted the space, by pushing this wall in from the outside; driving before them, of course, all the included fish. Many, however, found safety by jumping over the wall of weed, but some, jumping short, fell on it and were speedily transferred to the fishermen's baskets. When the weed was pushed up to the cages the latter were lifted up, and each was found to contain some fish about three inches long, a few sluggish barbed fish like our loach, and some shrimps or fresh-water prawns. The total capture was miserably small compared to the labour; but the fishermen seemed to be satisfied with the result.

February 9th.—Chiturpur.—For this and the two succeeding days we were confined to camp by a steady downpour of rain. At the weekly *hát* or market I bought 5lbs. weight of native brass and pewter jewellery, such as is worn by the women of the Sontal and other tribes. Some of the bracelets were of a shape almost exactly similar to the forms of the well-known gold ornaments which have been found in the bogs and elsewhere in Ireland.

February 12th.—Chiturpur.—To-day being fine we visited the Hundru Ghag water-fall on the Subanrika river, distant about twelve miles. The height of this fall is stated to be about 300 feet; it proved to be an object well worthy of a visit; but almost more beautiful than the fall itself is the view which is obtained from above, of the river winding through cliffs and densely forest-clad banks below. There is not a sign of any human habitation, no villages being situated in this part of the valley, and the wild grandeur of the scene is quite unequalled by that of any of the numerous other falls of smaller dimensions, but in themselves beautiful, which are scattered about through the hilly regions of Chutia Nagpur.

February 15th.—Chutter.—To-day I parted company from my colleagues, and started off on my lonely explorations. Rain continued to interfere much with out-door operations during the next succeeding few days. At this season I found myself often able to remain out for from seven to nine hours, having fully recovered from the weakness consequent on my fever. This recovery I mainly attributed to the good tonic effects of a course of Bass's beer.

March 4th.—Kurma to Bussutpur.—Hearing that my late companions were at the second-named place, I made a very long cross-country ride to visit them. The camp at Bussutpur was in a grove which had in former times been used by the Lurka Kols as a cemetery, and contained a number of ancient stone monuments. The major part of these had a sort of truncate pyramidal shape, and were marked superficially with groovings, which may possibly have some signification; they recalled to my recollection the ancient Ogam inscriptions of Ireland, though not actually similar to them in form. In this neighbourhood too I saw an ancient cross; but regret to say I do not retain any description of it, as I did not, at that time, fully recognise the importance of the symbol occurring otherwise than in connection with the Christian religion. The assumption that it is the exclusive property of

Christianity is clearly unwarranted, however, by certain now well-established facts.*

March 5th.—Returned to my own camp at Kurma. The large yellow blossoms of the torch-wood tree (*Cochlospermum gossypium*, D.C.) constitute a marked feature in certain parts of the jungle at this season. The tree has received its name from the fact that immediately after being cut, when still quite green, the wood burns freely like a prepared torch. With the fall of the leaves, caused by the dryness of the atmosphere at this season, the jungle commences to open out, and the range of possible vision vastly to increase. The first animals I saw, as a consequence of this clearance, were a pair of Nilgai; but the bullet which I sent in their direction was diverted by an intervening twig, as often happens in that kind of shooting, and the animals escaped unharmed.

The warm weather had now fairly commenced, and it brought with it a plentiful supply of mosquitos, from which pest I had been free during the previous months. But, I may here state, that mosquitos do not seem to be so abundant, in even damp places in these jungles, as they are in and near the large cities, where your water-jug furnishes them with the element necessary for the early part of their existence, and from whence, in their fully developed and voracious condition, they rise every night in swarms.

March 19th.—Murpa.—In the neighbourhood of this place the mhowa tree (*Bassia latifolia*, Roxb.) was very abundant. The singularity of the genus, of which this is but one of the species, consists in the fact that not only are the fruits made use of as articles of food, but the fleshy deciduous corollas are likewise largely employed for the same purpose, and, in point of fact, constitute a staple and sometimes almost the only article of diet available to the poorer classes during several months of each year. Towards the end of February or the beginning of March as the crop of

---

* *Vide* Proc. Asiatic Soc. Bengal, 1877, p. 189; and Jour. Asiatic Soc. Bengal, 1877, Vol. XLVI., part ii., p. 179.

mhowa flowers approaches ripeness, the corollas, becoming fleshy and turgid with secreted juices, gradually loosen their adhesion to the calyx, and fall to the ground in a snowy shower. The duty of collecting the fallen blossoms is chiefly performed by women and children; at dawn they may be seen leaving their villages with baskets and a supply of water for the day's use. Before the crop has begun to fall, they take the precaution to burn away the grass and leaves at the foot of the trees, so that none of the blossoms may be hidden when they fall. The gleaners generally remain under the trees all day, alternately sleeping and collecting the crop, and the male members of the family visit the trees once or twice during the day, in order to carry away what has been collected. At night bears, deer, and other animals visit the trees to take their share of the crop. In the early mornings, and late in the evenings, the less frequented trees, on the borders of the jungles, attract numbers of jungle and pea fowl. Cattle also are very fond of the flowers, and cow's milk has in consequence, at this season, a strong flavour of mhowa.

It often happens that the people who collect come from a considerable distance, in which case they erect with the branches of the Sál a temporary encampment of huts, in which they live until the crop is all gathered in. In front of each of these huts a piece of ground is made quite smooth and hard, for the purpose of spreading out the flowers to dry in the sun. When perfectly dry they have a reddish-brown colour, and in size they have lost three-fourths of their original dimensions, and about half their original weight. It is the custom with some of the natives, before spreading them out to dry, to pull off the ring of minute foliaceous lobes which crowns the fleshy corolla. It is very difficult to obtain any trustworthy statements as to the yield of the mhowa trees. A first-class tree, I have been told, will continue to shed its blossoms for fifteen days, at the rate of 120 pounds a day; but this estimate is, I believe, at least double what it ought to be. The rent of the trees varies with the abundance of them in the district, the quality of the previous rice harvest, and various other circumstances affecting the demand and supply. Two-pence to four shillings were the extremes of prices which, in various places, had, I ascertained, been actually paid for permission to collect. As does the rent of the trees, so the saved crop varies much in price—the limits being from 120 to 480 pounds for the rupee or two shillings; but when, as is most frequently the case, the exchange is in kind, the merchants only give a small quantity of salt and six or eight pounds of rice for a maund (80 lbs.) of mhowa. During the famine in Manbhum the price of mhowa averaged about 24 lbs for the rupee.

Two maunds of mhowa are stated by some to furnish a month's food to a family consisting of a father, mother, and three children. It is, however, seldom eaten alone, being mixed with the seeds of the Sal, or with the leaves of jungle plants; sometimes a small quantity of rice is added. It is the custom to cook but once a day, and each member of the family helps himself whenever he feels hungry.

When fresh the mhowa has a sweet taste, with an odour somewhat suggestive of mice; when dried it presents some resemblance to the inferior kinds of figs. Cooking renders it vapid, and utterly devoid of flavour. On distillation the newly-dried flowers yield a highly intoxicating spirit called *daru*, this is generally diluted with from five to ten times its bulk of water, and is then sold at about the rate of a penny for a quart. Its odour is most offensive to Europeans, but British soldiers have been known to secure for themselves the pleasures of intoxication, by drinking it with held noses, as a child takes a nauseous draught. By careful distillation it is possible to get rid of the essential oil which causes the unpleasant flavour. From the seeds a sort of oil is expressed, which is used for cooking purposes and to adulterate ghi. Although the natives protect such mhowa trees as exist, I am not aware that they do anything to increase the number.

March 20th.—Murpa to Juggasur.—To-day, while scrambling along the steep face of a hill, I almost knocked up against a bear, who took himself off very leisurely through the rocks and jungle, while I was beckoning to my chuprasi to bring me my gun. The man seemed glued to the ground with terror, and on my admonishing him for not having hurried up with the gun, he offered an excuse more ingenious than true. He said he was afraid of making haste down the hill for fear he might fall and so injure the valuable weapon. I endeavoured to track up the animal, but failed to see him again, and so lost my first chance of shooting a bear.

At this season the jungle fires served to clear away the undergrowth, and so render movement and vision through the forest more easy, but the absence of shade, and consequently a more direct exposure to the sun, counteracts the benefit to a great extent, and tends to lessen the tale of work which it is possible to accomplish during the day. Some Europeans in India appear to have got an idea that these fires are occasionally due to spontaneous combustion; this view, I need hardly state, is completely erroneous, and altogether without foundation. The lighting the fires is the deliberate act of the people, the principal object being to obtain a fresh crop of herbage for the cattle. The removal of the undergrowth also facilitates transit through the jungle.

March 27th.—Gangpur.—This day, having assembled about 120 Sontals, I tried to beat the hill where I had seen the bear; but, owing to my being badly placed by the man who professed to know the line the animals would take, I saw nothing, though I heard one bear in close proximity, and, according to some accounts, five in all had been seen by the beaters. The hero of the gun incident, above related, came up with his clothes torn, and sundry scratches on his person, and declared that one of the bears had caught him and rent his garments. He was, however, a more cowardly than veracious personage, and I heard from eye-witnesses that the damage had been caused by a fall which he had had when bolting while the bears were still a long way off.

March 29th.—Kusumdih.—A very good specimen of the native pariah dog, which had attached itself to the camp, used to follow me during my daily rambles, which were too long and tiring for my bull-terrier Joe. To-day he routed out of some bushes a wild cat (*Felis chaus*, Guld.) which I shot.

By way of aid in the collection of supplies there was a Sepoy of the Ramgurh Raja's establishment attached to my camp, most of the villages being in the Raja's territory. Several times I had had to warn this man for his misconduct; but to-day I was compelled to dismiss him with ignominy, in consequence of his having gone to a head man of a village and taken some rupees on the promise that he would not requisition him for his quota of supplies. The man paid the money under pressure, and straightway came to me to complain, upon which I compelled the Sepoy to disgorge, and then turned him out of the camp.

March 30th.—Kusumdih.—To-day some bird-catchers brought a number of Pippits and Larks for sale. The method of capture was ingenious. Sheltering themselves under a screen of leaves they would creep to within about thirty feet of where the birds were running about. They would then push forward a series of bamboos which fitted one another like the joints of a fishing-rod, the top one being provided with a prong-like twig, smeared with bird-lime. This, on coming in contact with the bird, would, of course, hold it fast.

April 3rd.—Khoka.—I was much inconvenienced again about this time by a succession of heavy thunderstorms, which rendered work in the rivers particularly troublesome. I had now completed my revision of the Ramgurh coal-field, and set about returning eastwards from the district of Hazaribagh to Manbhum, to continue the examination of the metamorphic rocks there.

April 7th.—Tenú to Barlodih.—As I was riding across the sand in the bed of the Damuda this morning, I observed a rat running along with a very peculiar gait. I was for some moments at a loss to account for the sight, until I saw that it was being pursued by a snake, which descended from the bank and glided rapidly after it. The peculiar gait, which was quite unlike the usual scamper of a rat, I can only describe as a sort of crippled canter.

It was doubtless caused by fear, as it is scarcely possible that the snake had in any way maimed the rat and then let it go again.* I was most anxious to witness the *dénouement;* but the snake, either seeing or hearing me, turned and fled to regain the jungle on the bank; but he was intercepted by one of my men and slaughtered.

April 14th.—Chundra to Sojadih.—To-day a mishap occurred owing to the stupidity of my Jemidar, Madaran Khan. I directed him to take the camp eastwards to the village of Budgaon, instead of which he took it northwards to Bargaon, and thence onwards to a village called Sojadih. The result was, that when I arrived at mid-day at Budgaon, wearied with heat and fatigue, I not only did not find my tent awaiting me, but I did not even know where to look for it. At last, hearing of the existence of the place called Bargaon, I got on the track, and ultimately reached camp at 10 p.m., in a frame of mind that resulted in a tableau, in which the guilty parties in the matter figured conspicuously. I shall not describe that tableau here; but I may say it was one which made an impression on the minds of my followers, since in after years it was more than once alluded to as an era with reference to which the time of occurrence of minor events was calculated. The tramp, which lasted from about six in the morning till ten at night, with but short intervals of rest, proved rather severe on my horse, and altogether too much for the faithful Pariah dog, as, overcome with heat and fatigue in the afternoon, it simply sat down in a tank of water and refused to follow any more. I was quite sorry for the loss of the poor beast.

April 15.—Sojadih.—This was a well-earned day of rest. In the afternoon I for the first time saw the *Singhara* nut, or water-chesnut, which affords in parts of India a not unimportant article of diet. Two of the species, the two and four-spined

* The late Mr. Waterton, however, asserts positively that no snake ever pursues its prey should it fail to capture it at the first dart.

Singharas (*Trapa bispinosa* and *T. quadrispinosa*) occur here. I have frequently seen numbers of people—men, women, and children—groping in half dried-up tanks for *Singhara*, fresh-water snails, and small sluggish fish, which latter are caught by dragging on shore the weed in which they lie concealed. From the produce of a morning's collection of these miscellaneous articles, a dish is cooked which is perhaps the only food upon which a family have to subsist for the day.

From the above, and from what I have said regarding the Mhowa, and the labour which is undergone in order to procure a handful or two of minute fish, the reader may gather some idea of the state of destitution of the lower stratum of the population in these highland districts. Further illustration of this will appear in the course of these pages. Captain Burton, in his work on the lake regions of Central Africa, writes as follows: * "The assertion may startle the reader's preconceived opinions concerning the savage state of Central Africa, and the wretched condition of the slave races, negroid and negro; but it is not less true that the African is, in these regions, superior in comforts, better dressed, and better fed and lodged, and less worked, than the unhappy ryot of British India." Captain Burton is here, doubtless, referring to the ryots of the cultivated tracts; had he taken for comparison the semi-nomadic tribes of the jungles, the contrast would be still more striking. For their normal condition, with their scanty cultivation, reaches a depth of poverty barely removed by the narrowest of margins from absolute destitution. In short, there are in India probably many millions of people whose means of subsistence are almost identical with those of the beasts that inhabit the jungles where they also live. The same wild fruits and leaves furnish the staple food of both. Those whose sympathies are often directed towards the Khedive's subjects—the fellaheen of Egypt—would do well to remember these, their fellow British subjects in India.

* Vol. II., p. 278.

One thing may be pointed out, however, as being in their favour when compared with the cultivating ryots—they are less affected by famines. The jungles produce their ordinary food, whether there is drought or an abundant rain.

April 16th.—Soradih to Poradih.—Under this date I find the following remark on the temperature, which may serve to convey some idea of camp life in the plains in April. "The heat has immensely augmented during the past few days. No more refreshing breezes can be expected. Breezes there are, but O how hot! Everything in the tent feels hot to the touch: chairs, tables, papers, edibles, tumblers, &c." Daily, for a week subsequent to this, the interior temperature of my tent at mid-day averaged 105° F. The jackals seemed to suffer much, and I frequently came upon pairs of them either lying in or sneaking off from water in which they spent most of the day, instead of being hidden away in holes, as they usually are.

April 20th.—Tadgaon.—About this date a species of *Cicada* commences to sing during the heat of the day, sometimes even beginning at sunrise and continuing till sunset. Whether the species has yet been named or not, I cannot say; it is about an inch and a-half long, and of a subdued brownish colour. Taking up a position on the trunk or branches of a Palas tree (*Butea frondosa*, Roxb.) it whirrs away incessantly. So far as I know, it is the only species of cicada found in these jungles, though on the damp slopes of the Himalayas there are possibly hundreds of distinct species of the family to be found. It is said that the male cicada alone sings, and hence the couplet:—

> "Happy the cicadas' lives,
> Since they all have voiceless wives."

April 27th.—Anarah to Bhowridih.—I think the first mad Hindu I had seen belonged to the latter village. He was a Brahmin, and since the death of his wife, two years previously, had been out of his senses. He was perfectly harmless, but spent the whole time I remained at Bhowridih singing close to the camp. I have since observed this propensity of stopping about the habitations of Europeans to be strongly developed among the native mad and idiots. The reason I cannot pretend to explain. Possibly it is akin to that common feature of madness which causes lunatics to believe that they belong to a social rank much higher than their own by birthright, and that they are the fit associates of, if not actually identical with, royalty.

April 28th.—Bhowridih.—There was a heavy fall of hail in the afternoon which served to cool the air. The hailstones were not spherical, as is usually the case, but were either compressed spheres or truncated cones. Of the former, I picked up one over an inch in diameter. There were also some discs which were thicker at the edges than in the centre. One hears in India often of hailstones as large as pigeon's eggs and even cricket balls: regarding such I can only say *non vidi.* I do know of one well authenticated case, however, where an English nurse had her wrist broken with a hailstone when she was, with outstretched hands, endeavouring to protect the heads of her young charges from an unexpected and furious shower of hail.

May 5th.—Chara to Purulia.—To-day I marched into the civil station of Purulia, the geology of the neighbourhood of which I had to examine. The chief amusements of the officials consisted in playing cricket in the evening, hot as it was, and bathing in an embanked reservoir (the so-called Purulia lake), which includes two well-wooded islands, and has no small claim to be considered beautiful.

May 19th.—Bara.—While at work yesterday on a small group of hills, the principal of which is called Sotabi, I met with indubitable evidence of the existence of bears, and accordingly arranged with one Ram Manji, the head of the Sontals, for a beat to-day. At 6 a.m., about a hundred men having been assembled, I rode off to the scene of action. Two *machans* had been erected upon the west side of one of the hills. I took up my position in one of them, the other being occupied by a man called Gopinath Singh, who was armed with an old "Brown Bess," and whom I employed as a sort of shikari to shoot small birds. The beaters had reached the crest of the hill from the opposite side, and were in full view before anything save a hare had made its appearance. Then, however, a fine bear rushed out close to Gopinath Singh, who fired at it and missed, as also did I, firing at long range.

A few moments afterwards I heard a shout directing my attention to something, I could not at first see what, but on turning on my shaky perch I saw a second bear, which must have run close under me and so escaped my sight. I missed him with both barrels, to my great disgust, and the beaters did not take any trouble to conceal their opinion that I had made a mess of it. However, I felt pretty certain that the bad shooting was due to my constrained and rickety position rather than to any fault of my own; so, as both bears had sought refuge in another of the hills, I took up my position at the foot of it, under the shelter of a tree, and sent the men round to beat back towards the first hill. Soon after the shouting and tom-toming had commenced the larger bear again appeared as before close to Gopinath Singh, who fired at it but missed, without my catching sight of it at all. Shortly afterwards, however, I heard a rustling in the bushes in front of me, and as I prepared to receive a charge, out galloped bear number two, who passed close to me, receiving a broadside from both barrels, which tumbled him over dead. Then advanced two Sontals cautiously to the carcase, and before I could stop them, or knew what they were about, one nearly sliced off the nose with his battle-axe, and the other stuck his spear into the back, thereby seriously injuring the skin as a trophy, while at the same time they made most insulting remarks about the bear's relations and ancestry.

Again we beat the first hill and the larger bear came down close to me; but, unfortunately, a crowd of spectators I had not previously noticed were in the line of fire on the other side, and I was afraid to shoot, though I had an otherwise excellent chance of killing him too. The beaters were now hot and thirsty, so we returned to camp, where I gave them a decoction, consisting of a bottle of brandy, a bottle of sherry, and *aqua quantum suff;* each man received his portion in a cup made of leaves, but from their faces I concluded that the dilution of the spirit did not meet with their full approval. Having received the usual copper coins, amounting to about two-pence per man, they departed. I have given the incidents of this my first successful interview with bruin in more detail than perhaps the subject deserves; but everyone who has shot large game must look back to the time when he killed his first large beast with a certain degree of satisfaction.

May 21st.—Barah to Kalidah.—The heat had by this time become so great that, when on foot, I used to be often quite exhausted by nine o'clock; and even on horseback the sense of extreme fatigue and exhaustion prevented any detailed work of real value being done after that hour. Often it took me several hours to recover in any degree from the condition of prostration I used to find myself in on return to camp. Libations of the hottest tea I have always found to afford the most effectual means for restoration; but they are apt to produce a nervous irritability which is especially troublesome in the hot and weary afternoons, quite preventing sleep. I have, however, no hesitation in commending hot tea in moderate amount as the most useful "pick-me-up" after hard exertion in the sun.

May 26th.—Dhukera to Ranigunj.—To-day I marched into Ranigunj; and was fully prepared to enjoy the comforts of civilized life and friendly intercourse with my acquaintances. On the last day of the month I returned to Calcutta, from which I had been absent on this tour since the 25th of November.

The Ramgurh coal-field, the revision of the geology of which had occupied a portion of this season, occupies a part of the valley of the Damuda river, within the limits of the district of Hazaribagh. The total area does not exceed forty square miles. From its position it is not likely ever to be of much importance as a source of fuel. It includes four distinct groups of sedimentary rocks, one of which only is coal-bearing. The seams in the eastern portion of the field are often thick, but the quality is very variable. In the west the coal is of better quality, and some of the seams are of workable thickness; but the areas they occupy are small, and they are much cut up by faults.*

The crystalline or metamorphic rocks, which were also examined during this season, I shall not here further describe, as they were singularly devoid of features of general interest.

---

* For description of this field, *vide* "Mem. Geol. Surv. India." Vol. VI., p. 109.

CHAPTER III.

MANBHUM.

1866-67.

START FOR RANIGUNJ — ACCOMPANIED BY A NEW COLLEAGUE — CAMP AT SEARSOLE — FAMINE WAIFS — MARCH SOUTH — NATURE OF WORK —SUSINIA HILL—GAME ON HILL—BANKURA—VEGETABLE MATRIMONY—REPTILIAN FOSSILS—MERGANSERS—HYÆNAS AND BEARS—SONTAL SACRIFICIAL OFFERING—CHRISTMAS FESTIVITIES—DR. KURZ ARRIVES—A BEAR IN THE SUGAR CANES—ADJUTANTS—GEOLOGY BECOMES DIVERSIFIED—GOLD AND IRON—CAVE ON KHATRA HILL—POT-STONES—THE BENGAL POLICE AGAIN — KOSSAI RIVER—CREEPERS — TRACKS OF WILD ELEPHANTS — ADVENTURE WITH A BEAR, TAKE THE CUB—"GOLD MINE"—RATS AS AN ARTICLE OF FOOD—GOLD WASHERS—"COAL," IRON, AND COPPER—THE KERIAHS—BARE FEET—A SPECIES OF WILLOW—THE KURMIS—A STANDARD OF RESPECTABILITY—MY COLLEAGUE BECOMES TOO ILL FOR FIELD-WORK —WOLVES—COW KILLED BY LEOPARD—SIT UP OVER CARCASE—THE CRY OF THE JACKALS — ELEPHANT IN DANGER — JHULDA — DOME AND CONE SHAPED HILLS—NATIVE CHRISTIANS—ALBINOS—FOOD OF BIRDS—BROKEN WEATHER AND FEVER—JUNGLE PRODUCTS USED AS ARTICLES OF FOOD—WOUNDED BEAR GOES MAD—SHOOT A BEAR WHICH HAD ATTACKED ONE OF MY MEN, FAIL TO CAPTURE CUB—CURIOUS INSTINCT OF CUB—RETURN TO CALCUTTA.

I LEFT Calcutta for Ranigunj, on the 8th of November, to commence my third season's field-work. On this occasion I was accompanied by a colleague, M. H. Ormsby, who had recently joined the Geological Survey, and who had to pass through a preliminary experience of camp life similar to that which I had myself undergone in my first tour. The work to be accomplished during the season consisted in the continuation of the Geological exploration of the district of Manbhum, of which about four thousand square miles still remained to be examined and mapped. Our camps had been already formed at a place called Searsole, where I had sent the men and tents. Crossing the Damuda south of Ranigunj, we first marched to Medjia, a village situated in close proximity to a large Jheel, or lake, on which, at times, a considerable variety of waterfowl were to be seen. In this neighbourhood our examination of the metamorphic rocks, beyond the limits of the coal-field, at once commenced.

While we were still encamped at Searsole, we were daily surrounded by sights of the most harrowing description, in connection with the assemblage there of hundreds of homeless waifs, the last victims of the great famine of 1866, better known as the Orissa famine. Large numbers of those who arrived there had deferred leaving their homes till too late, and were too far gone to be saved by any attention they were likely to receive, either at the relief-houses established by the Government, or at the one belonging to the wealthy native colliery proprietors at Searsole. They came in only to drop and expire, and increase the number of skeletons which, in a field close by, constituted a *Golgotha*. Deeply imprinted on my memory is the recollection of the ravenous, parchment-like faces of some of those who were daily assembled to receive their dole of boiled rice and *kunji* water. The number of inexpressibly miserable, silent, seldom begging, candidates for aid, and their often scarcely human physiognomies tended, I afterwards thought, to render us callous, and I fear we did not do all that we might have done to ameliorate the distress. This was, perhaps, partly due to the local civil officer deprecating indiscriminate charity; there being, he asserted, ample provision at the relief-houses. But for suitable medical treatment and regimen for the vast number of cases requiring them, there was certainly a deficiency in the arrangements. I write, not in condemnation of the officials, nor of the Government, knowing full well that no possible agency can be applied with complete efficiency to these wide tracts of India, when stricken by a real famine. The physical difficulties; the corruption, laziness, and indifference of any native agency that can be employed, and the difficulties arising from caste and various social customs, must always tend to interfere with the accomplishment of the designs of those whose business it may be to organize the relief.

For some weeks subsequently we not unfrequently came upon

the corpses of those who had fallen by the way. On several occasions also I most unexpectedly found bodies of those who had, so to speak, fallen out of the way; the miserable creatures having evidently dragged themselves, with their waning efforts, into the jungle, where they could breathe forth their last breath unexposed to the view of passers by. Soon the ripening crops afforded the survivors occasional stolen handsful of grain, which enabled them to travel back to their former homes.

November 22nd.—Susinia.—On this date we reached and encamped in the neighbourhood of the Susinia Hill, a remarkable-looking block of quartzite and granulit about 1,440 feet above the sea, or 1,100 feet above the surrounding country. The hill is an object familiar to travellers between Ranigunj and the Civil Station of Bankura. For many years it had been the site of quarrying operations by the so-called Burdwan Paving-Stone Company, and much material had thence been forwarded to Calcutta in former years; but latterly the use of artificial stone prepared at first by a French company, and subsequently, I believe, by the Calcutta Municipality, together with increased facilities for bringing down the more easily dressed Chunar stone, have almost, if not entirely, extinguished this Company.

On the north-east and south-west corners of the hill there are springs to which, in periods of drought, animals are compelled to resort, and watchers at night over them have thus been enabled to kill many animals. The resident manager of the works, an old Armenian, told me that he had, in the space of a few years, shot forty bears on the hill, besides other animals. Owing to the occasional visits of leopards, which did not hesitate at times to prowl through the verandah of the house, it was impossible to keep dogs here, and just before our visit one of the manager's pigs had been carried off bodily from its sty.

November 30th.—Bankura.—On this date we marched into the station of Bankura, a picturesque little town on the banks of the Dalkissur river. Much of its beauty was due to the way in which the principal roads had been planted with teak and other trees by a former resident.

December 18th.—Pabra.—In this vicinity there were some fine examples of vegetable matrimony between *Tal* palms (*Borassus flabelliformis*, Linn.) and certain species of fig, which latter clasp round the tall cylindrical stems of the palms in the manner which I have already described in the first chapter.

TAL PALMS AND FIGS AT PABRA.

December 21st.—Deoli.—Being in the vicinity, I paid a visit to this, the classic ground in Bengal, for certain reptilian and batrachian remains, which have been described by Professor Huxley.* While busy searching for the fossils, of which I obtained a large number, I observed a flock of mergansers† feeding in the Damuda river close by. They would first fly down stream for some distance, and then dive and swim back against the current. At a given moment all would disappear together, and then, after traversing some yards, would bob

* "Palæontologia Indica," Ser. IV., pt. I.

† *Mergus castor*, Linn.

up at the surface one after another. By diving against the current they no doubt found it easy to intercept the small fish drifting down with the stream. These birds I have always found to be exceedingly wary, and have shot but few of them; and, when successful, was so only because the ground admitted of a stalk within range. They are only winter visitants to these regions; their breeding places being in Central Asia.

December 24th. — Udaipur. — To-day we rode over in the morning to a village called Behari, at the foot of Beharinath Hill, to enquire about some bears said to be in that neighbourhood. We found that they were in the habit of coming to a banyan fig-tree in the evenings, and of occasionally amusing themselves by hunting the natives, one of whom told us that a few days before, he had been chased and had taken refuge in a tank, having had to wade out till the water was up to his neck, in order to escape.

In the afternoon we beat the Garangi Hill, which proved unproductive. The Sontal beaters did not expect anything, owing to the omission to provide a fowl for a votive sacrifice. In the absence of a fowl the Sontal chief or Manji did what he considered to be next best in efficacy. Placing a few grains of rice on a leaf in front of him, he proceeded to draw blood with a thorn from various parts of his person, commencing with his left great toe and proceeding upwards to the ear. As each drop of blood was squeezed out, it was received on a grain of rice, and the whole, when thus prepared, was placed as an offering to the Guardian Spirit of the Hill. Our seeing nothing in the beat was, I have no doubt, attributed to neglect of what these Sontals regarded as as an essential preliminary—the sacrifice of a fowl.

December 25th.—Udaipur.—The only Christmas festivities we indulged in were Sontal *naches* round a blazing log fire, during the progress of which a well-known Indian botanist, the late Dr. Sulpiz Kurz arrived. He had come up from Calcutta to spend a few days with me, in order that he might examine the flora.

We had hardly settled in bed when news was brought in that a bear was committing havoc in a sugar-cane field about a mile off.

In the hurry of preparation my bearer supplied me with a flask of coarse rifle-powder, with which I loaded my gun. On approaching the field quietly, we could hear bruin tearing down the canes and munching them up with great rapidity. Ormsby and I having taken up positions at two of the probable points of exit, we sent a man round to drive. After a few stones had been thrown, out walked the bear close to the tree where I was standing. Snap, snap went two misfires, instead of the broadside I had intended for him, and off he bolted unscathed into the darkness. Owing to my having made use of the coarse rifle-powder, I lost the best chance of successful night shooting I have ever had.

During the next few days Dr. Kurz accompanied me during my day's work, and collected several plants hitherto unrecorded as occurring in Bengal. These were chiefly small herbaceous species which he found in the moist paddy fields. Like everyone else, he was much astonished at the dryness of these jungles and the absence of that tropical luxuriance which one would expect to find in this latitude.

January 2nd.—Cherudih.—In this neighbourhood we found a colony of the Giant Stork or Adjutant breeding in trees. Unfortunately at that time I had not taken up the study of ornithology regularly, and am not quite sure which of the two species it was that had the nests. Both species were occasionally met with. Their nidification, though one of them (*Leptoptilos argala*) is so common in Calcutta at non-breeding seasons, is still very imperfectly known.

From the villagers and my servants I picked up some curious superstitious beliefs regarding adjutants. It is stated that in the pouch-like throat appendages of the older birds, the fang of a snake is sometimes to be found. This, if rubbed above the place where a poisonous snake has bitten a man, is supposed to prevent the venom spreading to the vital parts of the body. Again, it is believed that a so-called "snake-stone" is contained within the head of the adjutant. This, if applied to a snake bite, attaches itself to the punctures, and extracts all the venom. When it has done so efficiently, but not before, it falls off.

Specimens are said to be rare, since it requires a great deal of skill on the part of the Shikari to obtain it; for, should the bill touch the ground when the bird falls struck by shot or arrow, the stone is said to dissolve or disappear. When this contingency is avoided, it may be taken out of the head, and is at once ready for use. To remove the poison which the stone has absorbed from the wound, it is only necessary to steep it for a short time in milk, which becomes black. In size the stone is about equal to half the top joint of one's little finger. Its colour is black, and its weight equal to a two anna piece. My informant told me that he possessed one of them, which had been the means of saving the lives of two members of his family. He procured it from Balasore.

There is still another use made of the adjutant by native quacks. A small portion of its flesh is administered to be chewed daily with pawn in cases of incipient leprosy; this it is said, will effectively drive the disease out of the system.

January 3rd.—Cherudih to Selanpur.—By zig-zag marches, covering a wide tract of country in which metamorphic rocks alone occur, we gradually pushed our work of exploration from day to day towards the south-east corner of the district of Manbhum. In some places we met with tracks of leopards and tigers, and near the rocky hills, torn up ant-hills and deep holes in the ground testified to the presence of bears. From the people it was seldom possible to get any trustworthy information regarding the haunts of these animals, and having no spare time, we were obliged to limit our sport to what the tanks, which were often covered with duck, could afford.

January 10th.—Supur.—On our arrival in this neighbourhood, we found to our delight that we had come into an area where quite a new series of rocks awaited examination. The everlasting monotony of the gneiss and other metamorphic rocks of the country further northward and south of the Ranigunj coal-field, was about to give place to some very interesting geology. The new series belonged to a formation to which in India the term *sub*-metamorphic has been applied, as indicating the fact that the lithological characters of the rocks denote a less alteration of the structure of the materials forming the original sedimentary beds than is to be found in the crystalline or metamorphic rocks proper.

Instead of gneisses of more or less granitic character, with mica, schists, &c., which characterise the metamorphic series—the principal rocks of the sub-metamorphic series consisted of quartzites, chloritic and other varieties of magnesian schists, and hornblendic rocks. We soon obtained abundant evidence that these rocks belonged to a younger unconformable series resting on the metamorphic series. This the less metamorphic structure in itself led us to anticipate would prove to be the case. Analogy, and the experience gained in other countries besides India, led us further to anticipate that these rocks would prove also to be more prominently metalliferous than the older series. The event proved the correctness of this expectation. Rumours of the occurence of gold were met with everywhere, and iron ores, both magnetic and red and brown hæmatites, the latter along the line of fractured junction between the two series, were discovered forming deposits of exceptional richness and abundance. Further south, in the adjoining district of Singhbhum, copper and manganese ores were found, as I shall describe in a future page.

January 11th.—Supur to Dumria.—Before setting off on our work we ascended a large hill near the village of Khatra, to visit some caves near its summit, which were said to harbour wild animals. While standing at the mouth of the largest cave, which, from the bones lying about, had all the appearance of being occupied by hyænas, if not leopards, a strange and weird sound, which issued from the inmost recesses, puzzled me a good deal. At last I guessed it to be caused by bats flapping their wings as they hung suspended from the roof. This proved to be the case, and on throwing in some stones several flew out. While we stood there a large wood owl (*Ascalaphia Bengalensis*) eyed us from a tree on one side, while a group of monkeys on the other manifested considerable interest in our proceedings.

January 12th.—Dumria to Khatra.—In addition to the metalliferous ores above mentioned, the rocks of the sub-metamorphic series contain other mineral products of economic value. The principal of these are several varieties of pot-stones and impure soap-stones. These are in many places quarried and manufactured into plates and bowls, which are apparently preferred by the Hindus to vessels of pottery, and large quantities of these articles are despatched from Manbhum to Burdwan, and thence to Calcutta. In the Ranigunj coal-field similar platters are manufactured from a fine sandstone, but these are less highly esteemed. The natives have found out that the vessels made of certain varieties of these pot-stones will stand heat, and these are of course more valued than those which crack on being placed upon the fire.*

In the afternoon a crowd of people was seen advancing from the village towards the tent. Some of the servants supposing it was the Raja of Khatra, an impoverished Zemindar in the clutches of the money-lenders, placed a seat at the door of the tent; upon which I, in my innocence, invited the individual, without making any enquiry, to seat himself. After I had spoken to the man for some time, supposing him to be the Raja's brother, I dismissed him, and then found out that I had been giving a reception to none other than the head constable, in plain clothes, of the neighbouring police-station. Having thus been given a seat in my presence, and treated with courtesy, though I caused it to be communicated to him that it was under a mistake, his subsequent conduct was characteristic of the true Bengali: he showed not the least attention to our requisitions, and obstructed our servants in every way, the result being that I had to report him to his Superintendent, and afterwards received information that he had been fined. Though the source of no little annoyance to us, he also afforded us some amusement. Among other ways of showing his independence he rode close past the tent on a led pony. The pony

---

* The explanation of this is probably that the principal component magnesian mineral in the frangible varieties includes water in combination.

being let go for a moment kicked up its heels and deposited him on the ground in a most undignified position.

January 16th.—Rodara to Ranga.—The latter portion of this day's work lay through the finest jungle I had yet seen. It was more like a primeval forest than any I had before encountered. The large creepers (*Butea superba* and *Bauhinia Vahlii*) were developed on a magnificent scale. Some were of great length, and formed tangled arches stretching from top to top of the highest trees. In this forest I met for the first time with tracks of wild elephants, and was told that the elephants visit this part of the country in November, and do much damage to the rice crops in the neighbouring cultivated tracts. When they are discovered to be in the fields at night the inhabitants turn out *en masse*, and by means of drums and torches frighten them away.

January 18th.—Ranga to Kudum.—To-day, hearing of a new locality for gold, I went to visit it, and was pointed out a dried-up stream, where the people told me that the professional gold-washers, a tribe called Dohras, or Dokras, were in the habit of washing for gold during the rains. I was then informed that a bear had taken up its residence in a patch of jungle in the immediate vicinity of the village, and was a cause of terror to all around, as it used to charge out on passers-by, and prevent wood-cutters going into the jungle. I went to the spot indicated, and was just thinking the whole story to be a myth, when out charged the bear close to me, but an intervening bush made me reserve my fire for a more favourable opportunity, which never arrived, as the beast disappeared like a flash. I had been advised by a friend when charged by a bear to allow it to rise on its hind legs, and so expose its chest, before I fired. I had done so on this occasion; but the advice is not good, as though I have seen bears rise in that manner the cases have been exceptional.

Descending into a dried-up stream-bed to look for the animals' lair, I found it in the side of the bank, and inside the hollow was a very young cub, which I secured. Being about nine miles away from camp, I did not care to wait for the chance of shooting the old bear on its return at night. In its flight it had crossed some ground where it had given chase to a herd in charge of cattle, but had not caught him. I subsequently, some days later, sent to know if it had returned, but was told that it had deserted the place.

The cub was taken care of by the men, who spoon-fed it for some weeks, till it was able to take care of itself. It became a great pet, and was taken by my Jemidar, to whom I gave it, to his own country, where, on its becoming somewhat unmanageable and savage, he sold it to a professional bear-tamer.

On the map of this neighbourhood the words "Gold Mine" were inserted, and on the spot was an old excavation, from an examination of which nothing could be learnt. The natives had some rather vague and not very intelligible tradition about certain gold and silver figures of bulls having been found there. During the rainy season gold is here washed from surface scrapings taken from the roads close by.

The Sontals, and some others of the Kolarian tribes, in hard times like the present, are enabled to procure a means of subsistence by digging out rats from their holes in the embankments of the paddy-fields. These they eat, and often cook with this flesh-meat the rat's hoard of grain, which is said to amount sometimes to five or six pounds' weight.

January 21st.—Kudum.—With the assistance of a Dohra or professional gold-washer, we washed for gold in the Tutko river, and were all so far successful that we obtained visible specks of the precious metal. The implements used by the Dohra were a wooden dish hollowed towards the centre, measuring about three feet by two, and resembling an exceptionally broad butcher-boy's tray, and an iron hook fixed in a handle. With the latter he scraped together the sand and pebbles into the former, which he then placed in the water, kneading the contents with his hands and oscillating the dish to and fro till all the larger pebbles and light silt having been removed, some black sand, with a few scattered specks of gold alone remained. These specks being picked out the black sand was thrown away, these people not understanding the use of mercury to collect the very minute and invisible portions.

January 23rd.—Gowalpara.—On the map upon which we were laying down our geological lines the word "Coal," in large letters near this village, had for a long time attracted our notice, and though we had good reasons for supposing it to be very improbable that any coal-measure rocks existed in this part of the country, we were not without considerable curiosity as to what could have given rise to the idea, and caused the surveyor to write coal on his map. On arrival at the spot we found a quantity of both red and brown hæmatite or iron ore, forming a lode along the line of fractured junction of the two series of rocks; but not a trace of coal, or, indeed, of any sedimentary rock. Close by there was an old worked-out vein of copper ore, which had been long deserted, and of which we failed to obtain any history. Some fragments of malachite, &c., served to indicate what ore the excavation had been made for.

January 28th.—Satsule to Mussgarah.—While exploring the Jolhari hills, I came upon the huts of a wild race of people called Keriahs, whom I had not met with before. The following account embodies my enquiries regarding their habits and customs, made on some subsequent interviews as well as on the present one; but it may be appropriately inserted here:—

In the special Ethnological number of the Asiatic Society's Journal, Colonel Dalton has given an account of the Keriahs. He says that they are most nearly allied to the leaf-clad Juangas or Putoons, both forming branches of the Munda family.* They are quite distinct from the Korewahs, another branch of the same family. A few colonies of this last mentioned race are, I believe, to be found in Manbhum. They will be described in a future chapter.

* In Vol. XI., p. 203 of the Journal, Lieut. Tickell described a race called Bendkars of Keonjur. They did not know of any relationship existing between themselves and the Keriahs, but they are, in many respects, a similar race, living in the same kind of houses on hill tops, and deriving their principal subsistence from the same kinds of roots and fruits.

The position of the Keriahs having been thus established on the best authority, it is unnecessary for me to allude to it further; my simple object being, in connection with my discoveries of stone implements in Chutia Nagpur, to draw attention to a race who owe to their Aryan conquerors what little traces of civilization are observable amongst them. I have had singular opportunities of seeing the Keriahs in their homes, in the recesses of the jungle, where they live shut out and hidden from the surrounding world. If we are disposed to regard these people as savages, their Sontal and Bhumiz neighbours do not treat them much better, *ban mánus* (Jungle-man or monkey) being a term commonly applied to them.

The Keriahs show a marked dislike for civilization, constantly leaving places where they have any reason for supposing that they are overlooked. Their houses, generally not more than two or three together, are situated on the sides or tops of the highest hills; they stand in small clearances; a crop of Indian corn and millet being sown between the fallen and charred trunks of trees. Close to the south boundary of Manbhum, there are a succession of hill ranges, of which Dulma (3,047ft.), the rival of Parisnath, is the highest point. On this hill I saw three or four neat little Keriah cottages made of wattled bamboo, which, together with a small standing crop of millet, had been deserted. Further west, just outside the boundary of Manbhum on a plateau formed of trap, where there was a good water supply, the small Keriah villages had assumed a somewhat permanent appearance. Occasionally Keriah cottages are to be seen on the outskirts of villages; but this is a departure from what is one of the most characteristic customs of the race.

Besides the Keriahs, there is another race called *Paharias*, of somewhat similar habits, living on Dulma hill range. One of them told me that the people of his race were superior to the Keriahs, with whom they could neither eat nor drink. One of the chief distinctions between them appeared to be that the Keriahs do not eat the flesh of sheep, and may not even use a woollen rug. It would be exceedingly interesting if this custom could be traced to its origin;* I do not remember to have seen it stated of any other race. In other respects the Keriahs are not over-fastidious feeders. Both races eat cattle that have been killed by wild animals, and very possibly too those that have died from disease.

The first Keriahs I met with were encamped in the jungle at the foot of some hills. The hut was rudely made of a few Sal branches, its occupants being one man, an old and two young women, besides three or four children. At the time of my visit, they were taking their morning meal, and as they regarded my presence with the utmost indifference, without even turning round or ceasing from their occupations, I remained for some time watching them. They had evidently recently captured some small animal, but what it was, as they had evidently eaten the skin, I could not ascertain. As I looked on, the old woman distributed to the others, on plates of Sal leaves, what appeared to be the entrails of the animal, and wrapping up her own portion beween a couple of leaves, threw it on the fire, in order to give it a very primitive cooking.

With regard to their ordinary food, the Keriahs chiefly depend upon the jungle for a supply of fruits, leaves, and roots. I got them to collect for me specimens of the principal species they used. In addition to these, however, the Keriahs eat rice, which they obtain in the villages in exchange for several jungle products, such as honey, lac, *dhona* from the Sal, *tusser* cocoons, Sal leaves, and bundles of bamboo slips called *khúrki*, wherewith the leaves are stitched into plates. That the rice which they thus obtain in exchange, though small in amount, forms an important portion of their daily food seems apparent from the fact that a large number of them are said to have died in the 1866 famine. I can only explain this by supposing that they lost heart on being deprived of what had been a regular source of supply, and failed to exert themselves

* Since the above was first written I have had reason to believe that the sheep is the "totem" of the particular clan I met with.

in the collection of an extra quantity of roots. An explanation somewhat similar to this was given to me by a Sontal, who said, speaking of his own race, that those who underwent the labour of searching the jungles escaped, while those who sat in their houses wishing for better times, as a matter of course, died. The roots which they obtain in the jungle are dug up with considerable labour from the rocky ground, by means of an instrument consisting of an iron spike, firmly fixed in a wooden handle. The point of this frequently becomes blunted, when to avoid the necessity of taking it to be sharpened, perhaps half-a-dozen miles to the nearest blacksmith, the Keriahs have invented for themselves a forge, the blast for which is produced by a pair of bellows of the most primitive construction. They consist of a pair of conical caps about eighteen inches high, which are made of leaves stitched together with grass; these are firmly fixed down upon hollows in the ground, whence a pair of bamboo tubes or *tuyers* convey the blast (produced by alternate and sudden elevations and depressions of the caps) to a heap of ignited charcoal; in this the iron spikes are heated, until they become sufficiently soft to be hammered to a point by a stone used as a hammer on a stone anvil. The Keriahs never make iron themselves, but are altogether dependent on the neighbouring bazaars for their supplies. It is to this point that I wish more particularly to draw attention. Had they at any period possessed a knowledge of the art of making iron, conservative of their customs as such races are, it is scarcely likely that they would have forgotten it. It is, therefore, not unreasonable to suppose that there was a period, anterior to the advent of the Hindus, when iron was quite unknown to them; and when, owing to the absence of cultivation in the neighbouring lowlands, they were even still more dependent on the supply of jungle food than they are at present. In those times their axes and their implements for grubbing up roots were in all probability made of stone, and their arrows had tips made of the same material.

Owing to the timidity of the Keriahs, I have not had many opportunities of speaking to them; frequently, on my approach to a house, the whole family fled, and hid themselves in the jungle; at other times I have found the houses empty, all the family having gone out to collect food. On several occasions, however, I have had the men brought into camp, when I have questioned them as to their language and customs.

In their persons, the Keriahs are very dirty, seldom, if ever, washing themselves. Their features are decidedly of a low character not unlike the Bhumiz; but there seemed to me to be an absence of any strongly marked type in their faces or build, such as enables one to know a Sontal, and even a Kurmi, at a glance. They undoubtedly belong, however, to the races who excited so much disgust on the part of the Hindus, when they first came into the country, and whom they described as "The black-skinned, human-sacrificing, flesh-eating forest tribes."

January 31st.—Mussgarah to Manbazaar.—Owing to the difficulty of getting boots which, while being light, would be sufficiently strong for walking in water along river courses, of which there was much to be done, I often did my day's work in bare feet, and continued to do so now and then for several years until I was compelled to give up the practice in consequence of several severe cuts which lamed me. When the feet become properly hardened there is great pleasure in walking bare foot, even over rough and stony ground. There is a springiness naturally about the foot which boots, of the best construction, must always hamper. In adopting the custom I was following the practice of some of my friends who have done much walking bare foot in India.

On the banks of the Kossai I was pleased to meet with a species of willow (*Salix Roxburghii*) which reminded me of the old familiar friend of temperate climes.

February 6th.—Jubla.—The central part of Manbhum is chiefly inhabited by an industrious race of cultivators, known as Kurmis. Their harvesting having been completed at this season, they were devoting much of their spare time to marriage festivities. Almost nightly we could hear the tom-toming going on in the surrounding villages, and during the day we often met processions of people going as deputies, from one village to another, in order to arrange the preliminaries of new alliances. The name of Kurmi is well known in Upper India as belonging to a Hindu caste; but the Kurmis of Manbhum, though undoubtedly Hindus, are separated from their namesakes by a wide gulf, from the fact that they eat and rear fowls. It often happened to me in these regions, when hearing the name of a new race for the first time, to receive for reply, on asking what kind of people they were, "they are of low caste—they eat fowls." This reply was often made by people who knew full well that fowls were made use of in my library.

People in England who often talk glibly about our being stand off, and not on friendly social terms with the natives, little realize the many items which go to place a bar between Anglo-Indians and the natives, whether Hindu or Mahomedan. Not to speak of other trifles, the fact that we eat one dish—ham and eggs—is alone sufficient to alienate us from both the above large sections of the community. The Hindu regards the egg of a fowl as defiling: while a Mahomedan's disgust for an eater of pork is too well known to be a matter of special comment. Curiously enough Hindus of high caste (*e.g.* Rajputs) will sometimes eat wild pig; while Mahomedans do not hesitate to eat fowls and eggs.

It may be of interest to add that Mahomedans not only do not eat turkeys, but Mahomedan servants will not accord to them the ordinary *coup-de-grace* with a knife, when killing them for their masters' tables; but put them to death, it is said, in some cruel manner.* Some Hindus will eat goose eggs, while others regard them as unclean.

February 22nd.—Situlpur to Purulia.—My companion and colleague had become so ill with fever that I was compelled to take him into Purulia, the civil station of Manbhum. As it seemed improbable that he would recover if he remained out in the field, he started for Calcutta a few days afterwards, leaving me to continue my work alone, for the remainder of the season.

---

* Cutting the throat of an animal makes it *halal* or lawful for food.

March 6th.—Nuguria.—Shortly after I left camp to-day I heard a great shouting in a neighbouring village, and on looking up saw three wolves leisurely trotting across the fields. I ran for about a mile hoping to intercept them, and so get a shot; but they, perceiving my movements, put a safe distance between me and themselves.

March 10th.—Gund Bazaar.—A cow was killed this morning close to my tent, on the edge of the grove in which I was encamped. That a leopard had done the deed there was no doubt, so I had a seat made in the branches of a tree overhanging the carcase, and took up my position there in the evening. Having waited several hours without hearing or seeing anything, the moon at last set, and thick banks of cloud, indicating a coming storm, gathered, making so complete a darkness that I could not even distinguish the cow's body at the foot of the tree. I then heard an animal tearing the carcase, and the villager, who was perched above me in the branches, gently touched me to apprise me that the leopard had come. After waiting for some time, hoping to obtain a glimpse of the animal, I at length fired, and then, for a moment, against the sky line, saw the leopard sneaking off. A second shot, taken when I could not see the sight of my rifle, was equally unsuccessful with the first. I was much astonished at the noiseless tread of the leopard, for although the ground was covered with dry crackling leaves not the least sound indicated his movements.

Some jackals in the neighbourhood made, while the leopard was about, the peculiar *pheou* cry, which as is well known by many sportsmen, though disbelieved in by others, is a sure indication of the fact of one of the larger *felidæ* being in the vicinity. In subsequent years I have had abundant opportunities of proving to my own satisfaction, that this cry may nearly always be taken as the sure sign of the presence of a tiger or leopard; but on one occasion, I had reason to believe that the jackals set it up on suddenly seeing an elephant tied under a tree.

March 15th.—Nagrah to Mugunah.—To-day when going through heavy jungle, I saw what I supposed to be the hide of a

Plate II.]

VILLAGE OF BUNDU ON THE KANCHI RIVER.

(*From a Photograph by T. F. Peppé, Esq.*)

bear through the bushes, and had levelled my rifle, when I just discovered in time that the black object was none other than the head of an old woman who was collecting sticks.

March 16th.—Mugunah.—Owing to lameness, the result of a sprained ankle which I had not been able to rest for some time, I was now compelled to do my work from the back of one of the elephants, which to-day I very nearly lost, owing to its having got bogged in a narrow *khal* or ditch, from which it was extracted after much time and trouble had been expended.

March 19th.—Jhulda.—This is an important village on the road from Purulia to Ranchi, in which a considerable business in grain and jungle products is done by native merchants. In its vicinity there are some remarkable bosses and cones of porphyritic gneiss, which form a striking feature in the scenery. They present perfectly smooth and bare surfaces of rock. The cones, in some cases, are symmetrical in shape, and rise, in one instance at least, to a height of about 400 feet above the surrounding country.

March 21st.—Jagra.—At this village there was a small colony of native Christians in connection with the German Lutheran Mission at Ranchi. Among the school children there was one little albino girl who, save for a slight tinge of colour in the cheeks, was almost perfectly white. Her eyes being grey, I thought, perhaps, at first, she might possibly have some European blood in her veins; but the whiteness of her hair dispelled this idea. Her brothers and sisters were like their parents, of the ordinary dark mahogany colour. Previously, I had seen in these regions, at wide intervals, several other albino children and one adult. As a rule, I should think, albinos in India are not long-lived. Their skins seem to be particularly susceptible to disease and unable to stand exposure. The pink-eyed children seemed to suffer much from the direct glare of the sun; but the grey-eyed girl did not complain of weakness of sight.

March 23rd.—Tholen to Kulma.—Some birds which I shot to-day afforded me occupation in the afternoon, in ascertaining the nature of the food upon which they principally subsist. It has often been remarked that grasshoppers, and allied orthopterous insects, afford the principal food of a large number of Indian birds. A specimen of the common Paddy bird which I dissected contained the recognisable remains of sixty of these insects, and an at least equal bulk of semi-digested legs and wings, &c. ; now, as the average length of these grasshoppers was about one inch, the whole number, if placed head and tail, would have extended over a length of ten feet. Another bird, the so-called crow pheasant (*Centropus rufipennis*), which belongs to the family of cuckoos, although it does not lay in other birds' nests, was supposed, from native testimony, according to Jerdon, to rob other birds' eggs. That it really does do so was rendered extremely probable from my finding the egg of a dove in one which I dissected.

For the month succeeding this, broken weather, and constantly recurring attacks of fever, interfered much with the progress of my work. A collection which I had been making of the wild vegetable products (fruits, roots, and leaves) received some considerable additions during this period, and on my return to Calcutta I published * an account of them, in which I have described the great importance of these articles of food to the poorer classes.

April 22nd.—Sindurpur.—To-day, I halted at Sindurpur, in the hills near which I had, on a previous occasion, ascertained the existence of several caves which were occupied by bears. Towards evening I went to the hills, and was posted near a path by a man who said that the bears were in the habit of descending by it to drink every evening at a neighbouring tank on the north side of the hill. Sending away my gunbearer, I prepared to await the coming of the bears, when back he came, post-haste, to say that two bears were out on a sloping face of rock, on the south side of and below the steep culminating peak. I accordingly ascended this peak,

---

* Jour. Asiatic Soc. Bengal, 1867. Vol. XXXVI., Part II., p. 73.

having to take off my boots in order to scramble over the slippery surface. On reaching the summit, and peeping over the large blocks of syenitic gneiss, I saw two full-grown bears playing about some sixty yards below. One of these I shot, and, as he rolled head over heels down amongst the rocks, I thought there would be no difficulty in retrieving him; but as soon as we got to the place where we had seen him roll to, it became apparent that he must have picked himself up, and got into some of the neighbouring caves. We failed to find out which, and darkness coming on had to give up the search. About a year after I heard the subsequent history of this bear, which was that he had, on the following day, appeared in the village of Chutter, a few miles off, where the inhabitants thought him to be mad, and sent off to give notice in the civil station of Purulia. Several of the officers stationed there immediately rode out; but upon arrival found that the natives had already despatched him.

The next morning I took up a position at the entrance to the principal cave an hour before sunrise; but waited in vain till it was quite light. Having searched then for the wounded bear without success, I was just about thinking of descending the hill and returning to camp, when, as we were standing near but not on the edge of a steep cliff, formed of blocks of syenite, a shepherd in the jungle at the foot of the hill called out that there were two bears below us. They were quite hidden from our view in consequence of the cliff overhanging. Accordingly I descended one side expecting to get a shot, and was just about to peep round the corner, when a shout of *bhal! bhal!* attracted my attention to the place I had just left, and in another moment Sahib Jhan, my chuprasi with the spare gun, and the bear came tumbling down the path together. Without going over the cliff, I had only just room to move out of the way of the bear which, as it passed, received the contents of both barrels—the muzzle of my rifle being almost in contact with its body. However, it scrambled off, head over heels, down the slope. I had then to look after Sahib Jhan, who was a good deal hurt, both by the fall and the bear's teeth, having been severely bitten in the thigh. After despatching him to camp, we searched for the bear, and at last found it lying in a cave, into which a small hole at the top fortunately enabled us to see. A shot fired down through this hole drove the bear to the entrance, where it soon after died. It proved to be an enormous female—the largest I have ever seen. Her cub we found in another cave under the cliff from whence the bear had made her vicious charge up hill, but we failed to take it alive, as it was big enough to be an ugly object to tackle without any appliance, such as a net or cloth, and so, as I did not care to shoot it, it was allowed to escape, being sufficiently large to take care of itself. On the carcase being taken to camp it was shewn to the pet cub which, strange to say, though weaned in early infancy, immediately commenced to suck.

Three days later I reached the railway station at Barakar, whence I left for Calcutta, thus concluding my third tour.

Shortly afterwards I was again appointed to the charge of the Geological Museum which, with other duties, prevented me leaving Calcutta again for about six months.

In September, the despatch of a military force to the Nicobar Islands to punish the inhabitants for piracies committed by them, was on the *tapis*, and I applied to be allowed to accompany the expedition as naturalist, and was nominated for the purpose. Ultimately two of her Majesty's vessels, the "Wasp" and "Satellite," were sent from the Straits' Settlements to punish the natives and assume possession of the Islands; in consequence of which the Calcutta force did not start. The published accounts of the Nicobar and Andaman Islands which I had studied, fired me, however, with a desire to explore the islands for myself; and this I accordingly did on the first opportunity which presented itself.

CHAPTER IV.

MANBHUM. SINGHBHUM.

1867–68.

INSTRUCTIONS FOR THE SEASON—BANKURA—RAJA OF BELAIDIHA—RAJA OF SIMLAPAL—CAMP GOES ASTRAY—BENGALIS—RAJA OF PHULKUSMA—BEAT FOR GAME—RAJA OF SHAMSUNDERPUR—AN UNEXPLAINED SOUND—MARRIAGE PROCESSION—ELEPHANT AT LARGE—WILD ELEPHANTS—BEAT FOR TIGER—CHRISTMAS FESTIVITIES—DISCOVER LEAD ORE—RECLAMATION OF FOREST—DHADKA TIGER—GOLD-WASHERS—WILD ELEPHANTS—DALMA HILL—QUICKSAND—COPPER ORES—UNITE CAMPS FOR SHOOTING—DURBAR—BEAT—TWO BEARS KILLED—OTHER BEATS—THE BAG—PARTINGS—PORCUPINE—BRAHMINICAL RUINS—ORIGIN OF THE CHIEFS—WITCHES—THE REFINING PROCESS—BHAGMUNDI OR AJUDIA PLATEAU—BHAGMUNDI POLICE AND ZEMINDAR—GOLD—AJUDIA—PURULIA—BURABAZAAR—FEVER AND AGUE—CHANGED ASPECT OF THE JUNGLE—KERIAHS—ELEPHANTS—NIGHT VISIT BY A BEAR—TIGER AT DHADKA AGAIN—CONCLUSION OF THE EXAMINATION OF MANBHUM—ENTER SINGHBHUM—BIRD MERCHANT—LANDU COPPER MINES—RAJDOHA—SAXON MINER—THE BHUMIZ—GEOLOGY OF CENTRAL BASIN—THE HOS—CHAIBASSA—MARCH TO SERAIKELA—SICKNESS AMONG MY FOLLOWERS—CATCH FEVER AGAIN—PURULIA—RETURN TO CALCUTTA.

MY instructions for this season were to complete the examination of the geology of Manbhum, and, if time remained, to endeavour to get a preliminary insight into the structure of the adjoining district of Singhbhum.

November 14th.—I started for Ranigunj, encamping, as before, at Searsole. After two long marches from Searsole I reached the already-described station of Bankura, which is thirty-three miles distant. On the road I met numerous pilgrims returning from Jugernath. They carried with them, as mementos of their visit and as evidence for their friends at home that they had actually accomplished the journey, umbrellas made of cane and palm-leaves, and bundles of painted rattan canes. Some of them, too, carried back-bones of cuttle-fish to show that they had been on the seashore. These they called by the poetic title of "ocean foam;" and, no doubt, firmly believed that they were solid, hand specimens of the great *Samundar* or *Kala pani*, possessing certain medical virtues.

November 26th.—Belaidiha.—Three marches southwards from Bankura over alluvium and laterite brought me to Belaidiha, where I commenced operations for the season. At Belaidiha the so-called Raja of the place paid me a visit. He was a fat, jolly old Hindu, who informed me that his affairs were in a very much involved condition, which fact he seemed to regard in the light of a joke. Thinking I might have some influence in the matter, he urged upon me to get the authorities to sell him up, so that he might be released from the annoyance caused by his creditors.

November 27th.—Belaidiha to Simlapal.—Simlapal is the chief village of another petty Raja, who also paid me a visit, being accompanied by an imposing cavalcade and preceded by coolies bearing chairs for the accommodation of himself and relatives during the audience. This little precaution is not uncommonly taken by natives when visiting officials in camp to avoid the possibility of their dignity suffering from a scarcity of furniture.

November 30th.—Hatiagurha to Bhitjuriah.—Owing to a confusion of similar names, and my camp not having gone to the village I had directed, I was for some hours at fault before I found it, and was beginning to make up my mind to spend an uncomfortable night away from it. The traditions of the Geological Survey record that one of my colleagues, under similar circumstances, in an uninhabited tract, spent a miserable night in the branches of a tree.

December 4th.—Goburdha to Phulkusma.—The people were principally Bengalis in this neighbourhood, and, as I again found on about the same meridian further south, excessively untruthful and difficult to deal with. In reply to simple questions about roads, &c., I often got a sulky answer, of which the formula was, "I don't know," "I haven't seen," "I haven't heard."

December 6th.—Phulkusma.—To-day the Phulkusma Raja

having promised to collect his people for a beat for large game, I started on an elephant for his "palace" at Ruspal, my Jemidar and chuprasies following on the other. The house was not finished, the Raja having only recently moved to this new site from Phulkusma. It was built on a small hill of laterite, which was isolated by a moat from the surrounding huts. Having crossed the moat, I entered the courtyard, which was very dirty and untidy. Arriving at the entrance to the building, I dismounted and was pointed out a shed where there were a couple of chairs and a sort of camp sofa, upon which a gorgeous velvet cloth, with gold and silver fringe, was spread. It was a "property" in marked discordance with the surroundings. As I passed into this shed an individual in rather soiled white clothes was introduced to me as the Raja by the Dewan. I was then invited to seat myself on the afore-mentioned sofa; but as it seemed to be a rickety, antiquated sort of affair, scarcely capable of supporting my weight, I preferred and took (I suppose in violation of etiquette) a more substantial-looking chair. As the Raja could only speak Bengali, and did not appear to understand a word of Hindustani, our conversation, but for the interposition of the intelligent Dewan, would not have been of a very animated description. When we had sat for some time, and at length exhausted all the topics common or otherwise between two individuals so different in sympathies and pursuits, the Raja asked for permission to depart in order to make some final preparations. While we were talking, a motley crowd of the unwashed stood round on all sides watching the performance and endeavouring to pick up what they could of what was said.

After the lapse of about half-an-hour it was intimated to me that it was time to mount my elephant, which as I proceeded to do and left by one of the exits, the Raja with his Dewan, seated on his own, left by another and followed in my wake. On arrival at a village about three miles off, we found that not a single beater had turned out in response to the Raja's summons. Seeing this, the old man himself mounted a pony and ambled off to some other villages to collect men; while I, with the remainder of the party, moved on to the village of Doodanallah, from whence the Raja's son rode off in another direction to beat up stragglers. Another long delay ensued, which, but for the soothing effects of a cheroot, was very nearly causing me to retire in disgust. At length the beaters began to drop in in batches from their respective villages; and, as each batch kept more or less distinct, they formed a series of picturesque groups; some of the men sitting, while others stood and rested on their bows or long staffs. At about 2.30 p.m. the Raja reappeared, and, as there were then about 100 men collected, he asked me to take up my position while he undertook, as soon as the remaining beaters came up, to set them at their work. Accordingly I started for the *machans*, or elevated stages, which were situated in a jungle about two miles further west.

Shortly after I had taken my stand, the tom-toms and cries of the beaters were heard in the distance, and a few minutes later a jungle-fowl flew over my head. Presently some pea-fowl made their appearance, creeping stealthily along and taking to the wing as they approached the *machans*. But as tigers, leopards, bears, and even elephants were in the bill of fare, the small game were allowed to pass unmolested. Before the beaters came up a pig passed close to some of the matchlock men, and this was the only four-footed animal seen during the day.

The jungle was then beaten from the other side, the only result being to stir up a couple of the pea-fowl which had before been driven across. The whole bag consisted of a young peacock, which was shot by an illegitimate son of the Raja's by a Sontal mother. A wearisome journey of about eight or nine miles ended in arrival at camp some time after sunset. I have given this account in fuller detail than the results justify, as being the first one of these ill-managed Rajas' beats at which I have been present, and because it is fairly representative.

December 9th.—Shamsunderpur.—In the evening, after my return from work, I received a visit from the Shamsunderpur Raja, who was a younger man than either of the others, but shewed less intelligence than they did. At 6.25 p.m., shortly after his departure, a most singular rumbling sound, resembling but clearly distinct from thunder was heard, the sky being at the time quite cloudless. There was no earthquake, neither was any meteoric flash observed, but that may have been in consequence of the daylight. Unless it was connected with the bursting of a meteorite, I can offer no plausible explanation of the phenomenon. The villagers on hearing it were evidently struck with its novelty, and one man having shouted out "*Ram* has spoken," the whole population joined in the cry.

December 13th.—Bishenpur to Chura.—At 9 p.m., I took up a position in a field of dhál (a sort of pea), to await the coming of deer, which were said to be nightly in the habit of visiting the locality. After remaining there on the watch for an hour, silence was disturbed, and the chance of a shot wholly destroyed, by the sound of bells from a Raja's marriage procession. Returning to the tent I watched the procession pass in the moonlight; it included six elephants, about a dozen horses, a number of palkis, and about 100 footmen. The contracting parties were, I believe, members of the Sirguja and Mohurbunj Rajas' families. The object of travelling at night during this, the cold season, was to prevent the females of the party from being seen by strange male eyes.

During this night an elephant, which had been at large for some years, passed at the opposite end of the village to that where my tent was pitched; the shouts of the people near whose houses it stood, apprising us of the fact. According to the chowkidar, who seemed to know something of its habits, it was not admitted into the fraternity of the wild elephants of the neighbouring jungle, being, so to speak, outlawed by them.

December 17th.—Churku.—North of the village of Sutan I entered very heavy forest, where there were abundant traces of elephants; some of these were so recent-looking that I was sorely tempted to spend a day or two in endeavouring to track up the beasts, which could not have been very far distant. But my battery was hardly suited for such game, while moreover by shooting one I might, so it was said, have rendered myself liable to a fine of £50, such being the amount inflicted in preserved tracts, though whether this was actually at that time included, no one, including the local authorities, seemed to know. The bark of the Sal (*Shorea robusta*) and the Golgol or torch-wood tree (*Cochlospermum gossypium*), appeared to be, together with young shoots of the bamboo, the favourite food of these elephants.

December 25th.—Dhadka.—Having intimation of the existence of a tiger in this neighbourhood, which had been doing mischief among the cattle, I made an attempt to celebrate Christmas by compassing his destruction. About 200 Sontals and Bhumiz were assembled, and we beat the jungle supposed to contain the tiger, but, as so often happens on these occasions, drew a blank.

At night the Sontals and Bhumiz danced their respective tribal dances round a huge bonfire, and a small Sontal boy created some amusement by wearing an ingeniously contrived mask made of his cloth, and some slips of bamboo, which represented a bird's head.

December 27th.—Dhadka to Rajgaon.—The head man of Dhadka having given me a small fragment of galena or lead ore, found in the neighbourhood, I spent some time in seeking for the lode, and was not successful till to-day, when I found it with the aid of a Lohar or iron-worker. After some little excavation we managed to obtain a series of fine specimens of the ore and gangue. These, on assay, yielded the unusually large proportion of 119 ozs. 4 dwts. 16 grs. of silver to the ton of lead. An account of the discovery was subsequently published,* but, as with many similar discoveries of mineral resources, nothing has up to the present been done to test the value of the lode.

December 31st.—Narsinghpur to Kuncha.—My work to-day lay in the ranges of hills which separate Manbhum from Singhbhum. Here I first became acquainted with the method employed by the Sontals and other pioneer tribes, for reclaiming forest lands and rendering them available for cultivation. The first thing done is to ring the trees throughout a wide area. These immediately die, the leaves drop off, and the effects of dry rot and white ants

* "Records of the Geological Survey of India." No. 3, 1870, p. 74.

soon become apparent. The first crop of millet or pulse is sown while the bared trunks are still standing: but in the next ensuing hot season these are set fire to at the roots, and, soon falling, smoulder away into ashes, which serve to improve the soil. Everywhere this process is going on in the central highland tracts of India, the almost inevitable result being that, so soon as the land becomes of value, the greedy Hindu money-lender steps in to reap the benefits of the aborigines' pioneering toil.

January 1st.—Kuncha.—Hearing that the Dhadka tiger had killed three cows this morning I went over there in the evening, and sat up over a goat tied up as a bait till 10 p.m., without seeing or hearing any sign of the tiger. Unfortunately the carcases of the cows had been removed so that I could not keep watch over them. This custom of removing the carcases is not only the cause of a much larger number of cattle being killed than would otherwise be the case—since the tigers must eat—but it also, no doubt, leads to many becoming man-eaters out of revenge, or merely to satisfy their appetites.

At this place I engaged the services of two gold-washers, man and wife, who were to accompany my camp and wash at the places I pointed out, by which means I hoped to be able to define the limits and distribution of the auriferous rocks. The agreement was that I was to receive all the gold, in return for which I paid them the daily wage of an anna, or three-halfpence apiece, which was all that they asked for. Each day's find was carefully wrapped up in paper and dated, and subsequently weighed. Although there were few absolutely blank days, the value of the total amount collected did not more than equal half my expenditure.

January 4th.—Jhonjka to Susdah.—I spent eight hours to-day steady walking in the hilly country to the south of these villages. In one place I came upon the site of a village which the wild elephants had made unsafe for the inhabitants, in consequence of which it had been deserted. In the broken-down huts there were traces of the elephants as though they had for some time remained in possession.

January 9th.—Punsa.—At Dhadka I had been told that the elephants would be found on the slopes of Dulma hill, near this place. Here the people told me that they had all departed for Dhadka, though they said that when the rice was ripe they were sometimes to be seen in the afternoons in the fields close by. From what I saw the herd did not appear to be in either neighbourhood then, as the marks were from a week to ten days old.

January 11th.—Pardih to Asunbuni.—To-day I ascended the Dulma hill, which rises to an elevation of about 3,050 feet above the sea. The path up to the saddle between the two highest portions of the hill is not very steep. On this ridge or saddle there were several neatly wattled huts, which stood in the centre of a small area of clearance. They had been temporarily deserted by their owners the Keriahs, in consequence of a want of water, the hill being excessively dry and, as far as I could see, containing no springs. This massive hill is formed of a volcanic trappean rock, which occurs as an enormous dyke traceable for many miles in both east and west directions.

The hills and rivers in this neighbourhood afforded beautiful series of sections, indicating a most orderly arrangement in the succession of the quartzites, schists, pot-stones and other rocks of the sub-metamorphic series, which are here penetrated by the Dulma trap.

January 21st.—Kulianpur.—In the Kulianpur hill I found some old copper mines, and slags from copper furnaces; but the indications seemed to point to a very inconsiderable deposit of ore.

January 22nd.—Kulianpur to Ichagurh.—To-day, according to a previous engagement, I joined the united camps of the Deputy-Commissioner of the district, and of my colleague Ormsby, who had been engaged in the exploration of an adjoining tract in the Hazaribagh district. It was our intention to take a holiday for a few days' systematic shooting. Having completed my morning's work, I rode off to this camp rejoiced at the prospect of meeting friends, and speaking my mother tongue, after two months' abstinence from its use. When crossing the Subanrika to Ichagurh,

Plate III.]

THE SUBANRIKA RIVER NEAR PATKUM.

(From a Photograph by T. F. Peppé, Esq.

the chief town of the Raja of Patkum, I saw a large flock of mergansers, whose occurrence in the Damuda I have already mentioned.

The party had been engaged, I found, in shooting ducks that morning in some neighbouring tanks, and had made a large bag, and "Jerdon's Birds of India" was in great requisition for identifying the different species. In the evening a durbar was held for the reception of two of the Rajas; he of the place, a most unpleasant ill-conditioned looking individual, and the Raja, or more properly Zemindar, of Bhagmundi, a fine-looking man who had come for the sport. On the former, however, devolved the duty of collecting the beaters, &c., which he did reluctantly enough.

A pleasant dinner, followed by a rubber or two of whist, kept us employed till a late hour, when we retired, wishing each other success on the morrow. Curiously enough one of the party whom I thus met in the jungle proved to be an old schoolfellow of my own, whom I did not know was in India.

January 23rd.—Ichagurh.—While we were at breakfast the beaters were assembled by a loud tom-toming and blowing of horns, and soon a vast crowd of seven or eight hundred collected. Many of them were very wild-looking creatures, and nearly all were armed with bows and arrows, axes or matchlocks. We then rode off to the first hill which was to be beaten, and took up our positions on the machans which had been prepared. The beat had gone on for some time, when three shots from the Deputy-Commissioner gave the rest of us notice that game was afoot. Presently, as the beaters set up a shout, two bears crossed a road which divided the jungle. Soon after the beaters came up, and we then sent them round to drive the jungle in which the bears had taken refuge. Ere long the Deputy-Commissioner again led off with a couple of shots, and one bear passed in sight of my position. With a tremendous shout the beaters again advanced, and the Deputy-Commissioner now took a shot at rather close quarters, his ball taking effect, and the doubly-wounded and enraged bear rushed towards him with open mouth into which a ball soon crashed its way, carrying with it a part of the jaw, after which the animal succumbed.

On consulting as to the advisability of hunting up the bear which had escaped, or going off to new ground, we decided in favour of the latter. An unfortunate casualty occurred during this beat—a lad, one of the beaters, having got an ugly clawing, and a black eye! from one of the bears. We despatched him to camp to be attended to by the native doctor.

We then rode off to a village at the foot of the next hill to be beaten; and, in a grove close by, proceeded to discuss our tiffin, which the servants, according to previous arrangements, had brought up. The scene, as we disposed of the cold ducks and teal, the Bass and the Bordeaux, was a curious one; for, as the beaters came up, they pressed forward to have a view of the Sahibs feeding. Ere long we found ourselves in the centre of a vast crowd of over one thousand men of various castes and races, including Hindus, Mahomedans, Kurmis, Mundas, Bhumiz, Sontals, and Uraons. A large supply of uncooked rice having been obtained was distributed among them, and each man taking his share in the corner of his cloth, dipped it in the water of a neighbouring tank, so that by the partial softening it might be more easily eaten.

After this we took up our places on the new line of machans and the beaters commenced their work. Just as they reached the crest of the hill two bears were seen crushing their way down through the jungle towards the central machan. A shot turned them down in my direction; on they came, at full charge, running for very life, till, catching sight of me, they halted suddenly, giving me a splendid opportunity; but, though I gave them four shots, I only staggered one of them, which however managed to make off with its companion. The occupant of the machan next beyond me, knocked over one, but it picked itself up, and they again ran along in front of the line, but this time higher up the slope of the hill, where their path was marked only by the moving jungle. Shortly after they separated; one of them broke past the end of the line, and was soon seen out in the paddy-fields galloping like a fiend, a few straggling beaters following and yelling in his wake. The Deputy-Commissioner and the Bhagmundi Raja then disposed of the second bear, which broke close to them, after which we returned to camp; our day's bag included, besides the two bears, a jungle cat and several hares. A poor enough one considering the number of men and guns engaged, but exceeding the general average results of such beats.

The beaters were then paid; the Government reward of 10 rupees for each slaughtered bear, being available to defray a part of the expense. The officials having to go into Purulia on duty, Ormsby and I arranged to occupy ourselves with work in the neighbourhood till their return.

January 27th.—The welcome sing-song of the palki bearers reached our ears this morning just as we were consulting what we should do in the event of our friends not turning up.

The arrival of the Zilla Sahib, or officer in charge of the district, was the signal for the court officials, the Raja, and the general tag-rag and bob-tail to reappear. The scene which for the last few days had been comparatively quiet, at once assumed a bustling appearance, and the tom-toms striking up, the beaters began to assemble.

Shortly afterwards we mounted our horses and forded the Karkari river, which bounded our camp on the south—a living stream of men, ten deep, following in our wake. The picture produced by this body of men, bristling with spears, axes, and bows and arrows, as they pursued a winding course across the river, with a back-ground formed by the grove in which our tents stood, and a general surrounding of forest and scrub-clad hills, was more effective than anything of the kind I had ever seen before.

After a short ride we reached our machans, in which, having taken our seats and sent away our horses, we patiently awaited the result of the beat. Beyond a couple of small deer, a hare or two, and a peacock, which were not fired at, this long beat, lasting over two hours, produced nothing in our direction. The beaters themselves were more fortunate, as with a couple of arrows from their powerful bamboo bows they managed to kill a fine boar.

A council of war having been held, it was determined to try a flat jungle close by, in which bears were said to have been seen within the past few days. The Deputy-Commissioner and Ormsby took up a position on a pile of *débris* from a soap-stone quarry, while I, putting myself under the direction of a villager who knew the ground, was placed with my Jemidar on the edge of a ditch-like ravine, along the bed of which it was considered probable that the animals might endeavour to steal away. I was myself armed with a rifle. The Jemidar held a powerful No. 10 smooth bore, and a cooly, with a No. 15 smooth bore, stood behind as a reserve. Shortly after the beat had commenced some animal, either a deer or a wolf, came down the ravine, and just as I saw the top of its nose, turned and scampered off. The beaters had come quite close ere they raised the shout of *Bhal! Bhal!* Bear! Bear! Immediately, some men whom I had placed in trees, gave me notice that something was coming along a path on the edge of the ravine, and upon which we were standing. The Jemidar and I accordingly fell back a few feet, so as to leave the path open, and we had hardly done so when three bears broke, and as they passed I gave them a broadside. My first shot struck the leader, and the second killed one of the others, which subsided on the spot. The leading bear, which was no doubt the mother of the two nearly full-grown cubs, being wounded, immediately charged the Jemidar. As it rushed at him he stood his ground manfully and fired in its face. This made it recoil for a moment, but again it rose at him with open jaws, and struck at him with its fore feet, and was so near doing him a mischief that its claws actually tore his clothes. However, he pounded it over the nose with the gun, and, as I was coming to his assistance, it made off. Had the man with the spare gun only stood to me I could hardly have failed to bag both bears, but at the critical moment he was not to be seen, and I had only my empty rifle wherewith to aid the Jemidar in his peril. Soon after, shots from others of the party were heard, but the bears managed to get off, though we tracked the big one by patches of blood for some distance. The beaters surrounding a deer, chased it into a tank of water, where they killed it. This day's bag then consisted of one bear, one boar, one deer, and several hares.

January 29th.—Ichagurh to Urmal.—To-day our camp was broken up, and after taking leave of one another we started off on our respective tracks, which were to different points of the compass. However, during the succeeding week, my colleague and I managed to keep within hail of one another, and to interchange visits. The feeling of loneliness immediately after such meetings was always more oppressive to me than at other times.

February 6th.—Gutihuli to Kutai.—During the day I came across some men who had shot a porcupine, and bought from them the head for my collection of skulls. They were very curious to know what I wanted it for, and I overheard one of my servants assuring them that it was for medicinal purposes, which appeared to them to be an all-sufficient answer.

February 8th.—Terel-Chanda to Dulmi.—In the neighbourhood of Dulmi there are a number of Brahminical remains, said to have been built by some Raja called Vikramadit. But rather than give my own imperfect account of what I saw, I prefer to quote a description of the place* by Colonel Dalton, Commissioner of Chutia Nagpur:—"The antiquities of Dulmi comprise the remains of an old fort, several large tanks, and the ruins of numerous temples dedicated to the worship of Siva and Parbuti, to the adoration of the *lingum*, and other objects of Brahminical idolatry. Crossing to the left bank of the river, the first object that strikes you is a colossal figure of Gunesh, amidst a confused heap of cut stones. The poor fellow has tumbled off his pedestal and lost his legs in the fall. If he had had fair proportions he would have stood twelve feet high, as his body measures six feet; but with such ridiculously short and thick legs as were assigned to him he only stood nine feet. His place was that of Janitor, and the heaps of stones near him are the remains of the old river gate

* "Notes on a Tour in Manbhum." Jour. Asiatic Soc. Bengal. Vol. xxxv., 1866, p. 191.

of the city. A little hill overlooking the river near this place, is covered with cut and carved stones, and occupying the place of honour in the foundation of what appears to have been the principal temple. Just here is a *lingum*, 18 inches in diameter, protruding the same length from the *argah*, in which it is embedded. The *argah* is circular and three feet in diameter. In a brick temple near this shrine of Siva, there is a stand for an idol, but the idol, which it is said was an image of Vishnu, has been removed. There were formerly, I am told, a great variety of sculptures at this place, but they are now scattered all over the country. The brick temple is probably of more modern date than the stone buildings, as it is partly arched on the radiating principle. Near the river are two mounds formed of the *débris* of two or more fine temples. The altar-piece of one was a ten-armed figure of Durga slaying the monster Mahisasur. There are two groups of this subject, one greatly mutilated, the other in good preservation, the arms and weapons all perfect and sharp cut. There are here two elaborately-carved door-pieces of the entrance to the shrine. The ornamentation, cut in a very hard stone, is as sharp and clear as if it had but recently been turned out of the sculptor's hands. It is like the wood carving of a picture-frame, so minute and neat are the borders and scrolls. Near the other temple I found a large altar, representing, I believe, Kamadeva and his wife. They are represented seated lovingly side by side, and are in a state of good preservation.

"Amongst the detached blocks were two figures, having in alto-relievo the Machowa and Cuchowa Avatars of Vishnu. The whole series of incarnations doubtless formed the chief external ornamentation of one of the temples. On a former occasion of visiting these ruins I noticed here an image of Vishnu *in propria persona*, with well-formed features, a highly-decorated conical cap, jewelled, extensive ear ornaments, and a manikin in his left hand. This image I did not observe on the last occasion.

"Not far from the temples is a stone image of a life-sized bull, Siva's bull, which appears to have wandered from the shrine into the field to graze. We next come to an extensive tank surrounded by a moat and ditch; but between the moat and the tank there is a considerable space, all round which was probably the site of houses, making this an entrenched tank square. In the centre of the tank there is a singular structure of stone, two small columns supporting a triple umbrella, from which the tank is called the *Chhata pokhara.* This indicates that the tank was dedicated to Siva, the king of heaven, as the trident on a post in most tanks shows that the blessing of Siva has been invoked on the work.

"In the village of Dulmi we have a collection of sculptures that have been removed from the ruins. There is a group of Vishnu and Lakshmi, a single figure of Vishnu, a smaller bull, and various other images. An uncle of the Patkum Raja, a venerable-looking old man, lives at Dulmi; but, strange to say, he could give me no information about the antiquities of the place. The people, though to this day worshipping Kali and offering sacrifices to a clay image of her in a shed, utterly disregard the ancient shrines, and care not for the desecration or deportation of the idol. It is the same with similar remains of Brahminical worship all over the country. We see that it was established in places that are now the haunts of wild beasts, or the abode of a race that know nothing of such a worship, and we see by the destruction of the temples and the mutilation of the images that equal zeal was displayed in uprooting as in establishing it. The destructive agency is generally supposed to have been put in action by the Mahomedan power; but I do not understand, if this were so, how it is that some tradition regarding the destruction is not retained. We may associate some of these temples with the hermits, rishis, or sages of the ancient days of Aryan progress—attempts made to establish religious colonies amongst the yet unsubdued aborigines. It would appear that even in the days of the 'Ramayan' the aborigines of this part of the country were called Kols. In the 'Ramayan' they are alluded to as fierce savages in a conversation between Sita and her mother-in-law, wherein the latter enumerates the various difficulties Sita would have to encounter if she accompanied Rama in his progress south.* 'The 'Ramayan' (says Lassen,) contains the narrative of the first attempts of the Aryans to extend themselves to the south by conquest, but it presupposes the peaceable extension of the Brahminical missions in the same direction as having taken place still earlier. Rama, when he arrives at the south of the Vindhya range, finds there the sage Agastya, by whom the southern regions had been rendered safe and accessible. The Rakshasas, who are represented as disturbing the sacrifices and devouring the priests, signify here, as often elsewhere, merely the savage tribes which placed themselves in hostile opposition to the Brahminical institutions.'† The 'Ramayan' depicts the Dasyas as infesting the hermitages or settlements of the Aryans, as obstructing their sacred rites, as enemies of the Brahmins, &c. It is true we do not hear that in these early days the worship of Siva had been established; but the Hindus of the Puranic times were not less zealous in proselytising, and may have followed the same system of pushing forward religious settlements amongst the unsubdued Dasyas. This would account for the Brahminical ruins, mostly dedicated to the worship of Siva, scattered about the wild regions of this province, some in picturesque secluded spots that a hermit would delight in, others in connection with fortified cities all now deserted. We may conceive that these colonies, gradually assuming a more aggressive policy, were, after severe struggles, finally extirpated by the progenitors of the Kols, Bhumiz, and Mundas of the present day; that the aborigines thus maintained their independence and autonomy; but that from a feeling of lingering admiration for the superior intelligence, higher civilization, and god-like beauty of the unsuccessful invaders, they retained some amongst them as their guides and instructors, and, it may be, in some instances, from the remnant thus retained, elected their chief. We might thus account for the Aryan features and

---

* From "Muir's Sanskrit Texts." Part II., p. 425.

† *Ibid.*, page 435.

Brahminical predilections of some of the chiefs whom we find ruling an alien people without any evidence that they had by conquest attained that position. * * * * The chiefs, who all aspire to be Kshetriyas, have each his tradition regarding his accession to power. These are generally fables devised by the Brahmins, and they may thank me for having given them a method of claiming an Aryan descent without having recourse to them."

A belief in the existence of witches, or rather, I should perhaps write, in the malignancy and magic power of certain persons who are not always old women, is very prevalent amongst the tribes of both the Dravidian and Kolarian families. In this fact there is perhaps nothing very remarkable, as I suppose there is no country where at least some portion of the population does not retain a remnant of this once very general belief. But, writing under correction, it is a peculiarity here that the belief is so thorough that even those who are accused of being witches or sorcerers do not deny the impeachment, but accept the position readily with all its pains and penalties.

Before the British Government established the strange and singular rule that killing a reputed witch was to be considered murder, and that such a murder would be followed by the usual consequences of that crime, the Lurka Kols gave but a short shrift to anyone who was ascertained by their Sokhas or witch-finders to be the author of any injurious magic. And, indeed, it is said that whole families were disposed of by being hacked to pieces like venomous reptiles, since it was supposed that the black art was hereditary and that it was advisable to scotch the brood. The practice is by no means extinct, as the following story, which was told me by the Deputy-Commissioner of the district, who tried the case, will serve amply to illustrate. A Kol, losing some of his cattle by disease, employed the witch-finder to discover the author of the mischief. After the usual incantations,* a certain old woman was

* These are fully described in Colonel Dalton's "Ethnology of Bengal," p. 199.

pointed out. On being charged with the offence, she calmly admitted that she was guilty of having (*lit*) "eaten" the cattle. She was, however, forgiven, but warned against causing any further injury. After a time the man's eldest son died, and the woman was charged with having eaten him. Again she admitted the charge, but this time added, "I was not alone in doing so, but was aided by three sisters." All the women of the village and neighbourhood having been assembled, they were made to sit down in a circle, and the old woman, walking round, dropped fragments of cloth behind each of the three whom she accused. These then were made to stand forth, and they likewise admitted that they had shared in devouring the young man.

The father then addressing the first old woman, said: "I forgave you for eating my cattle; but this I cannot forgive." Arming himself with a sword, he caused the four women to carry the bier upon which his son was laid down to the river-side, and then proceeded to kill and cut off the heads of the women, one after another, none of them seeking safety in flight, though the last took temporary refuge under the bier. Having accomplished the quadruple murder, the man forthwith delivered himself up to justice, and in his subsequent trial, detailed with full *minutiæ* all the circumstances of which the above is but a brief sketch. Sentence of execution was passed upon him, as he all through expected it would be.

During the disturbed times of the Mutiny, in 1857-58, when law was suspended in these regions, the Kols of Singhbhum and other parts of the Province availed themselves of their freedom to make a clean sweep of the witches and sorcerers who had accumulated in their midst, under the benign influence of British authority. Numerous murders were committed; but, after the re-establishment of order, the murderers were, in many cases, brought to trial, and punished with death. In some parts of India it would have been difficult to have brought the cases home, but the truthfulness of the Kols aided the investigations; and very probably many were condemned out of their own mouths.

February 14th.—Turang.—The village of Turang, and three

others in the neighbourhood—Soesa, Soso, and Kalimutti—belong to four Kol Zemindars, or, as they are called in the Kol language, Mankis. He of this village, who was excessively black, and I should say undoubtedly a Kol, told me that he considered himself a Hindu, and added that the Brahmins were his priests. His seemed to me a most favourable case of an incipient stage of the process of refining aborigines into Hindus, which of late years has attracted some notice. In districts where there is a strong Hindu society, and a correspondingly watchful public opinion, it would be scarcely possible for a family, however opulent, to raise their caste. And hence it is that we sometimes meet with men of position and influence whose low caste remains as a blot only spoken of with bated breath. But in these remote regions, where the few Brahmins could doubtless be bought over, and some impoverished Kshetriya or Rajput could be found ready to give his daughter in wedlock to the Raja, a gradual advance in status and improvement in features has been accomplished. Colonel Dalton, as quoted above, offers a different suggestion to account for the curious anomaly, that we find in many cases these aboriginal races headed by alien chieftains, whose families stand alone in their respective districts. But elsewhere Colonel Dalton's opinions show a decided leaning towards the process of refining as affording the true explanation; and, indeed, I believe to him is due its first promulgation. Thus he states that the Raja of Patkum, who claims to be a Kshetriya of royal descent, has no family annals, and that he is, in all probability, nothing more than a Hinduized Bhumiz; and the Rajas of Sirguja, and others of the Gurjat States, are regarded by him as having a similar origin.

February 17th.—Susu to Bhagmundi.—A long day's work on the western portion of the Bhagmundi plateau, an outlying spur which extends for twenty miles from the Ranchi plateau into the district of Manbhum, brought me to Bhagmundi, where I found that the usual supplies were not prepared by the Zemindar or Raja, so called, whom I had met at Ichagurh. The police stationed here were, as usual, indirectly insolent and unwilling to render assistance, so that on arrival at camp, fagged and wearied with the morning's work, I found my men in a very discontented condition, and I had at once to endeavour to set things straight.

In the evening the Zemindar came to pay a formal visit; and as he had been asked by the Deputy-Commissioner to give me some sport, if possible, he invited me to beat a neighbouring tract of jungle on the following day. The beat turned out to be a lamentable failure, and I rode away from it in disgust, leaving the Zemindar to follow on one of the elephants which I had lent him. During the remainder of my stay at Bhagmundi his manner towards me became more and more disrespectful, forming a great contrast to his genial though somewhat subservient bearing when in the presence of the head district official at Ichagurh. So it is ever with these Hindus, who have no idea of an intermediate demeanour between cringing subserviency and insolence. Chewing pawn and smoking in my presence were among the means adopted by him of showing that he considered there was a great social gulf fixed between me and the district officials. Only an Anglo-Indian can fully appreciate these niceties of behaviour. One could easily put up with them were they not so often accompanied by a complete disregard of necessary requisitions for supplies. The worst about it is that sometimes I have found individuals of this type adhering to the mere letter of orders they have received regarding me from the district officials, while to me personally they have been insolent, thus cunningly leaving me nothing upon which I might found a complaint, though I have had cause for much irritation, and the progress of my work has been seriously interfered with.

February 19th.—Bhagmundi.—Copper and tin ores had been reported to occur in this neighbourhood, but on visiting the localities I found there was no trace of either; the idea in the case of the former having been originated from the discovery of a green mineral called epidote and some bronze-coloured mica; and in the latter, from some crystals of a mineral called ilmenite, in association with magnetic iron.

The gold-washers with me found here the largest piece of gold they had yet come across; it weighed 1·9 grains. This somewhat excited the Zemindar when he heard of it. He asked me what steps the Government would take in consequence of the discovery.

February 20th.—Bhagmundi to Ajudia.—As I intended to spend a night on the plateau at the village of Ajudia, I had arranged to take the elephants only, lightly laden, with me, while the bulk of my *impedimenta* was to travel round to a village at the eastern foot of the spur; but for this some additional carriage was requisite. Early this morning, however, notwithstanding promises made over night by the police and the Zemindar that carts (locally called "suggurs") and coolies would be ready, neither the one nor the other were forthcoming. After great delay, and numerous messengers having gone and returned without effect, I caused all the extra baggage to be loaded on my own carts, and then went to the police station, where I took down the names of the constables present, with the intention of reporting them, and then went to find the Zemindar. He came up from the tank where he was engaged at his morning ablutions. I asked him then for an explanation of his not having rendered me proper assistance, as he was bound to do. He, however, treated the matter in a very off-hand manner, and said the coolies would come shortly, &c. Finally, after hours of valuable time had been lost, I had to make the best shift I could, and proceed about my work, heartily glad to leave the locality.

I then ascended the plateau to Ajudia, which is about 776 feet above Bhagmundi, or 1,500 feet above the sea. There were on the highlands open spaces of meadowy-looking grass-land, interspersed through the jungle, which produced a very pleasing effect. I found here a colony of iron smelters, who used as an ore the magnetic iron-sand, which they obtained in the beds of rocky streams, and laboriously separated from siliceous and other impurities by washing. The iron produced contains, not improbably, a trace of titanium, and is of particularly good quality.

February 28th.—Chakultore.—After a fifteen miles' walk in the morning I rode into Purulia, which was only six miles off, to spend a day or two with my friends there. This ride was accomplished with not a little difficulty, owing to a tremendous gale which, in some of its more violent gusts, made the horse stagger, and threatened to blow him over altogether. However, by keeping him at a canter I managed to accomplish the distance without mishap. I met in Purulia one who had had some experience of Australian gold-washing, to whom I showed a sample of Manbhum gold, the result of many days' washing. He, supposing it to be the result of a single day's panning, remarked that if so much were found in prospecting, it would be considered barely sufficient to justify regular operations. This was not encouraging for the future development of my gold-bearing tracts.

March 14th.—Bura bazaar.—At this, the chief village of a *purguna** named Burabhum, I remained for several days, and enjoyed the use of a comfortable bungalow which had been built for the use of the district officials. The change from a tent was pleasant, as it was now already very hot, and in the afternoons it was necessary to use a *kus-kus tatti* (or screen made of the roots of a particular kind of grass, and which, when wetted, gives out a pleasant perfume), in order to cool the heated breezes from the west. On the walls of the bungalow there were numerous nests of wasps, which consisted of clusters of five to eight cells, made of a sort of papery substance, and are attached by a common stalk or peduncle. Each cell contains an egg which, hatching into a grub, feeds on the torpid, partially-stung (?) caterpillars, provided by the parent wasp, which remains on guard for some time after the cells are sealed up.

March 26th.—Chaiturma.—I was troubled, at this time, by attacks of fever and ague, the first of which came on the 24th, the exact anniversary of my last year's seizure.

April 1st.—Koniani to Joba.—I was now in the neighbour-

* A purguna is a fiscal division corresponding to our barony.

hood of Dulmi hill again, and the general appearance of the country presented a remarkable contrast to that which it had on the former occasion. Then the Subanrikha river was full of water, and the foliage of the surrounding jungle was dense and luxuriant; now the river was nearly dry, the trees leafless, and the undergrowth burnt and charred by the fires. In so far as geological work is concerned, this state of things, were it not accompanied by a vastly increased temperature, would be a real boon, as one can now travel with comparative facility straight across country, and the rocks are all bared and visible where they were before often concealed from view.

April 4th.—Mungla.—In this neighbourhood I interviewed the Keriahs, and obtained from them much of the information which I have given by anticipation on a previous page.

I met here the Dhadka Bubu, who told me that the tiger I had tried to circumvent on Christmas Day had since been shot by a native, who had accordingly received the government reward.

April 6th.—Kantagora.—This village is surrounded by jungle, and the inhabitants, owing to the incursions of wild elephants, have, in a great measure, given up cultivation as an unprofitable speculation. I was told that one evening they had seen thirty elephants all together.

Owing to the heat at midnight, I was lying awake on my bed, when I heard one of my men whisper outside that a bear had just passed. Jumping up and seizing my rifle, I rushed outside, and, it being bright moonlight, saw the bear disappearing in a trench. Loosing my three dogs I started them in pursuit, hoping that they would keep the bear at bay till I, in my slippered feet, could manage to get across the intervening rough ground. I am sorry to be compelled to add that my two bull-terriers, and an Australian kangaroo hound, on the bear making a rush and grunt at them, shewed a craven spirit, and scuttled back to the tent as fast as they could, while the bear himself bolted off before I could get within shot.

At this place the gold-washers, who had been with me since the 1st of January, took their departure. The results of their operations are given in a published paper, and may be here briefly epitomised.*

The experience of generations of gold-washers has enabled them to define the boundaries of the area within which washing is remunerative, and this area I found to correspond exactly with that of the sub-metamorphic rocks. Gold was not, however, absent in the more crystalline metamorphic rocks. Comparing the results, first by the number of successful days, it appeared that the productiveness of the former is to that of the latter as 2·5 to 1, while, comparing by the daily average of gold obtained, the proportion becomes 3 to 1. We may therefore conclude that the sub-metamorphic rocks are from two-and-a-half to three times as productive of gold as are the metamorphic rocks, so that since the gold-washers only find it possible to obtain a bare subsistence from the former, it is obvious that operations in the latter would not pay them.

The daily averages from which the above proportion was deduced were respectively 0·46 and 0·16 of a grain. The greatest amount found on any one day was 2·2 grains.

The above averages should not be taken as being indicative of the absolute amount of gold to be found by a regular system of working, where the washers would of course be set to work at the most favourable spots, and would not have to spend a considerable portion of their time daily, as was the case with those employed by me, in making marches before they reached the scene of their labours. I doubt very much if the ordinary earnings of these gold-washers amount to one anna a day. This may partly be due to the fact that, like many other orientals, they are apt to knock off work when sufficient for the day's bare subsistence has been obtained. They themselves describe the trade as one which simply affords them *pét bhur*, or a bellyful.

In the districts which adjoin Manbhum on the west, I met

---

* "Records of Geological Survey of India," 1869, p. 11.

GOLD-WASHING IN MANBHUM.

with other gold-washers, and throughout Chutia Nagpur the tribes who are engaged in this occupation may be classified as follows :—

First.—The Dohras, or Dokras, of Manbhum, who are allied to the Kumars, and profess to be Hindus. Among them both sexes wash for gold.

Second.—The Ghasis of Singhbhum, among whom the men only wash for gold. The Ghasis are also musicians, and only certain families, or sub-tribes, engage in the former occupation.

Third.—In the hilly country, west of Singhbhum, among certain of the Kol or Munda tribes, the women wash for gold during the rains; but the men regard the occupation as unworthy work for their sex.

The methods employed by these different tribes appear to be identical in all essentials, and similar to the process I have already described. Each occupies a distinct tract, and poaching on each other's favourite streams is not indulged in to any great extent.

April 7th.—Kantagora to Dhadka.—The Dhadka tiger having been killed, I was somewhat surprised when news was brought in at mid-day that two cows had just been killed close at hand by a tiger. Orders were at once given for the erection of a machan near the carcases, and at sunset I took up my position. The full moon soon rose and threw her pale glare over the ghastly white carcases and on the trunks of the trees around. For six hours, or until twelve, I remained watching and listening to the cries of night jars, owls, koels, &c., while rapacious mosquitos tapped my life blood. But no tiger came, and I returned to camp with an awful thirst, the result of which was that I made such libations of tea that sleep was banished from my eyelids for the rest of the night. The tiger's non-appearance to reclaim what he had killed was explained by the subsequently-ascertained fact that after killing the two cows he went to an adjoining village, where he killed a buffalo, which afforded him a dinner.

With my arrival at Dhadka on this occasion I had concluded the geological examination of Manbhum. My own share of the work lay chiefly to the south of the river Damuda; the coal-fields of the Damuda valley and the area of crystalline rocks north of the river having been explored in previous years by other members of the Geological Survey.

It being, though very hot, too soon to go into summer quarters, I determined to take a preliminary scamper through the adjoining district of Singhbhum, in order that I might form an idea of the work before me for the ensuing season. On this subject I was not, however, completely in the dark, as Colonel Haughton had published an excellent sketch-map and account of the geology; and several papers having reference to the copper-mines, of which more hereafter, gave me some idea of the geological features.

Leaving Dhadka on the 9th of April, I crossed the steep ranges of hills which separate Manbhum from Singhbhum, and, as the steepness of the Ghât proved to be somewhat severe on the elephants, I encamped at the small village of Narsinghpur at the foot. The appearance presented by the jungle in this vicinity was very different from what it had been when I last saw it. The trees had lost all their leaves, and the undergrowth had been burnt up. The wild elephants, traces of which were so abundant before, had evidently retreated to their fastnesses in the southern jungles. The following day I marched to a village called Ichara. On the road I met a *mahajan*, or native merchant, jogging along on a pony, and accompanied by half-a-dozen coolies carrying large cages full of young paroquets (*Palæornis eupatrius*, L.) for the Calcutta market. Some of them had scarce a feather on their bodies; but they are remarkably hardy birds. The nests of this species of paroquet are generally made in hollows, which the bird excavates in the soft trunks of the silk cotton tree (*Bombax*). Some of these trees are very lofty, and access to the nests is obtained by the natives by means of a bamboo, or series of bamboos, which are attached to pegs driven into the bark. This merchant had also a number of flattened-out skins of king-fishers (*Halcyon smyrnensis*), which I learnt were destined for Burmah, where the bright blue feathers are of considerable value for the ornamentation of head-dresses, &c.

On the 12th I left the regular made road to Chaibassa, which is the Sudder station of Singhbhum, and struck north-wards. Sending the camp to Landu—which was formerly one of the principal localities where the operations of the copper companies, of which mention will be found on a following page, were carried on—I first made my way to a village called Rajdoha, which was the place where the furnaces, dwellings, &c., of the copper works had been situated. On the way we encountered the bed of a torrent, which was crowded with large masses of rock and boulders, through which I endeavoured to lead my horse; but on the smooth face of a bed he lost his footing, and slipped into a cleft between two boulders, from whence he was rescued only with the greatest difficulty, and sent on to camp. On arrival at Rajdoha I found, to my astonishment, living in a tumble-down bungalow, a Saxon miner, who, after the collapse of the last company, had lived on in the old place. At first he had found some employment in collecting and despatching coolies to a Calcutta agency for Assam tea-gardens; but, the remittances not coming in regularly, he had to give up this occupation, and was, at the time I saw him, living a solitary life in the jungle, but looking forward to obtaining employment in some of the coal companies at Ranigunj. Subsequently I was glad to hear he had obtained the post he wished for. Under his guidance I visited the old workings. There were several inclines, and a shaft, but none of them going to any great depth. In some of them there were abundant traces of copper ore in the form of azurite and malachite. Some pyrites, too, had been struck in the shaft. In the engine-house lay a blast engine, which had cost many hundreds of pounds to bring to its present position. Owing to neglect, theft of the metal mountings, and the effects of the climate, it was fast becoming worthless. I then started for my camp at Landu, and, my horse having been taken to camp, had a trying walk of seven miles in the mid-day April sun. My boots being uncomfortable, I took them off and walked in bare feet. This I had often previously done for much greater distances; but on this occasion the heat of the ground was so great that the soles of my feet were badly blistered. The following morning I examined the old workings at Landu, which were more extensive than those at Rajdoha. Some of them had the appearance of great antiquity.

The people of Landu were of the Bhumiz tribe. Whether the works had demoralised them by bringing employment to their doors, to the destruction of their agricultural pursuits, I cannot say, but they seemed to be in a very wretched condition.

In a range of hills to the south of Landu, a local industry afforded occupation to people of the surrounding villages. This was a pot-stone mine and dish factory, similar to those already described in Manbhum. At the time of my visit the operations seemed to be in a rather languishing condition.

The next day I returned to the Chaibassa road, encamping at a village called Hesul. From this vicinity a general bird's-eye view of the geological structure and resultant physical features of the Singhbhum basin can readily be obtained. The central area consists of highly granitoid rocks, which are traversed by long and sometimes lofty trap dykes belonging to several series, which intersect one another at more or less regular distances, thus cutting up the greater part of the area into diamond-shaped plots, each of which is thus surrounded by natural walls, which serve as lasting demarcations between adjoining properties. Resting on the older metamorphic rocks of the central area is a group of schists, including the pot-stones and the copper-bearing beds. These latter, so to speak, cloak round the area, and as they rise to some height, form a distinct rim to the basin.

From Hesul I made a short march to Gundasai, mapping in the numerous trap dykes which are crossed by the road. In the evening I went to examine some hills in the vicinity of Gundasai, and on my return found that the villagers had swarmed out of their villages and were perched about on every "coign of vantage," in order to watch my proceedings. My examination of the rocks appeared to strike them as something particularly extraordinary. I had often been surrounded on previous occasions by numbers of people who had manifested much curiosity about my operations; but there was something in the manner and appearance of these individuals that shewed me they belonged to a distinct race from any I had before met with. This was soon confirmed by my finding that out of a group of some fifty individuals only one or two seemed to understand the questions which I put to them in Hindustani and Bengali. These were in fact, the Hos or Lurka Kols, who in many ways are one of the most remarkable races of aborigines to be found in Western Bengal. Here I first heard use made of the term *Gúmki*, a title of respect, which is the Ho equivalent of the Hindustani word Sahib.

On the following day I rode into Chaibassa, the Sudder station of Singhbhum, where I received a hospitable reception from a former acquaintance. The station is a small one, consisting of the public offices, a few private bungalows, and a small native bazaar. It is not altogether unpicturesquely situated, but there is an appearance of desolation in the surroundings, and one cannot help experiencing a feeling of being at the very outskirts of civilization when in Chaibassa. To the west and south-west one might travel through the wildest jungle for several hundreds of miles, without coming upon a single sign of any kind to indicate that the people have, in any way, been brought into contact with the British power—save, perhaps, that afforded by their quiet and undisturbed condition. As an outpost from which operations were carried on against the Kols and the turbulent Khonds, and other tribes of Sambalpur and Ganjam—Chaibassa was formerly of some importance from a military point of view. In more recent times, during disturbances in Keonjar, it also served as a basis of operations. Hereafter, should a direct line of rail connecting Calcutta with Nagpur be made, it may rise to some importance, but otherwise no great future can be predicted for it. I remained for one whole day in Chaibassa, and during the early morning hours was enabled to examine the geology of the immediate vicinity of the station. There was good reason for my not prolonging my stay; all the officers stationed there were down with, or were only just recovering from, fever. My men were falling sick too.

On the night of the 19th I started off the camp to Seraikela, a village situated about fourteen miles to the north, and followed it up the next morning myself. As the road ran nearly with the boundary separating the two series of metamorphic rocks above-mentioned, I was enabled to fix some points on the map, which subsequently proved very useful. Seraikela is situated on the banks of the Khorkai river. At it is the residence of a Raja who is semi-independent and pays no tribute; the said residence is by no means an imposing structure, being hardly distinguishable from the other mud huts in the village.

The following morning the camp started before sunrise for Kandra, I following later, in order to see all that was to be seen in the vicinity of the road. Riding along I was pained to find that some of my followers had become so enfeebled by fever that they could hardly crawl along the road; among these was the native doctor, who looked the most miserable of the lot. They had omitted to make an early start, and were in consequence feeling the heat. All managed, however, to reach the camp before evening. The tent was pitched in a small grove of mango trees, a thick layer of decomposed leaf-mould being first removed. This disturbed several snakes and scorpions—the former were seen at the time, the latter made their appearance after the tent was pitched, crawling up the walls. The imprudence of sleeping in such a tainted atmosphere was fully demonstrated before the night was over. I awoke, feeling the first indications of fever, and these became fully developed ere I reached the next halting-place at Chondil on the following day. For the whole of that day I remained in that semi-delirious condition characteristic of these fevers, and in which there is a feeling of double identity, which is very puzzling and annoying. I remember, after a long struggle between the two conflicting parties, experiencing a sense of relief on casting my eyes to the corner of my tent where the guns stood, and being able to fix myself, or rather a part of my entity, as their proprietor.

During the three following nights and early morning hours the march was continued to Purulia. Being too weak to ride, and no other means of carriage being speedily available, I used to get myself hoisted on to the top of one of the elephants' loads.

At Purulia I remained for two clear days with my friends to recover myself and servants. After which, four short marches took us through well-known country to the railway station at Barakar, whence I started for Calcutta. On arrival in Calcutta I was appointed, together with my friend and colleague the late Dr. Stoliczka, joint-Curator of the Indian Museum—the Curator, Dr. Anderson, having gone with the expedition to Western China, *viâ* Bhamo and Yunnan.

With the exception of a short trip down the river to the Sandheads—which was necessitated by my not being able to shake off the effects of the fever—I remained in Calcutta until the 11th of November.

CHAPTER V.

SECTION I.

SINGHBHUM.

1868–69.

INSTRUCTIONS FOR SEASON'S WORK—MARCH FROM SEARSOLE TO PURULIA—ADVENTURE WITH A TIGER—ASCEND THE CHUTIA NAGPUR PLATEAU—RANCHI—THE MISSIONARIES IN TROUBLE—START FOR SINGHBHUM—URAON NACH—MUNDAS—CHRISTIAN CONVERTS—PERWA GHAG WATERFALL—PARASITICAL PLANTS—CHERT-FLAKES—TUSSER COCOONS—KOL VILLAGES—CHRISTMAS AT CHAIBASSA—TOM-TOMS—SHIKARIS OR BAGH-MARS—SICKNESS IN CAMP—TIGER KILLED BY WILD DOGS—FIND A "CELT"—POST GOES ASTRAY—ANCIENT COPPER MINES—THAKUR OF KHURSOWA—BEAT FOR GAME—SUPERSTITION—INTERNATIONAL DANCING CONTEST—CHERT-FLAKES—RAJA OF SERAIKELA—GEOLOGY OF SERAIKELA—BEARS AND HYÆNAS—COPPER AND POT-STONE MINES—RANGAMATIA HILL, A REPUTED VOLCANO—TIGER'S HOUSE—KERIAH SIGNALS AND TRAPS—BEHURS—SECTIONS IN SUBANRIKA—HEAVY RAIN—SMALL BIRDS—RUAM—TRACKS OF WILD ELEPHANTS—RAJA OF DHALBHUM—BEAR SHOT BY SONTALS—OPPOSITION BY GUIDES—GOLD-WASHERS—POT-STONE MINES—KERIAH WEDDING PARTY—FRUIT-EATING PIGEON—COMMENCEMENT OF HOT SEASON—FIND DEAD BEAR—ENTER MIDNAPUR DISTRICT—DISTURBANCE WITH VILLAGERS—QUARRELSOME BENGALIS—BEAT FOR GAME—A LADY TRAVELLER—RIDE INTO MIDNAPUR—IRRIGATION—LATERITE—RETURN TO CAMP—PHULKUSMA RAJA—ADJUTANT—VULTURES—FORD SUBANRIKA—BOMBAY ROAD—ELEPHANT KEDAH—MOHURBUNJ—SUBANRIKA SECTION—NATIVES UNTRUTHFUL—RETURN TO SINGHBUM BASIN—CARTS—SHOOT A BEAR—ACCIDENT TO HORSE—NATIVES FEED ON DISEASED MEAT—BHAGMURIA HILL—BURSTING OF PODS—SONTAL COLONY—SEPULCHRAL RITE—PIGMY CATTLE—SNAKES—BEARS—VILLAGE PRIEST—SONTAL ANNUAL HUNT—INTENSE HEAT—LURKA KOLS—MENHIRS AND DOLMENS—KOL NAMES OF BIRDS—CLOSE WORK FOR THE SEASON—GEOLOGICAL RESUMÉ—ANCIENT COPPER-MINERS—MARCH AT NIGHT ON ACCOUNT OF HEAT—PLAGUE OF FLIES—PURULIA.

THIS season I was directed to commence the detailed geological examination of Singhbhum, and to pay especial attention to the copper dêposits which were known to occur there. On taking the field in November, I first went into camp at Searsole, near Ranigunj, where I remained for two days, and then marched for Purulia. Having no geological work to do on the line of route, I occupied my time principally in shooting small birds, thus providing employment for a bird-skinner whom I had brought out with me on behalf of the Indian Museum. At Sindurpur, the last stage before Purulia, I revisited the bears' caves, but waited in vain for the appearance of any bears. The natives accounted for their absence by saying that at this season they were living in the low grounds.

On arrival in Purulia, I found that the Deputy-Commissioner, with two others of the residents, had gone the previous day a few miles out from the station, on the report of the villagers that some wild animal—they could not say what—had concealed itself in a field containing a growing crop of rice. Having reached the place, they discovered some footprints, which clearly indicated the nature of the animal they had to deal with. It was, in fact, a tiger, which had evidently been travelling during the night, and with the break of day had found itself too far distant from suitable cover, and had accordingly taken refuge in the crops. A slight movement in the rice, as the party approached, indicated the position of the animal; but they had no means for driving him out into the open. The Deputy-Commissioner took up a position on an embankment of the rice-field, and called to his companions to throw some stones, so as to rouse the animal. They at first protested against his exposing himself; but as he would not return they threw a stone, when out sprang the tiger and flung itself upon him, knocking him down and biting his shoulder. At this critical moment, when it would have been dangerous for the others to fire, a half-bred bull-terrier, which had done good service before with bears, attacked the tiger in the rear, and so effectually distracted its attention, that they were enabled to fire and disable it. The Deputy-Commissioner, at the time quite unconscious of the extent of his injuries, picked himself up and helped to give the finishing shots to the animal. On examination it was found that he had been much bitten about the shoulder-joint, and the wounds at one time threatened serious consequences. His pluck, good constitution, and the favourable season of the year, all conduced towards a speedy cure, which took place in the course of a few months. Subsequently, I believe, in a different part of the country, he again experienced the sensation of being in the jaws of a tiger. Joe, my own bull-terrier, the companion of many rambles, had become so ill in Purulia, where I had left him, as to be permanently deaf, and otherwise enfeebled. Among my servants he was believed to have been the dog which had attacked the tiger as above described; and in spite of my telling them that such was not the case, they industriously spread abroad the report wherever we went, adding that the Deputy-Commissioner, out of gratitude for the rescue, had given him a collar of gold.

As four or five of my servants were already attacked with fever, it was several days before I could resume my march.

November 22nd.—Purulia to Jhulda.—I followed up my camp, which had started the previous day, and got as far as Jhulda, a considerable village about thirty miles off to the west. The following day I marched to a place called Sili, which is situated on the west bank of the beautiful Subanrika river. Between Sili and the next halting-place, Jona, the road gradually ascends the flanks of the Ranchi plateau, traversing a very fine piece of forest, in which may be seen some species of trees which below occur as small bushes, and others which are found only on the tops of the outlying hills. Sometimes the road crosses picturesque glades and rocky streams. A stage further on, at Lukum, the jungle is left behind, and the level surface of the top of the Ranchi plateau, studded with mango-groves and occasional patches of uncut jungle, opens to the view. A portion of the road, lined with fine old trees, resembles an avenue such as one sees in a well-wooded demesne in Europe.

November 26th.—To-day I reached the *Sudder* Station, Ranchi, where reside the Commissioner and the Judicial Commissioner of the Chutia Nagpur Division, and the local officers of the district of Lohardugga. The station is somewhat picturesquely situated in a plain, studded by a number of rounded, bossy, and conical hills of granitic gneiss. About the centre of the area occupied by the houses on the western side is a piece of artificially-enclosed water, generally known as "The Lake," which, with its wooded islets and causeway running three parts round, presents a very charming appearance. Two miles, or rather less, to the south of the civil station, lies Dorunda, where the military cantonments are situated. This is the most northern station garrisoned by Madras Native Infantry on the eastern side of India.

On the occasion of this, my first visit, I found that there was some commotion in the station, in consequence of the old German Lutheran missionaries—who had been established in Chutia Nagpur for many years, and who had, there is reason to believe, done much good and solid work amongst the Uraons—having recently been superseded by young men, who were sent out by the home society at Berlin. The latter were reputed to be more highly educated than the old pioneers, who by their judicious management of the affairs of the mission, had, I believe, rendered it nearly self-supporting. That young men, having no knowledge of the people, country, or language, should be placed over them they considered to be an act of great injustice. At a meeting held in Ranchi it was decided to support the old missionaries while the matter was pending, and to write to the society in Berlin the views on the matter entertained by the residents. These were to the effect that the old missionaries should be left to superintend the work they had hitherto performed so successfully. The society refused to alter the decision, and a schism was the result: several of the older missionaries were ordained into the Church of England, joined the Church Missionary Society, and took over with them a certain number of their converts.

At this time Ranchi was famous for its croquet and *chota-haziri* or early breakfast parties; these being arranged for different days of the week, constant reunions of all the members of the station took place in the pretty grounds attached to some of the houses.

November 28th.—To-day I started southwards for the Singhbhum district, the Civil Surgeon of the station accompanying me for a few marches. One evening we had a Uraon nach to celebrate his departure on the following day. It was markedly distinct from any dance I had seen by the Sontals or other races. The girls, carefully arranged in lines by sizes, with the tallest at one end, and the smallest at the other, firmly grasp one another's hands, and the whole movements are so perfectly in concert that they spring about with as much agility as a single individual could. Having been started at dancing on our account, they kept it up on their own for the greater part of the night at their regular dancing-place, or *akhara* in the village. Such dancing-places, surrounded and shadowed by trees, generally tamarinds, and with the ground well-beaten down, are to be found in the vicinity of almost every Uraon village. The vigorous dancing at night does not apparently prevent work on the following day.

December 5th.—Bandgaon.—This being a large village in a central position, I remained for a few days to examine the neighbourhood, which was within the limits of my season's work. While here, my camp was joined by a chuprasi from the Singhbhum Deputy-Commissioner's office, who proved to be most useful, as he understood five languages, spoken by the different tribes and races in the country I afterwards entered.

Some of the small villages in the hills in this neighbourhood were inhabited by Mundas, a tribe allied to the Hos and Sontals, and therefore quite distinct from the Dravidian Uraons, who occupy the plateau further north. These people often knew only two or three words of Hindustani. Very wild they appeared to be, and much given to drink. In one village I passed through, every soul—man, woman, and child—appeared to be drunk. With their faces whitened with wood-ash, they danced about in a half-frantic state, and the scene presented to my eyes was more of the nature of an African orgie than my previous experience led me to expect in India. When in their cups these people are fortunately good-humoured with Europeans, and their conduct is marked rather by the profundity of their salaams than anything else. With Hindustanis, however, when in this state they are apt to become unmanageable. Occasionally a passer-by on the road would salute me by saying *Esus*, at the same time pressing forward to touch my hand.

This proceeding I did not understand until it was pointed out to me that these persons were Christian converts who had been taught to salute in this manner by the missionaries. So far as my observation went, in none of the Christian villages were such scenes as I have above described ever to be seen. Indeed the missionaries seemed to have established a somewhat methodistical code of life. Dancing is strictly prohibited,—this could only be justified by the fact of its having been found impossible to alienate it from concomitants which might, perhaps, be with reason objected to. Not only do the Uraon converts abjure dancing, almost as an article of faith, but they avoid even being present when dancing by others is going on. Such being their view of the duty of a Christian, it was with unfeigned astonishment that some time after the period of which I write, they heard that the Bishop of Calcutta, the highest dignitary of the Church which some of them had joined, asked, on the occasion of a visit to Ranchi, to be shown a Uraon nach. Much were they scandalized, and it must have taxed the full powers of the missionaries to explain this act of the Lord Padri Sahib's—as he is called by the natives.

While at Bandgaon I paid a visit to a famous waterfall called the Para or Perwa Ghag, which is about eleven or twelve miles to the west. I was particularly anxious to see this fall, as a certain amount of mystery attached to it, in consequence of its having been stated by the natives that its waters completely disappeared in a deep hole or cave. Arrived at the Karo river, I went along the northern bank, but found, that from that side the full view was hidden by a projecting cliff, so I was compelled to swim across to the other side, and, from a rock on the edge of the basin hollowed out by the fall, was able to command the whole scene. The water tumbles over a steep face of granite, into an extensive basin cut in the solid rock, and over the edge of which it surges in regular pulses, so feeding the river below. There is no disappearance of the waters, as stated by the natives.

In this part of the country my attention was again attracted by the numerous diseases to which the forest trees are subject by the various parasitical plants. Among these there are two species of *Loranthus*, two of *Viscum* (mistletoe), and two "Dodders," all of which affect more or less the vitality of the plants upon which they settle.

In the heavy jungles which I passed through, in descending from the Ranchi plateau to the district of Singhbhum, I saw specimens of the so-called elephant creepers (*Bauhinia Vahlii*) of enormous size, the diameter of the stems being occasionally as much as ten inches.

December 19th.—Chukerdhurpur.—In the vicinity of this village, which is in the district of Singhbhum, I found a number of flakes of cherty-quartzite lying on the surface, which, quite apart from the fact of their resemblance to the well-known flakes of human manufacture, required particular notice and investigation, since they were found resting on granitoid gneisses, and at a distance from the rock source from whence they had been derived. Although I had seen specimens of flakes collected in this district before, and had indeed published a notice of the fact,* this was the first opportunity which I had of examining the circumstances of their origin for myself. It was perfectly clear that they had been transported at least three miles, as the nearest possible source of the material is situated at that distance from some of the spots where I found them. The levels at which they were found, and their angular and unrounded condition, rendered it almost improbable that the transporting agency could have been other than human. Such being the case, I think it safe to conclude that these objects are really of artificial origin. (*Vide* Appendix B.)

In the more open parts of Singhbhum a large portion of the waste land is studded with trees of the Asan (*Terminalia tomentosa*), upon which numbers of the *Tusser* caterpillar are reared. The silk yielded by the cocoons of this caterpillar is becoming so well known in England that it may be of interest to give an account of its cultivation.

---

* Proc. Asiatic Soc. Bengal, July, 1868.

The trees which it is intended to stock are carefully pollarded before the rains, and in early spring the leaves are stocked with young caterpillars which have been hatched in the houses. The men in charge erect wigwams and remain on the spot, isolated from their families, who regard them for the time being as unclean. During the daytime they have full occupation in guarding the large green caterpillars from the attacks of kites and other birds.

The cocoons are collected soon after they are spun, and boiled in a lye of wood-ash, and the extracted chrysalids must then be *eaten* by the caretakers, who have to undergo certain ceremonial rites before they are readmitted into the society of their fellows. The effect of the boiling in the lye is the removal of the glutinous matter, which renders it possible to wind off the silk. But this is not done until some time after, when the cocoons, having first passed through several hands, reach the manufacturer. The fabric produced is renowned for its extraordinary durability; the only objection to it being, in fact, the extreme difficulty which ladies experience in wearing out dresses made of it. The cocoon sliced into strips is employed by the natives for various purposes where great strength is required. Thus the barrels of matchlocks are secured to the woodwork by bands of this substance.

Some of the Kol villages in this neighbourhood presented a very untidy appearance as compared with respectable Hindu villages, numerous pigs and dirty children being seen wallowing together in the dust, as they do sometimes, it must be admitted, in a certain island 7,000 miles to the westward.

December 24th. — *Chaibassa.* — In the evening I rode into Chaibassa in order to spend Christmas with the limited circle of officials in the station. Some changes had taken place, I found, in the *personnel* since my previous visit. Those officers who have mastered the Ho language and have become intimate with the people, like this station; but with the executive services of Bengal generally, it is regarded much in the light of a penal settlement. One of the residents had so far identified himself with the Hos that he had learnt to play their national airs on the tom-tom, and used himself to join at times in their national dances. His house was open to all who came into the station to market. I believe his knowledge of and intercourse with these people, were the means of his often acting as adjudicator in disputes, which among Hindus and under a less patriarchal system would have blossomed into cases before the court. Thus a great amount of vexatious litigation which would give rise to ill feeling, to be perpetuated perhaps for generations, was put a stop to at an early stage. In domestic matters even of a most delicate nature, my friend was also often the referee, and the amount of confidence and attention paid to his *ex-officio* decisions was simply marvellous.

I have alluded above to tom-toms, and therefore take this opportunity of saying, in spite of an opinion which is very prevalent to the contrary, that there is a great deal of spirit and character in some of the airs played on them by the different tribes. After some experience of them I found that when hearing these tunes at night I could not unfrequently identify the race to which the performers belonged.

According to many, tom-toming consists of inane hammering away at the drum with the simple object of making a noise. Such is, however, really not the case; there is room for the exhibition of much skill in the performance, and the best performers are highly esteemed in their respective villages. I do not by the above mean to commit myself to an opinion that Europeans should cultivate the art of playing the tom-tom, nor do I blame them for not enjoying this particular kind of music. It has caused me so very much annoyance that I am never likely to become an advocate for its increase and further development. The whole subject of native music is one beyond my powers to discuss, but is an interesting one for those having special knowledge. It is stated that the natives admit our superiority in every art and science save only in music; our system being as distasteful to them as theirs is to us.

December 28th.—On returning to camp to-day, after my day's work, I found that some Shikaris, otherwise called *Bagh mars*, or tiger slayers, had brought in the carcase of a female bear with two live cubs. They had shot her with a set-bow and poisoned arrows. The contrivance is an ingenious one and worthy of description. It consists of a strong bamboo bow, to which additional strength is given by several splints firmly lashed on. The string is a stout rope. It requires two men standing on the bow and pulling the string to set it, and it is kept set by means of a stick provided with a cleverly-contrived trigger in which the string is hitched. The bow is then laid on stones, so as to give it the right elevation and command the path which the animal is known to frequent. A string attached to the trigger is fastened to an iron peg, which is driven into the ground at the opposite side of the path. Two arrows with poisoned barbs are then fixed in position on either side of the trigger stick, and all is ready for any such animal as a tiger, bear, or leopard, which passing along the path cannot fail to press against the string, so releasing the arrows, one, if not both, of which is sure to strike, and, in consequence of the strength of the bow, to penetrate deeply. An ingenious arrangement provides against the risk to the lives of cattle and men, which would otherwise be involved in the placing of these instruments near pathways. To the right and left, strings are stretched from the trigger and bound to convenient trees at such an elevation that a tiger or smaller animal would pass under them, and so proceed onwards to the lower string above mentioned. But a cow or a man would strike the higher string, so pulling the trigger and causing the arrows to be discharged well in front, so that no injury could ensue.

December 31st.—On taking stock of my servants on this, the last day of the year, I found that out of twenty-seven men only three had escaped fever during the short time I had been in camp. This, with my experience of Singhbhum in April, afforded strong evidence of the unhealthiness of the district.

January 1st.—Rabo to Gomria.—To-day, when returning to camp through some dense jungle, I met my friends the Shikaris in the act of finding the body of a remarkably fine leopard, which had been shot by their *kul* (engine) or set-bow. The poison must have operated quickly, as the animal had scarcely strayed 100 yards from the place where it was struck.

From these Shikaris I had most positive assurance that tigers are occasionally killed by packs of the wild dog (*Cuon rutilans*). One of them told me that upon one occasion he heard a tiger roaring in the jungle close to a house in which he and his friends took refuge. When the noise ceased he crept out and found a number of the dogs round the carcase of a tiger which they had just disembowelled. The balance of evidence seems on the whole to favour the probability of such an event sometimes taking place, though it is difficult to realise the fact of the tiger becoming so crippled by fear, as he assuredly must, as not to be able to lay low any number of such assailants. However, parallel cases of small, insignificant animals overcoming others vastly more powerful by force of numbers and activity, are not wanting.

January 2nd.—Gomria to Boghar.—To-day I was fortunate in finding a still more satisfactory trace of pre-historic man than the flakes above mentioned. This consisted of a well-shaped and partially polished "celt," regarding the artificial origin of which not a doubt could be entertained. It was of particular interest as being the first example of the so-called neolithic type which had been met with in Bengal.*

January 7th.—Bundnon.—With the assistance of the Purdhan or head man of this place, I found some old excavations for copper which had been reported to exist in this neighbourhood. They were in themselves small and unimportant, but were of interest as being at the most western extremity of a deposit of ore which I subsequently traced for about eighty miles, and which may yet prove to be of some economic value.†

January 8th.—Khursowa.—On arrival here I found the young Thakur or Raja awaiting my coming. He represents the youngest branch of the Porahat family, which was at one time supreme in these regions, at least so far as the not-very-manageable Lurka Kols or Hos would admit. His estate is a small one, but he

---

* Proc. Asiatic Soc. Bengal, 1870, p. 125.

† *Vide* "Records of Geological Survey of India," 1870, p. 86.

enjoys a sort of semi-independence, and is vested with magisterial powers for the trial of the less serious offences. His welcome was cordial and unaffected. He had learnt to shake hands, as have also most of the Rajas in this part of the country, unlike many of those I had previously met in Manbhum. Apparently the custom had been handed down from the instructions given by some former Governor-General's agent at Chaibassa. He was much struck with my breech-loading rifle, not having ever seen one before, as none of the district officials were sportsmen. For the purpose of producing an effect he came up to my tent in a pony-phaeton drawn and pushed by coolies. This and another conveyance which he had purchased from some official leaving the country could not have been much use to him, since he did not possess a road upon which he could drive.

January 10th.—Khursowa.—To-day I accepted an invitation from the Thakur to a beat for large game. When starting I was surprised to find that we did not take the route to what I considered the most likely ground—the Akarsuni hill and its surrounding jungle, and remonstrated accordingly. The Thakur, however, declared that where we were going was the best place for game, by which I was for the moment pacified; but we drew a blank and saw no signs of any animals such as abounded near the Akarsuni hill. I afterwards found that the reason why the Thakur did not beat there was because it was considered sacred, and that a prophecy existed to the effect that if any animals were killed there the destruction of the house of Khursowa would ensue. Similar beliefs I found to be very prevalent in Singhbhum, and the people in many places proved to be most unwilling to aid me in sport.

January 12th. — Govindpur. — Towards the afternoon an enormous crowd of people assembled near my tent to witness the celebration by dancing of the principal day of a Kol festival. It might indeed almost be called an international dancing contest, as a variety of different races, among whom the Sontals were conspicuous for want of grace, performed their characteristic dances. There were also some sham fights, the performers being armed with swords and shields. As with other wild people, the feints and dancing about are considered to be a most important feature in the combat. All the spectators were dressed in their best, so that the whole had a very gay and festive appearance.

January 15th.—Govindpur to Seraikela.—During to-day's work near the village of Hadua I discovered some more well-formed flakes and cores of chert. They occurred in broken ground, subject apparently to the action of floods, and lay in drifts mixed up with fragments of kunkur, laterite, mica, schist, and jaspery-quartzite.

The Raja of Seraikela drove up to my tent in a pony-carriage to pay a visit, a great mob of the villagers following and cheering in his wake. He was an old man, but remarkably clear-headed and intelligent. He freely gave me all the information he could about his estate. On his arm he had a handsome and massive bracelet made, he told me, of gold found in the streams on his own property. The Seraikela family is a branch of that of Porahat, and originally the proper title of the head member of the branch was only Kour, or prince; but, in consequence of good service rendered to the British, the Kour was in 1856 raised to the dignity of Raja Bahadur by the Government. In 1857, during the mutiny, he again did good service, for which he received a *killut*, or robe of honour, and a rent-free grant in perpetuity of Koraikela, a *Pir* or district which had been taken from the Porahat Raja, who was deported to Benares in consequence of his mutinous conduct at the same time.

The Khorkai river, on the banks of which, in a most picturesque position, Seraikela is placed, abounds in magnificent sections, which illustrate the geological structure in a very striking manner. Huge trap-dykes abound in the granitic gneisses, which in this vicinity are overlaid by a younger series of rocks, the members of which, though also metamorphic, are readily distinguished by their lithological characters. They consist chiefly of quartzites, pot-stones, and schists.

January 29th.—Gopinathpur.—Yesterday before I returned from work, Saidon, the Jemidar, went off on his own account to investigate the truth of a rumour that the neighbouring hills, through which I had innocently taken a quiet stroll on the previous evening, were full of bears. He came back with an account of his having seen a *bagh*, which might have been either a tiger, a leopard, or hyæna, and abundant traces of bears. In consequence of the information I arranged to pay the hills a visit before sunrise this morning. Rising about two hours before dawn, I went off to the hills in the moonlight. Having reached the south-eastern extremity, where a spur formed of huge boulders of trap, piled up in massive confusion, ran down into the plain, I was just preparing to ascend when I heard a rustling amongst the rocks, and my guide called out "Sahib, there are the bears!" For some moments, owing to the darkness, I could not distinguish their black bodies from the masses of black rock amongst which they were scrambling. At last, by the glistening of their silky coats in the moonbeams, which contrasted with the gloomy reflection from the lustreless trap rock, I was enabled to make out two bears, but at what distance exactly from the point where I stood I could not tell with accuracy. However, I took two shots, one of which caused a bear to howl, but the other was a palpable miss, since I heard the shell burst on the rocks. After this they made off, and as they rose on the crest of the ridge I could see them, together with a young one which I had not before observed, their outlines being well defined when the sky, and not the black rocks, formed the background.

Running round the spur in the hope of getting another shot at them before they could reach their cave, I saw two objects at the top of the ridge which I thought might be the bears' heads, but I could not be sure. After a minute or so they moved, and then one of the bears stood out in full profile against the sky. Whether the shot I took had any effect or not I cannot say, as it was so dark that I could only point my gun in the direction without attempting to take proper aim.

We then went to take up a position in front of two caves, belonging respectively to bears and hyænas, the occupants of which it was expected would be about returning at this time from their night's prowlings. As I approached the spot I saw some animal stealing through the jungle, which I have no doubt was a hyæna. While waiting here the night-jars and other nocturnal birds flitted about, screeching and whistling, and from the depths of the cavern in front came the mumbling sounds which bears make when sucking their paws. Gradually the chorus of the different birds which in this country welcome the rising sun waxed loud, if not melodious. As soon as it was light enough for us to see our way about we started off to a neighbouring hill, whence we hoped to be able to descry some straggling bear coming up from the plains. The active guide then ran off to the highest peak, and after scanning the horizon in every direction, came running back in breathless haste. At first I thought from his manner that he was pursued by some animal. He soon, however, pointed out a bear, which about a quarter of a mile off was sniffing about and leisurely making his way to the hills. Running as fast as the broken nature of the ground permitted, we ascended a ridge from the west, while Bruin scaled it by its eastern slope. On catching sight of him I gave him two shots and he rolled down to the bottom, apparently killed, but he soon picked himself up and made off across the plain. From his limping gait I thought it would be an easy matter to overtake him; so, loading as I ran, I started in pursuit, but whenever I stopped to take a shot the bear would be sure to be concealed by rocks or trees. The pace though not very fast was very trying from the nature of the ground and the numerous obstacles, and three times I tripped up and measured my length on the ground. Having run about a quarter of a mile or more, Bruin made a vigorous spurt for the hills, and when I came to the foot of the rise I found myself too much blown by the run and the falls to ascend, so, handing my rifle to Saidon, who had discharged his gun and thrown away his ammunition in the scrimmage, I told him to follow up, and that I would be after him in a moment as soon as I could get breath. He lost an easy chance of a shot, and when I got up I found that the bear had disappeared in a cave. This was a great disappointment, for, but for my falls, I should have been able to have ranged up alongside of him and given him a broadside. The extent of the caves rendered it impossible to make any attempt at smoking out the bears with the least prospect of success.

In the afternoon I started off again from camp for these hills, the scene of the morning's adventures, and took up a position in front of the caves. I must have remained there nearly half-an-hour without anything appearing. My attention, however, was fully occupied with watching the birds which, as I remained quite still, came close without fear. There were little *Prinias* and *Phylloscopine* birds, and a *Thamnobia* would now and then dart out from the rocks. The spot soon became a point of attraction to a number of other birds, as a cloud of termites rose to take their short and only flight. Crows, rollers, king-crows, kites, and a pair of black-necked storks, appeared on the scene, and formed a whirling greedy crowd pouncing with avidity on this favourite food. As each termite passed into the mouth of a roller, there was a loud snap caused by the rapid closing of the bird's mandibles.

A little before sunset I heard a couple of shots from Saidon's gun, he having gone off to some other caves, which were separated from those where I was by a north to south ridge of low hills. On reaching the top of this ridge I heard a rustle in the bushes on the eastern flank below me, and presently a hyæna broke into the plain below, and for some moments stood looking up at us, uncertain what to do. I might then have taken a long shot at him, but did not do so, as from my previous experience I had resolved to confine myself to close shots. Moving then up to some other caves which were in the east and west range close by, I took up a new position accompanied by two coolies, one of whom held a spare gun. After waiting some time, till it was quite dusk, I observed a movement amongst the stones in front, and then saw a hyæna which I hit, but he managed to scramble off. While trying to trace him up I heard a new rustling in the bushes of the north to south ridge, and presently, with that peculiar *woof* sound, which is neither a howl nor a growl, a bear rushed straight in the direction where I was standing. Fully expecting that he was going to dispute the passage with me, I reserved my fire for close quarters, thinking a shot so taken would be more effective. Unfortunately I had no opportunity of putting this plan into execution, as he turned off sharp and was immediately lost to sight behind rocks and jungle. It was now dark, so we had to make for camp empty-handed.

The man who had acted as my guide in these expeditions was a Mussulman, and a very plucky young fellow. As I was marching away he came to me to complain that the Bengalis and Bhumiz who lived in the village had been abusing him for taking me to the hill, as they believed the bears to be possessed by evil spirits who, if offended, would visit with wrath and utter destruction those who interfered with them. They assured the man that he would certainly be killed some day by a tiger or bear for his misconduct.

The badness of my shooting on this occasion, and indeed I may say all the time I remained in Singhbhum, was in a great measure due to the high trajectory of a new heavy breech-loading rifle, which never suited me, and which I got rid of as soon as possible afterwards. With the Express rifles of the present day, and perhaps somewhat steadied nerves, I should have made a very different bag.

January 30th.—Gopinathpur to Landu.—To-day I marched to Landu, where the old copper mines, mentioned on a previous page, are situated. I spent a couple of days in their exploration, and also in the examination of extensive pot-stone mines. In this neighbourhood I got a hint as to the probable identity of the ancient copper-miners: the result of my enquiries I give on a subsequent page.

February 2nd.—Landu to Rajdoha.—Since my last visit to Rajdoha the Saxon miner had taken his departure, and there was no one to look after the deserted engine and buildings left by the Copper Company. From this place I ascended the Rangamatia Hill, which Colonel Haughton in his geological account, already alluded to, describes on native authority as a fire-mountain. His own recorded observations clearly shewed that there was no real foundation for the story, which asserted that from a cavity on the face of some cliffs about half-way up, unearthly noises issued at times, and that in some years *after heavy rain* fire was poured forth from it. Colonel Haughton could not "detect the odour of any gas exhaling from it, and the cave itself had no appearance of igneous action about it." The natives with him could not be induced to approach it. Those with me could not, or would not, point out the exact spot, but I satisfied myself that the only foundation for the belief was that, after rain, a steamy cloud of vapour was often to be seen curling up from the summit. The appearance is not uncommon in these hilly regions, and is spoken of by the natives as being caused by *dhunan*, which is the term ordinarily applied to smoke, but also signifies vapour.

From the summit of this hill there was a remarkably fine view, the contrast between the country on either side being very striking. On the north there is a broad zone of jungle, in which the cultivated areas surrounding villages are few and far between. On the south, however, in the central Singhbhum basin, cultivation, dotted with villages and mango-groves, and a few small hills, prevails, while a few patches of jungle are seen at rare intervals. An old, apparently exhausted, copper-mine which I found on this hill, testified to the assiduity with which the ancients had searched the ground.

February 5th.—Ichinda.—On leaving camp this morning I first ascended the hills to the south-east, where I found along the crest of the main range constant traces of old copper-workings, there being upwards of twenty distinct mines. I then paid a visit to a place called *Bagh ghura*, or the tiger's-house, where it was believed that a tiger was in the habit of dwelling. The place was picturesquely situated on the banks of a small stream, the trees growing on either bank of which joined their branches together above, and were further bound together by a number of large creepers. The tiger's den was under an overhanging ledge of rock. It looked a likely place enough, but if ever inhabited by a tiger the proprietor on this occasion was not at home. However the picturesque wildness of the place was, in the absence of a chance of a shot, a sufficient recompense for the trouble of getting there. On the path leading to it, one of the coolies with me noticing some flat stones, turned them over, and disclosed under them some grains of parched Indian corn. These were either offerings made by the Keriahs to the evil spirits of the place, or, as was suggested by some of the men, signals to their friends according to some code. Such signals are, as is well known, often employed by gipsies. In one place I found a flat stone arranged for a sufficiently obvious and practical purpose. It was supported by an arrangement of twigs, similar to the schoolboy's figure of 4 trap; some grains of parched corn were laid as bait in this primitive trap, which had no doubt been set for jungle fowl. I sprung the trap to see its method of working, and, by way of repaying the owner for his disappointment, placed some small copper coins underneath. I fancy when the man found these he must have been not a little perplexed to account for their presence, and not improbably attributed it to supernatural agency. A Keriah whom I afterwards met told me of a race of people whom he regarded as still wilder than his own. These people, called Behurs, I had previously heard of, but the following particulars regarding them were new to me. It appears that they are without fixed home, and travel from jungle to jungle, no man knowing whence they come and whither they go. Their chief employment seems to be catching monkeys, which furnish them with a staple article of diet. The method of capture is popularly supposed to have an element of magic in it. A net is first placed in position, and the monkeys, on being driven from tree to tree, are stated finally to take headers into it, under the influence of the spells. Becoming entangled, they are then beaten to death with clubs.

February 8th.—Banki.—For some days about this time my work chiefly consisted in examining the sections in the bed of the River Subanrika, which involved much heavy trudging in sand and wading in water; but the beauty of the scenery, and the variety in the fauna and flora, made the labour a pleasure when, as not unfrequently happened, the geology was deficient in much of real interest. With regard to the flora, I noted particularly that the heath-like *Jow* (*Tamarix ericoides*), which is common in most of the other rivers I had examined, was here replaced by another bush (*Phyllanthus simplex*), which, though presenting a generally similar aspect, is a really very different plant, belonging to a distinct natural order. It is also sometimes called *Jow* by the natives. These bushes, which grow in the beds of the rivers, are seldom found except where there are rocks which enable them to hold on fast enough to resist the current of the river when in flood. The species of Tamarix found in the beds of the Ganges and Indus, and many other rivers, do not require such aid, although they are often completely submerged.

February 12th.—Dulduli to Moholia.—To-day I came upon a large tract in the jungle occupied by a common euphorbiaceous flowering shrub (*Grislea tomentosa*), with red tubular blossoms. These were now in their prime, and had attracted large numbers of the tiniest of Indian birds—flower-peckers, honey-suckers, wren and tree-warblers—all of which were busily engaged in quaffing a morning draught of nectar, or in capturing the insects attracted by the same. Only once have I seen a similar sight of equal animation and beauty. It was in the Nicobar Islands, where an *Erythrina* tree attracted a number of little honey-suckers—in this case Nectarineas—for the same purpose. The air of intense satisfaction of some of these little birds, as they elevated their bills after a long and deep draught was delightful to behold.

February 13th—Moholia.—To-day I ascended a fine hill called Sideshar, from which a most commanding view of the surrounding country was obtained. The hill rises to a sharp peak, and is formed of quartzite, in which I found traces of the green carbonate of copper, or malachite. Old excavations for ore occur in the jungle close by. At a place called Ruam, which I visited during the day, I saw remains of old tanks, and other indications of a former civilization, such as heaps of old copper slags.

February 14th.—Moholia to Ghatsilla.—At one place in the bed of the Subanrika I saw a large troop of brown monkeys

Inuus (*Macacus*) *rhesus*, which are not very abundant in these jungles. Shortly afterwards I came upon the tracks of wild elephants, which had been made, I was told, in December. The herd had evidently for the time taken up their position in some hills bordering the Subanrika, from whence they made nightly descents on the rice crops of the neighbouring villages. At this time they were reported to have departed southwards into the heavy jungles of Mohurbunj.

Ghatsilla being the chief town of Dhalbhum, I received in the evening a visit from the Raja, a child of seven years old, whose estate was in the charge of the Court of Wards. His father had died two years previously, leaving him and a brother to be protected by the Government, who had placed him under the charge of a guardian. The procession which came up to my tent, from the closely adjacent "palace," was designed to produce an imposing effect. In front was a gilt Palki in which the Raja and his brother—a pretty pair of children—were seated. Then came two elephants clad in gay-coloured trappings, and a single horseman, followed by a miscellaneous crowd of individuals on foot. I shook hands with the small Raja who did not seem to quite understand the process. He and his brother being seated, I carried on a conversation with the guardian, from whom I obtained a considerable amount of information regarding the Copper Companies, &c.

On the visit being concluded I went out for my usual evening stroll; but, before the procession was lost to view, my attention was drawn by the sounds of a drum to another which was approaching from the opposite side. It proved to be a party of Sontals carrying the carcase of a bear, slung on a pole. They related the following story regarding it. The day before yesterday, at the village of Teringa, some four miles off, a leopard or tiger had killed and eaten one of the village cows. Whereupon one of the Sontals, armed only with his bow and arrows, went off for the purpose of seeking the marauder, and avenging, not only the loss of the cow, but also the deaths of sundry villagers, who had from time to time been killed. Suddenly he found himself in close proximity with a bear into whose side he discharged an arrow, with such effect that it nearly went through the animal's body, and must have penetrated its heart; for, according to the man's statement, the bear tottered forwards only for about twenty yards, and then fell dead. I asked him whether he would have fired in the same way had it been a tiger; he replied, "Certainly. I should have killed it in exactly the same way." I was so pleased with the old fellow that I gave him a present of ten rupees—a larger sum, probably, than he ever possessed in his life before. This little story is interesting as shewing how this isolated colony of Sontals maintain their national characteristics of bravery and love of sport which, according to my experience, form but very small elements in the composition of the Lurka Kols and Bhumiz of Singhbhum.

The next day, in the course of my work, I visited Teringa in the hope that these Sontals might put me in the way of some sport, but I could obtain no information from them of a sufficiently definite character to be of any practical use.

February 16th.—Ghatsillah.—I frequently, in this part of the country, experienced considerable opposition from the villagers, whom I used to take with me as guides, when I wished to leave the beaten tracks and strike into the jungle, or ascend the hill sides. They would say, "There are no paths;" to which I would reply, "Then we will make one." "There is heavy jungle." *A.*—"I like heavy jungle." "There are lots of wild beasts." *A.*—"I'll shoot them if I see them." "There are big rocks and stones." *A.*—"It is for the purpose of seeing the rocks which I have come, and see them I must." After this they would reluctantly, and often sulkily follow in my wake; but, from time to time, they would insidiously attempt to turn me from my bee-line-cross-country direction towards a path leading to some village, perhaps miles out of my course, where they hoped to be exchanged and released from their attendance.

On the banks of the Subanrika, south of Ghatsillah, there was a hamlet occupied by Dohras and Kumars, who have no cultivation and depend for their subsistence on gold-washing during the rains, and fishing during the rest of the year. During the day I ascended a lofty peak called Dulmi, near the foot of which I saw further traces of wild elephants.

February 18th.—Ghatsillah to Ramchundpur.—To-day I visited a village called Tikri in the vicinity of which there are numerous pot-stone quarries and mines. Only five were now open; they belonged to the same number of Bengali Mahajuns. The slackness of work was due, I was told, to want of hands, large numbers of Sontals and Bhumiz having died during the famine. The Mahajuns said they could not afford to bring in and teach outsiders. They further told me that those who had survived the famine had been kept alive by their bounty. This statement, however, I had reason to believe was not founded on fact.

February 19th.—Ramchundpur to Budrasai.—When passing through one village I found that the Purdhan or head man had a severe scalp wound, as though from the cut of a sword. He told me it was caused by a *bagh* (leopard or tiger) which had dragged him out of his house at night, and only released him when his sons awoke and frightened it off.

At a Keriah village I saw a very wild-looking party collected to celebrate a marriage. As they were very shy, and I had a long way to go, I did not wait to see any of the ceremony; but a feed was evidently in contemplation, as each man had a platter of stitched sal leaves on the ground in front of him.

February 20th.—Budrasai to Rautora.—To-day I passed through a fine piece of forest, between Budrasai and Khakajor, where I saw specimens of the large fruit-eating pigeon (*Carpophaga ænea*). Subsequent explorations in areas to the north and south have enabled me to define very exactly the range of this bird which, since it is a powerful flier, may be considered a most remarkable case of limited geographical distribution.

It is not found either to the east or west of a zone, perhaps rarely more than from twenty to fifty miles wide, which stretches southwards for four hundred miles, from the Ganges through the Rajmahal hills, and the hills separating Manbhum, Singhbhum, and Midnapur, through the Orissa highlands to Jaipur in the

Madras presidency, whence it spreads over a wide area to the west and south. I am perfectly satisfied that this limited distribution is not wholly attributable to peculiarities in the vegetation, since one fruit-bearing tree (*Semecarpus anacardium*,) which affords a favourite food, is found in the jungles to the west of this zone. The deep sonorous coo of this pigeon can be heard from a considerable distance, and if the birds are present in a tract of forest one soon becomes aware of the fact.

February 22nd.—Rautora to Matia-bandih.—At this early date in the year many of the usual only too well-known symptoms of the approach of hot weather began to make themselves apparent. The Mhowa blossoms were formed and commencing to fall. Many trees too had shed their leaves, and the fires which glowed on the hill-sides at night testified to the dry condition of the lower vegetation. The heat at mid-day also became very oppressive, and on this date the thermometer registered 92.5° F. in my tent at 4 p.m. Either Singhbhum is an unusually hot district, or this was an abnormally hot season. Both suppositions are probably true. The prospect of a proportional increase during the succeeding two months was not pleasant to contemplate. In the evening I visited a cave said to be inhabited by a bear. On reaching the entrance I found some of his black hair, and on further searching, some of his bones which had been gnawed by Jackals. This is one of very few occasions where I have found the remains of one of the larger wild animals which had, in all probability, died a natural death.

February 25th.—Simulpal.—This place, to which I marched yesterday, is situated across the Singhbhum boundary, in the district of Midnapur, and the village, with some others in the neighbourhood, was included in an estate leased by an Indigo Company.

Just as I was about to start off for my work in the morning, one of my chuprasies, who had been sent into the village, ran back saying that the villagers had risen against him and chased him with sticks in their hands. On sending to enquire the cause, I found that a cheeky Bengali had come to find out who I was, having been sent for that purpose by the Naib or head native official of the Indigo Company. The result of his enquiries was, as I was told, that I was a copper-miner, and as such, not being a district official, a suitable object for annoyance, and a safe one to level insolence at.

On my calling him up he moderated his tone very considerably; but presented a long paper of charges in excess of what had been already willingly accepted for supplies, and a list of payments to be made to villagers who had assisted in the usual voluntary manner to pitch my tent, &c. I allowed him to read through this list in spite of Saidon's remonstrances, and then, taking the document, tore it into small fragments, which I presented to him as an acquittance. He then made a charge against one of my men of having given him a shove. This charge was evidently a frivolous one, though no doubt founded on fact, as my men had received great provocation in hearing me spoken of in the disrespectful terms used by this man. Had it not been that during the course of the day I made the acquaintance of the European assistant indigo planter, who proved a very good fellow, I believe these Bengalis would have trumped up a case against my men which would have involved their going off to be tried at Midnapur, sixty miles distant, and possibly some weeks' delay and no little inconvenience to myself.

March 2nd.—Sildah.—To-day I joined the indigo planter in a beat for large game. The beaters were numerous, but the tract of country surrounded was so large that there were breaks in the line, and nothing was shot save a rare species of mongoose (*Herpestes monticolus*), which I knocked over towards the termination of the beat.

March 4th.—Bhimpur to Dhaijuri.—This day's march brought me well off the rocks into the laterite and alluvium of Midnapur. In the afternoon, the wife of the Deputy-Commissioner of Singhbhum, with three children and ayahs, passed in palkis on their way to Midnapur. The journey through such wild country, without a single rest-house in the whole eighty miles, was a sufficiently formidable and uncomfortable undertaking for anyone.

I mention the fact simply to illustrate what can be and is done by English ladies in India.

March 5th.—Dhaijuri to Midnapur.—To-day, leaving my camp behind, I rode into Midnapur, twenty-four miles distant. At Chandu, where I had sent forward one of my horses for a change, I unexpectedly found another indigo planter, who had a messenger on the road to carry me off to his house for breakfast.

The station of Midnapur, which is about sixty miles distant from Calcutta, is situated on the banks of the Kossai (or Cossye) river. It constitutes a town of respectable dimensions for lower Bengal, and is, I believe, popular with officials as a residence. I spent two days there, during which time I made the acquaintance of the residents and examined the irrigation works, which form a part of the scheme for connecting Orissa and, I believe, Madras too, by canals with the Hugli and Calcutta. This system of inland water carriage and irrigation was instituted by a company after the 1866 famine, which, having spent all its capital, was taken over, block, stock, and staff, by the Government, the shareholders receiving, in consequence of this providential arrangement, the whole of their capital, instead of losing it altogether as they assuredly would have done.

The laterite rock as seen at Midnapur is a very remarkable deposit. From the fact of its being unfossiliferous, its origin is still a matter of much doubt and speculation. Its appearance seemed to me strongly to favour the view of its having been formed by the deposition of volcanic ash in water. Its highly-ferruginous composition is its most characteristic and constant feature. In structural characters it varies a good deal, being sometimes pisolitic and sometimes cellular. Its distribution is so singular as to render it one of the most peculiar of known deposits on the earth's surface. Not only does it occur as a marginal or fringing zone at the foot of the highlands of the peninsula, but it is also found capping some of the highest hills and plateaus in the interior with layers of from 100 to 300 feet in thickness. The balance of evidence seems to favour the view that it at one time covered over the greater part of the peninsula as with a film, which accommodated itself to the outlines of the country, which were probably not very different from those prevailing at present, the actions of denudation and erosion since the consolidation of the laterite having been chiefly instrumental in laying bare the old surfaces.

March 8th.—Midnapur to Dhaijuri.—To-day I returned to my lonely camp, after my short holiday of two days' duration in civilization. On the road I encountered the Phulkusma Raja, whom I have mentioned on a previous page. He was travelling towards Midnapur, where he was going to enjoy the luxury of a big and costly trial regarding some land then in the holding of the before-mentioned Indigo Company. It is amazing the fascination which litigation seems to have for all classes of natives, but more particularly Hindus. Many Rajas and Zemindars may be met with who make an open boast of the number of cases *sub judice* in which they have an interest.

March 9th.—Porhati to Bend.—A heavy thunderstorm came on just before daylight, and the tent was thoroughly wetted, while the men in their *suldaris*, or small single-roofed tents, had a bad time of it, all their traps being drenched. On the sky clearing at about 10 a.m. I ordered a march, and arrived at Bend about 1 p.m. The road through the soft alluvial soil proved very difficult. Shortly after arrival I shot a giant stork or adjutant, which, together with some vultures, was feeding on the carcase of a buffalo. Immediately the head man of the village applied for the snake-stone which he said would be found in its head. I gave him permission to take it if he could find it.

In this neighbourhood there was a great epidemic of small-pox among the cattle, and I was surprised to observe how the vultures rose to the occasion to do their duty as scavengers. Although the only hills where they can roost are a considerable distance off, every carcase had dozens of birds around it. Had there been no carcases one might have travelled many miles in all probability without seeing a single vulture.

March 16th.—Kumerara to Sirsa.—To-day I had to cross the Subanrika, an operation which, owing to the amount of water in the river, required some little management. Two sets of three *dungas*, or dug-outs, lashed together, served for the conveyance of the baggage, and the elephant, horses, and bullock-carts, managed to ford the river, but the last-mentioned not without considerable difficulty.

March 17th.—Sirsa to Makai.—From Sirsa, the old direct postal road from Calcutta to Bombay plunges into the wild hills and forests of the native state of Mohurbunj. Leaving my men behind, I cantered along this road for a distance of about eight or ten miles, in order to get an idea of the country. Mohurbunj is so-called after the peacock (*Mohur*), which is religiously preserved throughout the state. During my ride I saw several fine birds, one of them crossing the road deliberately in front of my horse, Such a sight would not be seen at mid-day in any of the adjoining districts. At the furthest point reached I rather unexpectedly came on the dismantled remains of what had a few years previously been the head-quarters of the government elephant-catching establishment, or kedah. The operations were very successful, as something like eighty head of elephants had been captured here. The skulls and bones which I saw lying about testified that at least some of the captives had never left their native home. Of the remainder, I believe, not a few succumbed during the subsequent training. Broken-heart is said to be the cause of many deaths, before elephants become accustomed to their new life.

March 20th.—Asunbuni.—The examination of the Subanrika section was very laborious work here, owing to the density of jungle on the banks and the quantity of water in the channel. A very few miles accomplished represented a hard day's work. Here, as also near Kumerara, I found traces of copper ores and old workings, thus proving their extension from the point where first encountered over a lateral distance of little short of eighty miles. I experienced much trouble from the inveterate untruthfulness of the people. Most positively they would at first assert that there were no old workings in the hills; yet on pressure being applied, they would sometimes guide me straight to large excavations. Out of Singhbhum I have rarely met the same untruthfulness and disinclination to enter the jungles.

My course now was back towards the central basin of Singhbhum, through the hills at its south-east corner. How the bullock carts managed to get through the country unprovided with cart-roads is a mystery to me to this day. Though slow, carts, as being easily packed and capable of being got ready over night, have a great advantage as a means of carriage. Subsequently to this period, as I shall have to relate in the account of my journeys into still remoter regions, I have had to employ pack-bullocks, and often regretted the carts which did such wonders on this journey.

March 29th.—Mandpur.—To-day I had intended to give myself complete rest after the great amount of fatigue and roasting by heat which I had incurred in the previous days, but it was not to be, as the head man (Purdan) of the village came up to say that there were bears to be had in some neighbouring hills. I accordingly arranged for the assembly of beaters in the afternoon. Out of the second hill which was beaten, a splendid bear broke close to where I was standing, and I bowled him over at a few feet distance, and the man with me set up a shout supposing he was killed. Bruin, however, thought otherwise, for picking himself up he made off, and we followed his bloody tracks for a long distance, till darkness compelled us to give up. The following day further tracks indicating great loss of blood were discovered, but we never found the bear. This was but another case of my finding a shell less effective than a solid bullet would have been.

March 31st.—Dudkur.—To-day I very nearly lost one of my horses in the following manner. Between me and camp towards the end of the day's work, was a lofty ridge, which I wished to cross, but instead of sending the horse a long way round as I ought to have done, I thought I would attempt to take it with me. The ascent from the eastern side of the ridge was effected without much difficulty, but when we came to the descent we found in one place a steeply scarped face. While halting for a moment to see whether we could find an easier track, the sayce leading the horse got frightened, and communicating his fear to the horse the animal gradually subsided into a sitting posture on its haunches, and, as it began to slip, suddenly broke from and knocked over the sayce; and had I not fortunately seized the bridle and brought it up on a narrow ledge off which I was just able to back it, it would inevitably have been smashed to pieces. A strained shoulder was the only evil consequence which resulted to the animal from this perilous scramble.

April 1st.—Dudkur to Potka.—This morning I observed a lot of vultures when passing the Mandpur jungle, and at once concluded that they had discovered and come to feed on the carcase of my bear. The remains of a cow had, however, I found been the attraction. From the numerous temporary fire-places all about it was also evident that some of the villagers had come out on the sly to have a quiet gorge on the diseased meat. I have in the Kol countries not unfrequently seen parties of people so engaged, and I believe the practice is more common with these tribes than they like to admit. One fact I have noticed is that the meat is generally cooked and eaten close to the spot where the carcase lies, and I should not be surprised if it were the case that none is taken home, and that the women and children are not permitted to take a share in the banquet. With regard to cattle killed by wild animals I am not aware of any similar custom prevailing. The meat is generally disposed of by some of the low caste tribes.

April 3rd.—Sarjamdih to Tengra.—In the evening I ascended a lofty hill called Baghmuria, which is 1,997 feet above the sea. It is itself formed of an enormous trap dyke, and from its summit commands a view of a network of trap dykes, referable to four very distinct series which traverse the granitic gneiss of the central Singhbhum basin. The decomposition of the granite has left the trap standing out in walls, some of which are of considerable height. The appearance is unique, or nearly so, in India, and cannot fail to attract the notice of travellers in the district who are even not geologists. While on the top of this hill my attention was attracted by a succession of sharp reports like those of a saloon pistol in the jungle below. These I found were due to the bursting of the large pods of the giant creeper (*Bauhinia Vahlii*).

April 6th.—Sinju to Pondripani.—In this neighbourhood, on the frontiers of Mohurbunj, I found some extensive villages exclusively inhabited by Sontals. I learnt that it is the custom of these Sontals, at three stated periods in the year, to make up parties consisting of a member of each household where a death has occurred. Each of these representatives carries with him in an earthen pot a portion of the ashes of the departed, which are cast into the Damuda river, the sacred stream of the Sontals. The journey to-and-fro, involving a walk of about two hundred miles, is sometimes shirked by the responsible individuals; but not for long, as Sontal public opinion will not regard lightly neglect in such a matter. The cattle belonging to the Sontals were a peculiar miniature breed, unlike any I have elsewhere seen in Bengal.

April 9th—Latu.—In the open stony country in this neighbourhood, I saw a number of snakes basking in the sun. Two specimens of the deadly Russell's viper, and two large pythons were killed.

April 10th.—Latu to Govindpur.—In the early morning I saw four bears entering their caves, and in the evening I revisited the Gopinathpur Hills, where I again saw several bears, but did not succeed in bagging any. In no part of India have I seen so many bears as in these hills, and in no part have I been so completely unsuccessful in my attempts to kill them. It was intimated to me that the reason of my want of success was that I had not bought over the aid of the village priest, who professed himself, I was told, to be ready for a consideration, to ensure me any amount of sport. He even said that he could cause the bears to come out of the cave at his bidding. Had I given him a present and then been successful, I should have felt myself guilty of perpetuating a superstition. Owing to the number and depth of the caves, which consist of fissures in the trap, produced by cooling of the molten rock, the chances in favour of a bear's escape, if not killed on the spot, are considerable. For many years none of the resident officials have been sportsmen, and, according to the villagers, even the sportsmen of former times, whose names are remembered, never killed any bears in these enchanted hills. To slaughter some is, I feel, a duty which I shall not fail to attempt, should circumstances lead me into that country again. As a matter of fact I believe I was the cause of the death of three, if not four, bears in Singhbhum; but I bore away no trophy from that field. The natives, indeed, seemed to regard my failure very much as a matter of course, and their confidence in the powers of the *Bhúts*, or spirits of the hill, has no doubt been augmented.

April 12th.—Govindpur to Kumdih.—To-day I met several parties of Sontals going to their annual chase for large game, which was to take place at a locality some miles off. Each man carried a supply of food with him, and it was expected that there would be a great assembly of these hardy hunters from a wide extent of country. The weather was too hot, and the distance too far for me to think of joining them; but I could not help regretting that I had not had their aid instead of that of the Bhumiz and Lurka Kols in my recent beats.

April 13th.—Kumdih to Nakasora.—To-day was so intensely hot that a number of night-herons (*Nycticorax griseus*) came at mid-day to stand in the water of the river, on the banks of which my tent was pitched. I have never before or since seen these birds abroad while the sun was above the horizon; but just after sunset or before sunrise they may be seen winging their way to-and-fro between their roosting-places and feeding-grounds.

April 14th.—Nakasora.—Being now in the country of the Lurka Kols, my camp was the centre of attraction to a vast crowd, principally of the female part of the population. The sights were myself, the elephant, the two young tame bears, and some other domesticated animals, and the dogs of English breed. The young bears on such occasions, strangely enough—as their appearance ought to be familiar to the people of these regions—claimed the largest share of public notice, and their antics were no doubt often amusing. To an onlooker, less accustomed to the sight than I had become, the appearance of some of the spectators would perhaps have proved the most novel, I do not say the most attractive, sight. The female Lurka Kol, when at her prime, is perhaps, when she appears in public, more often decently clothed than not; but the exceptions to this rule are numerous. After she arrives at a certain age, and loses, what it must be admitted, is often a very perfect figure, she begins to economise cloth, and by the time that the rounded outlines have given place to wrinkles, and other signs of advancing age, the sole garment worn has assumed almost microscopic dimensions, being scarcely larger than the leaf affected by the ladies of the Andaman islands. My Mahomedan servants used to profess themselves horribly shocked at the sights they saw, but the females, though probably as virtuous and proper as any in India, were unconscious of any shame. To them the strange appearance presented by myself seemed to afford a source of considerable amusement, and they often roared with laughter as I passed through their villages. Such conduct among Hindus would have been considered highly reprehensible, but with these simple people no particular meaning attached to it.

April 16th.—*Jaipur to Pokaria.*—The Lurka Kols,* or as they prefer to call themselves, the Hos, are, with rare exceptions, only to be found in the portion of Singhbhum known as the Kolehan, or Hodesum, as it has been called. There they live shut out from all Aryan influences, observing a most rigid conservatism with regard to the language and traditional customs of their race. Notable among these customs, as being one that must force itself on the notice of every traveller in the district, is the erection of stone tablets and slabs (Menhirs and Dolmens) over the graves, and to the memory of the deceased. Although it is only within the limits of the Kolehan that these monuments

* The following account of the Ho monuments formed the substance of a paper contributed by me to the "Indian Antiquary" for October, 1872.

Plate IV.]

HO (KOL) GRAVE-STONES, SINGHBHUM.

(From a Photograph by T. F. Peppé, Esq.)

are erected at the present day, they are to be found scattered throughout Chutia Nagpur and to some extent in the Orissa Tributary States; in some cases in localities upwards of one hundred miles distant from the Kolehan, which, in all probability, have not been inhabited by Hos for many centuries. There are few parts of the Kolehan, where an extensive view of several villages can be obtained, which do not include several groups of upright monumental stones. These groups may include any number, and there is no restriction to odd numbers, as is said to be the case in the Khasia Hills. The stones selected for erection are generally more or less rectangular or cylindrical in form, but sometimes they are of very fantastic shapes. These latter, however, it is important to observe, are not due to either freak or design on the part of the people. They are the natural forms of the flags, which they assume in their exposed positions in the rivers. Beyond being prised from the beds by means of crowbars, they are not, as a rule, touched with any tools. I have often come across the spots in the river sections, whence stones for this purpose, and also larger ones, intended for Dolmens, had been raised. The geological formations in the Kolehan consist in part of schists and slates, which supply an abundance of flags suited to the purpose.

In portions of the country not now occupied by the Hos, where the rocks are granitic, and flag-like masses can seldom be obtained, the ancient monuments are less tabular in shape, and of smaller size. I cannot help thinking that the geological formation may have had something to do in determining the selection of the Kolehan as the final resting-place of the race.

The rivers where the stones are raised are not unfrequently several miles distant from the village near which the Menhirs and Dolmens are erected. The transport of the stones is effected in the following manner. Partly according to the estimation in which the deceased was held, partly according to the amount of refreshments—chiefly rice beer—which the surviving members of the deceased's family are prepared to stand, a greater or less number of men assemble, and proceed to the spot where the stone is to be raised. If the flag selected be not very heavy it is placed on a wooden framework, and so carried on men's shoulders to its destination. When, however, the stone is of large size, it is placed on a kind of truck with enormously massive wheels, which is specially constructed for the purpose. Sometimes it is necessary to make a road for the passage of such a truck; at others, the pushing and pulling with ropes is sufficient to carry it over all the obstacles which are encountered on the way.

The history of the group of stones in the accompanying illustration, as told to me, was as follows :—The stone on the left was erected to the memory of Kundapathur, *Manki*, or head-man of the village of Pokaria, which is situated a few miles south of the station of Chaibassa. The next two stones were erected to Kunchi and Somari, daughters, and the fourth to a son of Pasingh, the present Manki, who was my informant.

For some reason there is no memorial here to Pasingh's wife, Seni; I rather think, however, there was one standing by itself somewhat nearer to the village. But in the centre of the village, under the shade of some glorious old tamarind-trees, a Dolmen, conspicuous among many others from its great size, covers her ashes, and affords practical evidence that respect for her memory was not wanting. Its dimensions are 17 feet 2 inches by 9 feet 2 inches by 10 inches, or 132 cubic feet in solid content, equal to a weight of about nine tons. The groups of Menhirs which occur scattered throughout the Kolehan are, so far as my observation went, in no way limited as to the number of stones. I have counted as many as thirty in one group, and my impression is that I have seen more than that number. A circular arrangement is seldom seen; generally the stones are either ranged along a straight line, or form the arc of an ellipse. The only localities where I have seen an attempt at sculpture on stone monuments is in the western part of Hazaribagh, on the borders of Palamow, and at Bussutpur, in the same district, as I have related in Chapter II. In both places the stones had the appearance of great antiquity; and, whether rightly or wrongly, were attributed

MENHIRS AT POKARIA.

by the people of the neighbourhood to an ancient settlement of Kols.

After examining these memorial-stones at Pokaria, I turned out my collection of bird's-skins, and took down the names for the birds in the Ho language. In subsequent years I obtained similar lists in other languages, and the whole were afterwards published in tabular form, the comparison tending to indicate that such names had a less stable character in languages allied to one another than have ordinary words, including, for instance, the names of domestic animals.

As space is not available for a full ethnological account of the various races mentioned in these pages, I have been obliged to limit myself very much to those habits and customs which have more particularly come under my cognizance. Among these is one which is, to the best of my belief, quite unique in India. It is that the Hos regard cows' milk as unclean, and unfit for human consumption. The cows in some parts of the Kolehan are used for ploughing, and where they are not in the charge of Hindu herds are never milked. Many a struggle used my servants to have before they could get the cows to submit themselves to the unaccustomed operation.

April 19th.—Sika to Chaibassa.—By this date I had walked myself dead lame, and the heat was so great—upwards of 100° F. in the tent daily—that I was compelled to close my work for the season, and march into Chaibassa, whence, after a day's rest, I started on my return journey. The geology of the immediate neighbourhood of this station is very interesting, as the two series of metamorphic rocks about to be described meet there. In the younger schists there are numerous quartz reefs, which I have reason to believe will prove to be auriferous. Lodes containing both ores of manganese and iron are also abundant. A great future may be in store for this country, should the project for connecting Calcutta with Nagpur in the Central Provinces be ever carried out. Although Singhbhum has the disadvantage of not including any coal-fields, its richness in other mineral deposits is perhaps not inferior to that of any other region in India.

As a *resumé* of the geology of this district, it may be stated that the rocks of Singhbhum, so far as they are known, are referable to two distinct series—the metamorphic, consisting of granitic and foliated gneiss, schists, &c. ; and the sub-metamorphic, consisting of slates, quartzites, and schists, the last-mentioned being sometimes not lithologically distinguishable from those belonging to the metamorphic series. The sub-metamorphic rocks occupy a large area in the south of Manbhum, as has been indicated in speaking of that area, whence they spread southwards into the district of Singhbhum, where they cloak round irregular areas occupied by the metamorphic rocks. The principal of these areas lies east of the station of Chaibassa; the rocks seen are coarse, granitic, and porphyritic, boss-forming gneisses, which are traversed by a perfect network of trap (diorite) dykes. This combination produces a very peculiar effect, which, as seen from the top of a high hill, has been aptly compared to a chess-board. North and north-west of Chaibassa there is another area of the same metamorphic rocks, which is, however, free from trap, or nearly so. The appearance presented by the area in which sub-metamorphic rocks prevail is very different from that just described; it is characterized by being traversed by long ranges of hills, with deep intervening valleys, the latter corresponding in position to those of the softer varieties of rock of which the formation is composed. It is in this formation that the copper ores occur disseminated through schists and quartzites rather than as actual veins. I shall now give the results of my enquiries regarding the identity of the ancient miners who probably worked the copper.

The existence of copper ores and ancient copper-mines in the district of Singhbhum was first prominently brought to notice by Colonel Haughton, who published an account of the mineral resources of Singhbhum in the Journal of the Asiatic Society for the year 1854. The result of this communication was that some Calcutta merchants deputed Dr. Emil Stöhr to examine the ground, and a company was formed in 1857 to work the ore. I shall not here discuss or further allude to the brief and unfortunate history of this company, or of that which, raised on its ruins, met with a similar fate.*

Commencing to examine the copper-bearing rocks at the foot of the Chutia Nagpur plateau, and proceeding thence eastwards, I found that at nearly every point where traces of ore occurred there were ancient excavations. These increasing in size, and being found in every conceivable situation—at the tops of hills, in valleys, in the thickest jungles, and even in the middle of cultivation where the rocks are obscured by superficial deposits—my curiosity was aroused as to who the ancient miners could have been, who have left such imperishable evidence of their skill.

Before proceeding to detail the conclusions at which I have arrived, it will be necessary to allude to what, so far as I have been able to ascertain, are the only published opinions on the subject. Colonel Haughton states: "There was no local

---

* In a paper published in the "Records of the Geological Survey of India," I have given an account of these copper deposits. *Vide* Vol. III., pp. 94–103.

tradition as to when or by whom the diggings had been worked, and it was a matter of doubt whether they were really made for copper." Dr. Stöhr, since his return to Europe, has published two papers, one in Zurich* and the other in the Jahrbuch for 1854. In the former he suggests a connection between these relics of ancient civilization and the rock temples of Orissa and the ruins of the town of Dulmi. He also repeats the only tradition known to the natives. This, as it was also told to me, I shall again refer to. In the latter paper he conjectures that the mines are of the eleventh century, when the kingdom of Orissa flourished.

In Singhbhum proper, the replies to my queries were of a negative kind. No one could make the least suggestion as to who the miners were; and with regard to the age of the mines, the answers were that they had not been worked during the past three, four, or five generations. From the local Rajas, called respectively the *Koer* of Seraikela and the *Thakúr* of Khursawa, though they seemed willing to communicate all that they knew, I received similar replies. In Dhalbhum, the *Purdhán* of Landú having been asked his opinion as to the ancient workers, replied that he did not know, but added, "The Seraks formerly possessed the country." This belief of the Seraks having once occupied the country is recorded by both Major Tickell and Colonel Dalton. Having thus had the name of the Seraks suggested, I was enabled to give a definite form to my queries, the result being that not only were several tanks pointed out as the work of Seraks, but, as I proceeded further eastwards, the mines were all attributed to the same ancient people.

East of the Kapergaddee ghât, on the Midnapur and Chaibassa road, there is the site of an old town called Ruam. From the *ghâtwal* of Ichinda, and independently from the Zemindar of Pairaguri, I heard the only tradition known in connection with

* Vierteljahrschrift der Naturforschenden Gesellschaft in Zurich, Vol. v., p. 329.

this place. It is that a Raja who lived there formerly possessed two tongues (*do jib*). This is the story which Dr. Stöhr also heard, and to him must be accorded whatever credit is due to priority of publication. Dr. Stöhr's interpretation is that he must have spoken two languages, and was therefore a foreigner. Colonel Dalton, to whom I communicated the story, has very kindly given its explanation as follows: "The legend of the two tongues shows that the potentate to which it alludes must have been a Nag, or one of the serpent race. There can, I think, be little doubt that by the serpent race, the Kols are really meant, and as the great bulk of the population of Dhalbhum are Bhumiz, *ergo* Kols, it is not unusual to find the legend of two-tongued Rajas among them." Hence this place has probably been inhabited by Kol Rajas since the time of the Seraks. But whether the copper was worked by the former, the latter, or by both, the remains at present to be seen do not decide. They consist of a ridge or moat of clay, which it is said enclosed the *gurh* or fort, but which now encloses and is itself enclosed by a jungle of remarkably fine trees with dense undergrowth. Close by are three old Serak tanks, and a great accumulation of copper slag, indicating that this must have been one of the centres of operations. Following the direction of the strike of the rocks, which from this point trends to south-west and south, old workings and slag heaps can be traced for many miles further, the last being about three miles north of Kamerára, on the Midnapur and Bombay road.

All along this line, wherever the people were sufficiently intelligent to reply to the enquiries, the mines were invariably attributed to the Seraks. At Ghâtsillah, where the Dhalbhum Raja (a minor) lives, I received the same information. Here I also heard of some remains at Karra-Mounda, six miles east of Kumerára. This locality I afterwards examined. On entering the village the eye is at once attracted by a number of rings of vitrified clay, which are thickly scattered over the surface throughout an area exceeding in extent that covered by the houses; on removing the surrounding clay and rubbish, I found that these rings were the sections of small furnaces, which had become covered up. The most plausible conjecture was that this place was a depôt in which the rudely-smelted copper brought from the hills was refined and prepared for market. Several tanks in this neighbourhood are said to have been the work of Seraks. Here for the first time did I hear mention made of any definite age. Several respectable villagers assigned to the furnaces a minimum age of 700 years, but admitted that they might be much older.

In the jungle east of the village of Khúrsi, a ridge of clay was pointed out to me, which was said to be the embankment of an ancient tank, with which assertion I was obliged to be satisfied, as the thickness of the jungle prevented more than a few feet of it being seen at a time; close by there were two or three slabs of cut laterite without ornament of any kind. These are attributed to the Seraks, and are regarded with a certain amount of awe, but no reverence. At Panrasoli there is a tank with a *chhatah*, or stone umbrella, in the centre; this I did not visit. At Bend there is what looks like the capital of a pillar with cogged ornamentation; this is also of laterite, and is said to have been brought from Panrasoli and to belong to the Serak period.

It is due to the ancient miners to give them credit for considerable mining skill; and the slags furnish conclusive evidence of their proficiency as practical metallurgists. They seem to have searched the country with wonderful care; even at remote points in Manbhum, where alone copper ores are known to exist, there are ancient excavations.

In a paper on Arabia Petræa, by Mr. H. Bauerman,* it is suggested that the ancient copper-mines therein described were in all probability worked with stone implements; such a supposition cannot for a moment be entertained in reference to the larger excavations of Singhbhum as they at present stand; but whether the very earliest outcrop excavations may not have been effected with instruments of stone, it is impossible to decide.

---

* "Quarterly Journal Geological Society." Vol. xxv., part i., p. 17.

Although it is evident that these ancients worked the ore with profit, it does not by any means necessarily follow that it would pay an English company to work them now. Not only could the ancients work economically, whereas every European administration involves a primary heavy expenditure, but in those early times, long before the metals arrived at their present relative values, copper may have been regarded as a precious metal.

In India, where there are few trustworthy records, even such evidence as has been given in support of the Seraks having been the ancient copper-miners is not usually obtainable. In Singhbhum there are in operation at the present day extensive pot-stone mines; and gold-washing is carried on by certain of the lower races. The unknown discoverers of these productions must be relegated to that class of mythical individuals who, in all countries, have pointed out the specific virtues of many drugs, and the particular properties of many natural productions.

All the published ethnological papers having reference to Singhbhum or the adjoining districts refer to the prevalence of a belief amongst the Hos and Bhumiz that their country was formerly in possession of the Seraks.

Major Tickell says "Singhbhum passed into the hands of the Surawaks, a race of Bengali Brahmins (?) now almost extinct but then numerous and opulent, whose original country is said to have been Sikrbhum and Pachete * * * the oppressions of the Surawaks ended in their total expulsion from the Kolehan."

Colonel Dalton has described several Jain temples and Buddhist emblems in subsequently-Hinduized temples which are found in Manbhum. He considers it "probable that these shrines mark the course taken in his travels by the great saint Vira." It may be that Vira did not visit Singhbhum, hence the absence of temples. Or, on the other hand, the Yatis, or clerical Jains, may not have extended beyond the ranges of hills which bound Manbhum on the south, the more adventurous Seraks, or lay Jains, having alone penetrated the jungles, where they were rewarded by the discovery of copper, upon the working of which they must have spent all their time and energy, as, with the exception of the tanks above mentioned, the mines furnish the sole evidence of their occupation of that part of the country. It is scarcely conceivable that the Hos, when they drove out the Seraks, could have utterly destroyed all trace of buildings. Colonel Dalton* estimates that the Jains were driven out by the Hos more than two thousand years ago.

Without the least desire to stretch or force an analogy, one cannot but be struck by the fact that the history of the earliest Aryan colonies in several other countries is connected with mines and mining, or, to quote the words of the author of the "Annals of Rural Bengal"—"A distant colony of the same race (Aryans) excavated silver ore in pre-historic Spain; and the earliest glimpses we get at our own England, disclose an Aryan settlement, fishing in its willow canoes and working in the mines of Cornwall."†

April 21st.—Chaibassa to Tolko.—This march brought me to the northern edge of the Kolehan—the extreme limit of the tract inhabited by the Hos. In the afternoon I had a regiment of small boys from the village busily engaged in searching for natural history objects. Land and fresh-water shells, snakes, lizards, birds' eggs, centipedes, &c., formed a part of their miscellaneous collections.

April 23rd.—Dugni to Chainpur.—The great heat compelled me to march at 1 a.m. The afternoon at Chainpur (a village in the district of Manbhum), with the temperature at 103° F., was spent in a battle with a plague of insects similar in appearance to those which are commonly called frog-hoppers. They invaded every corner of the tent, and found their way into hair, mouth, eyes, &c.; and, if not speedily removed, inflicted severe bites. I have, during the rains in Calcutta, seen similar invasions of an insect allied to, if not identical with, this one; but I never have found them to bite as these little wretches did. So great was the annoyance and irritation which I suffered that I was, as a last

---

* Jour. Asiatic Soc. Bengal. Vol. XXXV., part ii., p. 164.

† "Annals of Rural Bengal," p. 91.

resource, compelled to have a ring of smoky leaf fires lighted all round the tent. This gave some relief at last.

April 26th.—Modali to Purulia.—In this pleasant station, where I generally found friends, I remained for a three days' rest—the first, I may say, I had had since November, when I took the field. I afterwards marched to Ranigunj, and reached Calcutta on the 5th of May.

CHAPTER V.

SECTION II.

FIRST VISIT TO THE ANDAMAN AND NICOBAR ISLANDS.

1869.

START FOR RANGOON—FELLOW PASSENGERS—ALGUADA LIGHTHOUSE—KRISHNA SHOAL LIGHTHOUSE—RANGOON RIVER—FIRST IMPRESSIONS OF RANGOON—TRIP IN THE SUBURBS—THE SHUE-DAGON PAGODA—PIGEON-ENGLISH—AMERICAN MISSION SCHOOLS—BAZAAR—BURMESE MONASTERY—RELIGIOUS RITES AT SHUE-DAGON PAGODA—EMBARK ON STEAMER "ARAKAN"—NARKONDAM ISLAND—FIRST VIEW OF ANDAMAN ISLANDS—PORT BLAIR—EMBARK ON "QUANTUNG" FOR THE NICOBARS—RUTLAND ISLAND—LITTLE ANDAMAN—TILLANSCHONG—TRINKUT—HISTORY OF THE ANNEXATION OF THE NICOBARS—CHARACTER OF THE NICOBARESE—NEW SETTLEMENT—NANKOWRI HARBOUR—THE HULK "BLENHEIM"—VISITED BY THE NICOBARESE—APPEARANCE AND COSTUME OF THE NICOBARESE—"PTOLEMY'S TAILED-MEN"—VISITING NAMES OF THE NICOBARESE—THE VILLAGE OF MALACCA—EFFECTS OF PAWN CHEWING—CHARACTERISTICS OF THE NICOBARESE—NATURAL HISTORY COLLECTIONS—THE FOREST—HERMIT CRABS—THE ROCK-POOLS—BÊCHE DE MER—SEA MANTIS—SEA ANEMONES—SEA-WEEDS—CORAL REEF—DREDGING—KAMORTA—SHELL AND BIRD COLLECTING—KAMORTA—HO-HO BAY—GRASS—WILD BUFFALOS—THE MOUND-BUILDER—RETURN OF "QUANTUNG" FROM KAR NICOBAR—WESTERN ENTRANCE TO NANKOWRI HAVEN—VISIT SEVERAL VILLAGES—FRUIT OF THE PANDANUS—GUARDIAN DEITIES—CONSTRUCTION OF HOUSES—A SICK NATIVE—WOMEN AND CHILDREN—EXPLORATION OF TRINKUT—PIRATES' HOME—KLING TRADERS—CHINESE DELICACIES—CREEKS ON TRINKUT—DREDGING—CORAL REEFS—THE GAR FISH—VISIT VILLAGES ON N.E. OF NANKOWRI—CAPTAIN JOHNSON—CERTIFICATES—MALAY SONG—MUSICAL INSTRUMENTS—KITCHEN MIDDENS—GRAVE YARDS—THE NICOBARESE COMMUNE—PRIESTS AND WIZARDS—DEPORTATION OF EVIL SPIRITS—A CASUS BELLI—LABOURS OF MISSIONARIES—ORIGIN OF THE NICOBARESE—START FOR PORT BLAIR—WATERSPOUT—VIPER ISLAND—CONVICT SERVANT—COCOA-NUT CULTIVATION—VISIT THE ANDAMANESE HOME—SHELL HUNTING—MOUNT HARRIET—FEVER—FOREST—BIRDS—RETURN TO VIPER—DETERMINE TO RETURN TO CALCUTTA—GEOLOGY OF PORT BLAIR—SAIL IN "CZAREWITCH" TO RANGOON—RANGOON GAOL—A WARDER PUNISHED—MURDER OF DR. MAINGAY—BUDDHISM—SHUE-DAGON PAGODA—SAIL FOR CALCUTTA.

IN the summer of this year (1869) I was enabled, during a period of two months' leave, to carry out my intention of paying a visit to the Andaman and Nicobar Islands. At that time there was no direct communication between Calcutta and the Andaman convict settlement, as there is at present. It was therefore, necessary for me to go *viâ* Burmah, a circumstance which caused me no subsequent regret, since it gave me an opportunity of seeing something of Rangoon and the manners and customs of the Burmese.

On the 9th of July I started from Calcutta for Rangoon in the British India Steam Navigation Company's steamer Bushire. Our passage down the Bay was a rather rough one, but unaccompanied by any incident worthy of particular record. Early on the morning of the 12th we sighted the Alguada Lighthouse, a very solid structure, which rises to a height of 130 feet. Owing to the fact that the foundations were only laid bare at low tide and were exposed to much bad weather, the difficulties encountered during its erection were enormous. In spite of all these, and the misconduct of some of the subordinates employed, the engineer was able after three years' unremitting toil to report the work as completed. All the stones and other building materials were brought from Penang, and the total cost amounted to £95,000.

The Alguada Reef is a continuation of a line of elevation coincident with the position of the Arakan hills, and indicated in a southernly direction by the positions of Preparis, the Cocos, the Andaman, and Nicobar islands, and beyond these again in Sumatra, Java, &c.

During the afternoon we passed the Krishna lighthouse, which consisted of an iron lattice pile, on a shoal 6 fathoms deep. This somewhat frail-looking structure was also constructed with great difficulty; but, as affording little resistance to the waves, was regarded as a sufficiently stable edifice. During the past year (1878), however, it was one day missed from its place by a passing steamer. It had been simply swept away and submerged, not a soul among the four or five occupants having survived to tell the tale of the disaster. There is something peculiarly melancholy in the idea of such a fate befalling those whose lives were spent in a service devoted to ensuring the safety of others.

July 13th.—Having taken a pilot on board, we steamed up the Rangoon river this morning. I was told that last night, when about to anchor off the mouth, we nearly ran on the wreck of a ship called the "Maraquita," which had been sunk there a few days previously, and of the existence of which the captain was not aware. Fortunately, the commander of the pilot brig seeing where we were going, had made known the danger we were in by burning blue lights.

On arrival I was met by a colleague of my own, who was then engaged in the geological examination of Pegu. His account has since been published.*

My first impressions of Rangoon were not altogether favourable to it, regarded as a place of residence. The houses occupied by Europeans are generally, after the manner of the country, built of wood, and present with their external staircases and balconies, a strong resemblance to Swiss chalets—with this difference, however, that they are raised on posts, the ground floor, if it can so be called, being often unenclosed, and commonly used as a coach-house. As dwellings these houses appeared to me, owing to the lowness of the eaves, to be dark, and from the nature of the floors and walls unpleasantly noisy. Even the crossing of a room by a bare-footed servant is sufficient, except in houses of the very best construction, to cause a reverberation and trembling through the whole house.

The intense moisture of the climate and the abundance of mosquitos, accustomed as I was to the same causes of discomfort in Calcutta, appeared to me incompatible with any real enjoyment of life in Rangoon. However, residents who know it well are to be found ready and willing to sing its praises.

July 13th.—Rangoon.—To-day I made a round of calls on the principal official residents, and afterwards visited the native town. The portion of it which interested me most was the Chinese quarter. This is inhabited by a curiously mongrel population,

* "Memoirs of the Geological Survey of India." Vol. x., part ii.

since the Chinese being unprovided with wives of their own nation —the emigration of women from China being interdicted—have taken unto themselves partners from amongst the Burmese, Hindustanis, Madrasis, and Eurasians. The result is a most heterogeneous collection of people, in some of whom the Mongolian type is distinct, while in others it is hardly perceptible or wholly absent.

July 15th.—This morning I accompanied Dr. Maingay on a trip into the country surrounding Rangoon on the east. I shall allude to this officer's unhappy fate on a future page. His repute as a botanist, and his interest in other branches of natural history, gave promise that when moved to another more congenial sphere than that of Superintendent of the Rangoon Gaol, he would have attained considerable distinction in the scientific world.

We first drove out for about three miles on the Prome road, and then struck into a jungle of Jack fruit (*Artocarpus integrifolia*) trees, under the shade of which pineapples were so thickly planted as to have a semi-wild appearance. At intervals along the roads carts were stationed, and were being packed full of pineapples, which were brought in hundreds by women and girls. During the day we seemed to have seen a sufficient number to have supplied every man, woman, and child in Rangoon with a single pineapple. As we proceeded the full luxuriance of this tropical jungle became more and more apparent, and we soon found that owing to the tangled mass of vegetation it was absolutely impossible to leave the beaten paths.

Most of the trees were unknown to me, but of many I could guess the genera, and some few were identical with species familiar to me in Bengal. In the undergrowth species of *Curcuma*, *Hibiscus*, *Clerodendron*, and *Arum*, were the most common forms which were recognisable. In the hedges a *Smilax*, a *Vitis* with bunches of small grapes, and a climbing fern (*Lygodium*) occurred in abundance. A very common shrub is *Melastoma malabathrica*, which I have also met with in certain parts of Bengal and Orissa, and on the slopes of the Sikkim Himalayas. Its rhododendron-like blossoms attract attention at once.

On leaving this jungle we passed through some open rice cultivation and then through two Burmese villages, where the picturesquely-clad people smiled pleasantly at us, in a manner very agreeable after the extremes of either cringing servility, open insolence, or rude indifference, that one often encounters in Hindu villages.

We then walked along the Khiouk road for about four miles, to its junction with the main road to Prome, by which we had another five miles to walk before we regained our conveyance; *en route* we encountered a step or plateau of laterite, which rises to a level of at least 100 feet above Rangoon. This laterite is precisely similar in character to the typical rock of Midnapur and Orissa.

Accompanying this deposit was a flora * much more like that of south-west Bengal than was that of the just-mentioned moister jungle. But many species common in Bengal were conspicuous by their absence. Two species of bamboo are common, as also several species of acacia and allied genera. The finest tree by far in these jungles was the wood oil (*Dipterocarpus lævis*, Buch.); the most showy, *Lagerstræmia reginæ*; another handsome tree is a species of *Castanea*, or chesnut.

In the station of Rangoon the common trees planted near the roads are, for the most part, identical with those found in similar situations in Bengal, as for example, the Mango, Jack, Fan Palm, Pipul, Banyan, &c.; but there are others which do not seem to thrive so well in Bengal, and are seldom cultivated.†

During the day we saw a number of birds characteristic of the Burmese fauna, and shot specimens of the beautiful little Pigmy Falcon (*Hierax eutolmus*), the curious black magpie (*Platysmurus leucopterus*, Tem.), the Racket-tailed Drongo (*Dissemurus grandis*), several species of Bulbul, &c.

---

* Among familiar forms I noted the following:—*Holarrhena antidysenterica, Phyllanthus emblica, Lagerstræmia parviflora, Zizyphus œnoplia, Ficus religiosa, Bombax malabarica.*

† E. G. Teak, *Tectona grandis*; *Pterocarpus Indicus*; *Xylia dolabriformis*; *Lagerstræmia reginæ*; *Cassia florida*; and *Berrya mollis.*

July 16th.—This morning I visited the great Shue-Dagon pagoda, which, with its surroundings, and the ceremonies I witnessed at it, struck me as being one of the most remarkable monuments consecrated to religion which I had ever seen.

In the afternoon I went into the town to make some purchases, and in the English stores was surprised to hear the excellent manner in which some of the pig-tailed Chinese assistants spoke English. This experience prepared me to understand, what I have since been told, that the Chinese can learn to pronounce and speak English really well, and that the barbarous jargon called "Pigeon-English" is sometimes directly fostered and encouraged by Englishmen at the China ports, who object to their humbler employés and servants becoming accomplished in English, lest they should understand too much of what is said in their presence.

I afterwards visited the schools attached to the American Mission to the Karens, a race who appear like Kols, Sontals, and other aboriginal tribes of India, to be more susceptible to the reception of the doctrines of Christianity than are the Buddhists of Burmah and the Hindus and Mahomedans of India. The vagueness of the tenets of these devil-worshippers, as compared with the elaborate systems of the followers of the three great religions, very probably accounts for this difference in susceptibility. There are, probably, many hundreds, if not thousands, of converts from such tribes, for every one taken from the Buddhist, Hindu, or Mahomedan ranks.

On arrival at the Karen school, we were surprised to find the state of advanced knowledge which the scholars had reached. An algebra! class had just concluded, one of the pupils being, I found, a pretty-looking girl whose photograph I had previously purchased at one of the shops in town. In permitting and encouraging the converts to retain their picturesque and suitable native costumes, the missionaries had, I think, shown better taste than have those who insist on their disciples donning a mongrel European dress, which is never becoming to them.

N 2

July 19th.—Rangoon.—To-day I paid a visit to the native bazaars, where cloth and articles of food are sold. The stall-keepers were women and young girls, some of them extremely good-looking, and almost all dressed in clean and bright clothes. Many of them had red roses tastefully displayed amongst their raven locks, and not a few carried cylindrical ear ornaments in holes made through the distended lobes of their ears. When not of more valuable material, these cylinders, and the solid truncate cones, which are used for the same purpose, are made of glass in capital imitation of amber and jade. The viands offered for sale were of the most miscellaneous description. There were large dishes full of broken fish and crustaceans, seeds, fresh and dried fruits, spices, and the ingredients of pawn (pink-coloured lime, betel, and cutch). There were also exposed on some of the stalls various cosmetic powders, which are used by Burmese ladies for giving themselves fair complexions, or at least modifying the tone of their brown skins.

The cloth stalls contained gay-patterned cottons and silks, which I noticed were mostly of European manufacture; but the patterns and style were evidently expressly selected and made with reference to this market.

July 20th.—Rangoon.—To-day the Deputy-Commissioner of Rangoon took me to see a *Phungi Kyoun*, or monastery, near his house. Some of the wood-carving on the outside of the buildings was exceedingly beautiful,—animals and men being depicted with marvellous skill and vigour. It was pointed out to me that the introduction of camels, which appeared in these modern carvings, was an innovation, and was to be attributed to the fact that these animals had never been seen in Burmah till within the last few years. No part of the establishment was set apart as private, and we found ourselves free to go even into the rooms occupied by the monks. The Chief *Phungi*, or Abbot, received us in a civil but unemotional manner, not hesitating to continue his occupation, which happened at that moment to be the preparation of a mouthful of pawn for his own consumption. Afterwards he threw back a curtain, and disclosed to our view a great pile of manuscripts, each one being carefully wrapped up in cloth and labelled. All the monks of lesser degree were out on the tramp, making collections of food in the town for the day's subsistence. To live thus on daily alms is, I believe, the usual custom in these Burmese monasteries.

July 21st.—Rangoon.—The early morning I spent in the Shue-Dagon pagoda, watching the various services going on there. In one of the buildings, with gilt interior, three Phungies seated on carpets, recited long orations, to which their audience, all kneeling and with clasped hands, listened with rapt attention. Outside the circle of men knelt a few gaily-dressed women, whose hair was ornamented with gold chains and roses. After this service was concluded, all repaired to an adjoining building, where a refection was served. Offerings of fruits, vegetables, and ghi were made to the Phungies.

At mid-day I went on board the Government steamer, "Arakan," which soon after started down the river, bound for the Andaman Islands.

July 22nd.—On board the "Arakan."—During this day we passed within a short distance of the extinct volcanic island called Narkondam. I pressed the commander of the steamer to allow me to land, but on nearing the island he considered that the surf was too violent, and would endanger the safety of a boat, so that I had to content myself with taking a distant sketch. On a subsequent occasion, as will be related on a future page, I had an opportunity of partially exploring this seldom-visited island.

July 24th.—On board the "Arakan."—Early this morning we first sighted the Andaman Islands, and at about 8 a.m., we passed close to the three small islets called North, Middle, and South Button. These and some of the larger islands, owing to the luxuriance of the vegetation, and the brightness of the white coral strands, presented on that lovely morning a scene of beauty which I have rarely seen surpassed in any part of the world. Shoals of porpoises playing about in the blue waters gave an animation to the scene which would otherwise have been somewhat wanting. In the Middle Andaman a considerable range of hills, perhaps 1,500 feet high, forms the backbone of the island. This range is densely clad with forests, from the highest summit down to high-water mark, without a single break of any kind. A few hours later the steamer ran into Port Blair, where the leading features of the scene which opens to the view are Ross Island, at the entrance, where most of the officials reside; Mount Harriet, with its forest-clad slopes, which rises on the right-hand, or northern side of the port to a height of about 1100 feet above the sea; the cleared areas of Aberdeen on the southern island, or mainland as it is called, and the picturesque little Chatham Island, at the elbow of the bay.

The evening after my arrival I devoted to a preliminary examination of the geology of Ross Island.

July 25th.—Port Blair.—It having been settled that the Government steamer "Quangtung"—which was stationed at Port Blair for the purpose of keeping up communications with the Nicobars, aiding distressed ships, and on occasions pursuing escaped convicts—should start on the morrow for Kamorta, in the Nicobars, I devoted to-day to necessary preparations for taking a passage, by this opportunity, to the ultimate goal of my expedition. The Chief Commissioner of the Andamans kindly arranged that four convicts should be specially told off to accompany me as boatmen to pull me about at the Nicobars, and assist me generally in my explorations.

July 26th.—Steamer "Quangtung."—To-day I started from Port Blair in the "Quangtung," the only other passenger being the Deputy-Superintendent of the settlement, who was going to visit Kar Nicobar with the object of enquiring into the circumstances of a murder committed in that island by the crew of a native ship from some port in British India. The "Quangtung" gunboat, having been built for the North China seas, with stoves below for heating, was about as uncomfortable a craft for navigation in these tropical seas as could be conceived of. But, as we slept on deck, the character of the cabin accommodation was not a matter of much importance.

During the day we coasted along the South Andaman and Rutland Islands, and passed at some distance away from the Little Andaman, an island regarding which not much is known, owing to the treacherous character of the inhabitants, who have on several occasions proved themselves unwilling to admit of intercourse with the outer world. They seem to be in many respects distinct from the races found in the other islands, and are more particularly characterised by the fact that they erect commodious houses of bee-hive shape, which are said to be large enough for the accommodation of 100 men. These houses are not, however, raised on stakes, as are those presently to be described in the Nicobars.

July 27th.—Steamer "Quangtung."—Shortly after dark we sighted the island of Tillanschong. It had the appearance of being very hilly and steep, the cliffs in some places rising abruptly out of the sea. From this cause (the absence or, more correctly, limited extent of the coast whereon cocoa-nuts might grow) the fact that the island is uninhabited is probably due. There is a native story that the island has been at times used by themselves as a Botany Bay to which they transported their criminals. Generally it would seem, however, that they employ a more summary method for the disposal of obnoxious persons.

July 28th.—Steamer "Quangtung."—At an early hour this morning we found ourselves in proximity to the island of Trinkut. It is for the most part covered with vegetation; but there are some clear spaces. As we approached it we could distinguish strips of cocoa-nut palms along the coast.

Before proceeding any further with this journal, it may be well here to describe the circumstances under which the Nicobar Islands were, during the present year (1869), taken possession of by the Indian Government.

A history of the previous European occupation of these islands by the Danes, Austrians, and Dutch—the first settlement having been made by some Jesuit missionaries on the Great Nicobar in the year 1711—will be found in the account of the voyage of the "Novara,"* in Dr. Rink's "Geographical Sketch of the Nicobars" and in the "Selections from the Records of the Government of India."† Coming down to the history of the islands during the past few years, it was only so recently as 1866 that the crew of the native brig, the "Futteh Islam," when lying off the island of Trinkut, were most treacherously murdered. In July, 1867, two of Her Majesty's vessels, the "Wasp" and "Satellite," under the command of Captain Beddingfield, with a detachment of the 35th Madras Native Infantry, were sent by the Governor of the Straits' Settlements to punish the offenders.‡ All the villages on Trinkut, Kamorta, and Nankowri were visited, and 211 houses and 261 canoes were burned. The prisoners captured confessed to having seen four piracies committed in Nankowri harbour within the previous two or three years. The crews were all murdered, the women, in those cases where there were any on board, were made prisoners, and the ships taken outside and scuttled, so as to leave no traces of the deed. Probably many of these attacks have been caused by misconduct in the first instance by the ships' crews. Among the Nicobarese themselves, theft, if speedy restitution be not made, is said to be punished with death. It is, therefore, not unnatural to suppose that, when victimised by cunning traders, they may have felt justified in applying the same system of punishment to them. It is possible that this retribution may not always have fallen on the guilty parties, but on the offending nationality, whether Malays, Burmese, Indians, or Europeans.

The Rev. Mr. Barbe gives a circumstantial account of several piracies accompanied by murder which took place between 1830 and 1845. Whether the inhabitants always had the same bad character or not is uncertain. In 1795 they were thus described

* Vol. II., pp. 1–16. † Vol. XXV. p. 6.

‡ It had been originally settled that the punitive expedition was to have been fitted out from Calcutta; in which event I had been ordered to hold myself in readiness to accompany it.

by Lieutenant Colebrook.* "The Nicobarese are hospitable and honest, and are remarkable for a strict observancy of truth and for punctuality in adhering to their engagements. *Such crimes as theft, murder, and robbery are unknown to them;* but they do not want spirit to revenge their injuries, and will fight resolutely and slay their enemies if attacked or unjustly dealt with."

Dr. Rink states that though they rob vessels sometimes, they have been known to treat persons saved from shipwreck very well, supplying them with all necessaries.

In the month of March of this year (1869) the Nicobarese became British subjects, the islands having been formally taken possession of in the name of Her Majesty the Queen by Captain Morrell, of H.M.S. "Spiteful." A site for the new settlement was first selected on the island of Nankowri. This was subsequently, however, decided to be not so suitable as the undulating grassy country on the opposite island of Kamorta. If the selection had been made solely on strategical grounds, and for the purpose of mounting guard over the pirates of Trinkut and Nankowri, none could have been better. But it being also in view to form, if possible, a self-supporting colony, the selection does not appear to have been a judicious one. The poor character of the soil and its unsuitability for cultivation are made at once apparent by the large areas which, under the most favourable tropical conditions for luxuriant growth, are only able to supply dry unnutritious grasses. Owing to the peculiarities of the geological structure, it is only in the valleys and on certain hills that dense jungle flourishes. From another point of view, too, exception may be taken to the site. It is thus referred to in the account of the cruise of the "Novara." "Hemmed in on all sides, and with the welcome sea-breeze frequently ceasing to blow for a week together, it was speedily pronounced a riddle, impossible to be solved, how

* "Asiatic Researches," Vol. IV., p. 129.

this harbour came to be once and again selected by German and Danish missionaries for the purposes of colonization. Unless the key to its mystery be found in its secure situation, the exquisite beauty of the mountain landscape, and the numerous clear spots around." In all the southern islands of the group the rocks are similar to those of the Andamans, and form a generous and prolific soil, in consequence of which fact a dense and uninterrupted mass of lofty forest spreads from the highest peaks to the margin of the sea. It has been suggested that these grass-covered areas are the result of artificial clearing by some of those who formerly settled in the islands. How such a conclusion has been arrived at it is difficult to understand, since the rapidity with which jungle in this climate spreads over neglected clearings and reclaims them as its own is sufficiently notorious. Anyone who reflects upon it cannot fail to recognise the existence of some innate cause which determines this peculiarity. An examination of the sources from which the soil is derived reveals the fact that they consist of magnesian clay rocks, which invariably yield a poor soil. In April the first actual steps were taken towards the formation of the settlement and the permanent occupation of the islands by the British. The Superintendent or Chief Commissioner of the Andamans and Nicobars, accompanied by the heads of several of the departments in the Andamans, sailed from Port Blair on the hulk "Black Prince," in tow of the "Quangtung." The settlement, as then established, included three officers in civil charge, a guard of eighty sepoys and their officers, an apothecary, and 262 convicts whose terms were nearly completed, and would therefore not be likely to attempt to escape.

The scene which opens to the eye as the steamer rounds Trinkut Island, and enters Nankowri harbour, is one of great beauty. The calm sea, which is only disturbed along the outer line of the coral reef where a line of breakers is formed; the varied indentations of the coast line; the beaches of glistening white coral sand; the bee-hive-shaped houses of the Nicobarese nestling in the groves of cocoa-nut-palms; and the background of forest, broken at intervals by the grass-covered hills, all combine to form a most charming view.

On the "Quangtung" coming to an anchor, I transferred myself and belongings to the hulk "Blenheim," the "Black Prince" having become water-logged, and was hospitably offered share of the limited accommodation available on board by the Assistant-Superintendent in charge of the settlement. Shortly after our arrival, a number of the Nicobarese paddled up in their outrigger canoes and came on board. They seemed rather anxious to see what was going on than to do much bartering, although they brought some vegetables, &c., with them. They possess such an abundance and varied supply of food, including cocoa-nuts, the fruit of the screw-pine, vegetables, fish, pigs, and poultry, that they are quite independent of extraneous supplies. They seemed, however, to have taken a great fancy to rice, and willingly took it in exchange for fruits, vegetables, poultry, or whatever else they brought to the ship. They appeared not to care for rupees, but would coolly ask for the coat off one's back in exchange for a few shells, a bunch of plantains, or a cocoa-nut. For rum and tobacco they have nearly all acquired a strong liking.

Before leaving Rangoon I was advised to lay in a good stock of hooks, two and four-anna pieces, and tobacco for purposes of exchange. I found, however, that they would not accept the hooks on any terms, as they spear all their fish by torch-light at night. The spears are either made of iron, the pattern being similar to that of the spears universally used throughout India; or they consist of a bamboo split at the extremity into a number of prongs, each of which is barbed. The small silver coins are chiefly used to let into small cylinders of palm wood which the men carry in holes made through the distended lobe of the ear, in the same way as the already-described ornaments of the Burmese are worn. Under ordinary circumstances, in their own homes, and when at work, the costume of the men consists of a narrow strip of blue cloth or other material with which they tightly brace themselves.

When visiting ships, however, they invariably wear some articles of European clothing. A favourite costume appears to be a pea-jacket, a Burmese lungi or skirt, and a straw hat. The first man who attracted my particular attention wore a peaked French cap, and a coloured chintz coat, from beneath which a "tail" of blue and white bunting hung down and trailed on the deck. To the latter I am inclined to attribute the origin of the very ancient tradition as to the existence of tailed races of human beings on some of the islands of the Indian Ocean. Thus in Ptolemy's map of these regions, there are represented a group of islands which bear the following inscription:—"*Satyorum insulæ tres quarum incolæ caudas ut sunt Satyorum habere dicentur.*" Three islands of the Satyrs of which the inhabitants are said to have tails similar to those possessed by the Satyrs. The same idea is expressed somewhat differently in other editions of the map. Again, Koeping, a Swede, who sailed to the East Indies in a Dutch ship in the year 1647, and anchored off the Nicobar Islands, relates that he discovered "men with tails like those of cats, which they moved in the same manner."*

Nothing more ludicrous can be imagined than the appearance presented by the Nicobarese, when sauntering about with these tails dragging on the ground behind them. It is not difficult to believe that early navigators afraid to land or go into close contact with the natives, may, when coasting along the shores of the islands, have really thought that they were gazing on tailed men.

Another man who came on board wore an Oxford hat with a band of crape on it, a coloured waistcoat, and a pair of white *pyjamas.* His hair hung down over his shoulders in straight, smooth, and glossy locks of true Malayan type. His visiting name was "Capstan." Another ill-looking individual told me complacently that his name was "Garrotter." In the course of my trips in the neighbourhood, I made the acqaintance of various other local celebrities, the names of whom, as given

---

* "Asiatic Researches." Vol. III., p. 151.

by themselves, were Captain Smith, Captain London, Captain Johnson, Yak, Tungyup, and "Old Hat." In Kar Nicobar the names are more pretentious. Most Englishmen could afford to laugh at the practice by former visitors of conferring such names; but the compiler of the account of the voyage of the "Novara" apparently considered such a proceeding a fit subject for protest, as he writes:—"Captain John was surrounded by a considerable number of natives who presented themselves as Captain Morgan, Captain Douglas, Dr. Crisp, Lord Nelson, Lord Byron, Lord Wellington, and so forth, having been indebted to the singular whimsies of some English captains to confer on those filthy brown people the illustrious names of the hereditary and intellectual aristocracy of Great Britain."

VILLAGE OF MALACCA, NANKOWRI ISLAND.

In the evening, after the departure of the "Quantung" for Kar Nicobar, I crossed the harbour to the village of Malacca, on Nankowri Island. As seen from the hulk, this village has a very picturesque appearance, as may be concluded from the accompanying illustration.

The bee-hive-shaped houses are all supported on posts near the high-water line, the height of the floors above ground being from six to seven feet. The village is surrounded by a grove of cocoa-nuts which is itself backed by a dense jungle of large trees* and luxuriant undergrowth. The handsomest trees to be seen in this neighbourhood are undoubtedly the areca palms (*Areca nibong*). There is a fine clump of them consisting of trees fully eighty feet high close to the new settlement.

On our landing on the beach near the village, several of the natives came forward to meet us, while others merely peeped lazily out of the apertures which serve for windows in the houses. They seemed to be supremely indifferent as to what the object of our visit might be. A number of pigs, dogs, and poultry, ran about between the posts supporting the houses. The first mentioned much more closely resemble the English than they do the Indian animals—they are said to be of Chinese origin. Throughout the jungles there are wild or semi-wild pigs, believed to be of similar breed. The small species which occurs in the Andamans (*Sus Andamanensis*) has not been obtained in these islands. But wild pigs are known to occur in some of the uninhabited islands, as Preparis and the Cocos. The dogs are perhaps smaller, but otherwise undistinguishable from the Indian and Burmese "pariahs." They are of great assistance to the natives in their hunts after the wild pigs.

On platforms near the houses there was a plentiful supply of one of the Nicobarese staple articles of food—the fruit of the screw-pine or pandanus (*P. mellori*), which is called *larum* by the natives.

Numbers of valves of clams or *Tridacna*,† and cockles

---

* The principal trees are *Calophyllum inophyllum*, *Barringtonia speciosa*, various species of *Ficus*, *Dipterocarpus*, and *Terminalia*.

† The clams, though damaged themselves, were often found to have perfect specimens of *Camas* and other shells with *Serpulæ*, &c., adhering to them.

(*Arca scabra*) were scattered about. There were also specimens of a *Dolium*, and a very fine *Murex*, from which the animals had no doubt been extracted and eaten.

The people struck me as being the most unprepossessing I had ever seen; the round-faced jolly-looking Andamanese being handsome as compared with them. Owing to the incessant habit of chewing pawn their teeth are intensely black, the incisors of the lower jaw often protruding in an irregular manner like tusks. The tongue, too, is more or less black, and in the mouths of some there appeared to be horny growths or accumulations, which prevented them closing their lips. They are generally broad-shouldered and powerfully-built men, and of a somewhat absent and phlegmatic temperament. The high cheek bones, partially oblique eyes, and flowing hair, point to a Malayan affinity, but there may perhaps be a Burmese element or strain in their blood.

They are excessively indolent, and since their daily wants are readily supplied, they spend many hours of the day in sloth, doing nothing. I often noticed them when they came to the ship apparently in a fit of abstraction, gazing intently into space. The efforts of the missionaries of various faiths and nationalities who have resided on the Nicobars, though their lives were in most cases sacrificed owing to the climate and want of suitable food—were totally without permanent result. Indeed, according to some of them, they utterly failed to make even a transient impression on these people.

Having seen the village of Malacca, I at once commenced an examination of the geological structure in its neighbourhood. It soon became apparent to me that I should have abundant opportunities of making collections in various branches of natural history during my stay, the shells on the beach and adjoining reefs, and the plants in the forest alone, threatening to afford an *embarras de richesse* overpowering to a single collector.

Close to the village there were pointed out to me some bushes of a miniature lime (*Triphasia trifoliata*), with fruits about the size of a small marble. This was not indigenous in the islands, having been introduced by some of the former settlers. On my return to Calcutta I took with me seedlings, some of which throve weil, and the small trees when in full fruit were very beautiful objects.

As I wandered through the forest close to the village, I found that many of the branches of the trees were heavily laden with thickly-matted orchids and ferns; some of the former were pendent, and so formed festoons of blossom of marvellous beauty. The fallen trunks near the water's edge were covered with *Litorinas*, feeding on the decaying bark, while hermit crabs of different sizes scampered about in all directions. They appeared to feed on the roots of mangroves, cocoa-nuts, and other trees which occur near high-water mark.

July 29th.—Kamorta.—This morning, after a cup of coffee, followed by a glass of fresh-drawn toddy, I went out to search the rock-pools at Red-cliff Point, which lies to the east of the settlement. The tide was too high for making a large bag of shells, but the few I did find, and the many other treasures of the rock-pools which I saw and collected, more than satisfied me. A black *Onchidium*, which reminded me of our *Doris*, was very abundant on the rocks close to high-water mark. In most of the pools and under the stones there were large black *Holothurias*, or *Bêches de mer*, which are called *tripang* by the Chinese. Another less common species was striped pink and white. According to Dr. Rink there are in all thirteen distinct species in these islands. Under the stones, too, I found brittle stars (*Ophiocoma*), and an annelid covered with silvery hairs, which proved very irritating when coming in contact with the hands. I collected about seven or eight species of crabs, one of which burrowed in the sand with astonishing rapidity. Perhaps the most curious crustacean was the so-called "sea-mantis," of which the fore-part is singularly like that of the insect from which it derives its name. It can inflict a very painful wound with its fore-feet, which it flips about with great force and velocity, making the bottle in which it may happen to be confined, ring with the violence of the taps.

I observed several species of sea anemones; one of the

"plumose" group was fully 8 inches in diameter. Another, too, was particularly notable, having beautiful light purple tentacles and a pea-green centre.

Sea-weeds, as I believe is not uncommonly the case in tropical seas, were very rare. The only varieties which I observed were a species of *Fucus*, a red weed, a peacock's tail or *Padina?*, and a gelatinous weed, which might answer as a substitute for carrigeen. Two species of a grass-like marine flowering plant occur inside the coral reef, where they form submarine meadows. These plants are very similar in appearance to the *Zostera marina*, which, under the name of *Alva*, is collected at many places on the coasts of the British Isles, and is, when dried, used for stuffing mattresses. The fringing reef of coral extends, except at a few points where it runs further out, to a distance of somewhat less than a quarter of a mile from the shore. At many places the sea forms a line of surf along the outer margin of the reef, while all within is still water. Within the reef there is shoal water, which rarely exceeds a fathom in depth. Outside there is an abrupt descent into from six to ten fathoms of blue water.

On my way back to the hulk for breakfast, I made several casts with the dredge on the reef. The ground did not prove to be very productive; however, I got a few fine specimens of living shells, especially several species of *Mitra*. Owing to the irregularities on the surface of the coral, dredging is here a matter of no little trouble, and requires much care and patience.

In the afternoon, in company with two of the officers of the settlement, I went to examine some passages through the mangroves that encircle the northern side of Blenheim Bay. We landed at a native path on Kamorta, which led us into a dense and moist jungle, in which pigs seemed to abound. Very few of the plants were in flower, but we brought away some living specimens of an exceedingly beautiful little fern, which proved to be *Trichomanes javanicum*. I also picked up some land shells belonging to the genera *Cyclophorus* and *Helix*. Birds were very scarce, we only saw two during the whole afternoon. We had not time to follow the paths to their termination, which was evidently on the opposite coast of Kamorta.

July 30th.—In the early morning I resumed shell hunting at yesterday's ground, and, as the tide was lower, with better success. I also shot specimens of the following birds:—Paroquet (*Palæornis erythrogenys*, Blyth), Oriole (*Oriolus macrourus*, Blyth), Honey-sucker (*Nectarinea pectoralis*, Horsf.), Kingfisher (*Toderamphus occipitalis*, Blyth), and Bulbul (*Hypsipetes virescens*, Blyth). All these birds are peculiar to the Nicobars, more or less closely allied species being found in the Andamans.

In the afternoon I crossed the hills on Kamorta, which intervene between Blenheim and Ho-ho Bays. On landing from a small boat at the corner of the undulating grass-covered country which lies to the north-west of the settlement, we soon found a native path which led us round by the crest of the highest ground to the opposite shore. The grass below was very long, in some places being up to our necks: but on the slopes of the hills the poverty, or rather absence, of soil, was made apparent by the scanty vegetation—a sort of "brake" fern (*Gleichenia dichotoma*) being the only plant to be seen. In places where this was abundant, my companion and myself were simultaneously reminded of the heathers and downs of home. The illusion was quickly dispelled, however, by a glance down the sides of the hill, where screw pines were freely scattered about. At the bottoms of the valleys there were clumps of forest in which the areca palm was the most prominent form.

In the grass-covered stream-courses, a species of climbing fern (*Lygodium scandens*) was abundant. I also obtained a ground orchid in the same locality.

On arriving at the coast line of Ho-ho bay a heavy shower of rain came on. While sheltering ourselves under the trees we picked up a number of land shells, including species of *Helix Cyclophorus* and *Spiraxis.*

The grass on the hills is coarse and hard, and, therefore, most unfit for grazing purposes. It is of prime importance, with a view to the prosperity of the settlement, that some endeavour should be made to replace it by more succulent varieties. The cattle which had been sent down hitherto have not thriven on the herbage. They are pot-bellied and sunk in the loins. It is still a matter of doubt whether the wild buffaloes, which are found in Kamorta, are indigenous, or have run wild. According to Pastor Rosen, they have not been introduced by European colonists. If this opinion be correct, then the fact of the occurrence of so large a mammal on this island is one of very great importance, viewed from the point of view of the geographical distribution of animals. To my mind, the probability of their having been introduced is principally based on the fact that, so far as is known, they do not occur on any of the other islands, except Kamorta, which was the scene of several of the early colonization schemes. The tendency of the buffalo to revert to a wild state under favourable conditions is well known. At this time none of the European officers of the settlement had seen them, and the natives whom I interrogated could not give much information on the subject. But I have since seen skulls which were picked up on the coast, and quite recently the live animals have been seen by visitors to the interior.

July 31st.—Kamorta.—This morning I went out to shoot in a piece of forest close to the settlement, and was fortunate in obtaining three specimens of a most interesting bird—the mound-builder (*Megapodius Nicobariensis*, Blyth.) The bird is rather smaller than a hen jungle-fowl, and there is but little difference between the plumage of the sexes, a fact of unusual occurrence among gallinaceous birds. As may be gathered from the generic name, the megapodes are provided with enormous feet, with which they scrape together the materials which form the mounds. In these mounds, as I shall subsequently explain, the eggs are hatched without the aid of the parent birds. The megapode runs freely, but seems to be easily put up. The first which I shot flew into a tree, not far from where I was standing, much in the same way as jungle-fowl will do when suddenly startled. The call, or note, is not easily describable, being a peculiar prolonged chuckle, which commences with a croak resembling that made by bullfrogs. I also shot specimens of the Nicobar Imperial Pigeon, which is quite a distinct species from the Andaman bird, the latter being identical with the peninsular species (*Carpophaga ænea*, Lin.)

Later in the day the Nicobarese came alongside the Blenheim in their canoes, bringing cocoa-nuts, crabs, and fowl, and, to my delight, two large light brick-coloured eggs, which I at once concluded to be those of the megapodius. On my producing one of the recently-killed birds the natives confirmed my supposition.

In the afternoon the "Quangtung" returned from Kar Nicobar, the objects of the visit having been accomplished. These were to inform the natives that they had become British subjects, and to make enquiries into the circumstances of the murder of a native, which had been committed by one of the crew of a trading vessel.

The natives of Kar Nicobar appeared to their visitors to belong to a race superior, both physically and intellectually, to those of Nankowri.

August 1st.—This morning, in company with one of the officers of the Settlement, I went in a boat to the western entrance of Nankowri haven, from which a view of the island of Katchall is obtained. After examining the geological structure of the cliffs at the entrance, we went to pay some visits at the neighbouring villages, and to see what we could effect in the way of barter for curiosities. The first village we landed at was called Deryah, the chief's name being Tungyup. He came forward to meet us on the beach, and on our expressing a wish to see his house he invited us to ascend the ladder leading up into it. We found there the two female members of his establishment, with whom we shook hands. They were, we thought, on the whole, more hideous in appearance than the master of the house. They were engaged in the manufacture of their staple article of food—the farinaceous part of the fruit of the pandanus, or screw-pine, which they call *larum*, the Malays *nung-kwan*. The process is as follows: the fruit, which in external aspect is not unlike a giant pine-apple, is pared and placed on a staging to dry and ripen. When ready it is broken up and boiled in a large earthen vessel. The pieces are then taken out and the softer, farinaceous portion is scraped off on the edge of a clam shell. The bundle of fibres remaining forms a sort of natural brush. In the building works going on at Kamorta they were found to serve as very economical substitutes for paint and whitewash brushes. The stuff which remains in the clam shell is made into a kind of pudding, which is wrapped up in leaves, and suspended from the roof of the house ready to be taken down and used as occasion may require. It has a slightly acid but not unpleasant taste. The Nicobarese eat it in combination with fish and cocoa-nuts.

These people presented us with a couple of pairs of polished cocoa-nut water vessels; but were unwilling to part with any of the spears which were arranged on the walls of their house. One of the "properties" hanging up was an old silk chimney-pot hat. This we placed on Tungyup's head, and, showing marked pleasure at our attention, he paraded about with it until we took leave of him.

We next sailed across to Bijohar, Captain Smith's village, on the west side of the haven. The old man with a cloth cap on his head, and a tall hat, which time had changed from black to bronze, on the top of that, was seated in a house surrounded by a circle of his friends and acquaintances, all of whom were stretched in reclining attitudes, resting against the poles which supported the beehive roof. We shook hands all round, each man, without moving from his position, merely stretching out his hand. This appeared to me a rather *infra dig.* proceeding on our part; but my companion assured me it was all right according to Nicobar manners. One of the men was a victim to elephantiasis. It struck me afterwards that he was possibly a notorious scoundrel named Acheup, who had been mentioned in the published narrative of the "Wasp" and "Satellite" expedition as being afflicted with that disease. From the centre of the roof of this house a very good model of a gar-fish, carved in a light white wood, was suspended. It was cleverly painted with a few simple colours. There were also some screens formed of the *spathes* of palms and the *glumes* of bamboos, in which various designs were cut or punctured. Over the door was a sort of pigeon-hole framework, in which the lower jaws of a number of pigs, trophies of the chase, were neatly arranged. Just above the trap-door entrance was a wooden figure, about three-quarters life-size, in the attitude of a man about to hurl a dart at any intruder. These figures are carved with amazing skill and boldness, and the faces are generally smeared over with vermilion or some other red pigment. They may be regarded as the guardians of the houses, and their hostile attitude indicates the character of the reception which an intruder would receive. On either side of the entrance, supported by a framework, were the spears which, with their knives, or dahs, are the only weapons possessed by these people. Fishing spears and paddles were neatly arranged against other parts of the walls.

Though deficient in courtesy, the Nicobarese seem to be not unmindful of the duties of hospitality to visitors. Captain Smith presented us with some cocoa-nuts and citrons. With some difficulty we induced him to part with one of his spears, which he at length did for two rupees. The younger men in the house, however, did their utmost to prevent him from letting us have it. These spears are somewhat roughly made out of scrap-iron, and are fixed in light and slender handles, about eight or nine feet long. They are evidently only used for hurling. I saw none fit for receiving a charge. Captain Smith presented me before leaving with the finest pig's jaw in his collection.

In some of the houses in this village we saw European articles, which had been either received from traders in exchange or taken from wrecks. Some of them may not improbably have been stolen from the vessels which have from time to time been piratically seized and destroyed by these islanders. The houses are carefully constructed of bamboos and other similar materials, and being for the most part thatched with pandanus-leaves, are quite water-tight. They are dark, but pleasantly cool, as compared with the glaring coral sand beneath. From this village we sailed across to another, called Etoe, where a man met us on the beach with a beautiful branch of red coralline in his hand. On our ascending into one of the principal houses we found that the owner was sick, and that a large circle of his friends and neighbours had assembled to assist at his cure. Men, women, and children were all seated round the central room. From the roof various carvings, offerings of fruit, bunches of leaves, &c., were suspended for the purpose of appeasing the evil spirits. The principal ornament was intended to represent the mast, ladder, and yards of a ship, the latter being manned by a number of figures in European clothing and tall hats. On this occasion I had the sole opportunity afforded to me during my stay of seeing some of the younger women and children. Among the former, a few were just passable for a place where ugliness prevails to so great an extent; but the elder women had the same repulsive mouths, full of hideous black tusks, as the men. The next house which we visited was not of the ordinary bee-hive pattern, but was rectangular in shape. No one was at home. It belonged to Captain London, who arrived before we left. Both this and another house which we peeped into looked very clean and cheerful inside, the smoke from the fires not having had time to begrime the walls. Captain Yak, of the village of Malacca, who was showing us the different houses, now announced the arrival of Captain and Mrs. London, so we went down to meet them as they landed from their canoe. The captain is a broad-shouldered jolly-looking fellow, with a much less disfigured mouth than is commonly seen. His costume consisted of a straw hat, a pea-jacket, and a Burmese lungi. He had with him a basket, from which he produced his best coat, which he puts on when about to visit ships. It is a naval officer's blue coat, with gilt buttons. Mrs. L.'s appearance was not pleasing. Her costume consisted of variously-coloured Burmese and Madrassi cloths.

August 2nd.—To-day we made up a party to visit the Island of Trinkut. On reaching the coast we soon found a creek on the west side, up which we rowed till it brought us to a village on the site of one of those which were burnt by the "Wasp" and "Satellite" expedition. The people of this island are believed to have been the principal offenders in reference to the murders and piracies of former years. The population at present seems to be very small. It is supposed that some of the former inhabitants, finding that piracies can no longer be committed with impunity, may have migrated to Katchall, or some of the other islands. The advent of a steamer still causes some consternation and a stampede on the part of the remaining inhabitants to their hiding-places in the jungles. The position of this pirates' village at the end of a long winding creek was well chosen. It almost realised those described in romance. At the point where we landed there were two or three houses, which were apparently mere temporary dwellings for those who looked after the crop of cocoa-nuts. Here we met a party of Kling traders, who belonged to a ship which was lying off Nankowri. They had brought for exchange for cocoa-nuts the most utter trash. Among other things we noticed small squares of looking-glass, packets of sugar, biscuits, hooks, stuffs, earthenware-whistles, and beads—all of the very worst kinds. In Kar Nicobar there seems to be a regular rate of exchange; for in the account of the voyage of the "Novara,"* the value in cocoa-nuts of the articles commonly used for barter is given. The Klings told us that but for the existence of the British settlement they would not have dared thus to come on shore. Formerly they were obliged to observe the precaution of preventing more than one canoe at a time coming alongside their vessels, from fear lest the natives should swarm up the sides and overpower them. A short walk took us to the opposite shore of the island, where there is a beautiful sandy beach. Lying off this side of the island was another ship. A party from her were on shore, trying to do business, which, however, they complained of being very slack. Afterwards we heard that these Klings had been taking advantage of the fear with which the natives, since their punishment, regard the British, and had been helping them-

* Vol. II., p. 19.

selves to cocoa-nuts. Besides the trivial articles mentioned above, rice, rum, and rupees are also sometimes given in exchange for cocoa-nuts. The principal use made of the coins is to fashion the silver into ornaments.

During the north-east monsoon, Malay, Burmese, and Chinese vessels visit the Nicobar Islands for a miscellaneous cargo of cocoa-nuts, areca and betel-nuts, tripang or *bêche de mer*, edible swallows'-nests, and ambergris.* It is stated that the ambergris, which is collected on the coasts, is sometimes adulterated with vegetable resins by the Nicobarese. In Rangoon I was told that the Chinese impose upon their brethren by making artificial birds'-nests out of gelatine, which cannot, except by the most practised eye, be distinguished from the genuine article. In the same place, too, I was shown, besides sharks' fins beaten out into isinglass, a very singular article of food, said to be largely used by the Chinese. It consisted of split and dried cuttle-fish.† Close to the houses I shot some birds, and, on the mud-flats laid bare by the falling tide, I obtained examples of two species of the genus *Cerithium* (*C. palustris and C. telescopium*), which is remarkable for its wide distribution through space and time.

Returning down this creek, we entered another, which penetrated a mangrove swamp in a southerly direction. Here we saw a flock of whimbrel (*Numenius phœopus*), and a single example of the common Indian paddy-bird (*Ardeola leucoptera*), perched on the trees. After poling for about a quarter of a mile, our further progress was prevented by snags and fallen trunks.

August 3rd.—This morning I went out to dredge along the northern shore of Blenheim Bay. As before, it proved to be very

---

* In the second trip to these Islands, described in a subsequent chapter, we failed to find the true edible swallows'-nest in the Nicobars; but we collected a number in the Andamans. The German name for ambergris, *ambra*, appears to have given rise to the idea with some authors that amber was also found in the Nicobars.

† I see in a recently published work, "A Search for Fortune," that the Chinese in Australia make considerable use of the same article of diet.

difficult work, owing to the coral. The dredge generally brought up a quantity of fragments of shells, smashed by the surf, scattered through which débris there were a few whole and live shells. Even if I had returned to the ship empty-handed, I should not have considered that I had wasted the morning, as I had a leisurely view of that most marvellous of sights—a coral reef under water. There were corals which in their living state are of many shades of fawn, buff, pink, and blue, while some were tipped with a magenta-like bloom. Sponges which looked as hard as stone spread over wide areas, while sprays of coralline added their graceful forms to the picture. Through the vistas so formed golden-banded and metallic-blue fish meandered, while on the patches of sand here and there the Holothurias and various mollusca and crustaceans might be seen slowly crawling.

In the smooth water of Nankowri haven the strange-looking green-boned gard or gar-fish are very abundant. They possess a remarkable power of darting along above the surface, and often traverse distances little short of those accomplished by flying-fish. Starting from the water, they obtain fresh impetus after every few feet by a vigorous wriggle, which carries them forward, until, after a distance of about fifty or sixty yards, they dive down and disappear.

After breakfast I joined a party to visit some of the villages on the north-east of Nankowri. We landed first at some cliffs west of the village of Alta-Koang. The rocks of which they were formed proved to be a diallage and serpentine gabbro or trap. From thence we walked along the beach, seeking for shells, till we reached the village, where we ascended into the principal house, where a circle of most ruffianly-looking men were assembled. One of our party conversed with them in Malay, a language which they appeared to understand perfectly.

The circular room was boarded with large, smooth, and well-polished planks, which had probably been obtained from some wreck. If not, they must have been hewn from solid trees with great labour. Near the trap-door entrance there were several of the already-mentioned pandanus-fruit brushes, which were expressly placed there for the purpose of brushing off the sand which adhered to the feet of those who came up from the strand below. A further indication of cleanliness was afforded by the fact that at regular intervals there were small diagonal holes cut in the floor, which enabled the men to rid themselves of the red saliva produced by pawn chewing without soiling the boards.

One of the men of this village, Captain Johnson by name, had recently been taken on a visit to Calcutta by the Commander of the "Czarewitch." His fellow villagers, though he had not returned with us, made no enquiry about him and expressed no anxiety about his return. The reason for this was, I believe, that he is regarded by them as a traitor, in consequence of his having given information to the officers of the "Wasp" and "Satellite" expedition, which resulted in many other houses being burnt, while his own was spared. I was told that, like many other savages, he appeared to take everything shewn him in Calcutta very much as a matter of course. In the Museum he pointed out several animals as being found in the Nicobars, and among these was a crocodile. This was an interesting confirmation of a then somewhat doubtful fact, which has since been amply proved.

From one of two men who met us on the beach, I obtained a pair of ear ornaments, consisting of two four-anna silver pieces fixed on cylinders of palm-wood. In this particular example the effigy of Her Majesty had been effaced, but in others which I have seen it has been left intact.

The other man shewed us some certificates of good character and trustworthiness, which we were not a little amused to find had been given by European and Eurasian convicts, and which, on enquiry, proved to have been paid for with cocoa-nuts.

After we had descended from the house, and were seated on an old canoe, refreshing ourselves with cocoa-nut milk, the men above began chanting a Malayan dirge in a minor key. Save for a nasal twang, it would have been positively agreeable to listen to. As it was, it was much more in accordance with European ideas than the vocal music ordinarily heard in India.

On this occasion I did not see any form of musical instrument in the houses which I visited; but, according to Dr. Rink, the Nicobarese have flutes and a kind of guitar made of bamboo. On my subsequent visit to the Great Nicobar I obtained an example of what would be more correctly described as a flageolet than a flute, since it was a hollow bamboo, blown through at the end, with a reed tied over the first hole.

Close to these villages there are refuse-heaps, veritable kitchen middens, in which cocoa-nut husks, the débris of pandanus fruits, clam and cockle-shells, and hog's-bones are thrown together. Generally, too, there are graveyards in the vicinity. Over each grave crossed sticks are erected, upon which the clothes and other property of the deceased are suspended. Alluding to this custom, Dr. Rink writes:—"When I first came to the village of Malacca on Nankowri, the manner in which the natives had ornamented the grave of an English sailor boy (who had lived with them several years, and had adopted their customs) with his axe and his open trunk, made quite a touching impression." The complicated and singular funeral ceremonies of the Nicobarese are described by Dr. Rink and in the account of the "Novara" voyage. Unfortunately I did not witness these, and can therefore neither add to nor confirm the already-published statements.

August 4th.—To-day was chiefly occupied in packing collections. Some shells were brought in for me by the natives, who had previously been unwilling to take the trouble of collecting for me. One of the officers of the "Quangtung," too, added to my collection of birds some interesting specimens, including the large black-and-white fruit-eating pigeon (*Carpophaga bicolor*, Scop.), the large hill maina (*Eulabes intermedia vel Javanensis*, Osbeck), and a ground-thrush (*Geocichla innotata*, Blyth).

Before concluding this journal of my first visit to the Nicobars, I shall give a brief abstract of what is known regarding these people, who are now British subjects.

It is believed that there are no chiefs, properly so called, among the Nicobarese. The old men are, to a certain extent,

Plate V.]

GROUP OF NICOBARESE, NANKOWRI ISLAND.

(From a Photograph by Capt. J. Waterhouse.)

respected, but do not appear to exercise any particular influence in consequence of their age. The community of power extends even to domestic affairs, as it is said that many of the houses are the joint property of several families. According to Dr. Rink the women possess considerable influence over their husbands, and are consulted on all matters of importance.

Certain of the men take upon themselves the duties of priests, and are called Malves or Minlovens according to Rink and Barbe respectively. This may perhaps be derived from the well-known Mahomedan title of Mulvi. They fill the united offices of priests, physicians, and wizards, and in each of these capacities their whole energy seems to be concentrated on the exorcism of evil spirits, to the malign influence of which the Nicobarese are in the habit of referring all the evils which may befall them.

The Rev. Mr. Barbe's account of the manner in which the Minlovens carry out this duty is very interesting. Should a Minloven in his capacity as physician, be unsuccessful in his cases, and several patients die while under his treatment, the people agree to kill him, and he is forthwith murdered.

In spite of various modes of propitiation and every effort to keep them at a distance, it is found that evil spirits manage to find their way into villages, one causing sickness, another forcing a man to commit murder or some other crime, and so on, till matters become so unbearable that it is determined to force them to depart.

At certain festivals a clearance of these evil spirits, who may thus have taken up their quarters in a village since the period of the last previous expulsion, is effected by carrying about a raft on which by various incantations the Minloven compels them, terrified by his gesticulations and howlings, to take their seats. The raft is then taken to the sea-side, where it is towed out some distance and cast adrift, and the villagers believe that if the ceremony has been properly performed, they are thus completely freed from the causes of all sickness and trouble. Sometimes it happens that rafts with their cargoes of devils are driven on shore close to a neighbouring village, and as it is believed that they take the opportunity of transplanting themselves, the inhabitants consider that they are aggrieved, and that they have a *casus belli.* Accordingly, we are told,* "A village invaded (by devils) sends a challenge to the one from which they have been ejected, and a day is fixed for the battle. The captains of all the neighbouring villages having met in consultation the combatants are chosen, and as there are others who wish to take advantage of so just a mode of settling their disputes, they are summoned to appear: one has stolen something, another run off with his neighbour's wife—and the like. All these people now meet, both the injured and the guilty, and each being provided with a sufficient supply of sticks, they proceed to the place of rendezvous. There the captains examine the sticks, and those that are too thick are thrown away. This being done two of the combatants step out and lay about each other's back and head till one is obliged to give up. A second couple follow, and after them others, till in a proper space of time the whole company has got a good drubbing. The most innocent among them are generally the worst handled; however, the business is now decided and all are convinced that whoever was first obliged to give up was the offender. Peace is thus restored, both parties being perfectly satisfied with so just and wise a decision."

The missionaries who resided in the Nicobars found that the inhabitants had no idea of a supreme beneficent Being, and they in vain tried to shape their minds into a capability of even comprehending such an existence. Elsewhere in these pages I have described a similar state of creed among certain aboriginal races in India, but with some of them the missionaries have been more successful.

The origin of the Nicobarese is still shrouded in much obscurity. According to themselves they all came from the Great Nicobar. They are said to possess two traditions as to their primary origin, the first being that they are sprung from ants,

* I am unable to vouch personally for the accuracy of this account, which is by the Rev. J. G. Hænsel.

and the second that they are descended from a man and a dog—the sole survivors of a great inundation. This latter, however, may very possibly be a comparatively modern idea, derived from some jumbled account of the Noachian deluge taught them by the earliest missionaries. To what I have already said as to the probable affinities of the Nicobarese with the Malays and Burmese, I would here add that I have noticed among them certain traits which seem to me to point to an affinity between them and two tribes of Dravidians, with whom I have some acquaintance, these are the Malés, or Rajmahal Paharias, and the Sowras, or Savaras, of the tributary states of Orissa. The grounds for this identification are not, it is true, very definite; but when visiting the villages of the Malés many little things, such as the erection of ornamental bamboos to ward off evil spirits, and the store-houses raised on posts, recalled to my mind similar objects in the Nicobars. In order to test this supposition I have compared lists of Nicobarese and Dravidian words, and the result is that some few have proved to be identical, or nearly so.*

Possibly among other tribes, if search were made, apparent affinities of equal strength would be found. It is worthy of notice, for instance, that among the Garos the word *Nakoba* is used to denote a freeman, and since the country occupied by the Garos extends nearly to Cape Negrais, in Arakan, a connection between them and the Nicobarese would seem to be a not unnatural probability. But I forbear from wandering further into this line of enquiry, and shall leave the above hints to be worked out by others more accustomed to philological research than myself.

---

* *E.g.*—I	is in Nicobarese	*tjuen*	in Malé	*en.*
He	,, ,,	*ané*	,, Sowra	*ané.*
Eye	,, ,,	*olmat* or *emat*	,, ,,	*amét.*
Head	,, ,,	*Koi*	,, Malé	*Koku.*
Stand	,, ,,	*achicienga*	,, ,,	*chien.*
Run	,, ,,	*tjeng-ga*	,, ,,	*veng-hen.*

In the Nankowri dialect *Omjah* means a chief, or head man. Among the Uraons there is a functionary who is called *Ojha,* who is consulted on matters connected with the spiritual world.

Of course what I have above suggested merely points to a derivation by a different route, through the Dravidian instead of the Malayan branches, of the same original Thibetan stock.

August 5th.—Steamer "Quangtung."—This morning we started on the return journey to Port Blair. Having passed Tillanschong we witnessed the formation of a water-spout at some miles distance. At the surface of the sea there was a great commotion and boiling up, and, as we watched, a sort of finger or pointer stretched down from an overhanging mass of intensely black cloud. A junction having been thus formed, the waterspout assumed the well-known spiral aspect which is represented in works on meteorological phenomena.

August 6th.—Steamer "Quangtung."—As we approached the Andaman Islands we entered a region of rain and squalls,* which contrasted with the fine weather we had been enjoying in the Nicobars. Shortly after arrival at Port Blair I started for Viper Island, five miles up the bay, where my host, the late Dr. Curran, lived, being in medical charge of the convicts who were imprisoned on that island; in other words, of all the greatest scoundrels in the settlement, since to Viper all such were consigned. My friend's house, built in the already described Burmese style, was situated on the highest point of this small island, whence there was a commanding view of all the other buildings on the slopes below.

Dr. Curran's principal domestic was not only a life convict, but a murderer. He was, however, a most excellent servant, and when one heard that he had got into trouble for murdering the seducer of his sister, his offence against law did not appear to be one meriting so severe a punishment. As many of the warders and other petty officials on the island were also convicts, the company of Madras troops quartered there formed the bulk of the free population.

---

* It is in this neighbourhood, I believe, that the disturbances generally originate which result sometimes in the cyclones which prove so destructive in the higher parts of the Bay of Bengal.

August 7th.—Viper Island.—This day was spent in cleaning and putting away my Nicobar collections. In the afternoon I visited the reefs near Chatham Islands, where I obtained some good shells. I was surprised to find how well the cultivation of the cocoa-nut has succeeded in the Andamans, though the tree is, I believe, nowhere indigenous in the islands. Its absence is particularly remarkable, since it occurs in the Cocos Islands to the north, and the Nicobars to the south. Such a fact would be very apt to tempt a naturalist given to theorizing, to propound an explanation for this peculiar distribution, and some must of necessity exist; but what it may be I cannot venture to suggest.

August 8th.—Viper Island.—In company with Mr. Homfray, who was in charge of the "Andamanese Home," and Dr. Curran, I started from Viper Island, in Port Blair, to visit Port Mouat and the Home at Mount Augusta. Close to the landing-place, at Homfray's Ghât there is an old kitchen midden, in which the valves of oysters, *Arcas* and *Cyrenas*, were abundant. Mr. Homfray told me that the present race of Andamanese do not eat oysters—a rather singular fact, which suggested the possibility of there having been different inhabitants of this part of the island at some former period. The road to Port Mouat runs along by the side of a mangrove swamp, in which *Cyrenas* abound. These molluscs are eaten by the Andamanese, and the valves, possessing sharp edges, are used as substitutes for knives. Shortly after arriving at Port Mouat, we left in a boat for Mount Augusta. As we approached the shores near to which the Home is situated, a swarm of little woolly-headed Andamanese struck into the waves, and, swimming and diving under and about the boat, so accompanied us to the shore. On reaching the Home, we found that out of the 200 individuals who were said to be availing themselves of the shelter and the ration of 2 lbs. of rice per head per diem which Government gives them, the greater portion of the men had gone out in their large canoes to another part of the island to hunt for pigs. The sight presented to our eyes on entering the Home was a most singular one, and one not readily to be forgotten. At intervals along both sides there were a number of family groups, variously occupied. Some were boiling rice; others were engaged in cooking pork, which they effect by placing small strips in a hollow bamboo, which is then laid on the fire, and the meat, when scarcely more than warmed, is taken out and eaten. Mr. Homfray assured me that the Andamanese, so far as he knew, never eat meat in an actually raw condition. Of the men present in the Home, several were smoking—that being one of the few accomplishments they have learnt from their contact with civilization. *Calcutta poko*, which is the Andamanese name for tobacco, is in great demand with them now. After a little preliminary shyness had worn off, they did not hesitate to search our pockets to see if we carried any with us.

The simplicity of the clothing arrangements of the Andamanese is well known, the elaborate toilets of civilization being represented by a leaf, which is worn by the women suspended from a girdle of rattan or pandanus fibre. Sometimes this pandanus fibre is so beaten out as to form a bushy tail.

Of the various ornaments worn by the women, none seemed more extraordinary than the skulls of their defunct relatives, festooned with strings of shells, which some of them carried suspended from their necks. Those who had recently lost relatives were in mourning, which consisted in their being shaved, and covered from head to foot with a uniform coating of white clay. Non-mourners were more or less adorned with red clay.

Several of the men were amusing themselves manipulating, with pieces of string, the puzzles of the cat's cradle. Trivial a circumstance as this at first sight appears to be, it is really one of some importance, as it may be used as evidence in favour of a primitive connection between the Andamanese and races inhabiting the Malayan Archipelago. Mr. Wallace found the Dyak boys in Borneo more skilful than himself in the mysteries of cat's cradle. He says, regarding this accomplishment—"We learn thereby that these people have passed beyond the first stage of savage life in which the struggle for existence absorbs the whole faculties, and in which every thought and idea is connected with war or hunting, or the provision for their immediate necessities." These remarks cannot be applied with the same force to the Andamanese, whose rank in the scale of civilization is lower than that of the Dyaks.

Mr. Homfray pointed out one old woman who, he said, possessed great influence over the tribe, and acted as arbitrator in all disputes. Until the rule was enforced in the Home of making those who came to it give up their bows while remaining there, quarrels not unfrequently led to two parties being formed, who discharged their arrows at one another, even within the walls. A man on either side being struck was the signal for a cessation of hostilities.

Notwithstanding such outbursts, the Andamanese possess great affection for one another. Almost every one who has written about them has borne witness to this trait in their characters.

I had proposed to myself one subject upon which to make special inquiries on the spot: this was their method of making flakes of flint and glass, which they had been reported to be in the habit of using as lancets. My attention, however, was so taken up by other subjects of interest that I should have forgotten to investigate the point, had it not fortunately happened that on reaching one of the family groups I observed a woman engaged in making flakes, which she skilfully chipped off a piece of dark bottle glass with a quartz pebble. Having struck off a flake of suitable character, she forthwith proceeded, with astonishing rapidity, to shave off the spiral twists of hair which covered the head of her son. Mr. Homfray informed me that the Andamanese can still manufacture the flakes of flint, which they effect by first heating the stones in a fire, that being found to facilitate the breaking in the required directions. Thus we have, at the present day, a race who practise an art, the widespread knowledge of which in pre-historic times, is proved by frequent discoveries in all quarters of the globe. The Andamanese are, however, advancing beyond their stone age. In one corner of the building, a woman was occupied in polishing and wearing down into shape an iron arrow-head. It was a most formidable affair, heart-shaped, and from 2½ to 3 inches in diameter.

In the centre of the Home there was a trophy formed of the bones of pigs, dugongs, and turtles, together with some bundles of human ribs, which latter had been deposited there after having been carried about by the relatives of the deceased. All these objects were covered with red clay. Mr. Homfray said that he had encouraged the occupants of the Home in the formation of this collection, as it served to attach them to the place, and to make them really regard it as their home. I made some selections, with Mr. Homfray's permission, from this trophy. The strings with which the objects were tied were severed by a cyrena valve; this shell, as I have above noted, furnishing the ordinary knives.

In hunting for dugong and turtle, the practice appears to be to run the canoe close to where the animal lies asleep, or basking on the surface of the water. The striker, grasping the spear or harpoon firmly in both hands, springs forward on to the animal's back, the weight of his body serving to drive in the weapon further than could be done by mere hurling. A tussle in the water ensues, at which other men jumping from the canoe assist.

As to the reported cannibalism of the Andamanese, Mr. Homfray told me that he had interrogated the natives themselves, and they manifested the greatest repugnance to the idea, and denied most emphatically that such a custom existed amongst them. Further, some few years ago, thirteen men who landed from a ship on the Little Andaman, for the purpose of searching for water, were all murdered. An expedition was, on the arrival of the news, despatched from Port Blair, to visit the scene, and ascertain the circumstances. The members of this expedition, together with some of the Port Blair Andamanese, landed on the island. They were received with the most determined hostility, which the unruly and aggressive conduct of the Port Blair natives

—who, it was hoped, would act as go-betweens—served greatly to intensify. The bodies of the thirteen murdered men were discovered on the beach, slightly covered with sand, so that no cannibalism had taken place in this case. It may be added with reference to this expedition, that the boats had to be regained through a heavy surf, and under cover of musketry, as the natives, for whom firearms had no terrors, and the effects of which they could not at first realize, closed round in great numbers, and discharged hundreds of arrows.

I am therefore inclined to believe that the reputed cannibalism of the Andamanese is more than doubtful. That such a belief should be prevalent is no matter for surprise, considering their admitted hostility to all visitors to their coasts, and the general tendency there both was and is, on the part of travellers, to attribute such propensities to savage races about whom little is known.

August 9th.—Viper Island.—The next four days were spent collecting shells and other marine animals on the coral reefs laid bare at low tide, and in examining the geological structure of the neighbourhood of Port Blair. Some of the evenings were spent in the pleasant society which was gathered together at the station mess, where all the unmarried officials used to dine.

August 13th.—Mount Harriet.—To-day a party consisting of Dr. Curran, two other of the resident officials, and myself, started for Mount Harriet, where we purposed remaining for a few days' change in the comfortable bungalow at the summit. Landing at Hope Town, the locality where the horrible tragedy which deprived India of one of her greatest and most beloved of Viceroys was subsequently enacted, we ascended by a steep road through a magnificent forest in which the long straight stems of the wood-oil trees (*Dipterocarpus lævis*) were conspicuous. The undergrowth was so dense as to be absolutely impenetrable. Among the branches of the loftiest trees, and occasionally low down, a considerable variety of birds was to be seen from time to time. These included paroquets, pigeons, scarlet minivets, orioles, woodpeckers, fairy blue-birds, blue fly-catchers, kingfishers, king-crows, and several species of bulbul. In ascending this hill an unaccountable weakness rendered it difficult for me to keep up with my companions. I had no idea then that it was caused, as the event proved, by incipient fever.

August 14th.—Mount Harriet.—In the morning I walked along a newly opened-up road for about three miles into the interior. At several points, where the vegetation was somewhat open, capital views were obtained. An unlimited extent of dense forest-clad hills seemed to stretch before the eyes. I shot some birds, including a little tree-pie (*Dendrocitta Baylei*, Blyth) which is peculiar to the Andaman Islands. I also collected some four or five species of land shells. After my return to the bungalow I was struck down with a violent attack of fever and ague, which did not leave me till late at night.

August 15th.—Mount Harriet.—In the morning I shot birds, and while engaged in preserving them was again attacked by ague, and had to resign the task to my servant-boy, whom I had trained as a taxidermist.

August 16th.—Mount Harriet to Viper Island.—Descended the hill in a shower of rain. A very bad night succeeding, on my return to Viper Island I determined to take my passage in the "Czarewitch," which was about to sail in a few days for Rangoon.

August 17th.—Viper to Ross.—To-day I was busily occupied in packing up my collections, many delicate shells requiring care for their proper preservation. My host at Ross had as a guest in his house the Nicobarese "Captain Johnson," who was very ill with inflammation of the lungs.

The results of my geological observations made on this visit, in the Nicobars and Andamans, are given in two papers published in the Journal of the Asiatic Society of Bengal.*

In the Nicobars my opportunities for examination were limited to small portions of the islands of Nankowri, Kamorta, and

---

* Vol. XXXIX., part ii., 1870, p. 27; and *id.*, p. 231.

Trinkut. The rocks of these three islands which determine the character of the soil are:—

1st.—Coral rocks all round the coast, and forming raised beaches in places.

2nd.— Magnesian claystones with interbedded conglomerates belonging to an undetermined tertiary horizon.

3rd.—Gabbro, diorites and serpentinous rocks, which are seen on the highlands east and west of the village of Alta-Koang on Nankowri.

The coral rocks, together with the sea-drift and vegetable humus, have formed a soil in which the cocoa-nuts thrive. I have already, on a prévious page, pointed out that the magnesian claystones form a soil incapable of supporting more than a crop of grass. In the valleys, where this formation occurs, the accumulation of vegetable matter, &c., brought down by the streams has proved sufficient, in many cases, to support a forest of large trees; but in the hot-house climate of the Nicobars, the poverty of the soil is so great that the tops of some of the hills are quite bare, or are only able to support a fern (*Gleichenia dichotoma*). The presence of a conglomerate bed has the effect of locally improving the character of the soil by the decomposition of its contained pebbles of igneous rocks. The igneous rocks, gabbro, and diorites, where they occur, produce a much better soil, which is capable of supporting a dense forest. In the southern islands of the group, the rocks are similar in character to those of the Andamans described below, and hence the forests there, as in the Andamans, are not broken by bare spaces. The traces of coal which have been found in these southern islands appear to be of similar character to those in the Andamans. In the Andaman Islands, in the neighbourhood of Port Blair, there are sandstones which appear to be of tertiary, possibly Miocene age, and identical with rocks occurring in Arakan. Fossils, however, have not as yet been obtained, and we are, moreover, still unable to place these rocks in their position in reference to the magnesian clays of Kamorta, &c. Dr. Hochstetter has suggested that the different rocks of the Nicobars which, as I have said, include some like those of the Andamans, are simply "petrographically different products of one and the same period of deposition." Until the islands have been much more thoroughly explored it will be impossible to say whether this supposition is correct. It was not Dr. Rink's view, and it does not commend itself to me as probable. In the paper already alluded to will be found a description of the physical geology in the neighbourhood of Port Blair. Traces of coal have been met with on Ross and Viper Islands, and at Navy Point. It occurred in small nests in the sandstones, which were speedily exhausted, and no seam appears as yet to have been discovered. It consists of a sort of lignite, which, though of excellent quality as ascertained by assay, can scarcely be regarded as an economic product of value, owing to its small amount. The other useful products furnished by these rocks are ornamental serpentine and building stones. In some of the earliest accounts of the islands, mention is made of quicksilver as occurring in the Andaman Islands, but up to the present no confirmation of this has been obtained.

August 18th.—Sailed for Rangoon early this morning in the "Czarewitch," a vessel belonging to the Indian Government. On the 19th we passed Narkondam again. The sail was very enjoyable, and all the pleasanter from the absence of the noise and smell from the engines which I had experienced in the steamer voyages. It served to check, though not wholly to cure, my fever, as it broke out again after my arrival in Calcutta, thus showing how persistent are the fevers contracted in these islands. We reached Rangoon on the evening of the 21st.

August 23rd.—Rangoon.—This morning I visited the Rangoon Gaol in company with Dr. Maingay. The native convicts number about 1,500. Owing to the desperate character of a large number of these, and the persistency of their efforts to escape, a much stricter discipline is necessary than is in force in most Indian gaols. The native prisoners turn out some capital furniture and wood-carvings of grotesque designs suitable for panels, screens, &c. The Europeans, of whom there were about thirty, were engaged in breaking stones. While I was at the gaol, one of the warders, a Madrassi, was brought up for trial. It appeared that in the copious folds of his enormous pugari or turban he had been in the habit of conveying tobacco and other comforts to certain of the convicts whose friends outside felt for their privations. Judging from the profusion of jewellery on this man's wife, who came to intercede for him, the trade was profitable in proportion to its risk. A summary sentence of two months' imprisonment with hard labour was inflicted; and the contrast between the man's crestfallen appearance on hearing this award, and the air with which he at first strove to brazen out the charge, was considerable. Close to the spot where this scene was enacted Dr. Maingay a few months later lost his life in the following manner. The only guard at the gaol consisted of a body of specially-enrolled Madrassis, whose soldierly qualities consisted in wearing a uniform and carrying rifles. On the occasion in question some of the Burmese chain-gang were employed in carrying blocks of stone from the road outside through the principal entrance. Suddenly one of them knocked over the sentry with the stone which he carried, and seized his rifle. Another of the guard threw away his loaded rifle, which was picked up by a second convict, when the valiant guard immediately retreated into their room leading off the porch, and, closing the door, commenced to fire against it in a vague way, in the expectation that the bullets would penetrate the timber and possibly hit a convict outside. The European gaoler, hearing the disturbance, hurried out from his office, when a convict immediately levelled a rifle at him; but another well-disposed convict, rushing between, received the bullet in his heart and fell immediately. Just then Dr. Maingay appeared, and was instantly killed by a ball from the second rifle. The gaoler, seeing that the guard were of no use, bethought him of obtaining the aid of the European prisoners, and they, on being summoned, came forward and at once overpowered the Burmese, who were preparing to free themselves and friends of their chains, so that they might decamp *en masse*. But for this timely assistance, since cantonments were nearly a mile off, the greater number of the 1,500 convicts would, in all probability, have been free to depart, and what the consequences would have been may be imagined. As it was, the death of Dr. Maingay left many mourners both in Rangoon and elsewhere, where his repute as a naturalist was fast spreading. Amelioration of sentence was, I believe, granted to some of the Europeans who had done such good service.

Having seen the Shue-Dagon Pagoda on the occasion of my former visit, as I have already related, I availed myself of every opportunity which remained to me of further examining this extraordinary monument, and watching the crowds of worshippers that flocked to it. Even a superficial acquaintance with the doctrines and tenets of Buddhism cannot fail to leave an impress on minds not wholly given up to a narrow belief in their own religious systems. If it has no other effect, it should at least give rise to a charitable feeling towards the creeds of millions who are commonly spoken of as "heathen," living wholly in outer darkness, and destined to eternal damnation. Even the Jesuit fathers Gabbet and Huc were compelled to admit that there was much of good in Buddhism, and to offer as an explanation of the resemblance between certain of its rites and symbols and those of the Catholic Church, that they must have been the invention of the devil for the express purpose of keeping so large a section of mankind from adopting the true faith. Admitting for a moment the influence of his infernal majesty, it must not be forgotten that the Buddhist religion is of far greater age than the Christian, so that his operations, according to the theories of the two Abbés, must have been of a precautionary character, in anticipation of the birth, growth, and development of the Christian religion.

The pagodas of Burmah, of which the Shue-Dagon is one of the finest examples, are solid tapering cones of masonry, which are generally highly ornamented and crowned by a *Htee*, or golden umbrella. Not unfrequently sacred relics and treasure are built up in the centre, owing to a belief in which many of them were broken into by British soldiers during the last Burmese war.

The Shue-Dagon Pagoda was built by successive additions, and attained its present height of 320 feet in 1768, when the *Htee* was placed on it.

A few years ago the King of Burmah presented a new *Htee*, which, being made of solid gold and ornamented with rubies and other precious stones, was supposed to have cost a very considerable sum. In consequence of the probable disturbing influence of an old tradition current in Burmah to the effect that whoever raised the new *Htee* to the top of the pagoda should within a year rule Pegu, a condition was imposed by the Indian Government—namely, that the *Htee* should, on its arrival, be received by the local British authorities, and be made over by them, and not by the king direct, to the Buddhist priests. This proposal was for some time demurred to; but at last the condition was accepted, and the *Htee* was received with a grand ceremonial.

The removal of the old *Htee*, a work of no little difficulty, was accompanied by some accidents, which excited the superstitious fears of the Burmese. On the first day, when it was being lowered, a Burmese workman had two of his fingers cut off, and on the second day a Shan workman fell from the scaffolding at the top and was killed. It was proposed to build a new pagoda for the reception of the old *Htee*.

The approach to the elevated platform on which the pagoda is built is by a covered staircase, on the walls of which are a series of pictures, the subjects being of the most varied character. In the representation of the tortures to be hereafter awarded to the wicked, the artists have exercised much originality of conception coupled with boldness of treatment.

With regard to the religious services carried on, the perfect openness and tranquility of everything connected with them struck me as being the most remarkable feature. An absolute freedom to visitors to walk about through the ranks of the kneeling crowds seemed to be largely availed of and never resented. The worshippers themselves were often provided with long cheroots made of tobacco rolled in leaves, and puffing and praying alternated with one another, with the most perfect absence of any suspicion of impropriety.

The most singular sight I witnessed was the inauguration of one of the large brazen images of Gaudama by a party of Madrassis who had presented it to the pagoda. Being unprovided with Hindu temples in Burmah, the Hindu immigrants from India not uncommonly repair to the pagoda, where, in close contiguity to the silently-praying Burmese, they sing their own sacred hymns, and accompany the singing by a loud clanging of cymbals and beating of drums.

August 26th.—This morning at sunrise I left Rangoon in the British India Steam Navigation Company's steamer "Arabia," and arrived at Calcutta on the 30th, so bringing my trip to the Andamans, Nicobars, and Burmah to a conclusion. The collections I had made included birds' skins, shells, corals, weapons, and other objects illustrative of the habits of the people I had seen, photographs, and a few living plants.

CHAPTER VI

SECTION I.

BIRBHUM, RAJMAHAL HILLS, BHAGULPUR.

1869-70.

INSTRUCTIONS FOR SEASON'S WORK—START FOR RANIGUNJ—MARCH IN COMPANY WITH A COLLEAGUE.—ROCKS AT DUBRAJPUR—OBSTRUCTION BY POLICE—SURI, THE CAPITAL OF BIRBHUM—TUNGSULI COAL-BASIN—MAHOMED BAZAAR IRON-WORKS—NATIVE IRON-FURNACES AT DEOCHA—THE RAJMAHAL AND RAMGURH HILLS—PROGRAMME OF OPERATIONS—VALLEY OF THE BRAHMINI—THE SONTALS—HINDU MONEY-LENDERS—WOLVES—WILD ELEPHANTS—THE LAST RHINOCEROS—REST-HOUSES—SCENERY ROUND MUSUNIA—MAL PAHARIAS—SPEAR GRASS—USUL PAHARIAS, OR MALÉS—TRAP FOR PIGS AND PEA-FOWL—MHOWA-GURHI HILL—SICKNESS IN CAMP—VISIT CALCUTTA FOR CHRISTMAS—BIRDS COLLECTED—THE IMPERIAL PIGEON—PACHWARA PASS—TROPICAL VEGETATION—ALEXANDRINE PAROQUET—PAHARIA VILLAGE—INTOXICATED SONTALS—THE SWINGING FESTIVAL—DESCRIPTION OF THE SONTALS—ALBINO—MEET THE ASSISTANT-COMMISSIONER—HYÆNA AND CUBS—BEAT FOR TIGER—VALLEY OF THE GUMANI—KHARMATAND—COLUMNAR BASALT AT TELOBAD—PAHARIA ORGIE—COAL-MEASURES DISAPPEAR—OLD VOLCANO—MUNJWA PASS—SIGNS OF HOT SEASON—FOSSIL PLANTS—PAHARIA LANGUAGE—FIRST VIEW OF GANGES—OPEN COUNTRY TO THE EAST—IMPROVED CULTIVATION—CAMP VISITED BY A TIGER—COLGONG—ROCKY ISLANDS—CHANGES IN THE BED OF THE GANGES—PATHARGHATA—HINDU TEMPLES—FOOT PASSENGERS TO CALCUTTA—INDICATIONS OF A CHANGE IN THE FLORA—PINK-HEADED DUCK—SAHIBGUNJ—MY SANITY DISCUSSED—MAHARAJPUR FALL—HINDU FESTIVAL—SUPPOSED COAL-SEAM—DUCK AND PARTRIDGES—BUFFALOES AND TIGER—ZAMIN MUSJID—TALJHERI MISSION SETTLEMENT—UDWANALA—SKIMMERS—STONE QUARRIES—SCENERY NEAR BHAWA—ROAD-MAKING—A BURNT CHILD—BURHAIT—MAHADEO'S CAVE-TEMPLE—HINDUISM AND THE ABORIGINES—THE NATHS—WATERFALL—LUKRA-GURH—BEHURS—GREAT HEAT—SONTAL FESTIVALS—MHOWA CROP—TEPID SPRING—TIGER TRAP—NORTH-WESTERS—CALCAREOUS TUFA—JUNGLE THIN AT THIS SEASON—THE PARADISE FLY-CATCHER—YELLOW-BREASTED GROUND-THRUSH—THEFT IN CAMP—"JOE" IS LOST—BEAT FOR GAME—LEAVE SONTALIA BEHIND—RETURN TO CALCUTTA.

MY instructions for this season included the revision of old work done in former years by the Geological Survey in the Sontal Purgunas,* more particularly in the Rajmahal Hills,

* The nearest English equivalent to a Purguna is a Barony, a Zilla corresponding to a county.

and the region immediately surrounding them which is called the Daman-i-Koh. Owing to the interruption to work during the Mutiny in 1857, and the great Sontal insurrection in 1855, the examination had not been completed, and as in the eleven years which had elapsed considerable additions had been made to our knowledge of Indian formations, it was considered advisable before publication that the whole area should be re-examined, and the information brought up to date. On the 4th of November I left Calcutta for Ranigunj, and on the 8th, in company with my colleague, the late M. H. Ormsby, I marched northwards fifteen miles, to the village of Badinathpur, on the banks of the Adjai. The work to be done by him was included in the districts of Birbhum and Bhagulpur, on the south and west of my area, and consisted in the revision and preparation for publication of the maps of a wide tract, in which metamorphic rocks principally occur. This was the last work upon which he was engaged, as he died a few months after his return to Calcutta.

November 9th.—Dubrajpur.—Our second march was to Dubrajpur, a large village, to the south of which there is a hard ridge of granitic gneiss, which has been eroded into huge piled blocks and tors that stand out in a striking manner from a sea of alluvium, no other rocks being visible in the vicinity. Many of these large blocks having the rounded appearance of rolled and travelled boulders, some observers have concluded that they are so, and I have seen it stated somewhere that the "geologists" have confessed themselves utterly unable to account for the phenomenon. No geologist accustomed to the appearance and mode of weathering of certain of the hard crystalline rocks of Bengal could hesitate about referring the origin of these blocks to its true cause. They are simply the portions of a massive rock which have resisted decomposition, while the remainder has been gradually removed by atmospheric action and the waters of a river which at one time, in all probability, surrounded and partially submerged the ridge. As is commonly the case with all masses of rock and hills which seem to be out of a natural position in India, the Hindus regard them as fragments dropped by Rama when conveying materials for the construction of the bridge which was built for the conquest of Lunka or Ceylon.

There being at Dubrajpur a police-station, it was no cause for surprise that on our arrival we found that we were to be subjected to the usual Bengali insolence and annoyance. Our men, sent on before, had been refused all assistance by the villagers, and the grain-sellers had shut up their shops. The police, when referred to, said they had "no orders;" and we had indubitable proof that they were largely instrumental in producing this unpleasant state of things. It was with the greatest difficulty that grain could be obtained for the absolute necessities of the camp. I have in so many places in these pages alluded to the obstruction received from petty Bengali officials, that I shall not further enlarge on the subject, merely adding that a complaint to the Superintendent of Police resulted in the Dubrajpur Inspector being fined for his misconduct, and the grain-sellers were punished by the magistrate.

November 11th.—Suri.—Two more marches brought us into the station of Suri, the capital town of the District of Birbhum, where we put up in the Circuit House, one of the most comfortable residences for official travellers which I have seen in Bengal. Owing to the number of fine trees along the roads, and the gardens surrounding many of the houses, this town presents a most pleasingly bright aspect. Being, like Bankura, built on a lateritic gravelly soil, it is drier and more healthy than most of the towns in Lower Bengal. It is within the range of the hot winds, which some people, however, consider an advantage, since they *can* be artificially cooled, while the moist atmosphere of Calcutta cannot.

November 13th.—Suri to Tungsuli.—My first march from the station was to the village of Tungsuli, four miles N.W. of Suri, where there is a small basin of coal-measure rocks, occupying an area of about two square miles. The sections were sufficiently perfect to show that these beds do not include any workable thickness of good coal.

November 15th.—Tungsuli to Deocha—This morning I visited

Mahomed Bazaar, the site of a factory erected fifteen years previously by the Birbhum Iron Company. The works were carried on at a loss for several years, were closed and re-opened, the several attempts to establish the manufacture on a profitable footing proving unsuccessful. At the time of my visit I found a European on the spot, who had been employed by the native landlord to see if he could not re-open the works once more. But the niggardly way in which supplies were doled out did not render it probable that any real start could be made; and since none of the parties concerned seemed to have much knowledge of the subject, not even realizing a fraction of the difficulties connected with the manipulation and smelting of ores, certain failure and loss of whatever money was expended was inevitable. Within the past few years another attempt was made by a Calcutta company to re-open the works again, but though it was demonstrated that the ores were good, difficulties in reference to fuel and flux, and other circumstances connected with the market value of iron, have caused this last effort at resuscitation to be abandoned.

In the Ranigunj coal-field, in the vicinity of ore, fuel, and flux, and on the line of railway, iron-works have been started with a much better prospect of success, and the result of the experiment is at present anxiously watched, both by the Government and by capitalists who may be tempted to embark in similar undertakings. In the present condition of Indian finances, the desirability of keeping in the country as large a portion as possible of the money which is annually sent out of it for the purchase of iron is sufficiently obvious. But the prospects of manufacturing iron profitably in India are subject to the fluctuations of price in the English markets, the cost of production remaining nearly constant in the former country since nearly all European labour in India can only be retained by contract at a fixed and high rate of wage, and native labour is even less susceptible of reduction, the ordinary rate of remuneration being so low.

November 16th.—Deocha.—In this village there are some native iron-furnaces, the sole surviving remains of an industry now well-nigh extinct in this part of the country, owing to the restrictions placed upon it by the Birbhum Company which bought up the sole right to manufacture, and owing also to the royalty subsequently inflicted by the native landlord. To the best of my belief these furnaces are, for their size and the magnitude of their results, by far the largest and most important in the whole of India. Each furnace could make about 15 cwt. of iron per week; and the total estimated out-turn in 1852 from seventy of these furnaces was put down at 1700 tons by Dr. Oldham. The Lohars or iron-makers here were Hindus; but further to the north, in the vicinity of the Ramgurh Hills, there is another race of iron-makers, who use the ordinary small furnaces, and are called Kols. It is probable that they are identical with the Aguriahs of Hazaribagh and Palamow, whom I shall describe on a future page.

November 20th.—Sydachatore to Dhurumpur.—I was now daily engaged in examining the sections of the south-west corner of the hilly country which extends from the Dwarka river northwards for 170 miles, to the Ganges at Sahibgunj. These highlands may collectively be spoken of as the Rajmahal hills; but a portion of them, situated south of the Brahmini river, should properly be distinguished as the Ramgurh Hills. This division is, as I shall subsequently explain, coincident with an ethnical distribution.

My programme was to march northwards to the Ganges, along the western margin of the hills, branching off from that direction where the existence of valleys and passes cut by rivers from west to east yield opportunities for obtaining cross sections of the central plateau portion; and then, having rounded the hills on the north, to return southwards along the eastern margin.

November 22nd.—Panchbaini.—The first pass, of the nature just described, was that through the valley of the Brahmini river. The floor of this valley is formed of the coal-measures in which there are several coal-seams of inferior value, though worked in former times. These coal-measures are overlaid by a group of coarse sandstones in certain places; and these again, unconformably by vast sheets of basaltic trap, with which thin beds of mud-stones alternate, and often afford evidence of intense roasting by the overlying basalt, and frequently abound in beautifully preserved fossil plants. On the top of the basalt again, there are often widespread and thick beds of laterite, which slope from the edges of the western scarps down to the level of the plains on the east.*

I was much pleased by the simple hospitality of the Sontals in this vicinity. They were seldom sufficiently well off, and their stocks of stored grain were too inconsiderable, to afford much aid towards the supply of grain required for consumption in my camp, which had therefore to be obtained, often with the very greatest trouble, from the Hindu traders and money-lenders to whom the crops had in many cases been hypothecated. These vultures, who were the cause of the Sontal insurrection in 1855, and of several subsequently threatened disturbances, notwithstanding their former ejectment from the limits of the Daman-i-Koh, had flocked back again, and with the British courts to support them, as they knew every turn of the law while the Sontals knew nothing of it, they had resumed their usurious practices, causing, in many cases, the recipients of petty loans to become their bond-slaves for life. Here, and in many other parts of the country, Sontals or people belonging to similar simple aboriginal tribes, have poured forth to me the troubles which oppressed them from the exactions of these Hindu Shylocks. It is perhaps not too much to say that from north to south, and from east to west throughout the peninsula of India, the money-lenders' nets are spread, cramping the labours of the masses, and keeping them in a condition which is scarcely above that of starvation—*per contra*, it may be said with very great justice, that these people are themselves hopelessly improvident; that they will raise money for the expenses of a marriage or other festivity, which there is no chance of their ever repaying, and that the money-lenders, by their advances, render it possible for them

---

* An account of the geological structure of these hills will be found in the Memoirs of the Geological Survey of India, Vol. XIII., part. 2.

to obtain seed in some years when without such aid no cultivation could take place.

It is easy to condemn the authorities for this state of things, but it is very much less easy to suggest a practical remedy. A law or laws for the recovery of debt which may, in the abstract, be just, will not meet the case. An executive, however strong in numbers, if compelled, as it must necessarily be, to employ a subordinate native staff, which is sure to be corrupt and bribable by the richest party, is clearly incapable of dealing with millions of ignorant victims, who themselves are unlikely to take the initiative and come forward to state their cases. Within the last decade, the unrest of the Sontals and other tribes has, in different parts of India, been the cause of special and local legislation, with the merits of which the political economist and jurist are alone competent to deal.

The hospitality of the Sontals which touched me was the spontaneous way in which they would bring in, often from a distance, without being asked—one man a couple of eggs, another a jar of milk, another an ounce of ghi, sometimes on presentation simply saying the word *khao* (eat). Even my servants, who were not endowed with any unusual fineness of feeling, were often struck by this simplicity, and instead of dealing with the contributions in the ordinary way, would bring the bearers to my tent in order that they might have the gratification of making the present in person. With many of them, I believe, it was the case of the widow's mite; yet not unfrequently they would refuse to receive a return present of any kind, saying that what they did was out of respect for the Sirkar or Government.

Close to Panchbaini I saw a couple of wolves; but met with no others during my trip. Indeed, the hunting proclivities of the various races in this region have almost resulted in the extermination of all wild animals. Strangely enough, however, there were two wild elephants living somewhere in the neighbourhood of the Brahmini, as I frequently came upon their tracks, but they appeared to be great wanderers, in consequence probably of the rarity of cover sufficiently dense for their concealment. They were the sole existing representatives of the herds of elephants, which, as is described by the author of the "Annals of Rural Bengal," * committed serious devastations in Birbhum. Having mentioned the injury and loss caused by tigers in the years 1789-90, Dr. Hunter writes:—"The ravages of the wild elephants were on a larger scale, and their extermination formed one of the most important duties of the Collector for some time after the district passed directly under British rule. In two parishes alone during the last few years of the native administration, fifty-six villages with their communal lands 'had all been destroyed and gone to jungle, caused by the depredations of the wild elephants.' And an official return states that forty market towns throughout the district had been deserted from the same cause." At no very distant period the rhinoceros occurred in the vicinity of these hills, but there are none to be found south of the Ganges at the present day.

November 24th.—*Mosunia.*—A custom prevails within the limits of the Daman-i-Koh which I have not met with in any other part of India. It consists in the erection near the larger villages of thatched bungalows with mud walls, to the repair and support of which the Sontals of the surrounding circle of villages contribute labour and materials. These rude bungalows are intended as rest-houses for officers on tour. I often found them fairly comfortable, and occupied them as a change from the monotony of a tent. Not unfrequently, however, they were tenanted by swarms of wasps and hornets, whose nests rested on or hung from the uncovered beams of the roof. But Indian wasps are much less pugnacious and vindictive insects than their English representatives, and I never knew them to sting except under great provocation.

Before taking leave of the hilly region south of the Brahmini river, it will be convenient here to state that the Ramgurh hills, as

---

* First Edition, p. 66.

they are called, are inhabited by a race called the *Mal* Paharias, and are altogether distinct in appearance, customs, and language, from the *Usul* Paharias, who occupy the Rajmahal hills proper. My superficial acquaintance with the appearance and mode of life of the people of the former colony, led me to the belief that they were allied to the Keriahs or some similar wild Kolarian tribe, but an examination of their language* has shewn that there is no linguistic authority for this supposed affinity, and that in point of fact they afford an ethnological puzzle which has yet to be solved.

December 6th—Pujadih.—The day-to-day work in these hills was very arduous, owing to the great distances I had to go away from my camp, which it was impossible to take with me into the highlands, and it was only on rare occasions that I could use an elephant or horse. I suffered a good deal too from the spear-grass, which being sometimes seven feet high, would shower down upon me its barbed seeds in such a way that no part of my body was safe from the torture caused by them. Many a time I would have to stop to have them plucked out of my clothes by the men who accompanied me. In this neighbourhood I first made the acquaintance of the Usul Paharias, or as they call themselves *Malé* (according to some authorities *Mulair*, but I write it as it sounded to me, being nearly the same as Malay). Some of the villages were very picturesque, and in their neighbourhood vast hill clearances were occupied by crops of Indian corn, millet, and sirguja.† I shall, however, reserve my account of the people of this outlying Dravidian colony till I come to speak of the localities further north, where I had greater opportunities of becoming acquainted with them. But I may state here that their villages are situated almost exclusively on the tops of the hills, while the Sontals, with completely distinct language, customs, and

* "Descriptive Ethnology of Bengal," p. 274.

† *Guizotia oleifera*, D. C.

PORCUPINE AND PEA-FOWL TRAP.

physique, occupy the surrounding country up to the foot of the slopes of the hills, and all the intersecting valleys. I here first met with a form of trap for porcupine and pea-fowl which I have since found in use in regions hundreds of miles to the south. The accompanying illustration will, I trust, serve to explain its method of working. The bamboo-fence on the near side has not been represented, so that the trigger and lever arrangement by which the weighted trees are supported may be more distinct. When an animal enters and treads on the foot-board, the little pin attached to the string is set free, and the whole thing tumbles down, crushing the animal flat.

December 15th.—Simra.—To-day I explored the Mhowagurhi Hill, which some years previously had been suggested as a site for a sanitarium. The project, a palpably absurd one, was fortunately never carried out. The elevation above the sea being only 1,659 feet, is too inconsiderable to have much influence on the temperature, and the surrounding valleys are notoriously unhealthy, except just at the end of the cold weather. Even during this month of December I had often as many as six men down with fever at the same time; and for two days I was *hors de combat* with the same malady myself.

December 22nd.—Kushkira to Pakour.—Leaving my camp at Kushkira, a long journey on the elephant in the dark morning hours, and afterwards on horseback, brought me to the railway station at Pakour, from whence I took the train for Calcutta, where I went to spend a few days at Christmas, and be present at some of the festivities in connection with the Duke of Edinburgh's visit to India.

December 29th—Pakour to Kushkira.—On arriving at camp, after my return from Calcutta, I was glad to find all well, and that the invalids had shaken off their fevers. My bearer, who was a good shot, and the bird-skinner had prepared between them a nice little collection of the birds of the neighbourhood, many of which had not been obtained before.

December 30th—Kushkira to Pachwara.—Close to the village of Pachwara, in the valley of the Bansloi river, there is an ancient mango-grove, in which I found a colony of the large fruit-eating or imperial pigeon (*Carpophaga œnea*, Linn.), of the peculiar geographical distribution of which I have written on a previous page. The Pachwara pass, or valley of the Bansloi, is physically and geologically a repetition of that of the Brahmini. In both cases the rivers have denuded away the basalt, and laid bare the underlying coal-measures.

January 3rd.—Silungi.—Sometimes, when following up streams into the inmost recesses of the hills, I found in the sheltered nooks vegetation of a more tropical aspect than was to be seen outside. In such localities the large leaves of a wild plantain were generally conspicuous, and, with the change in the vegetation, there occurred certain species of birds which were thus confined to a very limited range. Particularly to be mentioned in this respect was the Racket-tailed Drongo (*Dissemurus grandis*, Gould).

January 9th.—Domra to Chudma.—On the hill-tops to the east of this line of march of my camp I passed through several very comfortable-looking villages of the Paharias, one of which was surrounded by a grove of Tal palms. The granaries, consisting of huge baskets made of split bamboos and elevated on posts gave an air of prosperity to the village never to be seen in the villages of the Sontals. Tame peacocks strutted about and perched on the roofs in every direction. As in the Nicobar islands, long bamboos were to be seen planted outside the villages for the purpose of keeping off the much dreaded evil spirits.

January 12th—Chudma to Paharpur (*Rampur*).—All the afternoon of to-day, after my return from work, parties of smiling but intoxicated Sontals were coming up to the tent as deputations on one pretext or another. Among other requests, they asked me to give them permission to perform the *Churuk Puja*, better known to English readers as the swinging festival, which has been forbidden in British India. They said that in consequence of the *Bhut*, or evil spirit, not being appeased, their women and children were dying from sickness, and their cattle were being killed by wild beasts. When I replied that I had no authority to give them such permission, they then became most urgent that I should send a petition to the Government (vaguely spoken of by them as Kampani Bhadur, *i.e.*, the Most Powerful Company) representing the hardships they suffered in consequence of the prohibition, and praying for its repeal. I did not attempt to argue with them, as I knew it would be useless. In their estimation the evidence afforded by the losses in their families and flocks would have been conclusive against anything which I might urge. Both in Manbhum and in the Daman-i-Koh I frequently saw the old timbers of the *Churuk* set up near villages, and I often observed in the small of the back of the men who preceded me to point out the road in my daily rambles the old scars left where the hooks used in the swinging festival had penetrated. These men were not unfrequently the *Chowkidars* and *Goraits*, or village watch, and I am inclined to believe that they must have had an *ex officio* claim to occupy the honourable position. Some of the scars looked so recent, and the men so young, that I suspect surreptitious *Churuks* have been erected in the remoter tracts since they were forbidden by the British government. As well as I can remember, in every case where I made enquiry I was told that the weight of the body was not supported by the hooks but by a cloth *kumarbund*, or waist-band.

I am well aware, however, that eye-witnesses have stated that the weight of the body was in some cases supported by the hooks which penetrated the interscapular muscles. Possibly these observers were not mistaken; but the men I alluded to above shewed no signs of permanent injury having been occasioned by their suspension. With regard to this, as also to some other Indian customs, highly-coloured narratives have, I fear, been drawn up for the especial benefit of the charitably-disposed among the British public.

In a small isolated scrap of French territory, it is said that the Zemindar derives a considerable revenue from the Churuk Puja and various other attractions forbidden in British territory, to which the people flock from all the surrounding districts, and are of course made to contribute their mites, which go to swell the Zemindar's annual receipts.

January 13th—Dhumani.—At this place I was amused by the conduct of the head Sontal, who bore the local title of Purgunite. He was in a genial phase of intoxication, and employed himself most of the day in singing my praises as the father and mother of his clan, the ruler of the country, and superior to all the Rajas of Hindustan. Suddenly he turned to one of his audience, a Bengali, who was not assenting to all his propositions, and forced from him, by his threatening manner, a full acquiescence. In the evening he came to me in a confidential way and asked for permission to be allowed to make then all preparations for the morrow's supply for my camp, in order that he and his people might have a clear day for performing their Puja and getting properly drunk.

A party of the women danced before my tent after dark in the usual grotesque fashion, which is not nearly so finished a performance as is the dance of the Uraons. Among the onlookers I noticed an adult Albino, whom, on enquiry, I learnt belonged to the *teli* or oilman caste of Hindus.

A few general remarks on the Sontals may fittingly be introduced here. As a rule, Sontal villages are quite distinct and separate from those occupied by Hindus. Indeed the Sontals have but little love for Hindus, and it is said they will not eat of food which has even been cooked by a Brahmin.

At a glance it is generally possible to distinguish a Sontal village from those of all other tribes, owing to their custom of ranging the houses, whatever the number, along either side of one long street. I have occasionally seen villages thus stretched out for nearly a mile without a single cross street or alley. They are further distinguished by the forms of the houses and the enclosures in which they each stand, and by having planted near them a certain tree (*Moringa pterygosperma*, Gärtn.), the leaves of which are used as a pot-herb. These villages are generally untidy and dirty, but the individual houses are often fairly clean, and it is not uncommon to see the mud walls ornamented with grotesque paintings, or geometric figures, in bright colours.

The Sontals are somewhat low in stature, being below even the average of jungle races. They are often excessively dark in colour, and not unfrequently approach the negro in blackness. Their features are of a coarse type, and it is rare to find in either sex any approach to beauty, though exceptions do occur. The nose is broad and depressed, the cheek-bones somewhat high and prominent, and the lips thick and slightly pouting. They do not, as a rule, cultivate beards. Although joyous enough at times when in their cups, and at their frequent festivals, where dancing and religion are combined, the Sontals generally lead lives of great toil and enjoy but poor fare. Their omnivorous propensities secure for them food (such as it is), however, where a man of caste might starve. As with many others of the tribes, the Sontals constantly sustain a load of fear in consequence of their belief in the ubiquitous nature of evil spirits, whom they suppose to be ever ready to injure them. They believe too in the existence of good spirits, and perhaps in that of one supreme deity, whom they connect with the sun as a visible presence. But as they consider that these good spirits will not injure them, their whole or principal ceremonies are designed to ward off the malign influences of the evil spirits. It is stated that some of the first missionaries who come in contact with the Sontals failing to understand this, though they had acquired some knowledge of the language, made use in their translations and addresses of the name of the greatest and most powerful spirit known to the Sontals, as being, they thought, the nearest equivalent to our idea of the Creator. It was not for some little time that they discovered he was much more nearly allied to our idea of the devil. Offerings to these evil spirits may often be seen. Sometimes they consist of clay images of horses and elephants, &c., which are offered on the sylvan shrines. Sometimes they are eggs, or a handful of grain placed on the path, as though to bribe the spirit not to enter the village, while sometimes they are merely wisps of grass, which are suspended to trees on the confines of the jungle.

One of the most curious points about the Sontals is the vagueness of their ideas as to distance. Other natives of India I have generally found have wonderfully accurate ideas on the subject; but a Sontal seems wholly incapable of saying whether a place is ten or three miles distant. Their mode of estimating distance traversed is, so far as I know, unique. On starting for a walk they pluck a branch of the Sal tree, which they carry with them; when the leaves have become so dry and crisp that they can be broken to pieces by crushing in the hand, it is said that a *kos*, or two miles, has been accomplished. According to this method a *kos* would be shorter in hot or dry than in cold or damp seasons.

The Sontals, when in good circumstances, generally clothe their women liberally, though their own raiment may be scanty. They also love to adorn them with a multitude of heavy bracelets and anklets, which are made of brass and white metal. Captain Sherwill records that he weighed some of the ornaments of a

Sontal damsel, and concluded that the total weight of a complete outfit could not be less than 34lbs.

In the stories of the creation, as related by their strolling bards, the Sontals assign a position of great honour to the English—one, in point of fact, next to that occupied by themselves,—but the Hindus are relegated to a very degraded position. I have been told that some of these bards carry about a sort of panoramic representation of these stories. I believe it to be the case that the Sontals retain no tradition of having ever been ruled by a king or supreme chieftain; and such also appears to be the fact with reference to some of the other tribes.

January 18th.—Puharpur.—To-day the Assistant-Commissioner of Godda brought his camp here to join mine for a few days. This was an unexpected meeting so far as I was concerned, but proved to be none the less pleasant on that account. During the day some Sontals brought in a slaughtered hyæna, with two young cubs. It appeared that a lad, when straying near her den, had been charged by her. Fortunately he carried an axe in his hand, and knew how to use it, since he cleft the animal's head in two. The body of a young boy who had been killed by a leopard or tiger was also brought in for inspection, as is required by the law.

January 19th.—Puharpur.—To-day, from 400 to 500 Paharias and Sontals having been collected, we beat a hill which a tiger was believed occasionally to visit. We saw nothing of him; but some peacocks were run down by the beaters, who, before we could stop them, plucked the feathers from the living birds and adorned their back hair-knots with them.

Puharpur and Dhumani are in the valley of the Gumani river, which has cut through and eroded the basalt and laid bare the coal-measures, as the already-described Bansloi and Brahmini rivers have done in their valleys.

January 21st. — Puharpur to Kharmatand. — To-day the Assistant-Commissioner and I parted company, our routes lying in opposite directions.

From the tops of the hills to the east of Kharmatand there

were several splendid views of the surrounding scenery. In some of the scarped faces of the plateaus the beds of intertrappean clays could be seen cropping out, their light colour contrasting with the dark reddish brown weathered surface of the basalt.

January 30th.—Telobad.—I remained at Telobad, where there is a bungalow, for several days, as there was much intricate geology to be worked out. The basaltic trap was here more distinctly columnar than it is in most other parts of the hills.

I was witness to-day to a Paharia orgie, which took place in a village I passed through. The people crowded round me and invited me to stop, which I did for a few minutes, but was soon compelled to retire from the neighbourhood of the unclean crowd and the savour of the ill-smelling liquor. The dance which was going on was principally notable for its obscenity.

February 3rd.—Simra.—Near this place, a little to the north, the coal-measure rocks which I had been tracing all along the foot of the hills and in the denuded valleys, are covered up and disappear under the Gangetic alluvium. I had met with numerous seams of coal, most of which had been partially worked by contractors and others during the construction of the East Indian line of railway. I have not thought it necessary or advisable to give any account of these in the preceding pages, since what is known on the subject is elsewhere published.

Close to Simra is a peculiar-looking group of small conical hills,* formed of trachytic-porphyry, which I believe to have been correctly identified by Dr. Buchanan, who wrote the first geological account of these hills, as the remnant of an ancient volcano. Indeed, I think it is possible to point out the position of the crater.

February 5th.—Simra to Meghi.—Close to Meghi is the entrance to the Munjwa Ghât or pass through the hills, a place of some historical interest, since it was the route by which the

---

* The name "Gundasuri" was possibly given in reference to the existence of a sulphur *(gunduk)* spring which has now dried up.

forces of the Great Mogul used to enter Lower Bengal. It is at present a considerable thoroughfare. Large droves of cattle and buffaloes were being driven through it on their way to the *churs* of the Ganges, the dry weather having left no grazing in the country to the west. I was amused to see one of the drovers complacently seated on a large buffalo, and holding up before him a calf of too tender an age to walk, which he was too lazy to carry.

An early hot season seemed on this date to have commenced, being inaugurated by an all-pervading haze, which completely obscured the view.

February 12th.—Murrero.—This is one of several localities where beautifully-preserved fossil-plants are found in the indurated mud-stones, which alternate with the great flows of basalt, forming the mass of these hills. The character of this *flora* has served to identify this formation with the Lias of Europe.* The morning was spent in excavating a series of these fossils. In the afternoon, I devoted some time to taking down a vocabulary of the Paharia language from a Sirdar or head man of that tribe. The poor man worked himself into a terrible state of nervousness, and, ere long, I found was answering the questions very much at random. At length, in order to put some Dutch courage into him, I suggested that he should take a mild libation of brandy. It was with the greatest difficulty that I could make him understand that he was not asked to put the terms of the offer into the Paharia language, but to actually quaff the proffered cup.

As to the dual and plural forms of substantives, and the tenses of verbs, or, generally speaking, the grammatical construction, I found on this, as well as on many other occasions, that the attempt to obtain them by direct questioning is a hopeless task. These, and names for abstract ideas, can only gradually be picked out of phrases, and are scarcely within the range of acquirement

* Mr. W. T. Blanford, however, considers the *flora* more nearly allied to that of the Rhætic or lower oolite of Europe. *Vide* "Manual of the Geology of India," Vol. I., p. 146.

by a traveller who cannot attain to sufficient familiarity with individuals. How insufficient as a test of the affinities of languages mere vocabularies are, is now pretty well known and recognised.

There can be no doubt that the Rajmahal Paharias are merely an off-shoot who have for many centuries been separated from their cognates, the Uraons. Their isolation on the hill-tops and plateaus of the Rajmahal group has caused them to retain many customs unmodified by any contact with those of other tribes. In the early settlement of the country they caused much trouble to the British in consequence of their raiding propensities. Periodically they would devastate the surrounding country, and would return to their hills laden with spoil. By raising among them a regiment of bowmen, and by making the head men custodians of the place, and paying them what is really black-mail, order was established. This black-mail is continued to the present day, and no land revenue is levied. The men are tall, clean-limbed, and lighter in colour than the average of Uraons. Their hair is chiefly collected in a knot at the back of the head, but two long locks are generally left free, and hang over the ears. The women often possess good figures, and, sometimes, pretty faces. Their dress is extremely graceful and effective. It consists of an ordinary skirt of coarse, dirty white cloth, to which is added a square of gay-coloured striped or banded tusser silk, one end of which is passed over the right and under the left shoulder, the opposite corners being tied in a knot; the lower margin is tucked in at the waist. Red coral necklaces are worn in great profusion, but metal ornaments, such as the Sontals delight in, are not worn. The marriage ceremony is a simple affair, and has been thus described:—On the day fixed for a marriage the bridegroom with his relations proceed to the bride's father's house, where they are seated on cots and mats, and, after a repast, the bride's father takes his daughter's hand and places it in that of the bridegroom, and exhorts him to be kind and loving to the girl whom he thus makes over to him. The groom then with the little finger of his right hand marks the girl on the forehead with vermilion, and then linking the same finger with the little finger of her right hand, he leads her away to his own home.

The Paharias keep pigs, goats, and a few cattle. They do not cultivate rice or use it as food, as they say it disagrees with them. They live principally on Indian corn and maize. The language is similar to that of the Uraons, but has become somewhat modified in consequence of its isolation. Grotesque wooden idols of large size are to be seen in some of the villages; and, when game was more abundant, skulls and horns, trophies of the chase, were placed on elevated stages near the houses. Sketches both of the idols and the trophies are given by Captain Sherwill in a paper on the Rajmahal Hills.*

February 15th.—Bindrabund.—In some low hills to the north of this village is the most notable locality for fossil plants in the whole tract of the Rajmahal hills. I quarried out a large series of beautiful specimens of ferns, cycads, &c.

Meeting here some intelligent Paharias I checked the vocabulary previously taken.†

From the tops of the hills close by I obtained my first view of the Ganges. For, although I had been six years in India, I had not previously seen the river above the head of the Delta. The haze limited the view very much, and the season was altogether too far advanced for the Himalayas to be seen. In the cold weather the snows of the highest peaks are said to be sometimes very distinctly visible, though they must be about two hundred miles off. The whistle of the passing trains was audible from Bindrabund, and afforded evidence, otherwise wanting, of the vicinity of civilization.

February 18th.—Bindrabund to Ferazpur.—I was now about

---

* "Journal Asiatic Society of Bengal," Vol. x. I may mention that in a work ("*Les Rajahs des Indes*") published a few years ago, two of Captain Sherwill's illustrations have been obviously used in the concoction of a plate without any acknowledgment.

† It was subsequently incorporated in the lists published by Col. Dalton in his "Ethnology of Bengal."

to leave the main mass of the hills for a short tour westwards, as far as Colgong on the Ganges, in order to examine some small outlying hills in the alluvium. The road to Ferazpur soon left the irregularly-broken and imperfectly-cultivated ground of the Sontals, and reached a very beautiful country, every available portion of which was highly cultivated. The principal crops were wheat, barley, castor oil, flax (which is only cultivated for the linseed), and a small cruciferous aromatic plant, the name of which I forget. In the barley there was a wild pink, which reminded me of a weed common in the fields at home. The country is studded with groves of mangos, and *Tal* and date palms, both of which are tapped for their toddy. In these groves birds were abundant, and, it appeared to me that a greater number might be obtained in a day here than in a month in the hilly country.

As I was reading at night before going to bed I heard the village chowkidar talking to my man on guard about the nightly visits paid to the village by a tiger, and soon after I heard shouts from a neighbouring village where the people were evidently driving off some animal. Having told the men to call me if the tiger came near the tent, I loaded my rifle, and had only just finished doing so when I was told that the tiger was close by; and, on going outside, I could hear the animal, whether leopard or tiger I cannot say, snorting in the adjoining bushes; but the intense darkness of the night prevented me from seeing him. After a time he moved off, and I went to bed, but was soon after roused with the intelligence that he had returned, and appeared close to where my horses were tethered; again I made a circuit of the camp, but was again unsuccessful, though I heard him breathing heavily close by. Next morning when about to start I was told by the villagers, who persisted that it was a tiger, that it had its lair in the middle of a field of sugar-canes surrounded on all sides by houses; this seemed to me to be an improbable tale, but I was unable to stop, as all my arrangements had been made for the march forward. The only thing that made me think that the villagers were possibly correct as to the animal's domicile was that there was no other cover in the immediate neighbourhood. The idea of the people going about their daily avocations within a few yards of where the animal lay, or was believed to lie, during the day, was sufficiently curious to be worthy of record.

February 19th.—Ferazpur to Colgong.—On the road to Colgong I examined several hills of granitic gneiss, which stand out prominently above the alluvium. As the town was approached, fences of a formidable nature, and gates, shewed a more distinct assertion of proprietorism than is commonly seen in such out-of-the-way places.

Colgong is the anglicised form of the native name, which is really *K'hal ganw*, meaning the town of K'hal, *i.e.* the black ointment which is used by women to anoint their eyes. The town is situated on the banks of the Ganges, and is also a railway station, so that it is a place of some importance as a mart through which goods, brought from the opposite side of the river and the country to the south, pass ere they are despatched by railway.

February 20th.—Colgong.—This morning I took a boat in order to visit several rocky islands, which rise from the channel of the Ganges, opposite the town. Although the river both to the east and west of Sahibgunj, on the north of the Rajmahal Hills, washes the base of certain small hills—the rocks at Colgong are unique in one respect, namely, that from the point where the Ganges leaves the outer range of the Himalayas at Hurdwar for a distance of nine hundred miles, or till it reaches the Bay of Bengal, no other rocks are exposed in its bed. The piled bosses and tors of granite, or rather granitic gneiss, which form these islands, produce an exceedingly picturesque effect.

The islands were colonized by numerous birds which, rising as I landed, circled round the highest peak. Most conspicuous were flocks of blue pigeons which afford some pretty shooting; among other birds there were two species of heron and large wood-owls.

There are several idols carved *in situ* on the rock, one being a

Durga, but I did not notice any inscription. In places there are wedge-marks, showing where huge monoliths have been split off. In some cases the operations were not successful, the stone having broken off short. The following remarks, which I wrote a short time after my visit, will serve to record what is known regarding the physical history of these islands:—

The annual changes in the course of the Ganges in Bengal, though they frequently give rise to disputes and litigation, are seldom accompanied by any great loss to the agricultural inhabitants of the valley and delta as a whole. If old ground is swept away, the materials are not lost, but re-appear in *churs* and accretions to the banks at other places. For cultivation or pasturage, the new ground generally answers the purposes of a purely agricultural population as well as did the old. But with the introduction of public works, and the unavoidable expenditure of considerable amounts of capital in the vicinity of the river, such changes assume a much greater importance. The shifting of the channel of the river at the present day may in certain localities involve losses to be estimated by many hundreds of thousands of pounds sterling. If it be remembered that on occasions the Hugli has threatened to desert Calcutta, it becomes not difficult to realize the vast amount of the interests which are subject to the freaks of the Ganges and its numerous outlets. In Eastern Bengal, at Kushtia, the changes in the channel of the Gorai have rendered it necessary to extend the line of rail beyond the original terminus in pursuit of the retreating river. During the rainy season of 1872, the Ganges at Gogra, between Colgong and Bhagulpur, has been steadily cutting into the bank, and threatening the destruction of a portion of the embankment of the East Indian Railway at that place. It is reported that the river appears to be returning to an old bed. This is probably the fact, as may be gathered not only from the character of the section exposed in the river bank, which is now being cut into, but from the historical evidence which we possess of the oscillations of the river in that neighbourhood.

In a paper on the "Course of the Ganges through Bengal," by

Major R. H. Colebrooke,* the following passage occurs :—"The alteration of the river at Colgong may be reckoned among the most extraordinary which have ever been observed in the Ganges." In 1779 the granitic rocks which now form small islands in the bed of the river at Colgong were surrounded by land. In the year 1788 they were isolated, and the current ran between them with great velocity; boats, which were confined to this, the only navigable channel of the river, in the cold weather, underwent great danger of being wrecked. Soundings close to the rocks in that year gave a depth of from seventy to ninety feet of water. In the year 1797, owing to the formation of a large island, the river at Colgong had become little more than a stagnant creek, which was to a great extent unnavigable. Since that time various changes have probably taken place, and the one above recorded is likely to prove of as great importance as some of those which have preceded it. Though I do not intend to enter here into the general question of the formation of deltaic land, or the mode in which the Ganges or any similar river cuts out new channels for itself, still it may be remarked that such changes are little subject to the control of man. A sunken boat or a 'snag' is sufficient often to cause the deposition of a 'spit' of sand, which may ultimately become a *chur* of sufficient dimensions to cause a deflection in the course of the main channel. Artificially-placed obstructions are sometimes capable of producing similar results, but subject as the river is to an irresistible impulse to change, no one can venture to predict what the effect of such obstructions may be. Thus a spur which was thrown out in the hope that it might deflect the Gorai, which was eating into some costly foreshore works at Goalundo, has proved quite ineffectual for the purpose, having, in fact, been bodily washed away."

February 21st.—Colgong to Patharghata.—To-day I turned eastwards again, marching along the banks of the Ganges to a place called Patharghata, where I halted in order to examine the

* "Asiatic Researches." Vol. VII., 1801, p. 1.

geology of some hills in the neighbourhood. The small hill which has given the name to the place, namely, the Patharghata, or stone pass, affords, so to speak, a fair sample of the geology of the neighbouring hills. At the base there are metamorphic gneiss rocks; these are overlaid by coal-measure sandstones and clays, with horizontal bedding, which are themselves covered by basalt, and the latter by superficial detritus. A bed of white clay affords material for pottery works, which have been established on the spot; but I believe there has hitherto been no very great demand for the articles which are manufactured. There is also an indigo factory here. On the hill were several Hindu temples, and in certain places artificial caves had been excavated in the sandstones, in one of which the officiating Brahmin of the principal temple had his residence. I proposed to him to sell me some of the carved figures which were lying about in great profusion, but he declined to do so.

February 23rd.—Sealmari to Mirza-Chuck.—The road between these places lies parallel and close to the railway. With each passing train the elephant became very excited and difficult to manage, much to the delight of the engine-drivers, who maliciously turned on their whistles. A constant stream of foot-passengers from Upper India passed along this road. Whether they were forced by poverty, or had other reasons for not using the train, I cannot say. A native, to whom time is not of much value, could live at a less cost for a month, while he walked say 600 miles, than his fare for that distance, even at the low rates charged for third class, would amount to; and hence it is that many whose funds are low, start off on foot for Calcutta, where they hope to obtain service. In the evening I ascended the Sondur peak, which is about 630 feet above the Ganges, where I found the remains of an old fort, built of blocks of dressed laterite.

February 25th—Mirza-Chuck to Sahibgunj.—To-day I came upon bushes of a wild rose (*Rosa involucrata*), and the rattan cane (*Calamus rotang*), neither of which occur in the jungles further south; their presence here, therefore, pointed to there being a *flora* with a different facies in this vicinity. In the *jheels* passed

I shot some birds, including the pink-headed duck,* which is one of the most remarkable-looking species of the duck tribe. This is the only locality where I have been able actually to secure a specimen; though the bird is not migratory, as, unlike most of the ducks, it breeds in Peninsular India.

February 26th.—Sahibgunj to Maharajpur.—While examining some small hills on the banks of the Ganges to the east of Sahibgunj, and using my hammer to extract fossils, I heard an animated discussion going on among some native passengers in a ferry-boat which was well out in the stream, as to whether I was a lunatic or not. Although my action in hammering at stones seemed to indicate the probability that I was one, the fact that I was accompanied by a chuprasi was urged by others as evidence that I was a sane though eccentric individual. I have little doubt that similar remarks have often been made about me, though there has not always been water to waft the sounds of the distant conversation to my ears; possibly, too, the fact that the water acted as an effectual bar preventing my making any hostile demonstration, may have had its effect on this particular occasion in loosening the tongues of my commentators.

At Maharajpur I found a vast crowd, principally of women, assembled to celebrate a Sivoid festival connected with the worship of a dripping rock in a cave at the foot of a waterfall, which rejoices in the poetic title of the Moti-Jhurna, or pearl-shower. On visiting this fall in the evening I found some difficulty in making an examination of it, owing to the jealousy with which the crowd of worshippers, with their priests and fakirs, regarded my approach; indeed, the last-mentioned, who nearly stark-naked and adorned with white ashes, were seated on leopard-skins close by, did not hesitate to make impertinent remarks about me in a loud tone. The sacred spot was in a cave hollowed out in a carbonaceous clay, interstratified with the harder basalt. This

* *Anas caryophyllacea*, Lath.

carbonaceous matter was many years previously reported upon as coal, being, in fact, the first recorded discovery of coal in these hills. Such examination as I was able to make without offending the priests by entering the cave, fully satisfied me of its utterly worthless nature from an economic point of view. The waterfall, which is perhaps 250 feet high, is formed of several steps, which correspond to distinct beds of basalt, the topmost one having a columnar structure.

March 2nd.—Tarbunna.—In the evening I visited a *jheel* or marsh about two miles off, and found there not only an abundant variety of ducks and waders, but also on the banks three species of partridge—the grey, black, and the kyah. I know of no other place in Bengal where such a variety of feathered game may be obtained with so little trouble. Where I could not get a boat I employed an elephant to retrieve the fallen ducks which I shot. From the people I heard that when the freshes of the rainy season flood the *churs* and low ground near the Ganges, wild buffaloes and tigers take refuge in these hills. The former they describe as being very dangerous neighbours, and of a most relentless disposition.

March 6th.—Durgowa.—Some small hills to the south consist of sandstone with a covering of laterite. On the principal one of them is a fine old ruin called the Zamin Musjid. It consists of a large hall with four domes, and an arched roof in the centre. Around it there are a number of cell-like rooms. Pigeons and owls now find a home in this old building, which is surrounded on all sides by thorny jungle, and is consequently not very accessible. A piece of rising ground close by is called English Sigrampur, and is said to have been the site of a factory which belonged to the English in the early days of the "Company."

March 7th.—Durgowa to Taljheri.—To day I encamped at Taljheri, which is the site of a church missionary settlement, where a number of Sontal converts live and are educated. As none of the missionaries were present during my stay I had no opportunity of becoming acquainted with the internal arrangements, but I cannot forbear to notice one point which struck me about the converts with whom I came in contact, and that was that there seemed to me to be a familiarity and absence of courtesy in their demeanour which was very unpleasing. Christian converts not uncommonly exhibit this characteristic, which is due no doubt to the idea that a great gulf is fixed between them and their heathen compatriots, and that they are thus raised to a social equality with the Sahibs.

In the vicinity of Taljheri I examined a carbonaceous deposit similar to that at Moti-Jhurna. It was subsequently reported upon by a practical coal-miner as a most promising "indication," but I heard of this in time to be the means of saving an outlay that could not but result in certain loss.

March 10th.—Juskoti to Udwa-Nalah.—On reaching Udwah-Nalah, after my morning's work, I found there a bungalow belonging to the Messrs. Atkinson Brothers, who have the monopoly of the supply of road metal to the Calcutta Municipality; or, to be more correct, they furnish from their quarries at this place whatever is required over and above that which is brought into the port of Calcutta as ballast. The bungalow was situated on one of the branches of the Ganges, commanding an extensive view. In the evening, in company with the head partner of the firm, I went out in a boat and encountered, besides other birds, considerable flocks of skimmers (*Rhyncops albicollis*, Swains). This was the first occasion upon which I had met with these very singular birds, and since that time I have but once seen them, and that was in the Mahanadi river, near Cuttack. In general appearance they resemble terns, but are separated from all the other members of the family by the extraordinary form of their bills. The lower mandible is prolonged in a flattened spatula-like shape for about two inches beyond the upper. The plane of the flattening is at right angles to that of the gape, so that when the bird flies along as it commonly does with this prolonged portion dipping in the water, it presents a knife-like edge which strikes the fish or crustaceans upon which the bird feeds. The precise advantage of this arrangement is not clearly understood; and, indeed, Dr. Jerdon in his Manual of the Birds of India expresses some doubt as to the nature of the food upon which these birds live; but some of those which I dissected on this occasion contained vertebræ of fish. From the fact that when shot in the day-time the stomachs often prove to be empty, and from the crepuscular activity of the birds which I noticed, I am inclined to suggest as a possible explanation that the birds may be nocturnal feeders, and that the prolonged mandible enables them to feel fish on the surface of the water when they cannot see them.*

I was surprised to find from 1,200 to 1,500 men employed here in connection with the quarries and the transport of the stone by boat to Calcutta. The system with regard to payment was an admirable one, and the popularity of the work with the coolies, carters, and boatmen, &c., who often came from long distances to offer their services, afforded the best testimony of its efficacy. The secret of all this was, I believe to be explained by the simple fact that there were no native clerks, treasurers, nor *gomashtas*, between the coolies and the European staff, and hence the men's earnings were not taxed by those commissions which invariably stick to the fingers of native go-betweens.

The labourers were principally Uraons who are sometimes called Dhangas, from Chutia Nagpur, many of whom had come one hundred miles from their homes to seek employment. Strangely enough, however, the nearly allied Paharias or Malés of the neighbouring hills would not engage in what they considered such degrading service as stone-breaking. Another fact, which was probably not without its influence, was that, unlike the Uraons, the Malés cultivate their own land on the hill-tops without being subject to the oppression of alien Hindus, and they are, therefore, less willing to emigrate.

Close to Udwah-Nalah is the site of the battle of Plasgache, which was fought in 1763, after which the British did

---

* Another species, *R. nigra*, is figured in Darwin's "Naturalist's Voyage." Dr. Darwin records that he actually saw this species capture fish.

not encounter any very serious resistance in their progress to the north-west, up the Ganges Valley. To this day remains of old entrenchments are to be seen, and cannon-balls are sometimes turned up by the plough in the neighbouring fields. My course from hence southwards ran along the eastern base of the hills.

March 15th.—Bhawa.—Close to Bhawa the plateau dips down to the level of the Gangetic Valley, the slopes being covered with a rich vegetation, in which there are numerous fine mango and tamarind trees. On the edge of the plateau there are several Paharia villages, surrounded by groups of *Tal* palms. These sites command an extensive view to the eastward, and are themselves visible from long distances.

March 16th.—Bhawa to Kuchpara.—Near Kuchpara I met an engineer of the Public Works Department, engaged in making a road from the railway at Bhawa to Burhait, in the centre of the hills. The gradient on a road which had been made as a famine relief-work had been condemned, and a new one was being laid out which would cost a considerable sum, the more particularly as the number of labourers was absurdly small in comparison with the staff of overseers *et hoc genus omne.* The whole principle upon which roads in these wild regions are made, or rather commenced, for they are often left unfinished, is, I believe, unsuited to both the means available and the actual requirements. The great object should be to make a practicable road quickly and with a small outlay. Such might be effected by paying less attention to the bridges and gradients with the consequent expensive embankments and cuttings. Of course it would be advisable to clear the line and keep it clear of obstructions here and there, and cutting and blasting would be occasionally necessary; but I have in previous pages shewn what bad roads native bullock-carts can traverse. The great check to carriage is caused by the difficulty of traversing the sandy or muddy beds of rivers too wide to be bridged; and this, since the bulk of the annual traffic is squeezed into the dry months, might, in a great measure, be removed by laying down causeways, upon which the carts could be drawn speedily across instead of being stuck in the mire for half a day at a time. Less engineering skill would be required for such roads, and they could be speedily made. What now happens is that enormous sums are spent on earthworks which, if not (as they are not likely to be, in these tracts) kept in constant repair, are worse than useless, in spite of their low gradients; I have seen in various districts many miles of such work relapsing into jungle, while the traffic runs on in the old lines made by the carts. Were it possible to make and maintain in all cases properly bridged and macadamised roads, it would be well for the country, but as it is not, such rough and ready roads as I describe would subserve a most important purpose in developing traffic. In making these remarks I am not referring to the roads in low alluvial or swampy country, which must, of course, be raised above the level by earthwork, but at the river crossings along them even causeways would be preferable to the so-called *cutcha*, wooden bridges, which are seldom safe, and are generally in an advanced state of decay, causing often a serious obstruction to traffic, as they completely bar the way, and necessitate circuits being made across country to avoid them.

March 17th.—Kuchpara.—This evening a Sontal with choleraic symptoms was brought into the camp for treatment; as he had been brought there was nothing to be done but to administer suitable medicines, but the prudence of allowing the man into the neighbourhood of my own followers might be questioned. However, no evil results followed, and the man himself recovered. I was told that it is a custom with these people not to move a man from the place where he has been seized, and this one had been left for three days under a tree attended to by his friends until my arrival in the neighbourhood induced them to bring him for treatment. A few evenings before a Sontal had brought a little girl who had been most terribly burnt by her cloth catching fire. Some abominable native mess had been placed over the sore, which extended over an arm and a considerable portion of the side. It took the native doctor and myself more than an hour to remove this and prepare the surface for the application of a more suitable substance. The poor little creature was only three years old, but bore the pain extremely well.

March 19th.—Kuchpara to Burhait.—To-day I marched to Burhait, which is the principal village within the limits of the Rajmahal Hills. It is situated in a valley which has been scooped out of the main mass of the plateau, and well illustrates the operations of subaerial denudation. The main river, called the Morel, has pretty nearly accomplished all the work possible for it to do, and now merely oscillates from side to side in the bed of alluvium which it has laid down for itself; but the lateral tributaries still continue to wear away the material forming the surrounding hills.

On the way to Burhait, where I was glad to find a roomy and comfortable bungalow, I visited a Mahadeo's cave-temple, which is situated at the head of a valley to the north-east of the village. The cave is partly natural and partly artificial, and is in a flow of amygdaloid, the basalt, both above and below, being columnar. All the interior is smeared with ghi, red paint, and goats' blood. A young Brahmin priest was in charge, to whom an offering of a quantity of milk had just been brought by three Sontals, thus illustrating what I have elsewhere enlarged upon, the influence of Hinduism on the aborigines. The jungle grew so close around that it was impossible to select a point whence a favourable sketch of the cave might be made. At the entrance of the valley were the remains of a gate, which had been put up at the last festival, to facilitate the collection of toll.

March 21st.—Burhait to Nowgaon.—Near Nowgaon there was an encampment of the gipsy-like Naths, who profess to be Mahomedans, the chief evidence of which is that they practise circumcision. My Mahomedan servants, however, regarded them with great contempt. They have no language of their own, speaking Bengali among themselves. Their principal means of subsistence seemed to be derived from the manufacture out of slips of bamboo of the combs (I know not the proper technical name) used to support the web in looms. These, though they must take a long time to make, are sold for two annas or threepence.

March 23rd.—Burio to Poal.—About half-way to Poal I discovered on the east side of the valley a very beautiful waterfall over basaltic columns. Though much smaller than the Maharajpur fall, it is well worthy a visit by those in search of the picturesque. Indeed these hills abound in such scenes, which, though not difficult of access from Calcutta, are never likely to be well-known. The unhealthiness of this tract is such as would make me hesitate to recommend a visit to anyone wanting a change who was not acclimatised to a jungle life. There is, moreover, nothing to attract the sportsmen; so, for many years, they are likely to remain hidden from public view.

March 25th.—Poal to Burio.—I had now to retrace my steps southwards from the *cul de sac* formed by this central alluvial valley. On the way I visited an old fort called the Lukra-Gurh, which is surrounded by a deep moat. Regarding its history I failed to elicit any information. What interested me most about the ruins was the evidence afforded by them of the destructive effect of the Banyan and Pipul figs (*Ficus indica* and *F. religiosa*) on old buildings, which is only too well known to Indian antiquarians. Huge masses of the walls have been lifted out of their position bodily, and are clasped aloft in the plastic-looking stems.

At Burio I found an encampment of Behurs, whose monkey-catching proclivities I have described on a previous page. Here, as there were no monkeys, they must have had some other means of subsistence.

March 30th.—Kosmah to Dhumani.—The heat at mid-day in these valleys was becoming almost unbearable, and I was compelled to curtail my hours spent abroad and endeavour to exist as best I might in close proximity to a *kus-kus tati* in my tent. On arrival at Dhumani, for this the second time, the Purgunite appeared to be delighted to see me, and promised that supplies should be forthcoming, and then straightway went off and got drunk, and refused to come out of his house again. In almost every other village passed through the Sontals were to be seen dancing in their groves of Sal trees. The violence of their gesticulations seem to increase with the heat of the weather.

April 4th.—Paharpur.—The crop of mhowa flowers was now in full fall, and the Sontals were very busy everywhere collecting it. The great abundance of these trees is often scarcely realised while they are still in leaf. Not until the flowers are on the ground is attention attracted to them. I shot here two very beautiful birds which I had not previously met with in these hills. They were the scarlet minivet (*Pericrocotus speciosus*, Lath.), and the small-billed mountain thrush (*Oreocincla dauma*, Lath.); both these birds are supposed to migrate in the hot season to the slopes of the Himalayas; but, from observations made elsewhere, I am inclined to doubt their doing so *en masse.* Near Chundana there is a hot, or rather tepid, spring, the temperature of which I omitted to ascertain. According to the natives the water is hot in the cold weather, and *vice versâ.* This arises, probably, from the contrast caused by the temperature of the atmosphere at the different seasons; that of the water remaining constant.

April 8th.—Bokraband.—To-day I saw a form of tiger trap which I had not before met with. It belonged to some Paharias, and consisted of a large wooden framework heavily weighted with stones. One side rested on the ground, and the other was supported by a lever connected with a trigger arrangement intended to be sprung by the tiger when entering to seize the bait, a live kid. A sort of trap-door in the frame over the spot where the kid was tied was ingeniously contrived to prevent it from being crushed on the falling of the frame.

The weather at this time was often stormy and tempestuous in the afternoons, owing to a succession of north-westers. One night my tent narrowly escaped being blown bodily away. In several places in these hills, as on the Mhowagurhi hill, there are calcareous deposits which, as I mention in other places in these pages, are called by the natives *Asahar* or giant's bones, the rumour of which, in the early days of Indian Geology, raised an expectation of their proving to consist of the fossils of some large mammalia.

April 12th.—Belaidih to Nargunjo.—I was now re-traversing in a southerly direction much of the country which I had passed through on my march northwards at the beginning of the season. My object in so doing was to get a better view of the rocks, now in many places laid bare by jungle fires and the fall of the leaf, but which had been completely concealed by vegetation in the cold season. I frequently came across jungle, spur, and pea-fowl, which before I seldom saw, owing to the thickness of the vegetation. I also saw a few barking deer flitting through the dried underwood. Now and then, in the track of the fires, I found the burnt nests and roasted eggs of goatsuckers, which build on the ground. On this date I first met with one of the most beautiful and remarkable-looking birds found in Peninsular-India. It is the Rocket-bird or Paradise fly-catcher (*Tchitrea paradisi*, Lin.) The adult male, which is about the size of a canary, is of a satiny-white with black markings and delicate etchings on the wings and tail. The head and a copious crest are of a dark metallic green, very nearly approaching to black. The bare skin surrounding the orbits is lazuline blue which is very clear and bright during life, but soon fades after death. The two central tail-feathers are prolonged for about ten inches beyond the ordinary tail, thus forming two long streamers which, as they undulate with the bird's lively evolutions in pursuit of insects, have a peculiarly graceful effect. The females and young males when fully grown resemble the adult males in general structure, but differ from them in having a bright sienna-brown instead of a white body colour. At one time it was doubted whether the white and brown birds belonged to the same species. That they do so has now been fully ascertained; and, indeed, males in a piebald transitional stage of plumage are to be found in most collections. In the very young birds the elongated tail-feathers are not present.

In Bengal, Orissa, and the Central Provinces, I have never met with a single specimen before the end of March; but by the middle of April they are generally to be found if there be much forest about. It is believed that they migrate from Southern India and Ceylon to these jungles to breed, but the time of their return is not known. A closely allied species occurs in the Himalayas. With these fly-catchers there appears another bird which has, however, a more limited distribution. It is the sole peninsular representative of the group of birds called ground-thrushes, which in the Burmese and Malayan countries, and some of the islands, includes species having the most exquisite coloration. The yellow-breasted ground-thrush (*Pitta coronata*, Linn.) from its retiring habits is not often noticed. It has wrongly obtained the reputation of being a silent bird. Most of the specimens of it which I have shot were obtained in consequence of its not being so, as I was led to their whereabouts by hearing their notes when traversing thick jungle.

April 13th.—Belaidih to Narginjo.—One of the few cases of robbery which have occurred in my camp took place to-day, when one of the drivers of the bullock-carts walked off with the worldly possessions of my bird-skinner, who was plunged in the depths of distress. The thief was never again heard of. Considering the facilities for theft in the first instance, and escape afterwards, it is amazing how little is stolen from Europeans in India. I am, of course, only alluding above to the petty thefts of goods —the systematic robbery by servants of a percentage of funds entrusted to them for expenditure all suffer from, and those who try to protect themselves from it find it very difficult to obtain *respectable* servants. Thus from my having found it necessary to make my Jemidar bazaar supplier, I have seldom been able, even by the offer of quite exceptional wages, to engage a really good and efficient table-servant. As I have allowed my Bearer and head Sayce each to furnish separate accounts, they have remained in my service for many years, and enjoy the satisfaction of cheating me every month.

April 19th.—Saldiha to Musunia.—To-day the sweeper in

charge of my poor old bull-terrier "Joe," who had been the companion of my journeys for six years, being ill with fever, had loosed the chain, allowing the animal to follow him. Suddenly, Joe espying something in the jungle, gave chase, disappeared, and was never again heard of. Though he had become deaf, enfeebled, and perfectly useless, I could not but grieve over the loss of my old companion. The tricks I had taught him might, perhaps, have made the Sontals, unaccustomed to seeing educated dogs, regard him as something uncanny. Whether he found an asylum in some Sontal's house, or fell a prey to a leopard, I cannot say.

April 22nd.—Jellidobah.—Being now in the Ramgurh hills where there was evidence of the existence of animals, and receiving information that bears were known to live close by, I determined to have a beat. Accordingly, men were collected, and being chiefly Sontals who love sport, a goodly number were assembled. In the first beat I shot the only animals that came in my way, a pig and a peacock; I then heard that a bear, with two young cubs, had been seen, but had disappeared. Just as the men had been thrown out for a new beat, a Sontal rushed up to say that this same bear, with the two cubs on her back, had appeared in the open. After a pretty severe run up and across some cleared hills, I came in sight of her on a distant ridge, where she was resting after a steep climb. Pushing on, I endeavoured to get within shot, but some fleet-footed young Sontals, getting excited, burst from all restraint, and kept well ahead of me, shouting at the top of their voices, and brandishing their axes. So that after crossing several ridges I was still a long way out of range when the bear reached some cover in which she disappeared, and I had to give up the chase. My young Sontal escort seemed rather ashamed of themselves when I explained to them how their conduct had interfered with my chance of making a bag.

April 27th.—Jagutpur to Berazpur.—To-day's march produced a vast change in the country and the people. I had left behind me the simple Sontals, their dirty villages, and their hilly country, and found in their place crafty and quarrelsome Bengalis with their more prosperous-looking villages surrounded by groves of handsome trees.

April 29th.—Berazpur to Synthea.—To-day I marched to the railway station at Synthea, where I broke up camp, and on the first of May started for Calcutta. It was a great relief to me to have brought my season's work to a conclusion, for the perpetual marching, necessitated by the size of the area I had to revise, the trouble about supplies in many places, and the great heat of the past six weeks, had completely wearied me, though I was in better health and vigour than I have been at the termination of most of my journeys.

CHAPTER VI.

SECTION 2.

MAHENDRAGIRI IN GANJAM.

1870.

SEARCH FOR A SANITARIUM — ORGANISATION OF EXPEDITION — START FROM CALCUTTA—FALSE-POINT—THE SURF AT GOPALPUR—GOPALPUR TO BERHAMPUR—BERHAMPUR TO HURIAPUR—FIRST VIEW OF MAHENDRA—MANDESUR—ASCENT OF MAHENDRA—VEGETATION OF PLATEAU—WATER SUPPLY—FAUNA—INHABITANTS—TEMPLES—TEMPERATURE—ASKA SUGAR FACTORY—CHILKA LAKE—GANJAM—CAPTURE OF A CROCODILE—GOPALPUR —RETURN TO CALCUTTA.

IN the autumn of the year 1870 I was invited by Dr. Charles Palmer, one of the Presidency surgeons, to accompany him on a search for a sanitarium. Like many of the other Calcutta doctors, he had often to recommend a change of air to persons enervated by the Calcutta climate, or weakened by sickness. To people with large or comfortable incomes it is generally a matter of no great difficulty to act upon such a recommendation. The stations in the Himalayas and the Neilgherries, and various sea trips in steamers which leave the port of Calcutta, afford a sufficiently diverse choice to those for whom the expense is not a subject of primary consideration. But with the members of a rapidly-increasing class in Calcutta, whose means are small or moderate, any of these expensive trips were simply out of the question. Darjiling was not then accessible from Calcutta, as it now is, by a railway which runs nearly to the foot of the hills, and the journey thither was not only expensive, but of a very fatiguing nature, and such as few invalids could undertake without risk. The sanitarium on Parisnath had proved a failure, and the sole remaining alternative, a trip down the river to the Sand-heads in a tug steamer, though often producing most beneficial results, left much to be desired. After a careful examination of the most recent maps, Dr. Palmer came to the conclusion that Mahendra Hill, in the district of Ganjam (which is the most northern of the districts included in the Madras Presidency) was likely to afford the much-desired conditions for a sanitarium. Not only was the hill ascertained to be about 5,000 feet high, and therefore above the range of malaria, but it was found to be but thirteen miles inland from a small port called Barwah, which seemed admirably suited for the establishment of a marine sanitarium. Thus this locality appeared to afford the triple advantages of a sea voyage, a sea-side residence, and a hill climate within range of, and exposed to, the sea breezes. Detailed information regarding this locality, which seemed to be endowed with such unique natural advantages was, however, sadly wanting, though it was known that a former collector of Ganjam (the Hon. Gordon Forbes) had made trial of Mahendra as a sanitarium, and some very brief notices of the hill were found in several works. Under these circumstances Dr. Palmer determined to organise an expedition for the purpose of exploring the locality, and ascertaining how far the actual conditions would support the opinions which he had formed from such *data* as were available. It being holiday time, Captain Murray, Assistant-Surveyor-General, and I were able to accept his invitation to join him in this expedition. Our several labours were allotted as follows:—Dr. Palmer took the general and sanitary aspects of the question; Captain Murray the mapping and photography; the geology, fauna, flora, ethnology, and antiquities fell to my share.

The results of our united observations subsequently appeared in a volume copiously illustrated with maps and photographs. Favourable notices appeared in the papers, and then the matter dropped, and has not since been heard of, as neither the Government nor the public could be induced to evince more than a passing interest in the scheme. The peaks of Mahendra still rise from their sylvan environment unassailed by the sounds of civilization which we had fondly hoped would ere long be heard on the beautiful plateau.

Circumstances have prevented me from illustrating the following remarks by an adequate selection from the very perfect series of photographs taken by Captain Murray; but two of his series will be found in this volume—the first, of a temple on Mahendra; the second, of the surf at Gopalpur. His views of the other temples and summit of Mahendra, and of the Chilka Lake, had considerable claims to be reproduced; but they have had to give place to others.

September 20th.—The British India Steam Navigation Company, with a liberality which I experienced on another occasion also, having given us free return passages to Gopalpur, we embarked on the steamship "Satara" to-day. On the morning of the 22nd we made the harbour of False-point, which is situated on one of the mouths of the Mahanadi river. It is a very dismal-looking spot, formed of new deltaic land. A few native craft, some cargo-boats, a house on the beach, and a lighthouse in the distance which rises from scrub-covered sands, were the only signs of civilization in this wilderness of land and water. The lighthouse-keeper as well as the port officials came on board, and the former entertained us with accounts of the nightly pranks of the tigers in his cabbage-garden and some other details of his strange life. We left False-point in the evening.

September 23rd.—To-day we were out of sight of land till the afternoon, when a bold range of hills in Ganjam became visible. By sunset we were off the port of Gopalpur, but as there was no sign of the *masulah* or surf-boats putting off, we lay-to for the night. On the following morning the surf appeared to be very violent, and we saw one boat, as it was being launched, capsized and smashed by the heavy rollers. Soon signals were hoisted, which on interpretation proved to be "dangerous to land." However, in a short time several boats made their way to the ship, and we determined to risk a landing, since it would have completely disturbed our programme to have gone to any of the ports further south. The landing was effected without accident.

The accompanying illustration, reproduced from an instantaneous photograph by Captain Murray, will serve to indicate the nature of the surf, with which visitors to Madras and all the ports along the east coast of India are only too familiar. No European-built boat could stand the succession of thumps from the rollers, culminating in the final one, which throws a boat on the sand. Accordingly, the masulah boats, which may be described as tolerably water-tight wooden baskets, have to be employed for the transit of passengers and merchandise. The springiness of these craft, due to the fact that their timbers are stitched together with coir rope, is one of the reasons of their immunity from wreck; and another, no doubt, arises from the number of the crew, the dozen to a score of men which they carry being sufficient to drag the boat when stranded through the receding waters and out of reach of the next advancing wave.

Another craft, if it can so be called, which is even more capable of being employed in the transit through heavy surf, is the catamaran, which owes its ability to withstand the rude buffeting of the waves to quite another cause. Being formed of three logs pointed at one end, and strongly lashed together, it is simply unbreakable however it may be knocked about. Its navigator may be washed off it a dozen times during the transit, but he has no difficulty in regaining his position and ultimately paddling to sea beyond the outer line of rollers.

Gopalpur consists of a few houses and stores, which, with a native village, are all situated on shifting sand dunes. The glare from the sand, and the all-pervading grit, and a clamminess in the atmosphere, are not altogether pleasant features, but on the other hand there is the view of the sea, and daily sea breezes afford a welcome and refreshing alteration of the temperature.

September 25th.—To-day we drove from Gopalpur to Berhampur, a distance of about eight miles. Berhampur is the present chief town of the district of Ganjam. The former capital, which was situated nearer to the coast, was deserted some years

Plate VI.

THE SURF AT GOPALPUR.

(From a Photograph by Capt. W. G. Murray.)

ago on account of an epidemic, and the ruins of some houses and a fort (the former built in the luxurious and massive style of former days), alone remain to mark its position.

At night we started in palkis for Huriapur, a stage on the Madras road opposite the foot of the Mahendra range. Immediately we noticed a provincial difference between the customs of the palki bearers and those of Bengal and Upper India; instead of there being only eight men to a palki, four carrying at a time, the complement here was twelve, with six men at a time. Relays of about forty men awaited our arrival at each ten mile stage. The heat was very great during the night, but we accomplished the distance of about thirty miles by 8.30 on the next morning. Shortly afterwards the Dewan of the Mandesur Raja, whose territory includes the Mahendra range, made his appearance. He informed us that a tent was ready for our reception, and that all arrangements had been made at Mandesur, and in the afternoon we moved on there, the distance being only about four miles. Before leaving, however, as the morning was clear, we were able, after the mist had risen, to obtain from Huriapur a magnificent view of the goal of our journey—the highest peak of Mahendra. The main forest-clad range, with those subordinate to it, stood out with admirable distinctness, and the whole landscape was of a kind not commonly seen in Peninsular India.

I must not omit to mention the beauty of the trees on parts of the Madras and Calcutta road along which we had travelled to Huriapur. They are chiefly the two common species of *Ficus*, the banyan and pipul; in places their branches interlock above and afford the most complete and grateful shade.

At Mandesur we were visited by and paid a return visit to the Raja, who had made great efforts to give us a comfortable reception, a table in the tent being laden with a large assortment of European tinned provisions for our consumption, shewing an advance in civilization to which the Rajas of the interior have not yet reached. In an adjoining district further down the coast, there is a Rani who prides herself on the manner in which she provides for the creature comforts of

European officials who visit her territories, but she is a great upholder of the laws and privileges of official precedence. In the supplies for the consumption of her guests a bottle of champagne is allotted to the Collector, while his assistant only gets a pint. Brandy not being commonly obtainable in pints the distinction is preserved by furnishing two whole bottles to the Collector and one to the assistant.

September 27th.—This morning we started at 4 o'clock and by sunrise reached a village called Sopachola, or Souacotta, at the foot of the ascent. Here there is a fine grove, including tamarind, jack, mango, pipul, and banyan trees. The tamarinds occur for several hundred feet higher; they appear to have been introduced, but wild mangos are abundant on the slopes of the hill. The road, which is from six to seven miles long, maintains a steady rise throughout, and there are none of those tedious interruptions and descents which one has sometimes to encounter on the roads to other hill tops. The rocks observed on our walk up were all highly crystalline gneisses, &c., the characters of which it is unnecessary to specify more particularly here. I failed to find any trace whatever of limestone, though while we remained on the hill I kept a good look out for a deposit, since its discovery would be of great importance in the event of buildings being erected on the summit. Lime made of sea shells on the coast could no doubt be obtained in any quantity, but the cost of carriage would render it very expensive.

At an elevation of 2,400 feet we passed a piece of level ground covered with trees of mhowa (*Bassia latifolia*, Roxb.) This was the only place in Ganjam where I noted the occurrence of this species, though it may be not uncommon. The highest cultivation seen on the ascent consists of Ragi (*Eleusine coracana*, Gærtn.) and Indian corn. Scattered about were sago palms (*Caryota*), which have apparently been introduced. The plateau at the top of the hill is characterised by a flora quite distinct from that which clothes the steep sides. Immediately on reaching it we discovered some violets and the common widespread bracken fern (*Pteris aquilina*, Linn.) The whole aspect of the jungle too was completely changed: instead of forming one uniform covering to the surface, as is the case on the flanks and lower spurs, it is broken up into detached patches and lines, which follow and run with the stream courses. Throughout the remainder of the area, the surface—except where smooth faces of exfoliating gneiss defy vegetation—is covered with grasses of many different species, some of which are juicy and succulent and admirably suited for grazing, while others would answer for thatch and similar purposes. A small species of palm, with a stem rarely exceeding four feet in height, occurred scattered about in the grass. Bushes of a *Eugenia* and an *Indigofera*, were also found in the same situation. I collected several rare specimens of ferns and a number of herbaceous plants, together with specimens of the characteristic trees. Lists of these are given in the volume already alluded to.

In reference to the formation of a sanitarium on Mahendra, there was no question more important for our investigation than the character and amount of the water supply. The time of our visit being towards the end of the rains, when the ground is thoroughly saturated, there was of course no lack of water. Creeping along the surface of the rock it burst through the turf at many points, closely simulating genuine springs. Without having to draw conclusions from the character of the vegetation or the other circumstances which would be influenced by the regularity of the water supply, we have the evidence of visitors to the hill during the hot weather, as well as the testimony of the natives, that there is a constant and abundant supply of water all the year round. But perhaps the most conclusive proof is, that numbers of buffaloes and cattle are driven up to the plateau for grazing during the driest portion of the hot weather. The plateau has an irregular area of rather less than one square mile, which slopes in places somewhat steeply to the culminating ridge on the west. It is drained by two principal streams, one falling into the southern valley, and the other, after traversing a deep depression in the centre of the plateau, falling over the north-eastern edge, formed of blocks of granitic gneiss, whence the water, bounding from rock to rock, is lost to view in a beautiful wooded valley, at least five hundred feet below.

The central depression might easily be made available for storing water. The formation of a lake or reservoir, by throwing a dam or weir across the stream at a distance from the head of the fall, would be a simple matter, involving no very great expense. This, while ensuring a constant and abundant supply of water to the station, would add very much to the beauty of the plateau. On a ledge overhanging this depression a small bungalow has been built, and the further ascent to the highest peak crosses over wide and bare surfaces of exfoliating porphyritic gneiss, in which there are crystals of felspar, about two inches long. The highest peaks are composed of jointed prisms of granitic gneiss. From the summit the aspect of the surrounding country is magnificent. On the north-west and south the view is more or less bounded by ranges of granitic hills, which succeed one another like huge waves, while the passage of fleecy clouds from peak to peak produces an ever-changing scene. On the east the hilly ground gradually breaks up into spurs and outlying hills, and beyond them the surf, with the *masulah* boats passing through it, can be most clearly made out with the naked eye, even at the distance of fifteen miles. The granitic gneiss of which the hills are formed is an important component in the scenery. In some places it forms steep and noble cliffs, in others it gives a craggy outline to the hills, and occasionally it exposes considerable exfoliating uncovered surfaces on the flanks. North of the bungalow, the rock of one of the cliffs is much jointed; this has caused it to have a peculiar mural appearance, resembling a large fortress. The large animals inhabiting the slopes are of the ordinary kind to be found in such forests. There are tigers, leopards, bears, sambar, and spotted deer, &c. Birds were very scarce, and I observed none which were particularly noteworthy. My collection of land shells included some species of great interest and rarity.

Close to the base of Mahendra there is a rather sudden transition from a Uria to a Telegu-speaking population—although there is perhaps no very sharp distinction of race to be detected—conterminous with the limits of these respective languages. A large number of the people belong to the race known as *Buis*,* hereditary palki-bearers and fishermen, many of whom are to be found plying their trades in distant parts of India, and not a few emigrate to the Mauritius and elsewhere. The existence of such a class of hard-working men on the spot, and immediately available for service, is a fact of considerable importance in reference to the establishment of a sanitarium.

In the northern and western parts of Ganjam the hills are inhabited by the Khonds, but in the vicinity of Mahendra a perfectly distinct but almost epually numerous people make their appearance. These are the Souras or Savaras. As a wild, intractable race, these people have been known from very early times. They are now perfectly docile, though maintaining their independence against the Zemindars and Rajas, to whom they, in most cases, pay no revenue whatever. In appearance the Souras are small but wiry; they are often very dark in colour, and sometimes quite black. Their hair is generally tied in a top-knot, and sometimes it is cut short over the forehead, two long locks being permitted to hang over the ears. A few individuals have frizzled shocks, with which no such arrangement is attempted. Most of the men have small square beards. The nose is in general broad, with wide nostrils. Of those races in Bengal with whose appearance I am familiar, they reminded me most strongly of the Bhumiz who belong to the Munda family; but I could also perceive in them some points of resemblance to the Dravidian Paharias of the Rajmahal Hills. They have not, however, the manly bearing and good physique of the latter. Their houses of wattled bamboos, and their hill-side clearances, reminded me of the villages on the Rajmahal Hills. Unlike

---

* By Sir George Campbell and Colonel Dalton, the *Buis* are believed to be connected with the *Bhuias*, who are considered to belong rather to the Dravidians than the Mundas.—*Descriptive Ethnology of Bengal*, p. 139.

the Munda or Kolarian races, they make but little display of their weapons, and have but few personal ornaments. Their bows have not nearly the strength of those used by the Sontals and Kols. Their manner of dancing resembles that of the Rajmahal Paharias, as I have on one occasion witnessed it, rather than that of either the Sontals or Kols. The balance of this sort of evidence seems to favour their being referable to the Dravidian family; and it is the opinion of some ethnologists that this is their true position. On the other hand, some few of the words in the vocabulary which I took from the Souras of Mahendra are distinctly Kolarian with the prefix *a.*

The old Sivoid temples on Mahendra are of great interest from several points of view, and form quite a feature in the scenery of the plateau. There are four principal temples and a number of rudely-constructed cairn-like huts, which are for the most part built of uncut stone, and are generally arranged in groups. These may have been put up as huts for shelter by the pilgrims at the annual festivals; but some of them look as if they were of considerable antiquity.

The temple which crowns the highest peak of the hill, at an elevation of 4,923 above the sea, is a remarkable structure. It is built in five courses of huge bevelled blocks of granitic gneiss surmounted by a carved coronet. There is an entrance on the eastern side, which discloses the *lingum.* The height of this temple is something under twenty-five feet. The largest block of stone in the lowest course measures 9' × 3'.9" × 3', or over 100 cubic feet. The worshippers of the present day get over the difficulty of accounting for such a structure by asserting that it was built by giants, who could raise the blocks in their hands unassisted by any mechanical contrivance. It is evident that this temple is in a very unfinished state, and that it was the intention of the builders to dress and carve the stone into shape when in position, such having been occasionally, I believe, the practice in Orissa. The accompanying illustration will serve to convey an idea of this structure, and show how it has been split on one side by lightning.

The second temple, near the bungalow, is a more finished structure, but is far from complete. There are some inscriptions near the doorway, possibly in Telegu; but, owing to the rugosities of the granite, they are quite indistinct and illegible. In

TEMPLE ON SUMMIT OF MAHENDRAGIRI.

front of the entrance there is a much-mutilated granite bull; inside there is the *lingum.*

The third temple, which is represented in the frontispiece, is a still more finished work. It is situated in a picturesque dell on the banks of a limpid stream of ever-flowing water. The outside of this temple is ornamented with several figures, including a tolerable one of Ganesa. As will be seen, the roof is covered with vegetation. Opposite and close to it is the fourth temple, which appears to have been constructed out of the old materials of some pre-existing temple.

Dr. Palmer being obliged to return at once to Calcutta, Captain Murray and I remained on the hill for about a week, and succeeded, in spite of very broken weather, in obtaining the topographical and geological surveys of it which we required. We were also enabled in this time to make a sufficient number of thermometric observations to justify a partial comparison with the temperatures prevailing below. During five days the mean of the maximum temperatures between sunrise and 8 p.m. was 69.56° F., and the mean of the minimum was 64.9° F. At Mandesur the maximum temperature which we recorded was 90.3° F., and the minimum 81.3° F.; so that the elevation of the hill produced a difference of from 16° to 20° F.

October 3rd.—To-day we descended the hill to Mandesur where, on the following morning, Captain Murray took photographs of groups of Souras, and of the Raja with his following. Two long night journeys took us, *viâ* Berhampur, to Aska, where we had been invited to spend some days with Mr. Minchin, the manager at that time, and at present the proprietor of the Aska Sugar Works and Distillery. Our stay in his hospitable and beautifully situated house was very enjoyable after the damp and discomfort we had been subjected to during the previous ten days.

The sugar factory at Aska is the first at which the "dialysis process" for the extraction of the saccharine matter from cane has superseded the old system of expressing by mills. Mr. Minchin's application of this system, which is generally in use in France in the manufacture of beet sugar, secured for him a gold medal at the Paris Exposition of 1868. All the machinery at Aska was of the newest make, and was worked by a highly competent European and native staff. By the dialysis process, which consists in steeping the thinly sliced cane in water, it has been ascertained that, supposing the cane to contain ninety per cent. of saccharine matter, only seven per cent. is left in the refuse; whereas in the best mills from three to four times that amount is liable to be left, while in native mills, perhaps five to six times the same quantity is wholly lost. Whatever is left in the refuse at Aska is subsequently saved by distillation and converted into rum. Sugar of many qualities and degrees of impurity is brought by the natives for sale to the factory, and I was amused to hear that they always, when any difference arose as to the price to be paid, deferred to the decision of the saccharimeter; these impure sugars are, in the factory, chiefly employed in the manufacture of rum. By the natives they are generally preferred to the pure product of the factory—the employment of animal charcoal in the purification may perhaps prevent some from making use of it, but with many, the mere fact of any article of food having come out of a European factory would be sufficient to condemn it. Natives are, however, notorious for having a sweet tooth, as housekeepers find to their cost, and sugar is a comestible about which many of them must have very pliable consciences.

October 11th.—Ramba.—We arrived early this morning at Ramba, by palki from Aska. Ramba is a village on the southern bank of the Chilka Lake, which is a shallow piece of brackish water, the area of which varies with the seasons from 344 to 450 square miles. It is separated from the sea by a narrow spit of sand, except at one point where there is an opening, The lake is studded with numerous islands, and on the west is bounded by ranges of low, forest-clad hills, so that it presents a considerable diversity and some very beautiful scenery; the stillness of the water contrasts with the troubled roll of the surf outside the spit of sand.

At the southern end of the lake there is an enormous house containing twenty-six rooms, which was built in the good old times, and of which, if the true history could be told, judging from the fragments of tradition which remain, we should have some facts illustrative of the habits of Anglo-Indians of a bygone age, which would contrast very strikingly with the manners and customs of these latter days. It is said that from this castle a former Collector defied the Government, and resisted all efforts at ejectment with complete success for many months. When at last he was brought to bay, and was ordered to give an account of his stewardship,—of the rectitude of which more than a doubt existed—it so happened that all the documents by which he might have been brought to trial were placed in a boat, and it further happened that this boat was swamped in the middle of the lake, and though it is not recorded that any lives were lost in consequence of this accident, it is certain that the papers were. In this house, which is still in fair repair and quite habitable, a party consisting of the local Ganjam officials, the Commissioner of the adjoining province of Orissa, and our detachment from Aska, assembled and remained for two days, which we spent in boating and shooting. From Ramba we were conveyed by boat through a canal to Ganjam, where there are the remains of an old fort, originally constructed by the Dutch, and the ruins of the former station.

In the river close by there were a number of pelicans, the first I had seen in India—though they are not uncommon in some parts of the country.

In the Chilka Lake I saw several porpoises, but whether these are of the same species as those which are found in the Ganges* and some other rivers, or are true marine porpoises, I was unable to ascertain.

From Ganjam we rode to Chutterpur, a distance of about nine miles, where we dined with the Collector, and after dinner continued our journey in palkis to Gopalpur. During the night the bearers of one of the palkis encountered a crocodile† about six

---

* *Platanista Gangetica*, Lebeck.

† Many Anglo-Indians, both in speaking and writing, call the Indian crocodile an alligator, unmindful of the fact that the alligator is a wholly distinct animal, which is found in America. This is not, however, the only instance where the Western World has been drawn upon by residents in the East for an incorrect nomenclature. Thus the gaur, or wild bull, is called a bison; the scaly ant-eater, an armadillo; the hornbill, a toucan; the honey-sucker, a humming-bird; and so forth.

feet long, which was crossing the road in transit from one piece of water to another; having belaboured it well with their sticks, they slung it on a pole and brought it on to Gopalpur, where we found that it was still alive. The extraordinary tenacity for life which these animals possess was well exemplified by this individual, since although a hog-spear was plunged through both its head and heart, it still continued to crawl about for some time.

On the 15th of October we embarked for Calcutta, thus bringing our very pleasant trip in search of a sanitarium to a conclusion.

CHAPTER VII.

WESTERN CHUTIA NAGPUR, HAZARIBAGH, LOHARDUGGA, SIRGUJA, AND GANGPUR.

1870–71.

INSTRUCTIONS FOR SEASON—PURCHASE ELEPHANTS—THEFT IN CAMP—THE POLICE—ASCEND PARISNATH—CHOPÉ COAL-FIELD—HAZARIBAGH JAILS—RANCHI—PACK-BULLOCKS AND COOLIES—CHRISTMAS DAY—SHOOT A BEAR—ENTER SIRGUJA—OTTERS—PAHARIAS—HOAR-FROST—FIND THE COAL-FIELD—PERTABPUR—CAPTIVE ELEPHANTS—THE REGENT—DISCOVER COAL—BIRDS AND BEASTS—EARLY JUNGLE FIRES—BLACK BUCK—UNDERGROUND RIVER—ADVENTURE WITH A BEAR—PILKA HILL—MOHESRI PERSHAD—BIRDS IN THE RER RIVER—ASCEND PILKA HILL—BRAHMIN PILGRIMS—TENT ON FIRE—A LUCKY SHOT—A STUPID GUN-BEARER—BISRAMPUR—CEREMONIAL VISITS—TERRIFIC STORM—TENT IN DANGER—LUKANPUR—MEET A TIGER AT MID-DAY—CAPTIVE ELEPHANTS—KAURS AND SAONTARS—DESCENT FROM SIRGUJA HIGHLANDS—POST LEFT BEHIND—RABKOB—ESSAY AS A FARRIER—UDAIPUR COAL-FIELD—SNAKE BITE—A FALSE ALARM—DRUNKEN SERVANTS—RAIGURH AND HINGIR COAL-FIELD—GOURS—WILD BUFFALO—NEWS FROM THE OUTER WORLD—SUADI—RAJA OF GANGPUR—RETURN MARCH—CALCAREOUS DEPOSIT IN TIMBER—BURGAON—MAHABIR HILL—URAON KERIAHS—BEAUTIFUL BIRDS—TROUBLES ABOUT CARRIAGE—ARRIVE AT RANCHI—RETURN TO CALCUTTA.

My instructions for this season were to make a preliminary exploration of the western frontiers of Chutia Nagpur, with a view to the future allotment of detailed work. That a wide area existed there, in which coal-measures and other sedimentary rocks prevailed, was already known; but the actual extent of the several coal-basins and their mutual connections could only be vaguely surmised.

November 16th.—Calcutta to Assensole.—I was delayed at Assensole for some days, arranging for the purchase, on the part of the Government, of two elephants, which were to carry my baggage. Two females, the property of the East Indian Railway

Company, were selected; a very fine-looking tusker being rejected on account of the uncertainty of his temper, and the fact that he had, when *must*, killed an old woman who went down to the tank where he was bathing. The two which were purchased were called Anarkalli and Peari, the former a sedate old maid, and the latter a skittish, well-shaped, good-tempered young thing of about thirty-five years of age. Since then both these elephants have travelled some thousands of miles with me, and, except that Peari occasionally suffers from fits, they have proved an excellent investment, and have done their work well.

On the 22nd I pushed on to the oft-mentioned Barakar, where my servants had been waiting for me; and on the following day I marched to Govindpur.

November 24th.—Govindpur to Rajgunj.—This night, which we spent at Rajgunj, the tent of the native doctor accompanying my camp was robbed, the carpet-bags containing his clothes and the medicine-chest having been carried outside, and the contents rifled. Early next morning, when the theft was discovered, there was a great disturbance; and, after a search had been made, some of the property was discovered scattered about in the adjoining fields. Among other things recovered was an envelope, which had been torn in half by the thieves, but which, to the doctor's great delight, contained in the untorn portion, safely enough, a note for ten rupees. The police when sent for came and took down the depositions, and then proposed that the recovered property should be delivered to them, to be produced as "exhibits," and evidence, perchance, of their vigilance before the magistrate. This absurd request I, of course, did not listen to, as the articles, once out of the doctor's hands, would never have reached them again. If such be a general practice, it can be no cause for wonder if the natives when robbed sometimes prefer to keep quiet rather than solicit the aid of the police. The inspector, I learnt on the following day, threatened to seize the proprietor of my bullock-carts on a charge of complicity with the thieves. The man was a perfectly respectable individual, from whom I had frequently hired carts; but, being a person of some substance, was a fitting subject for the inspector to operate on. As the man was returning home he begged me to give him a certificate which he could show in the event of the inspector trying to terrify him into disgorging a sum of money. The real thieves, were, of course, not found. Had I not been marching forward, and had the evidence against the inspector been a little more complete, I should have reported him; but, as it was, I thought time would be uselessly wasted in an attempt to get him punished.

November 26th.—Nimia-Ghât.—To-day I ascended Parisnath, as it was six years since I had first visited it; and in the meantime the Sanitarium had come into existence and disappeared again. In the officer's bungalow I found an hotel had been established by its owner, who had purchased the building from Government. It was hoped that visitors from Calcutta would come in sufficient numbers to support the establishment; but this hope was not destined to be fulfilled.

December 1st.—Hazaribagh to Bindi.—To-day, in company with Dr. Coates, of Hazaribagh, who had recently brought to notice the discovery of coal at a point on the plateau seven miles to the west of the station, I marched to Bindi, from whence we visited the coal-seam, which, unfortunately, consisted of very poor stuff, scarcely capable of supporting combustion. Had the coal been good, the discovery would have been one of some importance, from the fact of its vicinity to the station. Geologically, the occurrence of coal-measures at this high elevation, the other known coal-fields being below the plateau, was of great interest. I shall not, however, here enter into a discussion of the physical changes by which the difference in level has been in all probability produced. After three days spent on the examination of this coal-field, on which the name Chopé was conferred, and which is one of the smallest in India, I returned to Hazaribagh, where I visited the European Penitentiary, which is designed to accommodate about 100 Europeans.

The then superintendent had many schemes in hand for teaching the convicts various handicrafts. Some of these were subsequently, I believe, not approved of by the authorities. A suitable employment for European convicts in India must ever prove a difficult thing to discover. In Rangoon, the Europeans, as I have mentioned on a previous page, were engaged in the rather degrading task of stone-breaking. But in Hazaribagh, supposing the men to have been put to similar work, it would have been difficult to know what to do with the stone when broken. One of the schemes was to establish iron-works, with a view to which the Lieutenant-Governor of Bengal appointed a gentleman to explore and report on the neighbourhood: and in due time a report appeared, containing a most enthusiastic account of the mineral resources, which I shall not, however, further criticise in detail, since better counsels prevailed, and the costly experiment was never made.

From Hazaribagh I marched southwards to Ranchi, taking five days to accomplish the distance, which involves a descent of about 1,000 feet from the Hazaribagh plateau into the valley of the Damuda, and an ascent of 1,200 feet again to the Ranchi plateau. At Ramgurh, where I made one halt, I had an opportunity of seeing some of my first year's work on the coal-field of that name.

December 10th.—Ranchi.—At Ranchi I was delayed for several days trying to get pack-bullocks, as the carts could not accompany me further; but the well known hospitality of the residents at that station made the time pass pleasantly. I had before me the prospect of not seeing any European for a long time; and, as the event proved, five months elapsed before I again had an opportunity of talking English.

December 14th.—Ranchi to Nagri.—Some inkling of the extent of my journey had leaked out, and consequently I found it nearly impossible to engage either coolies or bullock-men. At length, however, by promising about fifty per cent. above the proper rates, I effected a start for the west this morning and marched to Nagri. The next five days' marches averaged ten miles each. The country was mostly open and fairly cultivated by the Uraons, who constitute the bulk of the population.

December 20th.—Arengi to Kotaur.—The bullocks I had, in desperation, been obliged to take at Ranchi had, though lightly laden, already shewn themselves to be unfit for their work. Three of them to-day had taken over thirteen hours to accomplish about ten miles. The prospect was not a pleasant one, since away from the stations it is impossible to find people willing to take service or hire out their cattle. A district officer might or might not be able to obtain what he wanted; but with me it has generally happened that whatever arrangement regarding carriage I made at the commencement of my six months' tours had to be adhered to throughout the whole time, however unsatisfactory it might prove to be.

December 22nd.—Dorkona to Barwa.—Barwa, though not a large village, is one of the most important on the western frontier of Lohardugga. It is surrounded by plains, which are shut in on three sides by hills, some of which, being capped by laterite, present a peculiar flat and truncate appearance. I halted here for the 23rd, intending to proceed again on the 24th; but on the evening of the former day the appearance of the new moon caused a commotion among the Mahomedan portion of my followers, who forthwith came to announce that it would be their Eed festival, and asked me to give them another halt in order to celebrate it in a suitable manner. As the keeping of Christmas Day by one's self is but a sorry affair, I determined to let them have their wish, and to march on the 25th.

December 25th.—Barwa to Juragi.—To-day, for the first time in Chutia Nagpur, I saw some antelope, or black buck, but they were very wild, and I failed to get within range of them by stalking. Shortly after arrival at the new camping-ground at Juragi, news came in that a man and a buffalo had been attacked by a bear, which had first torn off one of the buffalo's ears, and then clawed the man, who had, to save his buffalo, struck the bear with an axe. I immediately went off to the spot where a patch of jungle was pointed out as the one where the bear had taken refuge. On entering the bushes, the animal made a rather feeble charge, but I dropped him with a bullet ere he could do any further mischief. We then found that the man had dealt a terrific gash on the bear's head with his axe, which fact, in so far as I was concerned, had made the sport of the thing somewhat tamer than it might otherwise have been.

This being the *Burra Din*, or great day, the fact of an animal being shot was interpreted by the men as a favourable augury of future success in the same line during the ensuing season. In the evening, all dressed in their best came to make a salaam, and receive the time-honoured buckshish. I took the opportunity of telling them that a very long journey lay before them, and that they must not grumble if they occasionally met with short commons; and I besought them (this I said feelingly) to avoid squabbling and contention amongst themselves. All promised to be good boys, pocketed their rupees, and were dismissed.

December 26th.—Juragi to Tinako.—This day's march carried me out of the district of Lohardugga, into the semi-independent state of Sirguja, which is managed by a Regent, the brother of the present Raja, who is a lunatic. As my comfort in travelling would depend very much upon this Regent, I determined to see him as soon as possible. The road by which I entered Sirguja is one of the rough and ready sort I have described on a previous page, having been, so far as it is made, the work of the Regent. It is, however, unprovided with causeways at the river crossings; but since there are no carts in the district, this is not a matter of present importance. Trees had been planted along it, but many, I noticed, had been killed by hoar-frost. The boundary is coincident with a well-defined ridge, which is traversed by a pass, the top of which is about 300 feet above the adjoining Lohardugga plateau; but the fall from it on the western side is not equal to the rise on the eastern, so that there is a kind of steppe, from which there is a further descent into the basin of Central Sirguja, which stands at an elevation of about 1,800 feet above the sea.

December 29th.—Umko.—Two marches from Tinako brought me

to Umko, where I halted for a day, in order to visit the country to the north, more particularly the valley of the Kunhur river, which traverses a deep gorge through a lofty range. The furthest point which I succeeded in reaching was the Poai-ghag waterfall. Being broken up into steps, the general effect is not so fine as is that afforded by some of the other falls mentioned in these pages, and it is impossible to obtain any standpoint below from whence a general idea of its form can be obtained; but the view from the top of the fall, looking down the densely wooded valley, is superb. While seated on a block of granite, enjoying this prospect, I saw a number of otters playing about in the deep pools at the foot, and chasing one another over the sand. I have the authority of a friend for saying that he on one occasion, in the Central Provinces, witnessed a somewhat similar scene, with the addition, that a crocodile, lying on the sand, was the centre of the otters' gambols, and was frequently bitten by them as they played about him.

December 30th.—Umko to Sernadih.—To-day I descended into Central Sirguja by the pass to which I have just alluded. So far I found everything go along very smoothly in Sirguja, the people being civil and obliging. The wishes of the Sirkar, as represented by myself, were promptly attended to. How different from what it is in wholly British Districts, especially those which profess to be the most civilized. In some that I have had experience of, it is necessary to get a magistrate's order before the man whose trade is that of a farrier will condescend to shoe one's horse, or before a carter or a coolie can be engaged. Send your own messenger to call these people, offer them above the market rate, they will not be induced to come—they prefer being ordered; and as for supplies, without a magistrate's order they cannot be obtained in many places at any price, and with one they are often not to be got without much trouble.

December 31st.—Sernadih.—To-day I devoted to an exploration of the hills south of Sernadih. The highest peak ascended proved a tough climb, owing to the absence of any path, and the consequent necessity of pressing through creepers and other

Plate VII.]

THE DASUM FALLS ON THE KANCHI RIVER, CHUTIA NAGPUR.

(From a Photograph by T. F. Peppé, Esq.)

undergrowth, while concealed holes made by the Paharias, when grubbing out roots, gave me more than one nasty fall. The tail of followers in my wake was a curious one to behold. Starting with two Uraons from Sernadih, at a village called Palsingh, we picked up two Ahirs, or shepherds. A little further on a wild and dirty-looking Paharia joined the party, and he subsequently brought five of as complete savages as I have ever seen from a village or cluster of huts on the hill. They were very black, and had thick lips and flat noses, but most decidedly straight hair. While resting, I took down from them a short vocabulary. The words were distinctly Kolarian, but the language is quite distinct from that of the Korewahs, who inhabit the same jungles.

January 3rd, 1871.—Kumdih.—For the last few mornings it had been very cold again, and everything appeared at sunrise clad in a thick coating of hoar-frost. Each day I had been out, chiefly on foot, from early morning till four o'clock in the afternoon. To-day I examined portions of the Mahan river—the scenery on which resembles that of the Subanrika—and the Gehur. The latter was very difficult to follow, owing to the deep pools in the bed, and the thorny, tangled nature of the banks. The effects of the hoar-frost were here very apparent: large patches of jungle having been killed by it, and the brown colour of the dead leaves contrasted in a most marked manner with the surrounding dark green.

January 6th.—Mukanpur.—This place is just within the limits of the coal-field I had been searching for, and to-day I not only met with the coal-measure rocks, but also several seams of coal. In the sands of the rivers, tracks of tiger, leopard, and bear were abundant, and the prospect of my being able to get good sport later on, when the jungles became lighter, seemed to be promising.

January 7th.—Mukanpur to Pertabpur.—To-day I marched to Pertabpur, where the Regent of Sirguja, Raja Bindeshri Pershad Singh Rai Bhadur, C.S.I., resided. I found on arrival that he had not returned from an elephant-catching expedition which had engaged him for some time; but that he was expected, with some of his captives, on the morrow.

Pertabpur is but a small town, with a bazaar of trifling dimensions. There are indications of an attempt to lay it out after the ordinary pattern of Bengal stations, with planted roads, &c. The way in which the general population were ordered about by the Raja's officials, and their willing and contented obedience, as well as their civility and attention to me, had already attracted my notice; but here, at the capital, it was still more strongly developed. Of course this sort of treatment may, and sometimes does, merge into shameful oppression. I had, during this day, traversed wide tracts of arable land, of which no use is made in this thinly-populated country, and no doubt a better system would attract cultivators to it. The ordinary run of ryots are, I believe, however, in these native states, quite as well off as are those in the adjoining districts administered by the Government; but what cannot fail to strike the visitor to them, is the absence of men of substance—all are at about the same level. It is difficult for any man to accumulate wealth, but should one do so, the fact that the Raja is his heir by custom, prevents him from leaving his savings to his family, so they again must start afresh without capital. In some states the process of squeezing is carried on more than in others, and in these no man thinks it worth his while to attempt to rise above the general level. Here, where there was not much law and but a modified degree of justice, although I heard complaints of oppression, I could not find that the general standard of contentment was lower than it is in British territory; indeed I believe the contrary was the case. In British territory, the facilities possessed by the people for obtaining justice, or rather for having recourse to the courts, on account of trivial matters, is a never-ending source of ill-feeling and discontent. "Having the law" of an enemy is a common custom enough in British police courts. But the lower classes in the British Isles are far behind the natives of India in ingenuity in getting up wholly false and bolstering up utterly trivial cases.

January 8th.—Pertabpur.—This morning the whole town was

in great excitement, and numerous guns were fired off, as it was announced that the Raja was about to arrive with the first batch of captives. It being Sunday I remained in camp, and awaited the arrival of the procession. At about twelve o'clock it made its appearance, headed by a camel bearing two enormous kettle-drums, the beating of which by the rider caused a terrific noise; then followed a crowd of matchlock-men, who fired salutes from time to time.

After them came three kunkis, or tame elephants, each having two small wild ones in tow, the cable or stout rope attaching them being round the neck of the captive, and tied to a strong girth on the kunki. In this way the young ones were hauled unceremoniously along. They, for the most part, showed no signs of resistance; but if any of them happened to do so, they were soon brought to order by a smart cuff which the kunkis administered with their trunks. Following these were two kunkis each leading a medium-sized wild elephant, and then a larger tusker to which it had been necessary to attach two kunkis. All these were marched into the large mango-grove where my tent was pitched, and I learnt that they were to be tied up to trees in close proximity to it. This I did not object to, as it would afford me a means of watching their demeanor, and the methods of treatment adopted for their subjugation.

Shortly afterwards the Regent rode up to my tent, and his appearance, more particularly his well-worn Shikari costume of the Anglo-Indian pattern, at once assured me that he was a good fellow, and very unlike the ordinary run of natives,—and such, indeed, I soon found him to be. He was a truly courteous gentleman, without any humbug, save at times a slight assumed servility of manner.

During the afternoon the elephants were watered, and sugar cane, as a tit-bit, was given to some of the small ones which were already showing signs of docility. Others, however, were still very vicious, and I narrowly escaped being struck by pieces of branches which several of them deliberately flung at me with their trunks as I passed. This may be thought by some readers to be a traveller's tale; but those accustomed to the habits of elephants know that not only in this way, but also by kicking up gravel and stones, elephants employ projectiles against those whom they cannot reach.

In the evening the Raja came up again to my tent for a second visit. He presented me with a "*dalli*"* of fruit of considerable dimensions. It included a number of dishes laden with dried Cabul fruits, walnuts, &c. He remained so long talking, that, my table being laid, I at length asked him whether he would or could join me at dinner. To my intense astonishment he replied that he would with pleasure, but added: "What about to-morrow?" I said that I should be glad to see him again to-morrow at my table. "What about the day after that, and all the days which follow?" Again I replied, that though I was going to move forward on that day, he should always be welcome. "Ah!" he said, "that will not be sufficient for me. If I eat with you to-day, I shall be outcasted, and my own family will have nothing more to do with me, so that I shall have to become your daily guest for the rest of my life, and then, perhaps, the day will arrive when you, wearied with my company, will say, 'Darwaza bund' (the door is closed) when I come for the accustomed meal, and I shall be left friendless and to starve." Thus, ingeniously, he avoided giving a direct refusal to my invitation, and, so to speak, transferred the onus to my shoulders.

In a subsequent conversation he asked me much about my own private affairs, which I mention merely in order to allude to the peculiar agricultural form of expression he used when inquiring about my inheritance. "How many goats *(bukri)* did your father leave you?"

January 9th.—Pertabpur.—Although the Regent had much to occupy him on his return after his long absence, and the elephants required his unremitting attention, he nevertheless

* A *dalli* or more properly *daliya*, means a flat basket or tray upon which gifts are brought for presentation.

RAJA BINDESHRI PERSHAD SINGH RAI BHADUR, C.S.I.

insisted on giving me a beat for large game. Nothing was seen but a bear, which I knocked over, but it picked itself up and made off. Afterwards I was taken through the outer courts and rooms of the "Palace" and adjoining grounds; the buildings were mostly in an unfinished condition. In the central court a *nach* was performed by some strolling dancers from Benares. The Regent has the reputation of being very liberal in his largess to people of that class, and on the occasion of any family celebrations I was told that they swarmed down upon Sirguja in hordes from Patna, Arrah, and other towns in the Gangetic valley.

In the evening seven more wild elephants were brought in by the kunkis, which had been sent back for them to a depôt on the road where they had been left. Many of these elephants had terrible sores on their legs, from the fraying of the unaccustomed ropes by which they were tied up. The Raja, since his return, had not, for some reason (awaiting favourable omens, perhaps), entered the interior parts of his house; but had had a wigwam erected in the grove, not far from my tent, where he remained all night. At intervals, during the night, it was considered necessary to strike up the band in order to keep the elephants from going to sleep, and accustom them to the sounds. Large bonfires too were kept burning. Of course I did not sleep much on account of the din, but the Regent considerately apologised for the inconvenience to me, and had beforehand asked my consent.

January 10th.—Pertabpur to Dhurumpur.—The Regent at first insisted that it would be his duty to accompany me to the next camping ground; but, as his presence would be embarrassing during the heavy day's work I had laid out for myself, I prevailed on him to take his leave on the banks of a river a few miles south of Pertabpur. For the week following I was daily engaged in exploring the coal-field, and succeeded in finding a number of coal-seams, some of them being of considerable promise as sources of fuel. In the way of animal life, peacocks, monkeys, and crocodiles (the latter generally seen basking on the margin of deep pools, which were full of fish, in the bed of the Mahan river), were frequently met with; and, on one occasion, I came upon a wild dog, which immediately retreated into the jungle. Tigers' footprints in the sands of all the rivers were daily seen. Where the river was bounded by sandstone cliffs, as was occasionally the case, vast colonies of blue-rock pigeons were invariably found.

In the holes in these cliffs two species of owls of large size * were also very common. Unlike most other owls, both freely

---

* The Rock-horned Owl (*Ascalaphia Bengalensis*), and the Brown Fish Owl (*Ketupa Ceylonensis*).

take wing during the daylight, and I have often noticed them preceding me, flying from tree to tree, for long distances down these narrow gorges. They are easy to shoot, and I soon had more specimens than I knew how to dispose of.

During this period a slight attack of fever stopped my work for a day; but the season was an unusually healthy one, and few of my men suffered; though on my second visit to this part of the country, there was much sickness in my camp, as I shall have to relate hereafter. Rain held off in a wonderful way, although clouds collected almost every morning and evening. The consequent dryness was evidenced by the fact that the jungle fires, which are ordinarily deferred till the beginning of March, had already commenced.

January 9th.—Dhuria.—In a grassy plain near this place I saw the first herd of black buck which I had met with in Sirguja. During the day I discovered an underground river, which flowed through a tunnel, in a massive bed of sandstone, resting on a seam of coal which was laid bare in the bed of the river. My attention was first drawn to it as I was crossing over it, unconscious of its existence, by a flock of blue-rocks rising out of a hole in the ground in front of me. On descending into the tunnel I found traces which shewed that its cool recesses were places of resort for bears, but there were none at home just then. Possibly they may have slipped off as they heard me coming.

January 22nd.—Kuranji to Burio.—My plan of operations for the day, was to examine a series of small hills in the intervening country. This would be a pleasant change, I thought, from the daily plodding along river beds, some of which were very difficult to examine, owing to the steepness of the rocks on either side, the density of the vegetation at the tops, and the depth of the water in the pools, which frequently occupied the whole channel.

On the map, one of these hills was called *Bhal Pahar*, or the Bear hill; such names are common, and I did not attach any particular significance to the fact. On reaching it I ascended it by a narrow path, in order to examine a protruding ledge of rock. On arrival at this ledge, and while standing on a steeply sloping face of bare rock, I noticed that there were some cave-like excavations in a stratum of white clay underneath it; these I thought had probably been made by the villagers for obtaining the clay to use as a pigment, and I was just in the act of asking the coolies who accompanied me, whether such was the case, or whether they were bears' dens, when by a side glance I noticed a movement in one of them, which I thought was caused by a bat, which had been disturbed by our approach, flying round inside. In another moment the true cause was only too apparent, as I found myself confronted, at very close quarters, by an open-mouthed bear. Being unarmed, except that I had a geological hammer in one hand, and an alpenstock in the other, I executed a strategic movement of one pace to the rear, forgetting where I was standing, and with the result that I fell backwards on the sloping rock, my head pointing down hill. Out charged the bear, and I thought that the tribe of Bruin was about to be revenged upon me for what I had done to it. However, she rushed past me through my men, who gave her as wide a berth as possible, and down the path by which we had ascended. Picking myself up, I called to my rifle-bearer to hand me the weapon; but he delayed doing so so long that, before I could get a shot, the bear was careering through the jungle at the foot of the hill. My first shot was a palpable miss; the second may have hit, but I was not certain. Be this as it may, the bear got off. While considering what should be next done, I heard a low squealing sound, and, on descending the path, encountered a young cub scrambling back to the cave. It had evidently been dropped by its mother, whether because she had been hit by my second bullet, or whether it had been brushed off her back as she ran through the jungle, I cannot say. Its capture was effected by my lifting it off the ground by its long hair in such a way that it could not scratch or bite. It did not take long for the coolies to lash its little paws to a pole, which they carried between them; and, after my day's work was completed, it was introduced to camp life. Afterwards when its walking powers became somewhat improved, it used to follow the men on the line of march, and continued to do so until the end of the season.

In the evening, although not a little sore and stiff from my fall, I revisited the hill, hoping to have an opportunity of settling accounts with the bear. On this occasion, knowing the ground, I ascended from the opposite side of the hill, coming out on the ledge overhanging the cave; but the bear had not returned, and I failed to find any trace of her. While on the hill I saw several nilgai and some small deer in the surrounding jungles. In the morning, too, I had seen a boar; so there was no lack of variety in the game about, though I could not, in consequence of the necessity of constantly pushing forward, avail myself much of the information so acquired.

January 24th—Burio.—Frequently in this region I came upon people who, from the astonishment depicted on their countenances at my sudden appearance among them, had, I concluded, seldom set eyes on a European before. To-day, when crushing down the side of a pathless hill towards a cleared spot, some men who were engaged in cutting grass raised a shout to drive off what they conceived to be an approaching wild beast. They looked rather ashamed of themselves when I stepped into their midst.

February 1st.—Latori.—During the past week I had been steadily pushing southwards, demarcating the limits of the coal-field, to which I subsequently gave the name of the Bisrampur Field. Under this title it will be henceforth alluded to. To-day I was enabled to make a preliminary examination of the Pilka Hill, an isolated block which had attracted my attention from the time I had first entered the Sirguja basin. It proved to be physically and geologically similar to those which I have described on a previous page as occurring in the coal-fields of the Damuda Valley. In the jungle at its base I came on the tracks of an enormous wild elephant. The people told me it was then no longer in the neighbourhood.

At this place I was visited by the Raja of Lukanpur, Moheshri

Pershad, a cousin of the Regent. Though not possessing the manly character of the latter, he was a remarkably good specimen of a native, endowed with a most prepossessing manner. Subsequently I had several opportunities of improving my acquaintance with him.

February 4th.—Jamnuggur.—This morning I spent in examining a portion of the bed of the Rer, the most considerable of the rivers in this region, which, before it joins the Sone, absorbs a number of the minor streams—draining, in fact, a very wide tract of country. In its vicinity bird-life was very abundant. Among other species which I noticed there were two species of black stork, black ibises, mergansers, brahmini ducks, cormorants, ring plovers, kingfishers, peacock, bush quail, black partridge, &c. The common or grey partridge does not apparently occur in Sirguja, and jungle fowl are very rare and restricted to limited tracts. Nilgai and sambar were very abundant in the thick cover near Jamnuggur. Often when at work I used to drop my note-book and hammer to seize my rifle, in order to take a flying shot; but shots taken under such circumstances are rarely successful, though I shall have to record some exceptions to this rule.

February 5th.—Pilka.—To-day I ascended the Pilka Hill, or group of hills, the flat-topped summit of which is almost exactly 1,000 feet above the village. In the steeply-scarped sides the characters of the horizontal beds of red and white sandstones and conglomerates of which it is composed, are clearly apparent. The lowest bed, in a manner which is not common with the rocks of this age in other regions, rests unconformably, not only on the edges of the coal-measures, but also on the lowest or Talchir group of the sedimentary rocks, passing from them on to the old metamorphic or base rocks of the area.

Game had appeared to be so abundant, that I thought a beat here could scarcely fail to be productive; yet, though a wide tract of jungle on the slope of the hill was beaten, I saw nothing.

I was surprised to meet here a number of Brahmins from Upper India, who in preference to taking the circuitous Grand Trunk route far away to the north, had struck across country to find a short cut to Jugernath. The mere fact of their being *en route* to that place seemed to justify their demanding of me an alms. Being well-dressed and stalwart-looking men, very capable of taking care of themselves, I simply referred them to their co-religionists for assistance, at which they were not a little disconcerted, as they seemed to consider that their right to be aided when on this pilgrimage was indisputable.

February 16th.—Puputra.—Rain fell to-day for the first time this season. Its coming was very grateful, as the heat by day was often very severe for so early a date. On the other hand, its advent was not without this drawback, that, by filling the river-beds, it made the examination of the sections more difficult and less satisfactory.

After dinner, when writing at an hour somewhat later than that at which I usually went to bed, my attention was attracted by a peculiar crackling noise, and, on looking up, I saw that the tent was on fire. Rushing to the place, I managed to quench the rapidly-spreading flame with the water in a brass basin standing close by. The whole thing was over before the servants knew of it. Had I been asleep, the consequences might have been most serious. This danger I had not often thought of, though, with the numerous inflammable substances about, and the frequent use of lights and log fires, not to speak of smoking, it might be expected occasionally to occur. Curiously enough, however, to-day, when engaged in making cartridges, my thoughts had, I suppose prophetically, run a good deal on the subject. What surprised me most about the matter was the speed at which the canvas burnt.

February 21st.—Bhiti.—While examining the heavy forest country at the south-east corner of the Pilka Hill, I suddenly came upon an open glade at the further end of which, about two hundred yards off, there were four or five deer standing together. Without attempting to stalk I fired two shots from where I stood, the second shot being fired at some of them as they made off. The result I could not see, owing to the long grass; but on going to the spot I found two deer, one fully grown or nearly so, and the other about half-grown, in their death struggles. Both had been hit by the same bullet, which had first gone through the big one and then striking the smaller in the neck, had travelled up and broken its lower jaw. Strangely enough they proved to belong to different species. The large one being a red deer or barasingha and the smaller a sambar. In spite of the speed with which my Mahomedan chuprasies set about cutting their throats, the sambar died before they could make it into lawful food. However, as the Hindus said they could not eat barasingha, while sambar was for them lawful food, both sections in my camp were well supplied with meat, as were also some of the villagers who carried off both the bones and intestines, so that nothing was lost.

February 22nd.—Bhiti.—One of my men who followed me as gun-bearer to-day was a particularly stupid individual, never up to time with the gun as I might require it; indeed, I have generally found that except men are regular shikaris, they are fearfully obtuse about seeing game; gun on shoulder they plod along following one's steps, and are so flurried when suddenly called upon to act that many a chance of a shot is lost. On this occasion I saw first a splendid peacock entangled in a bush for a moment; turning suddenly, I seized my gun, but the man clung to it with such tenacity that I could not raise it from his shoulder till the peacock was off. I then told him to carry the rifle and give the other man the gun. A little further on I nearly walked on top of a porcupine, which made no attempt to bolt; now my gun was thrust into my hand when I ought to have received the rifle; but being at close quarters I gave the porcupine a charge of No. 5 which killed it on the spot. Afterwards I came upon a boar, when again the gun was brought forward, and the rifle was nowhere, in spite of my calling for it, and so the boar escaped.

February 23rd.—Bhiti to Bisrampur.—To-day I encamped in Bisrampur, the capital town of Sirguja. Here reside the Raja and his family. The former being out of his mind, as I have already stated, the management of affairs is vested in the Regent, who lives at Pertabpur. In the evening I was visited by the Raja's sons, two nice-looking but delicate zenana-reared boys. The elder repeated the English alphabet for my edification, and the glorification of his instructor. On the following evening I paid a return visit at the palace. As I walked under a canopy which had been erected in the central court, I saw a singular-looking old man in soiled raiment shuffling on to a stool, while he motioned me to a chair. This proved to be the Raja. A couple of very seedy-looking girls then commenced to dance and sing. My efforts to look pleasant before the surrounding crowd of servants and loungers cannot, I imagine, have been very successful.

In a lucid moment the Raja confided to me that he had once been learned in several languages, but that now he was an idiot. Every now and then he would turn and pronounce some gibberish to a mace-bearer who stood behind his seat. This functionary would receive the order with closed hands and a becoming degree of solemnity. All the time I underwent this ordeal I felt conscious that I was being narrowly watched by the Dowager Rani from some of the windows which commanded the court. This old lady enjoyed a reputation as a person of no little intelligence and business powers. As a promoter and instigator of intrigues her name was much mixed up with the politics of the district. A firm conviction that the Regent was determined to murder the mad Raja's children, with a view to the promotion of his own eldest son, was the source, I believe, of much of the trouble which she caused.

Some time after the event, I heard that the first prince of the blood, the simple-looking lad who had repeated his alphabet, having found that my large black retriever had a talent for destroying chickens, had invited the sweeper to take the dog to the palace where, on the flat roof, he was set on to worry a goose to death. I was, on all accounts, very much annoyed about this, but the only thing I could do was to punish the drunken scoundrel of a sweeper.

March 1st.—Burgaona to Dumali.—I was now marching

southwards into a wild valley between two spurs from the Main pât or plateau.

During the night there was a terrible storm, and the tent narrowly escaped destruction from the falling of a huge branch of a magnificent tamarind tree under which it was pitched. Later on I awoke, and noticed that the door-curtain or *purdah* did not lie square to the doorway. On getting up to ascertain the cause, I found that the pegs on one side had all drawn from the ground, which had been reduced to the condition of mud by the heavy rain, and the tent was lurching over, and with the next gust of wind would have fallen. The man "on guard" was carefully stowed away under the eaves of the tent, and was fast asleep. His slumbers were somewhat rudely disturbed, and all hands called up to put things to rights. The pegs were replaced by long poles which, driven down into the mud, afforded sufficiently strong supports for the ropes for the remainder of that tempestuous night.

March 4th.—Kusu to Lukanpur.—To-day I marched into Lukanpur, the residence of the Raja Moheshri Pershad, who is also known as the Lal Sahib. The little town had a somewhat civilized appearance, being laid out with roads, gardens, temples, tanks, &c. The Lal Sahib being away catching elephants, I was visited by his son, who, like his cousins at Pertabpur and Bisrampur, was very well mannered and intelligent. A very liberal "dalli" of supplies for the camp, &c., was sent in the Lal Sahib's name.

March 5th.—Lukanpur.—As I was walking up the bed of the Rer river at mid-day, about six miles away from Lukanpur, I saw an erect object before me on the bare sand, about four hundred yards distant; I could not at first make it out, though it appeared to be animate. On its moving a little I saw its tail, and then first became conscious that I was steadily walking in the direction of an enormous tiger which, seated on its haunches like a cat, was looking intently in the opposite direction. Immediately I called the men who were with me under the shelter of the bank, so as to be out of sight. Then to my disgust I found that only one barrel of my rifle was loaded, and the cooly with the ammunition was loitering behind. I beckoned to him in vain. Either he mistook the signal or caught sight of the tiger. He stood still, and call him I dare not. Thus much valuable time was lost which might have been employed in stalking the tiger through the jungle which overhung the place where I had seen him seated. During this interval he had become alarmed, and when I pushed on to where he had been I saw him making for the opposite bank by fording the river about two hundred and fifty yards further down. When up to his belly in the water I let fly at him with the rifle, but not having estimated the distance to be so great as it afterwards proved, the ball fell short and ricochetted over his back. With a roar he bounded through the remaining water, and scrambling up the bank was immediately lost to sight in the heavy jungle. Going on a little further I met a herd of tame buffaloes which had evidently been the objects of the tiger's fixed attention, and which prevented him from seeing me. These buffaloes were being tended, as they stood and rolled in the water, by a little girl of not more than six or seven years of age. There was not a man to be seen in the neighbourhood, and the nearest village was about a mile off. Afterwards, on passing through the village, I enquired from the people whether they were aware of there being a tiger in the neighbourhood, but they declared that they were not.

March 6th.—Lukanpur to Jajga.—I had now completed my preliminary demarcation of the limits of the Bisrampur coal-field, and was about to march southwards in order to ascertain the extent and relations of the other coal-fields which I expected would be found in that direction.

On the road I met the Lal Sahib, who was returning after a nine or ten days' absence from home, in which time he had captured two fine elephants, one of which, a tusker, was being marched along between two tame elephants, to which it was lashed, while a third tame one carried a stout rope attached to one of the tusker's hind legs; the other wild one was simply attached to one tame one, with which it walked along quietly enough.

Besides the above, there were two which had been the Lal Sahib's share of the Regent's large capture; one of these, though it had two men on its back, was not sufficiently steady to go alone; the other, a very small one, in the two months or so which had elapsed since its capture had become perfectly tamed, and obeyed orders with alacrity.

March 8th.—Luchmangunj to Sair.—At Luchmangunj there is a country house of the Lal Sahib, but the village consists merely of a few miserable hovels. In the bed of the Rer I found a little coaly shale, which in all probability was the cause of the locality being marked "coal-field" on some of the oldest maps; though no reference of a similar character was made to the vastly richer deposits in the area to the north.

March 10th.—Kesma to Matringa.—Two more marches down the much-narrowed valley of the Rer, brought me to Matringa, not far from which there is a well marked watershed, dividing the tributaries of the Sone on the north from those of the Mahanadi on the south. Here I found a mixed colony of Kaurs and Saontars. The former, though little, if at all, removed from the aborigines, are a sort of mongrel Hindus, and speak the same dialect of Hindi as that which is spoken in the districts respectively where they dwell. The Saontars are, by some authorities, believed to be an off-shoot—perhaps, indeed, the original stock—of the Sontals. Like the latter, they call themselves Manjis.

Subsequently I met several other colonies. Some of them knew the Sontals by name, but claimed to be quite distinct from them. They did not appear to have any distinct language; the words I took down from them were certainly all Hindi, but I had a suspicion that for some reason they were not telling me the whole truth in the matter. They are dark, coarse-featured people, but without any strongly-marked type of countenance. Their villages are very dirty and untidy. The huts are small, and are seldom enclosed by fences; there is an aspect of migratoriness, if I may use such an expression, about their habitations, notwithstanding that the groves testify to a long occupation of the localities. The houses are scattered about without any of the arrangement into streets so characteristic of the Sontals. They keep a few cattle and goats, but I saw no pigs.

March 11th.—Matringa to Porea.—About half a mile from Matringa the crest of a pass is reached. Thence there is a steep descent to a village called Amuldih. The path traverses weathered faces of sandstone, at a very high gradient, and is the most difficult piece of transit for elephants and laden cattle which I have ever encountered. The bullocks broke down completely, and some of their loads were brought in by coolies, and although the actual distance traversed was not more than six miles, some of the cattle did not make their appearance at camp till the evening.

The loss of elevation caused by this descent was evidenced by a very much increased temperature. Indeed, when I stood at the top of the pass at 7 a.m., a hothouse blast from the lower levels gave full warning of what was to be expected. I soon found that this wild tract, which becomes still wilder further west, includes an area in which the geological structure is very complicated, and will require much difficult and detailed work; but, after noting the general features, it was necessary for me to push onwards, as I had still many hundreds of miles to accomplish before the end of the season. I had now passed beyond the range of post, and for two months I remained almost completely shut out from communication with the civilized world. The events of the Franco-Prussian war were to me for the time a sealed book.

March 14th.—Mirigurha to Rabkob.—To-day I reached Rabkob, the principal town of a district called Udaipur (Odeypoor), which had been bestowed upon the Regent of Sirguja in recognition of his services during the mutiny. There is an indescribable aspect of depression and inactivity prevailing throughout this country. The cultivation is insufficient for the wants of the people, though good land abounds. They account for this by saying they have no plough bullocks. As no farrier was obtainable within a radius of a hundred miles, the Raja's horses being unshod, I had to shoe my horse myself. The rocky nature of the ground, and the brittle condition of the hoofs from the heat and dryness of the atmosphere, rendered the risk of his going lame, if left suddenly without shoes, too great. Fortunately I carried spare shoes and nails, but proper tools were wanting; however, with a botanical knife and a geological hammer I managed to do all that was necessary, and the shoes did not require removing for a month. Subsequently I induced my head sayce or groom to learn the art, and, as I now always carry a full supply of the necessary implements, and have with me a man who knows how to use them, I am independent of the slender resources of the wild regions in this respect.

March 19th.—Ududa.—In the Mand river and its tributaries I discovered a number of promising-looking coal-seams, besides many which were worthless. This new field, to which I have applied the name of the district, Udaipur, may, together with that about to be described, be of great value should a direct line of railway ever be made from Calcutta to Bombay.

March 20th.—Ududa.—To-day, while searching the stream-beds for coal-seams, I entered one, near the village of Jamangri, which for nearly a mile of its course traverses a deep gorge cut in sandstones; so deep and narrow is it, that in places there is only just room to walk along at the bottom, between vertical walls, which are in places forty feet high. Shortly after I had emerged into a more open, partly grass-grown, portion of the bed, one of the coolies who accompanied me suddenly said that he had been bitten on the foot by a snake. I examined the place and found that there were indeed two punctures, but they were wide apart (about an inch and a-half), and were, moreover, torn at the edges. Further, they were on the sole of the foot, in a position where it would be impossible for a snake to bite unless it had first lain on its back. I asked the man whether he had seen a snake, to which he replied that he had not, as it disappeared in the grass or water before he could catch sight of it. I then felt certain that the wounds were simply due to his having trodden on a bramble, and accordingly took no steps to arrest the imaginary poison. The other cooly complacently remarked, "He will be dead in five minutes," whereupon the man began to tremble violently, and held on to a tree for support. The chuprasies asked him whether he felt the leg heavy, and he replied in the affirmative, and added that he experienced a painful constriction across the chest. Believing that my diagnosis was correct, and considering that at any rate it was best to encourage the man, and laugh him out of his fear, I assured him that the punctures had been caused by thorns, and made him follow me at a brisk pace. After we had gone about half-a-mile or so, I asked him how he felt, to which he replied that he was quite well.

Mentioning this circumstance to my jemidar in the the evening, I remarked that I believed the man might have died, out of pure fright; he replied, "That is quite possible;" and then told me the following story:—On one occasion, when in the police, he was quartered in a barrack with a number of men. Just as they were going to sleep one night one of them cried out that he had been bitten by a snake. Whereupon the others jeeringly told him to go to sleep, and that there were no snakes there. Nothing more happened just then, but towards morning a bird in a cage suspended by a string, began to flutter and scream, and on one of the men going to ascertain the cause, he found a snake making its way by the string down to the cage. The man who said that he had been bitten, thereupon cried out, "I told you there *was* a snake!" and though six or seven hours had elapsed, he straightway fell down unconscious, and shortly afterwards died. I could not help thinking that these stories afforded a clue to some of the cases of "cure" of snake-bite by antidotes. The subjects may have exhibited symptoms, but had very possibly not been bitten at all.

The temperature at this season varied a good deal from day to day. On some days I was completely exhausted by 10 a.m., while on others it was possible to work from early morning till late in the afternoon.

March 24th.—Khurgaon to Chithra.—During the night, after I had gone to bed, there was a terrible row, caused, I found out, by the sweeper, who, drink being available in the village, had got drunk and, as usual, became quarrelsome. I had him brought out in custody and sent to his own quarters, and had no sooner settled myself to sleep, than the cook, who was also intoxicated, set up such a hideous chattering, that I was fairly roused again. Finding that messages were of no avail, I called him up, having heard his voice a considerable distance from the cooking-tent. However, he turned up from its vicinity in a few moments, attempting to look as if he had just risen from sleep; and as he told me a lie to support this pretence, I administered some summary justice, as the only means of restraining him from placing the whole camp in an uproar. The following morning he ostentatiously packed up his bundle and walked off. On my return from work, when still about half-a-mile from camp, I spied an individual sitting in a pensive manner under a tree. On coming closer I found it was the cook, who, on my enquiring what he was doing, replied that it was his intention, in consequence of the reprimand and loss of his *good* name, to die of hunger in the jungle. I ordered one of the men with me to bring him on to camp, and he came only too willingly. Had I thought of what I was doing, and not thus been caught in a trap, I should have wished him a prosperous journey through the jungle, and allowed him then to sneak back to his work, without giving him the opportunity of saying that he had been brought back by force.

I was now entering a new area of coal-measures, upon which I subsequently bestowed the name Raigurh and Hingir field. As some years later I examined it in greater detail than was possible on this occasion, I shall reserve a notice of its value and characteristics for a future page.

March 29th.—Jogra to Munund.—In this neighbourhood there were, in addition to the Kaurs, a tribe called Gours or Gores, who appear to be local representatives of the well-known Gonds of the Central Provinces. Like the Kaurs, they have no language peculiar to themselves.

April 1st.—Koraikela to Taraikela.—Among footprints of tiger, leopards, deer, &c., in the sands of the rivers, I saw to-day, for the first time, tracks of a wild buffalo. They were probably made by a solitary bull, who, judging from the spread of his foot, must have been of enormous size. The footprint measured seven inches from the apex of the cleft to the front. At night a tiger made himself heard in close proximity to the tent.

By going out twice a day I managed, in spite of the terrible heat which prevailed, to explore a wide area, and roughly lay down the geological boundaries of the different formations. The hills and forests surrounding the coal-field basin simply teem with game of all kinds; but I had no leisure to devote to sport, and if I had had, the cover was probably too dense to admit of much success. From the people, especially the Urias, who were becoming more abundant as I marched eastwards, I could get little or no information on the subject. Not unfrequently they point-blank denied that there were any animals.

I shall have much to say about Urias and their caste in future pages. I shall here only mention in illustration of it, that one night at an Uria village—during a terrible storm—shelter in a cowhouse for my horse was asked for. The people said the horse might come, but that the men in charge of it should not defile their threshold by crossing it.

April 23rd.—Tikripara.—I received a welcome bundle of newspapers to-day from the Deputy-Commissioner of Sambalpur, a station about forty miles off. I had, by messenger, represented to him my utter destitution in reference to news, in consequence of my having had to stop my own post from coming after me *viâ* Sirguja.

April 26th.—Ojelpur to Suadi.—Suadi, which I entered to-day, is the chief town of Gangpur. In reality it is only a very moderately-sized village, picturesquely situated on the banks of the Eeb or Hira (diamond) river, which I shall have to describe hereafter. The Raja was away being married; but from his representatives I received a most surly reception—the Uria element prevailing strongly in the population. I was compelled to blow them up in no mild terms, and subsequently to report them for their insolence and unwillingness to render the ordinary assistance.

Since that time the Raja has been imprisoned, or put under restraint, away from his own territory, in consequence of his having superintended, or at least been present at, the murder of a reputed witch.

April 27th.—Suadi to Jurangloi.—My great object now was to push over the ground which intervened between me and civilization as quickly as the heat, the worn-out state of the cattle, and the difficulty of moving invalids would admit of.

The Tikidar of Jurangloi, a *Teli*, prided himself much on his being a Hindu. He told me that the Raja had given him the option of either paying a percentage of his rent to aid the marriage expenses, or attending personally in the cortège. He elected the former, and remained at home. He enlarged pathetically on the defilement which he, as a Hindu, suffered from his neighbour's hens straying into his premises.

On the line of march, near the road, I noticed a curious fact which I had heard of before, but had never actually met with. Some white marks on the cut stump of an Asan tree (*Terminalia tomentosa*, W. and A.) caught my eye, and these on examination proved to be the sections of laminæ of calcareous matter, which alternated with the ordinary rings of woody growth. How this calcareous matter found its way into such a position it is difficult to say; but its occurrence is perhaps not more singular than that of silica in the joints of bamboos, where, as is well known, it sometimes forms what is called "tabasheer." The rocks about were gneisses and schists, and I could discover nothing in the soil to account for the peculiarity.

About a year previously, or in April, 1870, the fact of the occurrence of calcareous masses in timber had been brought to the notice of the Asiatic Society of Bengal, by Mr. R. V. Stoney, who stated* that many trees in the Orissa Tributary Mehals have pieces of limestone (or calcareous tufa) in fissures in them, but principally Asan (*Terminalia tomentosa*, W. and A.), Swarm (*Zizyphus*

---

* Vide P. A. S. B., May, 1870, p. 135.

rugosa, Lam.?), Sissu (*Dalbergia sissu*, Roxb.), and Abnus (*Diospyros melanoxylon*, Roxb.) In some cases, irregular-shaped pieces, seven inches long by two inches thick, were met with in the trunks at a height of about six feet from the ground. By the natives the lime is burnt and used for chewing with pawn. On examination it was found that there was no structure in these masses which would justify a conclusion that they had been formed by insects. Some included portions of decayed wood seemed to be cemented together by the lime.* Though I have not had an opportunity of consulting many botanists on the subject I believe it to be the case that the occurrence of deposits of carbonate of lime in timber has not been met with elsewhere. Oxalate of lime is sometimes met with in vegetable tissues, but in the form of carbonate, I am informed by Professor McNab that there is no recorded case of lime having been found, and such also appears to have been the opinion of the late Dr. Kurz.

April 29th.—Burgaon to Koringa.—Burgaon is a fine village belonging to a family of Brahmins. It is surrounded by exceptionally large groves of mangos, in which the most complete shelter for the camp was obtainable. A peculiar-looking hill, or ridge, of fine schistose gneiss, called Mahabir, lies to the south. In the crevices many thousands of blue-rock pigeons had their nests, while from the most inaccessible parts of the cliffs combs of wild bees' honey hung down in great abundance. To try to cut off some of these with a few rifle bullets was a great temptation. But though I have not had personal acquaintance with the wrath of wild bees when thus disturbed, I have too often heard and read of it to care to add it to my other experiences. Peacock and jungle fowl abounded in the cover at the foot of the hill, and the vicinity had all the appearance of being full of large game.

---

* A rough analysis of a small sample yielded to Mr. Tween the following result:—Organic matter, 8.4; soluble (mostly carbonate of lime), 89.8; insoluble (*silica, alumina*, &c.), 1.8 = 100.

In the evening I took down a vocabulary of the language of a people calling themselves Uraon Keriahs. The Keriahs proper undoubtedly belong to the Munda family; but here were Keriahs speaking a Dravidian language, many of the words being identical with those used for the same objects by the Paharias of the Rajmahal Hills. It seems probable that these people are really Mundas, who for some reason have adopted the Uraon language.

May 2nd.—Raiboga to Kulamora.—In one glade near the line of march I came upon the most wonderful collection of the brightest plumaged and, some of them, the rarest birds which are known to exist in the Chutia Nagpur Province. There were ground-thrushes, Paradise fly-catchers, shamas, scarlet minivets, bronze-winged doves, orioles, and kingfishers. The ground-thrushes I had never seen before, and was delighted to obtain some specimens.

May 3rd.—Kulamora to Tingina.—To-day we accomplished one step of the ascent to the higher level of the Lohardugga plateau. An epidemic of small-pox in the village I had intended to halt in compelled me to give it a wide berth.

May 4th.—Tingina to Kolabira.—The last half of this march was through very beautiful country. Mango-groves and dome-shaped hills of granitic gneiss being scattered about in rich profusion. The scene was sufficiently striking to call forth the admiration of my men.

May 5th.—Kolabira to Keluga.—What had for some days been threatening happened to-day. The pack-bullocks, unfed and uncared for by the men in charge, who were servants of the owner, became wholly incapable of bearing burdens, and the necessity of providing other means of carriage involved not a little trouble. Nothing would induce the village cartmen, of whom there were a few, to undertake the job, and the only other resource was to impress cooly labour, which ordinarily speaking would not have been difficult; but just at this time the Uraons had, by a new settlement of the land, been released from their bondage to the Zemindars and established as independent landholders. They had therefore shaken off all allegiance to the Zemindars, and it was impossible to effect anything through the instrumentality of the latter. There was a complete absence of cohesion throughout the communities.

May 8th.—Tilmi to Lodma.—Four marches, aggregating upwards of fifty miles, brought me from Kolabira to Lodma, from whence but one march remained to Ranchi. In spite of the difficulties about carriage, which were surmounted somehow, I put on all speed for the run into civilization. Since the 14th of December, or for five months less six days, I had not spoken English, and for about two months I had been even deprived of postal communication. My anxiety to put an end to this long journey and enter again into the society of my fellows will therefore be readily understood.

This evening two officers from Ranchi came out to Lodma in the hope of interviewing some bears said to live in that neighbourhood. With them I speedily made acquaintance, though at first they seemed to regard me in the light of a wild man of the woods. The bears were not to be found. Afterwards at dinner, for which our forces combined, I heard first of the French Communists and many other items of intelligence which were new to me. The next morning I marched into Ranchi, where I speedily found a haven of rest in the house of friends.

After a few days' rest I set out for the railway-station at Barakar, and on the 26th reached Calcutta, six and a-half months after I had started on this journey, in which my camp had marched upwards of 1,000 miles.

Two months later I was on my way to Europe for an all-too-brief absence from India of only three months' duration.

CHAPTER VIII.

SIRGUJA.

1871-72.

INSTRUCTIONS FOR SEASON—FORM CAMP AT BARAKAR—A VICIOUS DOG—THE FOLLOWERS OF A MADRAS REGIMENT—HUNDRU GHAG—RANCHI—SHELL-LAC—LAC-DYE—JASHPUR—LATERITE—ECLIPSE—SICKNESS IN CAMP—WILD DOGS—RIVER EROSION—FLORIKIN—SHOOT A BEAR, ETC.—SCENERY ON THE RER—THE MALABAR WHISTLING-THRUSH—THE COMMISSIONER HOLDS A DURBAR AT PERTABPUR—THE REGENT OF SIRGUJA—CONNECTION BETWEEN GEOLOGICAL STRUCTURE AND VEGETATION—LEOPARD CAUGHT IN A TRAP—RUMOURED DECLARATION OF WAR—THE ILLAQUADAR OF PATNA—HYMENOPTEROUS INSECTS—MUHURRAM PROCESSION—THE RAMGURH HILL—THE LUKANPUR LAL—THE BUNDER KOT—THE MAIN PÂT—GAUR OR BISON—TREE-CAT—PANGOLIN—FEVER—THE BISRAMPUR COAL-FIELD—MARCH TO RANCHI—RETURN TO CALCUTTA—VISIT DARJILING.

MY work for this season was to make a final survey of the Bisrampur coal-field, and of as much of the adjoining country in Sirguja as time would admit of. I was to be accompanied by a colleague who had recently joined the Geological Survey, and who was about to make his first acquaintance with field geology and our particular mode of life.

November 13th.—Calcutta to Barakar.—To-day I started by train from Calcutta, in advance of my companion, in order to make preliminary arrangements at Barakar for our start. Several days were occupied in getting together our baggage, and the elephants and carts for its conveyance to Ranchi.

Among our dogs there was one (a bull-terrier) of whose temperament we knew little, but he availed himself of the first opportunity of enlightening us on the subject. Being loosed in the evening with the other dogs he refused to follow us, but took up his position in the verandah of the bungalow, from whence, when our backs were turned, he made a most savage and unprovoked onslaught on the cart-bullocks, one of which he at last pinned by the throat, and the terrified animal stampeded across country. With great difficulty we wrenched the dog's jaws open, and set the unfortunate bullock at liberty, and having given the dog a sound flogging let him go, whereupon he immediately repeated the whole performance, and, when taken off the bullock, attacked the horses which were tethered close by. One of them breaking its head-stall, and dragging the pegs to which its heel-straps were attached, got loose and galloped off into the plain with all the ropes dangling after it, and the whole of our dogs in pursuit. Fortunately the horse was recaptured without having suffered any injury, and we then proceeded to try the culprit. Taking into consideration that his next exploit might be an attack on the elephants, an event which might not improbably be attended with loss of human life, we pronounced sentence of death, which was shortly afterwards carried out.

November 17th. — *Barakar to Rugonathpur.* — To-day we started on a succession of long marches in order to get over the road *viâ* Purulia to Ranchi, 120 miles distant, with as little delay as possible. The weather was superb, the country between Purulia and Ranchi very beautiful, and the companionship of a colleague very pleasant to me.

On the banks of the Subanrika at Sili we found an encampment of the followers of the 10th Madras Native Infantry. The regiment itself, 600 strong, was under orders for Burmah, and the followers, numbering about 5,000, were being sent to a depôt in the Madras Presidency. This extraordinary disproportion between the fighting power and impedimenta is, I believe, a common characteristic of Madras Regiments. The 10th had been for seven years at Ranchi, where the families had increased and multiplied, and long strings of carts on the road were packed full of children. There were also numbers of old women on the road, some of whom, to judge from their appearance, might have been great-great-grandmothers. Some of the stragglers in the evening laid themselves down on the road near where we encamped, a few miles beyond Sili, and we had to make some arrangements for their safety during the night, as the place was in the beat of a man-eating tiger.

November 23rd.—Lota to Jona.—While our camp proceeded along the road we took a round of about twenty-five miles in order to visit the Hundru Ghag waterfall, which I had seen six years previously. The view from the foot of the fall is less effective than that from its top when looking down the valley. A refreshing swim in the hollowed-out basin at the base enabled us to accomplish our long walk without suffering from over fatigue. Two days later we reached Ranchi, where we were at once installed in the house of a friend. As no more cart roads would be met with we were compelled to dismiss the carts, and make the necessary arrangements for carriage by pack-bullocks. A better lot than those I had with me last season were fortunately obtainable. A severe loss was occasioned us at the last moment by the unexpected recall of one of the three elephants which had only been lent to us.

November 29th.—Ranchi to Lodma.—This morning, before leaving the station, we visited a shell-lac manufactory, and as the method by which that useful article of commerce is prepared, and the source from which it is derived are not generally known, I shall endeavour to convey what I know of the subject as briefly as possible.

Lac (or as it is called in Hindustani *lah*,) is secreted by an insect (*Coccus lacca*) on the branches and twigs of certain jungle trees. The principal of these are the khusum, plas, and bier.* The lac from the first-mentioned, the khusum, is more highly esteemed than that from the others. To some extent the lac is found occurring, so to speak, spontaneously, and is collected by the forest tribes, and brought by them to the fairs and bazaars for sale. Where, however, there is a regular trade in stick-lac, propagation of the insect is systematically carried on by those

---

* *Schleichera trijuga*, *Butea frondosa*, and *Zizyphus jujuba*.

who wish for a certain and abundant crop. This propagation is effected by tying small twigs, on which are crowded the eggs or larvæ of the insect, to the branches of the above-named species of trees. These larvæ are technically called "seed." The larvæ shortly after sowing spread themselves over the branches, and, taking up positions, secrete round themselves a hard crust of lac which gradually spreads till it nearly completes the circle round the twig. At the proper season the twigs are broken off, and we must suppose them to have passed through several hands, or to have been purchased directly from the collectors by the agents of the manufacturer. On arrival at the factory, they are first placed between two powerful rollers which, by a simple arrangement, admit of any degree of approximation. The lac is then crushed off and is separated from the woody portions by screening; it is next placed in large tubs half-full of water and is washed by coolies, male or female, who, standing in the tubs, and holding a bar above with their hands, stamp and pivot about on their heels and toes until, after a succession of changes, the resulting liquor comes off clear. Of the disposal of the liquor drawn off at the successive washings I shall speak presently. The lac having been dried is placed in long cylindrical bags of cotton cloth of medium texture, and which are about ten feet long and two inches in diameter. These bags when filled have somewhat the appearance of an enormous Bologna sausage. They are taken to an apartment where there are a number of open charcoal-furnaces. Before each of these there is one principal operator and two assistants. The former grasps one end of the long sausage in his left hand, and slowly revolves it in front of the fire; at the same time one of the assistants, seated as far off as the sausage is long, twists it in the opposite direction. The roasting before the glowing charcoal, soon melts the lac in the portion of the bag nearest the operator's hand, and the twisting of the cloth causes it to exude and drop into a trough placed below. The troughs which I saw in use were simply leaves of the American aloe (*Agave Americana*). When a sufficient quantity, in a molten condition, is ready in the trough, the operator takes it up in a wooden spoon and places it on a wooden cylinder some eight or ten inches in diameter, the upper half of which is covered with sheet brass.* The stand which supports this cylinder gives it a sloping direction away from the operator. The other assistant, generally a woman, now steps forward holding a strip of the Agave or Aloe between her hands, and with a rapid and dexterous draw of this the lac is spread at once into a sheet of uniform thickness which covers the upper portion of the cylinder. The operator now cuts off the upper edge with a pair of scissors, and the sheet is then lifted up by the assistant who waves it about for a moment or two in the air till it becomes quite crisp. It is then held up to the light, and any impurities, technically "grit," are simply punched out of the brittle sheet by the finger. The sheets are laid upon one another and the tale, at the end of the day, is taken, and the chief operator paid accordingly,—the assistants receiving fixed wages. The sheets are placed in packing-cases, and when subjected to pressure break into numbers of fragments. In this fresh state the finest quality is a very beautiful object having a rich golden lustre. On seeing it thus, one cannot help feeling regret that it is not nice to eat—the best Everton toffee never looked more tempting. The above is the history of shell-lac, from its birth in the jungle to its appearance in the world as the commercial article. From the manufacturer it passes through the broker's hands to the merchant, and from him again to the manufacturers of varnishes, sealing-wax, and other commodities of which it is an ingredient.

The dark red liquor resulting from the washing above described, is strained, in order to remove all portions of woody fibre and other foreign materials. It is then passed into large vats, where it is allowed to settle; the sediment is subjected to various washings, and at last allowed to settle finally, the supernatant liquor being drawn off. The sediment, when it is of

---

* In some places the freshly-cut, smooth, cylindrical stem of the plantain is used for this purpose.

the proper consistency, is placed in presses, from which it is taken out in the form of hard dark purple cakes, with the manufacturer's trade-mark impressed upon them. This constitutes what is known as lac-dye. By the addition of mordants, this dark purple substance yields the most brilliant scarlet dyes, which are not inferior, I believe, to those produced by cochineal.* The dye which is thus separated from the lac by washing is said to be the body of the insect, not a separate secretion.

In the above description I have given the methods in practice in Ranchi. At Mirzapur, Jabalpur, and elsewhere where lac is made, the details of preparation may be somewhat different. At first sight it would seem that some mechanical arrangement would be more efficacious and economical for washing and separating the lac from the dye than the present system; labour is, however, so cheap, that this is not the case. The pay of the women per diem is from one penny to three half-pence; and of the men, from three half-pence to two pence. I inquired whether the feet of the coolies did not suffer in this work, and was told that at first they did, but not latterly. Whether by a process of natural selection this result has been arrived at, or, like the historical eels, they have become used to it, I cannot say; be that as it may, I saw a number of women and young girls at work, who did not complain of sore feet. Owing to the sudden and enormous oscillations in the price of lac in the London market, the trade is a somewhat risky one, and the profit made one year may be more than swamped in the losses of those which next succeed it.

An account of another insect which occurs in Chutia Nagpur, may suitably be introduced here. The female, as is also the case with the lac insect, alone forms the secretion. The resulting substance is, however, of a very different character, being, in fact, a white wax, which is found in small masses on the twigs and

* The introduction of aniline dyes has served to depreciate the value of lac-dye to an enormous extent.

branches of several trees, more particularly on the arjun (*Terminalia arjuna*, Bedd). The name of the insect is *Ceroplastes ceriferus*, and it is allied to an insect called *Pela* by the Chinese, which is propagated in China, the wax having there a considerable commercial importance, being more particularly employed in the manufacture of candles which are used in Buddhist temples. The Indian wax-insect has never, I believe, been propagated, nor has the wild product ever been collected in quantity. It seems to be—though undoubtedly of value—a substance which would scarcely repay an expenditure of European time and capital; but were the natives to take up its cultivation they might very possibly make it a very profitable undertaking. The wax is soluble, or nearly so, in boiling alcohol, and also in benzine and ether, but is only very partially dissolved in turpentine and carbonic sulphide. Its composition is C_{13}, H_{26}, O. The above facts are chiefly derived from a report drawn up by Mr. F. Moore, of the British Museum, from specimens forwarded by Mr. Peppé to the India Office for examination. Mr. Moore mentions that the insect is described in a paper by Dr. J. Anderson, which was published in the Royal Society's Philosophical Transactions so long ago as 1791. I may add that I have found the wax at many widely-distant points throughout the division, but can call to mind none where it is more abundant or more suitably situated for experimental cultivation than on the arjun trees which grow upon the embankment of the Purulia Lake.

December 2nd.—Jeriah to Kamdera.—At Kamdera to-day, my companion secured for me a specimen of an extremely rare bird, which had not previously been obtained by me, though Dr. Jerdon, in his "Birds of India," had prophesied that it would probably be found in Chutia Nagpur. It was the spotted grey creeper (*Salpornis spilonota*, Frankl.). Subsequently I obtained specimens in Sirguja and Sambalpur; but the bird is still a rarity in collections, and is therefore deserving of prominent notice.

Daily marches, *viâ* Palkot, Marda, Lodam, &c., brought us to Jugdispur, the residence of the Raja of Jushpur, in whose territory some of the largest specimens of gold from alluvial washings hitherto obtained in Bengal have been procured. His estate is a small one, not yielding more than £600 a year, if so much; yet he manages, with the aid of two elephants, to keep up a becoming degree of state. Up to this place the principal rocks were coarse granitic and porphyritic gneisses, forming hills and domes with fantastic outlines. Here these outlines were much modified by a thick crust of laterite, the result being very tame scenery, and this became still more the case a few days later.

December 12th.—Sunkiari to Sanna.—Our route to-day lay along the winding valley of the Eeb, a river I have already mentioned on a previous page. The scenery is very drear and wild, owing to the sparse jungle on the laterite-crusted gneiss hills which bound the valley. When we had traversed about one-third of the way, we stopped to watch the great eclipse of the sun, which, it will be remembered, took place on this date. The limb of the moon reached to about the centre of the sun, and the valley looked very dismal while the light continued subdued. At Sanna, a miserable village, the Sirdar or head man welcomed us most hospitably. He had already been at our previous camp, but had gone on during the night to prepare for our reception. He presented us with a couple of pairs of *gaur** horns, one of which measured five feet, with the curve, from tip to tip. The *gaur* had been shot in the highlands of Jushpur.

December 13th.—Sanna to Champa.—The route to-day lay through a similar valley to that just described, the granitic rocks only cropping out here and there through the thick covering of laterite. Three miles south of Champa, we crossed an important watershed, which separates some of the sources of the Eeb, which flows south to the Mahanadi, from those of the Kunhur, which joins the Sone. I got a bad fall near the camping-ground, which crippled me for many days. In going across country after a fox, my horse put his foot in a hole which had been made by a bear searching for white ants, the result being that he came down, and

---

* The bison of Indian sportsmen—*Gavæus gaurus*, Ham. Smith.

before I was free of him I received a number of kicks all over the body, and one which laid my head open. This prevented me from examining the country in the vicinity of the line of march for the next few days, an unfortunate circumstance, as there were many points of geological interest to be worked out. Already my companion had had a slight attack of fever, and there were a number of men on the sick-list, owing to the extreme unhealthiness of the Jushpur valleys. The fever proved to be of an unusually stubborn type, and many of the men had relapses ere long.

December 17th.—Sawari to Kumdih.—To-day, as we were going along a road to the Mahan river, a party of seven or eight wild dogs (*Cuon rutilans*) bounded out of one strip of jungle, and were making for another when they caught sight of us, and immediately stopped and formed a group, all eyeing us curiously. We advanced on them; but until we were within a hundred yards or so they shewed no sign or intention of being disturbed in their contemplation. A short bark in the jungle ahead of them, from a terrified sambar, at once apprised us of the position of affairs, and that the dogs had been running him down when they were arrested by our appearance. We were now fairly within the Sirguja basin, and the examination of the coal-measure rocks afforded us abundance of work. Tiger tracks were to be found in the sands of every stream; but the people did not complain of any injury being caused by tigers. We did not fail to revisit the scene of my last year's adventure with the enraged she-bear, but found the cave unoccupied.

December 31st.—Kiunra.—To the north-west of Kiunra the Mahan river enters a gorge which cuts through lofty ranges of crystalline rocks, which limit the coal-field on the north. That this river, the Kunhur, and the Rer, should thus penetrate a solid barrier of hills by a series of gorges is a remarkable fact, which admits, however, of a simple explanation. In times, geologically speaking, not very far distant, the central Sirguja basin was filled up to a considerable height with sedimentary rocks, younger than the coal-measures; the elevation of these served to establish a fall in the drainage to the north, and the rivers cut deep channels for themselves from above. Subsequently the soft and easily-eroded sandstones were removed by the action of rain and rivers; but the hard crystalline rocks through which the passes had been thus established offered greater resistance to the eroding action, and survived to form the ridges which exist at the present day. It is certain that no river, by simply battering against this barrier, could ever have cut through it.

Near Kiunra I shot a Florikin (*Sypheotides auritus*, Lath.) This, though a common enough bird in parts of the Ganges valley, was never before obtained in Chutia Nagpur, and Dr. Jerdon had given it as his opinion that it avoided that hilly region.

January 9th.—Punri.—For some days our camp had been accompanied by a son of the Bhaya or Zemindar of Jhilmilli, who was very anxious to show us some sport while we remained in his neighbourhood. Hitherto we had been unsuccessful, but to-day, in the afternoon, after our morning's labours were completed, we had better luck. We first beat a small hill near the camp. Soon after the beaters had commenced their work, I saw a bear in a very unhappy state of mind scrambling up and down the hill. I then lost sight of him, but as the shouting of the men advancing to the crest of the hill drove him forward, he appeared close to my machan, just giving me time to turn myself round and get a shot at him, which luckily caught him in the shoulder; but as, in spite of the severity of the wound, he appeared to be making off, I got down, followed him up, and despatched him. In the next beat my companion shot a hyæna. On the following day we beat the same hill, and the beaters picked up the body of a young leopard, which had apparently been killed a short time before by another of its own species. It was marked with bites on the throat and other parts of the body. Our own bag consisted of some peafowl.

January 12th.—Chungaro.—In the evening some of the villagers—Kaurs they were, I believe—entertained us with a dance, which was very different from anything seen among the

Sontals or Kols. A number of men performed a kind of "lady's chain," striking together, as they passed one another, pronged sticks which they carried in their hands. By foot, hand and voice, the time given by a tom-tom was most admirably kept.

January 19th.—*Datma.*—My colleague, James Willson, had been suffering from constant recurrence of fever, and about this time I had also to go on the sick list with fever and ague for a couple of days. As I have mentioned on a previous page, last year's experience of this country had led me to suppose that it was healthy. This year it proved to be the exact converse.

In some of the grassy plains about here there are a few Antelopes or black buck, constituting a detached and outlying colony, of which there are several in this general tract. In the rivers, and occasionally in the swampy paddy-fields, there were vast flocks of black-backed geese.* When feeding thus on rice the young birds are very welcome additions to the larder.

January 31st.—*Jhilmilli.*—Leaving the camp with my companion at Jhilmilli, I went for a three days' tour northwards up the valley of the Rer to a village called Korpa, a place very difficult of access. The scenes I came upon in the beautiful gorges were often very animated. There were parties of otters fishing and diving in the deep pools, while here and there crocodiles tumbled into the water at the sound of my approaching footsteps. Now and then a troop of brown monkeys would be seen sunning themselves on the rocks, and from time to time peafowl would rise startled from the open spaces on the banks. In the trees above, flocks of the lovely scarlet minivet (*Pericrocotus speciosus*, Lath.) were often seen. A land tortoise of a rare species and of unusually large size was the great zoological capture of the day. The geology proved more intricate, and consequently more interesting, than I had anticipated; for, in addition to the sedimentary and metamorphic rocks, I met with

---

* *Sarkidiornis melanotus*, Penn.

great sheets of overflowing columnar basalt; this being, therefore, one of the outlying regions of that volcanic activity which during the cretaceous period covered hundreds of thousands of miles of Western India with basalt or trap.

February 7th. — Kharapara. — To-day when exploring the Manickmara river for coal-seams, and while ascending a series of step-like cascades over the beds of massive sandstone, I shot a specimen of the Malabar whistling-thrush (*Myiophonus Horsfieldi*, Vigors). This may at first appear to the reader to be a very trivial fact to make the subject of special record; but before this discovery the bird was believed to be found only in Southern India and Ceylon, and, together with a small mammal called a tree-shrew (*Tupaia Elliotti*, Waterhouse), is regarded by Mr. Wallace, in his work on the "Geographical Distribution of Animals," as a characteristic species of his Ceylon sub-province. The discovery of both bird and mammal over a wide tract of Peninsular India necessitates their exclusion from the list of forms limited in range to that sub-province.

February 9th.—Kharapara to Pertabpur.—News having been received that the Commissioner of Chutia Nagpur had arrived at Pertabpur, on his annual tour, I rode in there, a distance of thirty miles, in order to pay him a visit, and witness a ceremonial at which it was intended to reward the Regent for good services done a few years previously. My companion was too weak from fever to attempt the journey. The first ceremony I did not witness, as it took place in the interior of the palace, to enter which the Commissioner was alone invited. Here, in the presence of the Rani and other female members of the household, a handsome gold watch was presented to the Regent on the part of the Government of Bengal. A grand durbar was afterwards held, at which the chieftains of all the surrounding territories were present, and the Regent, who was got up in gorgeous apparel, was again presented with the same watch, while the "Bhaya" of Jhilmilli received a sword and shield. I could not help remarking that the crescent and other ornamentation on these weapons would have been more appropriate had the recipient been a Mahomedan instead of a Hindu. The Regent, though gratified at the recognition of his services, was not altogether satisfied with his gift—a watch being, he said, of no use to him—a cannon would have been more to his taste. Subsequently the Commissioner obtained for him a horse, a double-barrelled rifle, and an elephant. Now it may be thought that sending an elephant to him, when he was catching wild ones by the score, was like sending coals to Newcastle. But of all the gifts this was the one that gave him most pleasure, since the bestowal of an elephant by the paramount authority is, according to native etiquette in such matters, an act of special favour. The services for which these gifts and honours were bestowed were characteristic of this really remarkable man.

A few years previously (1868), the state of Keonjar, in Orissa, owing to disputes about the succession, was the scene of an insurrection or rebellion, and troops, under the orders of the Commissioners of Orissa and Chutia Nagpur, were sent to establish order. While operations were going on somewhat slowly, owing to the unsuitability of the Madras sepoys for the work, which consisted in hunting up the Bhuia rebels among the trackless hills and forests, Raja Bindeshri, Regent of Sirguja, marched into camp with some hundreds of his retainers, whom he had brought about 250 miles to take part in the war. Having made a salaam to the Commissioner, he expressed himself as feeling hurt at not having been bidden to the aid of the Government, and immediately asked for some work for himself and his men. He was given the charge of a pass, and he immediately commenced a series of attacks on the villages and hiding-places of the rebels. His men were quite at home in that kind of country, and to their operations the authorities attributed in a considerable degree the speedy termination of the war. What Bindeshri's commissariat arrangements were, and how he fed his men, were best known to himself. He refused all pecuniary assistance, saying that he had only been rendering the Government the service and aid he was bound to do, and which they had a right to expect from him. For his services in the great mutiny he had been previously created a Companion of the Star of India, and given the State of Udaipur. The nature of these services also merit record from one particular point about them. With his own men he captured a number of mutineers, some of whom he shot or hung, others he mutilated, cutting off their noses and ears. When, after the establishment of order, these facts were reported by the Commissioner to the Government, it became a matter of consideration how Bindeshri should be dealt with. The mutilation was considered by the then Lieutenant-Governor of Bengal to debar the Raja from receiving all reward, if it did not even render him liable to punishment. Taking the lives of his prisoners might have been a necessary act, but mutilation could certainly not be so regarded. In the end it was determined to overlook the latter, and Bindeshri received the title I have mentioned. In Bindeshri's death which took place about three years ago (1876) the Government lost a strong supporter in these wild highlands. Though a hard and unscrupulous ruler in his own territory, he was regarded with a considerable degree of admiration by the people of Sirguja, and his reputation was widespread throughout Chutia Nagpur.

February 12th.—Karapara to Badsari.—In the course of my work to-day, when following up the rocky bed of a stream in a secluded valley, I came upon a party of villagers who had just discovered the carcase of a fine stag sambar, which one of them had shot with an arrow four or five days previously. They were ultimately led to the discovery by observing the vultures soaring over and descending to this spot in the jungle. The meat was somewhat high, and had been torn by the vultures and jackals, but was evidently considered by the villagers to be still good for human consumption, as they were preparing for its removal to the village.

In this vicinity I noticed a very striking connection to exist between the geological structure and the vegetation. In the midst of general forest there were some areas upon which the olibanum or frankincense tree* held the mastery. These areas I found on examination coincided exactly with the limits of the outcrops of a particular group of rocks which underlie the coal-measures, and are considered to have had a glacial origin, or at least to owe their peculiar character to the existence of drift ice at the time of their deposit. This is by no means the only instance where I have found relationships of this kind to exist. Such cases serve to illustrate how a knowledge of botany may be of service to the field geologist.

February 16th.—Kusmussi.—My companion's constantly recurring attacks of fever had produced such weakness that he was now quite unable to do a hard day's work. With the heat increasing daily, and our line of march carrying us steadily further and further away from Ranchi, the nearest station, I could not but feel that his remaining in the field any longer would be attended with great risk. Accordingly I recommended him to set forth at once and get back to Calcutta as quickly as he possibly could. This morning, taking with him the native doctor, one elephant, and sixteen men, most of them invalids, who were to return to their homes, he took his departure, and reached Ranchi in about fifteen days. Thus, once more, I found myself left alone to carry on my work for the remainder of the season. For many days I felt severely the loss of my colleague's companionship.

February 19th.—Unchuri to Kalwa.—In the evening of this day the carcase of a very fine leopard was brought into camp. It had been killed at Kusmussi, where we had been encamped. For two nights successively it had visited the village, and on each occasion had abstracted a porker from a pig-sty. A trap made on the following principle was accordingly set for it. In a small circular enclosure, made with stakes, a dog is placed as a bait, and an outer circle of stakes, provided with a narrow entrance and door, opening inwards only, surrounds this inner one. The

---

* *Boswellia thurifera*, Roxb.

animal entering, passes round the circle, closing the door before it, and, as it cannot turn in the narrow passage, becomes a prisoner. During the night the leopard had been thus caught; and an old man who lived close by hearing its struggles, went out with a heavy cudgel with which he intended to deal the animal a mighty blow. Raising it with both hands over his head, he was just about to bring it down when the leopard sprang forward, and managed to reach and tear him on both elbows. Other men coming up the leopard was soon despatched. Having rewarded the old man and dressed his wounds, which did not appear very severe, I let him return to his home. Three days later I was sorry to hear he had died of tetanus.

February 22nd.—Gongoti.—This morning rumours were flying about that there was likely to be a disturbance in the country to the west, between Bindeshri the Regent, and the Raja of Rewa. It appeared that Bindeshri had become so keen about elephant-catching that he had become somewhat oblivious to the rights of *meum* and *tuum*, and had established a *kedah* across the frontier in the Rewa jungles. While away at Pertabpur to receive the Commissioner, his agent was called upon by the Raja of Rewa either to desist from the catching of elephants in his territory or give an undertaking to hand over half the captives. The representative replied that he was unauthorised to promise anything on behalf of his master, but that, in the meantime he intended to continue operations. The Rewa Raja thereupon arrested the whole party, and it was reported that Bindeshri was now going off post-haste to wage war upon Rewa and *vi et armis*, release his people. It was said that for this purpose he was taking his artillery, one brass gun, with him. The Sirguja people were in great distress at the prospect of being engaged in actual warfare. They thought it hard enough to be dragged away from their homes to aid in the elephant driving, some of them being absent for three months, during which time each village had to keep its own people supplied with food. What actually happened, however, was that Bindeshri made friends with the Rewa Raja and agreed to make over to him half the elephants which were caught, while the latter promised to render material aid. During the several seasons which were devoted to elephant-catching by Bindeshri, I believe something like one hundred were captured. When I state that this was effected with men and tame elephants who had had no previous training for the work, his energy will be all the more apparent.

February 28th.—Patna.—I was now in a Zemindari called Patna, where the Illaquadar received me well, and made arrangements for several beats. When returning from one of these I invited him to sit on my elephant in order that I might talk to him; besides, as he was an old and rather fat man, I did not like to see him hobbling behind. On his taking his seat I observed not a few significant smiles pass between the men of his establishment. When he came to my tent I had given him a chair, and the result of all this civility was that in a few days both he and his people changed in manner towards me, losing the respect they would have had for me if I had treated him more "*haut en bas.*" During the ceremonial at Pertabpur he had been kept very much in the background, Bindeshri treating him as being vastly his inferior. The principal races in his illaqua are, he told me, Kaurs, Rajwars, Gours, Pankas,* and Bhuias. Some of the last-named whom I saw were of an inky blackness, but were powerful-looking mountaineers. The Illaquadar is himself a Gour, which no doubt accounts for his degraded social position. He denied that the Gours were connected in any way with the Gonds of the Central provinces. In this opinion he was undoubtedly wrong; but his holding it illustrates what I have elsewhere alluded to as the difficulty of obtaining information on such subjects by direct enquiries.

The chief exports from this and indeed all the adjoining tracts

---

* The Pankas are weavers; both these and the Rajwars I found bury the bodies of unmarried persons, while those of persons who have contracted matrimony are burnt. In the hilly regions on the north I met with colonies of Baigas; generally these people are found singly in the villages of other tribes where they exercise priestly functions.

are ghi, dhuna (a kind of tar), obtained by ringing the sal tree, kutch or catechu, and tikur or wild arrowroot. Lac is not cultivated, but the wild lac is collected to a small extent.

February 29th.—Patna.—To-day my condition of isolation and defective postal arrangements was exemplified by the fact that three weeks after the event I first heard of the assassination of Lord Mayo. Wherever in the habitable globe the telegraph reached to, the details had long since been discussed, but to me the fact was only now made known.

March 18th.—Kandrai.—The weather had been very changeable up to this, some days being fearfully hot, while others were cloudy and fairly cool for outdoor work. Storms were not unfrequent in the evenings. At this season several species of hymenopterous insects were engaged in building cells for the deposit of their eggs and in which the larvæ grow. The nooks and corners formed by boxes and furniture afford them suitable places for the erection of these structures built of mud, which the insect brings in the form of small pellets and then fashions into shape making many journeys to the nearest moist ground. The cell when completed is stocked with a larder of grubs and caterpillars in a state of torpor, which is produced probably by a sting. The egg is deposited and the entrance closed by a last pellet of mud. In this neighbourhood I shot several rare species of birds for Chutia Nagpur, including two species of Bee-eater or Merops (*M. Swinhoei* and *M. Philippensis*) and the Small-billed Thrush (*Oreocincla dauma*).

March 20th.—Katona to Jamgala.—My Mahomedan servants, hearing that there was to be a Muhurram procession in Lukanpur to-day, asked for permission to go and take part. I was somewhat astonished to hear that the Lal, as also the Raja of Pertabpur, supply funds for the expenses—the Mahomedan population being too small and poor to furnish them themselves. Hindus and the general population of the district assemble from long distances to witness the ceremonies. This shewed an amount of religious toleration very creditable to the parties concerned.

March 23rd.—Khudri.—Early this morning I started with the

intention of giving the whole day to the exploration of the geology and antiquities of the Ramgurh Hill, which is a very prominent object in the scenery. Two miles south of Khudri we passed through a miserable Gour hamlet called Saontari, soon after which the path became almost obliterated. Proceeding through a tangled mass of charred and smouldering branches and logs, where a jungle fire had passed, we at last emerged on a piece of flat ground shaded by a few mango and ebony trees, and bounded on the south by a perpendicular wall of rock several hundred feet high. At the base of this wall an unusual luxuriance of the vegetation at once attracted attention, ferns, figs, and other moisture-loving plants being abundant. On advancing a little further the cause of this luxuriance became apparent, as a sort of grotto opened to view. There, from a fissure in the massive bed of sandstone, a constant stream of pure water gushes forth in so strange a way that it is no cause for wonder that the natives regard it as evidence of the divine presence. I found the water refreshing, but not cool, at the same time its temperature was not higher than that of the surrounding atmosphere. A previous visitor had described it as being so. Possibly the discrepancy may be accounted for by the fact that our visits were at different seasons: his being in the cold season, and mine at the latter end of March, while the temperature of the water may remain nearly constant. The massive block of sandstone out of which the water gushes rests upon a seam of inferior coal which is four and a-half feet in thickness.

Leaving this sacred grove and fountain, which are at the north-east corner of the hill, we proceeded round by the eastern base to the south—the general level, along the path, maintaining an elevation of about 2,600 feet above the sea, or 600 feet below the summit of the hill. High up on the scarped face of the rock at the south-east corner, water is seen trickling down till it is caught by a ledge, which doubtless serves to redirect its course, and causes its reappearance in the fountain on the north-east. On the southern face of the rock, further on, there were numerous pendent combs of wild bees' honey. At a point on the path about three-fourths of the way round, the attention is arrested by a rudely cut massive model of a temple, which is about four feet high. In the lower portion there is a cavity, intended apparently for the reception of a tablet; but if it at any time contained one there is now no vestige remaining. A few steps further on there is a block of sandstone which, if attention were not drawn to it, one might pass without remarking anything particular about it. It is, however, of some interest, being artificially hollowed, with an entrance facing to the west. This block measures externally 3'.5" × 3'.8" × 6', the entrance 1'.5" × 1'.4", and the internal length is 3'.10". Though more like a dog's kennel than anything else, it is almost certain that it was the den of an anchorite, and it is so designated by the natives, who call it *Muni gofar.* A little beyond this the ascent by the only practicable route commences near the south-west corner of the rectangular block. After a steep climb of about 400 feet the path passes under an arched entrance, shewing some skilful carving, into a small temple which contains an image of Mahadeva. Close by, as it were on the very corner of the hill, there is a cleared space of rock surrounded by a wall or breastwork, from which a magnificent view of the country to the south and south-west can be obtained. From this point there is a sheer descent of not less than 1,000 feet, and a pebble dropped over the breastwork would have to travel that distance before it reached the tops of the trees in the jungle below. A further ascent of fifty feet by a made staircase brings one to the remains of another old building containing two images of Durga. From thence a gentle rise along the ridge carries one a hundred feet higher to the summit of the hill, which is 3,206 feet above the sea. The last sixty or seventy feet are composed of a capping sheet of basalt or trap, which rests on the sandstone. Here was a favourable opportunity for testing a theory put forward by the late Captain Forsyth, in his "Highlands of Central India," that a trap soil will not support sal trees. There were a number of very fine sal trees growing on this trap; and I have met with similar cases elsewhere, though in the particular regions described by Captain Forsyth I have noted * that the rule does hold that the teak and sal tracts are in many cases conterminous with the limits of the basalt and sandstone respectively. On the highest point of the hill there is a very tumble-down old temple, of which, however, the inner wall still remains. Whether a disinclination to interfere with a structure which is said to be of supernatural origin, parsimony, or a want of religious zeal is the cause of the terrible state of dilapidation into which this undoubtedly ancient building has been allowed to fall I cannot say; but, in spite of the fact that an annual festival is held there, I do not think that the people have much reverence for the place. Otherwise the wretched, overgrown condition of the approaches, and the ignorance of the village Baigas, who profess to do Puja there, as to what the hill really contains, are perfectly inexplicable. Even the custodian of the temple, a *fakir* or ascetic, who I was warned beforehand would hurl big stones at me if I attempted the ascent, had deserted the place. Local tradition asserts that some Englishman was thus prevented from ascending, and, at the solicitation of the Lukanpur Lal Sahib, gave up the attempt. On a stand or altar inside the temple there are images of Luchman, Balsundri, Janki, and Raja Janak. They appear to be cut out of the local basalt, and are in good preservation; but I did not like to offend the feelings of those with me by making a very close examination of the material. A little below the temple there is a spring, which probably feeds the already-mentioned fountain. My guide did not know the position of an old reservoir said to exist close by, and as there was still much to be seen, I could not spare time to hunt for it. Leaving behind us the cool and refreshing breeze on the summit, we descended again, and on reaching the gateway I noticed that those with me, Mahomedans as well as Hindus, resumed their shoes, which they had left behind them on entering the limits of what they considered to be holy ground. All the party having refreshed themselves at the fountain, we

* *Vide* Chap X.

retraced our steps for a short distance, and then struck eastwards by a path running along a spur from the main mass of the hill. After walking about a mile we reached the north-west end of a tunnel called the Hathphor. It is situated on the north side of the spur, and is rather more than a mile south-west of the village of Udaipur.

This very singular tunnel is undoubtedly of natural origin, having been formed originally by the trickling of water through crevices in sandstone. I looked in vain, however, for any slip or dislocation of the strata, such as is a usual cause tending to the formation of caves. The stream having found its way through an immense mass of sandstone, has been at work for ages enlarging the passage, and the present result is a tunnel 160 paces long, and about 12 feet high and 8 feet broad. As I was about to enter its gloomy but cool recesses, I remembered that it had the reputation of being the dwelling-place of a family of tigers, so I took the precaution of calling up my rifle-bearer, to be close at hand in case of need. When about half-way through, I saw by the dim light some animate object, with a pair of glaring eyes, on a ledge of rock in front of me. It proved to be a young wood-owl, which clapped his bill in furious rage at the intruders, and then made several abortive attempts at flight. At the south-east end of the tunnel, on the south side, a face of rock appears to have been chiselled off for some purpose, possibly for the reception of an inscription which was never engraved. Close by there is a small cave, to which you ascend by a few steps. It has been partially enlarged artificially. Returning through the tunnel to the north-west, the stream is found to take its rise in a basin or horseshoe-shaped valley, of very singular appearance. On the south rises a cliff of sandstone, high up on the face of which are seen the entrances to two caves. A climb up over *débris* from the mouth of the tunnel brings one, after an ascent of more than 100 feet, to the foot of a double flight of stairs, cut in the solid rock. Ascending the stairs, you find yourself on the threshold of a rectangular artificially excavated chamber, cut in the rock. There appears to have been originally a natural cave here, at least the outer hollow shews overhead no sign of chisel markings. On the extreme right of the mouth of the outer cave, there are two footprints, somewhat rudely cut in the stone. The entrance to the inner chamber is 12 feet wide, expanding to 17 feet. To the right and left of this entrance the cave extends inside with perfect symmetry. The total length of the interior is 44½ feet; the breadth at the centre is 12 feet 10 inches, and the height varies from 5 feet 6 inches to over 6 feet. This is partly caused by the floor of the recesses to right and left being raised 6 inches above that of the central portion, and partly to curvature of the face of the stratum of rock which forms the roof. The interior has, throughout, been finished with cutting tools. All round the wall there is a raised bench, cut out of the solid rock. On three sides this bench is double, the inner portion being raised two inches above the outer. On the side facing the entrance the double bench is 8 feet 6 inches wide. In the recess portions of the entrance side there is a continuation of the lower bench, and on each side of the buttresses of the entrance small seats of rock have been left. On the right-hand side of the entrance there is an inscription in two lines, the last two or three letters in each of which are much damaged and illegible. The letters are about two inches high, but, though clearly engraven, they do not exhibit much skill. I forwarded a copy of both this and the other (to be mentioned below) to the well-known Sanscrit scholar, Babu Rajendralala Mitra, who replied that they are in the "old Pali or Asoka character, and the Pali language, but not of Asoka. They record something about one Devadatta, but what it is I cannot make out. Many of the letters appear to be doubtful." Although there are some broken idols resting on the bench, which represent, on the authority of the Baiga, Mahadeva, Parvati, and Bardeoli, there is nothing to connect them with the cave. There is no attempt whatever at ornamentation in the chamber, and the benches look so eminently suitable for sleeping purposes, that I am inclined to believe it was constructed for and used as a dwelling-place.

The second cave is at about the same elevation as the other,

ARTIFICIAL CAVE, RAMGURH HILL.

but to reach it you have to scramble up a face of rock by means of some rudely-cut steps. The interior shows little or no sign of artificial excavation, and the sole point of interest about it is that it contains a four-line inscription, in much bolder characters than the other.

The local tradition regarding these caves is that they were the residence of Ramachandra for fourteen years previous to the Expedition to Lunka, and that it was from this place that Sita or Janki, the Hindu Helen, was carried away. There can be little doubt, however, that the caves are a remnant of Buddhistic and not of Hindu times.*

March 27th.—Jajya to Lukanpur.—The Lal Sahib was again away elephant-catching on his own account, in the Korea country,

* In the "Indian Antiquary" (Bombay) for September, 1873, I have given a somewhat more complete account of this place, accompanied by plans and elevations of the cave and transcripts of the inscriptions.

to the south-west. However, he sent in his eldest son to receive me, and wrote a letter of welcome, in which he mentioned that he had just succeeded in capturing fourteen elephants. For this, I afterwards heard, he got into some trouble, as Bindeshri, getting jealous of these independent operations, complained to Government that he personally had received permission, while the Lal Sahib, Moheshri, had not. In a separate note he asked me for all the percussion caps I could spare, as he had exhausted his stock. On my enquiring subsequently whether I could obtain anything for him in Calcutta which he might require, he enumerated, with other things, "Olway Sahib ke dawa:" *i.e.*, Mr. Olway's medicine. It took some little time before I could recognize in this guise the name of a well-known vendor of ointments and pills, which, as this is not an advertisement, and as I have no wonderful effects of the use of the medicines to record, I leave it to the intelligent reader to guess.

March 31st.—Dumali.—To-day I ascended a hill called the Bunder Kot, or Monkey's Home. Its elevation is about 1,100 feet above the village of Dumali. The plateau on the summit is about a mile and a-half long, and only from 100 to 200 yards wide. The rocks of which it is formed are steeply scarped for the last 300 feet, thus forming an almost inaccessible natural fortress. There are, however, two points where there has been a sufficient accumulation of talus or *débris* to render an ascent possible. Such a place as this was not likely to be overlooked in former disturbed times, and, indeed, there are still traces of a tank or reservoir on the top, and local tradition affirms that during the raids of the Mahrattas and Pindaris it was used as a retreat for the women and children of the Sirguja Rajas, and that a mere handful of men was sufficient to defend it from assault. The sandstones at the top show traces of baking from an overlying layer of basalt, which has now been nearly completely eroded away. From the summit a number of similar flat-topped hills, including the Ramgurh Hill, are to be seen in the country to the westward.

April 1st.—Dumali to Patpuria.—Leaving my camp and most

of my followers below, I ascended the Main pât or plateau, this morning, and remained there till the 6th. The ascent by a fair track on the north, which a loaded elephant experienced no great difficulty in accomplishing, was commonly used and kept open by droves of cattle, which are every year brought during the hot weather for grazing from distant points in Mirzapur and other districts of the Gangetic valley. The features of the geological structure which give rise to the peculiar form of this plateau soon become apparent. On an irregular surface of the basal crystalline rocks there is a covering of sandstones of varying thickness, resting upon which there are several sheets of basalt, with a total thickness of about 400 feet, and these are again overlaid by about 150 feet of laterite. Up to the last 20 feet or so, which exposes an abrupt scarp of laterite, the slope is covered by a dense mixed forest; but after it is scaled quite a new type of scenery opens to the view. The laterite forms a wide-spread and nearly level surface, interrupted here and there by depressions which mark the position of the sources of the numerous streams which take their rise in the plateau. In these depressions a small quantity of soil has accumulated, and supports a delightfully green grass, which is watered by perennial springs. These are the grazing-grounds which attract the cattle from so far. To the Raja of Bisrampur they and some others in the valleys below are a source of income, as on every head of cattle a charge of something like four annas or sixpence is made, and the total amounts to several hundreds of pounds per annum. On the other parts of the surface a few scrub sal bushes and an occasional solitary fig or wild mango alone manage to support an existence. At this season the young sal leaves were just sprouting, and exhibiting the extraordinary range of tint from green to reddish-copper which characterises this plant. From the abruptly-scarped edges of the plateau some excellent views of the surrounding country are obtainable. Perhaps the most striking features are produced by the deeply-cut valleys which indent the plateau in many places. On their slopes the cornices formed by the different layers of rock stand out with admirable distinctness, and one is enabled, in consequence, to trace with the eye the geological structure of a wide area.

My camp was pitched near a hamlet occupied by the race called Majwars, or Saontars, whom I have already mentioned on a previous page. I immediately interrogated the head man as to the probability of my being able to get a shot at any gaur (or so-called bison), this being notoriously a spot where they are known to occur. He told me that I had no chance of seeing any, as they had all left the plateau in consequence of the cattle and the men in charge of them being about. I offered him a large reward if he would shew me their haunts, but he declared his inability to do so. This disinclination to aid me was due to the Hindu idea, which is shared also apparently by these aborigines, that these animals are too nearly allied to the sacred kine to be lawful for sport. And further, as I afterwards ascertained, they are supposed to be under the especial protection of the *Bhut*, or evil spirit of the hill, who would relentlessly avenge any injury to these his *protégés*.

The level of this village is about 3,700 feet above the sea. I found the air keen and invigorating, and while I remained there the maximum temperature did not exceed 80° F., while below it commonly reached to 100° F. In the afternoon I descended into one of the above-mentioned valleys, that of the Manchuri river, to a depth of about 600 feet below the edge of the plateau, and then walked up the bed for about two miles, intending to trace the section up to the head source of the river. Finding, however, that I should probably be belated if I attempted to carry out this intention, I struck up the steep side of the cliff so as to take the shortest cut back to camp. While laboriously scrambling through the dense undergrowth under a ledge formed by one of the cornices, I suddenly found myself confronted by a large animal, which gave a loud snort as it looked down at me through the bushes, and immediately disappeared, and was nowhere to be seen when I reached the ledge. I then fully satisfied myself by an examination of the "form" where the animal had been lying that I had been in close proximity with a gaur which, if it had been disposed to hostilities, might have charged down upon me from its advantageous position.

On the following morning, when walking along the edge of the plateau, I saw a barking deer picking its way along under the shadow of the forest, some sixty yards below, quite innocent of my presence above; he afforded me an easy shot, and I killed him by a shot in the neck. Shortly afterwards I heard a peculiar rustling hollow sound, which I at first thought was due to an eddy of wind playing through the bushes. It was not till I had walked some distance further, and had omitted to place myself in readiness, with rifle in hand, that I saw clattering over the hard laterite behind me, at full gallop, a herd of ten gaur drawn out into a long string. Two shots which I fired at a distance from them of 250 yards, did not produce any visible effect. Over the steep edge and down through the piled boulders they dashed, without any visible check being caused by these obstructions, which few other less sure-footed animals could have traversed. For some minutes I could hear the sound of their hoofs on the stones and the crash of the branches as they forced their way through the forest below. I was much struck by their game-looking heads and square build. The stride they put on when alarmed by my shots was, as I subsequently ascertained by measurement of the footprints, about twelve feet long. These footprints, in spite of the great size of the animals, which sometimes attain, according to Jerdon, a height of eighteen hands, are surprisingly small and neat, not much exceeding those of a large sambar. Before I left the plateau I became very familiar with their appearance, and have had no difficulty in distinguishing them, wherever subsequently met with, from those of all other animals, including domestic cattle.

During the succeeding three days I explored a series of the deep valleys, which cut into the plateau in a manner which may be compared to the gap left by the first cut out of a cheese. In each of these valleys at the outcrop of a particular layer of columnar basalt, there were more or less picturesque cascades, and in these spots I rarely failed to see one or more of the already-mentioned Malabar whistling-thrushes. To this bird, as also to a nearly-allied species, which is found in the Himalayas, falling water seems to be a necessity of existence, and the whistle of the birds is seldom heard out of reach of the sound of a cascade.

April 6th.—Parputia to Dumali.—To-day I left with great regret the cool atmosphere and quiet of the plateau, to descend to the heat and turmoil of my camp below. Due provision had been made for the supply of my followers by the Bisrampur people, otherwise they might have been starved out in the valley where I had left them. In these jungles I used occasionally to come across a curious animal called the tree-cat (*Paradoxurus musanga*). It is stated by Blyth to have received its generic name from a specimen with a malformed tail—the ordinary normal tail can be rolled up, but is not prehensile. In many other respects the species of this genus are, however, somewhat paradoxical; they are plantigrades, their dentition is very similar to that of dogs, while in general aspect they resemble the genets and civets. As their English and native names imply, they can ascend trees, and, indeed, they are wonderful adepts at climbing. I knew of one which lived in one of the most populous parts of Calcutta, where, since there were no trees, he used to manage to swarm up the lightning conductors, thus gaining access into the highest rooms in the houses, where he committed nightly depredations. For some months he baffled all attempts at capture, regularly helping himself to the bait placed in a gin-trap which he most cleverly avoided springing.

Another animal which occurs in these highlands, but which I have not hitherto mentioned since I never saw one wild, its habits being purely nocturnal, is the pangolin or scaly ant-eater.* Several of the native names, by which it is known, shew by

---

* *Manis pentadactyla*, Linn.

their etymology the prevalence of the belief that it is a land-fish. It is occasionally captured by being dug out of its deep burrows in the rocks, and live specimens have, from time to time, been forwarded to Calcutta from Chutia Nagpur; but it is difficult to keep it alive in confinement. It is covered over with broad overlapping fish or rather reptilian-like scales, and attains a total length of forty-six inches to which the tail contributes eighteen. It is considered by the natives that the flesh has aphrodisiac properties, and rings and amulets made from the scales are worn in the belief that they will produce similar effects.

A week after leaving Dumali I was struck down with fever; during the days which had intervened I had felt all the premonitory symptoms of steadily increasing weakness, and often after a mid-day sleep found myself in a condition of partial coma; after four days spent unable to do any work, I felt compelled to close operations, and set out on the return march to Ranchi, which was distant about 140 miles.

As the Bisrampur Coal-field has been described in the publications of the Geological Survey of India,* I shall only give a very brief account of it here. The total area occupied by the coal-measures is about 400 square miles. They occupy a well-defined basin which is bounded on the north, east, and partly also on the south, by ridges of metamorphic rocks which served to define the original limits of deposit. On the west and south, denudation has had the effect of producing a disruption between this area and others which occur in the adjoining country. The sedimentary rocks are referable to three distinct series. At the base we have the Talchir rocks which rest directly on the metamorphic or crystalline series, and are believed to have had a glacial origin, since some of them consist of fine silts which include large transported boulders derived from the older formation. Above these again there are the coal-measures, which are in India known as the Barakar

---

* Records of the Geological Survey of India, Vol. VI. 1873; pp. 25-41.

group of the Damuda series. Resting upon the coal-measures is a group of non-coal-bearing sandstones and conglomerates which must have been, at one time, at least 1,000 feet thick, and have filled up the basin to the level of the surrounding crystalline margins. At the present day the Pilka hill forms the sole remnant of this once wide-spread deposit. The general character of the coal, of which there are numerous seams, is similar to that of most of the Indian fields: the proportion of impurity averages about fourteen per cent., and the fixed carbon 51·5 per cent. The other mineral productions are of no great importance, so that should this tract of country ever be opened up by rail—a contingency not in itself probable, owing to the land-locked nature of the area,—coal is the only mineral likely to be of value, and this can only be to a very limited extent, since there are other more accessible coal-fields both on the north (in Palamow) and on the south (in Sambalpur).

The march to Ranchi I accomplished in ten days, or, to be more correct, in ten nights, for owing to the heat it was necessary to save the men and cattle as much as possible. We used generally to start at about midnight, and reach the next camping-ground by seven or eight in the morning. The moonlight was most brilliant, and enabled us to traverse jungle, and ford numerous rivers, without difficulty. In many places flakes of mica lying on the roads, and in the beds of the streams, reflected back the moonbeams in a manner which made them resemble so many fire-flies. One night when riding along half asleep, with my feet out of the stirrups and the bridle on the horse's neck, he suddenly caught sight of some animal, and gave a tremendous shy which unseated me; and the bridle, which I had just time to grasp, giving way, he galloped off into the jungle, and from the broken nature of the ground I feared he would never be seen again uninjured. However, he circled back to the road, and about a mile off meeting a party of the servants, headed by the native doctor on his pony, he stopped, and was captured, though when he rushed amongst them they thought some wild beast was upon them. On another dark night, before the moon had risen, he stopped suddenly, and refused to go forward, in consequence, no doubt, of there being some animal (a leopard, probably,) ahead of us. During this period I used to hear the mahouts actually causing the elephants to lie down, or putting them to bed, at eight o'clock, in order that they might obtain forty winks before being loaded for the march at twelve.

On several occasions we passed in close proximity to burning jungle, which crackled and flared on either side of the road. I retain a very vivid recollection of the appearance presented by one such fire which we saw below us when descending the pass on the eastern frontier of Sirguja. The flames from the burning undergrowth as they shone through the branches of the higher trees produced a most singular effect—the wreathing columns of smoke simulating weird and ghostly figures perambulating through the vistas.

Towards sunrise I used to notice the gradual transition from the cries of the night-jars and owls to the notes of the various birds which then struck up their usual harsh cries with a regular sequence—the king-crows being the first to commence the concert. During this march I recovered much of my strength, and, as the fresh young leaves which were now sprouting enlivened the jungle, I could not help feeling a regret that I had not remained for another week in Sirguja, to round off some work which I had left uncompleted. On the 3rd of May I rode into Ranchi at six o'clock, and found that some of my friends there hardly recognised me, so much had the exposure and fever altered my appearance. For nearly a week subsequently I had a relapse of the fever, and was not able to resume my journey for the railway station, *viâ* Purulia, till I was somewhat recovered. On the 19th of May I reached the station of Assensole, and after a day's rest there took train for Calcutta, where I remained till October.

In October, in company with two of my colleagues, Drs. Stoliczka and Waagen, I paid a visit to Darjiling. To my shame, it must be said, I had been eight years in India without once having seen the Himalayas. What the full measure of my loss of time and opportunity had been I did not at all realise till I had seen Darjiling. I shall never forget the impression made upon me in the early morning of the 10th of October, when the clouds at length dispersed and disclosed to full view the whole panorama of mountain ranges, culminating in the mighty mass of Kinchinjunga, with its 14,000 feet of perpetual snow. From the lowest point to which the eye can reach in the Rungit valley to the highest peak of Kinchinjunga, the vertical height is not less than five miles—such a thickness of earth crust being probably nowhere else visible on the earth's surface.

During the week which we remained at Darjiling we did not wander far from the station, but the immediate vicinity affords scenes of great interest or beauty; and even the bazaar, where many marked types of man may often be seen assembled, abounds with subjects for the student of ethnology. My companions chiefly devoted themselves to entomology, and Stoliczka's collection of cicadas, which his untimely death prevented him from ever working out, was of considerable extent and value. Among the cicadas were some very curious forms, which imitated in an extraordinary way the external characters of insects belonging to many wholly different families. Thus some of them might at a glance be mistaken for moths. The thrilling and all-pervading, but sweet silver-bell-like note which must attract the notice of every visitor to Darjiling as he ascends the slope, near Kursiong, is produced, I believe, by a species of cicada. The birds more particularly claimed my attention, and among them one species, which I saw for the first time, is likewise remarkable for its imitation of the form of another species belonging to a wholly distinct family. It is a cuckoo called *Surniculus lugubris*, Horsf., and the bird it so much resembles is the very common king-crow (*Buchanga atra*, Herm.) That it ever lays its eggs in the nest of the king-crow has not, as yet, I believe, been ascertained to be the fact; but it seems not improbable that such may yet turn out to be the case. Many other species of birds occurring here belong to genera which are either wholly unrepresented in Peninsular India, or if represented are so by solitary species which are found in hill tracts like the Neilgherries. Indeed, it soon becomes apparent that this tract constitutes a portion of a province or sub-region of the geographical distribution of animals quite distinct from any into which India, south of the Ganges, has been sub-divided. It belongs, in fact, to the Indo-Malayan rather than to the Indian region as defined by Wallace, Blanford and other authorities on this subject. The forests about Darjiling which have as yet escaped the axe of the tea-planter are some of them of very great beauty, and in certain spots they include magnificent tree-ferns.

Since the time I write of, the examination of the geological structure of this portion of the Himalayas has been undertaken by the Geological Survey, and some very curious and unexpected conclusions as to the age and origin of the crystalline rocks which form the main mass of the Darjiling hills have been arrived at.* A zone of coal-measure rocks at the foot of the hills of the same age as those at Ranigunj has been also explored, and in places coal-seams have been opened up, the result being that the coal has been found to be in the condition of powder in consequence of the crushing and disturbance to which it has been subjected. There is no great promise of its ever becoming available as a source of fuel for the railway, which now reaches nearly to the foot of the hills; but this is chiefly in consequence of the difficulty and danger connected with mining in such crushed rocks, since it has been found possible to manufacture the powdered coal into an artificial fuel of good quality. This railway, with the aid of a newly opened up carriage road, upon which it is proposed to put a steam tram, places Darjiling within easy access of Calcutta.

---

* *Vide* F. R. Mallet, "Memoirs of the Geological Survey of India.' Vol. XI.

My stay at Darjiling was so short, and my notes of what I saw are, I regret to find, so meagre, that I have not material sufficient to enlarge upon the subject as it deserves. By compilation from various admirable accounts of British and Independent Sikkim it would have been possible for me to have devoted a whole section to the subject, but as this work is not a gazetteer, and as it has already grown to such a size that all possible compression is desirable, I must refer my readers to the sources of information given below.* To all visitors to India who wish to carry away impressions of grand scenery, I would say visit Kashmir, Simla, Naini Tal, and Masuri, by all means, if you have time, but wherever you go be sure to make time to visit Darjiling.

---

* Hooker, Dr. J. D., "Himalayan Journals." Sherwell, Major J. L., "Journal of a Trip undertaken to explore the Glaciers of the Kinchinjunga Group in the Sikkim Himalaya." Jour. Asiatic Society of Bengal. Vol. XXXI., p. 457. Blanford, W. T., "Journey through Sikkim," and "Zoology of Sikkim." Jour. Asiatic Society of Bengal. Vols. XL. and XLI.

CHAPTER IX.

SECTION I.

BIRBHUM—CHUTIA NAGPUR—CENTRAL PROVINCES.

1872-73.

INSTRUCTIONS FOR SEASON—MINING SPECIALISTS—DIFFICULTIES IN CONNECTION WITH MINING ENTERPRISE IN INDIA—MAHOMED BAZAAR IRON-WORKS—RANIGUNJ COAL-FIELD—IRON-FURNACES NEAR BARAKAR—MARCH TO HAZARIBAGH—IRON ORES NEAR HAZARIBAGH—KARANPURA VALLEY—KARANPURA COAL-FIELDS—MAUDIH TEA PLANTATION—DALTONGUNJ COAL-FIELD—SONE RIVER—KAIMUR PLATEAU—AKBARPUR—ROHTAS GURH—URAONS—DEHRI — SONE CANALS — APPRENTICE SCHOOL — POOR WHITES AND EURASIANS—DEATH IN CAMP—SEND BACK ELEPHANTS—ARRAH—BREAK-UP CAMP—BENARES—JABALPUR MARBLE ROCKS—MOPANI COAL-MINES—OMERPANI IRON-MINES—TENDUKERA IRON-WORKS—RETURN TO CALCUTTA.

THIS season my duties were of a special and unusual kind; instead of being allotted a new area for original exploration, I was directed to accompany a gentleman who had arrived from England in order to prepare a report for the Secretary of State on the value of the principal iron deposits in India, and on the advisability of establishing iron factories in different parts of the country. From time to time India has been visited by specialists, who have been deputed to report upon Iron, Coal, Petroleum, Gold, &c. They are expected to traverse large areas in a brief space of time, and to give opinions on unopened deposits. In a general way the conclusions which they arrive at may be summarised by saying, that they discover that in India there are special local conditions surrounding every question of this kind, which render it well nigh impossible for them to come to any satisfactory conclusions. In India the profitable exploitation of the mineral resources depends not merely upon the absolute or comparative richness of particular deposits, but upon the climate, the great distances which the productions must, in most cases, be carried, and the land tenures and mining rights. Although these important elements are or ought to be known to every district official throughout the country, it has been generally left to these specialist visitors to find out for them-themselves the existence of such abnormal conditions.

A case in point is afforded by the experience of a specialist who is at present engaged in testing the value of the gold deposits in Southern India, and who is making a more thorough and practical investigation of his subject than was possible to some of the others. From a recently-published and apparently authentic source,* we learn that "Mr. Brough Smith and Mr. Laing came to India to determine whether gold is or is not to be found in this country in remunerative quantities, and they have settled that question beyond dispute. There is gold in abundance, but India will never be a mining country like Australia, and for this reason—it can never be properly prospected. It may be asked why it can never be prospected. The answer is very simple: it is broken up into too many proprietorships. What with rajas, zemindars, and planters, men whose profession and livelihood is gold-digging will never come out here to prospect, *because there are no mining regulations.* One of the first things Mr. Laing said to me was, 'India can never be like Australia because there are no miners' rights.' If the gold industry in India is intended to be developed for the benefit of the many instead of the few, then mining rules should be drawn up and copies forwarded to the 'Mining Departments' in the various colonies for publication. Of course landowners will do all in their power to oppose this, as they will say the mining rights are already theirs. But they will find it far more difficult to raise capital to work mines in

* Correspondent of the *Madras Athenæum.*

India than it would be in any other part of the world. Both Mr. Brough Smith and Mr. Laing agree that some of the gold that they have found is far richer than anything of the kind they ever saw in Australia, and they showed me a large number of very rich specimens. They neither of them believe much in the Wynaad as an alluvial digging except on Vellera Mullah." This quotation is given, *faute de mieux*, merely to illustrate the context. It is not within either my province or present means of reference to describe the recent gold discoveries here.

I might quote numerous cases to show that enormous sums have been paid by companies, and even in some instances by Government, to landholders for the mining rights, simply because the law is so vague on the subject. And such precedents having been established the difficulty in the future has become all the greater. These enormous sums have, in not a few of the cases, more than swallowed up the profits from actual out-turn which have been made, and the works have been either carried on at a dead loss, or have utterly failed and been closed. Once you have proved that a valuable, or even a promising, deposit is to be found on the land of a zemindar or raja, he is sure to demand for the right to work it a rent that is absolutely prohibitive.* This has already, I believe, been the case in the Wynaad gold regions. The sanguine promoters of a company may yield to such exorbitant demands, and the natural results follow—failure and loss. But more than this, there is another feature in the dealings between non-official Europeans and natives, and that is that they are almost inevitably accompanied

* The following which I quote from a native paper illustrates this, though the particular incident had, I believe, no foundation in fact. The *Umdutull Akbar* says, "that a gold mine has been discovered at Lustia, a place about twelve miles distant from Prosunda, in the district of Bhagulpur. Government has already placed there a force of fifty constables under a European officer, and offered to pay the owner of the land fifty lakhs of rupees (*i.e.*, half-a-million sterling) by way of compensation. But the latter demands that he should receive half the profits accruing from the mine; Government has not acceded to these terms. No final decision has been arrived at."

by harassing and chronic litigation. The manager of a mine or factory should combine the qualifications of a lawyer—and a very sharp lawyer—with a knowledge of his own particular business, and, as a matter of experience it will be found that more than a moiety of his time will be devoted to the former branch of his business. The old "interloper" idea is still strong in the land. And not only is the non-official European in remote districts, away from the presidency towns, an object at which the natives fire their incessant darts of petty annoyance, but he is also not unfrequently regarded with disfavour by the district officials, who are jealous of any influence existing in their districts which does not emanate from themselves. I know of numerous individual exceptions to this rule, where the officials are really anxious to aid and encourage independent commercial enterprise; but individual officials are constantly being moved, and the useful and profitable employment of capital in India is seriously affected by the rule, of the existence of which there can be no doubt whatever. District officials may very properly complain of the manner in which non-official Europeans, more particularly those belonging to the lower social ranks, sometimes treat the natives; but, on the other hand, it should be remembered that these people receive an amount of provocation and insolence from the natives which is simply inconceivable to any one who has not been witness of it. The wonder is that they, as a body, show so much self-control, and bear patiently, without the prospect of ever obtaining any substantial redress, the obstruction and impertinence, not only of the pettiest of native subordinate officials, but also of the general population, including not unfrequently their own *employés*, who are ever ready to hasten off to the nearest magistrate with the most trivial and childish complaints. Deplorable casualties occur sometimes, but at wide intervals, in consequence of Europeans under provocation taking the law into their own hands and committing assaults. Generally these casualties are due to the fact of the man assaulted being in a diseased condition of health which the assaulter is in complete ignorance of. Deaths from this cause occur as the result of combats, or more frequently beatings inflicted by natives on each other, but such cases are dealt with in the ordinary course, and not being trumpeted through the land by a disaffected native press, do not attract much public attention. The notice which this subject has received from the Government and in Parliament has of late years brought it so much before the public, that I shall not dwell upon it further here.

November 28th.—Calcutta to Synthea.—Mr. Bauerman, the gentleman who had come out from England to report on the iron ores of India, and I, started by train for Synthea, in Birbhum, this morning, and shortly after arrival went off to Mahomed Bazaar, and put up in a tent which had been pitched for us near the old Birbhum Iron-Works. On the following day we visited the principal iron-mines in the country to the north. Most of them had been deserted, and were full of water, as there was but little doing in the native furnaces. The information which was to be obtained from the inhabitants as to the thickness of the deposit was of the vaguest and most useless nature. Subsequent explorations in this region, and an attempted resuscitation of the works, have abundantly proved that the ore is not deficient either as regards quality or quantity; but there are difficulties there in reference to the supply of suitable fuel and flux, which seriously affect the prospect of profitable iron manufacture. But regarding this subject reference may be made to what has been published elsewhere.*

Leaving Birbhum we next moved to the Ranigunj coal-field, and during successive days visited the mines and works of the three principal coal companies, the iron deposits, and a large European pottery manufactory, which is the only one in Bengal at present. From Ranigunj we marched to Assensole, and thence to Barakar, examining the coal and iron at all points

---

* *Vide* Mem. Geological Survey of India, Vol. XIII., p. 241.

where they occur in the vicinity of both places. Since that time two blast-furnaces have been erected by a company near Barakar, and it has been satisfactorily proved that good iron can be manufactured from the materials available on the spot; but the present depression in the iron trade has affected the prosperity of the undertaking very materially.*

At Assensole five elephants belonging to the Commissariat Department arrived to convey our baggage to the country to the west. On the 27th of December we reached Hazaribagh after the usual marches up the Trunk Road, which proved unproductive of any incidents worthy of especial record. The four days next succeeding were devoted to the examination of the various iron-ore localities which had been previously discovered in the neighbourhood of the station. None of them appeared to be of any great promise, and in several cases the supposed iron ore proved to be simply a form of massive garnet, which, though conceivably of use for some other purposes, could not be employed as an ore of iron.

January 1st.—Hazaribagh to Badum.—To-day we marched southwards, descending 800 or 900 feet by a steep ghât or pass into the Karanpura Valley, where there are two coal-fields, which have been surveyed and reported upon by Mr. Hughes, of the Geological Survey. The track then existing, by this the Mutra ghât, was so steep that the load of one of the elephants slipped bodily over its head, and much damage was caused to sundry articles of furniture. The view of this valley, with the block-like mass of the Maudih plateau standing out in the centre of it, as seen from the summit of the ghât, is a remarkably beautiful one. Many of the villages are large, and a considerable proportion of the houses are tiled, while the tracts of terraced

---

* While these pages were passing through the press, news has been received that this Company has been wound-up. The cause of failure appears to have been the insufficiency of the original capital, which was only £100,000 instead of being half-a-million, as it should have been in order to secure success.

cultivation are here and there interrupted by splendid groves of mangos and fan palms. At Badum there is an old fort, said to have been the abode of the Ramgurh Rajas before they went to Ramgurh; but, judging by the appearance of the ruins at the latter place, I should say that it was the older of the two.

The Karanpura Valley is the seat of considerable native iron factories, and to an examination of these and the iron and coal deposits our time was devoted for several days. As I subsequently had further opportunities of enquiring into the position and particular features of the iron industry, not only here, but also in some adjoining coal-fields, I shall reserve my account of them for a future chapter. While in the neighbourhood we paid a visit to a tea-plantation which is situated on the Maudih plateau, at an elevation, I believe, of about 900 feet or so above the general level of the valley. The plateau, being formed of porous sandstones and conglomerates, similar to those which form the large isolated hills of Lugu in the Bokaro field and Pachete in the Ranigunj field, does not retain moisture long, and in consequence the surface on the top speedily becomes dry after the cessation of rains. It is with extreme difficulty that the tea-bushes are kept alive during the scorching blasts of the hot weather. When the rains come on they flourish and do well, but the plucking season is a short one. The teas manufactured are chiefly the varieties of green, and are I believe of good quality, commanding a high price. Labour is cheap, the coolies receiving only about half what they would in Assam or Cachar.

On leaving the Karanpura Valley our next destination was the Daltongunj or Palamow coal-field, the coal in which was at that time being mined, or rather quarried, for the supply of the works in connection with the Sone irrigation at Dehri. Eight marches took us to Rajharrah, near which the coal-mines were situated. At several places, more especially between Pugar and Sorodah, we saw groups of stone monuments, the sole remnants of former colonies of Lurka Kols or Hos. Some of these, unlike those erected at the present day, were dressed into shape with cutting tools, and one or two resembled a form commonly used for head-stones in English grave-yards.

After a few days devoted to the Daltongunj coal-field, we resumed our march westwards, reaching the village of Kabra, on the Sone river, on the 19th of January. From this point a splendid view of the river, with the Kaimur hills forming a very substantial background, is obtained. The Kaimur hills, which are the most eastern extension of the Vindhyan range, are formed of a group of rocks belonging to a series quite different from any occurring in Chutia Nagpur. This series bears the name of the range, and is believed to be the peninsular equivalent of the old red sandstone and Devonian formations of other countries. The Kaimur or Kymore beds are at the base of the upper of the two divisions into which the series is naturally separated.* They consist of sandstones, conglomerates, and shales, and are, like all the other rocks of the series, quite unfossiliferous, and therefore the age assigned has been deduced from a consideration of the relations which exist between this and other formations of ascertained position, rather than by direct evidence such as fossils would afford. The Kaimur beds at this eastern extremity shew little or no signs of disturbance, forming nearly horizontal strata which rest on the limestones and shales of the lower Vindhyans. They thus form the level plateau of Rohtas, which, with its steeply-scarped sides, affords, on the west of the Sone river, physical features of a type not anywhere seen to the east.

January 20th.—Kabra to Akbarpur.—To-day we forded the Sone and marched to Akbarpur, on the western bank, where we became the guests of a renowned bibliophil and friend of the natives, Mr. Davies. This gentleman's name is mentioned by Sir J. D. Hooker in his journal. We found that his library was of considerable size and value, and that although he had, I

---

* For a full report of the Vindhyan series, reference should be made to Mr. Mallet's report. Mem. Geological Survey of India, Vol. VII.

believe, been born in India and had never visited Europe, he possessed a marvellous acquaintance with modern literature and the progress of scientific research. The contents of books of travels in many countries were simply at his fingers' ends, and we had abundant evidence of his wonderful powers of memory. It was sufficient to mention any country, however remote and insignificant, to hear all about its polity, natural productions, &c. Not only is Mr. Davies looked up to as a father by the people all round, but he is in a measure a patron of the denizens of the neighbouring jungle, since he has quarters in which food is always placed, and which the wild spotted deer have learnt to enter as a haven of refuge where they can come and go as they please. Often they are absent for months, but return again with their fawns when in the hot weather herbage is scarce in the jungle.

Overhanging the village of Akbarpur, on the corner of the Rohtas plateau, there are to be found a number of old ruins of houses and temples, included in a fort.* We visited these and explored a portion of the neighbouring plateau, upon portions of which there is still a considerable amount of jungle. It was from this neighbourhood that the Uraons are, according to their own traditions, said to have spread into Chutia Nagpur, and this very probably was a halting place for some years, when with other Dravidian races they pushed into south-eastern India from countries lying to the north-west. To the present day there are some villages and hamlets occupied by Uraons on the plateau.

Two marches from Akbarpur we arrived at Dehri, the centre of operations in connection with the Sone canals, which are fed by the water accumulated in the bed of the river by means of a weir or anicut. A vast network of distributories convey this water over a wide area of country, both on the Patna or eastern side of the river, and the Arrah or western. There are also canals for traffic, which, as feeders of the East Indian Railway, may

---

* An account of these will be found in the Journal of the Asiatic Society of Bengal, Vol. XLVI., part I, page 27.

become of very great importance, more particularly should the coal-fields of Palamow be opened up. When I left India the question of enforcing compulsory water-rates was under consideration. Whether any determination has since been come to I cannot say, but it seems to be only common justice that the people who alone derive benefit from any particular irrigation project should pay for all the expenses of it. And it is likewise evident that the extension of irrigation to any particular tract should be settled upon by the Government, by and with the advice of their most competent experts, and that the matter should not be left to the decision of a parcel of ignorant landowners, and still less to a certain class of writers for the press, and public declaimers, who, whether in Europe or India, fail to grasp the main features and unusual difficulties of the question. Here and in Orissa, as I shall afterwards mention, the supply of water is much larger and less likely to fail in seasons of drought than in Midnapur, the irrigation works at which place I have alluded to on a previous page.

At Dehri there was much of interest to be seen, and in the workshops we were shown several machines patented by Mr. Fouracres, the Executive Engineer in charge, which had been designed to save labour and meet the particular circumstances of the works. Thus there was a very ingeniously-constructed dredger, which served materially to expedite the sinking of wells in the sandy beds of rivers. A self-acting water buffer, by means of which the shutters at the crest of the weir would open to allow of the sudden rush of water during floods, and close again after they had passed, was likewise a most ingenious device. In the workshops almost anything that can be made with wood or iron could be prepared on the spot. It is essential in India, to prevent delays which might be of the most serious nature, that every great public work shall have its own factories and mills. Hence one of the great primary causes of expense in these undertakings. In connection with the workshops, and likewise under the charge of Mr. Fouracres, there was a school where a number of apprentice lads of European and half-caste parentage receive a theoretical and practical education, such as would enable them to become artizans with a prospect, in certain cases, of rising to something higher. This school was at the time in an experimental stage, but it promised well, and, together with others, was destined to fulfil a very important mission, since it affords a future prospect of employment to the rising generation belonging to the classes mentioned. Such efforts, though but mere drops in the ocean of a vast and speedily-increasing population of poor whites and Eurasians, are deserving of every encouragement. The destitution, degradation, and terrible misery of some of these people is one of the most distressing subjects of contemplation in the present and future condition of India. Various projects of starting colonies for these people have been from time to time talked of, but the material is bad, very bad for the purpose. It is deficient in bone and sinew, and in energy; and in some cases, it is to be feared, vicious propensities render the subjects almost hopeless objects for amelioration. Shipping off batches of Eurasians to Australia, which is sometimes resorted to, is calculated, no doubt, to relieve India of an incubus; but the benefits to Australia, or even to the persons exported, are perhaps somewhat problematical. In India, any unskilled work which the majority of these people are capable of doing can be performed equally well, and at a cheaper rate, by natives, who are preferred by most employers of labour.* They, however, somehow manage to exist, and they rapidly increase and multiply, and their existence and numbers are facts which cannot be ignored, and must be grappled with.

January 24th.—Dehri to Nussergunj.—After going to bed I was disturbed by a moaning sound, and on enquiry found that one of the mates, or mahouts' assistants, was very ill with dysentery,—so ill that I could entertain but little hope of his recovery. However, I administered what remedies I could, but in a few

---

* The most recent legislation on the subject is unfavourable to the prospects of a career in Government employ opening up to the people of these classes, as all minor appointments are to be given to natives.

hours he was dead. About a week previously I had treated him for fever, and as I had heard nothing further I supposed he had recovered. I now learnt that he had been ill ever since, but that the mahouts had kept it secret from me, and though every one of the servants knew of it, none thought it his business to mention it. They preferred to consult the village doctors, who assured them that the boy was not really ill, but was possessed by an evil spirit, whom they sought to cast out by their incantations.

During the last few days, having been in an open, highly-cultivated country, great difficulty had been experienced in obtaining the usual tree-fodder for the five elephants, and on one or two occasions we were compelled to feed them on sugar-canes—a rather expensive diet, and not easily obtainable, as the proprietors of the fields could not always be found, and, in some cases, it would have required a formal judicial enquiry to have ascertained to whom the crop really belonged. I accordingly hired bullock-carts for the remainder of the journey, and despatched the elephants back to the commissariat depôt at Hazaribagh. These elephants had only been captured a few months before they came to us, and some of them, though amenable to orders, were by no means thoroughly tamed.

On the 28th we reached the station of Arrah, which has obtained a wide notoriety in consequence of the defence of a small house by a handful of Englishmen against the mutineers in 1857. We there broke up camp, despatching tents and horses to Calcutta, and on the following day proceeded by rail to Benares where we spent a morning visiting the various temples, the Observatory of Raja Maun Singh (the instruments at which are described and figured in Hooker's Himalayan Journals)—the Ghâts, the Minarets, the bazaars, and the various other sights for which Benares is so well known. These I shall not pause to describe, as accounts of them are to be found in many works; but shall merely allude to what struck me as the most remarkable feature in this holy city—the religious centre of Hinduism; it was that there was no objection made to our entering the outer chambers of the temples, and that the priests and people about were uniformly polite. The former, indeed,—till we stopped them—occasionally most unceremoniously swept away kneeling worshippers so that we might get better views of the altars.

In many out-of-the-way places, more particularly in Orissa, one is generally not permitted to enter the temples, and the custodians are often inclined to be discourteous. From Benares we went by train to Jabalpur from whence we purposed to visit the coal and iron mines of the Narbada valley. But while delayed at Jabalpur we availed ourselves of the opportunity of paying a visit to the famed "marble rocks" some ten miles distant. These marble rocks are traversed by the river Narbada, which has excavated a deep gorge bounded by sheer vertical faces of pure white saccharine marble, some of them being 120 feet high. The gorge is about two miles long, and affords a scene of still loveliness of a very charming character. In Peninsular India, south of the Himalayas, I know of none more worthy of a visit. Many descriptions of the locality have been published—none of them, perhaps, more graphic than that by the late Captain Forsyth.* The visitor traverses the gorge in a flat-bottomed boat which, as it is rowed or poled along, enables him to fully realize the extraordinary combinations of colours which the play of light on the rugged white surface affords, and which forms a striking contrast with the deep hues of the water beneath. But the elements for producing scenes of terror and death are not absent from this still retreat. If while in the centre of the gorge you cast your eyes upwards to the most inaccessible points on the cliffs, you will probably see a number of semi-circular objects hanging therefrom. These, you are informed, are the combs of the much-to-be-dreaded bees which infest the gorge, and the boatmen will warn you not to fire off a gun in their vicinity, and to be careful to do

* "Highlands of Central India," p. 38.

nothing else to excite their ire. Once fairly roused the bees swarm down upon all intruders, and there is no means of avoiding their cruel stings. Even good swimmers, who have sought to save themselves by diving, have not always been able to escape. Captain Forsyth records one such instance, and there have been others, I believe. When standing on the narrow gravel beach near the fall, over which the water plunges into the gorge, I put my foot on a bee, in order to secure a specimen, whereupon the boatmen at once protested, declaring that news would be carried by the other bees which were crawling about on the wet stones, and that we should most certainly be attacked; but of this, of course, there was no danger. Real danger may be caused by people firing at the combs, or at the rock-pigeons from above, while there are others in boats below, as these latter are likely, from no fault of their own, to become the objects of attack.

Visitors to Jabalpur should not fail to pay this locality a visit, and if they observe the precautions which the boatmen, for their own safety, suggest, they will not run any great risk. While at Jabalpur we were told that a party of Cook's "personally conducted" tourists had, a short time previously, passed through the station. The marble rocks were not included in their programme, and the tourists declined to go to the expense of carriages themselves, and so the books kept for the purpose at the bungalow had not, at that time, been honoured by the autographs of these distinguished visitors, who left India without having seen one of the most remarkable scenes of natural beauty which it contains. I may add that the bees have not got it all their own way, since, by means of long bamboo ladders suspended from the cliffs above, the natives manage to rob the honey at night, first smothering the bees with the smoke from torches. At the time of our visit there were a number of these frail ladders hanging in close proximity to where combs had been, and where others were again being made to replace them. This locality, like most others in India, which possess any very striking features of natural beauty, has been adopted as the site of several Hindu Sivoid temples, and is esteemed as a place of particular sanctity. The quality of the marble varies a good deal; but a selected block of it which was sent to the first Paris Exhibition was pronounced to be equal to Italian marble for statuary purposes.

February 4th.—From Jabalpur we proceeded on this date to the coal-mines of the Narbada Coal and Iron Company, at a place called Mopani, which we reached by a branch line from Gadawara, a station on the Great Indian Peninsular Railway. I shall again allude to and shall briefly describe these mines in the next chapter. We next visited some iron deposits at a village called Omerpani, to the north of Gadawara, and the native iron factories in connection with them at Tendukera. The privilege to work the iron has been conceded to the above-mentioned company; but hitherto their operations have been confined to the extraction of coal. The ore is brown hæmatite, or the hydrous peroxide of iron, and occurs in lodes in a much-crushed band of siliceous limestones. It has been very extensively mined by the natives—some of the inclines running to depths of from thirty to forty feet from the surface. There are likewise numerous galleries and irregular burrowings, by means of which ore has been extracted. A quantity of detrital ore is also obtained in the alluvium. From Omerpani the ore is carted to Tendukera where it is converted into iron in furnaces similar to those employed in Bengal, except that the bellows are worked by hand instead of by foot, and the metal, which is of good quality, is sold at a rate equivalent to about £6 a ton.

From Gadawara Mr. Bauerman continued his journey to Nagpur and Chanda to examine the iron deposits in the latter region, and I returned to Calcutta on the 12th of February, whence I set forth again in about three weeks on the expedition to the Andaman and Nicobar Islands, of which an account will be found in the next section.

CHAPTER IX.

SECTION 2.

ANDAMAN AND NICOBAR ISLANDS.

1873.

ORGANIZATION OF PARTY TO EXPLORE ISLANDS OF BAY OF BENGAL—CONVICT FELLOW-PASSENGERS ON THE "SCOTIA"—ARRIVE AT PORT BLAIR—START FOR MACPHERSON'S STRAITS IN A STEAM LAUNCH—INFLUENCE OF GEOLOGICAL STRUCTURE ON VEGETATION—BEAUTY OF SCENERY—SUBMARINE LIFE—ASPECT OF THE STRAITS—ACCIDENT TO BOAT—LAND AT ESCAPE BAY—LARGE STONE PLOVER—OTHER BIRDS—CALAMUS PALM—TAKE UP POSITION FOR NIGHT—FISHING—MORNING PLUNGE IN SEA—LAND AGAIN AT ESCAPE BAY—JOLLY BOYS ISLAND—BIRDS SEEN AND OBTAINED—EDIBLE SWALLOWS' NESTS—CRAB PLOVERS—FLYING FOXES—LAND AGAIN ON JOLLY BOYS ISLAND—CORAL REEF AT LOW TIDE—BÊCHE DE MER—BARGE BOARDED BY ANDAMANESE—THEIR APPEARANCE, DOINGS, AND SAYINGS—BARTER FOR WEAPONS AND ORNAMENTS—REJOIN THE "SCOTIA"—THE "PRINCESS" TAKES LEAVE OF US—LAND ON TILLANSCHONG ISLAND—GEOLOGY—SHOOT BIRDS—CURIOUS DISTRIBUTION OF THE COCOA-NUT PALM—REACH NANKOWRI HAVEN—THE SETTLEMENT—THE NICOBARESE VISIT THE SHIP—TWO OF THEM AGREE TO JOIN THE EXPEDITION—GALATEA BAY—LAND ON THE GREAT NICOBAR—GEOLOGY—TREES—HERMIT CRABS—BIRDS—THE MEGAPODE, OR MOUND-BUILDER—TREE-SHREW—A CANOE CAPSIZES—PURCHASE OBJECTS OF ETHNOLOGICAL INTEREST—LEAVE GALATEA BAY—THE GREAT NICOBAR—LAND ON KONDUL ISLAND—BIRDS—HOUSES OF THE NATIVES—THEIR CONTENTS—HIEROGLYPHIC SCREEN—MY ESCORT—GEOLOGY—LAND AGAIN ON KONDUL—BIRDS OBTAINED—INHABITANTS OF THE INTERIOR OF GREAT NICOBAR—MONTSCHALL ISLAND—CAUGHT BY THE TIDE—GEOLOGY—TREIS AND TRACK ISLANDS—BIRDS—GEOLOGY—BOAT CARRIED OFF BY CURRENT—MERU ISLAND—DR. STOLICZKA IS LOST—RELIEF PARTY FIND HIM—CAPTURE OF A ROBBER CRAB—CANOE UPSET—RETURN TO NANKOWRI HAVEN—KATCHALL ISLAND—HUNG-HUNG-SU—CAVES IN CORAL LIMESTONE—BIRDS—BURGLARY OF HUNG-HUNG-SU'S PENATES—BOMPOKA ISLAND—GEOLOGY—BIRDS—VILLAGE—THERESA AND CHOWRA ISLANDS—LAND ON BATTI MALVE—THE HOME OF THE NICOBAR PIGEON—GEOLOGY—RATS—KAR NICOBAR—THE NATIVES—BARTER—MANGROVE-SWAMP—VILLAGE—CROSS-BOWS—BIRDS—RETURN TO PORT BLAIR—MOUNT HARRIET—LITTLE BUTTON ISLAND—EDIBLE SWALLOWS' NEST—THE REEF HERON—TRACES OF A VISIT BY NATIVES—BARREN ISLAND—NARKONDAM—GREAT COCO ISLAND—BIRDS—TREES—GEOLOGY—LITTLE COCO—TREES—CORAL REEF—HYDROSAURUS—BIRDS—GEOLOGY—PREPARIS ISLAND—TREES—COCOA-NUTS NOT FOUND—BIRDS—WRECKAGE—MONKEYS—GEOLOGY—TURTLE CATCHING—RETURN TO CALCUTTA.

SHORTLY after my return to Calcutta I was invited to join an expedition to the Andaman and Nicobar Islands, which was then being organized by Mr. A. O. Hume, Secretary to the Government of India. Arrangements were made with the British India Steam Navigation Company by which the usual monthly mail trip to Port Blair and the Nicobars, and which ordinarily occupies about seventeen days, was to be extended to a month, thus affording sufficient time for us to visit most of the islands of both groups. Our party included Mr. Hume, the late Dr. Stoliczka, Mr. Wood-Mason, Mr. Davison, and myself, with half-a-dozen native collectors and taxidermists. Being all on leave, we were free to follow our own devices and enjoy ourselves as best we could. The elements of enjoyment proved to be not wanting, and I can now look back to that month spent among the islands of the Bay of Bengal as one of the most pleasant of my life. Although a thorough and, as far as possible, exhaustive examination of the ornithology of the islands formed the primary object of the expedition, other branches of zoology and geology came within the scope of our investigations. Even botany was not neglected, as two native collectors from the Calcutta Botanical Gardens were on board.

On the 1st of March we embarked on the steamer "Scotia," and by 3 p.m. got fairly started on our journey. By sunset we had only reached as far down the river as Budge-Budge, and were therefore compelled to anchor for the night. Together with other passengers on board we found seventy male and thirteen female convicts under the charge of a guard of Sepoys. Among the men were two distinguished from their fellows by a curious episode in their lives. Nearly a year previously they had escaped in a small boat from the convict settlement at Port Blair. After suffering much hardship, they were picked up by a Norwegian vessel and made over to the English Consul at Antwerp, by whom they were forwarded to London. At the Asiatic Home, where they remained for three months, their antecedents were ascertained, and they were sent back to India, and were now about to return to the life from which they had thus ineffectually sought to free themselves. With one of them, a Sikh, I had some conversation, and learnt from him some of his adventures. The subject he seemed most particularly to dwell upon was the fact of his having walked about London in European clothes. Another of the convicts had a short time before run *ahmak** in one of the suburbs of Calcutta, on which occasion he had killed several people and wounded others. Fortunately such individuals only make their appearance at rare intervals in the crowded thoroughfares of Calcutta. How this one escaped hanging, which he most richly deserved, I cannot say.

During the following day, owing to delay in crossing the dangerous James and Mary Shoals, we did not get far enough down to continue our voyage that night with safety, and were therefore compelled to anchor near Saugor Island. Thus some precious time was lost at the outset, and a slight modification of the careful programme of our trip, drawn up by our leader, became necessary. His prevision proved of great service, and the dates being subsequently strictly adhered to, we were enabled to carry out all our plans.

Before we reached the blue water next day, specimens of a herring gull (*Larus argentatus*) and a Tern (*Sterna Bergii*) were shot, and the steamer was stopped in order that they might be retrieved. In descending into a boat for this purpose our leader unfortunately strained his back, and was in consequence very much crippled throughout the trip.

On the gloriously bright morning of the 7th of March we ran into Port Blair, and anchored off Ross Island. I have on a previous page described the physical characters and beauty of this harbour and its surroundings. I noted that the clearance of jungle had progressed, and that new buildings had been erected since my first visit, but otherwise I saw no change. Soon the different officers of the settlement, with their convict crews, put off in boats from various points on the islands and

---

* This word is anglicised into *a muck;* hence, perhaps, the slang phrase, "going a mucker." The original simply means foolish, or mad.

came on board. Our rigid programme admitted of our making no delay, and we were therefore unable to accept their offered hospitality. Our leader, after a brief conference with General Stewart, the Superintendent of the Settlement, had arranged that we were to proceed at once in a steam barge to Macpherson's Straits, which divide the Southern Andaman from Rutland Island. During the day the "Scotia's" cargo was to be unshipped, and on the following morning but one she was to pick us up and proceed southwards to the Nicobars. A few hours' steaming in the barge along and close to the coast of the South Andaman brought us to the entrance to Macpherson's Straits. The island up to this point is densely clad with forest, the hills in some places running down almost to the sea, in others terminating on the sea-face in steep cliffs with no beach at foot. At the turning-point of the island there is a small promontory called Bird-nest Cape, formed of reddish, green, and grey serpentine, upon which, save for a few tufts of grass, there is no sign of vegetation. This is but one of many examples to be found in these islands where rocks containing magnesian constituents yield a soil unable to support forest vegetation. In some places the serpentine exhibits a pseudo-bedded structure, due probably to the intrusion of an igneous rock between deposited layers of sandstone and shales. I do not think, from the few sections that I was able to examine, that the original rock was contemporaneous, but that its intrusion was accompanied by the disturbance and crushing of the beds now so apparent. Like the original igneous rock, some of the shales have also undergone alteration, and are unctuous to the touch, from the presence of a serpentinous mineral.

On the full view of Macpherson's Straits opening to our view as we rounded the Cape, we were much struck by the wild beauty of the scene. Unlike that at Port Blair, not a sign of the presence of human beings was to be seen in any direction. Although there was a decided surf breaking along the shore line, the main body of the water was perfectly still (or appeared to be so), and, as we steamed along, visions of the splendours of the submarine world broke upon our view through the pellucid waters. Though the sight was not a new one to me, I believe I did not yield to those who had never seen it before in the amount of my admiration. I feel quite unable to attempt the task of describing, much less of conveying, an adequate idea of the exquisite assortment of colour of the varied forms of life which were included in every square yard of these tropical coral reefs. The most gorgeous combination of vegetable and insect life afford but a poor subaerial representation of these submarine gardens. And yet there are many who have spent most of their lives in the tropics, and who have returned to Europe, without once having given themselves an opportunity of seeing this most marvellous of sights.

As the small islands which occur near the western end of the Straits shut out the view of the sea, its aspect from the eastern entrance suggests the existence only of a bay, or deep indentation in the coast, and it is not until one is close to the Jolly Boys Islands, as they are called, that the channels to the open sea become apparent. On the north, the Straits are bounded by the hilly, forest-clad southern extremity of the South Andaman. On the south, Rutland Island, which includes one hill, rising to the estimated height of 2,000 feet, limits the view. Along the margin, much variety is caused by the alternations of white sandy beaches with rocky headlands and steep cliffs, and the mangrove-swamps which occupy the low-lying grounds of the estuaries and mouths of streams. On getting inside the Straits, some of the party, I among the number, left the barge and proceeded towards the shore in a row-boat. Our landing in Escape Bay was not effected without some difficulty. So still did the water appear, that our helmsman, an experienced sailor, in whom we trusted, ran the boat in between two rocks. In a moment the swell caught us, and a scene of much confusion ensued. With some it became a question of *sauve qui peut*, and they scrambled on shore through the water. The lascars who had been rowing lost their heads and jumped overboard, and the boat was on the point of being smashed, when some of us had just time to seize the oars and pole out into deep water before any serious injury had happened. After this little adventure, we who remained in the boat rowed round to a sandy beach, where there were no rocks, and walked on shore through the surf.

The first bird seen was a large plover, which I—in my anxiety to shoot the first bird—approached too rapidly, and frightened off before getting within range. It was not until near the end of the trip, when at the Coco Islands, that we got a chance of obtaining a specimen. The species proved to be not the common Indian *Esacus recurvirostris*, as we had at first supposed, but the Australian *E. magnirostris.* The party then separated, and I walked westwards, over rugged purple-and-green serpentine rocks. Birds proved to be very scarce. I only shot a specimen of the Andaman tree-stare (*Calornis Tytleri*), two specimens of the white-breasted kingfisher (*Halcyon saturatior*), and one of the red-whiskered bulbul (*Otocompsa emeria*). I saw one specimen of the Burmese stork-billed kingfisher (*Pelargopsis Burmanica*), flying over the sea, and also some flocks of the Andaman paroquet (*Palæornis Tytleri*). I also heard in the depths of the forest what appeared to be the hooting of a large wood-owl, and the note of a barbet; but the Andamans have as yet yielded no species of either.

Leaving the beach, I followed up a creek for some distance, through rank vegetation and fetid mud. It was a most unwholesome locality, pervaded by the odour of wild pigs, of which, however, I did not see any. The enormous length attained by some of the species of rattan-cane, or *Calamus*, in this jungle, attracted my particular notice. Often they might be seen stretched along the ground, like huge cables, for 80 and 100 yards, before rising to ascend the lofty trees, twining through whose branches they passed over incredible distances.

Rcjoining my companions, I found that they had obtained several birds which I had not seen, including two brilliantly-coloured minivets (*Pericrocotus Andamanensis* and *P. peregrinus*). We then rowed off to the barge, and our bags, added to that obtained by the party on board, sufficed to afford ample occupation to the taxidermists for several hours. The barge then steamed to a sheltered position, and anchored for the night. Almost immediately some of the convict crew commenced to fish, and in a very short time a number of brilliantly-coloured fish were captured; but as soon as the twilight was over, the fish ceased to bite, and no more were taken. Having done ample justice to an excellent dinner, provided by one of the "Scotia's" table-servants, we tumbled into our sleeping garments and on (not in, as in Europe) to our beds, somewhat wearied with the day's exertions.

Next morning, after coffee and a plunge in the sea, the same party landed again at Escape Bay. From thence I proceeded westwards, meeting with birds in much greater abundance than I had on the previous afternoon. The best bird—because new to the islands—which was obtained was the southern brown flycatcher (*A. latirostris*); besides which I shot about a dozen other birds, including the Andaman maina (*Temenuchus Andamanensis*), the Andaman oriole (*Oriolus Andamanensis*), the Andaman green pigeon (*Osmotreron chloroptera*), &c., &c. After a few hours we returned on board, and while discussing breakfast and the cheroot which followed it, the barge steamed through the picturesque islets at the western end of the straits. Of all the places I have seen in Europe, Killarney can alone convey an idea of these scenes. The blue waters, the luxuriant emerald-green vegetation down to the margin of the coasts, and the passing showers which brighten all the aspects of nature, have their counterparts here.

Near the end of the straits there is a small island, with a white sandy beach all round, and an enormous reef, which stretches far to the south, and over which at low tide the surf could be seen boisterously breaking. This is one of the islands mentioned above as the Jolly Boys, and for purposes of distinction it was christened by us Jolly Boy Junior. Landing on it in the afternoon, when the mid-day heat and glare from the sun had somewhat abated, the first birds we saw were crows (*C. Levaillantii*), but they were far too knowing, though at such a distance from civilization, to allow themselves to be shot. I then worked down through the centre of the island, only shooting a couple of black mainas (*Eulabes intermedia*) and a green pigeon, though I got glimpses of other birds, including a goat-sucker.

At the south end of the island, on the reef, I found our leader and others of the party trying to circumvent a flock of crab-plovers (*Dromas ardeola*). They proved to be very wary, and only one was knocked over, which, falling into the sea, was retrieved by a Lascar, who experienced much difficulty in struggling through the waves and heavy surf, but fortunately sustained no injury. Besides these crab-plovers, there were several other waders on the reef, including the grey curlew (*Numenius lineatus*), the turnstone (*Strepsilas interpres*), and sand-plovers (*Ægialitis Geoffroyi* and *Æ. Mongolicus*).

Returning by the west side of the island, we discovered several small caves, the floors of which are covered by the sea at high tide. In the largest of the caves we found a colony of one of the supposed species of edible-nest-building swallows, or rather swiftlets (*Collocalia Linchi*). Many of my readers have, doubtless, heard of the edible nests so much prized by the Chinese. This was the first occasion upon which I had seen one of the bird's breeding-places. We obtained a number of nests, and some eggs. The former consisted in every case of sea-weed or other vegetable matter, firmly agglutinated together by a more or less abundant gelatinous substance of dark colour, and altogether presenting a very different appearance from that of the ordinary commercial article, which, when of the first class, consists of a perfectly white gelatinous substance, unmixed with any foreign materials. The first idea was that the original nests had been removed by the Chinese, who farm the right from Government to collect nests throughout the Andamans for a sum of £200 per annum, and that, as is commonly stated to be the case, these were the second or third attempts at building made by the birds when their supply of pure material had been exhausted. Mr. Hume, in reviewing all the evidence before him, has concluded that this species is not one of those which produces the pure white nests. To what he has stated

I may add, that on Narkondam Island, which is never visited by nest-collectors, I shot, off the face of a cliff quite inaccessible from below, several nests of the same character as those above described. The only circumstance which gives rise to a doubt in my mind is that some nests collected by Chinese, and which I obtained at Port Blair, resembled, in their shape and small size, the nests of *C. linchi*, rather than those which we took on Button Island from a different species, as I shall mention further on.

Just at sunset, as we were about to go on board the barge again, we saw the crab-plovers, which had been very much disturbed by the shooting, settle down on two small table-like islets of rock, a mile or so up the channel to the north. These were, in all probability, their roosting-places. There was only just standing room for them, and they appeared as a white band, scarcely raised above the water-line. Our boat, with the leader in the bows, and Stoliczka and myself in the stern, immediately started off to interview the birds; and visions of a splendid bag appeared before our eyes. We in the stern understood that our orders were to reserve our fire until the birds rose on being fired into by our leader. On we crept, steadily approaching, and allowing twos and threes to pass us within easy shot. At length, when the boat was within range of the main body, our leader turned round and signalled to us, not daring to speak. His signals we failed to interpret; and while he was making them, the birds suddenly rose, and in another second were off, not a shot having been fired. Gentle recrimination, not unmingled with light chaff, passed from bows to stern, and back again. Our leader concludes his account of the transaction with the following:—"In vain I pleaded that politeness alone had kept my finger from the trigger—that I was waiting and waiting for them to shoot; they were deaf to all my blandishments, and could not or would not forgive my misplaced courtesy."

Passing the barge, we rowed along the east side of the Jolly Boy Junior, and as the shades of night commenced to fall, shot a few flying-foxes (*Pteropus Nicobaricus*) as they flew off to their feeding-grounds on the larger islands. Those that we killed dead sank like stones in the water, and were lost; while the wounded ones, flapping on the surface, were easily captured. This species differs very little in size from the common *P. Edwardsi* of India, but the fur is quite black, and there are, I believe, some other differences which justify its being regarded as a distinct species.

During the night we remained at anchor close to the Jolly Boy Junior, and with the dawn landed again, in order to catch the early birds, and make the most we could out of this charming little island. I first took up a position under an *Erythrina* tree, at the blossoms of which a number of honey-suckers (*Arachnecthra Andamanica*, Hume) were assembled, quaffing a morning draught of nectar from the brilliant corollas. Shooting several of these, I passed on to the cave, where I found one of the Lascars was taking a nest, and as I stood at the entrance, I knocked over one of the swiftlets with a stick as it passed me. Thence I moved on to the reef, where I found three of our party in pursuit of the crab-plovers. I endeavoured to cut off the birds on their retreat, but failed, as when disturbed by the guns they flew out seawards. Three specimens were, however, obtained in the first discharge. Wading about on this reef was very heavy work, more especially where the coral was covered with a foot or so of water. Most destructive it proved to our boots; but the variety of life which it harboured was an irresistible attraction. "Bêche de Mer," or sea-slugs, so much esteemed as an article of food by the Chinese, were here in great abundance and variety, some of them being over a foot in length. Large pinnas and enormous clams (*Tridacna*) were abundant, but difficult to sever from the reefs. Fine specimens of some other molluscs were obtained, and various handsome sea-anemones were observed, but were left undisturbed.

Returning to the barge we steamed off to the eastern end of the Straits, where it had been arranged that we were to rejoin the "Scotia." On our way we were boarded by several canoe-loads of Andamanese, who had been hunting pigs in the neighbourhood. They had been instructed on the previous day to collect shells, &c., and of these they brought a few. These savages, being away from the restrictions which are enforced at Port Blair, were in a perfectly nude condition, save that the women wore the customary leaf. Some had covered their bodies with a coating of red clay and grease; others—those in mourning for deceased relatives—were adorned with white wood-ash. In no case was the true ebony black of their skins apparent. Indeed, this can rarely be seen, except among the well-washed orphans of the settlement. The more an Andaman native washes, it may be said, the blacker he becomes. To this cause, I have no doubt, is due the difference of opinion of various authorities as to their colour. All, both men and women, had their heads shaved, and there was not a sign of hair on any part of their bodies. This party was headed by the Rutland Island chief. He was accompanied by his wife and several other people. The "princess," as we called her, having supplied herself with a half-smoked cheroot, taken from one of our mouths, looked pleasantly about her, and then communicated in the broken Hindustani which she had picked up at the settlement, the important intelligence that a prince of the blood might shortly be expected to appear on the scene. This was a grand opportunity for obtaining specimens of their bows, arrows, cooking utensils, necklaces, paddles, &c., &c., and a brisk trade was immediately commenced. Cheroots were the currency which we employed. To one of the ladies I offered a bundle of cheroots for two necklaces which she was wearing. They consisted of turtles' vertebræ and human collar-bones strung on a thread, and richly anointed with grease and red-ochre. With most commendable obedience to her spouse, she would not close the transaction without having first obtained his consent. On his signifying his approval, however, she showed that the interests of her family were not likely to suffer while under her management; for not only did she take the cheroots agreed upon, but also suddenly snatched from my left hand those which I had intended to reserve for further transactions. Catching sight then, for the first time, of a human skull suspended from the neck of one of the defunct individual's relatives, I endeavoured to deal for it with cheroots, but found it impossible to obtain it.

Anything else could have been bartered for; but to avoid further discussion on the point, the skull was taken away and concealed in one of the canoes, and it was evident that nothing would tempt the owner to part with it. Probably it had not been carried about for a sufficient time by the friends of the deceased.

The "Scotia" now hove in sight, and it was necessary that we should proceed to join her; but our visitors were not to be easily shaken off. On this occasion my conduct seems to have rendered me open to some animadversion, so that, rather than present my own account of it, I give that of the Leader and Historian of our trip, who has written:—"The men, when we succeeded in making them understand, went off one by one, but the ladies, especially the princess, would persist in laughing and jabbering *ad infinitum.* We lifted her gently on her feet, pointed to the men who were already in the canoes, and, in fact, did everything we could think of to induce her to go, but go she wouldn't. At last the geologist, in hopes of quickening her movements, gently prodded her from behind with one of the blunt arrows she had given him; the effect was magical! Each grade of society has its own special etiquette; clearly he had gone too far; even in the most innocent manner you must not, it seems, according to Andamanese etiquette, prod a princess's natural bustle with a blunt arrow. She turned round with a look of offended dignity, that no duchess, suddenly slapped behind by a passing street-imp, as she got into her carriage, could have surpassed, and stalked off statelily to her canoe; in another moment we were off."

We found it somewhat difficult to reach the "Scotia" owing to the strong current running into the Straits, against which we had a hard struggle to make any advance. At last, having cleared the shelter of the land, we were exposed to a strong breeze and rough sea, which made the old barge roll to a most unpleasant extent, threatening to send everything which was loose on deck overboard. My whole attention had to be given to my recently-acquired ethnological collection which there had been no time to secure below, and which was now sliding about in every direction. The old tub, admirably suited for its work within the harbour of Port Blair, was clearly not one to be depended upon as a means of safe transit in squally weather outside. However, without accident, we all got on board the "Scotia," and the barge, in the charge of its convict skipper and crew, steamed off to Port Blair, while we continued our journey southwards to the Nicobars. Early on the following morning we were off the Island of Tillanschong, and immediately landed on a small beach near the southern extremity. Inside the beach we found a neck of low ground covered with screw pines or *Pandanus*, which surround a fresh-water marsh. On the other side lay Novara bay, a very picturesque indentation in the coast line, but of limited area. The rock forming the headland on the north presents a singular resemblance to an old ruined castle. On the beach pebbles of a compact blue limestone abounded. I had not time to hunt up the source whence they were derived, but found a pinkish calcareous sandstone *in situ*. I did not meet with similar rocks in any of the other islands. On the higher parts of the islands there was a dense forest jungle, the more open *Pandanus* scrub being limited to the immediate vicinity of the marsh and the beach. Shortly after landing, eight guns began active operations against the feathered inhabitants of the island. On returning to the marsh, having first examined the opposite beach, I found that vicinity deserted by my companions, who had wandered into the highlands. Thinking the marsh might, small though it was, contain some good birds, I waded about in it backwards and forwards, and so obtained three birds, which are common enough elsewhere, but which had never been shot in or recorded from the Nicobars before. There were two small bitterns (*Ardetta cinnamomea*, and *A. Sinensis*), and the white-breasted water-hen (*Gallinula phœnicura*). Another species of bittern was obtained in a different part of the island; it proved to be the Malayan tiger-bittern (*Goisakius melanolophus*). Just as I was leaving the marsh I saw a pair of megapodes, or mound-builders, which were running away from the shooters above. Following them up I knocked one over as it rose, but immediately it picked itself up and made off; by good luck I got another shot at it just as it was disappearing in the jungle, and, on going up, I found it making its last struggles. Of other birds obtained on this occasion the following were the principal: the Nicobar imperial pigeon (*Carpophaga insularis*), quite a distinct species from the Andaman bird, the Nicobar bulbul (*Hypsipetes Nicobariensis*), the Nicobar paroquet (*Palæornis erythrogenys*), the white-collared kingfisher (*Halcyon occipitalis*), the Nicobar white-eyed tit (*Zosterops Nicobariensis*), and the black-naped azure fly-catcher (*Myiagra azurea*), which, strange to say, is identical with the Indian species, while the race found in the Andamans seems to be entitled to specific distinction. A gun fired on board the steamer warned us that our time was up, and we reluctantly hurried down to the landing-place, when we partook of the milk of fresh cocoa-nuts which had been collected by the Lascars from a few trees in the vicinity.

Tillanschong is quite uninhabited; it has long been regarded as a poor unproductive rocky island, and such is the aspect it presents from the eastern side; but where we landed vegetation was abundant. We all agreed that it was a very charming spot, and regretted that our stay there was so short. Possibly the limited supply of the all-important cocoa-nuts, and also, perhaps, the fact that this long narrow island is deficient in places for concealment, have prevented its occupation by the natives. While on this subject I refer again* to what appears to me one of the most singular and unaccountable facts connected with these islands. In the Nicobars and in the Cocos cocoa-nut forests of greater or less extent are found margining the coasts of all the islands; while in the intervening Andamans, I believe I am correct in saying, not a single tree of self-sown or indigenous origin has ever been met with. Even in the outlying island of Narkondam we met with several trees which were evidently derived from drifted nuts.

---

* *Vide* p. 209.

That there is nothing in the soil or climate of the Andamans to have caused their absence is abundantly proved by the fact that at Port Blair planted cocoa-nuts have succeeded well and bear an abundance of nuts. In Preparis again, to the north of the Cocos, there are no cocoa-nuts, though they are found on the nearest coasts of the mainland of Burmah.

Continuing our voyage we entered Nankowri haven in the afternoon, and anchored off Kamorta. Little time remained that evening for seeing the new settlement, and of that little time I fear I did not make the best use, as I fancied that on the return voyage we should have plenty of leisure at our disposal. However I had previously, on my first visit, explored the neighbourhood, and in so far as ornithology was concerned, Davison, who joined us here, had been collecting birds in the vicinity for the previous month.

Building at the settlement had progressed much since my previous visit, and the convicts and sepoy guard were all housed on shore; but the officers still continued to use the hulk "Blenheim" as their dwelling-place, it being found more healthy than the shore. All precautions, however, are not sufficient to enable those who reside there to escape fever. The junior officers from Port Blair who, in rotation, have charge of the Nicobars only remain there for three months, but seldom succeed in warding off an attack.

The ship was of course visited by the Nicobarese, and I had the honour of renewing my acquaintance with Captain London and some of the other local celebrities. After some little preliminary negotiation it was arranged that two of them, Captains Long and Short, should accompany us to the Southern Islands, bringing with them a canoe which would enable us to land through the surf on uninhabited islands. It was also thought that they would be useful as interpreters between us and the inhabitants. They proved very lazy and very drunken whenever they could get an extra supply of spirits. However, they occasionally did useful service, and at all times afforded us a good laugh by the comicality of their manner and remarks. On one occasion Captain Long was asked to go off to a reef to collect shells; to this he demurred. On being then asked if shells were to be got there, he quietly replied, "Plenty, you go take." On another occasion, one of our party seeking to renew a former acquaintanceship with the same Captain Long, recalled to his memory a certain expedition which they had been on together. Upon the acquaintanceship being thus established, Captain Long did not omit to improve the occasion, for he promptly replied, "Oh yes; you give me present."

The following morning we started for the most distant part of our trip, Galatea Bay, at the southern end of the Great Nicobar, and the nearest point in these islands to Achin, in Sumatra. It was our intention to work back through the smaller islands, accordingly, during the day, we passed Meroe, Track, Treis, Montschall, the Little Nicobar, and Kabra, without stopping anywhere. In the evening we arrived off Galatea Bay, but as the weather was squally and threatened to become tempestuous, our captain, not knowing the ground, would not venture inside, the more particularly as the Bay offers no protection from the south. Accordingly we remained on and off during the night, rocking on the troubled bosom of the ocean. The following morning we steamed in, and a favourable place for mooring having been found, about a mile distant from the nearest point on shore, the anchor was let go. At eight o'clock we landed near a small village on the east side of the Bay. I at once started along the coast for the mouth of the Galatea river, about two miles distant. Some of the party remained in the vicinity of the landing place, others took the same direction as I did, whilst the remainder crossed the bay in a boat, landing on the western side near a village where we subsequently joined them. The rocks which I met with on the beach proved to be bluish-grey sandstones, similar to those found at Port Blair. In places they were covered by coral, now well raised above the sea level. In many places I encountered the huge recumbent branches of a large *Barringtonia*, with pyramidal fruits three and a-half to four inches long. In order to pass these branches, as they were washed by the sea, it was often necessary to wade round their tops. Hermit crabs were in great abundance. They seem to be chiefly vegetable feeders, and may sometimes be seen high up on trees eating at the tender inner bark of certain species and the exposed rootlets of others. I saw very few birds, and only shot a specimen of the Paradise fly-catcher (*Tchitrea affinis*) and the black-naped azure fly-catcher. As in the case of the Tillanschong bird, this proved to belong to the Indian species (*Myiagra azurea*). Others of the party were even less successful than myself, and the bag at the end of the day was not one upon which we could congratulate ourselves.

At the northern end of the Bay, east of the Galatea river, I crossed a sandy beach over which a species of *Ipomea* grew in great luxuriance. The outer zone of the jungle here was occupied by a succulent shrub, the name of which I do not know. Inside came a zone of cycads, pandanus, and a few cocoa-nuts, then another of rattans, &c., followed by general forest trees. I saw here, for the first time, the breeding-grounds of the megapode, or mound-builder, and caught sight of a few of the birds themselves running through the jungle. The largest mound which I examined was about five feet high and twelve feet in diameter. I had no means of opening it up to look for eggs, but it had much the appearance of having been deserted. Our leader, who remained during the day near the landing place, devoted some time to a thorough examination of one, and as the facts regarding the hatching of this bird's eggs are so remarkable, and at the same time so little known, I reproduce his account here:—

"I saw a considerable number of these mounds, chiefly at Galatea Bay, and there I examined some of them very minutely. These were situated just inside the dense jungle which commences at spring-tide high-water mark. It appeared to me that the birds first collected a heap of leaves, cocoa-nuts, and other vegetable matter, and then scraped together sand which they threw over the heap, so as not only to fill up all interstices, but to cover over everything with about a foot of pure sand. I say sand, but this term is calculated to mislead, because it does not contain much silex, but consists mainly of finely triturated coral and shells. After a certain period,—whether yearly or not, I cannot of course say,—the birds scrape away the covering sand layer from about the upper three-fourths of the mound, cover the whole of it over again with vegetable matter, and then cover the whole with the sand. * * * * A small mound—one as I take it still in use, though I could find no eggs in it—contained a much greater amount of vegetable matter, and was sensibly warm inside. I could make no section of it, as it was too full of imperfectly decayed vegetation. I believe that the bird depends for the hatching of its eggs solely on the warmth generated by chemical action. The succulent decaying vegetation, constant moisture, and finely triturated lime, all combined in a huge heap, will account for a considerable degree of artificial heat. The eggs are usually buried from three and a-half to four feet deep, and how the young manage to extricate themselves from the superincumbent mass of soil and rubbish seems a mystery. I could not obtain any information from natives on this point, but most probably they are assisted by their parents, if not entirely freed by them, for these latter, so the natives affirm, are always to be found in the vicinity of the mounds where their eggs are deposited."*

Be this as it may, the chickens must be fully fledged, or very nearly so, when hatched, as a chick taken from the egg shews the wing feathers well developed. The size of the eggs in proportion to the birds is enormous. Large ones are equal to the eggs of the grey Lag goose (*Anser cinereus*), and the average run very little smaller, since the measurements of sixty-two eggs in Mr. Humes' collection give length 3.25 inches, and breadth 2.07 inches. Some of them from their elongated shape remind one rather of the eggs of turtles than those of any species of bird. The colour changes from a ruddy pink to a buffy stone as the chick developes, and about hatching-time it becomes a yellowish-

* "Stray Feathers." Vol. II.

brown. Although we do not know it to be a certain fact, the balance of evidence favours the view that the young megapode on its first appearance in the world is of such large size and so well developed that, unlike the young of most, if not all, other warm-blooded animals, it is able to take care of itself. Indeed, if it be true, as is supposed by some, that several pairs of megapodes deposit their eggs in the same mound, it would be a wise chick that could recognise its own parents. And the doing so would evidence a degree of early intellect still more remarkable than the early physical development.

Close to the mouth of the Galatea river I saw in some bushes a squirrel-like little mammal which I shot. It proved to be a species of Tree-shrew. The same animal was obtained by the Novara expedition, and it has been separated from the Indian species of the genus *Tupaia* and called *Cladobates Nicobarica.*

I then followed up the Galatea river for about half-a-mile, experiencing great difficulty owing to the heaviness of the jungle on the banks and the depth and tenacity of the mud where I was obliged to walk in the bed. I here secured a fine specimen of the male cone of a cycad or zamia, which presented a resemblance to and was three times the size of a large pineapple. Before I could make my way across the river a heavy storm came on, and I was soon thoroughly wet. The canoe for crossing had been taken away by one of the ship's officers, who had gone up the river and had been a long time away. Sending the Lascar Ali (who usually accompanied me to carry my spoils) to recall him, I resigned myself to the full downpour of the heaviest rain I was ever exposed to in my life. Shortly afterwards Davison appeared, and taking off his clothes swam across and brought back a crank old canoe, into which we both got with our guns and spoils, but no sooner had we reached the centre of the river than the canoe shipped water and sank, and we had to return ignominiously to the bank. After some time a native who was going on a fishing excursion appeared and ferried us across. I proposed to exchange a bottle of rum for his fishing-spear, but although I added some silver coins he would not close with the offer. We then heard that the ship's officer had rather come to grief. His canoe had capsized, and his gun, &c., had gone to the bottom in deep water. The gun was, however, recovered by the Lascar I had sent, who had to dive for it. We then walked along the western shore to a village where others of the party had been safely ensconced during the rain. Several objects of ethnological interest had been obtained by them. We refreshed ourselves with some cocoa-nut milk and brandy, and soon afterwards, as the weather shewed no sign of improving, walked through the surf to our boat, and went on board, arriving there in a thoroughly moist and limp condition.

In the evening I bought from the natives a large piece of bark-cloth, which serves as a covering, but is not quite water-proof. It is prepared from the inner bark of a tree which has been stated to be a species of *Celtis;* but I am not sure whether this is correct or not. In appearance it resembles coarse newly-tanned leather. It is both tough and flexible. As to the manner of its preparation I have no information. Some flute-shaped musical instruments of bamboo were obtained here. They are blown into from the end, as in a flageolet; but the "reed" is loosely tied over one of the holes.

The last to come on board that evening were Captains Long and Short, who had evidently found their way to their compatriots' cellars. There was much of the "Won't go home till morning" manner about them; but they had sense enough left to paddle out their canoe in safety, and to realize the chance of the steamer leaving them behind. If I remember rightly, they had managed to bring off sundry cocoa-nut-fed pigs, gifts from their admiring friends. The cocoa-nut-fed pigs yield probably as good pork as is to be found anywhere. It was always an acceptable addition to our commissariat.

We remained at anchor for that night in Galatea Bay, and the following morning, with the first streak of dawn, steamed off along the western coast of the Great Nicobar. On this side of the island the undulating ground rises gently towards the main range, which culminates in a high hill to the north-east of the island.

This by some has been thought to be a volcano, and it is even said that flames have, on one occasion, been seen to issue from it. Trustworthy evidence on the subject is, however, altogether wanting. The geology, fauna, flora, and ethnology of the Great Nicobar are, as regards their details, still quite unknown; and, owing to the risk of sleeping in the pestiferous forests are likely to remain so for many years.

We came to anchor, about noon, in St. George's Channel, between Kondul Island and the Great Nicobar, Soon afterwards we landed, or rather one detachment of our party landed, on Kondul. This, though a small island, was selected, as we knew that most of the previously-obtained specimens of the extremely rare paroquet (*Palæornis caniceps*) had been shot there. At the western side, where we first landed, there was no village, but we found that two Malays, belonging to a vessel now cruising about the island, had established a depôt there for the collection of cocoa-nuts. While standing near their hut, I heard a paroquet calling, which I thought must be *P. caniceps.* On going to the spot I found a splendid tame male bird in full plumage, perched on an ingeniously-contrived bamboo stand. The Malays were not at first very willing to part with it, but having given them much more than its value could ever be to them, I carried it off in triumph.

Though we caught glimpses of several birds here we did not succeed in shooting any, and as it was impossible to penetrate into the island, owing to the steep cliffs, we got into the boat again, and rowed round to the other side, landing close to a village containing three or four houses. Here we found birds plentiful, and before long nine or ten specimens of the rare paroquet, several of a beautiful little scarlet honey-sucker, since described as new by Mr. Hume, under the name (*Æthopyga Nicobarica*), besides a number of other birds, were brought to bag by our party. In one of the houses I also purchased two fine females of the paroquet. The subsequent fate of these three birds was a sad one. They reached Calcutta safely, and for two months I kept them there, and they proved to be most intelligent and beautiful pets. As the species, except on one occasion, had never before been sent alive to Europe, I, when about to leave Calcutta myself, sent them by the steamer "Dhulia," bound direct for London. At Madras I went on board to enquire for my pets, and found that all three had been found hanging dead from their perches one morning. That they had died either from poisoning or suffocation I had no doubt. As the ship's officer into whose charge they had been given had himself died from cholera in the river Hugli, they had, I suppose, been neglected.

On this island of Kondul I made some interesting additions to my ethnological collection. Among these were two cleverly-carved wooden images. If I have not been misinformed these objects are no more idols than are the portraits of our ancestors with which we are in the habit of adorning our houses. I availed myself of the opportunity of examining the interiors of several of the houses, as the natives were remarkably civil. Neither women nor children were to be seen. They, as we usually found to be the case, had been already concealed on the steamer being first sighted. In one house I obtained a spear-head of copper; and this is the only one of the kind I have ever seen. I was also given a curious specimen of Nicobarese hieroglyphics, or picture-writing. The material upon which the figures are drawn appears to be the spathe of one of the species of Palm—it is too large for the *glume* or sheath of a bamboo, which it otherwise resembles. It is framed with slips of bamboo, and from the lower margin are suspended offerings of young cocoa-nuts and dried meat. That it is intended to record some event, or is the record of some transaction is, I think, extremely probable. Nearly all the articles represented are well known objects in the domestic economy of the Nicobarese.* The sun and moon and a few stars are to be found at the head of all these paintings, however they may otherwise differ in details, and the presence of these male and female

* An illustration and description of this screen will be found in the "Indian Antiquary—Bombay." Vol. IV., 1875.

emblems suggests to me a possible connection with marriage. The figures in different attitudes, apparently giving expression to different emotions, do not fit in well with an idea that might otherwise appear plausible, namely, that the upper portion represents the property of the man, the lower the dowry of his bride. Some of these screens are divided into three portions—the upper including the celestial bodies and birds, the central, various terrestrial objects, and the lower, fish and other denizens of the waters. Supposing them to have a meaning, I trust ere long it will be decided how far the designs are conventional and how far realistic. As a rule these pictures are not readily parted with. The one I obtained was taken with the consent of the natives from an apparently deserted house.

For most of the day while I remained on the island I was closely followed by one of the natives lightly clad in a narrow strip of cloth, and the usual seedy black silk hat. On one occasion, when I sat down to rest on an old broken and rotten canoe, he came and sat by me, in closer proximity than was absolutely pleasant; but before I could remonstrate and suggest the removal of his somewhat odoriferous person to a distance, the seat gave way with the additional weight, and we were both sent flying on our backs.

The only rocks which I saw on this island were sandstones, which on the east were steeply tilted, but on the west appeared to be horizontal. I saw some traces of carbonaceous matter in them, but found no fossils.

Leaving the ship at six o'clock on the following morning we again landed on Kondul, and got a more complete series of the same birds as we had shot on the previous evening, and some few additional species, more particularly among which should be mentioned a cuckoo (*Cuculus striatus*, Drapiez), as being an addition to the hitherto known fauna of the islands. Of the paroquet (*Palæornis caniceps*) nineteen dead and five live birds were brought away. Our greatest prize, however, was the beautiful little new species of honey-sucker (*Æthopyga Nicobarica*, Hume). Altogether we were most successful on Kondul, and I think we all agreed, at the close of our trip, that it was one of the best islands for birds which we had visited.

I asked the people on this island about the "ourang-outang" or inland jungle race of inhabitants, and they at once pointed to the highlands of the Great Nicobar as being the place where they were to be found. My informants said they were very bad men, but that they themselves seldom saw them. From want of an interpreter, I was not able to obtain any detailed account. But I am convinced that they will prove to be people resembling the Andamanese, although a very good authority on the Nicobars, Mr. De Ropestorff, thinks otherwise.

In the afternoon we started for the uninhabited island of Montschall, and landed there soon after. Having shot some of the little shore-waders (*Strepsilas* and *Ægialitis*), I started to walk round the island, but soon found the undertaking much more difficult than I had anticipated. Passing some of the party who had given up the idea in despair, I pressed onwards, sometimes scrambling round the steep faces of precipices, again wading, once up to my neck, in the rising sea, carrying my coat and gun aloft; my attendant, the Lascar Ali, following with other traps. At length I was fairly brought to a stand in a small enclosed bay, from which it would have been very difficult, if not impossible, to climb up the cliff into the jungle. The rising tide not only prevented our advance, but our retreat also, except, of course, by swimming, which, with our traps, would have been, to say the least, inconvenient. The sun was now setting, and the prospect of wandering in the dark through the jungle, supposing we could reach it, was not a pleasant one. By a most fortunate chance, at this critical moment a boat, which some of the "Scotia's" Engineers had taken out for a row round the island, made its appearance, and I was glad to accept a seat in it; and I don't think Ali was sorry, as, though he did not say much, the prospect before us of fighting in the dark through a thorny jungle was not cheerful.

The rocks on this island are chiefly stratified limestones of peculiar aspect. Sometimes they look spongy and cellular, like quite recent coral reefs, but in places the alternating layers were not more than two inches thick; and small faults and dislocations in these were not uncommon.

The next morning we arrived at the small islands of Treis and Track. We first landed on Treis, where we found birds in great abundance, pigeons being particularly numerous. In a short time fifty-two specimens of the very handsome black and white fruit-eating pigeon (*Carpophaga bicolor*) were bagged. These birds were in greatest abundance near the centre of the island in the branches of a large species of fig—what species I cannot say; but certainly not *Ficus indicus*, as has been stated in some of the previous accounts. Having shot nine of the pigeons, and seeing numbers falling to other guns, I proceeded to examine the island, which is very flat; and I think, so far as I can remember, I found no rocks exposed. Certainly I noted none at the time. As I entered a nearly dried-up grassy marsh, a megapode scuttled out, giving me an easy shot. Startled with the report, a young white-bellied sea eagle then rose from the grass in front of me, and received the charge from my second barrel, which, though it only contained No. 8 shot, proved sufficient to bring him to bag also. Another specimen was also obtained on this island. I then tried several long, or rather high, shots at the Nicobar pigeon (*Calœnas Nicobaricus*), but without success, as the birds were very wary, and seldom were to be seen within range. Two, however, were shot by one of the ship's officers. In company with two others I then crossed to the small island of Track, where we saw a number of *Calœnas*, or rather, I should say, heard them; for they would make a heavy flutter in the topmost branches of the highest trees, and be off before one came within range. These birds, except in one instance, to be mentioned further on, were, I found, excessively wary, seldom affording chances of a shot. On Track there were sandstones steeply inclined to the east. Near the landing-place we found some temporary huts, which had no doubt been put up by Nicobarese when visiting for the purpose of collecting cocoa-nuts. In these several articles had been left behind, including a neatly-made earthenware cooking vessel, of an oblate-spherical shape, and about 14 inches in diameter. A gun was then fired from the ship, and we, with the exception of one of our party, Davison, who had started to return before we left the islands, reached the ship after a rather long row. Davison's boat was at first nowhere to be seen; at last we saw it rounding one of the islands. When he came on board we found that he had been carried away by a strong current, against which the Lascars' feeble rowing had made very little progress.

In the evening we anchored off the island of Meru. We had been all much fagged by the morning's heavy work; and for my part a want of cartridges, and the necessity of preparing more for the following day, afforded an excuse which I was not sorry to avail myself of for not going on shore, the more particularly as it was late, and the island did not present an attractive appearance. Stoliczka, however, said he would go for a stroll on the beach and return before dark. As he did not intend penetrating the jungle, he only wore light canvas shoes, and was otherwise quite unequipped for rough work. He was accompanied by Mackay, Executive Engineer of Port Blair, and two of the ship's officers. They had a pull of more than a mile to the shore, or rather to the outside of the surf, through which the ship's boat could not be taken; but some Nicobarese, who had come to the island to collect cocoa-nuts, landed them in their canoes. They then spread themselves along the coast in order to shoot whatever they could before darkness. When the time to return had arrived Stoliczka did not make his appearance; and, as the evening wore on, his companions on shore began to be anxious, and, as we afterwards learnt, soon started in two parties to search for him. After a couple of hours spent in this way, Mackay and the chief officer, who headed the two parties, returned without having found any trace of the lost Doctor. Seeing the lights carried along the shore, and hearing the firing, we on the steamer at first supposed that bats or some night birds were abundant on the island, and were being shot by the party. But this theory gave way to a growing feeling of anxiety that all was not right.

Accordingly the Captain despatched a boat with the second officer for tidings. A fresh breeze enabled him to make the trip to and fro in about half-an-hour. On his return we were startled by the intelligence that Dr. Stoliczka was *lost*, and that, as above mentioned, search for him had been made but without success. It was added that those on shore were thoroughly fagged and tired, but that they had expressed their intention of renewing the search when somewhat rested. We immediately felt the importance of rendering prompt assistance, the more particularly as the self-devotion of those on shore had already been severely taxed. Volunteers from all grades and classes on board the ship presented themselves, including one of two little English apprentice boys. The late Dr. Dougall, Superintending Surgeon of Port Blair, who had not taken part in our daily excursions, hastily making such preparations as might be useful in the case of an accident having taken place, joined us, and, with a good stock of blue lights and lanterns we rowed off for the shore, and soon after landed through the surf in canoes. While rowing on shore our thoughts dwelt upon all the possible accidents that could have happened to our friend. One suggested that he had fallen over a cliff; another, that he had shot himself, or his gun had burst; another, that he had been bitten by a snake. Any of these were more plausible than that he had been attacked by natives; for wherever we had seen them they had appeared civil and inoffensive. Our leader, though in a state of the greatest anxiety as to what could have happened to our lost friend, was unable, from the effects of his accident, to take any active part in the search himself; but before we left he drew up a code of signals by means of which, with our guns, we might convey to those on board, in the speediest manner, the results of our search. The first thing to be done was to enjoin upon all the necessity of not firing a single shot except under authority. As I carried a handy little Snider carbine, such shots as would be required were to be alone fired by me. It was now about eleven o'clock at night, and I shall never forget the appearance of the motley crowd of Europeans and natives that stood in the moonlight on that white coral beach. Captains Long and Short, our own Nicobarese, after a short conference with those camped on the island, told us that the latter were ready to cut a path for us through the jungle. They professed themselves able to find the lost one in such a confident way, that we unhesitatingly followed their leadership, and started with a pleasing assurance of success. We first walked for about half-a-mile along the beach on the southern side of the island, and then struck into the jungle, where we had to follow one another in single file in the footsteps of the Nicobarese, who rapidly cut the branches and creepers which they encountered. Sometimes we came upon partly-open spaces, where the trees and the rope-like rattans, stretching to the topmost branches, could be seen with clearness when the blue lights were ignited. Weird and strange were some of these scenes, and unlike anything I had ever before conceived of, much less seen.

After some time, calling for perfect silence, I fired a shot, but no response was heard, and we proceeded for several hundred yards; again I fired, waited a short interval, and then, with what joy did we welcome the sound of a distant shot in reply. This, the first assurance that our friend was alive, and able to use his hands at least, sent us forward with renewed energy. From this onwards we pursued a steady course, our shots, fired at intervals, being replied to, and, at last, our voices too. In reply to "Where are you?" came "I can't get out!" And such, indeed, we found to be the case on reaching him, for he was fairly immeshed by the thorny creepers, and was actually leaning against a barrier of them. Having supplied him with a drink, his parched throat was somewhat relieved, and he then told us that he had replied to our calls with the greatest difficulty. The story of his adventures was, in short, that, contrary to his intention, he had gone into the jungle in pursuit of some rats which he had seen running about, had lost his way, and wandered about until the darkness came upon him. At one place he pushed forward to where he could see the sea, but had to turn back, as he found himself on the margin of a precipitous cliff. After some time he heard the shots of those who first went in search of him; he had fired in reply to them, but as they were in two parties, this led to no definite result, he being unable to force his way out, and the respective parties not knowing which shots were his, or, indeed, that he had fired at all. When this firing ceased, he lay down on the ground, but did not long remain there, as certain ominous rustlings in the leaves were suggestive to him of snakes. He then climbed up a tree, and was in that position when he heard our first shot. His previous shooting had been so futile of results, that he did not reply; but, on our second report seeming to come from a less distant point, he got down and fired a shot, and continued replying to us until we had reached him. His clothes and hands were much torn by the thorns, and his canvas shoes had been cut to pieces and his feet torn by the coral. Probably, had he taken with him a Lascar, or even his own faithful Hindu collector, Bullaram,* this would never have happened; for natives in such emergencies often show a wonderful instinctive power of steering through trackless jungle.

When retracing our steps, the light of the lamp carried in front suddenly flashed on an object at the foot of a tree close to me. A gigantic spider it appeared to me to be at the moment. Calling for the light to be brought closer, I saw that it was a crab of enormous dimensions, and, as it showed some intention of making off, I placed my foot firmly down on the carapace, in such a position that it could not get at me with its claws. None of the party having any rope or string with him, Davison cut a creeper, and making a noose with it, passed it over the animal's body, and proceeded to carry it. He had not got very far before the crab, stretching out its claws, caught his coat, and was gradually working itself upwards, and in a very few

---

* Some months later, when seeing my poor friend and colleague off at the train, on his departure for Yarkand, I charged this same Bullaram never to lose sight of his master, and bring him back safe to India. Twelve months afterwards, when returning laden with his spoils, Stoliczka succumbed to the effects of his journey at high elevations.

moments there would have been a scene rivalling Victor Hugo's description of the sailor in the toils of the cuttle-fish. However, while I held the crab, Davison took off his coat, and when it was laid on the ground, the strain being removed, the crab speedily let go and tried to make off.

How to give an adequate description of this crustacean fiend, which rejoices in the title of cocoa-nut thief, and is called *Birgus latro* by naturalists, I scarcely know, but the accompanying illustration will serve to convey some idea of its terrific appearance and powerful structure. When stretched to the utmost, it is

THE COCOA-NUT THIEF (*Birgus latro*).
(*From a Photograph.*)

about two and a-half feet in diameter. Of the great power of its claws we had evidence, from the fact that with one it simply crushed into fibre the end of a stout oak stick which was presented to it. Whether, as is stated to be the case, it climbs cocoa-nut trees and cuts off the nuts, descending again to devour them at leisure, remains to be proved; but there is no reason for doubt that it lives principally on fallen cocoa-nuts. The species has a wide range, being found in some of the islands in the Pacific, as well as in those of the Indian Ocean, and in the former the habits have been more fully studied than there has been opportunity for in the latter. Although living in deep burrows at the roots of trees, it is stated that it at times takes to the sea and to a diet of shell-fish. The inhabitants of the Samoan group of islands regard the flesh as a delicacy, and dig the crabs out of their burrows, in which there is often to be found a quantity of finely-carded cocoa-nut fibre, which is made use of for various purposes. Our captive being taken on board, we inverted over it an iron tank, under which it was kept alive for several days. On our arrival at the island of Kar Nicobar, where there was abundant evidence of the existence of these crabs, afforded by the torn husks which lay scattered about in every direction, we showed the crab to some of the natives, and offered them rewards if they would bring specimens. When the tank was lifted up, they drew back with horror, and declined most distinctly to have anything to do with the capture of another; and some of them even precipitantly left the ship, as though they had just remembered that they had important business to transact at home.

Having discovered our friend, and on reaching the beach, we fired the preconcerted signal, by which those on board were to understand that all was well, and then we followed the shots by three ringing cheers, which conveyed to them an assurance doubly sure of the successful results of our search.

On our return to the ship's boat we crossed the surf in a canoe, which was so heavily laden that there was barely an inch above the water-line. The Nicobarese paddler brought us alongside, and we—three of us—stretched out our hands to catch the side. In a moment the canoe turned under us, and the outrigger was lifted round out of the water and on to the heads of those who were standing up to receive us. Fortunately we could all swim, and had our guns in our hands, so that beyond the loss of a few trifles we suffered no injury from this midnight immersion. On the "Scotia" a warm welcome, of course, awaited Stoliczka. Somewhere about two o'clock that night we sat down to supper, and though not many could eat, we were able to drink to the health of the universally-popular Doctor.

To some of those who may read this narrative, it may appear, perhaps, that too much has been made of this adventure; but I can assure them—and those who know the character of the

Nicobarese jungles will bear me out in saying—that our extreme state of anxiety at the time was fully justified by the circumstances. Even after Stoliczka was found, the effects of an attack from the severe and too often fatal Nicobarese fever was much to be feared.

The following morning we steamed off for Kamorta, reaching Nankowri haven at nine o'clock. I landed at the village of Malacca, on Nankowri, and got from the natives some spears and two large wooden models of a shark and dolphin. These, like all such objects tied up in Nicobarese houses, had small pieces of dried meat attached as offerings. They were given readily in exchange for some rum, and did not seem to be very highly valued by their owners. The only bird I shot here was a specimen of the chimney swallow (*Hirundo gutturalis*, Scop.).

At four o'clock we steamed out by the western channel, and anchored off the island of Katchall for the night. Early the following morning we landed on Katchall, near a village where resides a somewhat notorious character, called Hung-hung-su. Whether from a consciousness of his guilt, or from a knowledge that though innocent he is in police phraseology "wanted," this gentleman immediately leaves his marine villa for some hiding-place in the jungle, whenever the island is visited by English ships. The charge against him is that he was a ringleader in many of the piracies which took place before the occupation of the islands by the British in 1869. It is believed that a European woman with her child, the wife of a captain of a vessel, who had been murdered with all his crew, were kept for some days and brutally ill-used by this man, who afterwards murdered them. On the present occasion Hung-hung-su's house, into which I peeped, had all the signs of having only been just vacated. We first struck inland to see some caves which are about half-a-mile from the coast. They are situated in a bed of limestone, which seems to have been derived from coral, but is not I think an original reef. Its general appearance is suggestive of coral, but the more closely it is examined the less does its rugose and cellular structure, exposed on the surface, seem to represent original coral structure. Some portions resemble a form of travertine. I believe its rugose appearance is in a much greater degree due to the solvent action of the rain-water than to its original structure. The greatest length of the principal cave appears to be about sixty yards; but there are low passages leading off in different directions, which we had not the means of exploring. A small species of bat (*Miniopteris pusillus*, Dobson), abounds, and its droppings formed the floor. Of these bats we caught a large number in butterfly nets. There was no time for examination of the country further inland, and I did not see any of the sandstones which are said to occur. I am inclined to think that these caves have been used as places of resort by the natives, and a thorough examination of them might yield some traces of the pre-historic race, which there are some grounds for believing may have occupied the islands before the advent of the Nicobarese, who are undoubtedly of extraneous origin. I would commend the subject to the notice of those who may have opportunities of visiting Katchall.

Leaving these caves we struck off, each taking independent tracks, to search for the Nicobar pigeons, which were said to occur in the island. I came across several small parties, but could never get within range. Several times I heard megapodes clucking in dense undergrowth quite close to me, but I could not succeed in seeing one. In a stream I found a large *Neritina* in considerable abundance, but only brought away a few, for which I was reviled by the conchologists of the party, who told me it was a rare and valuable species. There was no great bag of birds made: those shot were of species of which many specimens had previously been obtained on the other islands. Something about this island that I cannot explain gives it a sombre and cheerless aspect. It may have been the weather on that particular day which caused the feeling. However this may be, my recollections of the island are less pleasant than those regarding any other upon which we landed.

On our return to the ship I heard that the two before-mentioned European apprentices had been allowed to go on shore. Coming across Hung-hung-su's house they had scrambled up the ladder, pushed the door aside, and soon after passed down a large, more than life-size, wooden figure of a man. Soon after returning to the ship with this prize, they were at once ordered to return and replace it by the captain. They pleaded, knowing my weakness for ethnological specimens, that they had brought it for me. This argument, however, was very properly not regarded as being sufficient to justify what might be called by a bad name; and the tutelar deity, or whatever these figures should be called, was duly returned to his post at the head of the ladder in Hung-hung-su's house.

About noon we sailed for the island of Bompoka, on the eastern side and landed in the afternoon. I must say that I failed to see a resemblance which this island is supposed by Dr. Rink to present to a volcano. Neither the state of the jungle, nor the time at our disposal, admitted of our penetrating far from the beach. The only rocks which I saw were sandstones *in situ* and loose fragments of serpentine. These sandstones are similar to those in the Great Nicobar. The higher parts, including the supposed volcano, only support a grass vegetation, like that in the highlands of Kamorta, and I fully anticipate that the rocks will prove to be of similar character in both localities. Just within the cocoa-nut zone I came upon several clearances where the natives had made strongly-fenced gardens, in which plantains, chillies, papayas, and limes were growing. I passed quite close to a man at work, but he was so intently engaged that he neither saw nor heard me.

I shot several specimens of the Nicobar bronze-winged pigeon (*Carpophaga insularis*, Blyth), and might have got a large number, but these birds were now rather a drug in our hands. I also shot some of the Nicobar collared kingfisher (*Halcyon occipitalis*, Blyth), and a specimen of the bush-thrush (*Geocichla albogularis*, Blyth). This last species, though I occasionally saw it on the other islands, I had always found difficult to obtain, from the simple fact that perching on the ground it could only be seen at very close quarters, too close to admit of its being fired at without being blown to pieces, and so hitherto I had allowed it to escape. In the village I found a number of natives lolling about. Only one or two of them had articles of European clothing. They seemed to me to be cleaner-limbed, clearer-skinned, taller, and in every way better-looking men than the inhabitants of Nankowri and Kamorta. Their language is probably the same, or nearly so, as that which is spoken in the latter islands. The houses—both of the bee-hive and rectangular shapes—were remarkably well built; one of large size, and with well-laid smooth and polished plank flooring, since it did not contain any fire-place or domestic utensils, was, probably, a sort of meeting-house. These people were too lazy to climb the cocoa-nut trees, but kept a ladder which they readily used in order to supply us with as many nuts as we required. They did not seem to care much about rum, and the difference in their appearance may perhaps be due to their having more temperate habits than our more civilized acquaintances of Nankowri.

Returning on board the steamer while there was still light, we cruised along close to Theresa, a somewhat uninteresting-looking island, upon which we determined not to land. We then passed Chowra, a small island where the potters, who supply the whole of the Nicobars with cooking vessels, reside. During the night we steamed slowly towards the small island of Batti Malve, and by early morning circled round it at such a distance that it was impossible to see where a landing might be effected. Yielding to our entreaties, our ever-careful captain circled round again much closer in, and then we saw a little bay with narrow beach, which we thought might answer our purpose. During our first circling we had seen some parties of black birds with white tails flying from the island towards the south-east. At first we could not identify them; but when approaching the above-mentioned little bay, all doubt on the subject was set aside by our seeing, to our intense delight, a number of Nicobar pigeons feeding on the ground. We found that though it would have been quite practicable to land on the beach by wading from the boat, it would have been impossible to scale the surrounding cliff. Everywhere else there was a heavy swell breaking at the foot of the vertical cliffs which give this small island such a peculiar appearance. By choosing a spot on the west side, where this cliff was only about seven or eight feet high, and where the rock surface was sufficiently rough to be ascended by using hands and feet, and by anchoring the boat astern and then carefully working her bow on until within jumping distance, we one by one effected a landing, and, rushing off into the jungle, soon found that we had lighted upon *the* breeding-place and home of the Nicobar pigeon. In something less than two hours over sixty of these birds were shot, and many more might have been obtained, but that, owing to the somewhat critical position of the boat, the Lascars had to be left in her, and we had to carry our spoils ourselves; and this necessitated frequent returns to the landing-place, as it was impossible to carry a number of these heavy birds at a time without injury to their feathers. In one of these trips I had the misfortune to lose a hunting-knife which had all along proved invaluable for cutting a path through the jungle, and here especially, where the undergrowth was thorny. Had I been on an inhabited island I should probably have thought it had been stolen by the natives, as it often had excited their cupidity. It was made by Anachellum, of Salem, in the Madras Presidency, and was of much better quality and shape than any English hunting-knife I have had or seen. None of the trees on this island were of more than medium height. Many of them were covered with nests, some of which were only about eight feet from the ground; but we did not meet a single instance of a nest on the ground. In one or two Davison found eggs; but we were rather late for them, and young birds in various stages, from the newly-hatched to the fully-fledged, were to be found in most of the nests. Only one young one was found in each nest, and it would appear that but one egg is laid by this bird. In one place the old birds were feeding on the ground on some fallen seeds. Hitherto, on the other islands we had never seen a bird lower than the topmost branches of high trees, and I fancy that it must sometimes feed on fruits while still on the branch, and that it is by no means exclusively a ground-feeder. Previous accounts have either actually stated or indicated the probability that it breeds on the ground. I believe, however, the nests were never before taken by Europeans. It is probable that a large proportion of the birds which spread throughout the Nicobars come to this island to breed, but that all do not do so is evident from the fact that the natives occasionally have young birds for sale. Not unfrequently, too, they snare the old ones. The bird is a hardy one, and promises to do well in captivity. Some young ones which we brought away arrived safely in Calcutta, and one of them paired and bred with another subsequently brought from the Nicobars. In July, 1873, I saw about twenty of these birds in the Jardin des Plantes, in Paris, labelled from Cochin China. They looked remarkably healthy, and were in splendid plumage. In young birds the tail is not white as it is in the adults, but is of the same colour with the back. There are no hackles, and the general aspect is sombre and utterly fails to convey an idea of the splendour of the adult. Though generally a silent bird, those on Batti Malve kept up a constant croaking. This may be peculiar to the breeding season. When fairly started it is, I should say, a strong flyer, though the heavy and clumsy fluttering made by it as it leaves its perch at first gives the idea of somewhat feeble powers of flight.

Batti Malve appears to be formed of raised coral; but I think there are some sandstones at the northern base. I had no opportunity, however, of giving them a close examination. The remains of a hut and some fragments of broken earthenware vessels shewed that this island has been previously visited by someone; but there were very few cocoa-nuts, so it is difficult to say what the attraction may be—possibly the pigeons. At all times it must be difficult to land on it from native canoes, and when the slightest sea is on quite impossible, as there is no spot where a canoe could be beached. Probably the visitors were not Nicobarese, but the crews of Malay or other vessels.

On a gun being fired on board, our party, with the exception of Davison, all assembled. For about half-an-hour we waited, and as during that time we heard no shots from him, we began to fear some accident had befallen him. Just as we were about to start in search of him we saw him wearily walking along the rocks. It appeared that he had felt himself completely overcome by heat and exhaustion, and had lain down at the foot of a tree close to where the pigeons were feeding on the ground, and had availed himself of the opportunity of closely observing their habits.

Strange to say, I saw some rats on this small island. In the first pursuit of the pigeons I was so engrossed that I let them pass, and afterwards could not find one when I wanted to do so. None of the party obtained any specimens. The small mammals occurring in the Nicobar and Andaman islands do not appear to be numerous; but their examination, when a sufficient number shall have been collected, is likely to give results of high interest.*

Returning on board, we sailed for the large island of Kar Nicobar, and anchored in a bay at the southern extremity. Our arrival was the signal for the crews of two large native vessels to hoist sail and make off. Whether they had finished their business, or had guilty consciences and dreaded any questions being asked as to their movements, we did not find out. Soon canoes put off from the shore, and the natives, with a narrow strip of red calico round their loins and a band or cincture of palm-spathe binding their flowing locks, pressed up the companion ladder. Ladies being on board, they were not allowed at first to come on deck, upon which Captain Snooks, their leader, looking very much disconcerted, stretched out his hand and exclaimed, "Why are you so unfriendly?" Afterwards the Captain of the "Scotia" took him into his office cabin to do business: in other words, negotiate the purchase of some pigs and fruit. We were not a little amused to observe that the Captain arrayed himself in a staff officer's old cocked hat and feathers, which he proposed, in a fit of generosity, to exchange with other articles for fat swine. I rather think Captain Snooks was not much smitten by it, and considered an ordinary black silk hat, according to Nicobar taste, a more appropriate

* On this subject *vide* Appendix D.

head covering for a gentleman. I believe, however, he took the cocked hat, and will probably astonish future visitors by wearing it when paying them a visit. There were very few articles of European clothing among these people, Captain Snooks speaks English fairly. This knowledge of English possessed by the Nicobarese, of which we found evidence on all the islands, seemed to be remarkable, since the visits of ships with English-speaking crews cannot be very frequent. On one occasion I overheard the Lascar Ali talking English to a Nicobarese, though I had previously no idea that he understood a word of the language. We did not meet any of the personages bearing the distinguished and aristocratic names mentioned by the author of the "Novara" account, and alluded to on a previous page.

On landing I started up a creek which I endeavoured to follow, but after going about half-a-mile through mud, which was often up to my knees, and might at any moment have been up to my neck, I was obliged to stop. Had the tide been in, this creek would have been navigable. The only birds I saw were some whimbrel and curlew, but they would not let me get within range, The Nicobarese who followed me had all along been endeavouring to make me turn back. One man continually calling out "go road." I then, much to their disgust, and subsequently too to my own, struck off into the bordering mangroves, expecting to meet solid ground within a few yards; instead of which I had a weary tramp of nearly a mile through fetid mud and rotten mangrove stems, where I caught two water snakes, but saw no birds. The miasma which arose as I walked was fast beginning to affect my head. On reaching the jungle I went off with a number of natives to a village, where I drank some cocoa-nut milk and brandy, and began to shake off the evil effects, but for the whole of the day the fetid vapours seemed as it were to follow me. The village was a poor one; I only looked into one or two of the houses, and they did not appear to be nearly so comfortable as those on most of the other islands. The people are of much lighter build than those at Nankowri; their mouths, too, are less disfigured by pawn chewing.

How far these characteristics may be general throughout Kar Nicobar I do not know. It would appear from the published vocabularies that the language is, though of course allied, distinct from those used on the other islands. It has not as yet, however, I believe, been subjected to any very close analysis. In some of the previous accounts mention is made of cross-bows as being used by these people, and I was on the look-out for one, but did not see any in the houses. One of our party, after our return to the ship, told me that he had seen one. I cannot suppose but that this form of weapon was introduced by Europeans. A cross-bow is, however, I believe, used by a tribe in Western Africa. I got here, with some difficulty, two of the cane cylinders which are worn in the ears. The owners were most unwilling to part with them, but by offering three times their intrinsic value, and then setting the other natives to laugh at the men for refusing my liberal offer, I effected my purpose by means of their ridicule.

I then returned to the beach, and walked through the cocoa-nut zone, which is on this island very broad, where I shot two very rare birds, the Nicobar Tree-stare (*Temenuchus erythropygius*), and the Hawk Owl (*Ninox hirsutus*), besides several others. The first mentioned as it fell was caught in the leaf-stalk of an areca-palm at about sixty feet from the ground. I asked a man to go up for it and he immediately started. In his ascent he simply grasped the trunk with his hands and walked up. We saw many torn husks of cocoa-nuts on the ground which we supposed shewed the marks of the large crab; but the natives to whom the captive on board had been shown, resolutely refused to point out where one might be found. I saw nothing of the geology of this island, no rocks being exposed where we landed.

The following morning we reached Port Blair, where most of the afternoon was spent in calling on the residents. Early the next morning Stoliczka and I ascended Mount Harriet and shot a few birds. The view from the top of Mount Harriet which, as I have elsewhere stated, is 1,100 feet above the sea, is certainly very fine; but some indistinctness of demarcation between sea and land was caused by masses of clouds which, at that early hour, filled up the valleys.

By noon we had left Port Blair, and were steaming off northwards to the Archipelago, and in a few hours landed on an island known as the Little Button. In a cave on the south side we got a number of edible nests of a species of Swiftlet (*Collocalia spodiopygia*) as identified by Mr. Hume. These nests are made throughout of a gelatinous material without the admixture of any foreign substances. On the outer surface the material is in overlapping layers terminating in a sharp well-defined edge. Inside is a beautiful web of interlacing cross-stays of thread-like gelatine. These give to the nest great strength, and a certain amount of elasticity. The more regularly-formed had a horse-shoe shape, the flat side being that which was attached to the rock. Modifications of this shape were sometimes caused by the nature of the surface of the rock. They vary in breadth (long diameter) from two to three inches, and in depth from one-and-a-half to two inches. We shot several specimens of the bird; but the extreme rapidity of its flight and the rocking of the boat rendered it impossible to make as large a bag as we wished.

The abundance of the reef-heron on all the islands which we visited had been the cause of my diary up to this containing no notice of it, but it must not be altogether passed, the more particularly as it is of interest to remark that the species, which is normally of a slaty-blue colour, exhibits a marked tendency to albinism in a very similar way to that observable amongst rock-pigeons. According to my estimate, the proportion of white to blue individuals is from one-seventh to one-tenth. The birds when compared differ only in colour, and there can be no doubt that both belong to the same species. One white one which I saw on Little Button had distinct dark marks on the shoulders, which extended to some of the under-wing coverts. The white birds appeared to us to be unusually wary, and on more than one occasion I observed them to be the first to rise as I approached. This may not impossibly be due to some peculiarity of vision, a thing which *prima facie* might be expected to exist in conjunction with albinism. Under certain circumstances it is conceivable that this might lead to the preservation of the white variety, while the blue were exterminated. Even the numbers of the specimens in the collection made by us show to a certain extent the truth of this. Out of thirty-nine skins two only were white. Now if my estimate of the relative numbers be correct, and the white were not more difficult to shoot, there should have been four or five white ones out of the thirty-nine. As a matter of fact, I believe, most of our party, after a certain number of the blue birds had been shot, rarely fired at them, though they never lost an opportunity of trying to get a shot at the white ones,—certainly such was the case with myself. I believe double the number of the blue birds might easily have been shot for the same amount of trouble as was expended on the white.

Little Button Island is formed of a white calcareous rock quite unlike anything I have seen anywhere else in the islands. Some broken shells of nautilus, turbo, and trochus, a fragment of pottery, and an empty match-box! shewed that the natives occasionally visit this island in their fishing excursions. The pottery and the match-box pointed to the probability of their belonging to the Port Blair tribe.

Early the following morning we found ourselves close to Barren Island, in Lat. 12° 17′ N., and Long. 93° 54′ E. This volcano, and that of Narkondam, I have described fully elsewhere* so shall confine myself to very brief sketches of them here. As we sailed round the island, and the north-west side opened to view, it first became apparent that it does not consist, as might at first be supposed, of one solid mass; but of a circular ridge forming a huge amphitheatre which is broken down at one side to the

---

* "Records Geol. Surv. India," Vol. VI., 1873, p. 81; and "Geological Magazine," Decade II., Vol. VI., No. I., January, 1879.

level of the sea for a distance of perhaps 150 yards. The view obtainable through this entrance discloses a bare cone which rises from the centre of the island. Except at a sort of shoulder not far from the top, and at two peaks close to the summit, no rocks are seen on this cone, its smooth sides being covered with grey ash and occasional strings of shingle. Towards the top some whitish patches are seen—these are due to the presence of gypsum mixed with the ash.

The accompanying illustration, it will be observed, is somewhat diagrammatic in its character, being rather of the nature of a bird's-eye view, than a representation taken from an actual point

BARREN ISLAND VOLCANO.

of view. The total diameter of the island is, on the authority of Lieutenant Heathcote, 2,970 yards. The circuit of the island, from the time it took us to row round, I estimated at about six miles. The high encircling ridge is formed of somewhat irregularly deposited layers of lava, ash, and conglomerate, which dip away from the centre. A section of these may be seen on the left hand of the gap or entrance, and others at various points on the sea-face, no two of them agreeing exactly in character. These beds or layers generally dip at angles of 35° to 40°, which inclination appears to be continued steadily under the sea, as bottom, except at one place, has not been found with a line of 150 fathoms at a quarter of a mile from the shore. This steepness has been unfavourable to the formation of a fringing reef of coral of any magnitude, such as we find surrounding some of the islands of the Andaman and Nicobar groups. The elevation of this outer ridge varies somewhat in places, but it probably is nowhere much in excess of 1,000 feet. Its highest points are towards the south and west.

The appearance presented by the inner scarped face of this amphitheatre is very peculiar. In several places cornice lines mark the position of particular beds, but a purplish-grey, or in places brownish, ash spreads over the steep slopes, except towards the south-west and west, where there are some trees and shrubby vegetation. To the north, south, and east a few tufts of grass—generally arranged in long vertical lines, the first being a sort of protection to those below it—are the only plants which have managed to establish a footing in the loose ash. The outer slopes facing the sea are for the most part covered with a luxuriant vegetation, in which large forest trees may be discerned. These latter attract considerable numbers of fruit-eating pigeons (*Carpophaga bicolor*). From its composition and character, it is evident that this ring of cliffs is the remnant of the original cone which gradually rises from below the sea. Its top and a portion of the side were, no doubt, blown off by a violent eruption, and the present cone was subsequently formed inside. The gap or fissure in the surrounding walls bears about north-west-by-west from the centre of the island. It is the only place where an entrance can be obtained to the central valley.

For a long time Barren Island was considered by Von Buch and others of his school as a most favourable example of his elevation theory of craters. Since, however, the island is in reality only formed of volcanic materials elevated above the sea without a trace of any pre-existing rocks, it is evident that its peculiar form gives no support to that now exploded hypothesis.

Close to the landing-place, there is a hot spring which has been mentioned in several of the accounts of the island. Dr. Playfair found the temperature to exceed 140°,—the limit of his thermometer. Dr. Liebig's thermometer was only graduated up to 104°, but judging from the feel to the hands, he estimated it to be near the boiling-point. The Andaman Committee record it at from 158° to 163° F. At the time of our visit the highest temperature of the water where it bubbled out of the rocks, close to high-water mark, was 130° F. We therefore failed to boil some eggs in it which we had brought with us for the purpose. The water is perfectly clear and sweet,* and there was no trace of sulphurous vapours. Strange to say, where, though mingled with the sea, it was still too hot for the hand to be retained in it with comfort, there were a number of brilliantly-coloured fish swimming about.

Facing the landing-place is the termination of a flow of lava which extends backwards for about a mile to the base of the cone, round which it laps for perhaps three-quarters of the circumference. The height or thickness of this flow of lava is about ten feet at first, gradually rising to about fifty feet where it emerges from the base of the cone. The upper surface is deeply cleft and covered over with blocks of black cellular lava which rest upon one another in confused piles. Sometimes they are poised so insecurely one upon another that it is a matter of no little risk to attempt scrambling over them. Towards the base of the flow, the rock, from its slower cooling, is more compact and less cellular. In places it contains white crystals of a mineral resembling leucite. In others it is a true basalt with numerous crystals of olivine. As pointed out by Dr. Liebig, the older lava seen in the section of the ridge differs from this; it consists of a reddish matrix with crystals of felspar (probably sanidine), olivine, and augite. A somewhat similar rock occurs on Narkondam.

On our way to the central cone from the landing-place, we at first endeavoured to avoid the rough surface of the lava-flow by keeping on the slope of the gap; but after a short distance the bushes and unevenness of the ground compelled us to strike

* The Andaman Committee do not appear to have realised this fact, as they spent no little time and trouble in excavating a well without finding a trace of water.

down on the lava, where we were surprised to find a cleared path which must have been made by the committee sent from Port Blair to report upon the supply of grass. Arrived at the foot of the cone, we commenced the ascent from the west. The loose ashes and shingle rendered it somewhat toilsome work; and those in front found it difficult to avoid loosening fragments of lava which bounded down the hill in a most unpleasant way for those who were following. Dr. Liebig appears to have ascended from the north side, where it seems to have been equally difficult. About a quarter of the way from the top there is a shoulder of rock which shows very well in the photograph. This probably marks the position of an old vent. There is a good deal of firm ground about it. The summit of the cone is truncated, and contains an oval-shaped depression, one half of which is partly filled with *débris*, and the other, some twenty yards in diameter and fifty feet deep, has a circular bottom, which is filled with sand. This appears to have been the last crater formed on the island.

The two principal walls of the depression strike from north-west to south-east; they consist of ash permeated with fibrous gypsum (selenite); numerous cracks and fissures occur in this part of the hill, and the ground is hot. On turning over the surface, the sides of these cracks are found to be encrusted with sulphur, resting upon the rugosities of which small detached crystals of the same mineral were not uncommon. From the highest point on the northern wall a thin column of white vapour and sulphurous fumes is slowly poured forth. Even when standing in its midst, the fumes did not prove so irritating as might have been expected. On the southern side of the crater solid lava is seen *in situ*, and on the west there is a peculiarly-shaped mass which forms a conspicuous object from below. Portions of the lava here have a reddish matrix and are somewhat vesicular. I also found some basalt, the outer surface of which was weathered into a white crust. It seems probable that the nucleus of the cone is solid lava to a considerable extent, the ashes seen at the surface being only superficial. By following water-channels when they were to be found, and glissading over the ashes, the return to the base of the cone was effected speedily and without much difficulty.

By a small watch-aneroid supplied with a Vernier scale for feet, the height of the cone appeared to be 950 feet; but as one heavy storm of rain had passed, and clouds portended another, I am willing to believe that owing to the atmospheric disturbance the observation was not trustworthy, and that from 975 to 980 feet, given by Lieutenant Heathcote, Dr. Liebig and others, is the true elevation. The temperature on the top was 83°. The diameter of the base of the cone is 2,170 feet according to Lieutenant Heathcote. The slopes of the cone incline, according to my observation, at angles varying between 30° and 35°. Blair, as already stated, gave it at 32° 17′, or about the mean of these two. Other observers say 40° to 45°, but a photograph of the cone, which I possess, shows that the former are correct.

Dr. Liebig has discussed the question of the amount of sulphur obtainable on the island. He seems to think the chances of finding a permanent supply very doubtful, but recommends a preliminary trial. Considering the great expense which keeping up constant communication with the Andamans and the superintendence of convict labour would involve, I cannot see that there is any prospect of the collection and refining of the sulphur being made to pay. So far as is known, the substance occurs only at the summit of the cone, though doubtless, if the right places could be found, it does also occur lower down. But in such places, it could only be as an old deposit which, on being worked out, would not be replaced again. On the summit, deposition, so far as I could see, proceeds very slowly, certainly not with sufficient rapidity to keep labourers constantly employed.

In the paper above alluded to, I have given an account of the history of the island from all available records; and from these it would appear that the volcano has not been in a state of violent eruption since the years which closed the last and commenced the present century. The lava-flow, which stretches from the entrance, on the sea face, to the base of the cone, was probably poured out during this period, and raised the level of the valley some forty feet above its elevation in 1789, when Blair saw it. He makes no mention of a lava-stream in his time. If it did not exist then, it cannot—as has been supposed by some—have been instrumental in the formation of the entrance. I have pointed out in the above-mentioned paper the origin of some serious errors which occur in several Geological Manuals and works on volcanos regarding this island. These errors, having been unfortunately adopted in the works of Sir Charles Lyell and many others, have obtained a universal currency which will render it very difficult to wholly eradicate them from text-books.

March 23rd.—Slowly during the night we had steamed northwards, and at sunrise we saw and partly circled round the Island of Narkondam, at a distance which, while adopted as a safe precaution by the captain, did not commend itself to us, as we could not distinctly see the lie of the land, nor choose the best place for landing. Narkondam is situated in Lat. 13° 24′ N.; Long. 94° 12′ E. So little has been published regarding this island, that a few lines will suffice to dispose of all that has ever been recorded on the subject.

In 1795 it was passed by Colonel Symes,* when on his voyage to Rangoon, whence he started on his embassy to Ava. He speaks of it as "a barren rock, rising abruptly out of the sea, and seemingly destitute of vegetation."

Dr. McClelland, writing in 1838,† says:—"It is a volcanic cone, raised to the height of from 700 to 800 feet." He gives a sketch showing the figure of the cone, "the upper part of which is quite naked, presenting lines such as were doubtless formed by lava-currents descending from the crater to the base, which last is

* "Embassy to Ava," Vol. I., 1827, p. 167.

† "On the Difference of Level in Indian Coal-fields," "J. A. S. B.," Vol. VII. Also in the "Coal Committee's Report," and in "Corbyn's Indian Review."

covered with vegetation." No soundings are to be found at the distance of half-a-mile from the shore. This account is reproduced by Mrs. Somerville, Dr. Daubeney, Dr. Buist, and Mr. Scrope.

Horsburgh* says:—"Narcondam may be seen about fourteen or fifteen leagues from the deck, and appears in the form of a cone or pyramid, with its summit broken off. It is bold and safe to approach all round."

Dr. S. Kurz, in his report on the vegetation of the Andaman Islands, published by the Government of India, writes:—"Narkondam Island has an extinct volcano, remarkable for the great height of its cone, being twice as high as its outer wall. Owing to the great height of the cone (perhaps 2,000 feet) in proportion to the surrounding wall, this island must have sunk very much, or the volcano must have been formed from a considerable depth in the sea." The reasoning by which these alternative conclusions have been arrived at is not very clear. Dr. Kurz gives an outline sketch of the island as it appeared to him from a distance of twenty miles.

In a paper on the geology of the neighbourhood of Port Blair,† I made a few remarks on the appearance of Narkondam as seen from a few miles distance. I then accepted the height of the cone (2,150 feet) given on the chart as authentic. This, it will be seen by the sequel, I do not now adopt as correct.

Viewed from the north-west, at a distance of about four or five miles, the Island of Narkondam appears to consist of a tolerably regular cone, which rises from an interrupted ring of irregularly-piled masses. The apex is somewhat truncated, but has three distinct peaks. On the occasion, in 1869, when I first saw the island, a dense mass of cloud rested on the top. I was then unable to make out the character of the summit. But when subsequently seen, it was observed that there were three peaks,

* "Indian Directory," Fifth Edition., Vol. II. 1843, p. 55.

† "J. A. S. B.," Vol. XXXIX., part ii., 1870, p. 231.

as represented in the rough sketches published by Dr. Kurz and Dr. McClelland. The upper parts of the cone, and the sides for more than half-way down, are deeply furrowed by ravines, and what appears to be a very low scrub jungle spreads uniformly over the island, save upon some vertical scarped faces.

With the observers above-mentioned, who did not land, the conical form alone seems to have been accepted as sufficient proof of the volcanic character of the island. Dr. McClelland, as noted above, speaks of the lined appearance being "doubtless formed by lava-currents descending from the crater to the base." These lines are, however, simply the result of erosion, and mark the position of the watercourses. The elevation of the summit of the cone has been variously estimated at from 700 to 2,150 feet. Since however—according to Horsburgh—the island first becomes visible from the deck of a steamer at a distance of from fourteen to fifteen leagues, it is probable that about 1,300 feet would be nearer the true altitude, and such, indeed, judging by the eye, appears to be a very fair estimate. The general outline of Narkondam is extremely like that of Stromboli.*

We landed in a small bay on the north-west side of the island. At about 100 yards distance from the beach the water becomes so shoal, owing to a coral reef, that we were compelled to land on a raft. We soon found that the jungle, which in the distant view appeared to consist mainly of low scrub, was really composed of large forest trees, with a thick undergrowth. So dense was this, just above high-water mark, that at first it seemed probable that it would be impossible to penetrate it. Added to the natural density of the jungle, another obstacle was presented by the prostrate condition of many of the trees, which in their fall had carried down tangled masses of creepers and undergrowth. It soon became apparent that at no very distant period a violent hurricane or cyclone must have swept

---

* With the paper in the "Geological Magazine" already referred to, I have given a figure of Narkondam.

across the island. An entrance was at last found, and for three hours, cutting our way and making constant detours to avoid fallen trees, we endeavoured to force onwards to the summit, but were at length compelled to give up all hope of succeeding, and returned to the beach. Further evidence of the hurricane was there afforded by numerous fragments of a wreck which had been thrown up on the sand. Subsequently this storm was identified with one which took place on the 26th of October, 1872, and did much damage in the Coco Islands and other parts of the Bay.

The only rock seen where we landed was a conglomerate, or boulder-bed, some fifty feet thick. The boulders consisted of a trachytic porphyry, which contained sanidine, augite, and mica, in grey or pinkish matrices. We discovered no evidence whatever of recent lava or basalt occurring, though either or both may exist, as our observations were confined to one small bay. There is no historical record, so far as I am aware, of smoke ever having been observed to issue from Narkondam. It has, therefore, long been dormant, if not absolutely extinct.

Notwithstanding the luxuriance of the jungle, which included species of *Ficus*, Palms (*Caryota*), *Acacia*, *Calosanthes*, etc., no fresh water was discovered. We saw no traces of the goats and fowls which many years ago are said to have been let loose on this island. We shot two specimens of a hornbill, to which Mr. Hume has given the name *Ryticeros Narcondami*. We also obtained some bats, and saw swiftlets (*Collocalia linchi*) and sun-birds (*A. Andamanica*), and large water-lizards (*Hydrosaurus*). Much remains to be done in the exploration of this most interesting volcanic island. It is particularly desirable to ascertain whether there is really a crater at the summit, and whether there are any traces of recent lavas. Future visitors would do well to provide themselves with some wood-cutters. They should land near the northern spur, and getting then on the steady rise, they will probably find no insuperable obstacle on their way up. Owing to the fact of the physical geology of the Andaman and Nicobar Islands being as yet imperfectly known, I have not here discussed the connection which in all probability exists between their elevation and this adjacent line of volcanic activity.

Early on the following morning we landed on the east coast of the Great Coco Island. Just inside the beach there is a broken belt of cocoa-nuts, with cycad trees growing underneath their shade. In the breaks in the continuity of the belt where cocoa-nuts do not occur, the trees are pandanus, and occasionally mangroves. Passing through this outer belt I encountered some low sandstone hills covered with thorny shrubs, through which I was unable to make my way. I then traced up several creeks until they lost themselves in the jungle. Occasionally I caught sight of white-breasted water-hens, but besides the ordinary small shore-waders (*Ægialitis*, *Strepsilas*, &c.), the only common bird was a king-crow very closely allied to, but distinguished by its constantly larger size* from the Andaman (*Buchanga Andamanensis*). A good series of this bird was obtained. The other birds shot chiefly belonged to the more common Andaman species.†

Among the larger trees I noticed species of *Bombax* and *Dipterocarpus*, besides others with the appearance of which I was not familiar. A species of *Acacia* and sago palms (*Caryota*) also occur. I saw no trace of fresh water; it may however possibly be had by digging. All the rocks which I came across were sandstones of the same lithological characters as those of the Andamans. Dr. Stoliczka, however, told me that he saw near the highest part of the island some serpentine-diallage rock which was similar to that found in Macpherson's Straits. Through-

* It has been named *B.* (or *Dissemuroides*) *dicruriformis*, by Mr. Hume.

† In a recently published work, entitled "Sport in British Burmah," the author, Colonel Pollok, mentions having shot megapodes on the Great Coco. Mr. Hume also heard from the lighthouse-keeper on Table Island that they occur there. Now, if it be true, as is supposed, that they do not occur in the Andamans, then their distribution would appear to be the same as that of the cocoa-nut palms, and may possibly be due to the same yet undiscovered cause.

out the cocoa-nut zone fallen nuts of all ages strew the ground. Many of them have been hollowed out by rats and pigs, and some possibly also by the great crab. Land crabs and hermits here, as everywhere else where there were cocoa-nuts, were very abundant. I doubt very much if these islands are now visited by Burmese or other vessels for the sake of the nuts. We certainly saw no trace of anything of the kind, and the lighthouse keeper on Table Island told some of our party that he had never known any vessel to come to these islands for collecting purposes. From the same authority we learnt that the fallen trees on this island, and doubtless also those on Narkondam, had been thrown down by the cyclone of the 26th October, 1872.

I am unable, from want of space, to give an account of an early European settlement on the Cocos, but it may be of interest to state that last year (1878) the Governor-General in Council in the *Gazette* of India invited tenders for the lease of the island. The terms mentioned, which are otherwise hard, include the payment of a maximum sum of £2,000 per annum for the cost of the administration of civil and criminal justice. The sum is large; but the incubus of an establishment of petty native officials who, to prove their *raison d'être*, could not fail to make it their business to stir up disputes and litigation between employers and employed, would, to many experienced in Indian matters, be no doubt regarded as the hardest part of the contract.

The following morning we steamed over to the Little Coco, and landed at about ten o'clock. Here there was a similar zone of cocoa-nuts, with cycads growing in their shade, then a zone of brambly bushes and creepers. Inside were large trees without much undergrowth. One tree which I measured was close upon six feet in diameter. On the western side there is a coral reef which at low tide was uncovered for more than a quarter of a mile out from the land. Here there were several waders feeding, and among them a small flock of the large plover, which I had first seen at Escape Bay. I winged one of these, and as I was following him up came across a huge specimen, fully five feet long, of the great water-lizard (*Hydrosaurus*). As I did not care to shoot him, though I wanted to capture him, I threw stones at him, whereupon he hissed and lashed his tail in a manner that might prove alarming to any one not knowing the harmless nature of the beast. As I was pressing him into a corner he made a rush into the waves, but returned—apparently not liking the surf. Just as I thought he could not escape he made a sudden dart into the water, dived through the surf, and disappeared. I could not wait any longer, as I had to pick up the large plover. Another of the party secured a second specimen and an egg of this species, which turned out to be *Esacus magnirostris.* Among the birds shot on this island were the Paradise fly-catcher (*Tchitrea affinis*), the Malayan koel (*Eudynamys Maylayana*), the Andaman bush-thrush (*Geocichla albogularis*), Boie's grey thick-head (*Hylocharis philomela*), the brown fly-catcher (*Alseonax latirostris*), and several others. I caught a glimpse of one pig in the jungle, but could not get a shot at it, as it disappeared immediately.

The rocks are sandstones, which may possibly be in places penetrated by igneous rocks; but there is no foundation whatever for the statement made in an old account that this island is of volcanic origin.

The following day (March 26th) at about eleven o'clock, we landed on Preparis Island, the most northern of the group. The heat on shore was intense. I have never seen a more dangerous looking place than this island. Reefs stretch out from it in every direction—to the south, it is said, to the distance of eight miles. Taking a Lascar with me, I started through the jungle, steering as far as possible due west, in order to examine the opposite coast. I was joined by one of the ship's officers, and after a walk of about a mile and-a-half we reached the opposite beach. The undergrowth is for the most part light, there not being enough moisture perhaps to support thick shrubs; there are, however, plenty of fine trees. I saw no birds in the jungle, but I shot a grey squirrel. We heard a rustling in one thicket which we supposed to be made by pigs, but we did not see any. The outer zone of vegetation is formed of pandanus and mangroves, with an internal one of cycads. There is not a single cocoa-nut tree, I believe, on the island.

On reaching the western beach we found it had a reef very similar in character to that on the Little Coco. Where it was bared by the fallen tide there were numerous waders (*Ægialitis*, *Numenius*, *Strepsilas*, and *Ardea*). As the jungle had proved so devoid of bird-life, we determined to return by the beach round the southern point of the island. All along the high-water line there were numerous pieces of wreck, balks of timber (teak), several canoes, and portions of ship's boats. When about three-quarters of a mile from the south-west point, we saw some animals rushing across from the reef to the jungle. At first I thought they were pigs, but on reaching the place saw the foot-prints of monkeys. Subsequently we had a closer view of several parties of them which we startled on the rocks at the margin of the sea where they appeared to be feeding on crabs.* They were excessively wild, and I most unfortunately could not obtain a specimen. Altogether I must have seen fifty individuals. The occurrence of monkeys on this island is of particular interest, as none are known to exist in the Andamans. This seems to point to a more recent connection of this island with the main-land. What the species may be I am unable to say—possibly Blyth's *Inuus leoninus*, which occurs in Arakan, but it may be *I. carbonarius*. Some of the individuals I saw appeared to be almost

* I have elsewhere in these pages alluded to some of the late Mr. Waterton's positive assertions, and shewn them to be open to question. He states, "One traveller writes about apes feeding upon 'crabs, oysters, and other shell-fish,'" and then sneeringly enquires, "Did these fishes frequent trees in the forest?" On a preceding page of his work he scouts the idea of an ourang-outang feeding itself with a spoon, &c. All I can say to this is, that I have, like hundreds of other residents of Calcutta, seen an ourang take milk with a spoon from a cup, and put it most carefully into its mouth, and the man in charge said he had not taught the animal to do so. The same ourang "Jenny" was afterwards exhibited in the Regent's Park Gardens for some months, but was killed by last winter's severe frost.

black. At the extreme south point of the island we suddenly came upon a large sea-eagle (*Cuncuma leucogaster*). He was seated on a balk of timber busily engaged in eating a sea-snake. This was evidently a favourite perch, as there was quite a pile of snake vertebræ on the ground underneath. On rounding the point we were rejoiced to see the boats, although still some three to four miles off. Our long tramp over sand, loose coral, and rocks, together with the great heat, had so exhausted us, that we almost despaired of being able to accomplish the distance before nightfall. We saw no fresh water, but at about a mile from the south point we examined a superficially dried-up swamp, which is just inside the pandanus zone. The luxuriant condition of the grass seemed to point to the probability of water being found at no great depth from the surface. In one place the caked earth had been much disturbed, probably by pigs, though the way it was done seemed rather to suggest human agency. In this neighbourhood I saw a chestnut bittern (*A. cinnamomea*) and also the little green heron (*Butorides Javanicus*). Reef-herons were very abundant along the beach.

The most common rocks on Preparis are greasy dark shales. Sandstones are somewhat rare. I saw no fossils. Towards the southern end of the island there are some low hills, quite bare of vegetation. On one of them I noticed a well-worn path leading to the top; this had probably been in regular use by the monkeys, as they took that direction as they left the reef when startled by us. I was far too weary and exhausted to examine the ground closely then. On our rejoining the rest of the party we found that they had not wandered far from the landing-place, and that a large portion of their time had been devoted to the capture of sundry turtles, which they had discovered in pools in the reef. Altogether Preparis had not charmed us. There were few birds; the heat was excessive, and there were no cocoa-nuts to assuage our thirst. This island was the last place on our programme; so we steamed off for Calcutta, arriving there on the afternoon of the 30th of March, one day within our month's period of leave.

I remained in Calcutta during April and May; but on the 7th

of June was again on the move, having been appointed to take joint charge of the geological collections which were sent by the Government of India to the Vienna Exhibition. I remained in Vienna till the close of the Exhibition in November, and then returned to India for the next season's field-work.

CHAPTER X.

SECTION I.

NARBADA VALLEY, SATPURA HILLS, PACHMARI.

1873-74.

INSTRUCTIONS FOR SEASON—FORM CAMP AT JABALPUR—GADAWARA—BORINGS FOR COAL—VACCINATION—NARBADA VALLEY—FATAL ACCIDENT—DIFFICULT NATURE OF GROUND TO BE EXAMINED—TRACES OF FORMER CIVILIZATION—GONDS—BHURYAS—BIRMAN GHÂT—HINDU FESTIVAL—COPPER-MINES—NARBADA FOSSILS—SINKING SHAFT AT COAL-MINES—DUDHI VALLEY—RAJA OF HURRA—SAMBAR SHOOTING—BORING OPERATIONS STARTED—UNDERGROUND TEMPERATURES—ANCIENT RING-STONE—CAPTAIN FORSYTH ON THE DENWA VALLEY: ITS GEOLOGICAL STRUCTURE, FAUNA, AND FLORA—SHOOT A BEAR—THE BEAR'S CARCASE VISITED BY A TIGER—ATTEMPTS TO SHOOT TIGERS—SHOOT A SAMBAR—GAUR (BISON) AND ELEPHANT—TREE-SHREW AND MALABAR THRUSH—VISIT PACHMARI: ITS NATURAL BEAUTY AND ITS FITNESS FOR A SANITARIUM—RETURN TO CALCUTTA—THE COAL RESOURCES OF THE NARBADA VALLEY.

MY instructions for this season were to undertake the geological supervision, on the spot, of certain boring operations which had been started in order to test the extension of the coal-measures under the alluvium of the Narbada Valley, and under a series of sandstones, which are the only rocks visible in some valleys which traverse the portion of the Satpura hills included in the Narsinghpur and Hosungabad districts of the Central Provinces. Concurrently with these duties I had to carry on the systematic geological mapping of the hills surrounding the Denwa and Dudhi valleys to the east of the Pachmari plateau.*

Owing to my not having returned from Vienna (where I had

---

* I apply the term Satpura Hills to the whole range, though, locally, it is only strictly applicable to the western portion. The central portion, including Pachmari is known under the title of Mahadeo, and the extension thence eastwards is called the Mykal range.

been on duty in connection with our geological collection at the Exhibition) till near the middle of December, I was later than usual in taking the field, and did not start from Calcutta for Jabalpur till the 22nd of December—arriving there on the morning of the 24th, when I immediately set about buying a horse and hiring camels for the conveyance of baggage, in addition to that which was to form the load of the only elephant available. This elephant had been with me some years before in Bengal, when he was remarkably good-tempered as a rule, but he had since developed into a very dangerous animal, difficult to manage, and he had, I believe, killed more than one person. Already I had received some intimation of this change of temperament, and a trophy, in the shape of a portion of one of his tusks, which had a year or two previously been broken off as he tripped and fell when pursuing his mahout with murderous intent. For his management it was necessary to have three men on extra pay, and when he was loosed for watering or other purposes they all accompanied him armed with spears. During the season he did his work well, though he occasionally threatened the lives of his keepers; but, as the mahouts said, the greater his load the faster did he travel.

From Jabalpur I went on by train ninety miles to Gadawara, from whence I visited a boring which had been made at a place called Sukakheri. The object of this boring was to test whether the coal-measures of the adjoining Mopani field did or did not extend northwards under the alluvium of the Narbada Valley. The hole had been carried down to a depth of 343 feet without any solid rock having been met with; indeed, at this depth a running quicksand had been encountered, which prevented further sinking, as the tubing had already resisted all attempts to sink it lower than 333 feet, though it had been weighted with from twelve to thirteen tons of iron. Subsequently this boring, when better tools became available, was carried down to a depth of 491 feet, with only the negative result that no rock was met with, the base of the valley deposits not having been reached.

At Gadawara I had a conversation with a Mahomedan on various subjects; among others he introduced that of vaccination, and asked me its real object, stating that some of his co-religionists believed that the interest of the Government in the matter was due to the fact that they were anxious to discover the Imam Mundi, or Saviour of the World, who has still to come, Christ and Mahomet being merely prophets sent before. The Imam Mundi, it was believed, would restore the Mahomedans to power, and the object of vaccination was to examine the blood of all the infants born in the country, and when one with white blood should be found he would be immediately destroyed, and thus the British Raj would be preserved. He was somewhat astonished when I assured him that I had myself been vaccinated, as he had no idea that any but black children had to submit to the operation. This story is but one of many which might be told of the curious ideas which are simmering in the minds of the natives of India.

December 31st.—Gadawara to Thelwara.—On this, the last day of the year, I at length was able to commence camping, and march to the attack of the great bluff mass of hills on the south of the Narbada valley. The valley is here a highly-cultivated plain, about fifty miles wide, and is bounded both to north and south by steep scarps of rocks which belong to formations of very different ages. On the north there are quartzites and sandstones of Vindhyan age, which are overlaid by an extension of the great Dekan basalt sheet, while on the south there are sandstones, &c., referable to several groups of the great Jura-triassic Gondwana series. These likewise are overlaid by basalt.

Wide stretches of corn cultivation occupy the central valley, in which there is a rich black soil. Little or no rice is to be seen in this area. In lieu of fences, the corn near the roads is bordered by a zone of flax cultivation, the object of which is to avoid the loss which would be caused by passing cattle nibbling the heads of the corn. The flax, not being eaten by cattle, attains maturity, ultimately, however, affording, in the form of oil-cake, a valuable and favourite food for them. This Indian flax seems to be deficient in fibre. It is certainly never manufactured by the natives, who merely cultivate the plant for its oil-yielding seeds, of which large quantities are exported to Europe. The oil expressed from them in England is, I am given to understand on the best authority, largely exported to Italy, from whence, after undergoing some process, known only to the trade, it travels forth and is sold all over the world as the finest olive oil! a portion of it, no doubt finding its way back to India, as also do gin and other spirits which are distilled from Indian rice. Here and there throughout these wide plains parties of antelope or black buck are occasionally to be seen. As they are often shot at, and cover for stalking is rare, they are very wary, though on several occasions when riding I have been able to get very close to single bucks. On this first day I heard of the break-up of a shooting party in the neighbouring hills in consequence of an unfortunate casualty. A native police constable, having climbed into a bushy tree in the line of fire, was struck by a stray bullet, which passed through and shattered both thighs, and he fell out of the tree like a smitten bird, and died soon afterwards.

January 4th.—Chargaon to Chaluk.—The last few days having been spent in visiting the Mopani coal-mines, and examining the base of the scarp of younger rocks for possible outcrops of the coal-measures, to-day I obtained a first experience of the very difficult nature of the country I had to survey. The geology of the principal open valleys which intersect the great plateau masses of the hills had already, to a great extent, been worked out, so that, as supplies were not to be obtained at the small hamlets in these higher levels, and moreover the camels could not have travelled over the steep passes and stony paths, it was necessary for me to leave my camp below, taking the elephant, lightly laden with a small sleeping tent and other requisites. The first night was spent at the village of Chargaon, and next morning I sent the men and tent on to a village called Chaluk, intending to work up to it along the bed of the Sitariva river. With this object in view I descended about 1,000 feet into the valley, and immediately began to experience the very greatest difficulty in making any progress along the bed, owing to huge angular masses of sandstone which, having fallen from the steep bounding scarps, were piled upon one another throughout the breadth of the channel in massive confusion. At one spot, too, a trap-dyke, jutting out from the faces of sandstone on either side, proved a formidable obstacle, and I only succeeded in scrambling round it with the greatest difficulty. Having managed to traverse about a mile, we were at length brought to a stand in front of a waterfall, which fell over a sheer face of sandstone 80 to 100 feet high. To be compelled to return as we had come was not a pleasing prospect. At first I looked in vain for any place where the cliffs could be ascended. At length I saw a trap-dyke in one spot, which stood out vertically from the face of sandstone. Partly by ascending, after the manner of chimney-sweeps, a fissure left by the shrinkage on cooling of this trap-dyke, partly by scrambling up the exposed edge of the dyke, we were at length able to escape from the *cul-de-sac* to the level of the highlands, some 300 feet above. Still eight or nine miles of very severe up-and-down climbing remained to be accomplished before we got to Chaluk long after sunset. This was one of the hardest days' walking I ever had.

During the night I was awakened by seeing the flap of my tent lifted and a man creep stealthily in. On enquiring who he was and what he wanted, I found it was one of my own men, who said that he had heard a tiger close by and had come in for protection.

January 8th.—Baskera.—To-day I saw, but had not time to ascend, a massive block of sandstone called the Batkagurh Hill, upon which I was told there are remains of an old fort and tank similar to those I have described as occurring on certain hill-tops in Sirguja. That a civilization in advance of what is now to be found in these wild highlands, formerly existed, was further evidenced by a life-size carving of a curiously skirted figure which I found on a huge fallen block of sandstone in the bed of the Sitariva river. The present inhabitants of this tract belong to one or other of two tribes, the well-known Gonds and the Bhuryas.* To what other well distinguished tribe these last are most nearly affined I cannot say. Their only language is a bastard form of Hindi, and they do not as a rule understand the language of their close neighbours the Gonds. In appearance they reminded me of the Souras, who are among the lowest in the scale of races. It is not improbable that they are identical with a small tribe met with in Palamow, and called by Colonel Dalton Bhuihers.† Both the Gonds and Bhuryas are very migratory in their habits, constantly passing from one hill-side to another, where they cut down the forest and sow pulse, Indian corn, and millet, between the fallen and partially burnt logs. This *Dhya* cultivation, as it is called, is of course very destructive to forests, and to this cause it is in a great measure due that India at the present day is so ill-provided with timber, and is compelled to import sleepers for the railways from Australia and elsewhere. The Forest Conservancy now established in the Central Provinces will no doubt in due time result in India being able to supply her own wants to a great extent; but for the present the mischief has been done, and the growth of Teak, Sal, and some of the other timber-trees found in these forests is slow. In many places I found the maps of only a few years back afforded but little guide to the present habitations of these Gond and Bhurya nomads. The places that had known them knew them no more, and hamlets and clearances were met with where none were represented to exist.

From Chargaon I descended again to the coal mines at Mopani. Owing to the steepness of the pass it was necessary to send the elephant down unladen, the baggage being carried by coolies. I merely mention the above facts to show the difficulties

---

* Captain Forsyth, in his work on the Highlands of Central India, speaks of "Baigas," as inhabiting these regions with the Gonds. Daily I heard the name pronounced, and I have written it as I heard it, phonetically, and I have never, at any time, though familiar with the Baigas in Sirguja, met with any people whom I identified as such in the Satpuras.

† "Descriptive Ethnology of Bengal," p. 133

connected with the exploration of such a region of hills and deep valleys.

January 11th.—Mopani to Birman Ghât.—To-day, in company with the manager of the Mopani coal-mines, I went to visit and report upon a copper deposit which had been discovered and opened up by him on an island in the bed of the Narbada, close to Birman Ghât. A drive of nine miles from a station on the railway, called Kareli, brought us to the Narbada river at Birman Ghât, where there are several Hindu temples. Here an unexpected sight met our eyes. The banks of the river were crowded with numbers of pilgrims who had assembled in order to be present at some Hindu festival, and also for the purpose of bathing in the sacred river. The great display of colour in the costumes—turkey-red predominating—afforded a somewhat novel sight to me, accustomed to the appearance of crowds in Bengal where bright colours are seldom seen. Our tent was pitched on a commanding bank on the south side of the river, from whence we watched the assembling of the pilgrims. Each family party on arrival sought out for some unoccupied place upon which to encamp. A temporary bridge of boats across the river made both sides readily accessible, but for some reason the clay banks and masonry steps on the northern side attracted more people than the sands on the southern. Every ledge on the clay bank had its occupants, and very effective patches of colour were thus produced. On the sands on the southern side of the river booths were being erected for the accommodation of the petty merchants who were busily spreading out their wares. All the people had the appearance of being bent upon enjoying their outing. I have omitted, I find, to record the particular nature of this festival, but it was one of the minor sort. A very considerable *mela* or fair, is held here later in the year, when the assembled visitors number many thousands, and come from far distant parts of the country. On these occasions it is the custom of the European officials of the neighbouring stations to form an encampment and spend a week or so together. Close to this place the bed of the Narbada discloses pebble conglomerates, which are of great interest to the geologist, from the fact that in certain spots they have yielded bones of extinct species of mammalia, and at Bhutra the important discovery in these beds of stone implements, of undoubted human origin, was made by Mr. Hacket, of the Geological Survey; thus affording incontestable evidence of the existence of man at a time when now extinct species of elephant, *Stegodon*, rhinoceros, horse, *Hexaprotodon*, *Tetraprotodon*, deer, buffalo, wild cattle, tiger, and bear inhabited this region. The remains of the deer and buffalo shew a very close affinity, if they are not identical, with species found existing in India at the present day. It is considered that these remains indicate a Post-pliocene age for the gravels.* In the afternoon we visited the copper deposit upon which a trial excavation had been made. The ore, as I then saw it, permeated a thickness of about six feet of an argillaceous schist, and did not form a true lode; it chiefly occurred as the blue and green carbonates, azurite and malachite, but specimens of the grey and red oxides of copper were also to be seen. Assays of specimens of these ores gave results varying from 21.2 to 47.8 per cent. of metallic copper. Subsequently a large sample was sent to England (to Swansea I believe), and its sale paid all expenses, and it seemed at one time probable that the mine might be the means of developing a new industry in the Narbada Valley,† but as I have heard nothing lately on the subject I presume this has gone the way of the majority of such discoveries in India. While we were present I noticed that the workmen had some difficulty in restraining the pilgrims from walking off with samples of the handsome blue and green mineral. When our backs were turned we heard that they did a brisk trade in what natives might easily be persuaded to believe was a valuable medicine. Whether any cases of verdigris poisoning occurred in consequence we did not hear.

---

* *Vide* Lydekker—"Records of Geological Survey of India," Vol. IX., p. 87.

† "Records of Geological Survey of India," 1874, Vol. II., p. 62.

On the following day we returned to Mopani, and I spent another day in further examination of the mines, the result of which, together with some general remarks on the financially very important question of the coal resources of the Narbada Valley, I shall give at the end of this chapter. But here it will be convenient to mention one class of operations which were being conducted by the manager of the mines. The small area of coal-measures in which the mines are situated has been much disturbed by faults, and is completely cut out on the south by an east and west fault, and the edges of younger rocks are in consequence brought into contact with the coal-measures. By a number of borings it was sought to ascertain what the thickness of these younger rocks might be, and consequently at what depth coal might be looked for. But in the making of these borings, an unexpected—and, practically, very serious—difficulty arose, in consequence of the instruments having to traverse enormous beds of conglomerate, the hard boulders in which not only blunted, but sometimes broke, the cutting tools, thus rendering further work impossible. The manager fully and justly relying on the certainty that the coal must be below, though it might be at a depth of from 500 to 800 feet, or even more, it was decided to give up the borings, and to sink a shaft, without any further exploration. Such a shaft, with a timber lining, was accordingly started and carried down to a depth of some 60 or 70 feet successfully when, after passing through solid rock, the miners encountered a running quicksand, which, with the appliances available, proved quite unmanageable, as it swallowed up everything put into it. At length the manager was reluctantly compelled to relinquish the idea of sinking the shaft any further; but, anxious to save as much as possible of the timber, commenced removing it. A European overseer, who had been at the bottom of the shaft superintending this work, requiring a saw, came to the surface, and went off to his house to fetch it. On his return, he found a vast crater where the shaft had been. Not only had the men who were below at the time been engulfed, but several who had been seated or working at the winch above, and a sweetmeat-seller, with his stock-in-trade, had simply been carried down in the general subsidence. In all, about seventeen lives were, I believe, lost in this terrible catastrophe, and not a vestige of any of the victims of any kind was left above the surface.

Subsequently an attempt was made to carry down *pari passu* with the excavation, an enormous cylinder of bricks, twelve feet in diameter and two feet thick, and resting on an iron "crib," which, as it was undermined all round, gradually subsided till the quicksand was again reached; and the whole thing, ultimately, I believe, got tilted out of the perpendicular and had to be abandoned, after a considerable outlay had been incurred; thus, for the time at least, putting a termination to the hopes which had been entertained of a vastly increased area of workable coal being opened up.

From Mopani I marched westwards to a fine village called Bara, and thence southwards to Sali-Chowka, in the Valley of the Dudhi. In this neighbourhood I heard of game being about, including a tigress with a cub; and at night, two animals—hyænas, I believe—had a battle royal not far from the tent. A little bull-terrier, called Topsie, which I bought at Jabalpur, and whose name will again appear in these pages as the heroine of an adventure, here developed a talent for finding peacock in the jungle, and helped me to kill several.

January 18th.—Sali-Chowka to Bamini—Fixing Bamini as the head-quarters of my camp, I had to make a series of expeditions, each lasting for several days, into the hills, with a very much reduced establishment. The work proved intricate, and the difficulty of moving from point to point very great. The prevailing rock throughout a great portion of this tract is trap or basalt, and the absence of the steeply-scarped faces of sandstone which are seen elsewhere, produced a very different type of scenery. Teak grows in some abundance on this trap soil, which also supports a rank grass that attains a height of six feet. But, as a whole, the jungle on this trap is much thinner and lighter than it is on the sandstone.

In one of the rivers in this country, near a spot where the

water tumbled over a layer of columnar basalt, I met with the Malabar whistling-thrush, whose occurrence I have already mentioned in Sirguja. Curiously enough, it had just occurred to me that the situation was one eminently suited to the habits of the bird, when I heard its whistle, and soon after saw it flying up stream, well out of range. Occasionally I startled sambar in their mid-day lairs; but it was not always possible to get my rifle in time from the hands of my lagging men. However, I shot one stag, which had been lying concealed in the grass on the banks of the river Sitariva.

January 27th.—Ankawara to Bamini.—To-day I returned to my main camp from the hills, and in the evening the Raja of Hurra came to pay a visit. He is a Gond or Gore, pure and simple, his family not having undergone the refining process I have elsewhere spoken of as producing Rajputs from an aboriginal stock. He called himself a Gore, not Gond; but the two names are, as I have already suggested, in all probability interchangeable. He offered to provide a beat for me on the morrow, he being himself on a shooting trip. He assured me that there were gaur—or, as they are here incorrectly called, *Bun Bhainsa*—in close proximity to the village Ankawara, where I had last been; but the people there, whom I had particularly interrogated on the subject, had declared there were none. But I had heard a tiger roaring while there, and also the monkeys swearing at him as he passed along in the evening.

January 28th.—Bamini.—To-day I had a beat with the Raja, the result of which, though he had placed me in what he considered the best place, was that he shot a sambar while I saw nothing. On a second occasion upon which I went out with him precisely the same thing happened, and he expressed what I believe was genuine sorrow that he had not been instrumental in obtaining for me a shot; but one of the villagers came up to me in a confidential way, and explained the whole thing in a manner perfectly satisfactory to himself and those of my servants who heard him. It was that the Raja being a Gond, a dweller in the forest, was endowed with magic power over the animals, and drew them all to himself. Although on pleasure bent, the Raja had a frugal mind: for the people who beat for him complained that, with the exception of a quarter which was sent for my consumption, every scrap of the venison was "jerked" and packed up to be taken to his home as a store for the summer. This they looked upon not unnaturally as very mean conduct.

My regular work was now interrupted by its having become necessary to point out, actually on the ground, the spot at which the new trial borings in the Dudhi valley were to be commenced; the points selected being near the villages of Maneagaon and Khapa. The boring at one of these localities was ultimately carried down to a depth of nearly 700 feet without the coal-measures being reached. Some years later a series of observations were made* on the temperature in these bore-holes at various depths; the general result being that below a depth of 60 feet there was an increase of 1° F. for every 66 feet in depth. The bearing which such observations have on the question of a heated central nucleus to the earth will be perhaps sufficiently obvious to the general reader not to necessitate further remark.

One day about this time I rode over to Mopani to see how the shaft was progressing, and while going round the works I noticed that on an iron bolt which was used to connect some timbers a large perforated pebble was in use as a "washer." On removing it I found, as the first glance at it had suggested, that it was really an ancient stone implement that had thus been applied to a modern purpose. I heard that it had been picked up on the surface close by, and had been used as a handy substitute for a "washer." Subsequently I received news from the manager that a precisely similar one had been found. The form, which, as will be seen by those experienced in stone implements, is similar to that of objects which have been found

---

* By Mr. H. B. Medlicott, F.R.S., Superintendent of the Geological Survey of India.

in many far-distant countries, is figured and described in Appendix B.*

February 7th.—Chargaon to Umeria.—Having settled the matter of the borings, I was now free to continue geological work, and for that purpose to-day entered the Denwa valley, in the hills surrounding which, as the event proved, there was occupation for me for many days. This valley has been very fully described by the late Captain Forsyth in his able and interesting work on the Highlands of Central India. He has pointed out how the geological structure has had a marked influence on the vegetation, and again how the fauna is affected by the vegetation, and still further he alludes to a curious fact regarding the distribution of the inhabitants which seems to be likewise connected with it. Umeria occupies a nearly central position in the level portion of the Denwa valley. On the east there are irregularly-shaped hills and scarps which are intercepted by a broad valley ; to the south a low ridge, formed of basalt rocks and clothed with teak timber, rises close to the village, while some miles beyond it the lofty buttressed scarps of the Motur range give the valley the appearance of a huge amphitheatre, a natural colosseum. It requires but a very limited amount of geological knowledge to enable the observer to distinguish the hills and plateaus formed solely of sandstones from those into whose composition basalt also enters. The latter gives definition and angularity to the outline, while the former, owing to the unequal erosion to which they are subject, have a ragged and irregular profile no less marked than picturesque. On the west of the Denwa valley rises the mighty mass of hills which culminates in the Pachmari plateau. On the morning following my arrival at Umeria, at sunrise, a glorious effect was produced as the rays of light fell on the variegated pink and white sandstones exposed on the faces of the steep scarps and cliffs which in these hills rise from their deep green

* Since the above was written I have seen two remarkably fine ring-stones of very similar character fixed on wooden handles, which were brought from the Solomon Islands, where they are used at the present day as war maces.

forest environment. On the north of the valley the hills are low, but the view is limited by a well defined forest of regularly growing sal trees. Captain Forsyth has pointed out that in this region sal is alone to be found on a sandstone soil, or rather on soils which are not derived from basalt. As I have elsewhere pointed out, this rule is not of universal application; I have met with cases, in Chutia Nagpur and elsewhere, in which sal flourishes on trap rocks. Captain Forsyth points out that in this isolated patch of sal forest there occurs a single herd of the Barasingha deer,* and that within its limits the common red jungle-fowl † is found, instead of the rival species *Gallus Sonneratii*, which alone occurs to the south and west. These two animals, together with the wild buffalo, are characteristic examples of the fauna of the great eastern and northern sal forests. The remains of buffaloes in the Narbada bone-beds already alluded to, sufficiently proves the former existence of the animal in these regions. Captain Forsyth's conclusion is that this outlier was once in connection with the main sal tracts of the Vindhyan range, and that it became detached simply by the deforestization of the intervening Narbada valley. The same writer has recorded that a Kolarian tribe called Korkus range with the commencement of the isolated patch of sal forest; the bulk of the Kolarian tribes being found within the limits of the great eastern sal forests. This coincidence is, I believe, in all probability due to a wandering branch of the Kols having selected the locality in consequence of the presence there of their old familiar and almost sacred tree, the sal. Parallel cases might be given of settlers in America and Australia in search of a habitation seeing something in the natural features of the new country which reminded them of their far-distant homes, and caused them to select particular spots upon which they conferred the well-remembered names of their former homes.

* *Rucervus Duvaucellii.* † *Gallus ferrugineus.*

February 13th.—Harmung to Khairi.—It had again become necessary for me to leave my camp below, and for a few days preceding this date I had remained at a Bhurya hamlet, called Harmung, which is perched in a commanding position on the edge of a cliff overhanging a valley in which are situated the sources of the Dudhi river. In every direction deep canyons and gorges with vertical bounding cliffs of sandstone might be seen penetrating back into the great mass of the hills.

This morning, as I was peaceably smoking a cigar on my way to work, and while passing along a narrow path between two small hills, I heard a rustle in the jungle close by, accompanied, as I thought, by a grunting sound. On looking up the small hill on my left, I could at first discern nothing among the clumps of bamboos; but perceiving a very peculiar expression on the long-drawn countenance of one of the coolies who accompanied me, I rushed to his side, and followed the direction of his glances, till my eyes fell on a bear scrambling about over the rocks. Seizing my rifle, I gave him a shot with the right barrel which made him howl; but the second shot with the left was a palpable miss. On my firing it Mr. Bruin charged down the hill straight for me, and I had only just time to turn him with two charges of No. 8 shot, which he received at close quarters in the face. His retreat gave my chuprasi—who stood his ground manfully—time to find and hand to me a couple of bullet cartridges. The first of these which I fired caused the bear to make another savage and desperate charge, but the second knocked him over, and he soon after collapsed. I then looked for the two coolies who had accompanied me, but at first could not see them; presently I caught sight of them at the tops of two very slender trees, which they had swarmed up to a safe height with astonishing agility. The conduct of the chuprasi in not bolting deserved and received much commendation, and also something more substantial. Had he not given me the shot-gun at the proper moment I should almost certainly have been killed. How quick the whole affair was may be judged from the fact that at the end of it I found the cigar still in my mouth. The bear was very large and heavy, and it took eight Bhuryas five hours to carry the carcase about five miles to camp. In the evening, on my return from work, I superintended the skinning, and after my bullets had been removed there was found to be still another, which proved to be a hammered (not cast) mass of lead. It had been completely encysted in tissue, where it lay on the shoulder, and had doubtless been there for many years, since it had been fired from the matchlock of some native shikari. The way in which my spherical bullets, driven by about four drams of powder, had spread into jagged masses of lead, afforded the strongest evidence of the superiority of that kind of charge over conical bullets with a less quantity of powder. The Bhuryas were provided with knives in order to take off the skin, but they soon discarded them in favour of their small axes, which having removed from the handles, and placed their thumbs in the hafts, they employed with much greater efficiency than they could the knives, with the use of which they were not very familiar. I could not help thinking that the axes so employed represented the stone skin-scrapers of pre-historic times.

The skin and skull fell to my share in the division of the spoils, the grease to my men, and the meat to the Bhuryas; but there is still something to be told about the mortal remains of that bear. After the meat required by the Bhuryas had been cut off, the carcase was flung away at a distance of one hundred yards or less from my sleeping tent. Not long after dark my dogs began to bark, and I concluded that jackals or hyænas had come to the carcase. Several times I went out of the tent in order to see what the visitors were, but the night was very dark and I failed to distinguish anything. On the following morning, after the camp had started for Umeria, I struck back into the hills to look up a tract which I had left unexamined. I had not proceeded very far before I came upon the tracks of an old tiger and a cub, leading in the direction of the tent. A few hours later I returned to the same spot, and then tracked up the footprints into close proximity to where the bear's carcase had lain. I had already noticed in the morning that it had been removed. With the aid of vultures and crows I at length found it in the middle of some long grass, and as there was no sign of its having been dragged along the ground it was evident that it had been carried by some animal which could have been none other than the tiger. I then, too, heard for the first time that during the night a cow had been nearly dragged out of a cattle enclosure not far off, but that the tiger had released it on the men in charge setting up a shout. Had I known all this in time I should have remained on the spot for another day, hoping to get a shot in the evening; but my camp was already far away and I had to follow it up. There was every reason for believing that the tiger and cub had eaten a portion of the dead bear before the attack was made on the cow. At one time it was supposed that tigers would not touch carrion; but this is now known on the most complete evidence to be incorrect, and that moreover they will eat bodies of animals, which have not been killed by themselves, even when in an advanced state of decomposition. On arrival at camp at Umeria I heard that during my absence a cow had been killed close at hand by a tiger in the daytime, and that my jemidar had sat up over the carcase, which was visited by the tiger in the afternoon. He failed however to hit, though he had three shots at it, as the tiger did not move off at the first report, but actually, so the jemidar said, stood up on its hind legs against a tree in order to see whence the noise proceeded. I here picked up a local shikari who promised to show me at least one tiger, and for many nights we had cattle tied up as baits, but they were not touched, though one had been narrowly examined by a tiger, whose footprints were found the next morning. At first there was some difficulty in obtaining cows or buffaloes for the purpose, as no one would sell. However, a *gwala*, or herd, brought two buffaloes on loan, as he expressed it—not to sell, which would be an unlawful act for a Hindu. The contract entered into was that I should give him a present for the loan, and that if, by any chance, any accident should happen to the buffaloes, the present should be proportionately increased. Soon after these terms had been agreed upon, a Brahmin arrived from a long distance, having heard of the gwala's intention. With clasped hands he besought that one of the buffaloes, which he said was his own property, though left in charge of the gwala, should be made over to him. He said that 500 rupees would not tempt him to allow it to be used for such a purpose. On its being made over to him he rather coolly asked for a supply of powder, shot, and caps, for his own sport. This request I did not comply with, but asked him how he could expect help from me when he gave none to me.

On my way to work at dawn, I used to visit the baits with my rifle on full cock; but always found them either grazing or placidly chewing the cud. The fact of my having work to do on this, as well as on many other occasions, interfered with my chances of successful sport, which generally requires one's undivided attention. The shooting the bear, and the incident I am about to relate, occurred merely as chance and unexpected episodes in the course of my usual work.

February 22nd.—Jamundunga.—While walking under the shade of some trees which bordered the Denwa river, my chuprasi called my attention to the fact that a small herd of sambar was crossing to our side just behind us. As I took my rifle they first caught sight of us; but as they were more than half-way across the boulder-strewn stream, they made a rush forwards, and as they did so I selected one, a doe, not noticing at the moment a young stag which was in the party, and hit her fair in the shoulder. Together with the others, however, she bounded to the bank, while I, in the excitement of running to meet them, fired the second shot over their backs. As it was evident from the great splashes of blood that the doe was badly hit, we climbed the hill where they had all disappeared, and soon came up with and despatched her.

At Jamundunga I heard that somewhere on the southern slopes of the Mahadeo or Pachmari hills there is an elephant at large which escaped from some Raja's possession, and that it has formed a strange alliance with a herd of bison or gaur. The gaur are notoriously fond of feeding on bamboo-leaves, as also are elephants. According to my informants, this elephant pulls down the lofty shoots of bamboos, so enabling the gaur to obtain an amount of this food which would otherwise be inaccessible to them. In return they keep a good look out for enemies, and give timely notice to the elephant of the approach of danger. Subsequently, on trying to obtain some information about the whereabouts of the gaur, I was told that they had left this neighbourhood in consequence of a herd of them having been driven by the villagers down a narrow valley which terminated abruptly at the edge of a steep cliff. Several were said to have plunged over this, and to have been dashed to pieces on the rocks below. Altogether this valley and the surrounding hills contain, I think, a greater abundance and variety of game than any tract of equal extent which I have been in. As the jungles opened up with the fall of the leaf and in consequence of the fires, I frequently caught sight of deer and nilgai, and occasionally an ominous rustling in the bushes betokened the flight of some large animal startled by the noise of my approaching footsteps.

About this time the Chief Commissioner of the Central Provinces, Mr. Morris, passed through Umeria with a large army of followers, on his way to his summer residence at Pachmari, after a long tour to the most distant part (Sambulpur) of the wide area under his jurisdiction. As he did not remain for a second day at Umeria, I was obliged to postpone visiting him until I should be able to ascend to Pachmari.

March 2nd.—Jamundunga to Jhot.—I had again to leave my main camp behind in order to visit some rugged and difficult country to the south, on the slopes of the Motur plateau. My small tent was pitched at a Bhurya hamlet, near which I shot a specimen of the Madras tree-shrew (*Tupaia Elliotti*), to which I have already alluded. A few days previously I had shot two specimens of the Malabar whistling-thrush, which therefore ranges with the tree-shrew much further to the north in the peninsula than had been previously supposed. The bearing which these facts possess on the general question of the geographical distribution of animals I have already described in Chapter VIII. I shot a number of other interesting birds in this neighbourhood, including a good series of a beautiful little bush-quail (*Microperdix Blewitti*, Hume).

March 5th.—Jamundunga to Pachmari.—To-day I started to pay my first visit to the sanitarium of Pachmari. Riding from Jamundunga to the foot of the Mahadeo hills, I commenced the ascent on foot at the Tara Ghât. After we had accomplished about half the distance the path, which we had, I believe, taken by mistake, became very bad and steep, and my horse began to slip about and cut himself against projecting masses of rock. At last we put him at one spot where he completely lost his footing and rolled down the slope, being only arrested by the trunk of a tree. As he was much bruised and shaken, I sent him back to camp, and continued my climb upwards for another two miles or so, after which we reached a level road in process of construction, by which we arrived at the station, five miles distant, without further difficulty. As there was no public bungalow I was at first rather at a loss where to bestow myself; but it was not long before I discovered a haven of rest with a former acquaintance, the private secretary to the Chief Commissioner. House-room was then rather scarce, and several of the heads of departments of the Central Provinces were consequently living in tents. Since that time, I believe, great improvements have taken place, and Pachmari has become the regular resort of officials from Nagpur during the months of March, April, and May, when the dry heat below is of such a particularly trying nature. In short, it was at that time intended to make Pachmari to be for the Central Provinces what Simla, Naini Tal, Darjiling, the Nilgherries, &c., are to the respective provinces and governments in which they are situated.*

Under the most favourable auspices I was enabled to see and hear of the many advantages and beauties which the place possessed. The Chief Commissioner, Mr. Morris, took me to several of the principal sights, and as he had at that time more thoroughly explored the tract than anyone else, the two days I

* A project to expend £250,000 on Cantonments was at that time, I believe, under consideration, but has not been adopted.

remained there were very profitably and pleasantly spent. Even the Andeh Koh, a deep-cut canyon or ravine, which Captain Forsyth had stated in his book to have baffled him, and to be quite inaccessible, did not prove to be so to Mr. Morris, who had not only explored it himself, but had succeeded in exhibiting its weird recesses to a small party of ladies. The main level of the plateau is about 3,600 feet above the sea, or not more than half the elevation of the average Himalayan stations. But it is sufficient to produce a very considerable difference in the temperature, and the greenery and freshness of the vegetation after the dust and blackness of the burnt jungles below, must ever prove grateful sights to the visitor. Beautiful avenues and drives, several miles in length, have been laid out, traversing the park-like scenery of the plateau. To the west rises the massive sandstone peak called Dhupgurh, the summit of which is 4,380 feet above the sea. In the most unexpected corners one comes upon waterfalls or well-wooded glens, and a little research in the latter reveals the existence of tree-ferns, which, though of small size, are of considerable interest and beauty. I cannot lay claim, however, to having made this discovery myself, as I was shewn the dried fronds by a lady, to whom all the credit is due, the fact having been previously quite unknown and unsuspected by Indian botanists. I found that the Malabar whistling-thrushes were not uncommon near the station, and I was told that they increase in numbers as the rivers dry up below with the advance of the hot weather. Thus, since both this bird and also tree-ferns occur in the Nilgherries, the appropriateness of the title the "Northern Nilgherries," which has sometimes been applied to Pachmari, will, perhaps, not be disputed. The great want of Pachmari is a branch line of railway connecting the foot of the ascent with the main line of railway. I entertained a hope that the result of some of the borings might prove the existence of coal in a position which would be the means of furthering a project to construct such a branch line; but, so far as I have yet heard, none of these borings have been carried out to a successful issue.

March 7th.—Pachmari to Delakheri.—To-day I returned to my camp below, descending by the Kanji Ghât towards the north-east of the plateau. It took me just seven hours' steady walking, under a hot sun, to accomplish the distance, which was little short of twenty-five miles.

Three days later, on the 10th, I received letters and a telegram from Chindwara, where I had sent to post, ordering my immediate return to Calcutta. Accordingly I had to countermand the march I had intended to make southwards to the Motur Plateau. Two forced marches brought me northwards to the railway station at Bankheri, where I broke-up camp, and early on the following morning was *en route* for Calcutta.

In passing through Behar from Patna to Lakeserai I saw in the railway-stations and sheds, glutted with bags of rice, abundant evidence of the famine operations. The true history of that famine, if presented as an unvarnished tale, would contain some curious reading; but as I have no personal knowledge of the subject, I shall refrain from further remarks about it.

I shall conclude this section with a brief sketch of the coal resources of the Narbada Valley. The general geology of the area is of too complicated a character to be disposed of in a work like the present, and reference should be made, by those interested, to the recently published Manual of the Geology of India.

The Satpura field, the principal portion of which is covered by a great thickness of rocks belonging to formations younger than the coal-measures, has a maximum length of 110 miles, and a maximum width of forty miles, with an area of about 2,500 square miles.

On the northern margin of this tract the coal-measures are alone exposed at Mopani,* but further west some of the tribu-

---

* The seams at Mopani are :—

1 Inferior Coal	12'	not worked.
2 Good Coking Coal	20'	has been on fire.
3 Good	3' 4"	These are worked together.
4 10 feet Good	12'	

taries of the Narbada, as the Tawa, which traverse the mass of hills, have laid bare coal-measures in the bottom of the valleys.

The Mopani coal-field has for many years been worked by the Narbada Coal and Iron Company; but, as the area of working-face in the mines is limited, and, as I have explained, the efforts to increase it have all hitherto failed, the amount of coal raised has rarely exceeded 1,000 tons per month, and this amount, though the railway company pays ten rupees a ton at the pit's mouth, or from three to four times what is paid in Ranigunj, is barely sufficient to cover working expenses. The consequence is that the railways in Western India are, at present, chiefly worked by English coal, since there is a point where the rail-borne cheap Ranigunj meets the sea-borne English coal at equal prices. This point is, of course, not a fixed one, as it oscillates with the price of English coal and freight, the price of Indian coal, and its carriage remaining nearly constant. The high cost of fuel in the Bombay Presidency, and Western India generally, which results from this state of things has not only justified the expenditure on borings which have been made to prove the extension of the coal-measures under the younger formations, but would justify a still further expenditure in the future. The matter is one, indeed, of Imperial importance, and it would be a cause for regret if it were allowed to drop, as, under skilled guidance, there is good reason for believing that favourable results will be obtained.*

* Since the above was printed, news has been received from India of coal having been proved to exist to the south-east, and it seems probable that an extensive field will be opened-up.—*Vide* "Records of the Geological Survey of India," Vol. XII., p. 95.

CHAPTER X.

SECTION 2.

BILUCHISTAN AND AFGHANISTAN. AGRA AND DELHI.

1874.

DISCOVERY OF COAL IN AFGHANISTAN—APPOINTED TO REPORT ON IT —CALCUTTA TO MULTAN—MIAN MIR—MULTAN TO MOZUFFERGURH—FLOODS—HEAT—THE INDUS—DERA GHAZI KHAN—RIDE TO SAKHI SARWA —THIRST—ASPECT OF THE OUTER RANGES OF THE SULIMANS—ASCENT OF THE SULIMANS—REACH CAMP—OUR ESCORT—BILUCH MARES—START FOR THE INTERIOR—A BILUCH "CITY"—THE LUNI PATHANS—THE KISS OF PEACE—FIRST TRACES OF COAL—THE ROLL OF OUR ESCORT—THE COAL —WILD SHEEP AND GOATS—BEARS—THE CAMP—RETURN MARCH—BILUCH MARKSMEN—ASCEND JANDRAN—A SAMPLE RAIDER—THE KETRANS —HOSTILE NEIGHBOURS—KAFILAS—THE EXEMPT—ANCIENT POTTERY HEAPS—A SPY AND HIS VIEWS ON POLITICS—GEOLOGY—OUR TAIL OF FOLLOWERS DIMINISHES—EVIL PREDICTIONS OF A RENEWAL OF TURMOIL AND RAIDING—A CHIEFTAIN IN DISGRACE—FLOODS—RETURN TO DERA GHAZI KHAN—DELHI—IRON PILLAR—AGRA—SEKANDRA—WOLF-REARED CHILDREN—THE TAJ—SIMLA.

TOWARDS the end of June, 1874, correspondence regarding the discovery of coal by Major Sandeman, in the country of the Luni Pathans, about 100 miles west of Dera Ghazi Khan, led to a proposal that an officer of the Geological Survey of India should be sent to report upon the prospect of coal being found there in sufficient quantity to be profitably worked for the supply of the steamers and railways of the Indus valley. Although the locality was actually situated in Afghanistan*—the Luni Pathans

---

* A recent map represents the Luni Pathans' country as not belonging strictly to Afghanistan.

being more or less subject to the Amir of Cabul—Major Sandeman was sanguine as to the satisfactory adjustment of the political difficulty in connection with the opening out of a mine.

The climate of the Derajat* in July enjoys a somewhat evil reputation, and the Government of India most considerately declined to *order* any geologist on this mission, but granted permission to whoever might be selected by the Superintendent of the Survey to proceed or not at his own risk. The offer being made to me, was gladly accepted, as an opportunity of visiting such remote regions, beyond the British frontier, was not likely to recur, and the trip promised to be one of great interest, in spite of *désagrémens* inseparable from a journey at that time of year. The fact that I should not be alone, and the confidence that as I had already borne a good deal of exposure to extreme heat, I should now be capable of enduring as much as my companions, encouraged me not to hesitate about my decision. I therefore immediately made my preparations, and left Calcutta by train for Multan on the night of the 3rd of July. By travelling straight through, I reached Lahore at noon on the 6th. As the train for Multan does not leave until the evening, on account of the excessive heat by day, I employed the time at my disposal in visiting the city of Lahore and its neighbourhood. I shall not, however, here pause to describe what I saw, but continue the account of my journey. At 5.30 p.m. the train left for Multan. The carriages on this line—very different in construction from those in which I had come through from Calcutta to Lahore with great comfort—were divided into narrow compartments, and heavily cushioned, being apparently cunningly devised to intensify the sufferings of passengers. A slow rate of progression, frequent and long stoppages, and an abundance of flying sand, proved to be causes of further discomfort and irritation. I, the only European

---

* The Derajat is the strip of low-lying ground, *trans* Indus, at the foot of the Suliman range.

passenger in the train, passed a terrible night, and the natives seemed to suffer almost as much, as at every station the cries for water were unceasing.

For most of the way the soil is sandy, and only supports scattered bushes of species of *Capparis*, *Acacia*, *Euphorbia*, &c. Towards Multan, however, where there is some irrigation by means of Persian wheels, I saw crops of Indian corn, millet, tobacco, &c. The view of the cantonments at Mian Mir, across the bush-scattered sands to the south of Lahore, was most dismal. The change afforded by frequent trips to the hills can alone render existence bearable in such an abominable climate, and with such depressing surroundings. I arrived at Multan in the morning, and remained there during the day; but, owing to the heat, could not do much sight-seeing. I was met there by a native police-orderly from Dera Ghazi Khan, a most intelligent fellow, who made for me all the arrangements necessary for my subsequent journey. In the afternoon we took the train for Sher Shah,* the then terminus of the line, on the banks of the Chenab river. By the same train the Governor-General's agent and some other of the European officers of the flourishing native State of Bhawalpur, went down to a steamer which was awaiting their arrival. They kindly offered to put me across the river, but the flooded state of the opposite bank would have made it impossible to near the land, so that I crossed in the common ferry-boat, having for fellow-travellers a party of natives of all ages and sizes, who were grievously afflicted with boils. Landing on a slip of dry ground, I then had a mile's ride over a flooded road, to where a couple of gigs were in waiting, into which myself and goods were stowed. After a few miles' drive we reached the travellers' bungalow at Mozuffergurh about dark. The heat inside this building was simply unbearable; provision

---

* I see by a recent statement that the navigable channel of the Chenab river has, with the well-known inconstancy of Indian deltaic rivers, left the neighbourhood of Sher Shah altogether, and that the landing-place of steamers is now about six miles off.

was, however, made for this state of things by the erection of punkahs in the open, under one of which I passed a few hours, tossing about, and unable to sleep. At three o'clock we again started in the gigs, but before reaching the Indus were compelled to ride, as the flooded state of the country prevented wheeled vehicles traversing the road. The mail-boat carried me across the regular channel of the river. At this season it was possible to sail straight to the opposite bank to a place called Patun. In the dry season the channel is divided into two by a wide *chur*, or island of sand, which necessitates tiresome transhipment. The position of this *chur* was marked by the tops of the bushes of Jow (*Tamarix*) which grow upon it. At Patun, I was met by the Assistant-Commissioner of Dera Ghazi Khan, who drove me into that station, which was five miles distant. I was astonished to find the station so green and bright-looking. This is in consequence of the admirable system of irrigation, for the rainfall amounts to only about five inches per annum. The flooding of the Lower Indus is seldom due to local accession of water, but is generally attributable to the sudden melting of great masses of snow at the sources. During the year 1878, these floods were on a very destructive scale, and much damage was done to Dera Ghazi Khan.

Frontier politics I found furnished the officers of the Punjab frontier force with an unceasing topic of discussion. In several of the bungalows, maps showing the outposts of the Russians might be seen, with all the latest available information duly recorded on them.

It had been my original intention to press on, the night of my arrival at Dera Ghazi Khan, so as to join Major Sandeman's camp on the top of the Suliman range without delay, but I had earned a night's rest, and as it was necessary to fortify myself for a sixty miles' ride, I thought it better to defer my departure till the afternoon of the day following. The morning was spent seeing the sights of Dera Ghazi Khan, including the jail, in which there were a number of murderers of both sexes, belonging to the Biluch and other tribes. The radial arrangement of the buildings forming this jail reminded me of the Menagerie at Schönbrun, near Vienna.

Leaving the station at 4 p.m.. I reached Sakhi Sarwar, thirty-two miles distant, at about 8.30. The horses provided for me were the property of the Police-Sawars, one of whom accompanied me as orderly from relay to relay.

A short distance from Sakhi Sarwar, I was met by the head man, who had ridden forth to greet me. As he held out his hand, I saw in the dusk that it contained something, and putting down my hand towards it, observed that he closed his fingers upon a coin. This was his *nazar* or formal offering, which he of course expected to be remitted, but which my action for the moment, I suppose, made him think I was going to accept. To make such offerings, and never to appear empty-handed on making a salaam, I found to be the universal custom among the Biluch on both sides of the frontier. In most parts of India, though traces of the custom are met with, it seems to be gradually dying out.

On arrival at Sakhi Sarwar I found a partly-finished two-storied rest house occupied by a motley crew of wild-looking Biluch, several of whom had to be disturbed from their slumbers in the upper verandah to make room for the cot upon which I was to rest. They did not hesitate to grumble at this ejectment, but departed to search for other quarters. I had no sooner sat down in the bungalow, than I became aware that I was afflicted with an absolutely unquenchable thirst, and that my liver had been jolted into a condition which removed all desire for food, and rendered sleep impossible. Sakhi Sarwar's reputation being so well known, at Dera Ghazi Khan, ample provision of iced drinks had been, with much forethought and kindness, prepared for me, but without avail, for after consuming an amount of claret and soda-water which I am ashamed to record, I was still thirsty, and had, before I started, to drink some of the local brackish and almost tepid water.

Sakhi Sarwar is said to be the place of which it was remarked by some native that, it being in existence, it was unnecessary for the Creator to have made Hell also. There are, I believe, some other places which claim to have had this said of them, but its application to any of them can scarcely be more appropriate than it is to Sakhi Sarwar. The name is derived from that of a Mahomedan *Pir*, or saint of great sanctity, whose tomb close by draws many pilgrims. An annual festival in his honour, which partakes also of the nature of a fair, brings together many thousands of Hindus as well as Mahomedans.*

The great heat of this place at night is no doubt attributable to the radiation from the closely adjoining verdureless outer slopes of the Suliman range. Those who have not seen the arid hills bordering the Red Sea, or some similar scenery, could scarcely conjure up in their minds a landscape so desolate as that presented by these uniformly brown and arid-looking rocks. Sakhi Sarwar is stated to be about 926 feet above the sea.

At about two o'clock on the following morning I rode southwards for a few miles, and then about dawn turned westwards into the Siri or Sakhi Sarwar pass, which was an old Kafila route to Kandahar. I was mounted on a rather miserable-looking Biluch mare, but she proved a capital one to go, though the route, especially where it lay in the boulder-strewn bed of the Siri river, was a very rough one. Here my geological observations commenced; but, as the full results of my examination have been elsewhere published,† I shall not now dwell upon details, my object being rather to describe the people and general features of a portion of a tract of country to which considerable interest attaches at the present moment. The bed of the river in the plain outside the flanking range of hills, and for a distance of perhaps two miles inside it, had not a trace of water, but beyond that we came upon running water from

---

* A very complete account of Sakhi Sarwar and the fair is given by J. Macauliffe, Esq. B.A., in the "Calcutta Review," No. CXIX., 1875, p. 78.

† "Records of the Geological Survey of India," Vol. VII., p. 158.

the interior which suddenly disappears beneath the surface coincidently with a bed of conglomerate which dips downwards. Judging from the maps, this seems to be the fate of most of the rivers along this frontier, few of them finding their way to the plains, although the continuation of the *nullahs* or dried-up-water-courses indicates that they have done so formerly, or even may do so now under the exceptional circumstance of a heavy and long-continued rainfall. Such a rainfall took place a few weeks after my visit, and much damage was the result of this locally-fed flood in Biluchistan, and other parts of the Indus valley. At the end of the Siri Pass, which is about four miles long, a north to south valley opens to view in which numerous ridges formed of green and red shales or clays, and brownish sandstones, and further in, white nummulitic limestones strike from north to south. The open parts of this valley, though stony, support a certain amount of vegetation which is dwarfed and stunted in growth, but produces an agreeable appearance, after that of the dreary waste outside.

At Kudji I found a fresh horse in charge of a Biluch Sawar, and with him and Ali Bux, the police constable, who had been in close attendance upon me all through, I commenced the ascent of the main range of the Sulimans, by a track which had been opened up by Major Sandeman. Before reaching the next relay I began to feel much fatigue, and a yearning for sleep, which I was compelled to gratify, by dismounting and lying down under a sheltering ledge of rock, for an hour. When I mounted again I became conscious of serious damage to my integument, otherwise known as loss of leather, which had been caused by the steepness of the climb, and the saddle not suiting me. The rest of the journey, up seemingly endless zig-zags, to the bungalow erected by Major Sandeman as a sanitarium, at an elevation of 5,880 feet above the sea, occupied several weary hours, and it was nearly four o'clock before I got to the end of it. The slow pace, however, had the advantage of enabling me to watch and note more carefully the geological changes than I should have been able had my bodily condition permitted me to ride as fast as Ali

Bux wished. I trust I have not wearied the reader by dwelling on my physical sufferings. Any allusion to them in a formal scientific record would, of course, be inadmissible; but to conceal them in an account of this nature would be a mistake, and only tend to give a wrong impression. They constitute, however, but a trifling shadow on the memory of one of the most interesting and pleasant of the many exploring expeditions I have made in India.

At the bungalow I found Major Sandeman and Captain Lockwood, and close by were the tents of the Biluch chieftains Jamal Khan, Emam Bux, and others, with their followers, all of whom were to accompany us across the frontier. The following day it was arranged that we should remain where we were in order that I should recover from the fatigue of the journey; and on the day after, in the afternoon, we made a short march of six miles westwards, descending from the main ridge of the Sulimans into the Rukni valley, so called after a village belonging to the Hudianis, a section of the Ketran tribe of Biluch. This flat valley, which is about 3,500 feet above the sea, has a remarkably fertile appearance, being covered with a green-sward of grass, scattered about in which there are bushes of wild plum or *Zizyphus*, &c. Of this but a small portion was cultivated in the immediate vicinity of the walls of the village. Though so near to the British frontier, raiding is carried on between the tribes, and only a few months previous to our visit the *Maris*, a tribe living further to the south, had swept through the country.

Our body-guard consisted at first of about 150 Biluch chiefs with their followers, mostly mounted. The armed cavalcade presented a singular appearance with their swords, shields, matchlocks, and flowing white garments. Physically they are powerfully-built and handsome men. As a rule the chiefs shew in their bulky frames the superiority of their food and nurture over that attainable by the mass of their tribesmen. Each mounted Sawar carried a matchlock slung across his back, and a sword suspended by a more or less richly-embroidered shoulder-strap, not by a belt.

Other portions of their equipment consist of cartouche cases, brass châtelaines, from which are suspended powder measures, small horns for priming-powder, turnscrews, &c. Their commissariat arrangements are simple. A sheep's skin full of water is slung under the horse's girth, and a skin full of flour is strapped in front or behind the saddle. For days together the food of these men may consist only of lumps of partially-kneaded dough baked on the embers of wood fires. When on the raid the meat of stolen sheep is added to this simple fare.

It will be convenient here to describe the Biluch horses, of which before many days were over I had seen nearly a thousand. The true Biluch will only ride mares; a few entire horses are kept for breeding purposes, but the majority shortly after birth are simply neglected and allowed to starve, not being thought to be worth the trouble of rearing. The reason of this strange custom is simply that in their raids, the actual fighting being accomplished by stealthy assaults on foot, it is of great advantage that one man should be able to hold a score of horses which will remain quiet and not give the alarm by neighing. Geldings might answer, perhaps, but would scarcely be so docile or quiet. However this may be, the Biluch does not try them. The mares perhaps average something under fourteen hands. They are fairly fleet and as active as cats on the steep, often trackless, hill-sides. The prices—from 300 to 500 rupees—asked for them by their often ragged-looking owners, seemed to me to be absurdly high. On the following morning we started at half-past four for the Taghar valley, the route exposing rolling beds of nummulitic limestones abounding in fossils. The clear sections of these rocks, which rest upon the older sandstones that form the main Suliman range, were very instructive. The freedom from vegetation enabled one to obtain most comprehensive views of the structure. A few scattered olives were the only trees which seemed able to maintain their existence on the dry ledges. We remained in the Taghar valley and rested during the heat of the day, resuming our route at 2 p.m. From this valley, which is 3,800 feet above the sea, we had to ascend and cross a ridge by a pass of about 5,200 feet elevation. On our descent into the Bughar valley we found ourselves surrounded by a most agreeably altered scene, in which were scattered about several walled cities * surrounded by cultivation. I went inside one of these cities and found it crowded with miserable hovels of stone and mud, with here and there a few mats to close the apertures. Dirt, untidiness, and squalor, prevailed to an extent I hardly anticipated from the appearance of the men. At each corner of the walls was a tower looped for matchlocks. My appearance created some excitement amongst the inhabitants—especially the female portion of it—who had never set eyes on a European before.

The following day we marched to Chamarlang, having a mid-day halt at Karer. The successive valleys, which we crossed at nearly right angles, have been generally formed by denudation along the broken crests of the rolling beds of limestone, and not as might be expected in the hollows of the rolls. During the day our cavalcade, which had been steadily augmenting, was increased by the advent of the Luni Pathans, into whose country we had entered. Their general appearance was very different from that of the Biluch, and the long lances which they carried served still further to distinguish them. The manner of reception which they would give us was up to the last moment a matter of some uncertainty, but Major Sandeman's extraordinary influence and prestige served to elicit from them a sufficiently respectful greeting. The principal chiefs in Major Sandeman's suite dismounted and embraced the Luni Pathan head man, after he had enacted the form of presenting his *nazar*. This "kiss of peace," which was gone through by the whole party on the occasion of each new chief joining with his levy, merits some description. Rushing into each other's arms in a most melodramatic manner, they would both repeat the word *Khúshi*, pleasure, several times. How far these demonstrations were

* So-called *Shahrs*. Village would be a more appropriate title.

sincere may be inferred from the fact that in less than a month afterwards the tribes represented by some of these chiefs were fighting with one another, raiding and murdering. Early the following morning we rode to the base of a scarped hill called Kuch Budi, where the first indications of coal had been observed. These proved to consist of a number of thin seams, none of which exceeded four and a-half inches, and most of which were not half that thickness—the whole being consequently quite valueless. Several other sections having been examined, we then rode on to another camp in the Chamarlang valley, close to which occurs the principal coal-seam which had been the goal of our journey, and upon which the hopes of everyone connected with the matter centered. The chiefs, who live in British territory, but exercise only a nominal authority over certain of the tribes beyond the frontier, hoped for a favourable verdict on the coal, foreseeing that were the country acquired by the British this authority would be strengthened, and might possibly become a source of profit, instead of being a mere barren honour—which involved indeed from time to time subsidies and presents to these wilful Ishmaelites. In this camp, on roll being taken, it was found that there were representatives from sixteen tribes, with their chiefs, in all about 1,500 men, about half of whom, or rather more, were mounted. Seven of these tribes were from British and the remaining nine from independent territory. There were also about 100 baggage camels, carrying supplies, &c. The elevation of this camp was about 3,900 feet above the sea. The next morning we visited the coal, and the appearance presented by some hundreds of armed Biluch perched on every coign of vantage, while I measured the seam and examined the coal, was one I shall never forget. Finding that the thickest part of the seam was only nine inches, and that the inclination or dip was 45°, it was impossible for me, in spite of the fact of the coal being of excellent quality, to pronounce other than a most unfavourable opinion. Regretfully I observed the disappointment with which the announcement was received, but there was no help for it, and all my subsequent exploration and enquiries convinced me that not only was there no better seam elsewhere, but none even so good.* This result was similar to that which has invariably been found to be the case where the coals occurring in the tertiary rocks on the north-west frontiers of India have been explored.

The remainder of the day I spent in examining the geology of the neighbouring hills and collecting fossils. While so employed, I met a Shikari who had shot a fine wild goat or *Markhor*. Two or three hills were pointed out to me as being inhabited by bears. They probably belonged to the same species as the animal called the *Mamh* of Biluchistan, which about two years ago excited considerable controversy in India, some writers maintaining it to be a mythological animal, others, from its small footprints, concluding that it was a monkey. A skin subsequently obtained has enabled Mr. W. T. Blanford, F.R.S., to describe it as a new species of bear, to which he has given the name *Ursus Gedrosianus*.

The day's halt appeared to be much enjoyed by the people, and not less by the mares, which scampered about in herds over the sward in the fulness of their freedom. Major Sandeman's camp occupied the centre of the valley, and the different tribes had been told off to occupy various points on the circumference of a surrounding circle about a quarter of a mile in diameter. In the vast assemblage I did not once hear anything like a squabble going on—not even high words. How different it would have been had there been only one-fiftieth part of the number of Hindustanis present! It seemed that for the time the British flag quenched all animosities, though the different chieftains could not entertain much love for one another, in consequence of old traditional feuds. Major Sandeman, however, encouraged the establishment

* In a letter from a correspondent to the *Pioneer* with the Thull Chotiali field force, dated April 20th, 1879, I observe that while an extract from my report is given, it is added that it was believed that I had subsequently modified my views as to the improbability of an abundance of coal being found. I take this opportunity, therefore, of saying that such has not been the case, no additional facts having been discovered which would justify my altering the conclusions arrived at from an examination of the ground.

of certain matrimonial contracts, which bid fair to heal the differences in some cases, and it was hoped would result in the war-hatchet being buried. The difficulty of bringing about such a state of accord is very great whenever one of the tribes counts a life still to be avenged.

While Major Sandeman was thus engaged in matters political, and I with the geology, Captain Lockwood was busily occupied in the preparation of an admirable sketch-map of the country. His finished work, extending over an area of about 700 square miles of previously unknown ground, has been inserted in the latest maps.*

Our position in Chamarlang was within about sixty miles of Thull Chotiali, quite a different locality from Thull, near the Khyber Pass, which recent events have made familiar with the British public.

On the following morning (17th), taking a new line for our return, we marched to a place called Hunki, crossing a section of rocks belonging to the coal horizon, in which there were some thin layers of coaly matter. We remained there for breakfast and for the examination of the neighbourhood, and then having got thoroughly wet in a heavy shower, rode on, skirting the Karvada range, to an open and fertile valley, called Pasta Mara, crossing *en route* the old Kafila road to Kandahar. From time to time during our journey we came upon piles of stones, some of which marked the spot where a man had been shot down. Among our following there was often to be found some one able to give the history of the murder.

In the evening the Biluch showed their excellence as marksmen. A man who made an indifferent shot—none shot badly—at once became the subject of ridicule by the surrounding crowd. A small cavalry Snider-carbine of mine was much admired for its handiness, and several of the chieftains, who had

---

* I must protest against the insertion of the words "Coal cliff" in one of these, that by Stanford, on the site of the thin seams of coal, since it is calculated to convey a very erroneous idea of the true nature of the deposit.

never fired a weapon of the kind before, made capital shots with it, breaking a bottle on the ground at a distance of 150 yards.

Leaving Pasta Mara on the morning of the 18th, we rode through a series of deeply-cut gorges, about ten miles in a south-easterly direction, to the Hun Pass, where Major Sandeman and I ascended a spur of the Jandran range, to a peak about 5,000 feet above the sea. Various stories were afloat as to the marvellous sights to be seen on the summit. It was said that a Jogi or Fakir had lived in a cave there, and that his cooking-vessels, &c., were to be found turned into stone. This suggested to me the possibility of the existence of some remarkable fossils in the rocks. On arriving at the summit, after a very steep and laborious climb, we failed to find the cave, and our guides professed to know nothing about it. One of them, named Jana, a very singular-looking individual, and a notorious raider and thief, with whom we conversed, admitted the impeachment that such was his character with the most unblushing effrontery. "Yes, Sahib!" he remarked, "without doubt I am a thief."

Descending the hill, we continued our march through the Hun Pass to the Barkan Valley, which is inhabited by a tribe called Ketrans, who, as their name indicates (derived from *ket*, a field), are cultivators. This and the neighbouring valleys having a perennial supply of water, are well suited for agriculture; but, unfortunately, feuds, which interfere seriously with the course of peaceful avocations, are not unknown. The head man and the inhabitants of the village or *city* of Mir Hadji, not far from where we encamped, were on the worst possible terms with the people of another village, not two miles off, and no opportunities for mutual reprisals were lost, so that it was impossible for them respectively to move away from the vicinity of their walls, save when armed in sufficient numbers to render an attack dangerous. For, as a rule, it must be said, attacks are generally made with overwhelming numbers, when there is little or no risk of loss on the side of the attacking party; and often a man falls, basely "potted" from behind a rock, being profoundly ignorant of the presence of his assailants, be they few or many.

From this valley we first saw kafilas of pack-bullocks, with grain, travelling eastwards. Whether on account of their service as traders, or because of their effeminate natures, the Hindu merchants in these regions are never killed in the raids; with them are spared the women and children, and all boys who have not donned the manly garb, or who are, in other words, *sans culotte*. The assumption of trousers by a youth carries with it the liability to be counted and shot at as a man.

On the 19th we marched to a place called Chowatta, but owing to heavy rains having soaked the tents, &c., could not start till ten o'clock, when they were somewhat dry. I employed the morning in visiting some mounds, believed to be of great antiquity. At first sight I thought they might be Buddhistic topes, but, save some fragments of broken ornamental pottery, I saw nothing to give a clue to their nature and origin. Possibly excavation might have revealed something, but for this there was no time. In consequence of the fact that pottery is not manufactured at the present day in Biluchistan, and, indeed, can scarcely be said to be used there, this pile of broken fragments was considered a remarkable sight.* The cooking-vessels are—so far as I saw—exclusively made of metal, and the drinking-vessels, &c., are made either of wood or leather. I also visited a garden belonging to one of the chiefs, Biluch Khan. It contained grapes, figs, and pomegranates, all of which appeared to grow luxuriantly.

A man from Thull, who turned up to-day, was admitted to Major Sandeman's durbar. His account of himself was that he had been tracking up some strayed cattle, and, hearing of our army, had followed us up. He spoke out his mind with a freedom from restraint which was particularly refreshing. Among other things, he professed incredulity as to the coal being the real object of the expedition, and said, "You are not wheeling

---

* Some ancient remains of pottery have been found in another part of Biluchistan (Mekran) by Major Mockler; in association with them were various other articles, including flint knives, &c. *Vide* Proceedings Asiatic Society of Bengal, 1877, p. 157.

about the country for nothing. We know full well that the Sirkar Angrez (English Government) is hankering after Kandahar and Kabul, but we will never submit to be called by the hated name of Ryots, nor will we be the servants of anyone, though we may perhaps consent to render you our assistance, should you at any time require it." How these prophetical remarks, made five years ago, have been fulfilled by recent events it is, perhaps, needless to point out.

The geological structure of this valley was beautifully displayed in a number of admirable sections, and the nummulitic limestones, especially at a place called Chukerani, yielded an abundant supply of fossils.

The next day we returned to the bungalow on the main Suliman range, and remained there for three days, in which period of grateful rest I was abundantly occupied in writing out my report on the geology, and collecting and observing the few species of birds to be found at this elevation.*

During the return march our army had gradually diminished to its original strength of about 150, as the various chieftains led off their forces to their respective homes. I was much impressed with a remark made by one of the subordinate chieftains to Major Sandeman. He said, in Hindustani, "We are sorry you are leaving the country. Henceforth turmoil and raiding will furnish the principal events in our daily lives." The event fully bore out the truth of this prophecy. One of the men—I think it was the before-mentioned Jana—said that he, with his small following, had been invited to join a raiding party, and most complacently asked for advice as to whether he should join it or not. The doubt in his mind seemed to be altogether due to a calculation which he had made of the cost, and the consequent uncertainty of its proving a paying speculation. It does not by any means follow that these raids prove formidable. Sometimes

* An account of these observations is published in the Indian Ornithological Journal "Stray Feathers." Vol. III. 1875.

the raiders are well thrashed; often they lose many of their beasts and some of their own lives, and when they arrive at home the division of spoil yields but a miserable pittance per man. After one long and wearisome raid, which was accompanied by much loss, I think I saw it stated that each man received only the equivalent of three shillings as his share.

Our return to Dera Ghazi Khan was accomplished without special incident, save that the principal chieftain got himself into disgrace with Major Sandeman for not conducting me to a place where coal had been found on the outer slopes of the Sulimans, as it had been arranged that he should on the day we descended. The following day, although the deposit was known to be insignificant, being also on the same geological horizon as that which had been examined, I wished to go to the place, but was assured that in the morning heat I could not visit the low valley in which it was situated except at an absolute risk of my life. Accordingly a messenger was sent, who brought some specimens, but did not rejoin us at Sakhi-Sarwar till the afternoon. He came back much exhausted, and told me, when I asked him what would have happened had I gone with him, that I should be still lying there under a tree.

The following night we slept at a village called Veddore, in the plain. A grateful shower of rain, of which there had been an abnormal amount, cooled the air sufficiently to render sleep possible. But we were disturbed during the night by a terrible uproar in the village, caused by the floods bursting through a retaining embankment, which necessitated all hands turning out to save the precious fluid for cultivation.

July 29th.—After two days' rest in Dera Ghazi Khan I started on the return journey to Calcutta, and rode to Mozuffergurh. For several miles on the eastern side of the Indus our route was through water. At one place where the mounted orderly who accompanied me was at fault we got a villager to wade in front of the horses, and I was rather surprised to observe that he left the high-road and struck across the fields and waste lands, as they, he said, were covered by a less depth of water.

At Lahore, which I reached on the morning of the 31st, I visited a large musjid or mosque in the centre of the town, and the native bazaars, which are more like those of Egypt than any to be seen in Bengal. A large proportion of the people struck me as being remarkably unclean in their persons, and the flies and evil odours which abounded rendered the visit far from pleasant.

On the following morning I arrived early at Delhi, and devoted the day, in spite of the very great heat, to visiting the various interesting sights in the city and vicinity. But as descriptions of these are to be found in many works, not to speak of guide-books, I shall, consistently with my programme, avoid describing them here. I must remark, however, that to my mind by far the most wonderful sight there, is the great wrought-iron pillar at the Kutub. It is 23 feet 8 inches long, with a diameter at base of 16.4 inches, tapering to 12.05 inches at top. These dimensions indicate a weight of 5.7 tons. The capital and a bulbous protuberance at the base would probably make the total weight not less than 6 tons. It is supposed by Mr. Fergusson * to be 1,400 years old. It affords, therefore, evidence of

---

* In Mr. Fergusson's "History of India and Eastern Architecture," is to be found, I believe, the only accurate account yet published of this pillar. He writes :—"One of the most interesting objects connected with this mosque (Kutub), is the iron pillar which stands—and apparently always has stood—in the centre of its court-yard. It now stands 22 feet above the ground, and, as the depth under the pavement is now ascertained to be only 20 inches, the total height is 23 feet 8 inches. Its diameter at base is 16.4 inches, at the capital, 12.05 inches. The capital is 3½ feet high, and is sharply and clearly wrought into the Persian form that makes it look as if it belonged to an earlier period than it really does; and it has the *Amalaka* moulding which is indicative of considerable antiquity. It has not, however, been yet correctly ascertained what its age really is. There is an inscription upon it, but without a date. From the form of its alphabet, Prinsep ascribed it to the Third or Fourth Century; Bhau Daji, on the same evidence, to the end of the Fifth, or beginning of the Sixth Century. The truth probably lies between the two. My own conviction is that it belongs to one of the Chandra Rajas of the Gupta dynasty, either consequently to A.D. 363, or A.D. 400.

"Taking A.D. 400 as a mean date—and it certainly is not far from the truth—it opens our eyes to an unsuspected state of affairs to find the Hindus at that age

the existence of an amount of metallurgical skill at that early period which could not have been equalled in Europe a few years ago. It is only within a very short space of time that it has become possible for the iron-forges of England to manipulate equally large masses of metal. It is believed by those competent to form an opinion that this pillar must have been formed by welding lengths together; but, if so, it must have been done very skilfully, since no marks are left of any such welding. Analyses of the iron have been made both by Dr. Murray Thompson, of Rurki College, and Dr. Percy, of the School of Mines. They have found it to be pure malleable iron without alloy. I recently stated the above facts to some iron-masters in South Wales, and they expressed great astonishment, and admitted that even now it would be a matter of considerable difficulty to forge such a mass.

From Delhi I pushed on to Agra, arriving there on the morning of the 3rd of August. Having seen some of the sights of the city, I drove to Sekandra, in order to visit the Orphanage, and avail of the opportunity for the first time afforded to me of making enquiries on the spot regarding the reputed finding

---

capable of forging a bar of iron larger than any that have been forged in Europe up to a very late date, and not frequently even now. As we find them, however, a few centuries afterwards using bars as long as this lât in roofing the porch of the temple at Kanaruc, we must now believe that they were much more familiar with the use of this metal than they afterwards became. It is almost equally startling to find that, after an exposure to wind and rain for fourteen centuries, it is unrusted, and that the capital and inscription are as clear and as sharp now as when put up fourteen centuries ago.

"As the inscription informs us the pillar was dedicated to Vishnu, there is little doubt that it originally supported a figure of Garuda on the summit, which the Mahomedans of course removed; but the real object of its erection was as a pillar of victory to record the defeat of the Balhikas near the seven mouths of the Sindhu or Indus.

"General Cunningham was at first told that the depth below the surface was 35 feet by the man in charge. On excavation it proved to be only twenty inches. Just below the surface it expands in a bulbous form to a diameter of two feet four inches and rests on a gridiron of iron bars which are fastened with lead into the stone pavement."

of boys living with wolves as their foster parents. A year previously, as I shall presently show, I had been instrumental in drawing attention to the cases of wolf-reared children which had been reported, and I was most anxious to examine one of the boys myself. But before giving an account of the results of my enquiries, and a *resumé* of the existing literature of the subject, I wish to say, by way of preface, that I have found that this subject is one of those which the majority of people seem unable to discuss without prejudice. They make up their minds that the whole thing is a myth, before they have heard what evidence can be adduced in its favour. I am, unfortunately, not in a position to give any personal testimony of importance; all that I can do is to place the evidence available before the reader. In the first published communication on this subject which I made to a learned Society,* I advocated, as I also do now, that the matter should, on the first recurrence of an opportunity, be most strictly enquired into, and that it should not in future be approached in the hostile and incredulous spirit which has hitherto prevailed. My paper, which was presented during my absence in Europe, met with some opposition, but subsequently saw the light in the form of an abstract. It however attracted the attention of Professor Max Müller, who, in the pages of the "Academy," pointed out the importance of the subject, and quoted a selection from the recorded cases of wolf-reared children. At the same time he strongly urged upon sportsmen, naturalists, and district officials, the desirability of carefully investigating, on the spot, the probability and possibility of such cases being true.

The story of Romulus and Remus does not by any means stand alone. There are many other gods and heroes of antiquity who are stated to have been suckled by wolves, and whose histories are regarded as wholly mythical in consequence of the presence of this element. If the case of a child being suckled and

---

* *Vide* Proceedings of the Asiatic Society of Bengal, 1873, p. 128.

reared by wolves can be established as a physical possibility by a single well-authenticated case in India, such histories will assume a totally new aspect, and will have a chance of being accepted as true in their entirety.

Shakespeare alludes to the existence of a belief in such stories :—

> ANTIGONUS. "Come on, poor babe :
> Some powerful spirit instruct the kites and ravens
> To be thy nurses ! Wolves and bears, they say,
> Casting their savageness aside have done
> Like offices of pity."
>
> WINTER'S TALE, Act II., Scene 3, Line 185.

Most of the recorded Indian cases I believe come from the province of Oude. This is possibly in a great measure attributable to the fact that the number of children carried away and killed by wolves is greater there than elsewhere. According to a table which I possess, the loss of life in the province attributed to this cause for the seven years from 1867 to 1873 inclusive, averaged upwards of 100 *per annum.*

On the authority of Colonel Sleeman,* as quoted by Professor Max Müller, the number of little victims carried off to be devoured is so great in some parts of India, that people make a living by collecting from the dens of wild animals the gold ornaments with which children in India are always decked out by their parents. It is said even that these people are unwilling to take part in any wholesale destruction of wolves for fear of losing their livelihood.

The *modus operandi* adopted by the wolf has been thus described†:—" Night comes on, the wolf slinks about the village site, marking the unguarded hut. It comes to one protected by a low wall, or closed by an ill-fitting *tattie* (mat). Inside, the mother, wearied by the long day's work, is asleep with her

---

* "Journey through the Kingdom of Oude," 1858 (Vol. I., p. 208).

† Correspondent of the *Pioneer*, Nov. 25th, 1874.

child in her arms, unconscious of the danger at hand. The wolf makes its spring, fastens its teeth in the baby's throat, slings the little body across its back, and is off before the mother is fully aware of her loss. Pursuit is generally useless. If forced to drop its burden the cruel creature tears it beyond power of healing, while should it elude pursuit, the morning's search results in the discovery of a few bones, the remnants of the dreadful meal."

Shortly after this visit of mine to Agra, I read the following in the papers. The hotel mentioned was the very one at which I had stopped:—"On Saturday night while the chowkidar at Falmon's Star Hotel, was going his rounds, he observed a screen hanging before an open door moving, and something from the outside enter the house. On giving the alarm the wife of the hotel-keeper had only just time to enter a room and save a sleeping child from the mercies of two wolves which she found there."

It is remarkable that in some countries wolves rarely attack human beings. I have recently read an interesting work on Wolf-hunting in Brittany, in which the author describes the ravages committed by wolves among cattle and horses, but states that human beings are not attacked. He relates a strange but apparently well-authenticated story of a little girl, who followed up a wolf into the forest where it carried a goat which she had been tending. For six weeks she was lost; but at the end of that time presented herself at a charcoal-burner's hut. During this long period she had wandered through the wolves' strongholds, and had managed to subsist on berries. Be this story true or not, it is a fact that children are not carried away by wolves in Brittany as they are in Oude. It suggests itself that the Oude wolves are a local race of man-eaters, characterised by an exceptional liking for human flesh. That wolves in all European countries where they are found will attack and devour man, when in packs, in severe winter weather, is well known, and does not require further notice.

My attention was, in the first place, drawn to this subject by the following extract from the Report of the Sekandra Orphanage, which, towards the end of the year 1872, went the round of the Indian papers:—

"A boy of about ten *was burned out of a den in the company of wolves.* How long he had been with them it is impossible to say, but it must have been for rather a long period, from the facility he has for going on all fours, and his liking for raw meat. As yet he is very much like a wild animal; his very whine reminds one of a young dog or some such creature. Some years ago we had a similar child; he has picked up wonderfully, and though he has not learned to speak, can fully express his joys and grief. We trust the new 'unfortunate' may soon improve too."

I immediately wrote to the Superintendent of the Sekandra Orphanage for confirmation of the story, and for any further information on the subject. To this application I received the following reply from the Rev. Mr. Erhardt. * * * "We have had two such boys here, but I fancy you refer to the one who was brought to us on March 6th, 1872. He was found by Hindus who had gone hunting wolves in the neighbourhood of Mynepúri. Had been burnt out of the den, and was brought here with the scars and wounds still on him. In his habits he was a perfect wild animal in every point of view. He drank like a dog, and liked a bone and raw meat better than anything else. He would never remain with the other boys but hid away in any dark corner. Clothes he never would wear, but tore them up into fine threads. He was only a few months among us, as he got fever and gave up eating. We kept him up for a time by artificial means, but eventually he died.

"The other boy found among wolves is about thirteen or fourteen years old, and has been here about six. He has learnt to make sounds, speak he cannot; but he freely expresses his anger and joy. Work he will at times, a little; but he likes eating better. His civilisation has progressed so far that he likes raw meat less, though he still will pick up bones and sharpen his teeth on them.

"Neither of the above are new cases, however. At the Lucknow Madhouse there was an elderly fellow only four years ago, and may be alive now, who had been dug out of a wolves' den by a European doctor, when I forget, but it must be a good number of years ago.

"The facility with which they get along on four feet (hands and feet) is surprising. Before they eat or taste any food they smell it, and when they don't like the smell they throw it away."

WOLF-BOY.
(*From a Photograph.*)

I shall now describe the result of my visit to the orphanage. On my arrival there, Mr. Erhardt very kindly sent over for the boy to the school and he was led in by the hand. He presented an appearance not uncommonly seen in ordinary idiots. His forehead was low, his teeth somewhat prominent, and his manner restless and fidgety. From time to time he grinned in a manner that was more simian than human, the effect of which was intensified by a nervous twitching of the lower jaw. After taking a sort of survey of the room and the people in it, he squatted on the ground, and, constantly placing the palms of his hands on the floor, stretched forward in different directions, picking up small objects such as fragments of paper, crumbs, &c., and smelling them as a monkey would do. I was told that he depends much more upon the organ of smell than on that of taste for the identification of objects,* and his conduct while I watched him fully bore out the statement. On being shewn a guava he exhibited much excitement, writhing about and stretching out his hands for it. When it was given to him he first smelt it all over very carefully, and then holding it close to his mouth proceeded to gnaw it. He was then given some unripe *Karaunda* (*Carissa carandas*, Linn.) fruit. Having smelt them he shewed signs of uneasiness which were interpreted by those standing by as indicating a want of salt to allay the acridity—it having been given to him on previous occasions. He was a somewhat slenderly-built lad, standing about five feet three inches, and was considered by Mr. Erhardt to be about fifteen years of age, and had been then (1874) nearly nine years in the orphanage. He is described as being of a happy temperament. He has acquired some knowledge of locality and can go about the grounds by himself, but could not do so when Mr. Erhardt first took charge of the Orphanage. Without constant supervision it is found to be impossible to keep him to any work. He will for instance carry a basket while watched, but immediately drops it when left alone. The feature in his physical structure which above all others attracted my particular notice was the shortness of his arms, the total length being only nineteen-and-a-half inches. This arrested growth was probably caused by the fact of his having gone on all-fours in early life, as all these wolf-boys are reported to have done when first captured. Mr. Erhardt not having been in charge of the orphanage when this boy was brought in, could give no further particulars regarding his capture than those contained in his above quoted letters;

---

* In connection with this it may be of interest to quote a passage from Darwin's "Descent of Man," 1st Edition, p. 24. "The sense of smell is of extremely slight service, if any, to savages, in whom it is more highly developed than in the civilized races."

but a native guide in Agra whom I interrogated as to whether he had any knowledge of the subject, told me that rather less than nine years previously he was in the magistrate's court when this boy, the body of an old female wolf, and two wolf cubs were brought in. At that time the boy was a perfect *Janwar* (wild beast). He went on all-fours, refused all kinds of cooked food, but would eat any amount of raw meat. For some time he was kept by the Civil Surgeon of Agra, bound down on a *charpoy*, or native bedstead, in order to straighten his legs, and several months passed before he was able to maintain an erect position.

Regarding the boy which was brought to the orphanage on the 5th of March, 1872, Mr. Erhardt said that on his arrival he would not touch any food in the form used by human beings; at the same time he was too young and weak to have provided himself with any, but he would eat raw meat ravenously. Observing these facts and also sundry wounds and burns on the body, Mr. Erhardt sent for the people who had brought in the child, and then first heard that he had been smoked out of a wolf's den. While he lived at the orphanage, which was for only about four months, he used occasionally to get loose at night, when he would prowl about the ground searching for bones. Shortly after his arrival he made an effort to escape into the jungle, but was captured and brought back. During the whole time he uttered no sound save a melancholy whine like that made by young cubs. A strange bond of sympathy attached these two boys together, and the elder one first taught the younger to drink out of a cup. While the younger boy remained alive Hindus frequently came to the orphanage and applied for permission to make their salaam to him, being under the impression that by so doing they, through his influence with the wolves, would avert any loss or injury to their families and flocks. I shall now give some of the previously recorded cases.

A short notice on this subject was communicated to the "Annals and Magazine of Natural History,"* by the late Sir

* Vol VIII., Second Series, 1851, p. 153.

Roderick I. Murchison. It consists of an extract from the journal of the Hon. Captain Francis Egerton, R.N., who, on the authority of Colonel Sleeman, relates several stories of these wolf-reared children. Colonel Sleeman knew of five instances, in two of which he had both seen the children and was acquainted with the circumstances of the capture. One of these captures was made in the following manner:—"Some time ago, two of the King of Oude's sawars, riding along the banks of the Gúmptji, saw three animals come down to drink. Two were evidently young wolves, but the third was as evidently some other animal. The sawars rushed in upon them and captured all three, and to their great surprise found that one was a small naked boy. He was on all fours like his companions, had callosities on his knees and elbows, evidently caused by the attitude used in moving about, and bit and scratched violently in resisting the capture. The boy was brought up in Lucknow, where he lived some time, and may for aught I know be living still. He was quite unable to articulate words, but had a dog-like intellect, quick at understanding signs and so on." It seems probable that this was the same individual as the one mentioned in the letter from the Superintendent of the Sekandra Orphanage, above quoted. The following also occurs in Captain Egerton's journal:—"There was another more wonderful but hardly so well authenticated story of a boy who never could get rid of a strong wolfish smell, and who was seen, not long after his capture, to be visited by three wolves, which came evidently with hostile intentions, but which, after closely examining him, he seeming not the least alarmed, played with him, and some nights afterwards brought their relations, making the number of visitors amount to five, the number of cubs the litter he had been taken from was composed of. I think Colonel Sleeman believed this story to be perfectly true, though he could not vouch for it."

The following passages I quote *verbatim* from Professor Max Muller's letter in the *Academy*:—"A trooper, sent by the native Governor of Chandour to demand payment of some revenue, was passing along the banks of the river about noon, when he saw a large female wolf leave her den, followed by three whelps and a little boy. The boy went on all-fours, and when the trooper tried to catch him, he ran as fast as the whelps, and kept up with the old one. They all entered the den; but were dug out by the people with pickaxes, and the boy was secured. He struggled hard to rush into every hole or den they came near. He became alarmed when he saw a grown-up person, but tried to fly at children and bite them. He rejected cooked meat with disgust, but delighted in raw flesh and bones, putting them under his paws like a dog. They tried to make him speak, but could get nothing from him but an angry growl or snarl.

"So far the evidence rests on native witnesses, and might be considered as more or less doubtful. But the boy, after having spent a time with the Raja of Husunpur, was afterwards forwarded to Captain Nicholetts, the European officer commanding the 1st Regiment of Oude Local Infantry, at Sultanpur. Captain Nicholetts made him over to the charge of his servants, and their accounts completely confirm what was stated before. The wolf-child would devour anything, but preferred raw meat. He once ate half a lamb without any effort. He never kept on any kind of clothing; and a quilt, stuffed with cotton, given to him in the cold weather, was torn by him and partly swallowed.

"In a letter, dated the 17th and 19th September, 1850, Captain Nicholetts informed Colonel Sleeman that the boy had died at the latter end of August. He had never been known to laugh or smile. He formed no attachment, *and seemed to understand little of what was said to him.* He was about nine years old when found, and lived about three years afterwards. He would run on all-fours, but occasionally he walked uprightly. He never spoke, but when he was hungry he pointed to his mouth. Only within a few minutes before his death, the servants relate that he put his hands to his head, and said it ached, and asked for water; he drank it and died.

"Another instance is related as having occurred at Chupra. In March, 1843, a man and his wife went out to cut their crop of wheat. The woman was leading her boy, who had lately recovered from a severe scald on the left knee. While his parents were engaged, the child was carried off by a wolf. In 1849, a wolf with three cubs was seen, about ten miles from Chupra, followed by a boy. The boy, after a fierce resistance, was caught, and was recognized by the poor cultivator's widow by the mark of a scald on the left knee and three marks of the teeth of an animal on each side of his back. He would eat nothing but raw flesh, and *could never be brought to speak. He used to mutter something, but never articulated any word distinctly.* The front of his knees and elbows had become hardened from going on all-fours with the wolves. In November, 1850, Captain Nicholetts ordered this boy to be sent to Colonel Sleeman, but he got alarmed, and ran to a jungle.

"The evidence, therefore, of this case rests, to a certain extent, on native authority, and should be accepted with that reservation. The same applies to a third case, vouched for by the Raja of Husunpur, which adds, however, nothing essential, except that the boy, as seen by him in 1843, had actually short hair all over his body, which disappeared when he took to eating salt. He could walk on his legs, but he could not speak. *He could be made to understand signs very well, but would utter sounds like wild animals.*

"Another, a fourth case, however, is vouched for again by European witnesses. Colonel Gray, who commanded the 1st Oude Local Infantry, at Sultanpur, and Mrs. Gray, and all the officers of the place, saw a boy who, in 1843, had been caught while trotting along upon all-fours, by the side of a wolf. *He could never be made to speak*, and at last ran away into the jungle.

"A fifth case rests on the evidence of a respectable landowner of Bankipur, in the estate of Husanpur, called Zulfukar Khan. Here, too, the boy—who had been six years' old when carried off, who was ten when rescued—*could not be brought to speak*, though it was easy to communicate with him by signs.

"One other statement of a wolf-boy is given by Colonel Sleeman; but as it rests on native evidence only I will merely add that this boy also, when caught, walked on all-fours, ate raw meat, and smelt like a wolf. He was treated kindly; but though he learnt to behave better and walk uprightly, *he never could understand or utter a word, though he seemed to understand signs.*

"There are other cases, but those which I have selected are to my mind the best attested. They all share one feature in common, which is of importance to the student of language more even than the student of mythology, viz., the speechlessness of the wolf-children. It was this fact, more than the bearing of these stories on a problem of mythology, which first made me collect the evidence here produced; for as we are no longer sufficiently wolfish to try the experiment which is said to have been tried by a King of Egypt, by Frederic II., James IV., and one of the Mogul Emperors of India (*Lectures on the Science of Language*, 7th Ed., Vol. I., p. 394), viz., to keep babies in solitary confinement, in order to find out what language, if any, they would speak, these cases of children reared by wolves afford the only experimental test for determining whether language is an hereditary instinct or not."

Supposing the above stories to be true, the only suggestions which I can offer to account for the preservation of the children from the ordinary fate, are that, firstly, it may be that while one of a pair of wolves has brought back a live child to the den, the other may have contributed a sheep or goat to the day's provision, and that this latter proving sufficient for immediate wants, the child has been permitted to lie in the den, and possibly to be suckled by the female, and has so come to be recognised as a member of the family. Secondly, and, perhaps, more probably, it may be that the wolf's cubs having been stolen, the children have been carried off to fill their places, and have been fondled and suckled.

There is one curious point common to all the stories, to which attention has not been previously drawn; it is that all the children appear to have been of the same sex—namely, boys. There is no record, I believe, of a wolf-reared girl.

I am fully aware that much has been written and said in ridicule of this subject. Not very long ago I had an opportunity of asking an eminent and well-known surgeon, who formerly resided in Oude, what he thought of these stories, and his reply was, "I don't believe one of them."

According to the law of averages, the next few years ought to produce a case, and it is to be hoped that should one occur, it may be made the subject of the very strictest enquiry by a joint committee of judicial and medical officers. Till such an event happens, I trust that my readers will at least recognise the justice of suspending judgment.

Before taking leave of Agra,* I must say a few words about the Taj. I paid it a second visit at night, and was charmed with the effect produced by burning a few blue-lights in the interior. I then tried the echo: it is so quick, and at the same time the reverberations are so prolonged, that a sequence of notes produces a somewhat jumbled effect; but by running up or down the diatonic scale, allowing each note to gently die away before the next is sounded, the effect is really marvellous. The first echo seems to intensify the original sound, then follow a series of warbling sounds, which gradually and almost imperceptibly fade away in the glorious dome. Even should the original sound be in itself harsh and unmusical, under this mellowing influence soft and musical notes are produced. In this way it was, that when I first entered the Taj, I heard, as I supposed, a beautiful chant going on, the original source of which I found to be the chattering and squabbling of some of the attendants. Although I did not burst into tears, nor did even the moisture rise to my eyes—as, according to the guide-books, it should have done—I believe I did not fail to be impressed with feelings suitable to the occasion of this visit to what must be admitted to be the most splendid monument ever raised by the hand of man.

---

* For one of the best accounts of Agra reference should be made to "A Handbook for Visitors to Agra," by H. G. Keene, Esq. Calcutta: Thacker and Spink.

After this visit to Agra, I returned to Calcutta, but in October was directed to go to Simla, in order to take charge of the zoological and geological collections which had been made on the Yarkand Expedition by Dr. Stoliczka. His death, on the return journey, has already been recorded in these pages. The material and notes which he had so carefully amassed were not destined to be worked out by himself. However, while recognising the great loss to science occasioned by Stoliczka's death, it is satisfactory to be able to state that a series of volumes, descriptive of his researches and collections, by the ablest geologists and zoologists in India, is now in process of being issued.

For an account of Simla and Simla life, I would refer the reader to such authorities as the authors of "The Chronicles of Dustypore" and "Imperial India," &c., &c. The subject is neither within my powers nor province.

CHAPTER XI.

SINGHBHUM, SAMBALPUR, ORISSA.

1874-75.

WORK TO BE ACCOMPLISHED—NATIVE APPRENTICE—THE 1874 FAMINE—PURULIA—SUBANRIKA RIVER—SERAIKELA—CHAIBASSA—GOLD—ANCIENT STONE IMPLEMENTS—HO DANCERS—PACK-BULLOCKS—CUSTOMS OF THE HOS—THRESHING-FLOORS—HO MARRIAGES—IRON-SMELTERS—SAL FORESTS—URIA COLONIES—ROUTE FOR DIRECT LINE FROM CALCUTTA TO NAGPUR—GOLD-WASHERS—FEVER—BIRDS—WILD BUFFALO—SAMBALPUR—DISCOVERY OF LEAD ORE—COAL-SEAMS—SHOOT A SAMBAR WITH SNIPE SHOT—DEWAN OF KODIBUGA—WATER-BEARING STRATA—A CARNIVOROUS PLANT—THE TREE-SHREW—OFFICIALS OF THE RAIGURH RAJA—STONE-BORING SPIDERS—BEARS VISIT CAMP AT NIGHT—BEAR KILLED BY TIGER—HINGIR—PEOPLE INSOLENT—GAUR AND WILD BUFFALO—TELLINGAS, A STROLLING PARTY OF VATICINATORS—THE COAL-FIELD—SMALL GAME—ARRIVAL OF SUMMER BIRDS—MONSTER SNAKE—NAVIGATION OF MAHANADI AT THIS SEASON DIFFICULT—THE RAJA OF RAMPUR—THE URIA IN HIS NATIVE HOME—UNGUL—RAJA OF INDOLE—MEET A KANDAHARI—COMPLETE CHANGE IN THE VEGETATION—CUTTACK—IRRIGATION—NIRAJ—MUDAR SHRUB—SAIL FOR CALCUTTA.

My work for this season was to complete the geological examination of a portion of the District of Singhbhum, which I had been obliged to leave unfinished in the year 1869, and then to march on to Sambalpur in order to take up the detailed survey of the Raigurh and Hingir coal-field, the limits of which I had only roughly demarcated when I visited it in 1871.

I left Calcutta for Barakar on the 5th of November, arriving there next morning, and on the 7th started to march southwards for Chaibassa *viâ* Purulia. Some little difficulty was experienced in crossing the Damuda River, owing to the quantity of water still remaining in it; but the elephants managed to ford it with their loads, and the horses swam across, the men going in boats.

I was accompanied on this occasion by a native apprentice, who was to be instructed in field geology. The fact that in the

Geological Survey alone, of all Indian departments, there were no native subordinates, had attracted the attention of Lord Mayo and his Council. Accordingly it had been determined to establish a grade of apprentices, to whom the prospect of ultimate promotion to the higher appointments should be open. Owing to the arduous nature of the work, it was considered that natives of Bengal, from deficiency of stamina and manliness, were not likely to be suited to it, and therefore the appointments were offered to Sikh students of the Lahore College, who, before being permitted to go to the field, had to attend courses of lectures in several branches of science in Calcutta. This process of manufacturing geologists, of course, wholly ignored the fact that, as a rule, those who take to scientific pursuits as a profession, and certainly those who cultivate them with most success, start with a natural taste for them. Hitherto the natives, however intellectual, and however well they may have been educated in various scientific branches, have shewn but little capability for undertaking original scientific research, and, indeed, they seem to be deficient in synthetical powers to an extraordinary degree. It is moreover not uncommon to meet with really clever natives, who, when they have to describe ordinary natural phenomena, make use of the most grotesque and unreal language, rendering themselves thereby supremely ridiculous. This first Sikh apprentice, who was entrusted to my care for instruction, proved to be neither intellectually nor physically fitted for the work. He seemed to be unable to grasp the rudiments of the science of geology, and as he was physically incapable of hill-climbing, the prospects of his being of any service to the Department seemed to be slender. As he has since died, I do him no injury by saying so much, which I might illustrate by half-a-dozen stories about him in the course of the following pages; but I forbear from giving them. There are at present, however, two of his compatriots in the Survey who have done good work as fossil collectors.

At Indipur, where I made my first halt, I found the rooms of a small bungalow filled up with bags of rice, this place having been one of the depôts for the distribution of relief during the 1874 famine. I here heard many particulars about the famine. The portion of the people upon whom the scarcity pressed most were the women, and among them chiefly the widows, of whom large numbers assembled for relief. The Hindu part of the population, as in not a few other districts in Bengal, according to the report of the Commissioner to the Government, were most unwilling to work on the roads, such work being, in their estimation, degrading to their gentility. They were, however, anxious to get whatever they could in the way of assistance, and seemed to think that it should be delivered at their doors. So far as I could learn, there had been no deaths from starvation. Had there been no relief, it seems not improbable that the same would have been the case, as the scarcity was hardly so great as to cause a real famine. Many of the local well-to-do landlords were most unwilling to subscribe to the relief fund. This was more particularly the case with the Raja of Pachete.

The following day I marched to Rugonathpur, where I remained with the officer on special duty in charge of the relief. This was the head-quarters of his circle, and was the site of several newly-built bungalows and a series of *golas* for storing the grain, much of which was still on hand, though there was then no further necessity for it, as the early crops were being reaped. A real change in the weather to-day seemed to mark the long-deferred commencement of the cold season.

I arrived at Purulia on the 10th, and remained there for a few days, making some final arrangements for the march. The lake at Purulia afforded, as on previous occasions, when I had visited the station, a great resource for occupying spare time. I derived much amusement from paddling out in a canoe to the islands and watching the proceedings of the water-birds, which roost and breed upon them in great numbers. The colony included cormorants, snake-birds, night herons, purple herons, egrets, and black, white, and shell ibises; besides these there were four species of maina or starlings, including the rosy pastor; and among birds of prey there were kites, marsh-harriers, and a pair of fishing eagles (*Polioaetus ichthyaetus*). The young shell ibises were sufficiently fledged to fly off with the old birds to their feeding-grounds. In the adult shell ibis (*Anastomus oscitans*) the bill gapes in a peculiar way. This was, at one time, supposed to be due to attrition of the edges caused by the nature of the food upon which the bird is generally believed to subsist, and from which it has received the above name. Dr. Jerdon, however, stated* that the bill of a young bird which he had examined exhibited the same gaping. This I did not find to be the case with any of the large number which I saw. The bills were very much smaller than in the adult birds, were conical in shape, and the edges were in distinct apposition, or slightly overlapping, throughout. The change does not appear to me to be due to any loss of material of the bill by attrition, but to a structural bowing or arching of the mandibles. This may facilitate the grasping of the round *Ampullarias* or apple-shells, and *Unios* or fresh-water mussels. Small thin-shelled fresh water snails and frogs also form a portion of this bird's food. Sundry remains of birds on the islands shewed that the eagles by no means limited themselves to a fish diet. And one morning I saw one of them strike a young shell ibis, and then, grasping its head in its claw, fly off to its perch, trailing the unhappy victim along the surface of the water.

I found in trees on the islands some nests of the snake-bird (*Plotus melanogaster*, Gmel.), so called from its long snake-like neck, which it rears high above the surface when swimming along with the rest of its body deep down in the water. The nests contained young birds, which were for the most part covered with soft white down, and, with their long necks, presented a very comical appearance.

On the 13th I left Purulia, halting first at a village called Urma, twelve miles to the south. The two following marches to

---

* "Birds of India," Vol. III.

Burma and Chondill, over a partly-made embanked road, brought me to the banks of the Subanrika, which I crossed the following day. This river, like the Damuda, containing a good deal of water, some trouble was caused by the necessity for unloading the carts and transporting the baggage by means of boats; but the elephants managed to ford the stream with their loads. At Kandra, the next halt, there is a grove of sal-trees (*Shorea robusta*), in which I found a colony of the large paroquet (*Palæornis eupatrius*, Linn.), and shot some specimens. This handsome bird is the least common of the three species of paroquet which are found in this part of the country. In the large primeval forests further south I found it to be more abundant than it is near cultivated tracts.

The next march was to Seraikela, fifteen miles. The road, though only a district one, was in much better condition than the embanked one in Manbhum, which had been for years under construction by the Public Works Department. On the banks of the Subanrika, near Seraikela, there are several groups of monumental stones, which were erected formerly by the Lurka Kols, and are similar in general appearance and character to those which have already been described and figured on page 165.

The next march brought me to Chaibassa. On this occasion I felt more than ever convinced of the auriferous character of the rocks in this part of the district. In lithological characters they are strikingly similar to some of the most prolific which are gold-producing in Brazil. There are earthy slates and shales with magnesian schists and numerous quartz veins. That they do actually contain gold there is no doubt whatever, since a section of the population make a livelihood by washing for it, as I have already explained on a previous page. Close to the station of Chaibassa I found a considerable deposit of manganese-iron ore. This may hereafter be of importance for the manufacture of *Spiegeleisen*, should the country ever be opened-up by a direct line of railway from Calcutta to Bombay.

While at Chaibassa the Superintendent of Police gave me a remarkably fine stone adze, which presented a close resemblance to the peculiar forms which had previously only been known from Burmah. Subsequently I received from the same gentleman two others, one of which was also of the same adze-shape, and the other more nearly of the ordinary type of European celts. I here insert a portion of a note upon them, which I read before the Asiatic Society of Bengal.

"The large adze was found about two years ago by one Baidonath, purdhan of the village of Kyma Pattra (on the west side of the Subanrika river, and not far from that river) in his sugar-cane field, embedded in the earth about three feet or so from the surface. The purdhan's story is, that during the night preceding the finding of the implement, there had been a violent storm with thunder and much lightning, some of which flashed unpleasantly close to the village. On going into his sugar-cane field next morning he found the cane within a radius of ten feet or so all burnt, singed, and scorched-up in a most surprising manner. He considered that the destruction had been caused by lightning, as no doubt it had. His curiosity being excited by the crater-like appearance of the soil at the very centre of the circle of destroyed sugar-cane, he dug down with the view of ascertaining what might be there, and found the adze in a vertical position, edge downwards. It was then in the same condition, with broken edge, as it is now. (*Vide* Plate II. fig. 11, Appendix B.)

"The smaller adze has no particular history attached to it. It was obtained from a villager who could only say that his father—now dead—had found it somewhere in the jungle.

"With regard to the wedge-shaped stone, the Superintendent, on the authority of the Head Constable of Kokepara, states that 'it was found by a man of Guru Banda (west side of Subanrika) embedded in the very centre of the lower part of the trunk of a middling-sized Mhowa tree (*Bassia latifolia*) which had evidently been struck by lightning and split in twain from top to the very lowest extremity of the trunk.' The popular notion is that all these stones are thunderbolts. The same opinion is held by the people in Burmah regarding the very similar implements found there.

"The larger shouldered specimen is formed of dark green, excessively dense and hard, quartzite, with a wavy structure, and includes some pebble-like masses of different composition. The other shouldered adze is made of a black igneous rock, shewing a minute crystalline structure; it can be readily scratched with a knife. The wedge-shaped stone mysteriously disappeared from my possession * and I only retain a sketch of it; but so far as I remember, it appeared to be made of the same material as the larger adze.

"In reference to the origin of these implements, their mineral composition is not, I believe, inconsistent with the view that they may have been manufactured originally in the part of the country where they were found. The source of the material from which the flakes I formerly exhibited to the Society † were manufactured occurs within the district of Singhbhum. It is a bed of dark chert-like quartzite, and from it the material of the large adze might very possibly have been obtained. Again, the very numerous dykes and intrusive masses of trappean rocks in Singhbhum may contain a material identical with that from which the smaller adze was manufactured.

"On the other hand, the close resemblance in form which they bear to the implements of Burmah cannot fail to suggest a foreign origin for them. Unfortunately the stories of their discovery given above do not help us in forming an opinion as to their antiquity. It would be of course useless to attempt any speculation, on the strength of such data alone, as to an incursion or immigration of Burmese races into that part of Bengal in pre-historic times; but the fact now recorded may hereafter be of importance should evidence of another character tending in the same direction be by any means established."

Some time after this note was published, General Sir

---

* It was probably stolen by one of my servants, who may have considered that it possessed medicinal properties.

† These are described on p. 136. Also see Appendix B., figs. 14 and 15.

Arthur Phayre pointed out to the society, *in epist.*, that the valley of the Irawadi, in Burmah, where the stone implements have been chiefly found, is inhabited by a race called *Mun*, whose language presents affinities with that of the *Mundas* of Singhbhum. Hence the probability of an early intercourse having existed, and possibly of an identity of origin between these now widely-separated peoples, becomes very great.

These facts have led me to generalise on the whole subject of the geographical distribution of stone implements in India, and to compare the results with the present distribution of the so-called aboriginal races, and the theories of their migrations into India which have been deduced from a study of their languages and customs. My paper on this subject has been published in the Proceedings of the Royal Irish Academy, and a *resumé* of it will be found in Appendix B.

While at Chaibassa I was told by the Deputy-Commissioner that, a few weeks previously, when the Governor-General, Lord Northbrook, was on a visit to Ranchi, in the adjoining District of Lohardugga, it was determined that he should be entertained by a series of characteristic dances to be performed by the different races inhabiting the Chutia Nagpur Province. My informant, anxious that his subjects the Hos should appear to advantage, gave sums of money to a number of the best dancers in order that they might obtain suitable outfits for their journey to Ranchi, and for the performance which was to take place after it. Having, as he thought, settled the matter, he was surprised to notice that the people held aloof from him for some days; but one night the male relations of the village maidens, who had in the meantime been engaged in concocting and discussing the most absurd reports, came to his house and indignantly flung all the money into his verandah, and my friend became subsequently the object of a storm of female indignation and abuse. It was not that they objected to be sold outright, but they considered that the sums which had been given them were under their value, and they accordingly considered themselves insulted. What the marketable value of a wife is in Ho land, and how the high figure asked has resulted in there being among these people, unlike most if not all other races in India, a number of spinsters of mature age, I shall presently explain.

Beyond Chaibassa it was impossible for me to take carts, and pack-bullocks (though most objectionable) afforded the only form of carriage to be obtained supplementary to the two elephants.

Some time was devoted to negotiations with proprietors of pack-bullocks, all of whom were at first unwilling to hire out their cattle for the journey which I contemplated making. Finally, however, I concluded a bargain for eight bullocks with two men in charge of them, and on the 21st November plunged into the wild jungles which stretch between Chaibassa and Sambalpur in the Central Provinces. The march, however, was not commenced without a scene which drew an admiring circle of the populace. The bullocks had been out at grass for some time, and as each one was loaded he proceeded to kick up his heels and divest himself of his unaccustomed burthen. At last I found it necessary to appear upon the scene, and establish some system by which the beasts should be restrained. Finally they started in a somewhat orderly fashion; but at the first river I came to, as I followed an hour later, I found two of the loads, much to the injury of their contents, deposited in the water, and the bullocks scampering over the country.

During the following fortnight I was engaged in the geological examination of an area to the west of Chaibassa, which had not been quite completed on the occasion of my previous visit. The rocks all belonged to the younger metamorphic series already briefly described. Iron ore is abundant in some places; both magnetic and brown hæmatite forms were found, and manganese-and-iron ore, similar to that nearer Chaibassa, also occurs.

The people of this tract chiefly belong to the Ho or Lurka race of Kols, and I found my slight knowledge of the language of considerable use. But for communication with them I had the assistance of the polyglot Chuprasi Sidú, whose services had again been placed at my disposal by the Deputy-Commissioner of the District. The Hos are still in a very primitive state; few of the women wear more than a cloth round their loins, and in some cases the allowance for that purpose was most limited. Ram Singh, the native apprentice, professed himself to be terribly shocked, as in the Punjab such a costume, or rather such a lack of it, is quite unknown. The custom is not due to poverty, as it is to be seen in practice by the members of families where the men are provided with a good substantial cloth, and are otherwise known to be well-to-do farmers. Near most of the villages in this tract there were a few memorial stones, but I did not observe them anywhere in great abundance. It is not unusual to see a number of men assembled for cock-fighting. The birds generally, I think, belong to a different breed from the ordinary domestic fowls. Some of them even resemble the wild birds in plumage, and it seems not improbable that they may have a strain of jungle-blood, which is possibly renewed from time to time. Hawking is also a favourite pastime with these people.

The Hos, indeed, are fond of amusing themselves in various ways, and the stronger sex appeared to me to do the smaller share of the hard work. Certainly females were more numerous than males as reapers in the fields. In some of the villages cattle were scarce, and I occasionally saw women, children, and old men employed in treading out the corn, thus performing one of the duties usually assigned to the kine. I find I have not described these threshing-floors, so may here appropriately introduce the subject. They consist of spots of ground which are specially prepared for the occasion by moistening the earth, and then spreading the resulting mud, mixed with cow-dung, evenly, and allowing it to be baked by the sun to a smooth and hard surface. At the centre a stout post is driven into the ground, round and round which from three to half-a-dozen cattle attached to one another by halters are slowly driven, the rice or other grain in the ear being under their feet. The scriptural injunction "Thou shalt not muzzle the ox that treadeth out the corn," is observed, and the cattle are permitted to help themselves at their own discretion. The grain is winnowed from the chaff and dust by throwing it up into the air from shallow basket-work trays, when the breeze carries the lighter portions away from the heavier, each forming separate heaps. The grain is stored, sometimes underground, sometimes in huge boxes built of mud and straw, and sun-dried; or it is placed in baskets made of split bamboos covered with a layer of cow-dung. The Sontals and some other tribes generally use ingeniously-contrived spherical baskets, three feet in diameter, which are made with straw ropes.

As I shall not have further opportunity in this volume for alluding to the Hos or Lurka Kols, I shall here point out one or two of the more salient features in their economy which may be taken as being supplementary to what I have said in preceding chapters on the same subject.

So recently as the beginning of this century the Hos were a scourge to the surrounding country. It was not until 1819 that measures were taken for their subjugation. Major Roughsedge, who was in command of the force detailed for the purpose, wrote:—"The Raja and Zemindars of Singhbhum, who are in attendance on me, have so formidable an opinion of the power and ferocity of these savages that, notwithstanding the considerable force under my command, they are much alarmed, and have made a formal protest against the danger of the march." It is related that in the subsequent operations a small party of them, with only their battle-axes in hand, stood to receive a troop of cavalry in an open plain. Few of them, of course, escaped.

Not the least interesting among their customs are those connected with marriage. Both Hos and the nearly-affined Mundas are divided into tribes called *kilis*, and a man must not marry a girl of his own *kili*. Marriages take place much later in life than in most oriental countries, and, owing to the fact that the bridegroom has to pay a considerable number of cattle—in some cases forty or fifty—the marriageable spinsters on hand, relatively to the rest of the population, are nearly as numerous in Singhbhum as they are in some of the countries of Western Europe. Elopements are not considered respectable. "Tell a Ho maiden, that you think her nice-looking, she is sure to reply, 'Oh, yes, I am; but what is the use of it? the young men of my acquaintance don't see it.' Even when a youth has fully made up his mind to marry, it may happen that fate is against the happiness of the young couple; bad omens are seen, that cause the match to be broken off, or the father cannot or will not pay the price demanded."* In consequence of this distressing state of things, the Deputy-Commissioner of Singhbhum, in the year 1868, convened a meeting of the head men, and it was agreed in words, though (as the event proved) not in hearts, that a lower tariff should be substituted. Two oxen, a cow, and fourteen shillings was to be the price for a maiden belonging to the higher ranks, and the same amount of money, without the cattle, for the poorer classes. It is said, however, that there has been no practical result from this conference. The old conservative parents hold out for the old prices, and their daughters remain unwedded. Supposing, however, a marriage to have taken place in spite of all obstacles. After three days of wedded life it is the correct thing for the bride to leave her husband, and for the husband to carry her home again, while she strenuously resists with kicking, screaming, and biting. This performance, which I have once witnessed, should be enacted as though there were no shamming about it. It is considered, with much probability, that this is a relic of former times, when wives were snatched from other tribes by the immigrant Hos.

At one village I found a colony of Kumars, or iron-smelters. There were about ten houses belonging to them, and the same number of furnaces. Formerly, so far as I understood, they were more numerous; but a number of the people died during the famine of 1866-67. One of the furnaces I found to be in blast. As the people in charge of it complained of want and great hardships, I told one of my servants to give some copper coins to a small boy who was standing by, while his mother

* "Descriptive Ethnology of Bengal," p. 192.

worked the bellows. On the coins being produced and offered to the little fellow a most unexpected scene ensued. The child began to whimper, and his aged and decrepid father snatched him in his arms, refusing the tendered coin as though it had been offered as the price of his own flesh and blood. No explanation that we could offer had the least effect in putting matters straight. The father walked off with his child to the village, but the mother could not leave her station at the furnace. We left the coins for them to pick up at their leisure; and I fear we also left a not altogether favourable impression regarding our intentions.

The forests on these hills were very fine, and included many large sal trees, most of which, not being under forest conservancy, had been ruined for timber, owing to the practice of "ringing," to tap the tar-like *dhona*, or, as it is called commercially, *damar*. Sometimes the jungle was so thick along the tracks which my camp had to pass that it became necessary for the people to turn out of their villages to cut down the trees, which would have obstructed the loaded elephants; and in one place I was compelled to leave my camp altogether behind, and go for several days into the hills with a small tent.

Such fine forests as these were naturally not deficient in bird-life, and I here for the first time in Chutia Nagpur saw on the wing the handsome black or hill maina (*Eulabes intermedia*, Hay). The showy scarlet minivet (*Pericrocotus speciosus*, Lath.) and the large hornbill (*Hydrocissa coronata*, Bodd.) were both very common. There being plenty of dead and dying timber in the jungles, wood-peckers and *Sittas* were also abundant. I also met with the swallow-shrike (*Artamus fuscus*, Vieill.) in one large flock. It is a singularly local bird, and I have seen it on but a few occasions, and then always near dead timber in forest clearances.

December 6th.—Orjanpur to Daraikela.—In this neighbourhood I found that we were passing out of the region occupied by the Lurka Kols, into one where outlying colonies of Urias of the gwala or cow-keeper caste prevailed. My servants were rejoiced to meet with people with whom they could converse after a fashion. With the Hos a very few words had had to do a great deal of duty. On one occasion I carried on for a long time a most animated conversation with an old Ho, who was most profuse in his politeness, neither of us understanding a word the other said.

It distressed me much to find that long-continued carrying of heavy loads had very seriously affected the pace at which the elephants could go. From about three miles an hour on a good road, it had fallen to two, and was now barely one and a-half. This was often the cause of serious discomfort on these long marches, as it involved tedious delays before my tent was ready.

While travelling along this road I paid a good deal of attention to the question of the suitability of the country between Chaibassa and Sambalpur, as a route for a direct line of railway between Calcutta and Nagpur, so avoiding the present circuitous route *viâ* Allahabad. It would be of little interest to my readers perhaps to give the details of these observations, but I may say that I embodied them in a report, in which I pointed out that there were no serious engineering difficulties to be encountered, and that the following advantages would accrue from the construction of such a line. In the first place the possession of an alternative route could not fail to be of great strategical importance. Secondly, from six to ten hours, according to the actual route taken, would be saved on the journey from Calcutta to Bombay. Thirdly, the cheap grain of the Central Provinces could be brought to the port of Calcutta. Reference to the map will show the route I propose for this new line.

December 8th.—Derwa to Dhipa.—The camp to-day was pitched on the banks of the Koel river. In the same grove was a colony of Dohras, their huts being mere miserable piles of branches. These people were very black and their hair was somewhat frizzled; their nostrils were much distended, but their general appearance was not of a negro or negroid type, as might hastily be concluded perhaps on a mere casual observation. Although their three-fold occupation as ferrymen, fishermen, and gold-washers, all brought them into contact with water, they were personally in a hideously dirty and unwashed condition. In the evening I got them to wash some gold for me. The "pay dirt" was taken from a small island formed of the river drift which lay under the shelter of some ridges of rock. The quantity of gold found after several washings was almost microscopic in size, consisting of very minute specks.

The forest through which the road passed to-day was lofty and dense, and had a more tropical aspect about it than any which I had previously seen in Chutia Nagpur. Although much injury had already been done by the "ringing" of the fine sal trees, I could not but feel that it was the greatest pity that something in the way of conservancy should not be applied to this forest, with a view of its becoming hereafter a source of timber supply in the event of the railway being made.

December 12th.—Kukuda to Garjan.—I rose this morning with a severe headache, and before leaving Garjan had a sharp ague fit, which nearly shook me off my horse. In consequence of this attack, and in order to give the doctor a chance of treating successfully the other invalids in camp, I remained at Garjan for three days, although the locality itself was not a healthy one in consequence of the heavy mists which rose from the Brahmini river, near which we were encamped. During one of the nights some small scops owls (*Ephialtes*) had a terrific fight in the tree over my tent, and the next morning one was picked up dead as the result of the conflict. The inhabitants here were Uraon Keriahs, with a few houses of Brahmins.

December 14th.—Garjan to Laingurh.—Near Laingurh there are said to be some old ruins, but my weakness, consequent on the fever, compelled me to keep quiet, so I was unable to explore them. Both my horse and myself were now dead lame, and the walking I was compelled to do in order to save him nearly resulted in serious injury to myself.

December 15th.—Laingurh to Lobloi.—Both the above places are in the Gangpur district, and at the latter I found the residence of a relative of the Gangpur Raja. The camping-ground was one of the prettiest I had been in for some time. There are some fine trees, and birds appeared to be abundant and in great variety. One which I shot was of considerable interest to me, as I had not previously obtained it in Chutia Nagpur; it was a species of hornbill (*Hydrocissa albirostris*), which here encroaches or overlaps into the domain of another species (*H. coronata*), which is very common in these regions, and hence onwards to Sambalpur; with it ranges another, but very different, species, the grey hornbill (*Meniceros ginginianus*, Shaw). Traces of wild buffalo were very abundant all about. Although I had been told that there were buffaloes in the neighbourhood I did not realise that they were so close by, and apparently so easy to be got at, until I was marching away, or I should in spite of my weakness have endeavoured to have got a shot at them. The next day I entered the Sambalpur district, encamping at a village called Songra, thus having passed from Bengal into the Central Provinces. I was met by two chuprasies sent to attend upon me and arrange for supplies, by the Deputy-Commissioner of Sambalpur. To-day I first met with traces of the eastern extension of the coal-field which I was in search of, but the general lie of which I had ascertained in the year 1872, when I had bestowed upon it the title of Raigurh and Hingir field.

December 23rd.—Sasun to Sambalpur.—To-day I marched into Sambalpur, which I found, most unexpectedly—as it had not borne a good repute—to be a particularly prettily-situated station, having an unusually pleasant and sociable, though small, circle of official residents. The native town stretches for about a mile along the northern bank of the Mahanadi river, which here runs from west to east. To the east of the town lie the houses of the officials, which command a splendid view of the wide and rocky bed of the river, with hills rising in the distance beyond the opposite bank. Occasional boats traversing the narrow, rock-bound channels, and the movement of a considerable quantity of water, confer no little animation upon the scene. Further inland are situated the lines for the accommodation of the wing of a Madras regiment which is always quartered at this station.

Under medical advice I was compelled to remain in Sambalpur till the 4th of January, when in company with Major Bowie, the Deputy-Commissioner, I marched to a village called Jhunan, ten miles higher up the river, where operations had been in progress with the view of re-discovering a lode of lead-ore or galena, the history of which was as follows:—On my arrival at Sambalpur I was shewn some fragments of galena, which had remained in the possession of some of the residents since before the British occupation of the district in 1850. They were said to have been brought from Jhunan, where the lode had been discovered in the Raja's time and was worked to a small extent, the galena having been used as a substitute for *surma* or antimony for anointing the eyes. Suddenly, however, Narain Singh, the Raja, becoming afraid that the discovery might attract the notice of Europeans, had ordered the excavation to be stopped and the lode to be covered up and concealed. Ultimately we found the lode in the bank of the river, and some large samples of ore were taken out, in which traces of antimony and copper also occurred. On assay the galena was found to contain 12 oz. 5 dwts. of silver to the ton of lead. This, though a small percentage, would be sufficient under favourable circumstances to yield a profit on the cost of extraction. Some little money was expended in endeavouring to prove the further extension of the lode inland; but as there was no skilled miner to direct the operations on the spot, the results obtained were not satisfactory, and the matter was allowed to drop.

From Jhunan I marched a few miles northwards up the valley of the Ebe river, and soon found myself on the coal-measure rocks of the Raigurh and Hingir coal-field, the examination of which I commenced forthwith. I found the country and climate very pleasant, and, as the people were well-disposed, I experienced no trouble whatever from them.

January 25th.—Bindichua.—At Bindichua I ascended a sandstone hill, which had been weathered and eroded to a most grotesque shape; but I experienced much trouble in inducing the coolies who were with me to accompany me to the highest peak, which was, indeed, somewhat difficult to reach. One man positively refused, the other two were trembling violently the whole time, and without assistance would certainly have come to grief. They excused themselves on the plea that they did not know how to climb; but I believe some superstitious fear was the real cause of their reluctance.

February 13th.—Lukanpur.—By this time I had discovered several seams of coal, and ascertained the probability of the field containing a tolerable supply, but not of first-class quality. The country was very hilly and broken, and much covered by forest. Hamlets occupied by iron-smelters were met with in the most out-of-the-way places, and a considerable amount of iron is exported from hence. Many of the villages were occupied by people called Kultas or Kulitas. There were also some colonies of Uraons, who had doubtless wandered thither from Chutia Nagpur.

February 14th.—Lukanpur to Borkhol.—To-day, when walking along the banks of the Koilar river, I suddenly came across a pool of water in which a young male sambar was lying. My shot-gun, instead of my rifle, being put into my hands, I fired into his head, at rather close quarters, two charges of No. 6 and No. 8 shot respectively, which threw him back stunned into the water, and, before he could recover, he was caught, and his throat was cut with all due formality by my Mahomedan attendant.

February 23rd.—Kodibuga to Muchda.—The Zemindar of Kodibuga, who enjoys the title of Dewan, is a Raj-Gond—*i.e.*, a Gond refined by an infusion of Rajput blood, and an Hindu in religion. He proved to be a fine, manly fellow, fond of sport. His appearance reminded me of the Raja of Sirguja, whom I have described in Chapter VIII. In a beat which he gave me I shot a boar and a barking deer. To the north of Kodibuga, just inside the coal-field, there is a waterfall on the Jungmur river, which is regarded as being a spot of great sanctity by the people all about.

March 2nd.—Sambalpuri.—In this field, overlying the coal-measures, there is a considerable thickness of sandstones, the bedding of which is, for the most part, horizontal. Through these sandstones a number of rivers, which run from north to south, have cut deep gorges, and, since the sandstones are themselves water-bearing, the rivers contain a copious and perennial supply of water, while the rivers of the neighbouring tracts, where metamorphic rocks prevail, are dry for nearly half the year. This constant supply of moisture is not without a very visible influence on the vegetation; and I found that where the water filtered out on the faces of sandstone, a small carnivorous plant (*Drosera sp?*) was very abundant. Its sticky leaves were covered with the remains of insects.

To-day I picked up a dead specimen of the tree-shrew (*Tupaia Elliotti*, Waterhouse). Except a little blood about the mouth, it shewed no sign of injury. I had previously seen several in beats for large game, when I could not venture to shoot so small an animal. I have already mentioned in Chapter IX. that I obtained the tree-shrew in the Satpura Hills, thus proving it to have a vastly wider range in Peninsular India than had previously been known. A few days later I shot a specimen of the whistling-thrush (*Myiophonus Horsfieldi*), which, as I have also related, I found ranging with the tree-shrew in the Satpura Hills.

March 7th.—Gudgaon to Bagchoba.—Being now in the territories of the Raja of Raigurh, my camp was accompanied by a Muktiar or agent and some police of the Raja's establishment. I found that this Muktiar was himself receiving all the money paid by my followers for supplies brought in by the villagers. When I spoke to him on the subject he admitted that such was the case; but stated that he carefully credited the rent account of each village with the amount. Although I did not believe this altogether, still, as the practice was said to be the custom of the country, and the people made no complaints to me, I was unable to take any steps which were likely to be of much effect in altering this very objectionable system. And here I may say that I have found interference in such matters is often misinterpreted, and that an excess of anxiety to see that justice shall be done is apt to be regarded as evidence of weakness by people whose lives and traditions have made them accustomed to high-handed oppression. Your humanitarian efforts to lighten their burdens result sometimes in their refusing to bear any burdens at all, which may leave you in an awkward predicament. Indian servants and petty officials go on the principle of asking for much in order that they may receive a little, rather than of asking for a little, knowing that they are, in response, likely to receive nothing at all.

March 21st.—Kolam to Milupara.—While examining the interior of a bear's cave, in a massive bed of sandstone, near Milupara, my attention was attracted by numerous small holes in the rock, which was of a loose and friable nature, and could be cut with a penknife. In the older-looking perforations I found the remains (cast skins) of spiders, and portions of web, but in the fresh-looking perforations I found bag-like webs, or rather nests, with a trap-door entrance, which small spiders closed behind them as they retreated. The holes were about the size of a crow-quill, and from half to three-quarters of an inch deep. I have no doubt whatever that the holes were the result of the removal, grain by grain, of the loose sandstone, and that the spiders themselves had made them. I saw no holes unoccupied by either dead or living spiders. Since there were no webs, properly so called, these spiders probably lived by hunting the small flies, which, attracted by the bears, and the comparative coolness of the cave, were abundant on the walls. The spiders were exceedingly agile, and I found it somewhat difficult to secure specimens without having recourse to rough measures, which would have injured their soft and tender bodies. Those I did obtain were subsequently forwarded to the greatest authority in England on spiders, the Rev. O. P. Cambridge, who pronounced that they were a species of *Clubiona*, in an immature stage, and could not therefore be specifically characterised. He further expressed incredulity as to the spiders having made the holes themselves; but I am quite satisfied that they had done so.

March 25th.—Janjgir.—The village of Janjgir is situated in a flat valley, which penetrates for about two miles between some high sandstone ridges, covered with forest. There was abundant evidence of the presence of game, and at night two bears commenced to fight close to my tent. Hearing the noise, I rushed out, rifle in hand, before any of the men, including the one on guard, were awakened. There was brilliant moonlight, but the shot I took at the bears failed to stop them, as they made off to their caves. On the following day I came across the remains of a bear, which the natives said had been killed by a tiger, and as a *machan* had been erected in a tree for a Shikari, who is said to have sat over the carcase of the bear in the hopes of getting a shot at the tiger, I suppose there was some truth in the story. On several occasions in this country I sat over the carcases of slaughtered cattle, but as the tigers never visited them while I was on guard, though they sometimes did afterwards, the details would not prove of much interest to the reader.

April 1st.—Hingir.—This is the chief village of a small state of the same name, which is subordinate to Gangpur. As in Gangpur proper, I found the people of Hingir disposed to be insolent, and that they had made no preparations for my camp. I accordingly refused at first to accept a *dalli* which they brought as a peace-offering, after I had reprimanded them and had threatened to have them punished. Towards evening, on their earnest solicitation, I consented to receive it, thus making it impossible for me to report them. During the night I was disturbed by my dog, Topsie, making a vigorous demonstration, which was replied to by growling and spitting. On getting up to ascertain the cause, I found Topsie respectfully contemplating a wild cat, which ascended a tree on my approach, from whence I soon dislodged it.

April 7th.—Dolunga to Laikera.—For some days I had been seeing tracks of gaur and wild buffalo, and on arrival at Laikera, heard from some local shikaris that there were herds of both in the neighbourhood, and about mid-day, when it was very hot, they brought me word that they had marked down a small herd of buffalo in the jungle, about a mile distant. On going to the spot, I found that there were half-a-dozen buffaloes, taking a *siesta* in a sheltered glade where there was a pool of water. By careful stalking I got within eighty yards of them, and unfortunately selected an Express rifle wherewith to attack them. I wounded one, but it made off with its companions, and though we tracked it by blood for about three miles, we failed to find it. Subsequent experience with buffaloes has satisfied me that an Express bullet of ·500 guage is not well suited for killing them, a large solid ball from a heavy rifle being much more effectual. On the following evening, when roaming through the jungle on the chance of a shot at deer, I came upon three gaur or bison. They allowed me to creep within forty yards, staring intently at me all the time. I then fired again with the Express at the one standing nearest to me, which also appeared to be the largest, and hit him behind the shoulder, but they all bolted off as though I had missed, but soon stopped again, and as I fired with the other rifle the wounded one lay down. Passing him, I went in pursuit of the others, but did not succeed in stopping them. The young bull, as he proved to be, was, I found on my return, quite dead. Covering the carcase with leaves, we left it, as the sun had set, till the next morning, when I had the whole skin removed, with very great trouble, intending to have it set up in Calcutta, as mounted specimens of this animal are very rare. Unfortunately, the skin, the carriage of which, on account of its great weight and awkward size, was a source of no little inconvenience, was allowed to go to the bad during the rains. The height of this bull, measured from pegs driven into the ground at the feet and withers, was fourteen and a-half hands.

April 11th.—Durlipali to Charbatti.—To-day I followed the bank of the Ebe river for several miles. Owing to the reflection from the wide expanse of sand, the heat seemed to be greater than usual. Near one village on the river-side I passed an encampment of gipsy-like people, the men having beards, who called themselves Tellingas. One of the women of the party, seated on the ground, was swaying her body about, and with her hair all streaming, appeared to be working herself into a state of frenzy, probably for the purpose of performing some divination. A man accompanied or encouraged her gesticulations by playing on the tom-tom.

The Raigurh and Hingir coal-field, the examination of which

I had now completed, is the south-eastern extension of a vast tract of coal-measure and associated rocks, which, along the frontiers of Western Bengal and the Central Provinces, in all probability covers an area of about 5,000 square miles. The coal-seams which are exposed are neither very numerous nor individually of very promising quality; but the coal-measures are not only as a whole very slightly disturbed from their original horizontal position, but are much concealed by superficial deposits. The true or even approximate value of the field can only be ascertained by borings, but in the meantime it may safely be asserted that there is a fair prospect of this field proving to be of considerable value should a line of railway ever pass in its vicinity.*

April 13th.—Ektali.—In this neighbourhood, which is open country to the east of the Ebe river, there are some jheels and swampy grounds, where, though so late in the season, I found snipe to be tolerably plentiful. There were also three species of teal and black-backed geese. It was quite a treat to me to get some shooting such as these birds afforded, as I had been so long in hilly forest-country, but I am not quite prepared to defend the practice of shooting water-birds at this time of year.

About this time the jungle trees were putting forth their new leaves, and the consequent freshness and greenery were very pleasant to behold, after the absence of foliage of the last six weeks. With this change I noted the arrival of the Paradise fly-catchers and ground-thrushes, whose sudden appearance at this season I have already alluded to. I also saw some flocks of the large bee-eater (*Merops Philippensis*).

Mr. Motte, who visited Sambalpur to purchase diamonds in 1766, and to whose observations I shall have to refer in the next chapter, gives the following curious account of a monster snake.

---

* For an account of this coal-field *vide* Rec. Geol. Survey of India, Vol. IV., p. 101, and Vol. VIII., p. 102.

I believe the locality is still known, though the snake has been dead for many years :—

"On my return from this place (the Ebe river), I paid a visit to the Naik Buns, the great snake worshipped by the mountainous Rajas, which they say is coeval with the world, and which at his decease will be at an end. His habitation was a cavern at the foot of a rock, at the opening of which was a plain of 400 yards, surrounded by a moat. I understood he came out once a week, against which time such as make religious vows carry kids or fowls and picquet them on the plain. About nine in the morning his appearance was announced to me. I stood on the banks of the moat, opposite the plain. He was unwieldy—thicker, in proportion to his length, than snakes usually are, and seemed of that species the Persians call Ajdha. There was a kid and some fowls picqueted for him. He took the kid in his mouth and was some time squeezing his throat to force it down, while he threw about his tail with much activity. He then rolled along to the moat, where he drank and wallowed in the mud. He returned to his cavern. Mr. Raby and I crossed the water in the afternoon, and supposed, from his print in the mud, his diameter to be upwards of two feet." *

April 27th.—Jhunan to Sambalpur.—To-day I marched into Sambalpur, having concluded my season's work. As it was necessary for me to return to Calcutta as soon as possible, I was unable to accept an invitation to join the Deputy-Commissioner, who was engaged in making an enormous bag of game in country about 100 miles to the south. To have joined him would have involved my remaining in Sambalpur till the commencement of the rains in the middle of June, when floods in the Mahanadi would have rendered it possible to run down to Cuttack by boat in two or three days. My original intention was to attempt the voyage at this season, but I was told that owing to the small

---

* I give the above curious tale without comment as I omitted to ascertain the local traditions on the subject.

amount of water in some of the channels it would take me about fifteen days in a very small boat of light draught to reach Cuttack. The heat reflected from the sand I was further told would be terrific, so that I determined to march by land, and selected a route *viâ* Ungul, north of the Mahanadi, which is 158 miles long, in preference to the cart-road which follows the southern bank *viâ* Sonpur and Bôd, and is upwards of 200 miles long.

May 6th.—Charmal to Rampur.—Four marches brought me to Rampur, which is about 45 miles distant from Sambalpur. The Raja of the place came to see me in the evening, and I found him to be a garrulous and noisy old gentleman. He asked me a number of questions about various countries and the planetary system. My exposition of the laws of gravity did not serve to convince him that men would not fall off the earth if it revolved on its axis as he had been told it did by some former English visitor. There is a story related of some Bengali schoolmaster, who when expounding to his class the laws of planetary motion, explained to a friend that he did so only because it was a part of his duty, while from the evidence of his senses he believed the whole thing to be absurd. Among the stories told me by the Raja was one of a tiger which lived in the neighbourhood. According to his description it would have measured at least five feet high at the shoulder, and about a yard across the head. Whenever it attacked a herd of cattle it killed several before it left them. It had not then been heard of for some little time. The Raja possessed a remarkably fine breed of dogs, with which his people hunt deer during the rains. The huntsmen pursue on foot through the jungle and spear the deer when they are brought to bay by the dogs. I have not met with this sport elsewhere in India, but I understand it is practised by the Brinjaras.

May 8th.—Nuamunda to Kutada.—I had now entered the province of Orissa, and made my first acquaintance with the Uria in his native home. The Urias who come to Calcutta for service, chiefly as bearers or *valets*, often make excellent and orderly servants, whose appearance conveys but a very small idea of the rude material in the jungle. I had always considered the Bengali peasant to be a quarrelsome, noisy, untruthful, and discourteous specimen of the Indian native in the rough, but he is certainly outdone in all these respects by the Uria. They shout and yell at one another, often using most abusive language, in a way that is perfectly indescribable. Conversations about trivial matters are carried on in a key that is shrill to excess and hideous in the extreme. Anything like quiet seems to be unattainable near an Uria village. Admonitions to speak in a low tone are of no avail, and just as one has perhaps managed to fall asleep on a hot afternoon, a stridulent voice strikes up at a few yards distance and seems almost to penetrate one's brain, putting sleep out of the question.

The next day I marched to Ungul, which is the central town in these tributary states of Orissa. I found there a good and substantial bungalow in the occupation of the Tehsildar, or petty native magistrate. On my asking for two rooms to be placed at my disposal I was told by him that he had received permission from the Commissioner to occupy the house, and that being a Hindu with his family living with him, he could not accede to my request.* However, he pitched a tent for me, and as he was otherwise civil I presumed he was acting under authority, and I did not find out till afterwards that the permission granted to him included the reservation that he was to give up half the house to any official traveller who might require it. At most of the other halting-places I had made use of the small rest-houses on the road, which gave a more efficient shelter from the heat than that which my tent could afford, and saved my men the trouble of pitching and striking the tent every day.

May 12th.—Mydapur to Rasul.—At Rasul, in the evening I

---

* I merely mention this incident in order to further illustrate what I have said on previous pages about our social relations with the natives; but it is a text on which much might be written.

was visited by the Raja of a state called Indole. Together with his brother, both of them lads, they came riding straddle-wise on a baby elephant, which they said was only three years old. It had been given them as a reward a short time before for aid rendered to the Government Kedah, or elephant-catching operations in these regions. I had some conversation here with a traveller, a native of Kandahar, who had come to India with horses. He was now on his way home, and he told me that the only money in his possession was two peiss, or about three farthings. His disgust for the Urias, their language, manners, and customs, was considerable, and he complained much of their stinginess. Though so far away from kith and kin he had a light and merry heart, and was delighted to hear me talk of Thull-Chutiali, and other places which I had been at or heard of during my visit to Biluchistan.

May 14th.—Gutpir to Daiserah.—During the last few marches I had been noticing a steady change in the character of the vegetation. It begins to be most apparent near Ungul, but here at Daiserah the ordinary forms of jungle trees and bushes of the interior were completely replaced by an altogether distinct type of *flora.* Rattan canes and a species of *cycad* or *zamia* were the most prominent of the new forms which I could recognise, but there were also numbers of thorny bushes of species unknown to me, which form dense thickets in which jungle and pea-fowl abound.

On the morning of the 15th I reached Cuttack, having taken thirteen days to traverse the distance of 158 miles from Sambalpur. Heartily glad was I to have reached this stage on my journey. The site of the town of Cuttack, in the angle between two rivers (or rather, to be more correct, on a delta between two outlets of the Mahanadi), is one of the most unsuitable that could possibly have been selected. It has necessitated costly revetments and other protective works on the river face, and it will hardly be believed, though it is nevertheless the fact, that a large portion of the ground on which the town is built is seven to eight feet below the level of high floods. Were there no high lands out of the range of inundation there might have been good reason for continuing this station in the position which was probably adopted by the Mahrattas and their predecessors on stragetical grounds; but since there are good sites, both to the north and south of the river, the unwisdom of the retention of this site is fully apparent. At the same time it must be admitted that it is not easy to transplant towns; and each year, with the increase of expenditure on local buildings, it becomes still more difficult to do so. The houses occupied by the official residents are for the most part substantially-built and commodious residences, many of them standing in fine compounds, which are scattered over a wide area of three miles in diameter. The irrigation works in connection with the Mahanadi river have drawn to this station a number of engineers, while it is also the head-quarters of missionary establishments belonging to several different denominations, so that the circle of English residents is more numerous and diversified than are those to be found in many stations in Bengal. The irrigation works of Orissa are included among those Indian public undertakings which, by a figure of speech in use in the Financial Department, are classed as "reproductive." A very considerable amount of capital has been sunk upon them, and since taking the water has not been made compulsory * upon the cultivators they only pay for it when it suits their convenience to do so, and, as I was informed on the spot, the receipts did not cover the cost of collection, while the interest on the capital expended was being paid by the country generally; a state of things which might be paralleled by defraying the cost of waterworks of individual townships in England out of imperial instead of locally-raised funds.

May 17th.—Cuttack to Niraj.—As the steamer by which I

---

* It had not, at least, a twelvemonth ago, when I left India. But the levying of a water-rate was then being discussed, and legislation on the subject was in progress.

proposed to return to Calcutta would not leave False Point till the 22nd, I availed myself of the opportunity of paying a visit to Niraj, about six miles distant from Cuttack, where there is a weir by which the amount of water permitted to find its way into the Kajuri or southern outlet of the river is controlled. My principal object in visiting Niraj, was to enquire into the truth of certain reports as to the existence of indications of coal occuring in the rocks of that neighbourhood. The result of my examination was the discovery of some black shales which did not by any means render the occurrence of coal probable. Subsequently I found some fossil plants which shewed that these rocks belonged to a series which is younger than the coal-measures, and which has nowhere been found to contain workable coal itself. An excellent bungalow at Niraj is situated in a commanding position on the banks of the Mahanadi, and from its verandah it was possible to take long rifle shots at crocodiles and garials as they lay on the edge of the sand or floated on the surface of the water.

May 19th.—Cuttack to Taldunda.—Owing to there not being sufficient water in the canals for the Government steam-tender to come up as far as Cuttack in May,* it was necessary to make a journey of about twenty miles by night in a palki, to a place called Taldunda, where I went on board. At Karmassie, where we anchored for the night of the 21st, it was said that the jungles on the island contained numbers of spotted deer and some tigers, but though I took a long walk through them I saw nothing. A common shrub on some of these islands is the mudar (*Calatropis gigantea*), which yields a silky fibre that has often been favourably reported on by experts, but which has never, so far as I know, been manufactured on the large scale. The shrub is very common in many places, and there would be, I should think, no great difficulty in obtaining a constant supply of it.

* This month is selected for clearing the canals of weeds, and the water is kept at a low level.

Another common tree on the *churs* is a species of date (*Phœnix palustris*), which with its bunches of fruit at once attracts notice. At False Point I embarked on the steamer "Satara" and reached Calcutta on the 23rd.

CHAPTER XII.

SECTION I.

ORISSA AND SAMBALPUR.

1875-76.

INSTRUCTIONS FOR SEASON—LEAVE CALCUTTA BY STEAMER FOR GOPALPUR—RAJA OF VIZIANAGRAM—LAND AT GOPALPUR—CHILKA LAKE—PURI—TEMPLE OF JUGERNATH—SACERDOTAL DISPUTES—CUTTACK—ANCIENT KITCHEN-MIDDEN—COMMENCE MARCH—FOSSIL PLANTS—BRAHMINI RIVER—SHOOT A GARIAL—BEAR SHOT—TIGER WOUNDED—SAMBAR SHOT—URIA CONSERVATISM—THE SECRET OF HOW TO MANAGE THE URIAS—RAJA OF DENKENAL—RAJA OF TALCHIR—COLD SEASON IN ORISSA—ANCIENT STONE IMPLEMENT—BOTANICAL COLLECTOR—TELLINGAS—COAL AT GOPALPERSAD—BEATS FOR GAME—TALCHIR RAJA—CHARACTER OF THE URIA CHASAS—ENTER UNGUL—COAL AT PATRAPARA—HILLY FOREST-TRACK TO WEST OF UNGUL—VALUE OF THE TALCHIR COAL-FIELD AS A SOURCE OF FUEL—RARE BIRDS IN REHRAKOLE—FIRE A CHARGE OF SHOT INTO A LEOPARD—MAN WOUNDED BY A BEAR—A SPIDER LIKE THE COMMON RED ANT—SAMBALPUR—FEVER—NATIVE PANTOMIME—SMALL GAME—ROCKS OF THE MAHANADI VALLEY WEST OF SAMBALPUR—BRINJARAS OR GIPSIES—SAMBALPUR AND CHUTIA NAGPUR DIAMONDS—SAMBALPUR GOLD—MARCH TO ORISSA—BAD WATER—FEVER—UNGUL—ATHGURH SANDSTONES—KHURDA—HOT SPRING AT ATARI—CADASTRAL SURVEY—BUDDHIST CAVE TEMPLES OF KHUNDAGIRI—HINDU TEMPLES AT BOBANESHWAR—CUTTACK—CHANDBALLI—CHANDIPAL—RETURN TO CALCUTTA.

MY work for this season was to report on the quality and amount of coal in the Talchir Coal-field in Orissa, and on the prospects of making it commercially available. It had been thought by the local authorities, and by the Lieutenant-Governor of Bengal, that if the field could be profitably opened up considerable benefit would accrue to the Province of Orissa. Twenty years had elapsed since the field had been reported on by the Geological Survey.* Indeed, though difficult of

---

* "Memoirs of the Geological Survey of India." Vol. I.

access, its examination was one of the first pieces of work which was accomplished by the Survey. A rumour had been spread abroad that the field was really of greater value than the geological report had indicated, and an officer of the Public Works Department had been sent to open up some of the coal-seams, and to bring the coal down to Cuttack for experimental trial in steam-engines. I was further instructed to examine a basin of sandstones in the Mahanadi Valley, above Cuttack, and to give whatever time I could spare besides to the continuation of my examination of the geology of Sambalpur.

I left Calcutta in the British India Steam Navigation Company's steamer "Khandalla," on the 29th October. On our way down the river some little excitement was caused during our transit of the James and Mary shoal, where many good ships have been lost. The steamer drew eighteen and a-half feet, and as it proved there was only twenty feet of water over these treacherous sands. Had we touched, the Pilot afterwards told us, we should have immediately gone over. Among the passengers were the late Raja of Vizianagram and his son, together with a considerable following, both male and female. He was journeying from Benares to his own country, whence he purposed to proceed to Madras, to be present there on the arrival of the Prince of Wales. As being one of the most enlightened native members of the Governor-General's Council, the Raja was well known throughout India. It was therefore with some surprise that I learnt that he countenanced a superstitious belief, to the effect that the growth of indigo, or the employment of iron in the construction of buildings, &c., in his territory would be inevitably followed by epidemics of small-pox and other diseases.

On the following morning we anchored off False Point at ten o'clock. I had intended to land, but as the only boat available was taken up by the Raja and his followers, who being Hindus had to cook their food on shore, I thought it better not to intrude into their company, and accordingly gave up the trip.

Next morning I landed at Gopalpur. I have already described this sea-side town on a previous page. On the following day I drove into Berhampur, where I had an interview with the Assistant-Collector on the subject of a discovery which had been made of what were supposed to be fossil-bones, and which I had come to investigate. I then first heard that the locality was distant ten days' march in the hills, and the particulars I received convinced me that the deposit was none other than a calcareous tufa, similar to those I have described on p. 254, and elsewhere in preceding pages. I accordingly determined, after a visit of a few days' duration to Aska, to push on to Cuttack, where my servants and equipment were already awaiting my arrival.

November 5th.—Aska to Ramba.—I made the journey between these two places by night in a palki, and on arrival next morning at the latter, which I have described in a previous chapter, I could see, far away on the Chilka Lake, the Police boat which was to convey me northwards to Puri or Jugernath, slowly making her way towards Ramba. I embarked during the afternoon, and sailed throughout the night and following day, except where we lay to in order to land and get a shot at the antelope on the strip of sand which separates the lake from the sea, or took fishermen's small boats to go in pursuit of the flocks of geese and ducks which were just commencing to arrive with the beginning of the cold weather. I saw a number of pelicans and other birds, and I felt satisfied that a month or so later the sportsman or ornithologist, or, better still, he who combines both characters—and most ornithologists in India are sportsmen—would find the Chilka to be a perfect paradise for a week or fortnight's sojourn.

Owing to slackness of water we were unable to continue the voyage beyond a place called Urkata, from whence, after a second night spent on board, I travelled twelve miles by palki to Puri, which I reached by mid-day on the 8th. The houses of the English residents at Puri are on the sea-shore, in the middle of a zone of drifting sand-dunes, which at times threaten almost to bury them. The position seems to be not well-selected, since the glare from the sand and the grit in the air are very real sources of discomfort. The native town surrounding the temple of Jugernath lies further inland, and is surrounded by a luxuriant vegetation, which presents a markedly tropical aspect, owing to the presence of screw-pines and palms.

November 9th.—Puri to Cuttack.—In the morning, in company with the Superintendent of Police, I rode round the outer wall of the great temple of Jugernath, and through the suburbs of the town. I should be very glad to give a description of the temple could I do so at first hand, but since it is surrounded by a high wall, and no European is permitted to pass the threshold of the gates, information on the subject cannot be obtained by a personal visit. It is stated that it was under discussion among the priests whether they should not invite Lord Mayo to enter the temple when he visited Puri, as he intended to do, towards the end of the tour which was cut short by his assassination at the Andamans. The pilgrims whom I saw were a dirty and beggarly-looking lot; the female portion consisting, for the most part of decayed and excessively-ugly old women, who were clad in soiled raiments.

There was a bitter discussion and controversy going on in Puri in reference to the temple: it was a case of Church *versus* State; the Raja, in whom the guardianship and a portion of the revenues were vested by the Government, being on the one side, and the priests with a portion of the worshippers on the other. Under former Governments the paramount authority always secured for itself a portion of the revenues of Jugernath, as well as of other places of pilgrimage throughout the land; but it was not thought advisable that the British Government, or the Company before it, at least for many years back, should avail themselves of such sources of income, and hence they have devolved upon the Raja.

Although on bad terms with the priests, and compelled to obtain the interference of the local authorities to bring them to order, the Raja was regarded as a person of exceptional sanctity. About two years ago, however, he was sentenced to a term of penal servitude for a murder committed in his presence, and by his orders, which for cruelty in its details has perhaps not often been equalled. The punishment, nay, even the trial of this almost deified personage, who richly merited hanging, caused great excitement in Hindu society; an excitement almost equal to that which arose when, a century ago, the first Brahmin Nund Kumar was sentenced to death by the British, who had previously not ventured to make Brahmins amenable to the common law. One curious cause of discord had arisen just before the time I write of. In consequence of the insecure and dangerous state of the great central dome in the temple—of which, indeed, a portion had already fallen—it had been necessary to remove the image of Jugernath from its lofty throne, and place it in a sort of chapel-of-ease, or minor shrine, where there is no throne. One party of ecclesiastics maintained that so long as this state of things continued, and Jugernath remained away from his throne, the holy food, which is prepared for and distributed to the pilgrims, would be shorn of its sanctity and efficacy, and that no pilgrim would derive any benefit from a visit to the temple during the same period. This must have been rather distressing intelligence for those who had travelled many hundreds of weary miles from their homes. Other Pundits likewise learned in ecclesiastical law held a contrary opinion, and hence a very pretty quarrel was in progress.

November 10th.—Cuttack.—I arrived at Cuttack this morning, having travelled during the night by palki from Puri. I should have liked to remain there a day or two longer in order to visit the Black Pagoda, an extensive ruin situated on the coast a few miles further north; but I was anxious to push forward, and expected that two or three days spent in Cuttack would serve to enable me to make all necessary arrangements about carriage and some extra servants. I found, however, that Urias are not to be hurried, and, as I have previously remarked, and also subsequently found to be the case, Cuttack is a very difficult place to get out of when once you have got into it. During the week which I was thus compelled to remain there, I paid a visit to some laterite quarries at the site of an old town called

Chaudwar on the north bank of the main branch of the Mahanadi. My object in visiting these quarries was to examine the circumstances under which a bed of laterite, which was said to contain fragments of pottery, occurred. The specimen from these quarries which had attracted the notice of one of the engineers in charge of a section of the irrigation works, was a large block of laterite which had been rejected as unsuitable for building purposes. Although I could detect no very sharply-marked line of demarcation between the portion of the block which contained the pottery and that which was free from any trace of it, still it was apparent that, in so far as this particular specimen was concerned, the layer of pottery was superficial —in other words was *on* not *in* the laterite. On reaching Chaudwar, I found that throughout a considerable portion of the area occupied by the quarries, the cuttings down to the surface of the laterite disclosed sections of from one to three feet of a layer of broken pottery and bones,—in fact, the remains of an ancient kitchen-midden. The base of this layer, the portion in contact with the laterite, is firmly cemented by ferruginous matter; but higher in the sections the deposit becomes looser and looser as it rises to the surface. In some cases the pottery is so firmly attached to the laterite that it cannot be detached without fracture. It is not, I think, necessary to suppose that the laterite was in a soft or only partially formed condition when the pottery was first thrown down upon it. The percolation of waters from above, more or less charged with organic matter, may have acted upon its upper surface in such a way as to cause the solution and subsequent deposition of the ferruginous matter which now includes and binds to the laterite the fragments of pottery.

Had this been a *bonâ-fide* case of the occurrence of pottery *in* laterite it would have had an interest very much greater than it can be now said to possess. Although evidence, that of stone implements, has been found of the existence of man while one of the forms of laterite was being deposited, it still remains to be proved that man, so far advanced in knowledge of the arts as to manufacture pottery, lived in India at so early a period. As to the age of the deposit, the date of the founding of Chaudwar, the capital of Orissa, would only furnish a rough indication; but even it is not certainly known. Mr. Beames puts it at probably A.D. 350, other authorities so far back as A.D. 23.* Either is probably sufficiently remote for the completion of the operations giving rise to the phenomena above described and which belong most distinctly to the, geologically speaking, present period.

November 17th.—Cuttack to Kukkur.—At length, having completed my list of servants, purchased a second horse, and made other arrangements, I parted to-day from my friends in Cuttack, and made my first march, a short one in consequence of the river crossing, to Kukkur. On the following day I was fortunate in making a discovery of fossil plants in some sandstones which occupy the already mentioned basin to the west of Cuttack. These fossils have since served to determine the age of these rocks as being identical with that of those which occur interstratified with the basalt of the Rajmahal Hills. Two days later I reached Denkenal, the chief town of a native state of the same name. Here the Raja had provided a commodious bungalow for the accommodation of English visitors. In the evening I joined him in a beat for game close to the village, but nothing save a jungle-fowl was shot. There are animals in the neighbourhood, however, and my men sent on in advance, had seen two wild elephants. From Denkenal I marched to Bowlpur where I found two Greeks, the agents of a Calcutta house, engaged in collecting timber and country produce generally, such as oil-seeds, &c.

November 24th.—Kurakpershad.—Three marches along the banks of the Brahmini brought me to Kurakpershad, where I took a boat in the afternoon in order to try to get a shot at the crocodiles and garials which were very abundant in the river.

---

* See on this subject "Indian Antiquary," February, 1876, p. 55.

Plate VIII.

THE CAMP AT 6 A.M. AND 6 P.M.

One of the latter, which I hit with an Express bullet in the neck, was unable to reach the water near which he was lying in consequence of his fore-limbs becoming paralyzed, though he lashed about vigorously with his tail. He proved to be about ten feet long, and it was rather a difficult job to hoist him into the boat. At the next camping-place, Kumlong, the camp was prettily-situated on the banks of the river, and commanded a good view of the rocks which make the navigation of the Brahmini so difficult at and above this point. The river is most dangerous when in flood, as these rocks are then concealed beneath the surface, and should a boat come in contact with them, it immediately capsizes and is broken-up. This subject was one of importance for my consideration in connection with the subject of bringing the coal down to Cuttack, upon which I had to report.

November 30th.—Karpada.—To-day I arranged with the jemidar of the Denkenal Raja, who accompanied my camp to provide supplies, to have a beat for game in a range of hills to the north of Karpada. Men were ready in the afternoon after my return from work. I was placed in what was considered to be the most likely pass for the game, with some village shikaris with their guns thrown out on either flank. I saw no animals during the beat, but a shot was fired on either side of me. The first proved to have been at a bear, which was badly wounded, and to which I gave a finishing bullet. The other was at a tiger, which had also been wounded. Getting on its track, which was marked with blood, I followed it up, and in one place saw the jungle moving in front, but failed to see the animal itself, and the tracks were lost; but before I gave up a sambar crossed our path, and I shot him. On the following day I resumed the search, beating over the same ground, when I shot another sambar. But the men were very inefficient trackers, and we saw no more of the tiger. Some time afterwards I heard that the remains of a tiger had been found a few miles off, on the other side of the Brahmini river.

The jemidar whom I have mentioned above was a Mahomedan, and amused me by his stories of the Urias, whom he regarded with no little contempt on account of their uncleanly habits, their superstition, and their aversion to all change and improvement. He told me of some villages where in the hot months there was no water, and what was required had to be daily brought from several miles distant. The people were urged by the Raja to make wells for themselves, but declined to do so on the ground that their fathers before them had not had wells, and that therefore they would not have any. During the Keonjur war in 1868 the Raja of Denkenal was called upon by the local authorities to furnish carriage for the conveyance of grain to the troops, whereupon he invited the proprietors of pack-cattle to attend with their beasts; but they replied that they would rather be excused. The jemidar then asked permission of the Raja to be allowed to exercise his powers of persuasion on them. This being granted, he in a very short time had assembled more pack-bullocks than were required, and, on the Raja asking for his secret of "how 'twas done," he replied to him by telling a story, which was something to this effect:—Once upon a time a Raja had a favourite who took umbrage at something that was said to him, and retired to the forest in high dudgeon. The Raja became disconsolate, and sent a series of deputations, and even his own private palki as a conveyance, and besought the favourite to return; but he would not. At length one of the courtiers asked for permission to try whether he could not bring the favourite back. This being granted, he went up to him, and, removing one of his shoes from his foot, proceeded to give him a severe castigation with it, whereupon he cried out for mercy, and forthwith marched back to court. "Similarly," said the jemidar, "I gave one of the bullock-owners a thrashing, when not only he, but all the others, who feared a like treatment for themselves, brought their bullocks without further delay."

The Denkenal Raja, though possessing an establishment, it was said, of about sixty wives and concubines, was without male heir, and, at the time I write, was very anxious that the Indian Government should become heir, not only to his estate, but also to a considerable sum of money invested in Government securities. To this, however, the local authorities were opposed, and, under their influence, I believe, he adopted an heir from the neighbouring family of the Raja of Bôd, and this heir has since succeeded to the Raja. In view of the backward state of Denkenal (though one of the best managed of these estates) and its capabilities, it seemed to me to be somewhat unaccountable that the Government should have declined the offer of so valuable a bequest. However, there were probably good reasons for the action taken in the matter. There is no doubt that some of the Rajas of the adjoining estates regarded the prospect of its absorption into British territory with alarm, and several of them expressed to me, pretty openly, their views on the subject.

December 3rd.—Egaria.—I had now entered another state—that of Talchir—and I was at Egaria visited by the Raja, a young man of about one-and-twenty years of age, whose appearance and manner did not prepossess me much in his favour; but as I shall have to refer to him again, I shall reserve my account of him for the present. Several beats which he gave me for game were such miserable fiascos that I declined to join him in any others. The matchlock-men were so noisy that it would have been a miracle if any animals had broken in our direction. They were, moreover, far more numerous than the beaters, who were the worst I have ever seen.

I often longed at this season for the cool weather of the Chutia Nagpur highlands; for the cold season of Orissa is rather a delusion. At night I commonly slept with little or no covering and with both the doors of my tent open, while by day the heat was often very oppressive. At the same time I used to read in the papers how at the camp, then being held at Delhi, it was necessary, on account of the cold, to have stoves in the tents, and to wear great coats at dinner.

December 11th.—Kusramunda.—To-day I found an ancient stone implement of the chipped quartzite type, very similar to a form of which great numbers have been found in Madras.

Subsequently I met with a few others. These will be found figured in Appendix B.

I had promised the Superintendent of the Botanical Gardens at Calcutta to collect plants for his herbarium, and for this purpose when in Cuttack I had engaged a Mali or gardener to accompany me who was said to know something of wild plants. He had, however, played me false, and never joined my camp. On writing to the magistrate about him, I received in reply a note something to this effect:—"When you engage an Uria to do anything he has to pass through three stages—first, he gets fever; secondly, his mother dies; and thirdly, his sister gets married. After which he may begin to consider the propriety of fulfilling his contract. The mali has not yet got through the first of these stages."

December 16th.—Sundrapal to Chindipuda.—To-day the camp was visited by a party of acrobats, who called themselves Tellingas; though their professional language was Hindi, I heard them talking Uria among themselves. Considering that they had none of the usual European appliances, such as spring-boards, &c., their performances were marvellous; two of them turned complete summersaults, springing off the bare ground. They were of an inky blackness, and possibly belonged to a gipsy race.

December 19th.—Royjono to Gopalpershad—At Gopalpershad there is a considerable seam of coal exposed in the Tengria River, and some trial shafts had been sunk in it, and fifty tons of the coal taken to Cuttack for trial. It had proved to be very poor fuel, as might indeed have been concluded from an examination on the spot, and much more expensive than English coal considering the work it was capable of performing.

I had several beats here in the afternoon, in one of which two bears, a hyæna, and several deer were seen, but I did not get a shot at them, and none were bagged by Saidon or the matchlock-men, of whom a considerable number assembled. The people were very sad at this result, but attributed it to the deity who presided over the forest. It was hinted to me, as it had been under similar circumstances in Singhbhum, that he might be induced to withdraw his protection were I to present the local priest with some sweetmeats. This I declined to do, though I rewarded the beaters liberally as they had done their work uncommonly well for Urias.

December 25th.—Talchir.—Yesterday, after my arrival at Talchir the chief town of the state of the same name, the Raja called on me, and to-day I went to pay a return visit at the palace. I was received in the cutchery, or office. As I approached I could see preparations, being hurriedly made to give an appearance as though formal business, a trial, was going on. The whole thing was a stupid farce, and was wretchedly enacted. After I had witnessed it for a short time, I proposed an adjournment of the court, and we moved into what might be called, perhaps, in Mahomedan phraseology, the Dewan-i-Khas, or private audience-chamber. Dirt and squalor were prevalent all round, and the Raja's people were deficient in everything like courtesy of manner. All were supremely ignorant, or seemed to be so, of matters out of the province of Orissa. They did not know even the names of many notable places in India. I noticed in one corner a pile of Uria newspapers lying in their covers unopened. The paper is published in Cuttack, with the view of conveying information about public affairs to readers of the Uria language; but these people were too apathetic to take the trouble of reading it. The Raja had some slight knowledge of English, and blundered through a page of a two-syllabled class-book for my edification. The book belonged to an educational series consisting of first, second, and third books, &c., and I felt somewhat posed for an answer when he asked me how many books there were in the English language. He was apparently under the impression that the whole literature of England was arranged in a progressive scale of this nature.

About the only article of English manufacture, besides guns, which he possessed, was a telescope, which indeed he sent for my examination before he first called upon me. I presented him with a pocket sun-dial, to which he seemed to have taken such a fancy that I was somewhat disconcerted by his off-hand way of receiving it. Although his appearance and manner were not pleasant he must have some good points about him, as I have continued to receive up to within the last few months, and since my arrival at home, letters from him, which shew a decided improvement in his knowledge of English. The following is a specimen :—

TALCHIR FORT *25th May 1878*

MY DEAR V. BALL ESQ

I become more glad to receive your acknowledgment letter of the 13th Instant and felt rather than before to hear that you are in good health and immediately ready for marching to England for two years before leave. I Do not know where and in which plese being your own house. I request the favour of your informing me by the Post letter. The above requests before are after your going there.

I also beant to state you that I had lately been travelled to Moffussils for inspections and shootin some of animals as below 2 Deers, 4 Hogs, 1 Khoarung, 1 Tiger Totals 8

I am quite well hoping you and your householders are the same

Yours truely

RAM CHUNDER BEERBUR HURRI CHUNDUN
MOHINDER BHADUR, Raja of Talchir.

The dalli which he sent me during the day was a very considerable one, covering many brass trays, which were borne on men's heads. There was a lamb, fish, vegetables, and sweetmeats *ad nauseum* as far as I was concerned ; but they were very speedily divided and gobbled up by the servants. Before I left Talchir I had several more visits from him, but obtained little information of interest.

December 29th.—Kompur to Porongo.—To-day I dismissed the people of the Talchir establishment, who had been sent with my camp by the Raja to provide supplies ; they were a useless and ill-conditioned lot, being headed by a confirmed opium-eater, who used to precede the camp by way of making preparations, which he however never did make. I was heartily glad to pass from a State occupied by a population so debased and degraded into another, Ungul, where the people might be better, but could not easily be worse. And here I may as well attempt to describe the Chasas, or Uria cultivators of the Orissa tributary Mehals.

They are of a spare and weakly habit of body, their features hard, with high and prominent cheek-bones, and a generally forbidding aspect, the hair of the head is often completely shaved, save one lock on the poll. Frequently their gnarled-looking countenances reminded me of those representations of hobgoblins that one sometimes sees in old oak carvings in cathedrals. They are untruthful to the last degree. Writing of them many years ago, Lieut. Kittoe said:—"It is next to impossible to obtain any correct information even on the most trivial subjects. Every question put by a stranger is considered and re-considered ere a reply is given, and that too is an interrogation as to the object you have in asking it." I found this to be still quite true. Often in a village one man out of a crowd would tell me an obvious and foolish lie, and all the rest would invariably affirm the same to be the case. Their ideas as to their own personal sanctity, and the restrictions put upon them by caste, are not the least extraordinary points about them. In some of the villages the Chasas would refuse to hold a rope or help to carry a log of timber with a Chatia, though both were living as neighbours. I found it very difficult to arrange for the carriage of my sick, as these people generally refused to act as bearers, and moreover there were no charpoys or bedsteads in the villages upon which they might have been carried, while on the other hand my Uria cartmen refused to allow certain of the lower classes of the servants to sit with the baggage on the carts, as they said it would defile them, and cause them to be fined by their co-religionists. Their curiosity is insatiable: occasionally they would walk up to my tent and peer in at the door in a way that most other natives would hesitate to do. Sometimes when passing a village crowds would flock out like a troop of monkeys and squat down on and about the path I was taking, not offering to move out of the way till I almost rode or walked on top of them, when, without rising, they would simply draw themselves crab-like on one side. They never offered the customary salute or *salaam*, while a chance Mahomedan or up-country man met on the roads in Orissa would seldom fail to do so. Their stridulent voices, their eternal chattering and gossip, often carried on close to the tent, used to drive me nearly mad. They might be sent away to a distance, but, like flies, they or others would soon be back again, shouting at and squabbling with one another. It is a fact that two Urias engaged in *conversation* as they walk one behind the other along the road can be heard distinctly at a quarter of a mile's distance. Whether engaged at work, or in search of game, I naturally preferred to go quietly through the jungles, yet it was well nigh impossible to keep the coolies' tongues from wagging. Gossip is the salt of existence to most natives of India, but their tongues are generally under some restraint—not so those of the Urias.

January 2nd.—Durgapur to Handiguda.—I had now entered Ungul, which is a state directly under British management, there being no Raja. On arrival at Handiguda I was told that a cow had been killed, and that two tigers had been heard fighting over the carcase during the night. Early this morning the meat had been removed by the Chatias of the village for their own consumption. Men in sufficient numbers were not to be obtained for a beat, and no persuasion could induce the people to let me have a cow to tie up, though I entrusted the getting of one to a Christian Constable who himself should have had no scruples. I declined the offer to sit up over a couple of kids as I had previously had enough of that kind of thing.

January 6th.—Patrapara.—In the neighbourhood of Patrapara is one of the few exposed seams of coal in this field. The quality is somewhat better than that at Gopalpersad, but it is still very poor stuff. It can only become of value should a line of railway ever pass in its vicinity, connecting Cuttack with Sambalpur. To the west of Patrapara, extending thence into Rehrakhole in the Central Provinces, there is a wild tract of forest and hills in which gaur and buffaloes are to be found. On its margin I met with a colony of very black-looking people called Soundas, who are probably identical with the Sowras or Savaras of Ganjam and Southern Orissa. There were also some Khonds and Bowries in this neighbourhood. Up to the foot of the hills there were extensive clearances planted with castor-oil; the plants rarely exceeded three feet in height, and are generally not half that—being, therefore, very much smaller than the bushes which are grown near villages, and which sometimes appear to be perennial. Other oil-bearing seeds are cultivated largely in these tracts, and the yield must be considerable.

In a field of cotton at one place I saw a single house the proprietors of which were there and then, on the spot, engaged in spinning and weaving the cotton into a coarse fabric. If Manchester could only have her way altogether, such a sight would never more be seen in India. In Dacca and elsewhere where the finer fabrics used to be made in large quantities, the industry has been almost crushed out of existence.

The results of my examination of the Talchir Coal-field, which formed the subject of a special report to Government, may be stated in brief as follows :—

First. The known coal-seams contain fuel of a quality very inferior to ordinary Ranigunj coal.

Second. The thorough exploration of the field by boring would be very costly.

Thirdly. The coal consumption in Orissa is too trifling to support a regular mining establishment; and, further, were coal even to be found hereafter in Talchir, equal to that of Ranigunj, it could not, owing to expensive land and river carriage, compete successfully with seaborne coal, whether Indian or English, at the Orissa seaports.

I could not, therefore, recommend any further expenditure being incurred in reference to the development of this field.

January 12th.—Nakrideol.—I had now left the coal-measures of the Talchir field behind me, being on the way to Sambalpur. I was, therefore, rather surprised to find a large fragment of coal lying in the bed of the Tikaria river to the north of Nakrideol. The discovery first caused me to suspect that there might, perhaps, be another hitherto undiscovered field higher up the valley, but I afterwards ascertained that it had in all probability been brought from Patrapara, as a priest in the neighbourhood was in the habit of using coal, brought from thence, in his religious ceremonies. At Nakrideol, in a very ancient mango-grove, I shot a number of rare and beautiful birds, including a trogon (*Harpactes fasciatus*, Gmel.), only one specimen of which had ever been previously obtained so far to the north, the regular home of the bird being in the western and southern forests of the Madras Presidency.

January 16th.—Balum to Konchonpur.—To-day I took a shot at a jungle-fowl which rose out of a field at the foot of some hills; as he dropped wounded among the bushes, I ran forward to intercept him, and suddenly found myself within about thirty yards of a leopard which had apparently not been much disturbed by the shot, but proceeded to run off as he caught sight of me. There being no time to put in a bullet I rather imprudently let him have the charge of shot. He fortunately did not resent this, but disappeared in the cover without giving me another chance.

At this place a man came up to the camp who many years previously had been wounded by a bear. A more horrible disfigurement of the face I have never seen—one eye, the nose, and the front-teeth, had been torn away. It is said that bears when attacking more commonly injure the face than any other part of the body. Several other villagers here shewed me old wounds which had been caused by bears.

January 17th.—Konchonpur to Megpal.—While waiting at Megpal for the arrival of the camp, I occupied myself in watching a number of red ants (*Formica smaragdina*, Fabr.) which were scampering about among some rocks. What I at first supposed to be one of them had the abdominal portion somewhat shorter, and carried it higher than the others; a little closer examination shewed it was a spider—a veritable wolf in sheep's clothing. Even its way of running resembled that of the ants. Although I have in previous pages alluded to several cases of close imitation or mimicry in structure between very different animals, I have certainly never met with a more remarkable instance than this. I unfortunately lost this specimen, as it spun a thread, dropped from my hand, and disappeared amongst leaves. I have never since been able to find another like it, and I do not know whether it has ever been described or named.

Two days after this I reached the station of Sambalpur, where I was glad to meet with friends after my two months spent in the tributary States of Orissa.

January 23rd.—Sambalpur to Tabla.—I found the climate of Sambalpur very pleasant after the damp heat of Orissa; but ere long I had my usual attack of fever, which crippled me for some little time. The country which I was about to examine, in continuation of last year's work, lay to the north of Sambalpur, and east of the Ebe river. The inhabitants in this tract belonged to a great variety of different races, including Kultas, Bhumias, Gores or Gonds, Pabs, &c. At one place called Kudderbuga I was entertained by the villagers with a kind of pantomime. There were two young and good-looking boys, gorgeously appareled, who sang and danced very cleverly. Then there were various characters, such as the Raja with a huge wooden mask, the comic man, the fakir and his son, and other miscellaneous personages.

Tanks and jheels in this tract often afforded me some shooting, ducks, teal, and snipe, being occasionally met with. On the dry uplands two species of sand-grouse (*Pterocles*) were sometimes to be found, but they were not very abundant, being scarcely more than stragglers. In the sandy and rocky tracts of Western India they sometimes occur in vast flocks. I revisited Laikera, the place where I last year shot the gaur or bison, but could not find any more, nor did the buffaloes then appear to be any longer in that part of the country; the only animal which I shot was a nilgai which hardly rewarded me for so long a journey.

February 25th.—Bulwaspur to Sambalpur.—To-day I returned to Sambalpur, and, after a day's rest, marched south-westwards along the southern bank of the river, in order to make a preliminary examination of a series of rocks which occur there, and are intermediate in age between the coal-measures and the crystalline or metamorphic rocks. This series consists of sandstones, shales, and limestones, which, though unfortunately not containing fossils, may safely be identified with a portion of the great Vindhyan formation which occupies a large area in North-Western India. As I shall presently describe, the series includes some diamond-bearing strata.

From day to day I marched westwards along a narrow belt of flat ground intervening between the foot of the Barapahar hills, which are formed of these rocks, and the southern bank of the Mahanadi. Near the village of Kurumkel I shot two specimens of a very rare bird, the spotted creeper (*Salpornis spilonota*, Frankl.), which I had only once obtained in Chutia Nagpur. Ten years ago there were only two or three specimens of this bird in collections: of late years it has been found in several different parts of India; but it is still a treasure for the ornithologist.

March 11th.—Pudampur.—I had now forded the Mahanadi and crossed to Pudampur, on the northern bank, from whence I purposed returning eastwards. To-day when passing through the village of Labanatand, a sort of standing camp or depôt of the Labanos or Brinjaras, I was at once struck by the peculiar costumes and brilliant clothing of these Indian gipsies. They immediately recalled to my memory the appearance of the Zingari of the lower Danube and Wallachia.* In about two minutes I was surrounded by all the women of the place, who commenced to chaunt and escort me across the fields. This attention, however, I declined, as I was at work and did not care for their company, and they retired, somewhat crestfallen at my repelling them. Afterwards, however, in the evening two parties about thirty strong each, came to the camp and sang for an hour or so in the peculiarly melancholy minor key which characterises all the music of these people which I have heard.

---

* I was informed by a Russian Prince who travelled in India in 1874, that one of his companions, a Hungarian nobleman, found himself able to converse with the Brinjaras of Central India, in consequence of his knowledge of the Zingari language.

Later on, after I had returned from a cruise among the rocky islets of the Mahanadi, where I shot several birds which I had not met with before—further detachments, not only of Brinjaras, but also of other tribes, performed their respective dances and songs, so that the amount of *largesse* which I had to expend amounted to a considerable sum.

March 12th.—Pudampur to Kudibuga.—To-day I passed through another Brinjara hamlet, from whence the women and girls all hurried out in pursuit, and a brazen-faced powerful-looking lass seized the bridle of my horse as he was being led by the sayce in the rear. The sayce and chuprasi were both Mahomedans, and the forward conduct of these females perplexed them not a little, and the former was fast losing his temper at being thus assaulted by a woman; *nolens volens* they wished to persuade me to stop to listen to their singing again, but the previous day's performance had been quite sufficient for me.

From the Dewan of Kudibuga, whom I mentioned in the last chapter, I heard that according to tradition the Bairias, Chirus, and Bhils, were the earliest inhabitants in this part of the country, and that there are remains of old forts made by some of them. A few small colonies of these tribes still remain. The Kultas, who form a large section of the inhabitants, say they first came from Ajudiah or Oude. The Dewan also told me that the strong-minded Brinjara women are in the habit of inflicting severe chastisement on their husbands with very large sticks (*bara bara lathi*). A similar custom prevails in the Nicobar Islands. This fact, I find, I have omitted to mention when writing of the Nicobarese in Chapter V.; but I may, perhaps, though it is somewhat out of place, here quote Dr. Rink's remarks on the subject. Speaking of the women, he says:—"I have reason to believe they even occasionally exercise palpable authority over the men, and that a closer view of their matrimonial life would shew that the respect of these people towards the fair sex did not, strictly speaking, originate in the free-will of the men, and is not, therefore, to be considered a virtue."

A week after this I had completed the work of examination of the rocks in the valley of the Mahanadi, so far as time had admitted, and it was now necessary for me to march back to Orissa, where there was still much to be accomplished before my season's operations would be completed. But before passing away from Sambalpur I shall give an account of what I have been able to ascertain regarding the occurrence of diamonds in Sambalpur, together with a sketch of such historical notices on the subject as I have been able to trace. Already this account has in substance been published elsewhere,* but as diamonds have always an interest for the general reader I believe that I do not err in reproducing it here.

In Rennell's "Memoir on a Map of Hindustan," † the following passage occurs:—"On the west of Boad and near the Mahanuddy river, Mr. Thomas passed a town of the name of Beiragurh, which I take to be the place noted in the Ayin Acbaree as having a diamond mine in its neighbourhood. There is indeed, a mine of more modern date in the vicinity of Sambalpur; but this whole quarter must from very early times have been famous for producing diamonds. Ptolemy's *Adamas* river answers perfectly to the Mahanuddy, and the district of *Sabaræ*, on its banks, is said to abound in diamonds. Although this geographer's map of India is so exceedingly faulty in the general form of the whole tract, yet several parts of it are descriptive."

With reference to Beiragurh I can find no place of that name in Sambalpur, and the late Mr. Blochmann, to whom I referred the matter, informed me that the Beiragurh mentioned in the Ain Akbari is there stated to be in the *Subah* Berar, and was therefore probably not identical with the place mentioned by Mr. Thomas, according to Col. Rennell. In Ptolemy's map ‡ the Adamas flus flows into the Gangeticus sinus (Bay of Bengal),

---

* "Records of the Geological Survey of India." No. 4, 1877.

† "London," 1792, p. 240.

‡ Asiæ x. tab. "Geographiæ libri Octo, Gr. et Lat. Opera P. Bertii Lugduni." Bat. 1618. Fol.

mid-way between Cosamba (Balasore?) on the north and Cocala (Sicacole of Arrowsmith's map, the modern Chicacole). The Dosaron and Tyndis rivers probably represent the Godavari and Kistna, so that it is very likely that the Adamus may safely be identified with the Mahanadi. Ptolemy represented the Adamas as flowing through the district of Sabaræ, across which runs the following description:—"*Apud quos adamas est in copia*," which is otherwise given in an earlier edition of the map,* "*Sabaræ i his habundat adamas.*" Both sentences read strangely from a classical point of view, but mean that in Sabaræ the diamond occurs in abundance. The upper portion of the river passes through a district named Cocconage, which would include Chutia Nagpur. There are good reasons for believing that diamonds were found in Chutia Nagpur also. The following notices on the subject I quote from a paper by the late Mr. Blochmann †:—"Kokrah (the ancient name of Chutia Nagpur) was known at the Mughul court for its diamonds, and it is evidently this circumstance which led the generals of Akbar and Jahangiri to invade the district. I have found two notices of Kokrah in the Akbarnamah, and one in the Tuzuk-i-Jahangiri, from which it appears that Chutia Nagpur was ruled over in 1585 by Madhu Singh, who in that year became tributary to Akbar. He was still alive in A.D. 1591, when he served under Man Singh in the Imperial Army which invaded Orissa. Tuzuk-i-Jahangiri (p. 155):—'On the 3rd Isfandiarmuz of the 10th year of my reign (A.D. 1616) it was reported to me (Jahangiri) that Ibrahim Khan (Governor of Bihar) had over-run Kokrah and taken possession of its diamond-washings. This district belongs to *Subah* Bihar, and the river which flows through it yields the diamonds. When the river contains little water, tumuli and hollows are formed. The diamond diggers know from experience that

* Tab. X. "Cosmographiæ," libri VIII. Lat. Justi de Albano, Ulmae. 1486. Fol.

† "Journal Asiatic Society of Bengal." Vol. XL.

chiefly those tumuli contain diamonds over which insects hover, called by the Hindus *Jhingah.* They pile up stones on all sides of the tumuli, and then cut into them with hatchets and chisels and collect the diamonds from among the sand and stones. Sometimes diamonds are found of the value of a lac of rupees each. The district and the diamond river are in the possession of the Zamindar Durjan Sal. The governors of Bihar frequently sent detachments into Kokrah; but as the roads are fortified and the jungles impenetrable, the governors were generally satisfied with a tribute of two or three diamonds. When I appointed Ibrahim Khan Governor of Bihar, *vice* Zafar Khan, I told him at the time of departure to invade the district and drive away the unknown petty Raja. No sooner had Ibrahim entered on his office than he prepared himself to invade Kokrah. The Raja, according to custom, sent a few diamonds and elephants; but Ibrahim was dissatisfied, and invaded the district before the Raja could collect his men. When he received news of the invasion he was already besieged in the pass where he used to reside. Some of Ibrahim's men who had been sent out to look for him, found him with several persons, among them his mother, another wife of his father, and one of his brothers, concealed in a cave. They were deprived of the diamonds in their possession. Twenty-three elephants besides were taken. * * * The district is now subject to me. All diamonds found in the river are forwarded to court. Only a few days ago a diamond arrived which had a value of 50,000 rupees, and I hope many more will be added to my store of jewels.' The diamond river alluded to is the Sunk." To the present day a spot in the Sunk river* is pointed out by the inhabitants as the place where the diamonds were washed for.

Mr. Blochmann also gives a quotation from a history of the

---

* The geological structure of the valley of the Sunk river is at present very imperfectly known, and it remains to be seen whether the rocks resemble those of Sambalpur.

Maharajahs of Chutia Nagpur, in which is described a method of testing diamonds for flaws by affixing them to the horns of fighting rams, and states that, "Jahangiri says the diamonds which Ibrahim Khan had brought from Kokrah had been given to the grinders, 'They were now submitted to me, and among them is one which looks like a sapphire. I have never seen a diamond of such a colour. It weighs several *rattis*, and my lapidaries fix its value at 3,000 rupees, though they would give 20,000 for it if it were quite white and stood the full test.'"

Colonel Dalton (Ethnology of Bengal, p. 163n), states that the Raja of Chutia Nagpur's family still possesses a diamond valued at 40,000 rupees, from these now fabulous mines. As illustrating the methods by which English officials in the olden time shook the pagoda tree, the following will be read with interest. In the year 1772 the Raja appeared before Captain Camar, commanding a force in Palamow, and after exchange of turbans acknowledged himself as a vassal of the Company. "In regard to this exchange of turbans," writes Colonel Dalton, "the family annals tell a strange tale. In the Raja's turban were some very valuable diamonds, which, it is insinuated, had excited the cupidity of Captain Camar. The proposal for the exchange emanated, it is said, from him. He declared it was the English method of swearing eternal friendship, but the Captain had no diamonds in his head-dress, and the Raja evidently concluded that he had been rather 'done' by the Company's officer."

In comparatively recent times, so far as I have been able to ascertain, the first published notice on the subject of Sambalpur diamonds is to be found in the narrative of a journey which was undertaken by Mr. Motte in the year 1766.* The object of this journey was to initiate a regular trade in diamonds with Sambalpur, Lord Clive being desirous of employing them as a convenient means of remitting money to England. His attention had been drawn to Sambalpur by the fact that the Raja had, a few months

* "Asiatic Annual Register," London, 1799.

previously, sent a messenger with a rough diamond, weighing 16½ carats, as a sample, together with an invitation to the Governor to depute a trustworthy person to purchase diamonds regularly. The Governor proposed to Mr. Motte to make the speculation a joint concern, "In which," writes the latter, "I was to hold a third; he the other two: all the expenses to be borne by the concern. The proposal dazzled me, and I caught at it, without reflecting on the difficulties of the march, or on the barbarity of the country, &c."

In spite of his life being several times in danger from attacks by the natives, the loss of some of his followers by fever, and a varied chapter of other disasters, Mr. Motte was enabled to collect a considerable amount of interesting information about the country. Owing to the disturbed state of Sambalpur town, however, he was only able to purchase a few diamonds. After much prolonged negotiation, he was permitted to visit the junction of the Rivers Hebe (Ebe) and Mahanadi, where the diamonds were said to be found. A servant of the Raja's, who was in charge there, informed him that "it was his business to search in the River Hebe, after the rains, for red earth, washed down from the mountains, in which earth diamonds were always found. I asked him if it would not be better to go to the mountains and dig for that earth. He answered that it had been done, until the Mahrattas exacted a tribute from the country; and to do so now would only increase that tribute. He showed me several heaps of the red earth—some pieces of the size of small pebbles, and so on, till it resembles coarse brick-dust—which had been washed, and the diamonds taken out."*

The next mention of Sambalpur diamonds is to be found in Lieutenant Kittoe's account† of his journey, in the year 1838,

---

* This description suggests laterite as the matrix from which the diamonds were proximately derived. In this connection it may be noted that one of the principal sources of Cape diamonds is said to be a superficial ferruginous conglomerate.

† "Journal Asiatic Society, Bengal." Vol. VIII., 1839, p. 375.

through the forests of Orissa. He speaks of the people as being too apathetic and indolent to search for diamonds. His remarks on the localities where they occur seem to be derived from Mr. Motte's account, to which, indeed, he refers.

Although published in the same number of the Asiatic Society's Journal * we find a paper, dated two years later, or 1840, which was written by Major Ouseley, on the "Process of Washing for Gold-dust and Diamonds at Heera Khoond." In this we meet the following statement:—"The Heera Khoond is that part of the river which runs south of the islands. The diamonds and gold-dust are to be washed down the Ebe River, about four miles above the Heera Khoond; but as both are procurable as far as Sonpur, I am inclined to think there may be veins of gold along the Mahanadi." No mention is made by Major Ouseley of the system of throwing an embankment across one of the channels, which is described below; but from my enquiries I gathered that that method of washing was in practice for many years before the period of Major Ouseley's visit. He describes the operations of individual washers—not the combined efforts of the large number, which made that washing successful. The diamonds found became the property of the Raja, while the gold was the perquisite of the washers, who sold it for from twelve to fifteen rupees a *tola.*

In the *Central Provinces Gazetteer* it is stated that "during the period of native rule some fifteen or twenty villages were granted rent-free to a class called *Jhiras*, in consideration of their undertaking the search for diamonds. When the country lapsed in 1850, these villages were resumed." So far as can be gathered from the various sources of information, large and valuable diamonds have been occasionally met with; but the evidence on this point is somewhat conflicting. I do not think, however, that what we know is altogether consistent with the statement in the *Gazetteer*, that "the best stones ever found here were thin and flat, with flaws in them."

---

* "Journal Asiatic Society, Bengal." Vol. VIII., p. 1057.

Local tradition speaks of one large diamond, which was found during the Mahratta occupation. Its size made its discovery too notorious; otherwise it would in all probability, like many other smaller ones, found at that time, never have reached the hands of the Mahratta agent. It is said to have weighed two tolas and two mashas (at ten mashas to the tola),* which would be about 316·2 grains troy, or expressed in carats 99·3. It would be impossible, of course, to make any estimate of the value of a rough stone of this size, regarding the purity, colour, &c., of which nothing is known. Another diamond, in the possession of Narain Singh, is said to have weighed about a *tola*, the equivalent of which, calculated as above, would be 45·35 carats. Already one of 16·5 carats has been mentioned as having been sent to Calcutta in 1766. One large, but slightly flawed, diamond, which I saw in the possession of a native in Sambalpur, was valued in Calcutta, after cutting, at Rs. 2,500. Mr. Emanuel, in his work on "Diamonds and Precious Stones," gives some particulars regarding the diamonds of Sambalpur, but the limited information at his disposal does not appear to have been very accurate. He records one diamond of 84 grains having been found within the period of British rule, but does not mention his authority. There are said to be a good many diamonds still in the hands of the wealthier natives in Sambalpur. Of course, large diamonds such as those above mentioned were of exceptional occurrence; those ordinarily found are said to have weighed, however, two to four *rattis*, equal on an average, say, to the thirtieth part of a tola, or 4·7 grains = 1·48 carats. In the Geological Museum at Calcutta there is at present a diamond which was sent to the Asiatic Society of Bengal from Sambalpur by Major Ouseley. It weighs only ·855 grain = ·26 carat.

As is usual, I believe, in all parts of India, the diamonds were classed as follows:—

I.—*Brahman.*—White, pure water. II.—*Kshatrya.*—Rose or

* (One masha = 14·37 grains troy): properly speaking there are 12 mashas in a standard tola.

reddish. III.—*Vasiya.*—Smoky. IV.—*Sudra.*—Dark and impure.

From personal enquiry from the oldest of the Jhiras, or washers, at the village of Jhunan, and from various other sources, I have gathered the following details as to the manner in which the operations were carried on in the Raja's time:—In the centre of the Mahanadi, near Jhunan, there is an island, called Hira Khund,* which is about four miles long, and for that distance separates the waters of the river into two channels. In each year, about the beginning of March or even later, when other work was slack and the level of the water was approaching its lowest, a large number of people,—according to some of my informants, as many as five thousand,—assembled and raised an embankment across the mouth of the northern channel, its share of water being thus deflected into the southern. In the stagnant pools left in the former, sufficient water remained to enable the washers to wash the gravel accumulated between the rocks in their rude wooden trays and cradles. Upon women seems to have fallen the chief burden of the actual washing, while the men collected the stuff. The implements employed and the method of washing were similar to those commonly adopted in gold-washing, save only that the finer gravel was not thrown away until it had been thoroughly searched for diamonds. Whatever gold was found became the property of the washer, as already stated. Those who were so fortunate as to find a valuable stone were rewarded by being given a village. According to some accounts, the washers generally held their villages and lands rent-free; but I think it most unlikely that all who were engaged in the operations should have done so. So far as I could gather, the people did not regard their (in a manner) enforced services as involving any great hardship; they gave me to understand that they would be glad to see the annual search re-established on the old terms. Indeed, it is barely possible to conceive of the

* *Lit.* Diamond mine.

condition of the Jhiras having been at any time worse than it is at present. No doubt the gambling element, which may be said to have been ever present in work of the above nature, commended it to the native mind. According to Mr. Emanuel, these people shew traces of Negro blood, and hence he has concluded that they are the "descendants of slaves imported by one of the conquerors of India." They are, however, I should say, an aboriginal tribe, shewing neither in their complexions, character of their features, nor hair, the slightest trace of a Negro origin. And here I may note that a statement made recently by Professor Flower * to the effect that "The presence of a Negrito element in the population of India is based at present on very slender evidence," is wholly confirmed by the results of my observations in those tracts of the country which I have visited. I have never in India met with any race having the slightest resemblance to the Andamanese or to the Somali. Some writers who have suggested a Negrito or Negroid element in people whom they have described, appear to have given undue weight to the presence of a black skin, coupled with thick lips, and depressed and broad nostrils, all of which may occur in races quite distinct from each other and from the Negritos.

When Sambalpur was taken over by the British, in 1850, the Government offered to lease out the right to seek for diamonds, and in 1856 a notification appeared in the Gazette describing the prospect in somewhat glowing terms. For a short time the lease was held by a European, at the apparently low rate of two hundred rupees per annum; but as it was given up voluntarily, it may be concluded that the lessee did not make it pay. The facts that the Government resumed possession of the rent-free villages, while the Raja's operations had been carried on without any original outlay, materially altered the case, and rendered the employment of a considerable amount of capital then, as it would be now, an absolute necessity.

---

* Hunterian Lectures delivered at the Royal College of Surgeons, on the Comparative Anatomy of Man. *Vide* "Nature," July 10, 1879, p. 246.

Within the past few years statements have gone the round of the Indian papers to the effect that diamonds are now occasionally found by the gold-washers of Sambalpur. All my enquiries failed to elicit a single authentic case, and the gold-washers I spoke to and saw at work assured me that such statements were unfounded. Moreover, they did not appear to expect to find any, as I observed that they did not even examine the gravel when washing.

With regard to the origin of the diamonds, the geological structure of the country leaves but little room for doubt as to the source from whence they are derived. Coincident with their occurrence is that of a group of rocks, which has been shown to be referable to the Vindhyan series, certain members of which series are found in the vicinity of all the known diamond-yielding localities in India, and in the cases of actual rock-workings, are found to constitute the original matrix of the gems.

In several of the previous accounts, the belief is either stated or implied that the diamonds are brought into the Mahanadi by its large tributary the Ebe. It would not, of course, help the point I am endeavouring to establish to say that the Ebe, at least within our area, except indirectly,* is not fed by waters which pass over Vindhyan rocks, but I have the positive assurance of the natives that diamonds have not been found in that river, although gold is and has been regularly washed for. On the other hand, diamonds have been found in the bed of the Mahanadi as far west as Chanderpur, and at other intermediate places, well within the area which is exclusively occupied by the quartzites, shales, and limestones of Vindhyan age.

The fact that the place, Hira Khund, where the diamonds were

---

* By a few small streams which rise in an isolated outlying hill, called Gotwaki. It should be stated, however, that one of the tributaries of the Ebe, the Icha, far away in Gangpur, is said to produce diamonds; but the statement needs confirmation, and the geology of that part of the country is at present quite unknown. Near its sources, in Chutia Nagpur, I have heard the Ebe spoken of as the Hira Nad, or Diamond river.

washed, is on metamorphic rocks, may readily be explained by the physical features of the ground. The rocky nature of the bed there, and the double channel caused by the island, afforded unusual facilities for, in the first place, the retention of the diamonds brought down by the river; and, secondly, for the operations by which the bed could on one side be laid bare, and the gravel washed by the simple contrivances known to the natives.

It is impossible to say at present which the actual bed or beds of rock may be from whence the diamonds have been derived, as there is no record or appearance of the rock ever having been worked; but from the general lithological resemblance of the sandstones and shales of the Barapahar hills, and the outlier at Borla, with the diamond-bearing beds, and their associates at Panna in Bhandelkand, and Banaganpilli in Karnul, I have very little hesitation in pointing to these rocks as in all probability including the matrix. Above Pudampur, the Mahanadi runs through rocks of this age, and I should therefore strongly urge upon any one who may hereafter embark upon the undertaking of searching for diamonds in Sambalpur, to confine his operations, in the first instance, to the streams and small rivers which rise in the Barapahar hills and join the Mahanadi on the south. Besides the obvious advantage of being—as I believe would be found to be the case—close to the matrix, these streams would, I think, be found to contain facilities for obtaining a sufficient head of water for washing puposes. Such works would require but a few labourers, and could be carried on for a much longer period every year, say for eight or nine months, than would be possible in the case of the washings in the bed of the Mahanadi itself.

According to the accounts received by me, the southern channel of the Mahanadi used not to be emptied in the Raja's time; but from various causes I should expect it to yield, proportionately, a larger number of diamonds than the northern. In the first place the stronger current in it would be more efficient in removing the substances of less specific gravity than diamonds, while the rocks and deep holes in it afforded admirable means for the retention of the latter. Again, it is in direct contact with the sandstones and shales (presumedly diamond-bearing) of an outlying ridge near a village called Borla. Owing to the greater body of water to be dealt with, it would be found to be more difficult to divert than that which flows in the northern channel; but the result in a greater harvest of diamonds would probably far more than compensate for the greater expenditure incurred.

In the country to the south of Sambalpur, in Karial and Nowagurh, where rocks occur of similar age to those of the Barapahar hills, I have failed to find any traditional record of diamonds having ever been found or searched for. It is just possible, however, that the names of several villages in which the word *Hira* (diamond) occurs, may have reference to some long-forgotten discovery.

In addition to diamonds, pebbles of beryl, topaz, carbuncle, amethyst, cornelian, and clear quartz, used to be collected in the Mahanadi; but I have not seen either sapphires or rubies. It is probable that the matrix of these, or most of them, exists in the metamorphic rocks, and is, therefore, distinct from that of the diamonds.

Gold in all probability occurs pretty generally throughout those portions of the district in which metamorphic rocks prevail. So far as I have been able to gather from personal observation, the washers confine themselves to the beds of the Mahanadi and Ebe; but in the rains they are said to leave the larger rivers and wash in the small jungle-streams.

In the Ebe, below the village of Tahud, I saw a party of gold washers encamped on the sand. The places where they were actually washing were within the area occupied by rocks of Talchir age; but whether the gold was proximately derived from them, or had been brought down by the river, as is possible, from the metamorphic rocks a short distance higher up, I am unable to say.

There is, of course, no *primâ facie* improbability in the Talchir rocks containing gold. On the contrary, the boulder-bed, including as it does a large proportion of materials directly derived from the metamorphic rocks, might naturally be expected to contain gold. In the original description of the Talchir coal-field, the following passage occurs:—"Gold is occasionally washed in the Tikaria river, and was also a few years since obtained from the sands of the Ouli." The latter case is rather interesting, since the localities are in a sandstone country, through which the Ouli mainly flows.* In this connection it may be mentioned that in Australia, quite recently, a conglomerate bed of carboniferous age has been found to be auriferous.†

As to the methods employed by, and the earnings of, the gold-washers, the remarks already made on the gold of Singhbhum apply equally to Sambalpur, and need not be repeated here.

March 30th.—Rampur.—To-day I reached Rampur, the chief town of Rehrakole, having taken nine days by a somewhat circuitous route to accomplish the distance. I found a condition of anarchy prevailing in the State, and supplies and even guides were only obtained with the greatest difficulty, while the coolies who were employed would deposit their loads in the middle of the jungle and decamp. There is a deficiency of good drinking water on this route, and three days later, or on the 2nd of April, I had a sharp attack of fever, which I felt sure was due to the bad water I had drunk at night in consequence of thirst, brought on by the great heat at this season. Owing to this attack I was obliged to halt for some days in the bungalow, at Ungul, which, since my previous visit, had reverted to its legitimate purpose as a rest-house for travellers.

April 10th.—Daiserah.—At this place, in the neighbourhood of the basin of sandstones, in the Athgurh State, which I had still to examine, I dismissed the carts which had been with me for the past five months, and forwarded my heavy baggage to Cuttack, a dozen coolies being retained to carry such necessaries as could not be packed on the elephants. During the remainder of the month I was engaged in the examination of the sand-

---

* "Mem. Geol. Survey, India." Vol. I., p. 88.

† *Vide* "Geological Magazine," 1877, p. 286.

stones, both in order to determine their actual geological age, and to ascertain what probability there was of their overlying and concealing a deposit of coal-measures. Owing to the dense, thorny, and practically impenetrable thickets which cover the area, this work was not accomplished without much difficulty, which was further increased by a return of the fever. I can look back with no pleasure to the three weeks so spent. The heat at night was most trying and enervating, and it was difficult to obtain an adequate amount of sleep, and when to this I add that the people I had to deal with were Urias of the degraded type I have previously described, it is unnecessary perhaps to enlarge further upon the subject.

April 29th.—Mundasol to Khurda.—This morning I rode into Khurda, which is a sub-divisional station subordinate to Cuttack. The afternoon was devoted to the examination of some hills of garnetiferous gneiss in the neighbourhood, and the massive ruins of the fort and dwelling-place of the Khurda Rajas. On the following morning I rode out with the Settlement Officer to visit a hot-spring at a place called Atari, about seven miles distant. We found that the water rose in the centre of a rice-field, no rocks being visible in the vicinity. The discharge of water, which is caught in an artificial basin, is copious, and with it a quantity of sulphuretted hydrogen is given off. The temperature was 138°, or too hot to permit of the hand being retained in the water. Annually, at a particular festival, the spring is visited by numbers of people, and I was informed that scrambles for betel-nuts, thrown by priests into the mud, through which the overflow-water of the basin trickles, are a leading feature. The scramblers are principally barren women, and those among them who succeed in finding a betel-nut will, it is believed, have their desire for children gratified ere long.

At this time preparations were being initiated for making a cadastral survey of the Khurda estate on the scale of thirty-two inches to a mile. In the maps it was intended to represent every field and small plot of cultivation, and it was believed that the settlement of boundaries would prove to be a check to litigation in the future. So far as I could form an opinion the survey was of too costly a nature for the country, and out of all proportion to the annual revenue of the estate, which is wholly in the hands of the Government.

May 1st.—Mundasol to Jagamura.—To-day I visited the Gumpas, or cave-temples of Khundagiri, which have been described and illustrated in various works of late years, more particularly in Dr. Hunter's "Orissa," Mr. Fergusson's "History of Indian Architecture," and Dr. Rajendra Lal Mitra's "Antiquities of Orissa." Their age is not yet quite satisfactorily determined. Knowing that they had been carefully explored by experts, I did not make more than a cursory examination of them, giving my attention rather to the rocks, in which I hoped to find some fossils, but was unfortunately not successful.

On the following morning I visited Bobaneshwar, which is famous for the number of its temples, some of which are in good preservation, and are covered with well-executed carvings. The principal temple is enclosed, and not accessible to Europeans, but most of the others can be entered, and indeed many are suffering much from neglect. Great complaints were made to me by a Brahmin, who acted as my guide, of the maladministration of the funds intended for the preservation of the temples. In not a few cases trees of the Pipal, &c., have taken root amongst the carvings, and have caused steadily-widening fissures and cracks. All the temples which I saw were built of the local sandstone—laterite being employed only for walls, revetments of tanks, &c. Carvings of an indecent character are less common than is often the case on the temples of southern India, and those which do exist are generally in out-of-the-way niches, and are not given a prominent position.

May 5th.—Chundkar to Cuttack.—To-day I marched into Cuttack, having completed my season's work, intending to proceed at once to Calcutta, to enjoy a much wished-for season of rest, quiet, and iced beverages; but my experience on this occasion only served to further justify the remark I made in the last chapter as to Cuttack being a very difficult place to get out of once you have got into it. Two night-journeys on the 9th and 10th, with a halt during the heat of the day at Kendapara, which is a sub-divisional station about mid-way, brought me to Chandballi, a newly-opened port on the Dhumra River, one of the mouths of the Brahmini. The journey from thence to Calcutta, when the tides suit, can be made within twelve hours, and I expected to be in Calcutta by the following morning; but on arrival at Chandballi, I heard that the steamer had broken down, and that it would not be on the line for another week, so that I was perplexed as to how I should occupy the time. While considering whether it would be worth my while to pay a visit to Balasore, which was seventy-five miles distant, the arrival of a party of officers from Calcutta, who purposed spending some days encamped at a place called Chandipal, near the mouth of the river, turned my attention in that direction, so that I joined them, and though our morning and evening rambles in the *Tamarix* jungle, in search of game, did not result in a very large bag, still some few head of spotted deer, &c., were killed, and we managed in spite of the great heat to spend a pleasant week together. At last, on the 18th, the steamer from Calcutta, with an enormous cargo of betel-nuts and some piece-goods and metal, appeared, and having filled up with rice and deck-passengers, which are the principal articles of export from Chandballi, left again for Calcutta, where we arrived on the evening of the 19th.

CHAPTER XII.

SECTION II.

NAINI TAL.

1876-77.*

NAINI TAL AND ALMORAH—LUCKNOW—FAKIRS OR ASCETICS—URDU LITERATURE—PATNA—RICE GOLAH—SECOND VISIT TO NAINI TAL—ACCIDENT ON THE ROAD—MONKEYS AT MALWA TAL—MR. WATERTON ON MONKEYS—LEOPARD KILLED IN TRAP—SPORT AT BHIM TAL—POSITION OF THE KUMAON LAKES—NAINI TAL—BHIM TAL—MALWA TAL—NAUKACHIA TAL—SAT TAL—CONCLUSIONS.

In July, 1876, I took a month's leave in order to pay a visit to Naini Tal, in the Himalayas. While there, and also during a short trip which I made from thence to Almorah, I familiarized myself with the general geological features of the area, and availed of the opportunity of making a small collection of birds, which I supplemented by purchases from the local dealers, from whom also I obtained a series of heads and horns of the principal Himalayan mammals.

On the return journey, down-country, I stopped for a day at Lucknow, where I visited all the principal show places of that historic city; but these I do not propose to describe here. The buildings, being chiefly of brick and stucco, are not to be compared with the magnificent stone structures of Delhi and Agra. The great beauty of the place, which has been called the "Garden of India," is derived from the luxuriance of the vegetation

---

* For convenience the accounts of two separate visits to Naini Tal are combined in this chapter.

and the abundance of flowers. In and near the city I noticed several Fakirs or ascetics, who appeared to be objects of considerable adoration. One of them reclined on a heap of kunkur, which forms a couch about as luxurious as would be one made of engine-house clinker. Were it not probable that the bodies of these men have from exposure become almost devoid of feeling, such mortification of the flesh could hardly be endurable. Such ascetics, and those who allow their elevated arms to stiffen and wither, are seldom seen in Bengal—at least, such is my experience. Many early and some recent accounts of India have had the effect of causing the English public to believe that one meets with them, and also with cars of Jugernath, &c., all over the country and at every turn; but such is not the case at the present day, at least.

In the streets of Lucknow I bought several lithographed books in the Urdu language. One of these was copiously illustrated with a number of quaint pictures of mythical animals; it was, in fact, a sort of native zoology. The descriptions are not very explicit, nor are local habitations for the various monsters assigned; but many of them can evidently be identified with the chimerical animals of Arab literature. Thus there is a representation of Sindbad's roc; of the men with dog's heads, by whom the Andamanese were intended; and of the unicorn, besides many others of similar character, and some which were, perhaps, solely the creation of the author's pencil. The whole work reminded me of Aldrovandius' celebrated volume—"Concerning monsters."

At Patna, where I also stopped for a day, there is a lofty brick golah, or receptacle for grain, which bears some resemblance to a glass-factory cupola. It was erected, in 1786, to serve as a storehouse for grain, in order to prevent the recurrence of famines, or, more correctly perhaps, to mitigate their effects. On a tablet which states this, there is a blank left for the name of the person who might first fill the golah with grain; but neither blank nor golah were ever filled. As the door at the base opens inwards it would have been impossible to have opened it had the interior ever been filled with grain. Inside there is a most extraordinary echo. If you stand in the centre, your words, and even the noise of your footsteps, come back with a wonderful celerity and exactitude, the return wave of sound seeming actually to strike you on the top of the head. I could not for some little time believe but that there was some one mimicking me; and, indeed, at first I turned sharply round on the custodian of the place to rebuke him for what I conceived to be his impertinence. I could not help contrasting the echo in this building with that in the Taj at Agra. While the latter has a wonderfully mellowing and softening effect, the former produces a harsh and particularly unpleasant sound.

In September, 1877, I spent a week at Simla, and then went to Naini Tal for a second visit, where it was my intention to examine the Kumaon lakes, and, if possible, discover their origin. As it would have taken about three weeks' hard marching to reach Naini Tal from Simla through the hills, I was obliged to descend again into the heat of the plains to Umbala, from whence I went to Moradabad by train, and thence drove to the foot of the hills at Kaladungi; but this last part of the journey was not effected without the occurrence of an accident, which, though only causing inconvenience, might have been more serious. At about 4 a.m., just after leaving a changing station, I was disturbed by the rolling from side to side of the dâk ghari or sleeping carriage. Supposing, however, that a pair of bullocks or buffaloes had been yoked to the carriage, as is sometimes done, in order to draw it through the boulder-strewn bed of a river, I lay quite still. After one or two more lurches, however, the carriage went over on its side with a crash. As soon as I was able to disentangle myself from the *débris* and climb out by the window, I found that what had actually taken place was, that a pair of utterly-untrained ponies had, soon after starting, completely broken away from the control of the coachman, and had drawn the carriage off the embanked road down into a ravine, where the collapse took place. The carriage was extracted and placed on the road again with no little trouble; and I then found that I had been wounded in the foot by a splinter of wood. My servant had been flung off the top of the vehicle, but, though he lighted on his chin, sustained no serious injury. Having at length reached Kaladungi, I had an opportunity of seeing how these natives love one another, when the two local agents of other carrying firms came to me to beg me to send in a complaint against the one which had supplied my carriage with such dangerous ponies. The agent of the latter, however, was, I believe, ready to refund my fare had I asked for it. One of the former amused me by the persistence of his efforts to make me cause trouble to the opposition. He actually laid paper, pens, and ink before me in order that I might send in a formal complaint to the magistrate. Perhaps I ought to have done so on account of others, especially ladies, who might have to travel by the same route.

I remained at or near Naini Tal for nearly four weeks, during which time I visited most of the lakes and made the observations recorded below, and which I have thought may be of sufficient interest to some of my readers for reproduction here. Others will, no doubt, make use of the privilege of skipping, which, in all probability, they have already exercised with reference to other matters discussed in these pages. I make no attempt to describe the social life of Naini Tal, as that is a topic outside the limits which I have prescribed for myself.

When at Malwa Tal, which is one of the lakes where I spent a day, I was warned that in passing under a landslip which slopes down to the lake, I should be liable to have stones thrown at me by monkeys. Regarding this as being possibly a traveller's tale, I made a particular point of going to the spot in order to see what could have given rise to it. As I approached the base of the landslip near the road on the north side of the lake I saw a number of brown monkeys (*Inuus rhesus*) rush to the sides and across the top of the slip, and presently pieces of loosened stone and shale came tumbling down near where I stood. I fully satisfied myself that this was not merely accidental; for I distinctly saw one monkey industriously, with both fore-paws, and with obvious *malice prepense*, pushing the loose shingle off a shoulder of rock.

I then tried the effect of throwing stones at them, and this made them quite angry, and the number of fragments which they set rolling was speedily doubled. This, though it does not actually amount to throwing or projecting an object by monkeys as a means of offence, comes very near to the same thing, and makes me think that there may be truth in the stories of their throwing fruit at people from trees; but, be this as it may, the late Mr. Waterton's generalized statement that the act of throwing things does not exist in any animal except in man, whose reasoning faculties enable him to repeat the feat,* is certainly not correct, as I have, in Chapter VII., related that I have seen recently-captured and quite untrained elephants project branches of trees with the object of striking persons out of their reach.

Just before leaving Malwa Tal, when exploring the valley below the lake, I came upon a couple of men who had just taken the body of a remarkably fine leopard out of a trap very similar in character to that which I have described as having seen in the Rajmahal Hills (Chapter VI.). The leopard was very beautifully marked, and measured within half-an-inch of seven feet.

In the fields of Ragi or Murwa (*Eleusine corocana*), near Bhim Tal, quail and black partridge occurred in some abundance about the beginning of October. These, with Kalege pheasants (*Gallophasis albocristatus*), afforded me some very fair sport when not engaged in exploring the hills and lakes.

In so far as the outer and lower ranges of the Himalayas are concerned, the group or series of lakes about to be described† is quite unique. To many out of the thousands who have visited the beautiful part of the country where these lakes are situated the question of their origin must have presented itself.

Of the age of the unfossiliferous metamorphosed schists in which the lakes occur, nothing is certainly known. In the account of

---

* "Natural History Essays," by Charles Waterton, p. 153.

† The following is abstracted from a paper published in the Records of the Geological Survey of India, Part II., 1878.

the Geology of Kumaun and Gurhwal, by Mr. H. B. Medlicott,* will be found such information as exists on the subject. Some casual observations on the geology which bear upon the physical origin of the lakes will be found in their places below; otherwise I have no intention of giving a detailed account of the stratigraphy here.

This series of *Tals* or lakes is included in the Chhakata purguna of Kumaun†. They are by no means all of equal size or importance. They seem, however, to fall naturally into three classes, the members of each class having certain features mutually in common. So arranged, they would stand as follows:—

Class I.—Naini, Bhim, Malwa; Class II.—Naukachia, Sat; Class III.—Kurpa, Dhobie, Saria, Sukha, Khoorea, &c.

Naini Tal.—This lake, so call after a Hindu goddess, is situated about ten miles in from the southern slope of the hills. It lies at the bottom of a valley, which runs about north-west to south-east, and is surrounded on all sides, except at the outfall on the south-east, by lofty ridges, which serve to give an unusual amount of definition to the limits of the catchment area. The greatest length of the lake itself is 4,703 feet, the maximum breadth 1,518 feet,‡ and the elevation of the surface at high water about 6,409 feet above the sea. The principal peaks on the encircling ridges are Luria Kanta, 8,144 feet; Sher-ki-danda; Ulma; China, 8,568;§ Deopathar, 7,989; Iarpathar, 7,721.

The China (Cheena) portion of the ridge, at the head or north-west end of the valley, is steeply scarped above, with an under-cliff much concealed by talus, brought down by landslips. It consists chiefly of shales, with which there are some quartzites, and towards the crest there are limestones, which, so far as is

* *Vide N. W. Provinces Gazetteer*, edited by E. Atkinson, Esq., C.S.

† Excepting Malwa Tal, which is just outside the boundary.

‡ These figures are taken from a small table in the *N. W. Provinces Gazetteer*, article "Kumaun."

§ The highest point is somewhat in excess of this elevation, which is that of the peak nearest to the lake.

clearly seen, may partake either of the nature of beds or veins. Passing thence, round by north to south-east, the ridge is mainly formed of shales and argillaceous schists, which are much contorted and broken; but the prevailing dip is probably to south-west, the beds striking with the direction of the ridge. An obscurely seen trap-dyke seems to observe the same course. To these two facts—the dip of the beds and the existence of the rigid trap axis—the present form of the slope is, I believe, under the influence of subaërial denudation, to be attributed, and not to the friction of a glacier. It is true that there are no "subordinate ridges and spurs," but such is not uncommonly found to be the case where valleys run with the strike between hard beds bounding softer ones, which have been eroded to form the valleys.

Towards the end of the ridge, overhanging the depôt, limestones, which are clearly seen in section to occur as irregular lenticular masses—not as beds—become somewhat abundant. I shall have to refer to them again presently. The range, on the south-west of the valley of which Iarpathar and Deopathar are the culminating peaks, is formed of massive limestones, the bedding of which is generally very obscure. There is also some trap, the combined rocks giving a very rigid and steep outline to the range, which contrasts most strikingly with that on the north.

All the rocks of this basin, whether shales or limestones, are singularly unsuited to the retention of the minor glacial marks; and if glaciation did take place, it may be from this cause that no such traces are now found.

From an inspection of the large-scale map, it is apparent that the head of the valley has very much the form of a 'cirque,' as defined by Mr. Helland,* who argues with considerable force that the cirques of Norway and Greenland are due to glaciers. The Rev. Professor Bonney, on the other hand, describes Alpine cirques, which he believes to be formed by

---

* "Cirques are large spaces excavated from the solid rock, bounded on three sides by an almost semi-cylindrical steep mountain wall, and with a tolerably flat floor."—Quar. Jour. Geol. Soc. Vol. XXXIII. p. 161.

Plate IX.]

NAINI TAL.

(From a Photograph by Saché.)

streamlets pouring down the sides. It has often been remarked how some forms of our Indian alluvia, under the operation of heavy rainfalls, exhibit in miniature many of the forms of denudation and erosion. Among these forms, cirques and cirque valleys are not unfrequently met with. They are invariably due, not to denuding action from above, but to subterranean springs or streams. To a similar cause may, I think, be attributed cirque-like valleys in rocks formed of loose shales and, to some extent, even those where the rocks are limestones.

A section of the bed of the lake indicates a state of things very different from what might have perhaps been anticipated; but, however the lake has been formed, explanations to account for the peculiarity about to be described can be suggested. The soundings from which this section has been plotted have been taken from the Revenue Survey map, on the scale of ten inches to a mile. In some cases the exact character of the bottom is given, but not in all. A knowledge of this character is, no doubt, a great desideratum for the discussion of this question. It would be especially desirable to know the nature of the bottom all across the lake transversely to this line, at the point where the shallowest sounding occurs. As represented in the section, the lake consists of two basins, with the maximum depth nearly centrally situated in each case. They are separated by what appears to be a barrier. If it really be so, then it would lend considerable support to the glacial hypothesis. Indeed, if consisting of rock *in situ*, it would fairly prove the existence of a true rock basin, thus furnishing a strong argument in favour of the glacial origin. Supposing it to be so, the twin basins might be readily explained by the hypothesis that they had been successively excavated by the retreating end of a glacier. Unfortunately, the case is not susceptible of so simple an explanation, as the shallow sounding may be caused, not by a barrier, but by a mere hummock, which, if (as is possible, so far as is certainly known at present) occurring isolated by deep channels from the margins of the lake, would be on the other hand a strong argument against the glacial origin, as such an obstruction must assuredly have been swept away by a glacier capable of scooping out the deeper hollows. Still another view of the nature of the barrier or hummock, be it which it may, is possible. It may be that it is not really formed of rock *in situ*, but is merely the remnant of an ancient landslip.

In the present state of our knowledge, therefore, no certain conclusion can be drawn from it. But the peculiar character of the basin still remains a subject for some speculation, the more particularly so when it is remembered that the operations of the present day must tend steadily to obliterate these features by the deposition of silt in the hollows.

Passing from the lake itself, to examine the nature of the barrier at the outfall, we find that it is formed of a confused mass of *débris*, in which some very large rock masses, some of them ten feet in diameter, occur. Following down the bed of the stream, rock *in situ* is not met with till near the waterfall, or at a level which must be considerably below that of the bottom of the lake where deepest. I had neither the time nor means for actually ascertaining the elevation of the exact point where rock *in situ* is first met with in the stream. But it is an important point to be determined. The result would, I feel confident, completely dispose of any belief in the existence of a rock basin.

It has been suggested that the large blocks of stone are erratics, and that they may have been derived from the limestone at the ridge at the head of the valley (Deopathar). The source of these blocks I believe to be much closer at hand. In great part they have, I think, simply tumbled down from the Iarpathar ridge and its eastern prolongation, where not only is similar rock to be seen *in situ*, but similar detached blocks are found on the slopes; one remarkably fine example being seen in the compound of Welham house. Others, on the other hand, may have fallen from the ridge to the north of the depôt, where the already described lenticular masses of limestone occur. The remainder may, I think, have simply been eroded from their envelopment of shales at, or very close to, the positions where they are now found. Though it is convenient to speak here of these blocks collectively as-limestones, they vary much in character, and some are highly indurated, but only slightly calcareous, mud-stones. From these varying characters it may be possible, hereafter, to trace their origin individually with considerable accuracy. As to the other characters of the *débris* at the outfall, I in vain searched in it for evidence of a glacial origin, and am unable to point to any feature which is inconsistent with the idea of its having been formed by a landslip.

Further down the valley, near Joli, some 3,000 feet or so below Naini Tal, I observed, when on the road to Ranibagh, that the river has cut through an accumulation of boulders and finer *débris* to a depth of 200 feet or so, which at the time seemed to me as possibly of moraine origin. On reading Mr. Campbell's opinion of the same kind of deposit near Kalka, which I have also seen, I fear it would require stronger facts than I am in possession of to prove it other than diluvial. I merely mention it here in order to draw attention to the fact of its existence, with a view to its future examination.

Bhim Tal.*—This lake is situated about six miles, in a direct line, to the east-south-east of Naini Tal. Its elevation is about 4,500 feet above the sea, or 1,900 feet lower than Naini Tal. It lies at the bottom of a valley between two ranges, which strike from north-west to south-east. The northern one is largely made up of greenstone, which I traced from the neighbourhood of Bhuwali, through Bhim Tal, up to Malwa Tal. According to General Strachey's geological map, a continuation of the same outburst extends northwards up to Bhujan on the Kosi. The southern range consists chiefly of quartzites and shales, and rises to a height of 1,300 feet above the lake.

At the entrance to the lake, in the very throat of the gorge, occurs a small hill, about 80 or 100 feet high, which deflects the in-flowing stream, and the existence of which, if it is, as it appears to be, a stable prolongation of a spur, presents a serious

---

* So called after Bhim, Shib, or Mahadeo, to whom there is a temple.

obstacle in the way of a glacial theory. No one can, I think, controvert the opinion that a glacier capable of scooping out the lake could not have passed over, or on one side of, such an obstruction.

The determination of the fact, whether, or to what extent this hill consists of rocks *in situ*, is a point, I believe, of crucial importance in this enquiry. Bearing in mind the vast size of the landslips which take place in this region, no one should hastily venture an opinion on such a point. My examination of the ground was of too cursory a nature to admit of my coming to a final decision.

The maximum dimensions of this lake are, length 5,580 feet, breadth 1,490 feet, and depth 87 feet. It is, therefore, the largest, but the shallowest,* of all the series herein described.

Whether it be a historical fact or not I cannot say; but it is clearly, I think, *a fact* that the present outlet of the lake was not the original one. The waters now only escape through a sluice close to the temple, which is situated about midway on the eastern side; but that originally the water found its way out at the southern end, an inspection of the map alone is almost sufficient to determine.

This southern end is now stopped up by what appears to be the *débris* of a landslip. I was unable to examine the valley below, and the position and elevation of the highest rocks there remain to be determined. At the present outfall, the rocks *in situ* are apparently at a higher level than the bottom of the lake; but this, if it be the case, is a fact of no importance, if my supposition as to the position of the original outfall be correct.

Towards the southern end of the lake, on the eastern side, there is a boulder deposit, which extends along the bank up to a level of perhaps 10 feet above the water. The rounded blocks which it includes were possibly rounded by the waters of the lake when they stood at a higher level, but its appearance suggests a

* Sat Tal being excepted as regards depth.

moraine origin. The most remarkable feature about it, however, is, that it is backed by no high range on the east, so that, if derived from a landslip, the materials must have come from the west, and, of necessity, temporarily filled up a portion of the bed of the lake.

Malwa Tal.—This lake is situated about five miles, in a direct line, to the east of Bhim Tal; it lies in a deep valley, which strikes north-west and south-east, and is traversed by the Kalsa river, a tributary of the Gola.*

The elevations of the parallel bounding ranges on the north-east and south-west average upwards of 3,000 feet above the level of the lake, the height of which above the sea has been approximately estimated at 3,400 feet. The range on the north is formed chiefly of white and purple quartzites, with which there are some slates and shales. The dip of these beds is variable, but north-west at a low angle seems to be the prevailing direction. Much of the higher face of this range is steeply scarped, but landslips abound, and have, to a great extent, concealed the character of the lower portions. The range on the south consists primarily of an axis of greenstone, which stretches continuously hence from the neighbourhood of Bhim Tal. Associated with this greenstone are quartzites and shales, the beds in immediate contact often showing signs of much alteration and induration. Occasionally the effect of the former has been such as to cause the affected beds to assimilate to the character of the greenstone, and to be almost undistinguishable from it by mere examination of the outward lithological structure.

What the exact nature of the physical relations of this greenstone may be has not yet been fully ascertained; but that it does not exist merely as a single simple dyke is amply testified by the fact that branches from it cross the valley at both ends of the lake, and are cut through by the infalling and outfalling streams.

---

* It is perhaps worthy of note that the drainage of all these lakes is into the Gola river.

At the head of the lake is a boulder-bed through which the river cuts to a depth of eight or ten feet. This deposit consists chiefly of subangular fragments of trap and quartzite. At first I was inclined to attribute it to the effects of a retreating moraine. Temporarily this view was supported by the discovery of boulders of granite and gneiss—no *known* source for which exists within the present drainage limits of the Kalsa. It was impossible, however, to overlook the fact that there were no signs of polishing on any of the blocks, and that those which have come furthest (the granite, &c.,) are well-rounded and water-worn. Taking into consideration the professedly general character of the only existing geological map, it would be clearly unsafe to adopt the view that no source for these boulders exists within the watershed; and this the more especially as in the adjoining basin of the Gola on the north the occurrence of gneiss and granite is indicated on the map.

The importance of determining the source from whence these boulders have been derived is sufficiently obvious. If they have not come from within the limits of this catchment basin, then indeed it might be necessary to invoke the aid of an ice cap to account for their transport; but in the meantime it is impossible to assert that this accumulation of boulders at the mouth of the gorge is other than a delta of diluvial origin.

Now as to the character of the lake itself. Its maximum dimensions are:—length 4,480 feet, width 1,833 feet, and depth 127 feet. Unfortunately, as was the case with Bhim Tal, no series of soundings are available, and the form of the basin is, therefore, uncertain. The bounding ranges and their slopes, however, indicate the **V** (river) rather than the **U** (glacial) type of valley denudation.

Looking up the lake towards the course of the stream, the view just beyond the gorge is quite shut out by projecting spurs, which a glacier could have scarcely failed to modify, if not remove. At the outfall, no rocks are seen *in situ*. The barrier, now modified by a sluice, appears to be mainly formed of debris thrown down by landslips. The first rock which I detected *in situ* in the bed of the stream was the already mentioned greenstone, which will, I believe, prove to be at a lower level than the bottom of the lake. As I only had a single day to spend at this lake, I was unable to examine the characteristics of the wide and unusually straight valley below the village of Malwa Tal; its examination may throw some light on the subject.

Naukachia Tal. — This curiously irregular-shaped lake has received its name from its nine corners. It is situated about one mile and a-half to the south-east of Bhim Tal. It occupies a hollow on the slope, and is surrounded by low hillocks—not by pairs of distinct ranges, as are the previously described lakes. With a very narrow outfall on the north-west, its appearance, as seen from a mile distant, suggested its being little more than a shallow pond; and it did not seem to me to be advisable to curtail my already too short time at the other lakes by paying it a special visit. On returning to Naini Tal, I found, very much to my astonishment, that its depth is recorded at 132 feet, thus being the deepest of the series. If this be the correct depth, it renders the lake one of the most singular of all. Its shape, the nature of its surroundings, and the narrow winding course of the outfall, all seem inconsistent with the view that it is of glacial origin. Its length is given at 3,120 feet, its breadth 2,270 feet, and its approximate elevation above the sea 4,000 feet.

Sat Tal.—The so-called Sat Tal, or seven lakes, are situated about the same distance to the west of Bhim Tal that Naukachia is to the south-east. They are surrounded on all sides by steep hills; a narrow valley, 100 yards wide, at the outfall of the principal lake serving to carry off the drainage. What the maximum depth may be, I do not know; but two soundings, which I took in the western arm of the principal lake, gave depths of about 58* feet. An artificial dam and sluice somewhat increase this depth beyond what it would be naturally. At

* The maximum depth was subsequently ascertained to be 61½ feet.

the outfall there is a landslip, and I do not think any rocks are seen *in situ* till a much lower elevation is reached than 58 feet below water-level. When it is remembered that this curiously-shaped lake has but one narrow outlet, and that it is otherwise surrounded on all sides by hills, but without any considerable catchment area for a glacier to be formed and fed, the difficulty in the way of a glacial theory of origin becomes strikingly apparent. I have seen in parts of the Central Provinces, where no question of glaciers can arise, denuded hollows among hills, which, if closed by landslips, would form very similar lakes.

Of the smaller lakes enumerated above under Class III., I have nothing to say at present. They have not yet been specially examined. Very possibly there may be in connection with them various points of interest yet to be discovered.

Reviewing the whole of the facts which are enumerated above in reference to each of the lakes, and considering the limited zone in which they occur—the probability that they are all the result of one general series of operations impresses itself as being an hypothesis of primary importance. If one of the lakes, then, exhibits indications which seem to connect it with one particular mode of origin, while others of the lakes do not show such or similar indications, it becomes all-important to submit the former to the severest scrutiny. In this way, I think, the appearances suggestive of a glacial origin, which are perhaps strongest in the case of Naini Tal, lose much of their force when we find that other lakes exist of generally similar character, but in which the special indications are wanting. In the single character of the outfall barriers all the lakes agree; opinions may differ as to the origin of these barriers, whether they are remnants of moraines, or have been formed by landslips; but it is almost certain* that not one of them consists in any degree of rock *in situ*, and we therefore have not the positive aid of a rock basin to determine a conclusion.

---

* Careful levelling only can decide this point.

There is one point geologically which links the three larger lakes together, and that is the occurrence of trap dykes in the vicinity of each. Now, I do not think it at all probable that the lakes are due to the original outburst of trap. Indeed, the above described fact in reference to Malwa Tal, where both the inflowing and outflowing streams cut through trap, renders such a view untenable. But it seems not improbable that, when the great upheaval and disturbance of the rocks of this area took place, the existence of comparatively rigid lines of trap may have been largely instrumental in determining the form which the surface assumed, and that on their flanks the soft shales, &c., may have been so much crushed and broken, as to yield more easily to the subsequent operations of denudation, thus affording an abundant supply of material for landslips, which ultimately served to close the valleys, and form the lakes.* Or even supposing the outburst of trap to have accompanied the upheaval and disturbance, its effect in determining the subsequently established lines of denudation could not fail to make itself felt. This explanation seems to me more in accordance with the known facts regarding the whole series of lakes, than any glacial theory can be.

---

* It is possible that the basin of Naini Tal may be connected with some local faulting, the existence of which is implied by the sulphur spring at the outfall. That a fault occurs all along the centre of the valley is, however, scarcely probable, as, did one exist, it would show in the scarp of China, the beds forming which appear to be continuous across the head of the valley.

CHAPTER XIII.

SECTION I.

ORISSA, SAMBALPUR, PATNA, KARIAL.

1876-77.

INSTRUCTIONS FOR SEASON'S OPERATIONS—VOYAGE TO CUTTACK—FALSE POINT—ORISSA CANALS—FIRST MARCH—UNINVITED CAMP-FOLLOWERS—BANKI—CLIMATE OF ORISSA—JUGERNATH PILGRIMS—TOPSIE RESCUED FROM A LEOPARD—BARMUL PASS—ANOTHER LEOPARD—FOREST SCENERY—SALT CARTS—SUPERINTENDENT OF GURJAT POLICE—HOT SPRINGS AND TEMPLES—BÔD—THE GRASSCUTTER'S CASTE—THE URIAS—SONPUR—THE RAJA AND THE DELHI DURBAR—BINKA—MEET THE ASSISTANT COMMISSIONER OF SAMBALPUR—BEHREN—SCHOOL—BURPALI—DANCING BOYS—JACKALS—DUCK—BEAT FOR GAME—BEARS AND JACKALS AMONG THE SUGAR-CANES—PART FROM MY COMPANION—MADRASSI SERVANT—PATNA RAJA—PATHAN SETTLER, HIS LIFE AND ADVENTURES—KABUL POLITICS—BOLANGIR—DUCKS—TEMPLES—THE TEHSILDAR—BEATS FOR GAME—SHOOT A TIGER—KABUL MERCHANTS—ATHGAON—SHOOT A LEOPARD—DIAGAON—SOINTILA—DURAMGURH—WILD BUFFALO—THE GAONTIA A THAUMATURGIST—GRAPHITE—LAPIR—MONDOL—BRAHMIN BEATERS—SHOOT A SAMBAR—CASTE—GUMANI—GRAPHITE—TOADS IN A HOLE—ESCAPE OF THE ELEPHANTS—GUNDAMURDAN RANGE—LATERITE—NURSINGHNATH—CAVE OF SHIV—SITAMA—SCORPIONS—HARISHANKAR—BINJWALS AND BHUMIAS—RAIN—GAME—PAINTED PARTRIDGES—NURSINGHNATH—SERENADED BY A TIGER—ENTER KARIAL—TARNOT—GEOLOGY BECOMES MORE INTERESTING—LEAVE CAMP TO VISIT MARAGURA—JONK RIVER—BHIM-ER-LAT—JUMLAGOR—WATERFALL—SAMBAR—MAD DOG BITES AN ELEPHANT—DRENCHED BY DEW ON THE LONG GRASS—SPUR FOWL—TORBA—THE RAJA'S OFFICIALS—SUPPLIES GRATIS—FEVER—BIRD-CATCHERS—BEAT FOR TIGER—UNDER RIVER—TROGLODYTES—HEAR OF A HERD OF BUFFALO—ADVENTURE WITH THE BUFFS—NEWS FROM THE CIVILIZED WORLD—HOT SPRING—ISOLATED TEAK FOREST—SYMPTOMS OF THE HOT SEASON—BEAT FOR TIGERS—A DYING BOY—KARIAL—THE RAJA'S VISIT—TEMPLES OF RANIPUR-JURAL—LEAVE KARIAL.

MY instructions for this season were to explore as great an area as I possibly could of the wide region which extends from the Mahanadi river in Orissa and Sambalpur, to the Godavari river in the northern provinces of the Madras Presidency. The native states of Bustar and Jaipur were especially mentioned as places to be visited, but the routes I should adopt both in going and coming were left very much to my own discretion. As it happened, circumstances arose which caused me to modify in an essential manner the programme which I had drawn up for myself; for instead of marching to Vizagapatam, on the coast, as I had intended to do from Jaipur, I turned northwards for Raipur, and concluded 1,000 miles marching at Nagpur, whence I returned by train to Calcutta instead of by sea from the coast, as I had purposed to do. In view of the preparation of a general account and map of the geology of India it was an object of some importance to reduce as far as possible the limits of the blank space in the above indicated region, regarding which our geological knowledge was absolutely *nil.* Though from analogy it was possible to speculate on the formations represented, we did not possess a single fact or trustworthy observation on the subject. Fortunately excellent maps of the whole area were available.

On the morning of the 9th of November, I started from Calcutta for False Point and Cuttack, in the British India Steam Navigation Company's steamer "Satara,"—rather, however, I should say, intended to start, for owing to the immense amount of cargo to be taken on board we were unable to leave the moorings till late in the afternoon, while there was still time to drop out of the limits of the port, by which the penalty attached to a steamer's not leaving on the advertised date is evaded. On such occasions one of these steamers, as it drops down the Hugli river, stern foremost, presents a rather singular sight, as it carries with it a swarm of native cargo-boats, the process of shipping goods going on all the time, and the boatmen constantly struggling for nearest place to the receiving-gangway.

We did not reach the mud-locked apology for a harbour known as False Point until the morning of the 12th. Large steamers can now no longer go inside, owing to a bar across the entrance which has been thrown up by the Mahanadi.

Anchored outside, they have to await the arrival of the cargo-boats which are towed out by a tug. On this occasion one cargo-boat was pointed out to us which belonged to a proprietor unprovided with steam-power. This wretched craft had for six weeks been trying to fetch successive Calcutta steamers. Part of its cargo consisted of the private effects of an officer and his wife, who had been put to the greatest inconvenience by their non-arrival. While we lay at anchor, discharging cargo, a severe swell, due to the rising tide, began to affect the boats exposed on the weather side, and although there was neither wind nor a rough sea, one of them, from the intensity of its rolling, was for a short time in considerable danger of being swamped. The water-cask, though lashed to the deck with ropes, was carried away together with a number of spars. It was extraordinary that some of the Uria boatmen did not follow, but they managed to cling on like flies. All this may have been amusing to ordinary onlookers, but for my part I felt anything but comfortable, as all my stores, tents, &c., were on the deck of another cargo-boat on the lee-side of the steamer, which was gradually swinging round on her moorings with the tide. The prospect of seeing my belongings go adrift in the same way as the water-cask had done was far from pleasant. However, I had to satisfy myself with the assurance of the nautical authorities that as we swung round the swell would go down. The event proved that they were right.

Towards night the passengers who like myself, were bound for Cuttack, left the steamer in a steam-barge, and, having passed inside the outer bar, anchored for the night, there not being sufficient water on the inner bar for us to cross it, and also in consequence of the navigation among the islets of the delta being too intricate for night travelling. The box-like deck cabin was sufficiently commodious to enable our party of five to place our beds on benches, table, or floor. Fortunately there were no ladies in the party, or we should have been compelled, or at least expected, to resign this box to them, and to have "pigged" it out amongst the coals and miscellaneous crowd of native passengers and crew. Early next morning we steamed off to the entrance lock of the canal at Marsagai. On our way we passed through churs and islets densely clad with low jungle in which a small palm (*Phœnix palustris*) was conspicuous. At Marsagai another long and dreary wait ensued till the arrival in the evening of a small steam-launch from Cuttack enabled us to continue our journey. As we entered the canal it became quite dark, but we continued on our course, taking in tow one of the cargo-boats which had on board our servants and the baggage of some of the party. As the time for turning-in arrived, some little awkwardness arose on the subject of how we were to dispose of ourselves for the night, the accommodation in the steam-launch being limited to a narrow cabin with two benches, with a well or passage between them. It was perfectly clear that two of the party would have to take up their quarters in the cargo-boat. Two did go, but seemingly they went under protest,—at any rate they seemed to go with the deliberate and foregone intention of being as uncomfortable as possible, thereby establishing a claim to growl on the morrow. According to their own account they spent a rather miserable and sleepless time. About sunrise the next morning we realized that we were still about ten hours journey from Cuttack, and that we were unprovided with any commissariat. Starving, or broaching my cases of stores, were the alternatives: the latter seemed the more preferable of the two, and was accordingly adopted. We were not, however, compelled to rely wholly upon this source of supply, as near one of the locks where we were delayed stood the house of one of the irrigation engineers in charge of a section of the canal. Here we were hospitably entertained with *chota haziri*, and were thus enabled to continue our journey at the pace of about three miles an hour.

The canal-banks were very much like canal-banks in other parts of the world, and there is little to be said about them. During the day we passed the Government steamer bound for False Point with a number of irrigation officers on board. They were apparently somewhat amused to see us towing away at the unwieldy cargo-boat which would probably otherwise not have reached Cuttack for three or four days. In India especially, but also in many other parts of the world, time is, in the long run, actually saved by travelling with one's impedimenta. Personal presence may serve to counteract the ill effects of break-downs and delays caused by a multitude of trivial circumstances. I am not alluding to ordinary day-to-day travelling where there is a regular system established, and where, perhaps too often, native subordinates make use of means to expedite the arrival of their master's property, which means might not in all cases meet with the master's approval—but in anything like travelling out of the ordinary routine, personal presence on the line of march may save days of anxious waiting at the end of the journey.

Towards the evening we left the canal and steamed across the Mahanadi to Jobra, a suburb of Cuttack, just above the weir. Cuttack I have before described, and shall, therefore, say nothing further regarding it. I found my men, two horses, and four elephants, awaiting my arrival. Some few other servants of the minor sort had still to be engaged, and negotiations with these, and making final preparations for my start, occupied several days. However, on the morning of the 21st, everything was packed on the four elephants and despatched to the village of Ramchand, some ten miles off on the Sambalpur road. Late in the afternoon I followed up, and, as I had a wide expanse of water and sand in the Kajuri branch of the Mahanadi to cross, I did not reach my tent until some time after dark. On entering it I found that my faithful bearer had arranged all its contents with his usual neatness and care, and everything was in the exact spot to which, from long custom, it particularly appertained. A feeling of rejoicing filled my heart as I gazed through the gloom of the mango-grove, here and there illumined by the numerous fires of my followers. I had now fairly broken the last link binding me to civilization for a long season. I felt that my equipment was as perfect as the long experience I had previously had of the life could make it. Nothing that I was likely to urgently require had been left behind, and supplies of all articles not to be found in the jungle were, I was confident, in sufficient abundance to last me through the trip. The country I was about to visit could not fail to be interesting in many ways.

While reflecting on these topics over my first log-fire for the season, I became cognisant of the present of certain impedimenta in camp of whose existence I had not before had any idea. Female forms indistinctly seen over the fires and shrill female voices declared the presence of more than one representative of the sex as uninvited camp-followers. Calling up the Jemidar Saidon, I asked him who they were, and learnt from him that there were three of them—wives of two of the mahouts and one of the *charkuttas*, or mahout's mates. I then made the further enquiry whether they were the *pucka* (real) wives, and was assured that they were; whereupon seeing that it would not be altogether wise to insist upon their being cast adrift to find their way to their homes, which were many hundreds of miles off in the neighbourhood of Jabalpur, I was obliged to vent my indignation on the Jemidar whose business it was to have reported their presence to me. This may seem a trivial subject upon which to devote so many lines, but it must be remembered that I was starting on a very long and wearisome journey, that there was the prospect of these women breaking down from fatigue, and becoming an encumbrance. It had also been an object with me to keep down the number of followers as much as possible as there was every prospect of supplies being scarce. Moreover it required not the spirit of prophecy to enable me to tell that their presence would not conduce to the harmony of the camp. Sooner or later they were sure in some way or another to supply a *casus belli.* The event fulfilled both predictions.

A muster being called, I found that there were twenty-eight men, three women, four elephants, two horses, and two dogs, to be provided for daily, and besides these there were always several chuprasies or police, furnished by the local authorities to escort me through each district. The men so sent from Cuttack consisted of one chuprasi and two constables, one of these men together with one of my chuprasies always kept ahead of the camp in order to have the supplies ready.

The next march was to Patpur, a village belonging to the Domepara Zemindar, who shewed his independence by not having made any arrangements for supplies, although he had been specially written to on the subject by the magistrate. However, what was necessary for the camp was forthcoming from the village after the usual amount of Uria noise, squabbling, and delay. *En route* I visited a large jheel, where I shot a few snipe; but the birds were very wild, rising in flocks out of range. My bird-collection for the season was commenced by my shooting a honey buzzard (*Pernis cristata*) and a plaintive cuckoo (*Ololygon passerinus*). The latter is a rather rare bird in most parts of India, but abounds in the thorny zone of jungle to the west of Cuttack.

The next day I marched to Banki, passing off the sandstones of the Athgurh basin on to an area in which metamorphic rocks, much concealed by alluvium, prevail. Close to Banki there is a steep peak of gneiss, which was formerly the abode of a fakir, regarding whom various stories of his miraculous powers are still current. Banki is a Tehsil, or head-quarters of a Tehsildar. There is an excellent travellers' bungalow there, which is picturesquely situated on the banks of the Mahanadi. It is the only one worthy the name on the road. Most of the others are merely mud hovels, but they served sufficiently well for my purposes, and generally enabled me to dispense with my tent. Imperial pigeons (*Carpophaga Ænea*) and golden plover, and some smaller birds, especially the white-browed bulbul (*Ixos luteolus*), contributed to my bag to-day.

The next march was to Bydesur, thirty-seven miles from Cuttack. Most of the country was open alluvial land, but there are hills of garnetiferous gneiss close to Bydesur. On this, the 24th of November, the afternoon was exceedingly warm, the temperature at 6 p.m. standing at 81° F. This was, of course, abnormal; but I very much doubt if anything like a real cold season ever occurs in these parts.

Leaving Bydesur, the next march of thirteen miles brought me to Kontalu, in Daspala, where the Raja's Muktiar or agent was in waiting to receive me. Here there are several temples, which are sacred to Kali, I believe. They are built on a small hill, and form a picturesque group. From hence onwards the rest-houses were in a wretched condition, and the chowkidars in charge said that they were quite incapable of restraining the people from making free with the compounds surrounding them. The village of Kontalu is a tolerably large one. Among the inhabitants there is a colony of braziers, who seemed to be at work both day and night, to judge from the incessant tapping.

The next day's march to Belpara, ten miles distant, was through jungle, part of it more properly forest. In the densest portion I shot a fine specimen of the large Central Indian red squirrel (*Sciurus maximus*). Many pilgrims to Jugernath were passing along this road; most of them appeared to be badly off, and some, who were quite destitute, were begging for aid. Among them were some miserable old women, with their feet bound up in rags. They were dismally hobbling along at a rate, perhaps, of five miles a day, to their still distant destination.

In the evening, accompanied by my two dogs, "Topsie" and "Skinny," and carrying with me a shot-gun, I went to examine a small group of jungle-clad hills in the neighbourhood of the bungalow. While ascending to the main peak, the dogs rushed off in pursuit of some animal, but what it was I could not see. After a long time spent by me in whistling, they at length returned, and I resumed my walk to the top of the hill. As the sun set, I turned back to get to camp. Shortly before leaving the jungle, and just at the foot of the hill, Topsie, who was following behind me, gave a bark, followed by an angry cry, which showed me that some animal had caught her. Turning back, I followed the retreating cries as fast as I could, through the bamboo jungle up the side of the hill, and on getting close they ceased, and the poor dog, released from the jaws of the animal that was carrying her off, came running towards me, but dropped exhausted before she could reach me. Though I must have been within a few feet of the animal, I failed, owing to the undergrowth, to get sight of it. No doubt it was a leopard, and possibly it was the animal first pursued by the dogs, as a leopard will often fly before a small dog. If such were the case, he probably tracked us down the hill, and took a favourable opportunity for springing on the dog. His method of procedure was apparent from the wounds. A tear on the flank showed where he had struck her, in order to turn her into position for grasping her in his mouth by the neck. He had buried his four canines deeply in her neck; but thanks to her thick covering of fat, she had escaped receiving a fatal wound. Carrying her back to the bungalow in my arms, I then, with the aid of the native doctor, bathed and bandaged the wounds. For many days she was on the sick-list, and was unable to walk the marches for about six weeks. She proved on the whole a good patient, but began to hate the very sight of the native doctor when—owing to the too quick healing of the wounds, and suppuration setting in—it became necessary for him to use the lancet. Physically her recovery was complete, but I found that her spirits were affected, and she showed a marked disapproval of evening strolls in the jungle, particularly, it seemed to me, when she saw that I did not carry a gun. Poor dog! after this and other less stirring adventures and escapes, it was her fate to die miserably of distemper on my return to Calcutta. Those, and those only, who have had for the companion of their solitude an affectionate dog, with a good deal of character and intelligence (why call it otherwise), can appreciate the full measure of my loss.

The next march was to Barmul—thirteen miles. Close by is the famous Barmul Pass,* one of the great show places of Orissa.

---

* Figured in Hunter's "Orissa," Frontispiece, Vol. I. In the year 1803, a battle was fought at the Barmul Pass between the British troops, which were sent to subjugate Orissa, and the Maharatta forces. This was the last stand made by the latter, who were completely routed; in consequence of which the Rajas of Bôd and Sonpur came in and tendered their submission.

Its distance from Cuttack, upwards of seventy miles, prevents its being often visited, and the book at the bungalow contained but few names of tourists. I made a halt here in order to give my men and beasts a rest and afford myself a better opportunity of examining the pass than was possible on the day of arrival. The Pass consists of the narrowed and much-deepened channel of the Mahanadi, which runs here due N.W. S.E. for about eight miles between two parallel sugar-loaf peaked ridges of garnetiferous gneiss. The bedding of the rock is steeply inclined, at angles of from 40° to 80° to N.E. The scenery possesses some resemblance to parts of the lower Danube, but lacks the bold and precipitous outlines of the more striking views on that river. The only boat available for going up the stream was an exceedingly lubberly craft, which I found to be quite unfit for the purpose. I soon got tired of the tedious poling, and landed on the northern bank to examine the rocks. The jungle there seemed a likely cover for large game. In such places a sort of instinctive perception of the presence of game often seems, in an indescribable way, to pervade one's consciousness. Not unfrequently I have found the correctness of such perceptions fully established by some subsequent discovery.

On return to camp I heard that while one of the mahout's assistants was on the previous evening climbing up into the lofty branches of a banyan-tree by its pendent roots, a leopard came and sat underneath the tree. The man called out to the mahout, who, from the cries, guessed what was the matter, and took with him the elephant, which at first refused to enter the strip of jungle in which the tree was situated, and did not do so till the leopard had bolted off. Hearing this, I thought the occasion might afford an opportunity for avenging Topsie's injuries. Accordingly, I had a village dog tied up as bait, and sat up in a *machan* over it. At one time the dog seemed to see something in the jungle, as he growled ominously; but at sunset he quietly lay down to sleep, after which I waited for about an hour, and then got down from the tree and returned to the bungalow.

Ten miles beyond Barmul there is a bungalow at a place called

Sonakhani or Sonakulli, but no village. The road is a pleasant one through well-wooded hills. Here and there it overhangs the Mahanadi, affording glimpses of beautiful little bits of scenery. Some bamboos of unusually large dimensions occur in this jungle; and I saw some of the largest cut down by carters to make into oil-bottles and water-vessels. The pleasure of travelling through this beautiful section of the road was much marred by the presence of long strings of carts laden with salt from the coast, which were always in the way at the river crossing; and by constantly causing a dust and noise they proved themselves in other respects disagreeable adjuncts.

The next stage of ten miles brought me to Horbunga, where I found the Superintendent of Police, who was just returning to Cuttack from a tour in the Khond Malias, or hills inhabited by the Khonds. He described the country as being very difficult to travel through, owing to the impossibility of using any other carriage than coolies; and the people, from his account, appear to be in an unusually wild and unsophisticated condition. The geologist to whose lot it may fall to explore the belt of hills known as the Eastern Ghâts will have a very difficult task indeed to perform. In Bôd, the country I was just about to enter, he was, he told me, on one occasion in charge of the supply arrangements for a regiment. On the day they entered the State a peacock was shot by an officer, and the Raja immediately sent to claim the bird as being one of his royal prerogatives. The reply he received was an invitation to come for it himself, which he declined to do.

The next stage was Ramgurh, twelve miles. The country is open and uninteresting, and nothing occurred during the day worthy of record. On the following day, instead of proceeding onwards at once, I first retraced my steps for two miles, and then crossed the Mahanadi in a dug-out to a village called Woodasing. The antiquated boatman would have afforded a capital model for Charon. He was not unskilful with the paddle, but, owing to the swiftness of the current in the successive channels we had to cross, the transit took a longer time than I had expected. At

Woodasing the Pujari or officiating priest shewed me the way to the hot springs, which were the object of my visit. I found that there were several distinct springs in the jungle about a mile to the north of the village. The hottest of these springs has a temperature of 134° F.; others, rising into basins of already-cooled water, gave temperatures of from 90° to 100°, that of the air being 75° F. In the immediate vicinity there are several temples to Devi and Mahadeo. The original idol of Devi is said to be kept at the Raja's palace in Athmalik. These temples resemble the smaller ones of the Mahendragiri series. They were of especial interest to me, as the material used in their construction were sandstones, which shewed recognisable characteristics of the formations known to occur in the area of the Talchir coal-basin. The rocks of the immediate vicinity were gneisses and granites, and since the repairs to the temples had been effected with these subjacent materials, it is probable that the ancient founders brought the sandstones from distant localities. This locality is regarded as being one of considerably sanctity, and is called Deoljhari. A large *mela* is held there annually.

In several of the springs there was a curious felty confervoid growth, which in one place was covered with a cobalt-bloom looking substance. This was possibly of the nature of a *protococcus* growth. Unfortunately I omitted to bring any away for further examination. On the edges of the hottest spring there was an encrustation of common salt (*sodium chloride*); but I failed to detect any distinct sapid taste in the water. Possibly this was owing to the strong flavour of sulphuretted hydrogen. The vegetation of the immediate vicinity of these springs was peculiar, and quite unlike anything to be found in the surrounding jungles. Among the plants I noted a *Pandanus* and a fern (*Acrostichum aureum*), which is very common at the Salt lakes and generally within the tidal region near Calcutta. The whole aspect of the place was so singular that it suggested to me a train of thought in connection with the fossil floras of tropical aspect which have been found in countries which have now a temperate or even a frigid climate. I do not for a moment propose to explain all such cases by the existence of hot springs. What I mean is, rather to draw attention to the possibility of an abnormal activity of hot springs over a limited area producing locally a perennial hot-house climate, and thereby inducing the growth of plants other than those normal to the country and climate in which they are found. Not unfrequently it happens that fossil plants are found densely compacted in particular parts of particular beds, while the main mass of the same beds are totally devoid of fossils. It is conceivable that the places so abounding in fossils may have been in the immediate vicinity of hot springs.

I did not reach Bôd, where my camp had preceded me, till late in the afternoon. On arrival I soon found, from the dismal faces of my servants, that things had not been going smoothly. Bôd enjoys such an evil reputation for incivility among all those whom I had met who had travelled up the road, that I had hardly expected that my experience would be very different from theirs, though, to avoid any unpleasantness, I had applied to the Commissioner for special letters to be sent with and before me, and addressed to the Rajas respectively, requesting them to afford me all necessary supplies and assistance. On enquiry I found that my men had been treated with a very scant measure of civility, and that a flaunting yellow *nirik namah* or price-list had been affixed to a tree near the camp. As this price-list not only included articles—such as wood—which are usually supplied free of cost, but put down everything at rates higher than prevailed in the Bôd Bazaar, its object was only too apparent. Awaiting my arrival, my men had not attempted to cook their food, and refused to take anything on such terms. In this they were actuated by the belief, no doubt correct, that an acceptance of these terms would be an admission of inferiority. It may perhaps not be quite easy to the English reader who does not know India to understand why the conduct of the Raja's people should appear so objectionable; but the very different and most hospitable receptions I met with subsequently will perhaps serve to shew what, among the well-disposed Rajas, is considered to be the proper conduct on the occasion of a visit like this. It was soon apparent to me that the object was simply to adhere to the bare letter of the Commissioner's parwana, while shewing a want of respect to me personally. After some little delay, the man appointed by the Raja to arrange for the supplies made his appearance. He was, I believe, the chief officer of the Raja's police, and he proved to be a worthy specimen of the knavish and insolent Uria. I asked him first to tear down the flaunting price-list, and enquired as to the various items, regarding which his answers were short and unsatisfactory. He would not tell me what the bazaar prices were; but they were certainly lower, as my men took their supplies from the shops. In reference to wood, he said that it was charged for because Bôd was a city. This was news for me, as, having just ridden through it, I had seen more jungle than houses, and not a single building of any size. Straw for my horses had indeed been graciously supplied by the Raja. This was, however, a concession, as the travellers I have before spoken of had told me that, when passing through Bôd, no money would purchase straw or anything else, the people distinctly saying that they had the Raja's orders not to render assistance of any kind. I then ordered a supply of wood sufficient for the camp, and paid for it, and took from this policeman a receipt for the amount in the Raja's name. This, with most Rajas, would have been felt as derogatory; but I was disappointed in supposing that it would have any such effect here. My action had the result of shewing that I would not submit to the studied insolence and indifference of these people, and was the cause, I believe, of my receiving a visit from the Raja's son—the Raja himself, I was told, never leaving his house. The son proved to be a fat, uninteresting lad of a limited degree of intelligence. When about to start on the following morning no coolies were forthcoming to carry the basket containing the sick dog Topsie, and among my men not one, save the sweeper, could be found who did not consider he would be defiled by touching it. This although they all professed to have the greatest affection for the dog when well. I then ordered my two Uria grasscutters, who were Ghasias by caste, to take up the basket; but they refused, saying their caste would go if they did so. They admitted that their religious status would permit of their leading a dog by a chain, but not of carrying it. This was too preposterous, and savoured so much of insubordination that I inflicted a small fine, which I made a particular point of subtracting from their pay. Let those who would talk of respecting caste prejudices put themselves in my place, and then say what they would have done,—remembering, too, that had it been a sick child or a sick wife, instead of a sick dog, there would have been nearly the same difficulty had there been none of the regular bearer caste at hand. After some further delay in the village, two men were found willing to carry the basket.

I marched fourteen miles to Boira. The rocks, so far as they were seen, proved to be almost exclusively coarse porphyritic granites. In the tanks there were whistling, cotton, and common teal in some abundance; and on the uplands I saw parties of the graceful courier plover.* From Boira I sent back the Orissa Tributary Mehal chuprasi and constables, as the morrow's march would, I was thankful to feel, take me out of Orissa into the Sambalpur District of the Central Provinces, where, though the people are to a great extent Urias, and speak the Uria language, they are much less bigoted and more manly and civil than the deeply-religious, undefiled, but dirty and knavish, inhabitants of the Gurjat states of Orissa.

The next day's march brought me to Sonpur, ten miles distant. Sonpur is the chief town of the Gurjat state of the same name. On arrival I rode through the town, expecting to find a bungalow and preparations for my camp, but the only bungalow to be found was a small and not particularly clean one-roomed school-house, which I declined to occupy, and accordingly went off to a grove near the junction of the Tel and Mahanadi rivers. I then learnt that the Raja had, through some mistake, received no official intimation of my coming, and from what I heard, seemed to be

---

* *Cursorius Coromandelicus.*

rather offended that I had not written to him, instead of sending a verbal message; but if he had this feeling, better thoughts soon led him to send me as ambassador an old half-caste, bearing a civil message to excuse preparations not having been made, and to convey his intention of visiting me in the evening, and to express his hope that I would spend several days as his guest. Soon there followed a procession, bearing the usual and time-honoured *dalli* of fruit, sweetmeats, and a fat kid, together with all the supplies required for the camp. On the arrival of the elephants I wrote him a letter explaining matters, and received in reply a well-written English letter, in his own hand. For some reason—the state of his health, it was said—he did not pay the promised visit, but the next morning wrote to say he would call upon me at seven o'clock, if I would wait so long. To this I replied that it would suit me better to call upon him, on my way through the town, as my tents had been taken down. Accordingly I visited him in his cutcherry, and found him to be a handsome, well-set-up man, with a pleasant manner and a good knowledge of English. He was in great trouble on the subject of the Delhi Durbar, the time for which was then quickly approaching. Having consented to go, he had got so far as to send his camp to the opposite bank of the Mahanadi, but then his heart began to fail him. Rheumatism and fever, he said, were the causes of his changing his mind; but he added, significantly, that such assemblies were suited to men like Scindia, Holkar, Jaipur, and other chieftains of Rajputana, not to Rajas like himself. Had he gone, however, he would have found that the members of the group of feudatory chiefs to which he belonged were received with salutes of seven guns, and otherwise treated with a degree of honour they could scarcely—even important as they may think themselves—have aspired to. He asked me whether he would be likely to get into disgrace for not going. On this point I could give him no information; but I assured him that his changing at the eleventh hour, when all preparations had been made, could not meet with approval. Ultimately, he did not go, and the district officials were, I believe, far from pleased. From some of the natives I learned that it was their opinion that he had lost a great opportunity in not securing his right to the seven guns.

This day's march was a wearisome one of sixteen miles to Binka, which is situated at the point where the Mahanadi changes from its N. to S. direction to the steady N.W. to S.E. course which it pursues from hence eastwards to the sea. Here also there was no bungalow, and I had a particularly dreary wait for the elephants, which did not arrive till late in the afternoon. I arranged to stop here for a day, and then, leaving my camp behind, push on to the station of Sambalpur, where I had some final arrangements to make before starting for the native states to the south. The Mahanadi in the neighbourhood of Binka exhibits good sections of the rocks, and the day was spent in examining these, and in reading the pile of newspapers and letters which had just reached me. They were the first I had received for a fortnight. The next morning I started for Dama, about half-way to Sambalpur; but after walking five miles to Turam, I met the Assistant-Commissioner of Sambalpur, who had written to say that he was coming out to meet me. Finding from him that it would be possible for me to make the necessary arrangements about money, &c., without going into Sambalpur personally, we agreed to march across the Dakin-tir, or southern portion of Sambalpur, together.

On the following day, which we spent encamped at Turam, my camp, which I had sent for to Binka, came up. Our first march was ten miles to Behren, the residence of one of a group of semi-independent Zemindars occupying the Dakin-tir. Our camp at Behren—there being no regular grove—was pitched under a few trees in an unclean and noisy spot in the middle of the village; and, it being market-day, was soon surrounded by a shouting crowd.

In the evening we visited the school, which was one of those established under a system peculiar to Sambalpur, being supported by subscriptions, and unaided by Government grants, but supervised by the District Officials. In this and several of the schools subsequently visited, I noticed that, taken at the same ages, the girls were vastly more quick and intelligent than the boys. One young damsel of nine or ten years old, who particularly distinguished herself in ciphering, we shortly after noticed seated in charge of a stall in the market, putting her school acquirements into practice. Indeed it seemed that they were taught when set questions in multiplication to give the answer in rupees and annas, and many of the questions were solved mentally in a most creditable manner.

The next day we moved ten miles further west to Burpali, the Zemindar meeting us on the boundary, and accompanying us to camp, which was pitched in one of a series of very extensive mango-groves. In the afternoon we visited the town and schools, and later on, after dinner, were entertained by the Raja with a *nach*, the performers being small boys. In addition to the dancing, one of the boys possessed an extraordinary snake-like flexibility of spine, which permitted the musicians and other attendants to do almost anything with him but tie him in a knot. Female dancers are seldom seen amongst the Urias.

The following day was a day of rest for the camp, and we devoted part of it to shooting, our bag including teal, quail, and snipe—of the latter we had daily come across some during the march. While we were shooting, the dog-boys in charge of my companion's pack, loosed two couples after a pair of jackals. Hearing the noise we rushed to the embankment of a tank, below which we had been shooting. We there found that two of the old dogs had gone away altogether, but that the pups had first driven into the water, and afterwards apparently "killed." On examining the *dead* jackal, I thought he winked at me, and turned round to say so, when lo! he bolted, and took refuge between two haystacks, but was soon dislodged, finding immediate refuge in a neighbouring field of sugar cane. Afterwards he was routed out of this; but the pups failed to get sight of him, and ultimately he got clean off and escaped. The other dogs, we found on our way back to camp, had accomplished the death of their jackal. The dog-boys, of course, got into trouble for their misconduct in thus wildly loosing their charges without orders.

The next march was to Bijapur—eight miles. On several of the tanks near the road there were large flocks of duck, especially on one of them, where there appeared to be some thousands of pintail and gadwall. Owing to the difficulty of retrieving we carried away a smaller bag than we should otherwise have done. At Bijapur there is a remarkably fine sheet of water, formed by an unusually massive bund, faced with cut laterite, which has been thrown across a valley. We much enjoyed a swim in its deep clear waters in the evening.

The following day we turned southwards to a small village called Louamunda, nine miles distant, and on arrival we heard news of a tiger at a village about five miles off, which we set out for after breakfast. With the aid of the villagers we found the beast's lair, and some tolerably recent footprints. We then determined to try a small beat, and about a score of men were soon collected; but, save a few spotted deer, no other animals were turned out.

The next day we marched ten miles, still southwards, to Gainslot. When passing through some of the villages the people, more particularly the women, cheered us, wagging their tongues from side to side of their mouths, in the same manner as some of the African tribes are said to do. I have never elsewhere met with this custom in India.

At Gainslot we shot a number of quail—grey, black-breasted, and button—and saw one specimen of the florikin, an extremely rare bird in these parts. Our camping-ground proved to be on the first unaltered sedimentary rocks which I had met with since leaving the neighbourhood of Cuttack. The early part of the next day was devoted to their examination, and in the evening we had a beat for a bear, which my companion had tried to track up while I was at work. That bears were tolerably abundant was evident from the destruction caused by them among the sugar canes; but even here, as well as in the more open country we had come through, the people did not so much complain of the injury done by the bears as of that of which jackals were the authors. By careful watching the bears might be kept off, but no amount of watching could save the crop from the insidious attacks of the jackals, who would bite across ten canes for one that they would eat. Our beat was unsuccessful, the only animal seen being a boar. As yet, therefore, I had had no chance of trying the effects of a new "Express" rifle I had bought before leaving Calcutta. Next morning the Assistant-Commissioner returned northwards to Sambalpur, where he had to go in order to make arrangements for the Imperial rejoicings on the 1st of January.

After another day devoted to the geology of the neighbourhood of Gainslot I marched to Jornapali, six miles. On the road a Madrassi servant I had recently engaged, and who was represented to me as being a model servant, was found by the rear-guard helplessly drunk. On my remonstrating with him he excused himself by saying it was his "first chance"—meaning, I presume, first offence. When crossing one of the streams on the road, some of the men reported having seen a bear taking a sand-bath.

At Kusm, the next halting-place, two days were spent examining the neighbourhood. I had a visit here from a Babu, a relative of the Patna Raja, who was then under supension on account of misconduct and oppression of his ryots; his territory being administered by a Tehsildar under the Deputy-Commissoner of Sambalpur. On entering my tent the Babu flung a couple of rupees down on the table. This in itself was an indication that I was entering among a people with somewhat primitive habits, as the custom of making such offerings on ordinary occasions is now becoming obsolete in British India.

At the next halting-place—Simlia, on the Sokethel river, I was surprised to find a settler, an old Pathan, who had first come into this part of the country many years previously as a merchant. He related to me a long story of his vicissitudes of fortune. Just before the mutiny he had, he said, amassed a considerable fortune, but lost it all during those disturbed times. He had many stories of ill-treatment by the Rajas. The land and village which he now occupied had been given him by the Patna Raja in acquital of a debt of long standing; but after he had spent money upon it, and made a tank, the Raja again resumed possession of it, and threw him into prison. After his release he appealed to the Deputy-Commissioner who satisfied himself that the deed granting the land was a genuine one, and reinstated him, though the Raja declared it to be a forgery. One of his ventures in his travelling days was a rhinoceros which he bought in Calcutta for a thousand rupees, and marched down at the rate of from six to eight miles a day, driving it, as he described it, like a cow, before him. Finally he disposed of it to the Raja of Jaipur for the fancy sum of sixteen thousand rupees, which sum, however, he declared he was never paid, though fed on promises for several years. The old man did not disguise his dislike to the Uria-speaking people among whom he lived. He said he would migrate to some other part of India if he could afford to do so. By his wife, a Benares woman, he had a number of children who were growing up uneducated, as he would not allow them to learn Uria—the only language taught in the neighbouring schools. On Kabul affairs he waxed eloquent, and insisted on the fortification of the Khyber Pass as the great point to which the Indian Government should address itself.* He expressed some disgust with the Amir for imprisoning his son Yakub Khan.

The next march was to Bolangir, six miles. I had a long day's work in the intervening country. At one village the people complained to me of the excessive damage caused to their rice crops by wild geese, ducks, and teal; and, indeed, I could see that whole fields of grain near a tank had been totally destroyed. I diminished the marauders by half-a-dozen, when they flew off to other pastures.

---

* Recent events have shewn what a good knowledge of the "situation" this old man possessed.

At a village called Santpur I saw some old temples which were rather elaborately carved; but I know nothing of their age or origin: probably they were only a few centuries old. Their chief interest to me consisted in the materials of which they were built—enquiries, subsequently made, led to the discovery of two localities whence the stones may have been brought.

At Bolangir I found a subdivisional station in process of formation, and a Tehsildar installed as dispenser of justice in place of the dethroned Patna Raja. This Tehsildar, a somewhat learned Pundit, whom I had previously seen in Sambalpur, proved to be very much more civilly disposed than are most of his race to those who are not in immediate authority over them. He had got together for my inspection a small collection of the mineral productions of the neighbourhood. This included some crystals of quartz, graphite, garnets, &c. Subsequently I visited the localities where these had been obtained and got better specimens. One of the quartz crystals I dug out was upwards of a foot long, and three inches in diameter. This had been one of the favourite shooting-grounds of a former Deputy-Commissioner, Major Bowie, whose large bags of tigers and other game were among the most considerable made in the Central Provinces. The Tehsildar having collected information, with a view to my visit, was prepared with news regarding several tigers and a herd of buffalo. Shikaris, trained beaters, and game, being all present, I thought I could not do better than spend my Christmas in endeavouring to get a shot at something. Accordingly, while I ranged the country geologizing for a couple of days, *garrahs*, or cattle for bait, were tied up in likely places. On the morning of Christmas Eve a kill was reported, and the beaters having been collected, we moved off to the spot, which was about two miles distant from camp. Markers were posted in the trees on either side of the one in which I was perched, and a pair of elephants on the flanks of the line. The beaters then entered at the opposite end of the jungle. After a short time it became apparent that the tigress—for it was a female well-known to the shikaris—was afoot. Soon after there was a loud shouting by the beaters as they caught sight of her, and as she was crossing in my direction the man in the tree on my right, unmindful of all the instructions he had received, made such a hideous noise that she turned without my having seen her. The men were then again put round the jungle, and the beat recommenced; but the tigress had in the meantime managed to sneak off without being seen. Many were the invectives cast by the beaters and shikaris at "*Sali-gachia*," as he was called, for spoiling sport. For some little time I could not think what the term meant, but I at last remembered that the individual in question had been seated in a Sali (*Boswellia thurifera*) tree, and that its interpretation was, therefore, "He of the Sali tree."

For my part I was disgusted and depressed, as it seemed to be my destiny never to get a shot at a tiger. The shikaris then proposed we should beat a small rocky hill not far off, to which, therefore, we adjourned. My seat was a native charpoy or bedstead, lashed in the branches of a small tree; this I have found to be the most convenient way of keeping oneself and spare guns together whenever it is advisable to use a tree. As the beaters reached the crest of the hill, an ominous rustling in the bushes was followed by the appearance of a civet cat, which leisurely trotted under my tree. But it was evident that it was not the cause of the noise, as there was some animal still moving about. Presently the man in the tree next to me, notwithstanding what had been said to *Sali-gachia*, began to enquire in a stage whisper whether I saw the tiger; after he had called out half-a-dozen times I told him to be silent; but apparently he did not hear me, as he continued to call out until a tiger made its appearance on the path leading down to the foot of my tree. Keeping it steadily covered till it was within about five yards, I then gave it a ball in the neck as it turned its head on one side. The effect of the Express bullet was marvellous; the animal simply subsided without a struggle, and was only just able to grin at me as I called out to the beaters to be careful how they approached. In another moment it was dead, of which I satisfied myself by hitting it with the empty brass cartridge-case before I allowed the men to come down. The carcase was soon hoisted on to one of the elephants, and started off for camp, being taken *en route*, by special request, for the examination of the ladies of the Zemindar, who were temporarily occupying a neighbouring village. The tiger proved to be a moderately-sized one, only nine feet long. After it was measured, the elephants were introduced to it. Three of them were particularly anxious to kick it, and were accordingly gratified to an extent consistent with the preservation of the skin from damage. But the fourth, "Anarkalli," simply trumpeted, and would not approach the carcase. The next day, Christmas day, I had a series of beats in a tract of country to the east, where a tiger was reported to have been seen on the previous day. However, nothing larger than a hyæna was seen, which I just caught a distant view of, as it scampered up the steep face of a boss of granite. On the day following I had another series of beats; the only animal seen by me was a young male sambar, which I shot. One of the beaters declared that he had seen a tiger, which broke back, but the truth of his statement was doubted. All this time *garrahs* had been tied up, but there had been no kill, though the tigress was still about, the natives saying that they had heard her calling for the male which had been shot.

Some Kabuli merchants bound for Jaipur with elephants—including one only a few weeks old—a most amusing baby—passed through Bolangir to-day. The next march was to Athgaon, where I found the grove of trees where my camp was to be, occupied by a crowded *hât* or market. However, it was an early one, and by the time the elephants arrived business was nearly concluded. I was rather surprised to observe the women present at this *hât* come up in parties to make their salaams. It shewed clearly enough that they were not Urias, who if they cannot run away adopt the graceful custom of turning their backs on a sahib should they meet one on the road. They all I believe, in fact, belonged to the tribe called Binjwal. In the evening the Zemindar paid me a visit; he seemed to be half idiotic, but his brother or cousin appeared to be a sensible lad enough. A neighbouring ridge of hills was said to harbour a large colony of bears, so a beat was arranged for the following afternoon. Towards the end of the first beat I caught sight of a leopard and got a shot at it as it ran past a gap in some rocks, behind which it was sneaking off. After I had fired it hurried on as if nothing had happened. However I thought I heard a fall followed by some growling. Presently I just for a moment saw another larger leopard, the male, almost under the feet of the beaters. I did not fire then as I thought he must come down my way. Unfortunately there was a break in the line where he disappeared. I called to the men to beat down in that direction, which they did after some delay, but in the meantime the brute had managed to slip off unseen by any one. Getting down from my tree, I soon found some blood which led up to the body of the first, which proved to be a leopardess quite dead. The Express bullet had gone quite through her, making a considerable wound on the off side. The distance she had travelled, and the pace she had gone at, spoke volumes for the vitality of these large cats. In the second beat nothing was turned out. I then heard for the first time that the great place for the bears was at the extreme east of the range which we had been beating, but as it was then near sunset we were compelled to return to camp.

The following day I marched to Diagaon, another small zemindari, where I put up in the school-house, which had been swept and garnished with a carpet for the purpose of my reception; but was unprovided with means for closing either doors or windows.

December 30th.—Diagaon.—Early this morning, before sunrise, I went off in the hope of intercepting some wild buffaloes, before they left the crops upon which they were in the habit of feeding every night. We got on the tracks of one small herd, and while following them up we heard another lot crashing through the jungle, but failed to get sight of either. At one place there were some splashes of blood on the bushes, which the shikaris attributed to one of the buffaloes having gored another with his horns. The next march was to Sointila, and I traversed a considerable area of country, also examining a portion of the section of the Tel river, where I found an outlying patch of sedimentary rocks belonging to the Talchir series.

On the 1st of January I marched from Sointila to Daramgurh. During the day I heard of the occurrence of buffalo in several places. They appear to be especially abundant in the neighbourhood of a hill three miles south of Sointila. On arrival at Daramgurh the head man or *gaontia* made his appearance. He wore the garb and marks of a Fakir, and enjoys a far and wide reputation as a thaumaturgist. Saidon had picked up, and no doubt believed, various stories about him. Among other things he told me that he was reputed to be invulnerable to wounds by arrow or bullet. Whereupon I asked whether he would stand up as a cock-shot for my rifle. To this Saidon made some reply which I did not quite catch, but he evidently regarded my question as little short of blasphemy. I had a long talk with the old man, who speaks a dialect of Hindustani, which was very agreeable to my ears after the horrible jargon of half-Uria, which had for some time back been my means of communication with the people. In the evening I examined a deposit of graphite close to the village. The rock is a foliated schist, and the graphite is not very pure. It did not appear to exist in any great abundance, but the outcrop was much concealed. I scarcely think it probable that graphite, however abundant, could, in a spot so remote and difficult of access, ever possess any economic importance.

From Daramgurh I marched eight miles to Lapir. Though a short march, the elephants were much delayed by over-hanging jungle. Sal timber is very scarce, but Sali and Asun or Saj (*Boswellia thurifera* and *Terminalia tomentosa*) are abundant. The road constantly crossed the winding bed of the Burabailat river. In one place I saw an encampment of people engaged in the collection of what they called *bockli*, which I understood to be the root of some tree which is employed in dyeing Tusser silk. I failed to get specimens of the leaves of the tree, and was therefore unable to identify it.

Lapir being a small village, supplies were brought in from about a dozen neighbouring hamlets. The *gaontias* came in a body to make their salaam. They most positively and distinctly declined to receive any payment for their contributions, saying it would be a disgrace to them to take money from the Sirkar. Poor men, to judge from the scantiness of their raiment, they were not in affluent circumstances.

The next two marches were to Duabota and Mondol. Mondol I had been led to expect was one of the best places for tigers in the country. Circumstantial accounts of a family of four tigers which were said to be almost daily carrying away cattle, became modified by successive steps of a descending scale as I approached the place, and on arrival I found, quite close to where my camp was pitched, that a cow had indeed been killed, but by a leopard. The people of the village proved to be Brahmins; they seemed to know nothing about the existence of any tigers in their neighbourhood. To my surprise, however, a number of them turned out as beaters, when I announced my intention of devoting the afternoon and evening to a beat for the leopard in a neighbouring tract of jungle. Towards the end of the beat a doe sambar passed me. Just as she was disappearing from my sight she looked so sleek and fat, and so eminently fitted for the pot, that I could not resist the temptation of a snap shot which knocked her over. My good intention of giving a feed to all was frustrated in this wise. Firstly the sambar was killed by the bullet, so could not yield lawful food to the Mahomedans. Secondly, after she was skinned, and a portion of meat cut off for my use and that of the Brahmin *gaontia* of the village, the Ghasia grasscutters and the sweeper proceeded to help themselves; and, having touched the carcase, caused the Hindus to raise a shout that the meat was contaminated, whereupon all of that persuasion likewise refused to make use of it. The result was that the Gond beaters and musicians had a larger share of the remains than would otherwise have fallen to them.

The next march was to Gumani, fourteen miles. I had

a long and wearisome wait for the elephants till 4 p.m. On the following day I visited another graphite locality at Domaipali, about seven miles off. On having an excavation made into the bed, I was rather surprised to see several peculiar globular-looking, thin-skinned toads, thrown out from a depth of about three feet beneath the surface. It was marvellous to see such helpless-looking animals in such a position. They doubtless managed to burrow down while there was still water on the surface, but the hard, gritty nature of the soil could never have been, one would think, very favourable to such operations.

On my return to camp I heard that three of the elephants, Mowlah, Anarkalli, and Peari, had most improperly been allowed to graze, unwatched, on some bamboos close to heavy jungle and had disappeared. No one could tell what direction they had taken. I immediately despatched men to search on all sides, but without success, till about sunset, when news came from a small hamlet that they had been seen. Soon afterwards they were found by the mahouts, who brought them back to camp, and then received a reprimand from me for their neglect. As if this had not been enough, the remaining elephant, Bhari, broke her chains during the night and made off, and was not captured until mid-day, when it was too late to march. This straying of the elephants in heavy jungle, although generally quickly followed by recapture, always caused me a good deal of anxiety. I knew that if not captured the same day, each day would increase the difficulty by a rapidly augmenting ratio, owing to the larger radius of country that would have to be searched, and the greater wildness and intractability of the elephants as they had further opportunities of enjoying freedom from all restraint. The old female, Bhari, was incorrigible; she would frequently spend the greater part of the night trying to break her chain. At one time she was so bad that it became necessary to tie her in such a way that she was prevented from lying down. According to the mahout, when loose she showed an extraordinary degree of cunning, and would hide herself behind a tree or bush, and remain quite still when she saw him coming to look for her. I have heard, however, of a still more cunning elephant, which is reported to have been seen, in open country, lying down behind the embankment of a tank, in order to baffle its pursuers. While on the subject of elephants, I may mention that the mahout above alluded to told me that elephants generally lie down to sleep three times in the night, each separate nap being about an hour's duration. The intervals are chiefly devoted to eating. I fancy that individuals differ much in this respect, and that there is no general rule. However tired, an elephant never lies down to sleep during daylight.

The next march was to Nandupalla, at the foot of a fine flat-topped range of hills which separates the Patna district from Bodosamar, and is known as the Gundamurdan range. The following morning I ascended the plateau by a steep and rough path over the vertical edges of a considerable variety of garnetiferous gneiss rocks, capped at the top by about 100 feet of laterite, which forms, at an elevation of about 3,000 feet above the sea, a level plateau very similar to that of the Main Pât in Sirguja. My intention had been to descend the opposite side of the range, in order to visit a locality called Nursinghnath, which is of wide repute throughout the country as a place of pilgrimage. I found, however, that it would scarcely be possible to accomplish the two ascents and two descents in a day; so, instead of attempting it, I followed my guides to what they considered to be the great sights of the plateau. The first place to be examined was a huge cave in the scarped face of the laterite, known to the Urias as *Bhim-er-munda*, or the Cave of Shiv. The dimensions are about thirty feet high, by fifty feet long, by forty feet wide. Owing to a portion of the roof having fallen in, a sort of natural sky-light illumines the interior. The subdued light caused by the masses of vegetation and fallen blocks near the entrance, gives to the cave a weird aspect, which no doubt evokes the awe of the pilgrims. In the valley below this is the head source of the waters which make the falls at Nursinghnath. The locality is called *Sitama.* One of the branches of the stream rises in a spring which makes its appearance among the roots of a lofty mango-tree, which is accordingly an object of special veneration. On the top of the plateau, under the loose fragments of laterite, I found numerous scorpions, and my followers were somewhat surprised to see me picking them up. But soon entering into the spirit of the thing, they improvised tweezers with twigs, and came running to me with wriggling scorpions in great abundance.

On returning to the foot of the hill I visited a temple at a spot called Harishankar. Here there is a fine cascade over the vertical edges of the gneiss. There was nothing remarkable about this temple, save that it was built of sandstone, which must have come from a considerable distance. The amount of water falling from various parts of this range is very considerable, and testifies to the storing powers of the laterite. On parts of the slope, where the water trickled down, there were gardens, containing oranges and plantains, which belonged to the Pujaris or priests of the temples.

The next march was southwards to the village of Koripani, six miles. I had hoped to have been able to cross from this westwards, but found that the road was quite impracticable for laden beasts. So on the following day I was compelled to march still further south in order to round the end of the range, and encamped at Potrapali. At Koripani the people called themselves Bhumias, those of a good many of the previous villages I had stopped at having been Binjwals, whose ethnic affinities I did not succeed in ascertaining. At Potrapali, during the night and following morning, there was a heavy downpour of rain, which prevented me from marching on the following day. From this date, 13th of January, commenced a season of broken, rainy weather, which, with short intervals, continued up to the end of the first week in May. Such a season has been quite unparalleled in my experience; but, great as was the inconvenience of constant drenchings of the camp, it was more than compensated by the frequency of cloudy days, which rendered an amount of work possible in March and April which could never have been even attempted in ordinary years.

The next march was to Sindkela, six miles. I took a wide

sweep round, but did not meet with anything of particular interest. In the evening I went out again to examine the country to the west, a curious, wild tract, the low cultivable portions of which were covered with grass which was, in some places, six feet long and upwards. Game appeared to be very abundant. I saw several barking-deer (*Cervulus aureus*), and nearly trod upon some large animal in the long grass, which made off, however, without my seeing what it was. Peacocks were very abundant, and, with the aid of my dogs, I bagged a couple. Poor Topsie had almost recovered from the effects of the leopard bites, and was very keen after everything that moved. She came back, after a private pursuit of one of the barking-deer, with her lip cut and bleeding, as though the animal had given her a kick in the mouth with one of its hoofs. Here, for the first time, I came across painted partridges (*Francolinus pictus*), whose peculiar calls resounded from every patch of grass towards sunset. In this area they replace the nearly-allied black partridge (*F. vulgaris*), which is the species found in Chutia Nagpur.

On the following day I started on a long journey of twelve miles to Nursinghnath, returning to Sindkela the same afternoon. The temple is situated on the south bank of the stream, the source of which, near the top of the plateau, has been already described. Above the temple there are a series of cascades, with hollowed basins at their bases, each of which bears a separate name, as *Sitá-Kún*, &c. Ascending by a series of steps, which are roughly hewn in the face of the rock, we reach the pool known as the *panch panda*, from the figures of the five *pandas* which, together with that of the elephant god *Ganesh*, are sculptured on the rock on one side, while on the other are figures of the triple god Brama and of Narain, with attendant satellites. The principal figures, which are of more than life-size, are vigorously wrought in the hard granite rock. Nursingh is said to be an image resembling a cat which was found by a Khond, and the shrine was erected in its honour by a Raja of the Gung-bansi dynasty. Here, no doubt, we have a traditional record of the absorption of an aboriginal deity into the Hindu Pantheon. The guardian priest I found to be a Benares man, who had, some eight years previously, been in the employment of Moheshri Pershad, of Lukanpur, in Sirguja. At first he made what looked like a hostile demonstration, on my expressing a wish to see the temple; but afterwards we became very good friends, and he sent in a boy to light up the image, while I remained outside. Over one of the pools, and under a cascade, there is a bamboo staging, upon which the pilgrims are expected to sit and take cold *douches* —very cold, they are reported to be.

During the night a tiger, with attendant jackal, serenaded my camp. I walked round with my rifle, but could not see either of the animals. The sound of a tiger roaring at night had become so familiar a sound, that my men—even those sleeping in the open under trees—did not take any precautions for their protection, nor show the slightest sign of fear. Afterwards it began to rain, and continued to do so, with short intermission, for nearly forty-eight hours. As it cleared up on the second day, I made an afternoon march of eight miles to Sambasinghi, in Karial, and dismissed the chuprasies, constables, and shikaris, who had accompanied my camp through Patna. I was here met by a Darogah and Tehsildar of the Karial Raja; and their very civil reception augured well for my comfort while in this native state. The next day I made a short march to Tarnot, a village situated below the north-east corner of an extensive plateau, which, from its configuration as represented on the map, and as seen from the distant glimpses I had of it, would, I felt confident, prove to be of considerable interest geologically. The event fully justified this confidence. Two months spent in rapidly traversing wide areas in which, with unimportant exceptions, metamorphic rocks had alone been met with, made me hail with delight a new formation, regarding the limits and character of which nothing was known. But it is necessary, perhaps, for one to be a geologist in order to fully realize how such a discovery can afford pleasure.

Soon after my arrival at Tarnot, I set out to examine a scarped face of rock, which from below looked so easy to scramble up that I was tempted to ascend it. Having, with assistance, accomplished the first fifteen feet or so, which was a nearly perpendicular face of rock, I found that the further ascent was a much more formidable affair than I had expected, but as I could not get down again, I resolved to attempt to reach the crest of the hill, some 150 feet above. How I managed it I hardly know. In one place my whole weight was supported from a small fig-tree growing in the crevices, and while drawing myself up by means of it, my right arm was strained, and had it not been for a hollowed space below the crest, into which I crept and remained until somewhat rested, I believe I should have fallen through sheer exhaustion. The natives accompanying me were of course better able to make their way over the steep face than I was, but the mental and physical strain seemed to have told upon them also in no small degree. Arrived at the crest we found the slope on the other side covered with fallen blocks and jungle, and offering no serious obstacles to the descent.

The next day, leaving my tent and camp behind me, I took a small sleeping-tent and such articles as were necessary for a three days' absence to Maragura, a village rather difficult of access, from being surrounded on all sides by hills, but conveniently situated as regards the plateau, which I proposed to ascend and examine. The locality of Maragura is, I believe, otherwise called Manickgurh. I found here a fine tank with the remains of an old temple. The present village is a miserable collection of huts, but some of the men were fine sturdy fellows, though of what race I find I have omitted to record. Having pitched my tent on a suitable spot on the embankment of the tank, I shot a couple of teal, and then proceeded to retrieve them, and at the same time refresh myself with a bath. As the birds had fallen among weeds, where the water was out of my depth, I had an opportunity of realising how unpleasant must be the position of those who sometimes are sent in to fetch out birds. Not that I was in any real danger, but the feeling caused by the long stems twining about one is not agreeable, more particularly when, as in the present case, some of those stems happen to be covered with thorns.

In the afternoon I went out to examine the bed of the Jonk or Jong river where it debouches from the hills. It contains an enormous accumulation of quartzite boulders under and through which the water makes its way. But occasionally there are deep pools containing water of an opaline sea-green colour, which is a common appearance in the water flowing from this plateau. It has also been noticed as characterising the water flowing from rocks of similar age which are found far away to the south in the Madras Presidency. At one point on the banks there was pointed out to me a huge iron spear, about six feet long, with a spirally ornamented shaft 2½ to 3 inches in diameter. It must have taken a giant to wield it. Although stuck up in the ground, quite unprotected, it shews no sign of rust. It is called *Bhim-er-lat*, or the mace of Shiv, and is an object of adoration, and is noteworthy simply as a piece of native metal-work.

On the following morning I started to explore the plateau. The path at first led up the valley of the Jonk for about a mile, after which we commenced the ascent over the edges of horizontal beds of quartzite belonging to the Vindhyan series. A walk of about four or five miles brought us to an ancient fort called Jumlagor, which is situated at the head of a picturesque waterfall about three hundred feet high. The view from this point, including deep-cut gorges with the scarped and terraced edges of the plateau rising one above the other and crowned here and there by isolated peaks, made up a scene of great beauty, and one shewing very characteristically the manner in which the rocks of this formation are usually affected by sub-aerial denudation. A second waterfall higher up I was unable to visit owing to the badness of the weather, a heavy thunderstorm appearing to be imminent. The old fort must have been a formidable affair in its day, and was probably used as a place of retreat when there were disturbances in the plains below. The walls were built of stone, but bricks had also been employed in its construction.

With the exception of the walls, which enclose perhaps about half an acre, I saw no traces of any buildings. Both here and on the ascent we startled several sambar from their lairs. The plateau must be full of them, judging from the numbers I heard belling in the evening. Near the head of the fall too, I saw very fresh tracks of a tiger, which must have been roaming about there shortly before our arrival. From the people, and even from the Raja afterwards, I could learn nothing definite about these remains; in fact I found it difficult to get reliable information in these native states, in reference to simple enquiries about the present state of the country.

The next day I returned to my camp at Tarnot by a circuitous route, which brought me over some very rough ground on the outer slopes of the plateau. In many places I found remains of old fortifications now enveloped in heavy jungle. On arrival at camp I was greeted with the unpleasant intelligence that during my absence a mad dog had made his appearance and had sprung at Peari, my favourite among the elephants, and bitten her on the trunk. The attack was so sudden that she had been caught quite unprepared and unable to defend herself. Saidon took a gun and wounded the dog, which was afterwards killed with sticks by the chuprasies. For several days the possibility of Peari going mad caused me some anxiety; however, although marked by the bite she suffered no ill effects. About this time the male elephant, Mowlah, becoming *must*, began to give trouble, and to shew a particular dislike for the mate mahout, whom he several times knocked over.

The following day I devoted to the examination of the country to the west of Tarnot, intending to march on the day after, but was prevented from doing so by rain. The storm of rain was preceded by a rushing mighty wind which awoke me about midnight. On going outside the tent to see that all was right, I beheld, as I thought, a raging fire coming swiftly in the direction of the tent. My first impulse was to shout out for all hands, the effort rousing me from the half-asleep condition I was in, and enabling me to realize the true state of things. The strong gusts over the logs of the camp fire were driving flames and sparks in the direction of the tent, and there was just a possibility of danger, though the man on guard did not appear to think so.

The next march was to Balukona, eight miles distant. I had a rather severe day's work along the eastern flank of the plateau, and got thoroughly drenched by the dew on the long grass which I had to travel through in the early morning. Here I came across some spur-fowl and shot one. It proved to be the painted species *Galloperdix lunulatus*, Valenc. The red spur-fowl (*G. spadiceus*, Gmel.) I had previously shot near Cuttack and in Patna (Sambalpur). After another day spent in continuation of the examination of the line of junction between the metamorphic rocks and the Vindhyan quartzites of the plateau, I reached Torba, where I found an accession to those already in attendance on my camp on the part of the Karial Raja. They were headed by one Abdul Rahim, a Lucknow man, who was the chief inspector of the Raja's police. Having a good deal of power, he proved a useful adjunct to my camp, but used to annoy me at times by his plausible untruthfulness. Afterwards I found that he bore a very bad character, and I have no doubt his good conduct while he remained with me was in a great measure due to his desire to obtain from me a certificate which might be of service to him at some future time. He brought word from the Raja that while I remained in his territory no payment was to be taken for anything supplied to my camp. The Tehsildar of Tarnot had previously said that he could not *receive* payment for anything without the Raja's order, but I had insisted on his accepting it, as the custom was not a good one for my servants, and would be sure to involve some hardship on the people, though the Raja's officers protested that due deductions would be made them from their rental for whatever was supplied.

In the evening a feeling of weariness which I had experienced for the past few days became intensified, and I felt other symptoms of approaching fever, the cause of which I had little hesitation in attributing to the drenchings from dew off the long grass with which each morning, for some days past, I had commenced my day's work. The next day I marched six miles to the village of Rain, passing during the morning through a village called Manickgurh, where I had been falsely led to believe there were some ruins. Maragura must, I believe, be the Manickgurh about which I had heard. On arrival at Rain the fever fully declared itself, and I had to succumb to it and go to bed.

The following day I pushed on four miles to Kumuna, and, as soon as my tent was ready, tumbled into bed, where I remained, my head occupied with various strange fantasies, till late in the evening. In the evening the Inspector redeemed a portion of a promise which he had made, that, on arrival at Kumuna, I should find some hundreds of live birds ready in cages for my reception. I found that he had instructed a party of itinerant bird-catchers, called Pardis, to await my arrival. Thenceforth while I remained in Karial these people accompanied my camp; of men, women, and children there were about a dozen, all told; their mat tents they used to convey from place to place on their trained bullocks. During the time they remained with me their captures consisted of peacock, painted partridge, painted sand-grouse, and four species of quail.* The methods practised by these people are as follows:—For peacock, sarus cranes, and bustard, they have a long series of nooses, each provided with a wooden peg, and all connected by a long string. The tension necessary to keep the nooses open is afforded by a slender slip of antelope horn (very much resembling whalebone) which forms the core of the loop. Provided with several sets of these nooses, a trained bullock, and a shield-like cloth screen dyed buff and pierced with eye-holes, the bird-catcher sets out for the jungle, and, on seeing a flock of pea-fowl circles round them under cover of the screen and the bullock, which he guides by a nose-string. The birds feed on undisturbed, and the man rapidly pegs out his long strings of

---

* *Perdicula Cambayensis*, *Microperdix Blewitti*, Hume; *Turnix taigoor*, Sykes; *Cotunix Coromandelica*, Gmel.

nooses, and, when all are properly disposed, moves round to the opposite side of the birds, and then shows himself, when they, of course, run off, and one or more getting their feet in the nooses, fall forwards and flap on the ground, but are immediately captured by the man, who knows that if the birds are permitted to release the strain, the elasticity of the nooses is such that they would open and admit of the bird's escape. Birds of the size of partridges, and all smaller, are caught in long conical bag nets, which are kept open by hoops, and are provided with a pair of folding-doors. The bullocks are also used in conjunction with them, to walk through the grass and drive the birds towards the net, which has previously been fixed in the proper position. Very cruel practices are in vogue with these people with reference to the captured birds, which they wish to keep alive until a purchaser is found. The peacocks have a feather passed through the eyelids, by which means they are effectually blinded, while the smaller birds have both wings and legs broken. I, of course, endeavoured to put a stop to this system, but, from long custom, the men, were always trying to revert to it, and were specially disgusted when two or three birds, from not having been thus disabled, managed to effect their escape.

The early part of the second day at Kumuna I devoted to attempting to cure the fever, as there was a chance of its hanging about me for an indefinite period. In the evening I rode out to examine some hills to the east, and on the following morning, feeling much better, but unfit for hard work, I had a series of beats for a tiger, which was known to inhabit a tract of jungle not far off. In the first piece of jungle driven nothing came in my way, though the cover looked likely enough. But from want of experience, and owing to the absence of a shikari of authority, I saw that the beaters were not good for much. In the first drive a pig was shot by one of the Raja's police. The second drive was across a heavily-grassed plain, with a few scattered trees—most unpromising looking ground, I thought. Nevertheless, a tiger was seen by one of the people to escape towards the river at our backs. Having satisfied myself that the tiger had crossed the bed of the river, I took up a position on the opposite bank, telling the beaters to keep well together in the bordering strip. After a time I heard a shot, and was given to understand by a man who was in a tree, which commanded a view of the river, that the tiger had crossed back to its old ground. This, however, was not the case, as when I least expected it, the beast rushed past me with a roar, but quite hidden from me by grass and jungle. Another drive failed to find him, and I returned to camp in a very weak and feverish condition, and much disgusted with the whole business.

The next marches were to Korlapitta and Dedora, in all thirteen miles. At Dedora the deep-cut gorge of the Under river proved to afford, as I expected it would, a most instructive section of the plateau-forming rocks. This was the last day of January, and my latest news of the civilized world was of the 29th December. During the month my camp had marched 130 miles, and I personally had traversed about 450—most of it on foot, as I could seldom use my horses.

The next day, feeling much stronger, I started very early in order to penetrate the gorge of the Under river, as far as possible. I had not gone very far before I came upon fresh tracks of a very large solitary buffalo. However, I had no time to devote to an attempt at following him to his mid-day lair, which might have been a long distance up a cross valley, and quite out of the direction my work lay in. Proceeding along the bed of the valley I came upon two colonies of a wild race of people called Kumars by their neighbours. They were regular Troglodytes in their habits, dwelling in caves,* and existing chiefly on roots and fish. It is singular to observe how little the people of these wild races do to protect themselves from the inclemency of the weather. In one of these caves the sole protection from the air

---

* At Solon, in the Himalayas, below Simla, there is a colony of people also living in caves, who, I was told, call themselves Kunjwas, a name which is applied to the Khonds of Kalahundi.

was a lean-to of loosely placed branches. The people seemed to be very timid, hiding themselves on our approach. I did not, therefore, like to attempt an examination of their dwellings. After some calling on our part one man was induced to make his appearance. He was a most wretched-looking leprous object, having lost several fingers and toes. He could give no very definite explanation as to his means of subsistence. All he could say was that he lived "by picking up odds and ends, here and there." However, he seemed to be able to afford himself the solace of tobacco. A few cocks and hens at one of the caves, and a goat at the other, were the only domestic animals which I saw.

On return to camp I heard that the *gaontia* of a neighbouring village, Nakpara, had come in to report that a small herd of buffalo was causing damage to his crops, and that he could lead me to the spot where they were likely to be. It was too late and I was too tired to start then on such an expedition; but I told him I would go over to his village early the next morning. I asked him to set watches upon the movements of the buffalo. Rain in the early morning prevented my starting so early as I had intended; but when it had cleared off I took one of the elephants, Anarkalli, as she might, I thought, prove useful in the long grass. When near Nakpara I met the *gaontia* and some of his men. He said that the herd had not visited the crops that morning. But we found their tracks, and, thanks to the recent rain, were able to follow them into the jungle without any difficulty. After a short time a man was put into a tree, and he immediately reported that he saw five buffaloes (a bull, two cows, and two calves) feeding a short distance off and coming towards us. The *gaontia* proposed then that I should get up into a tree, while he and his people would drive them down towards me. To this, however, I would not consent, preferring to stalk up to them as being the safest way of securing a shot. I soon got in sight of them, and, at a distance of about thirty-five or forty yards, fired a couple of shots with the .450 Express into the bull. One ball struck behind the shoulder, a little far back, and the other took effect, but where exactly I could not see. Off the whole herd went, and I followed the broad track through the long grass, which was spattered here and there with blood. Several times I got close to them, but each time they started off again without my seeing them, owing to the grass, which was upwards of seven feet long. At length I found that the wounded bull had separated from the two cows with their calves; and, as it seemed impossible to get sight of the animals, I mounted the elephant and followed the bull's track, and after a time sighted him at a long distance. While taking a long running shot at him, one of the cows with a calf crossed in front of the elephant at pretty close quarters. I fired at her, and saw that she was badly hit, and rather unfortunately I determined to follow her up in order to give the bull time to lie down. After getting several other shots at her she lay down, and the men who had followed the elephant swarmed up trees all round her. Having fired or dropped all my Express cartridges, I fell back on my old muzzle-loading 12-bore rifle, and then advanced; whereupon the calf ran out, being soon followed by the cow, in full charge at the elephant. Anarkalli, not liking the aspect of things, trumpeted and turned tail, and put on a pace which fairly astonished me. All this time I had no little difficulty in keeping myself and four guns, &c., on the pad. However, as the buffalo came on I fired the heavy rifle at her with one hand while I held on with the other. The bullet hit her on the horn just as she was making a vigorous butt at Anarkalli's stern quarters. She then returned to her lair, and quite disappeared from sight by lying down. With some difficulty the mahout got the elephant back again; but, as she was very nervous, I got off the pad into the branches of a tree. Presently the cow stood up, and I then gave her a shot behind the ear which immediately dropped her dead. In all she had received seven bullets, one of the Express balls having, strange to say, broken one of her hind legs high up near its insertion with the pelvis. In spite of this she had run a long distance and made the gallant charge I have described. I was rejoiced, but at the same time somewhat surprised, to find that the elephant had not a scratch, though the buffalo's horns seemed once or twice to have touched. My ammunition being exhausted, I returned to camp, telling the villagers to track up the wounded bull. But they apparently feared to do so; for, though I promised a large reward, they never brought in the head. In the evening I went again to the gorge of the Under river, and found there the tracks of the second cow with those of her calf. She had evidently during the day made off along the bed of the river to the fastnesses where I had previously seen the tracks of the solitary buffalo. Could I have spared the time I should like to have made search for the latter, but the next day I was obliged to push onwards eight miles to Makarbal.

About this time I was rejoiced to receive a bundle of newspapers, forwarded to me by a kind friend from Raipur. To avoid their going astray I had been compelled to have all my own letters and papers forwarded to Jaipur to await my arrival in that part of the country.

From Makarbal I marched seven miles to Banskela, but, owing to rain, was not able to make a start till noon. A stiff climb of about 1,000 feet brought me to the top of the outer bounding ridge of the plateau area, descending from which into the internal valley beyond, I encountered another very complicated section; and on one of the lines of fracture found a hot spring; but, as the water rises in the centre of a large artificial basin, I was unable to ascertain the original temperature. A thermometer, thrust down to where the bubbles were rising, registered 84°, or about that of the air at the time. A lateritic conglomerate and a calcareous tufa occur close by, and the line of fracture is marked by a vein of hæmatite, which is continuous for several miles. A Brahmin from Benares is established by the Raja of Karial as custodian of the spring. He presented me with a basket of the produce of his garden, which, being watered by the spring, was in a luxuriant condition. A lofty mango which grows on the edge of the basin is almost wholly enveloped by a flourishing banyan, the roots of which are bathed by the warm water. According to the Brahmin, this banyan yields seven crops of fruit in the year, thus affording another instance of the local influence of hot springs on vegetation, to which subject I have alluded on page 561. At night, it was said, the water felt quite hot, and that the spring became intermittently energetic, at times rising like a fountain above the general level.

The next marches were to Dindubosa and Nilji. The Udet river, which debouches from the hills at Boidelpur, affords a section of the very complicated relations existing between the Vindhyan quartzites of the plateau and the metamorphic rocks which form the basal formation throughout.

Surrounding Nilji, on the north bank of the Udet river, there is an area of about ten square miles in which teak trees occur. I could not detect anything in the soil or the rocks from which it is derived to which I could attribute this peculiar insulated occurrence of teak. In the jungle surrounding there are no teak trees whatever, but in the southern parts of Patna, about thirty miles off to the north-east, teak is known to occur, and is thence carried to Raipur in some quantity. In Nowagurh on the west, towards the sources of the Udet, I met with a few scattered trees of teak growing in the midst of general jungle. For the most part, the trees in this Nilji forest are gnarled and rather wretched-looking specimens—apparently they suffer from heart-rot. To-day (7th February) a warm breeze from the west seemed to point to the early advent of the hot weather, and the mango trees being thus early in full blossom, and the mhowa just coming into flower, seemed to give further evidence of the same.

On arrival at Nilji I was told that four tigers lived in some neighbouring rocky hills, and accordingly had a buffalo tied up. When tying it up I heard what the people said was a tiger grunting in the neighbouring jungle; but I was not quite so satisfied as to the nature of the animal. Neither on that nor the following night was the buffalo touched, and in several beats of the small hills nothing larger than barking-deer, hares, monkeys, and pea-fowl was seen.

While at Nilji a poor lad in the last stage of tetanus was brought into my camp for treatment. According to the story of his accident, he had been out herding cattle, and was knocked down by them and had his head laid open as they stampeded away from a tiger which had suddenly rushed in amongst them. The next march (seven miles) was to Gondabahali, a few miles from the foot of the Chaoria Hill, a massive block which rises to a height of upwards of 3,000 feet. Bad weather detained me here for three days; on the fourth I marched eight miles to Korntori, and the day following five miles further to Karial, the chief town of the District, and the residence of the Raja. In the afternoon I had a visit from the Raja, who, accompanied by his son, came up to my camp at the head of a procession formed of his servants and retainers. Both father and son were mounted on elephants, and wore very gorgeous golden and jewelled crowns. The Raja's method of descending from the box-like howdah in which he rode was rather amusing than dignified, as he seated himself straddle-wise on the shoulders of a stalwart retainer, who walked with him towards the tent, and then stooping, gently deposited his royal burthen on his feet. He appeared to be an amiable old gentleman, with a peculiarly comical expression of countenance. His whole appearance was suggestive of the monarchs of burlesque. As I expected to leave on the morrow, I accompanied him to his house to pay a return visit. Notwithstanding the amount of state which he was able to keep up out of doors, I found his house, as is so often the case, in a very tumble-down and dirty condition. He spoke to me of the wretched poverty of his ryots, a *good* village yielding only, he said, seven rupees a year, and his whole income not exceeding 6,000 to 7,000. I do not suppose this included his receipts in kind, but these I fancy enable him to feed his establishment, and, perhaps, leave a margin for sale. The whole area of the chieftainship probably exceeds 1,500 square miles. It is said to have been given as a dowry by the Patna chief to a daughter who married one of the ancestors of the present Raja. By caste the Raja is a Chauhan; he speaks Hindustani with difficulty, Uria being the language of his household. The entertainment at his house consisted of dancing and singing by a party of itinerant Raj-Gonds from Sambalpur. This caste seems to furnish the only female dancers in Sambalpur. Their performances are not much encouraged by the true Urias, whose taste in these matters I have already alluded to.

From Karial I marched to Tukla, passing through an area crowded with magnificent bosses and tors, the smooth surfaces of many of these suggested the appearance of an ironclad—stern up.

From Tukla I paid a visit to a place, ten miles distant, called Ranipur-Jural, which is famous for its temples. I had not travelled very far before I felt so weak that I knew I was in for another turn of fever. However, I pushed on, passing through an open grassy plain with a few hills dotted about here and there. The site chosen for the temples which have given this place its celebrity is somewhat peculiar. Two bare, depressed granitic bosses have at least fifty small Sivoid temples (with the usual Orissa form of cogged capitals), perched about them in groups, over an area of about half a square mile. With one exception these temples are built of the local stone, a highly felspathic, garnetiferous, granitic gneiss. The exception is a brick temple of not unartistic design, which must have looked well when the stucco was in place. Near Ranipur there is a pillar and post sort of structure in a ruined condition, and, on the highest point of the most southern boss, there is a circular enclosure with upwards of sixty figures of four-armed females arranged in stalls all round. The heads are all different, and represent, I presume, various *avatars* of Kali. Besides human heads, those of an elephant, cow, deer, &c., are seen. Some of the figures are much damaged, and have fallen down from their stalls. What the age of these remains may be there is nothing to shew, but they may, perhaps, be several centuries old—they all, undoubtedly, belong to the Hindu period. Considering that the temples have been built without mortar, and merely rest on the smooth surface of the rock, it is marvellous how well they are preserved. I did not observe any signs of guardian priests being about the place.

The next march (five miles) was to Koirbari. As an example of the difficulty of getting at the truth about any matter in these parts, I may mention that I was told there were forty houses in the village—on arrival I found two! Supplies were, however, brought in from the neighbourhood. From this place I dismissed the crowd of Karial people who had been accompanying my camp, and I also paid and left behind me the party of Pardis, or bird-catchers.

Owing to the great length of this chapter I have divided it into two sections, and the account of the remainder of this journey will be found in Section 2.

CHAPTER XIII.

SECTION 2.

KALAHUNDI, JAIPUR IN VIZAGAPATAM, BUSTAR, NOWAGURH, RAIPUR, NAGPUR.

1876-77.

ENTER KALAHUNDI — OBSTRUCTIVE POLICEMAN — FEVER — BEAT FOR TIGER—INTERNATIONAL DISPUTE AMONG THE BEATERS — CHAORIA HILL — JUNAGURH — NACH GIRLS — EASTERN GHÂTS — THUNDERSTORM — A HANDSOME OFFER — RAMPUR — BIRDS — BLACK CATTLE — ELEPHANT BECOMES OBSTREPEROUS — KHONDS' "TOTEM" — MOULPATNA — CEREMONIAL VISIT — BAPLAIMALI PLATEAU — RAJA'S SECOND VISIT — THE PARAMOUNT AUTHORITY — FOREST ON THE ASCENT TO THE JAIPUR PLATEAU — BIRDS — POST AT LENGTH RECEIVED — ENTER JAIPUR—DUAL ADMINISTRATION — NEW RACES OF PEOPLE — NAORUNGPUR — PERSIAN HOSPITALITY CONTRASTED WITH INDIAN — BORIGUMA — VISIT JAIPUR — THE RAJA — HISTORY OF JAIPUR — STRANGE SOURCES OF REVENUE—MERIAH SACRIFICES—RAJA THE ROBBER CHIEF—THE GOVERNMENT ON JAIPUR AFFAIRS—CRIMINAL ADMINISTRATION ASSUMED—UNHEALTHINESS OF JAIPUR—REVENUE OF JAIPUR—CHANGE IN PROGRAMME—DISPUTES IN CAMP—KOTEPAD—ELEPHANT MERCHANT—THE SIAM ELEPHANT AT LARGE—EFFORTS TO CAPTURE HIM—MARCH TO BUSTAR—VISITED BY RAJA — BUSTAR ETIQUETTE — STANDING ARMY — WILD ELEPHANT — MAN KILLED BY SIAM ELEPHANT — RACES IN BUSTAR — BUSTAR *v.* JAIPUR — GREAT AMOUNT OF SICKNESS—WAR-DANCE—MAD DOG—DECOY FOR PEAFÔWL — MID-DAY MARCHING — SHOOT A BUFFALO—THE SWAMP-DEER—BRINJARAS — LEAVE MADRAS AND ENTER CENTRAL PROVINCES — GIANT CLIMBING PLANTS — FREQUENT STORMS — ENTER NOWAGURH — SHOOT A FLYING-SQUIRREL — FIND A DEAD TREE-SHREW — PAINTED PARTRIDGE — CAUSES WHICH MAKE LIFE A MISERY IN THE HOT WEATHER—MAN-EATING TIGERS—THE DOW—THE PEOPLE OF CHATISGURH—RAJIM BUILT OF STONE —RAIPUR—SEE WHITE FACES AGAIN — TREASURY — SALE OF OPIUM—EFFECT OF ABNORMAL RAIN ON GUINEA-FOWL—SET OUT FOR NAGPUR—CHICHOLA—SHOOT TWO BEARS AND A HYÆNA—LEAD AND COPPER LODE —TRANSPORT OF GRAIN—BIRDS—TROTTING-BULLOCKS—VALUE OF MONEY NOT UNDERSTOOD — BANDARA — NAGPUR — WARORA COAL-MINES — RETURN TO CALCUTTA.

ON leaving Karial the next march was to Manjer in Kalahundi, eleven miles distant. On arrival I found that, owing to the obstructive interference of a Brahmin police Darogah, my messenger, whom

I had sent on two days before, had been unable to get the *Gaontia* or head man of the village to make the usual preparations. The Darogah's position, like that taken by many of his rascally *confrères* under similar circumstances in British territory, was that he had received "no orders on the subject," and could not act without them. As, although the sun was very hot, I was shivering from ague, I was not in a mood for much parley, and so, in a very few and brief sentences, the purport of which he could not possibly misunderstand, I told him that I would make matters extremely unpleasant for him if he did not personally aid in giving assistance. This had the desired effect, and the *Gaontia*, who proved to be not a bad sort of fellow, soon produced what was required, and, somewhat to my astonishment after what had happened, prayed me not to pay for anything. Owing to the badness of the road, the elephants were not up till late. No sooner was my tent pitched than I had to go to bed and spend the afternoon in accomplishing the successive stages of the fever. In the evening, in response to a message I had sent on some days before, several servants of the Kalahundi Raja arrived and placed themselves under my orders while I remained in the district. The Raja himself was away at Delhi at the assemblage. The *Gaontia* then told me that on the previous night a cow had been killed by a tiger at the foot of a small rocky hill within a rifle-shot of my tent, and that if I liked he would undertake on the following day to shew me the animal, with whose habits he professed himself to be thoroughly acquainted. As I was very weak, and many of the servants, besides the native doctor, were down with fever, I thought it well to make a halt, and next morning beaters were collected; but, as men were scarce in the neighbourhood, I ordered the Karial Jemidar and constables, who had followed me in order to get certificates, to cross the border into their own district, and bring over a detachment of their own men. The beat took place, but nothing came in my way. Perhaps it was well that a tiger did not come, as I was perched on a rock easy of access, and my nerves, owing to weakness caused by the fever, were in by no means as steady a condition as was desirable under the circumstances. Presently I heard a row amongst the beaters, and the names of different animals were shouted out. On getting to the spot I found that a young leopard had been killed with arrows, and was the subject of a serious dispute between the Kalahundi men headed by the *Gaontia* and their neighbours of Karial headed by the Jemidar. The result of my enquiry into the matter was that I found that a Kalahundi man shot first, and that his arrow had simply passed right through the loose skin of the back without doing any serious injury, and that the Karial man then killed with a well-planted arrow. According to the rules of sport the Kalahundi man, who first drew blood, was entitled to the animal; but, as I wished to make things pleasant all round, I rewarded both men equally. This was the first indication I had observed of a bad feeling existing between the people of these adjoining states. I soon found that it was much stronger than could be due to mere clannish feeling. The Karial Jemidar and constables were refused food on the day of our arrival by the *Gaontia*, and had to be fed by my men, while Abdul Rahim, the inspector who had accompanied my camp in Karial, was, I was told, an outlaw from Kalahundi. The bluff Chaoria Hill, already mentioned, was a disputed property between the two Rajas. The ascent of this hill I was quite unable to attempt, as a steep scramble of upwards of 2,000 feet required more vigour than the fever had left in me. The next marches were to Daspur and Junagurh, nine and eight miles respectively. The name Junagurh means the old fort, and the place was formerly the residence of the Kalahundi Rajas, but was deserted some years ago. The permanent residence is twenty miles distant, though Junagurh is occasionally visited. In the evening some nach girls, with their attendant musicians, danced before my tent. The girls were most ugly and debased-looking specimens of humanity, though they evidently thought a good deal of their tawdry finery. I merely mention them on account of the peculiarity of the instruments used to accompany their excruciatingly inharmonious singing. These consisted of hollow cylinders covered with skin at one end. From the centre of the skin proceeded a string, which was held in the left hand and strained tight, the cylinder being kept under the arm, and with the fingers of his right hand the operator twanged out the hideous discord on the string. Having listened for ten minutes I dismissed the party with a reward about equal to the price of an opera stall, and I heard them murmuring as they went off, their discontent being due not so much to the amount of the reward as that I had not listened through the whole of their very ill-prepared *repertoire.*

From Junagurh I marched seven miles to Rajpur. Close by was the commencement of a series of ranges of hills, which run from north to south and spread eastwards to Ganjam, forming a portion of what are called the Eastern Ghâts. While out in the afternoon I was caught in a thunderstorm of unusual violence, which I found, on return to camp, had very nearly carried away my tent. Had it not been for some conveniently-situated trees, to which my Jemidar tied the principal ropes, this would have happened, as under the soaking rain the pegs had all drawn. What I had seen of the rocks was so curious and unexpected, that I did not want the additional argument of wet tents to make me determine upon a halt on the following day.

The next morning was devoted to an examination of the hills, which proved to be made up of an ancient group of volcanic rocks, whose characters had been completely modified by the general metamorphism of the rocks with which they were associated.

From Rajpur I marched eleven miles to Kalompur. I there received a visit from the brother of the Rampur Raja, a chieftain subordinate to Kalahundi. He was much pleased and astonished with my Express rifles and other weapons—so pleased, in fact, that he subsequently sent a message to say that he would like to receive one as a present. My servants, however, acting on my behalf, declined this handsome offer, and assured him that they were of enormous value.

On the following day I ascended the hills towards Rampur, a stiff climb of about 1,500 feet, bringing me to the elevation of the higher valleys. The road was very steep in places and covered with tumbled blocks of stone throughout. A fine forest abounding in large sal trees occurs on the outer face, but there is no teak. I heard the notes of many species of birds not commonly met with below. The shama (*Cercotrichas macrouras*, Gmel.) seemed to be particularly abundant, as I heard its sweet thrush-like notes resounding from the valleys. Owing to the thickness of the foliage I scarcely saw any birds, but I shot one, the black-crested yellow bulbul (*Rubigula flaviventris*), which is a rare species in this part of the country. I heard jungle-fowl for the first time since I had left the vicinity of the Mahanadi. On the plateau portion of the hills I noticed that the cattle exhibited a percentage of melanism very much higher than is to be found in the plains. Melanism is common, I believe, in all hilly countries, but I am not aware that the cause of it has ever been properly explained.

The next morning I marched eleven miles from Kalompur to Kundaimunda. While the male elephant, Mowlah, was being strapped up for his load, he suddenly attacked the mahout's assistant and, with a swing of his trunk, flung him rolling over the ground. The poor man who had already a leg damaged by a wound received previously, looked a most pitiful object as he squatted crying on the ground. A number of Khond coolies accompanied the camp to show the road and carry odd parcels. Not one of them, however, could be induced to carry a basket which contained the skin of the young leopard mentioned on a previous page. This, so far as I could make out, was because the animal was the *totem*, or sacred beast of the tribe. Again I felt symptoms of fever and I was forced to come to the conclusion that a single day's severe work in this country was sufficient to bring on an attack.

On the following day I marched to Moulpatna, leaving everything which I was not likely to require behind at Kundaimunda, together with half the men and elephants. The ascent of the ghât proved a much more serious affair than I had anticipated. However, the elephants managed, being very lightly laden, to accomplish it, though there were one or two spots which very nearly stopped them. I found that Moulpatna was about 1,300 feet above the last camp. It is situated in the valley of the Indravati river, which rises some miles further to the north. The village seemed to be a very small one, but the portion of it occupied by the zemindar, who is called, by courtesy, Raja, was hidden from view by clumps of growing bamboos, which are employed as a means of fortification in these wild parts. I was somewhat astonished to find a tent in very fair condition pitched for my accommodation, and still more so when the Raja, accompanied by his brother, came to pay a formal visit in the evening, as I had supposed that being subordinate to Kalahundi he was not likely to be a person of much consideration. The first intimation of the extent of the *cortège* about to approach was given by the arrival of half-a-dozen chairs for those of the Raja's suite and family who were to accompany him, and were by their position entitled to the dignity of a seat. The procession soon made its appearance with torches and music in the van, followed by a magnificent tusker elephant, surrounded by spearmen to keep him in order; then came the Raja and his brother, mounted on a pair of handsome piebald ponies, and surrounded and followed by standard and umbrella-bearers, matchlock-men, &c., &c. A salute was fired on his majesty reaching my tent. Both he and his brother were gorgeously attired with handsome gold and jewelled crowns, kincob dresses, and patent leather boots, and carried light English-made canes in their hands. The whole display was very complete and excited the approval of my servants. I certainly did not expect to see such a sight in a country chiefly inhabited by poverty-stricken Khonds (locally called Kunjwas), Suris, and Domes. The young men were at first rather timid, but as they gained confidence shewed themselves remarkably intelligent, and seemed to be specially interested in some astronomical topics which I explained to them. I found that they were aware of the fact that an eclipse of the moon was to take place that night.

On the following day I paid a visit to the Baplaimali plateau, which was about seven miles off. Having crossed the Indravati river, which owing to the rainfall of the previous week was very full, I passed through a series of north to south valleys and intervening ridges with Khond villages scattered about here and there. The ascent to the plateau was not very steep though the elevation attained is 3,587 feet above the sea. The surface is nearly devoid of vegetation, being of laterite, which forms a cap about 300 feet in thickness. From the view obtainable from the summit it is plain that this plateau is only one out of many having similar characters, which rise to elevations varying from 3,000 to 4,000 feet above the sea, and it can scarcely be doubted that the caps of laterite formed at one time a continuous bed. If such was the case, an enormous period must have elapsed while denudation has operated to produce the isolation of the plateaus.

In the evening the Raja again came over, but on this occasion he and his brother had laid aside their magnificence to a great extent. Our conversation was in continuation of that of the previous evening, and related principally to the stars. Some disturbance was caused during the day by the Kalahundi people wanting to exert their paramount authority in reference to supplies, while those of Moulpatna * jealous of such interference endeavoured to shew their independence. The dispute arrived at a climax when the Kalahundi man accused one of the Moulpatna men with deliberate attempt to poison my servants by supplying adulterated ghi, and threatened to make a prisoner of him and carry him off to Kalahundi. My servants were, however, very well entertained, and I believe some of them received presents of cloth and rupees, but that I did not hear of till some days later, or I should have endeavoured to prevent it.

---

* Moulpatna, together with several other neighbouring estates, was given, in the year 1712, by the Jaipur Raja to the Zemindar of Thuamal, whose daughter the Raja at the same time espoused; a quit rent of 300 rupees was paid for these estates up to the year 1862, at which time the independency of Kuripur, one of the estates above mentioned, was declared by the Governor-General.

On the following day I descended the same pass as that by which I had ascended, meeting *en route* streams of people heavily laden, and toiling up the steep ascent to take part in a weekly market which was held on that day. A crowd of Khonds, some of them very wild-looking fellows, accompanied me to Dansuli, where I found the men I had left below awaiting my arrival. I heard that during my absence the elephant "Mowlah" had broken loose, but had fortunately come back to camp of his own accord, after people had been searching for him in every direction.

From Dansuli I had intended to march up to Tetulkuti on the Jaipur plateau; but, finding the road very bad up to the foot of the ghât, I was compelled to remain at a small village called Pundi. A remarkably fine forest here clothes the slopes of the plateau, and I obtained or saw several rare birds, including trogons (*Harpactes fasciatus*), and black mainas (*Eulabes intermedia*).

In the evening I was rejoiced at receiving by the hands of a messenger, whom I had sent on some days before, my letters, &c., which had been accumulating at the Jaipur post-office for about two months. Not to speak of letters, books, &c., about seventy newspapers had to be gone through before I could venture to consider myself *au courant* with the course of events. To arrange them in order, and read the telegrams, beginning with the most recent, was the first thing to be done. The news was not of so startling a character as I had expected. It chiefly referred to the hanging fire of the Turkish conference.

Dismissing the Kalahundi men as I was about to enter Jaipur, I next day ascended the plateau by a not very difficult ghât at Tetulkuti. Here I found to my disgust that all the preliminary business about getting assistance from the local authorities had again to be gone through. In the present instance, too, I found a peculiar dual administration to exist of which I had previously no notice. The whole system of carrying on affairs in Jaipur is, as I shall presently shew, of an unusual character, and it is to be hoped, for the sake of the general body of ratepayers, that it is unique. The magisterial powers in the district are wholly in the hands of the Madras Government, represented by their agent at Vizagapatam, and his assistants, Tehsildars, and police, who are stationed throughout the country. These officials, however, have nothing to do with revenue matters, which are completely in the hands of the Raja. This being the case the government officials are not in a position to aid in reference to supplies. As, until some properly organised arrangements were made, I knew from the character of the country I should have endless trouble, I was compelled to push on towards Jaipur in order to get into proximity with the authorities. At Tetulkuti, where I remained for two days, the foreign character of the people as compared with those whom I had left behind became tolerably apparent. Both in dress and language the Telegu element was to a great extent apparent, though the latter was, I believe, nominally Uria.

The next march was (twelve miles) to Naorungpur, the residence of a Zemindar, the present one being a widow who is generally spoken of as the Rani of Naorungpur. Much of the country passed through is alluvial, a large portion of it being under cultivation. The jungle patches include some fine sal trees scattered here and there. The villages are large and clean. The people appear to be in good circumstances, and robust, but most of the women seen about were most hideously ugly. Dirty yellow, as in Orissa, is the ordinary colour of their *saris*, which are worn somewhat differently here. Although now the 5th of March, the weather was by no means unpleasantly hot.

Some distance from Naorungpur I was met by the head man of the Rani's establishment who conducted me to the camping-place, where a tent, in anticipation of the arrival of my own, was erected for my convenience, and *dallis* of fruits, &c., in great abundance were sent to me by her majesty, who enjoys the reputation of being an old lady of considerable intelligence and acumen with reference to the management of her estate. Save upon one occasion in Sirguja where the Raja had a sort of guest-house, Moulpatna and Naorungpur are the only places where shelter has been provided for me by native chiefs. In Persia we read that it is possible to travel hundreds of miles and to be daily accommodated in a good house—the owners temporarily vacating. In India, on the other hand, off the regular line where government rest-houses are established, and, perhaps, in the capital towns of Rajputana chiefs, a traveller, unprovided with tents, can only obtain shelter in dirty cow-houses; but even that class of lodging would often be denied to him by the stricter class of Hindus.

The next day I marched southwards to Boriguma, twelve miles. Here I found a *cutcha* bungalow, and the first indications of a made road which I had seen for months. But as I had arranged to stop here until some proper arrangements for the supply of my camp could be made with the Raja, it was rather perplexing to learn that the people of the neighbouring villages professed themselves to be able to furnish only one day's supplies, and there was no market or bazaar to which I could send for what was necessary. I despatched a messenger to the Raja with a letter requesting immediate assistance, and determined to have at least one day of rest in order to write letters, read my news, and give the men some chance of shaking off their fevers. Shortly after arrival I heard that there had been a kill near the village; on examination I could find no footprints near the carcase to indicate whether it had been a tiger or a leopard which had done the deed, and the people could not say. According to the rule believed in by some sportsmen that a tiger commences to eat the hind quarters, while a leopard begins with the fore, it ought to have been a tiger; but this I did not think probable, from the place, and from the fact that no tiger was known to live in the neighbourhood. As it was already raining, and there was no moon, I did not think it worth while sitting up at night, as I had been always unsuccessful at that kind of sport.

My intention of spending a quiet day writing letters and reading up the news to date was frustrated by the receipt on the following morning of a letter from Captain Blaxland, the Assistant-Agent in charge of Jaipur, inviting me to meet him at Jaipur where he expected to be for the day. Accordingly I set out at 10 o'clock to ride the fourteen miles which intervened, and found him on arrival, together with the Superintendent of Police, occupying a bungalow near the town. It was a great pleasure to me to meet them after having spent over ten weeks alone. In the evening the Raja paid a demi-official visit. He proved to belong to the heavy unintellectual type of chieftains who are completely in the hands of their creatures. So much was this the case that the Government was compelled to press upon him the appointment of a well-educated Dewan who, though not, I believe, liked either by him or the people, was enabled to keep matters straight and from lapsing into confusion.

The Raja rode on a pony which was an innovation on his usual custom of travelling in a palki, or, as it is more commonly called in Madras, a palanquin, and was accompanied by a small cavalcade, and a crier with a deep and sonorous voice who proclaimed the monarch's might and titles aloud as he approached. He had been with the greatest difficulty induced by the Government to attend the Delhi assemblage, in charge of the Assistant-Agent, and had made the grand tour of India from Madras to Delhi, and home by Calcutta and Jugernath. At Madras he had been introduced to the Prince of Wales who was much struck with a party of his paiks or swordsmen, who performed a war dance, and were photographed for his Royal Highness. From the Raja I obtained a copy of this photograph, and of some others representing himself and followers, which I regret being unable to reproduce here, as they illustrate some strange ethnological types.

Here it will perhaps be most opportune to leave the course of the narrative in order to give some account of the past history of Jaipur. According to the family legend, the Raja of Jaipur* is descended from a line of kings of Jambudesa. The eighty-eighth prince of this line, Vinayak Deo, was adopted by the old Sila Vansa Raja of the country, who gave him his daughter in

* The following facts are chiefly derived from the account published in the "Vizagapatam District Manual," by D. F. Carmichael, Esq., M.C.S.

marriage, and resigned in his favour. A more probable story is that the first of the line was an official at the court of the Gujpatis, at Cuttack, in Orissa. In the commencement of the fourteenth century the Gujpatis conquered the country southwards from Orissa, as far as the deltas of the Krishna and Godavari rivers, and in A.D. 1568, their kingdom was overthrown by the forces of the Mahomedan Governor-General of Bengal. It is supposed that in the interval which elapsed, the above-mentioned official, Vinayak Deo, a Rajput of the Lunar line, was established as the Jaipur chief by the Gujpatis, and that in order to strengthen his authority over the wild races of the highlands he took the last princess of the Sila Vansa rulers as his second wife. Be this the true origin of the family or not, it is known that in the year 1652 it was found by the Mahomedan general not only in possession of the present Jaipur Zemindari, but also of all the hill Zemindaris at the base of the ghâts. The tribute payable to the General was fixed at 24,000 rupees.

About this time the Vizianagram Raj was established, and grew so rapidly that in 1773-74, Sitaram Raj, brother and Dewan of the Vizianagram chief, aided by two battalions of Company's troops of sepoys drove out the Raja, who took refuge in Bustar; but finding the country to be unmanageable, he afterwards reinstated him, fixing the revenue to be paid to Vizianagram at 40,000 rupees. This state of things continued till 1794, when in reward for his not joining in disturbances which took place on the death of the Vizianagram chief, Lord Hobart granted a *Sannad* to Ramchandra Deo, the then Raja of Jaipur, for the possession of his estate to himself and heirs in perpetuity, on payment of an annual tribute of 25,000 rupees. This sum was further reduced to 16,000 at the permanent settlement of 1803, in consideration of remission of certain taxes which had been a source of revenue to the Raja; but the maintenance of which was considered to be objectionable by the Government. Traders of all kinds had been heavily mulcted—the transit dues for salt and other commodities being particularly heavy. The Raja used moreover to "sell licenses permitting the holders to assume the sacred thread common to the upper classes, to use the sectarial marks smeared by Hindus on their foreheads, to wear bracelets of the precious metals, and even to use an umbrella, provided always that it is of calico; for to do them justice it must be said that there is no charge where the article is of palmyra leaf only."

Meriah sacrifices, there is no doubt, used to be practised, and in all probability were a source of income. The boys and girls who were purchased by the wealthier classes, and reared up for this purpose, were called Toras and Torees respectively. There is "reason to believe that the present Raja, when he installed himself at his father's decease in 1861, sacrificed a young girl of thirteen years of age at the shrine of the goddess, Durga, at the town of Jaipur."* Thus we see evidence that a custom similar to those for which the kingdom of Dahomey has become so notorious, existed in India in a part of the country nominally under British supervision only a few years ago. The Raja was, moreover, it is believed, practically the patron of the robbers and thieves of his territory, and either directly or indirectly through his officials became the recipient of a share of the stolen property.

In one large taluk female infanticide was also a source of income. When parents wished to destroy a child they had to procure a license from an official (the Ameen) in charge of the taluk. This official, on the other hand, had to pay the Raja for permission to collect these fees. Moreover, "when any person wished to marry the widow of one of the Gour, Sundi, Dome, or Buttra castes, he had to pay a fee to the Raja, as these women were called the widowed daughters of the Raja."

From the time of the permanent settlement in 1803 up to 1848, beyond receiving the tribute of 16,000 rupees, the officers of Government took little interest in the affairs of Jaipur. On one occasion when the Raja was slack in his payments, it was even

* Report by Mr. Carmichael, "Manual," p. 105.

thought by the Madras Government to be too wild and difficult a country to enter with an armed force, and it was proposed "to transfer the Zemindari to the Nagpur State, but the offer was declined."

In the year 1848, rebellion and anarchy within the state assumed such proportions that it became necessary for the Agent, Mr. Smollett, to visit the district. The leaders of the party in opposition to the Raja were his eldest son, the present Raja, and his mother; they were supported by most of the influential men of the country. Mr. Smollett only visited the purgunas below the ghâts. His first report was followed by others, in which he strongly urged, as the only means of producing order and quiet, the location of a police force in the country. To this "the Honourable Court of Directors objected, that 'we never had exercised police control in the Zemindari; that it was cursed with a pestilential climate; and that it would be sufficient, if without meddling in the internal dissensions of such a tract, we repelled all incursions into the low country.'" Mr. Smollett strongly protested against this evasion of what he considered to be the duty of the Government.

In 1855, Jaipur affairs were again under discussion, owing to the discovery of the prevalence of both sutti and meriah sacrifices. Regarding the former, the Raja "having been questioned on the subject, admitted the frequency of the rite within his territories, but pleaded ignorance of any knowledge either of the unlawfulness of the act, or of the order of Government prohibiting it." After further enquiries the Madras Government, in 1855, authorised the Agent to assume "the control, both police and revenue, of the tracts above the ghâts, the taluks below being managed by the agency direct." But it was not to be, for Lord Dalhousie at once objected on the ground that "to do so, may involve the British Government in a protracted jungle and hill war, such as that of Gumsur." Mr. Smollett pointed out that the analogy to Gumsur did not hold, as in that case the Raja was deposed, while in the present instance the Raja's authority was to be established. He further held that the Zemindar was not responsible under the original *Sannad* for the suppression of crime, while the Government was.

In August, 1860, the old Raja, Sri Vikrama Deo, died, and was succeeded by his son, Sri Ramchandra Deo, the present Raja. It being found that the new Government was no more competent than the late one, it was at last settled to assume the direct administration of the country, and in January, 1863, two officers, Lieutenant Smith as Assistant-Agent, and Captain Galbraith as Assistant-Superintendent of Police, arrived in Jaipur. After noticing the jealous hostility which was, for a time, shewn to these officers by the advisers of the Raja, the Agent reviews the results of the first year's working of the new system in the following words:—"Truth to say we are working out in Jaipur an experiment which has never been tried before. Eighty years of independent native misrule have been succeeded at once, without compromise and without any exhibition of military or semi-military force, by an administration which aims at the same completeness as prevails in our oldest provinces. Not a shadow of their ancient authority remains to the Raja of Jaipur and his chiefs. * * * That we have met in Jaipur with no open menace, and with no higher degree of passive resistance than was reasonably to be expected, is first due to the fact that we commenced our reforms by restoring to the Raja the five taluks of Gunapur, of which we assumed the management during the Jaipur disturbances of 1855-6. This at once assured him and his followers that our object was not annexation. It is due secondly, perhaps, to the success of last year's tour, in the course of which every chieftain of note was visited, and a knowledge of the nature and difficulties of the country acquired; but it is due, lastly and principally, to the fortitude and temper with which the Junior-Assistant (Lieutenant Smith), and the Assistant-Superintendent of Police (Captain Galbraith), have met all the difficulties of a new and isolated position, in the midst of much sickness, discomfort, and privation."

Had I possession of the facts, I have no doubt that a long roll of suffering and even of death, might be recorded from among the histories of the succession of Executive and Survey officers who have resided since that time in this unhealthy tract. A solitary grave near Jaipur records on a granite tablet sent by his friends from England, that one young officer died thus at his post. The late Captain Basevi's narration of his preliminary survey of Jaipur, gives a thrilling account of the sufferings of himself and party. In one instance he describes arriving at an Assistant's camp and finding every one of the party prostrated by fever, and not having even sufficient strength left to pitch their tents.

It will be observed that Mr. Smollett's suggestion to place the revenues of the country also under the management of the Government officers was not adopted; and to this day, except in the form of tendering advice, the officers cannot interfere in these matters. If purely native management possessed a tithe of the qualities which are so freely ascribed to it by a certain class of writers, the condition of this state ought certainly to exhibit some evidence of them. It is difficult to say what the revenue of the country would be under British management, but I can scarcely believe that £20,000 nett would not be exceeded in the first year's collection, and as communications became opened up, and the ryots began to flourish under a lenient treatment, this sum would tend to increase steadily. But what do we find to be the case? On the one hand the Raja is robbed, and at times nearly insolvent, and unable to pay up to date the miserable 16,000 rupees, which is but a fraction of the expenditure disbursed by the Government on account of the magistracy. On the other hand, the population generally is in a very impoverished and wretched condition, and along the frontiers there are many people who are constantly moving from Jaipur into the neighbouring states to avoid payment of revenue, it being the custom to allow people to squat and cultivate for two years without payment; and so they oscillate backwards and forwards, yielding permanent allegiance to no one. At the same time, to be consistent with what I have elsewhere stated, I must admit that the advantages to the ryots in some tracts under direct British rule are by no means so manifest as might be imagined from the advance in general prosperity which follows from British administration, the effect of which is often to create a class of well-to-do farmers and merchants, rather than to elevate the lower strata of the population above their hand-to-mouth existence.

March 8th.—Jaipur to Boriguma.—I was unable to go into Koraput, the station where Captain Blaxland had his head-quarters, as I had left my camp where there seemed to be a deficiency of supplies, and my men might have got into trouble had they been left alone. Accordingly I returned to Boriguma, where, after giving full consideration to the subject, I determined to modify my original programme, and instead of working down to the coast at Vizagapatam, to march back northwards after visiting Bustar, to Raipur and Nagpur in the Central Provinces. It took the whole of this afternoon and that of the day which followed to bring myself up to the level of current events by a careful perusal of the already-mentioned seventy newspapers.

March 10th.—Boriguma to Sasahandi.—To-day occurred the most serious, though it was not the first, of the long foreseen troubles due to the presence of women in camp. One Mrs. Mahout came to complain that she had been turned away by her husband (Khoda Bux) in consequence of another of the women having said bad things of her in connection with Saidon, the jemidar. I accordingly called up the husband, and told him that he must take back his wife, as he appeared not to believe the accusations, and certainly shewed no enmity towards the alleged co-respondent. He said his own honour was affected by the imputation, and that his honour was dearer to him than life, and very much dearer to him than the woman. He continued to make remarks of this character, and to refuse to act upon my order, until I was at length compelled to chastise him. Now mark the sequel: next day, when on the line of route, and when the senior mahout, who was the husband of the mischief-maker, and who had charge of the troublesome elephant, was fully occupied, Khoda Bux, determined to be revenged, gave the old gossip a tremendous thrashing, and in the evening Kurim came to complain. Here was a pretty dispute for settlement. I could not but feel that already I had been the cause of a new phase of it by my interference. The only thing to be done was to assume, if I did not feel it, an excess of anger with all parties, and to *defer* judgment and the infliction of penalties—thus keeping the rod in suspense. Immediate punishment would certainly have been followed by further complications, and, as is commonly the case, in order to get one another into evil repute, the men would have taken good care that I should somehow be put to inconvenience.

March 11th.—Sasahandi to Kotepad.—Kotepad is a place of some importance in consequence of its being a border town between the territories of Jaipur and Bustar, and the scene of many contests in former years. I found the people civil, and the sub-magistrate, as representing the British Executive, and a functionary called a Nigoman, or revenue collector, on the part of the Raja, waited upon me, and the latter sent an extensive dalli of fruit, &c. The neighbourhood of Kotepad, owing to the lateritic character of the soil in the uplands is very sparsely covered with jungle. In the hollows there is a fair amount of rice cultivation.

On the following day I explored a wide area to the south of Kotepad, and in the evening, after my return, was visited by a young Kabuli merchant, who cried as he besought my aid. He told me that he and another Kabuli had with them an elephant which both the mahout and assistant had deserted during the last three or four days; that there was great difficulty in getting water for it, as the people of Kotepad would run away after taking prepayment for bringing it, and that it was wholly impossible to get any branches for it. He added that they were strangers in a strange land, and could not understand a word of the language of the country, which was Uria. His uncle, to whose party he belonged, had, he believed, gone on to Bustar by a southern route from Jaipur, and what he wanted from me was the loan of one of the mahouts' assistants to take on the elephant with my camp to Bustar. He represented it as being a poor-spirited creature which would go along with him if he only knew the words of command. I recommended him to send word to his uncle at Bustar, and get aid from him. To this he replied that there was a difficulty about getting any trustworthy person to send, and that the elephant would suffer great hardships from the delay. He then besought me so earnestly and persistently for aid, that, in spite of my knowing the risk attached to meddling with strange elephants, I so far yielded that I called up my mahouts and asked them what they thought of the matter. I found that they had already seen the elephant, and had even mounted him as he stood chained up. In reply to my question as to whether they could venture to bring him on, they said that if he would kneel when told to do so, they would have no hesitation in taking charge of him on the road. During the day he had not done so, but had permitted them to mount him as I have said. Not having seen the elephant save from a long distance, I had no means of forming an opinion as to the nature of the animal except from such information as I received from the Kabuli and my own men. I settled then that the best mahout (Khoda Bux) of one of my elephants, and the best mate (Domun) of another, should visit the Kabuli's elephant early the next morning, and that if they felt satisfied that there was no danger they should bring it on to the next camp.

March 13th.—Kotepad to Pirinji.—Shortly after the arrival of my four elephants with the camp, the merchant's elephant was brought in triumphantly by Khoda Bux. I then saw that it was, if not quite the tallest, certainly the largest, elephant I had ever seen. It had an enormous head and rather sloping quarters, and was of a somewhat reddish hue. Altogether its appearance was very different from any Indian elephant I had ever seen; and I was then told that it had been marched up all the way from Bangkok in Siam. That it was a remarkable elephant may be judged from the fact that the price asked for it was 8,000 rupees, or more than four times the price ordinarily asked for a good elephant in India. It seemed to be tolerably amenable to orders, and knelt down when told to do so. It was then taken off and tied up in a grove near the village. I heard nothing further about it till the afternoon, when news was brought that it had been taken down to water by the mahout, who, over-confident of his powers, had allowed the Kabuli to remove the chain-couplings from its feet. On reaching the water the elephant immersed itself at once, and the mahout, according to his own account, narrowly escaped a blow from its trunk as he swam to the shore. Having refreshed itself, the elephant walked on shore, and would not then permit anyone to approach it. Application was accordingly made to me to permit the three female elephants to be made use of to decoy it back to the grove. Shortly afterwards, when I went out to the scene of operations, I found that, aided by the females, the mahouts often got it close to the tree, but that when there it was most careful to prevent all attempts to tie it up, and it soon began to charge at everyone who went near it, including myself. At last as night fell nothing had been accomplished, and we were compelled to permit it to walk off in the direction of some heavy jungles to the southward, or whither else it listed; but the young Kabuli declared that it would not go far, as it had been reared in confinement in Siam, and would be afraid to go into the jungle.

March 14th.—Pirinji.—As it had been my intention to march for Bustar to-day, the tent was taken down at an early hour; but before starting I sent to enquire for the elephant, if it were still in the neighbourhood. Before the messenger returned the Kabuli servant of the boy merchant came in and gave us to understand, in his very limited Hindustani, that the elephant was then near a village about two miles off, and that during the night it had visited a grove where some of the Raja of Jaipur's elephants were tethered, which were thereupon loosed by the mahouts, who feared their being gored to death where they stood. Hearing all this I thought it incumbent on me not to desert the lad, but to do what I could to get the brute tied up. Accordingly I started with the three female elephants, and on the way picked up two belonging to the Raja, together with some of the men who were then on an elephant-catching expedition, and were supposed to understand the work. On arrival at the village of Amgaon we found the elephant with a circle of men round him in a grove of trees close by, which included a magnificent banyan. After the mahouts and Foujdar had, as they said, satisfied themselves as to the *rung* (*lit.* colour) of the animal, they loosed two of the kunkis or females, who, after a little preliminary timidity, fraternised with the big male. For about two hours or more I watched the attempts made to capture him by slipping a noose over one of his hind feet. He was, however, far too cunning to be so disposed of, and invariably picked up the rope with his trunk and broke it to pieces, while now and then he would charge viciously and put everybody to flight. In the meantime news of the old Kabuli (the uncle of the lad and the proprietor of the elephant) being at a village two miles off reached me, and I had sent for him. On his arrival the first thing he did, and before I could interfere, was to give the lad a severe cuffing. As he seemed to be pretty confident of his ability to tie up the elephant, and as the beast appeared to know him and took rice from his hands, I, being by that time in high fever, retired from the scene and returned to camp, where I had to remain in bed for the rest of the day. Before leaving I had advised the old Kabuli to offer a liberal reward to the Raja's men, in order to induce them to aid him in tying up the animal at once, as, if it remained much longer at large there was no telling what injury it might not do.

March 15th.—Pirinji to Jugdalpur or Bustar.—At a village about half way from Bustar I was informed that it was the Raja's wish that my female elephants should take a round to avoid the town as they had there a wild elephant, which had been decoyed in from the jungle by the Raja's kunkis, but which had not yet been tied up. I was met outside the town by a deputation, and was conducted through the fort to a grove in which my camp was to be pitched. Owing to the round which the elephants had to take, I had a long wait before they arrived. The Raja then sent to say he would pay me a visit in the evening; but a heavy storm coming on, it had to be postponed. A very urgent request was then communicated to me that I should prolong my visit up to the 19th; but I replied it was impossible for me to do so, as I had arranged to be at Kotepad on that date. Later on I was told by my servants that the Raja had, in a swaggering way, declared that it was not the "custom" in Bustar for visitors to leave without his permission, and that, as I had come to suit my own convenience, I should go when it suited his—even if I remained for ten days.

March 16th.—Jugdalpur or Bustar.—After a feverish night, which was rendered otherwise uncomfortable by heavy rain, I started early in order to examine the river beds in the country to the west for sections of the rocks, all being concealed by laterite and alluvium near Jugdalpur itself. In the afternoon the Dewan, a fine-looking old man, with some other officials, came to announce to me that the Raja might shortly be expected to arrive, and again to express a wish that I would prolong my visit. While waiting in my tent, which was filled with chairs, all other articles of furniture having been removed, I had a long conversation with the Dewan on various matters. Among other subjects he spoke of a strange race of people of whom he had heard, and from what he said about them I had no difficulty in recognising the Andamanese as being the race referred to. In all probability the stories he had heard had been told by some returned convict. I was able to shew him some pictures of the Andamanese which aroused his interest not a little. Some time after the Raja's procession made its appearance. It included horses, elephants, the regular army of about forty men, clad in old second-hand red coats, with the facings of a dozen regiments, and dirty white country cloth trowsers, and armed with brown-Besses and bayonets; mace-bearers, &c., and a numerous and miscellaneous crowd of irregulars. The Dewan then asked me to go out fifty paces from the tent to meet the Raja; but my jemidar, mindful of my dignity, whispered to me not to go more than four! However, I went to the spot where the Raja descended from his elephant, which was thirty or forty paces off, and conducted him to the tent. He proved to be a fine-looking old man, with a rather brusque manner, and a habit of not addressing any one directly. I did not observe until after I had shaken hands with him, that he was a leper, and the discovery made me feel rather uncomfortable during the remainder of the audience. As he was departing I made some remark about his army, when he immediately ordered the sergeant to put them through some evolutions. English words of command were used, and a very awkward squad indeed the forty men proved to be, and their knowledge of drill to be vague in the extreme.

On the following day I paid a return visit at the Palace, the Durbar being held in a tumble-down old shed, which was in close proximity to the Raja's stables. On this occasion the Raja alluded to an old-standing dispute about boundaries between himself and Jaipur, and mumbled out something about my declining to go on a shooting expedition with him on the 18th. After this audience, which bored me horribly, I was taken off to see the wild elephant, to which I have already alluded. He was standing close to three kunkis, which were picqueted close to the houses on the margin of the town. He seemed to be much attached to a little baby elephant, which trotted about from one to another. Although he would take sugar-cane from the mahout's hands, and would go to and fro to water with the kunkis, he had not then been chained up, though from various contrivances of poles, &c., which stood about, I concluded efforts had been made to slip on a noose. This elephant was at the time also a subject of dispute between the Rajas of Bustar and Jaipur; and the adjudication of the respective claims were then under consideration of the Madras and Central Provinces Governments. The whole history of the matter, so far as I could gather from very conflicting, and to some extent wholly contradictory statements was, that there had been for many years four elephants at large in the Bustar jungles; but whether they were the survivors of an original herd, or had escaped from captivity during the mutiny, as the Jaipur people maintained, opinions were much divided. At first Bustar gave permission to Jaipur to aid in the capture, and each Raja obtained one elephant, a third elephant died naturally, and the fourth was the one which had just been decoyed into Bustar, and which the Jaipur Raja's men had been waiting for at the place on the frontier where I met them, as before related, when I was attempting the capture of the Siam elephant. The Jaipur Raja was striving to get the Government to interfere, and in support of the claim that the elephant had originally belonged to his family, produced a roll in which the animal's "marks" were duly recorded. Altogether it was a very pretty quarrel, and the source of much bitterness between the adjoining States, which were from other reasons not on very good terms with one another. Whether the matter has been yet decided by the paramount authority or not, I cannot say.

News came up to-day that one of the Jaipur Raja's mahouts had been killed by the Siam elephant. It was said that he had been riding on an elephant past the place where the animal was still at large, and that on its giving chase he had thought it best to slip off from his seat and leave the two elephants together. While doing so he fell, and in a minute the animal was up and trampled him to death, and then tore him to pieces. But this was not the only death connected with this unfortunate business, for the Kabuli lad died of fever, brought on by the exposure and wear and tear to which he had been subjected. It will be best perhaps to state here the subsequent history of this elephant. A week afterwards I recommended the old Kabuli to ask the Raja of Jaipur's assistance. Accordingly he rode off to Jaipur, and, in an audience, the Raja said "I will give you 5,000 rupees for it, and you need not trouble yourself further about it, as my men can capture it." The Kabuli told me that he had accepted this offer, and went next morning to claim its fulfilment; but in the meantime the Raja's advisers had urged him not to waste money by giving the Kabuli anything, as the elephant being at large in his own jungles he could have it caught at his leisure. Subsequently I gave the Kabuli a letter to the Assistant-Agent, who prevailed upon the Raja to capture the animal, and long afterwards I was told that the Raja bought it, adding it to his already numerous stud of about forty. A further detail which I obtained about the matter was that the mahout who had deserted the elephant was still hanging about in the neighbourhood, enjoying the confusion caused by his misconduct. His leaving was said to have been in consequence of the Kabuli lad having struck him. Before going it was reported that he had administered some medicine which had made the animal go wild. Had my pity for the poor young Kabuli not caused me to act in opposition to my better judgment, I should not have had this tragical story to relate; and the moral of it all for you, my reader is, beware how you take charge of strange elephants, even though they be represented to you as being poor-spirited creatures.

March 18th.—Jugdalpur to Tarapur.—The principal inhabitants of Bustar, I found, belonged to races which were previously unknown to me, and since I had not time to make personal enquiries as to their peculiarities, I shall not pause here to quote other authorities regarding them. According to the Dewan, the following are the names of the principal of these races; they are said to possess distinct languages: Bhatra, Muria (= Gond), Purji, Gudwa (or Gudaba), Jhoria, and Mariah or Meriah.

This brief trip into Bustar had enabled me to get a general idea of the geological formation of a wide tract, but in the time available it was, of course, impossible to go into any minute details.

In the afternoon the Raja's Munshi came to Tarapur with a bundle of papers having reference to the long-standing disputes between Jaipur and Bustar. From these I learnt that the matter had been finally disposed of by the Governor-General, in 1862, by establishing the *statu quo*, without much reference to the past history; but, though I copied an abstract of the whole into my diary, I can scarcely suppose that it is likely to be of sufficient interest for reproduction here. But the impression was very strong on my mind that the decision dealt very hardly with the Bustar Raja, who had a large slice of territory taken from him, receiving, in lieu of the homage and tribute, a sum of 3,000 rupees annually from Jaipur. I could not give them any hope that this decision was ever likely to be reversed.

On the following day I marched back to Kotepad, in Jaipur,

where I remained for four days. The unhealthiness of this country may be gathered from the fact that, not to mention other servants, my six chuprasies and the jemidar, and seven men out of the eight in charge of the four elephants, *all* had fever at the same time. It need hardly be said that, under such depressing circumstances, and in places so remote from any real aid, it requires all one's resolution to enable the work of exploration to be carried on with success. I had one consolation here, however, namely, that there was postal communication, of a sort, between Kotepad and the outer world.

March 23rd.—Kotepad to Korenga.—The next two marches were northwards, twelve miles each, to Korenga and Dubgaon. At Korenga, while I was dressing in my tent in the evening, a mad dog ran through the camp and made a rush at my dog, Topsie, but was driven off by the men. I immediately gave chase, and followed it through the village, where, catching sight of it, I shot it. According to the villagers it had been going about in a rabid state for several days, but none of them had attempted to kill it. This was the second case of a mad dog coming into my camp on this journey. Although not a hot year, I heard of numerous cases of rabies subsequently. Generally they are of rare occurrence in India. At Dubgaon I remained for three days, making some long trips in the neighbourhood, to explore various hills and river sections. There are in this part of Jaipur long strips of sal forest, which are intercepted by grassy glades called *beras.*

While I was here the Superintendent of Police arrived, and one evening shewed me a native method of shooting pea-fowl, which he had adopted. On a brick-red cloth screen the figure of a peacock was painted in the rudest possible style of native art, and the sportsman had the screen carried before him by a cooly to the vicinity of the pea-fowl, when he fired at them through a loop-hole. On the first occasion I saw this used as I was watching from a distance, one peacock, which at first ran up to the edge of the jungle, suddenly turned and ran towards the screen as though to give battle to the intruder, when it was knocked over by a shot, though it was not bagged. The next two marches took me twenty miles further northwards to Jergaon, from whence I dismissed some Jaipur officials who had been with my camp to provide supplies, but who had not been particularly useful in that respect, the local Nigomans doing most of the work. I also sent away from here two Ganjam constables who had been sent to act as a guard, &c., in case I entered that district or Vizagapatam as was at one time probable. Having handsome uniforms, they had been useful "properties" to display in addition to my own men in my interviews with the various Rajas. Rain and attacks of fever interfered again much with my work, but I managed in the intervals of both to cover a good deal of ground, my method being to start early in the morning, sling a hammock and have some food cooked at the most distant point reached, remain there till the afternoon when the heat had somewhat moderated, and then return to camp.

April 1st.—Jergaon to Omerkote.—To-day I marched twelve miles, starting at mid-day to Omerkote, where I joined the camp of Captain Blaxland. In ordinary years to set out on a march at mid-day on the 1st of April would be little short of madness, but in this abnormal season of frequent storms and showers it was often necessary to march whenever one could without reference to the time of day. Near the road I saw two antelopes or black buck, and I afterwards heard that a small isolated herd of them lived in the neighbourhood.

April 2nd.—Omerkote.—Hearing that wild buffalo were in the neighbourhood I went to the spot, and after a long stalk got within 150 yards of a small herd of five or six cows, one of which I shot with a single bullet from the 12-bore rifle; the Express, as before, not serving to stop any of the others at which I fired as they retreated. The sport of the thing was very small indeed, and I resolved then that in future I would not shoot any more cow buffaloes out of a herd.

April 3rd.—Omerkote.—To-day I examined the Poragur range of hills to the south of Omerkote. It proved to be formed of hornblendic gneiss rocks with a cap of laterite, forming a narrow plateau. There were some tracks of gaur on the top, such lofty plateaus being a favourite haunt of these animals. On the ascent I saw a male specimen of the trogon (*Harpactes fasciatus*). It fluttered past me like a ball of flame into a bamboo jungle, and although I jumped off my horse and gave chase I failed to see it again. I had, as recorded, met with the dull-plumaged females of this species in the country further north, but this was the first male I had seen alive, and it would have given me as much pleasure to have added the specimen to my collection as it would to have shot a gaur, and very much more pleasure than I derived from shooting the above-mentioned buffalo.

April 4th.—Omerkote to Bera.—To-day I parted from my friends, but, owing to the wet, was again unable to make an early start. The country passed through was very wild, and tracks of animals were abundant, but I only saw one rib-faced or barking-deer (*Cervulus aureus*). Just after sunset an animal set up a hideous cry close to my tent. I supposed that it was a hyæna, but the people declared that it was a hind barasingha, or swamp-deer (*Rucervus duvaucellii*). Bera is the deserted site of a village. I met here a large encampment of Brinjaras, with from five hundred to six hundred pack-cattle on their way back from the coast with salt for Raipur and Nagpur. Along this route I met also many similar troops both coming and going, those coming carrying grain from Chatisgurh. These Brinjaras had with them a fine breed of large dogs, whose deep baying at night contrasted with the fretful and currish howls and barks of the ordinary Indian pariahs of the villages. It was interesting to observe the orderly way in which the Brinjaras stacked the bullocks' pads and loads, which formed, with the aid of canvas, a substantial shelter from the rain. After grazing, the cattle, many of which were very fine animals, were picqueted in lines along the sides of squares surrounding the encampments. In some cases the women and children travelled with the party, and the former might be seen immediately on arrival at a camp to set about their culinary operations while the men attended to the cattle.

April 5th.—Bera to Raigurh.—To-day I continued my journey ten miles northwards. I found Raigurh to be a more civilized place than I had been led to expect. As it was in a central position, I remained there for three days to examine the neighbourhood. The jungle looked very green and bright, and owing to the rain nothing had been burnt, which was both bad for geological work and for shooting. Besides barking-deer and nilgai I saw one hog-deer, which, in consequence of its horns being in velvet had come to the margin of the jungle to feed. It is probably a rare animal in these parts, as from enquiry I had failed to hear of it, and among a large number of horns in the possession of the Nigoman of Omerkote, there was not one of this species. I have no certain knowledge of its occurrence in Chutia Nagpur.

April 8th.—Hathgaon to Risgaon.—To-day I entered the Central Provinces leaving the Madras Presidency behind. I dismissed the Omerkote and Jaipur men who had been accompanying my camp. I found that a very loose system of payment in regard to supplies had been going on under my nose. In some places the Nigomans had received payment, in others they had said they were forbidden by the Raja's orders to receive anything. I found, however, that my bills for the keep of elephants, horses, and table expenses, were maintained as usual, and I had good reason for believing that Saidon, my jemidar, whom I had previously almost implicitly trusted, had been making a large purse for himself by inducing the Nigomans to make some charge so that he might keep his account running. The provisions having in many cases been brought from long distances to the uninhabited spots where I encamped, it was impossible to take any steps by which the actual suppliers should be refunded, and in these native states it would seem that it is the "custom of the country" that they should not be so refunded.

April 9th.—Risgaon to Sobha.—Leaving the camp to follow the direct route, which was only six miles, I struck eastwards for about ten miles, crossing some very broken country covered with long grass, which was drenched with dew. The forest which I traversed included a few fine teak trees, but sal was also present, both growing indiscriminately on the crystalline rocks. Other trees, such as *Sterculia urens*, *Boswellia thurifera*, and *Cochlospermum gossypium*, with other species less familiar to me, made up a very mixed jungle. I had recently been reading Darwin's work on "Climbing Plants," and I noted that all the specimens of the giant creepers (*Bauhinia vahlii* and *Butea superba*) twisted round the trees, some of which were nearly a foot in diameter, from left to right. I subsequently found, however, that this rule is not invariable, and only a few days later, indeed, I met with a curious case in which two thick cables of *Butea*, which apparently started from a common stock, immediately twisted round a large tree in opposite directions, and so continued their spiral courses upwards.

At 10 o'clock I slung my hammock under a bush on the banks of a stream, at a place called Amur; had my breakfast, and set myself to sleep through the heat of the day; but at 12 o'clock, a thunder-storm being imminent, I had to beat a retreat to a miserable Gond hamlet where I sheltered from a downpour. On the rain ceasing I started for camp, but was caught in a return shower, and had a most disagreeable tramp of nominally six miles through jungle, beds of rivers, and long grass. Within the forty-eight hours which preceded 12 o'clock on the following day, there were six distinct thunder-storms with copious rainfall. It will have been observed that in my previous journeys I had never experienced such bad weather as that which characterised this very abnormal season. I was almost inclined to believe that the rainy season had actually commenced, and as I had still about 350 miles of marching before me the prospect was not very pleasant. At the same time the clouds afforded a welcome shelter from the sun which would have been, and indeed was on clear days, very severe.

April 11th.—Sobha to Borgaon.—Borgaon is in the native state of Nowagurh, and I expected to be met on arrival, if not by the Raja, at least by some responsible person deputed by him. But there was no one present, and it seemed probable that I should have again to go through all the trouble I had experienced at first in each of the other states which I had traversed. On this, about the usual date, as I have alluded to in previous pages, I saw the first specimen, a fine male, of the paradise fly-catcher (*Tchitrea paradisii*), and on the following day I saw a number of the same birds, and also some specimens of the yellow-breasted ground-thrush.

While the camp was being pitched there was a loud crash heard in the jungle close by, the cause of which was the falling of a tree into which one of the *mates* had climbed in order to cut branches for his elephant. The tree proved to be a banyan, which was nearly thirty feet high and about two feet in diameter at the base; but it merely consisted of a shell enveloping the decayed remains of the trunk of some other tree, and was held in the loose and damp soil by soft roots, which had given way. The man, though much shaken, and at first I thought internally injured, sustained no permanent ill effects from his tumble.

April 14th.—Chuia to Doarpur.—At this place I found the Raja of Nowagurh residing in a temporary dwelling, which he had come to in consequence of sickness at his capital. In the evening he paid me a visit, and proved to be a snuffy-looking little old man, with dyed hair and very dirty clothes. He did not appear to be equal to much conversation; but his nephew, who bore the title of the *Dow*, proved to be very capable in that respect. On the previous day they had written me a letter, in which they gave one reason for not having met me on the frontier, and they now gave another, which was obviously equally untrue. As it was a serious matter to have found myself left to such slender resources of supply as the poverty-stricken Gond hamlets could afford, and as I had in consequence had to modify my route, avoiding a wild tract which I had wished to examine, I had already forwarded a complaint to the Deputy-Commissioner of Raipur, who subsequently called upon the Raja for an explanation; but in the meantime the Dow accompanied my camp to the frontier of Nowagurh, and, as he proved attentive, and I had no further trouble, I was able to intercede for them and prevent their being visited with the official displeasure which they had incurred by their first neglect to act upon orders they had received regarding me months before. During the audience I made enquiries about a family of man-eating tigers that I had been hearing of for some time, and offered to do my best to exterminate them if the Raja would render the essential assistance; but he received my offer somewhat apathetically, and even began to deny the truth of the stories about the depredations. Subsequently I visited the locality, as I shall presently relate. During the evening, at dusk, when sitting outside my tent, I saw a large squirrel climbing to the topmost branch of a tree close by. Calling for my gun, it was just put into my hands in time to arrest the course in mid-flight of the animal, which proved to be a flying-squirrel (*Pteromys oral*, Tickell), and which was soaring from its lofty perch towards some bushes. This is the only occasion upon which I have seen this animal; being nocturnal or crepuscular, it is doubtless seldom observed, and the Raja's people said they had never seen a *bird* like it before.

The next marches to Milkua, Datbai, and Mahuabatta were comparatively short ones, as there was a good deal of close and interesting geological work to be done along the boundary of two formations occurring in the vicinity.

April 18th.—Mahuabatta.—To-day I picked up a dead specimen of the tree-shrew (*Tupaia Elliotti*). It was quite fresh, and had doubtless been killed during the night. There were some punctures in its body, as though it had been caught in the talons of a bird, possibly an owl.

Painted partridge were very abundant here, and were to be heard calling from every other tuft of grass both in the morning and evening. The difficulty of flushing them is unparalleled in my experience of every other bird. One rose off a clear piece of ground, where the grass was burnt, after I had twice hunted for it with the aid of my two small dogs.

Among the many causes of annoyance which combine to make life a misery in camp in the hot weather, the cries of certain birds are not the least. One of these, that of the hawk-cuckoo

(*Hierococcyx varius*), caused me to use much bad language. By day and night it would reiterate its chromatic scale of seven or eight notes, with a monotony that was to me, when feverishly striving to snatch some much-wanted sleep, simply maddening. The koel, which is another species of cuckoo, the hoopoe, the coppersmith barbet, crows, and a few other species, are also sources of irritation. And if you add to these human voices raised in dispute, tom-toms, the lowing of calves, and a variety of other sounds, you obtain a total number of performers in the hideous concert which renders rest impossible to anyone whose nerves may have been unstrung by fever and the all-pervading heat.

April 21st.—Paragaon.—I came to this place for the express purpose of trying to interview a family of tigers, whose depredations had closed one main line of road, and had caused several small villages to be deserted, after the inhabitants had been more than decimated. The Dow had collected beaters, and this morning we beat a hill to the south-west of Paragaon. I felt confident that there was something in it, as the crows in the trees were very noisy; but nothing save a hare and some pea-fowl were seen by me. Some of the beaters said they saw a bear. In the second beat, which was through a likely strip of jungle, nothing was seen either; but the beaters picked up near a shaded pool the skin of a freshly-killed spotted deer. Everything save the head, feet, and skin had been eaten. The tiger must have somehow managed to sneak off unobserved, though I had placed a pair of elephants on the flanks of the line of trees occupied by matchlock men. The third beat included a small hill, and I was placed by the shikaris on the right of the line, on the flank of the hill. It was supposed that the animals would not follow down the hill to its extremity, but would break off in my direction. Owing to rocks and undergrowth, I could not command a view of the terminal slope of the hill. My own idea was to take up a position on the hill itself; but the shikaris dissuaded me from doing so. As events turned out, some animal passed down the slope and grunted in an indistinguishable way as it came near me; but it was hidden from my view. One of the mahouts saw some animal pass through long grass, and a man far out in the plain declared that he saw a tiger bounding from rock to rock. In the evening some of the beaters said that they had seen the tiger, but had not told me, as they were overcome with thirst, and wanted to get to water. The day was certainly terribly hot, as the clouds had all been dispersed. This result was a great disappointment to me, as I had felt pretty confident of success, and several human skulls and bones which we found near the hill bore testimony to the fact that one or more of the tigers were man-eaters; so that their destruction was much to be desired. I arranged for another series of beats on the following day in another tract recommended by the shikaris. On rising in the morning I felt very far from well, the previous day's exposure having brought back my fever. However, as men were collected, I could not draw back. In the beats which we had nothing was seen, and I returned to camp completely done. Taking into consideration the density of the undergrowth in the jungle, which had not been burnt, as it would have been in ordinary years, the great heat, the badness of the beating, and my own state of health, I felt it advisable to order a march forward for the morrow; but this I did with great reluctance, as I had really hoped to have been the means of ridding the country-side of the tigers which in one direction were stopping all traffic and cultivation, and also prevented the people visiting the jungle for firewood. As, a day or two later, the clouds again collected, I could not but feel that, had I waited, I might perhaps have had better success, since there was no doubt that the badness of the beating was in a great measure due to the exceptional heat of the two days.

April 25th.—Bourka to Panduka.—From Bourka, as I was entering Raipur proper, I dismissed the Dow, and as he had been civil I made him a present of a powder-horn and some other trifles, but refused to give him a certificate, as I could not overlook the neglect on my first entering Nowagurh. He left me looking very sad, and my servants told me that he wept bitterly for an hour afterwards.

Some three miles before reaching Panduka I left the hills and rocks behind me, and came into an alluvium and laterite-covered open tract, with good villages and fine groves dotted about. The people of Chatisgurh, as the whole area is called, were very different from those whom I had left behind. This was more notably the case with the women, who were to be seen going about in an open way, such as I had not seen elsewhere during my tour. They made some pretence of covering their faces on seeing a stranger, but at the same time took care to exhibit their features. Their costume, otherwise ample, is so devised as to leave bare their legs from the knee downwards, a dress, or want of it, which would be regarded with horror by the women of Bengal or Orissa. Their figures were plump and well-favoured. If report speaks truly they are very independent, and their lords are not their masters except when it suits them to be obedient.

April 26th.—Panduka to Rajim.—Up to Rajim I saw no rocks uncovered, and was therefore surprised on arrival there to find a good-sized town, many of the houses being built of stone. Such a sight I had not seen in the whole course of my journey; since in Cuttack the houses are built of brick, and everywhere else that I had been at, plain mud, or, in some few cases, sun-dried bricks were the only materials which I had seen in use. I was told that the stones had been taken from the ruins of a city which flourished 1100 years ago; but I understood from the Malguzar, or land revenue collector, who came out to meet me on the road, that the stone occurs at no great depth below the surface. It is a material admirably suited for building purposes, as it is a grey flaggy limestone, which can be readily chipped into blocks.

Two marches, aggregating twenty-five miles, over dry laterite plains, where there was no jungle, and where the principal fuel in use was dried pats of cow-dung, brought me at length to Raipur, where I was soon made comfortable in the house of the Deputy-Commissioner, and shortly afterwards joined a lawn-tennis party, where in five minutes I saw five times as many white faces as I had seen in the more than five months which had elapsed since the 21st of November, when I left Cuttack. Indeed, since that time I had met but four Englishmen, namely, the Superintendent of Police of the Gurjat States of Orissa, the Assistant-Commissioner of Sambalpur, with whom I had travelled for a few days, and the Assistant-Agent, and the Superintendent of Police of Jaipur,—the meeting of even these, save the second, being a mere chance. I might indeed not have happened to cross the paths of any of them, so little frequented by British officials are the regions through which I had marched upwards of 800 miles.

April 29th.—Raipur.—I was much charmed with the cleanliness of the town of Raipur. The Deputy-Commissioner, to whom this state of things was, I believe, altogether due, took me into what ought to have been, according to all analogy with other towns, oriental or otherwise, back slums redolent with filth; but they proved to be very clean lanes, with neat stone drains, and with nothing offensive about them of any kind. Several buildings of a useful or ornamental character were in process of construction, and as they were being built of stone, they bid fair to last for many a year, and perpetuate the memory of their founder. Public gardens and parks had been laid out with great taste, and were well planted with ornamental shrubs and beautiful flowers. Altogether I was much charmed with Raipur, and retain a very pleasant recollection of it. Among the public institutions which I visited was the Government Treasury, and what I have to say regarding it I mention as it was novel to me. Very possibly, however, similar practices may be in vogue at other treasuries throughout the land for anything I know to the contrary.

It so happened that in the Raipur treasury there was at that time a vast amount of silver, I forget how many laks of rupees. It was all done up in bags of net-work so that the silver could be seen, the object of which was that the native clerks, or sub-treasurers, should not have an opportunity of substituting copper for silver coins, as they have been known to do when closed cloth bags were employed. A serious defalcation by a native treasurer here some short time before had caused the Deputy-Commissioner to be mulcted in a large amount; not that criminal breach of trust by natives in the position of treasurers is a rare occurrence calling for special notice. Hardly a week passes that a case is not recorded from somewhere throughout the length and breadth of India. This fact has been specially brought to my notice since my return home, when I have been in the receipt of a weekly newspaper from India.

Everybody knows that the Government of India reserves to itself the monopoly of the sale of opium, and derives from it a considerable revenue; but I was not before aware that a chamber in the Court House was ever allotted for its retail to large customers—yet such I found to be the case at Raipur. I was told that the feudatory chiefs obtain it at a somewhat lower figure than that at which it is sold to British subjects.

A curious fact which I heard at Raipur in connection with the abnormal rainfall of this year, was that the guinea-fowls, of which large numbers were kept by some of the residents, had already commenced laying, though in ordinary years the first eggs are laid at the beginning of July, after which each bird lays daily for an average of one hundred days, after which there is a cessation for the remainder of the year. This fact, though it may appear to be a trivial one, is of interest, as showing how a modification of seasons or climate may produce a change in habits. That it does not always do so is exemplified by the case of an Australian goose (*Cereopsis*), which lays in the summer of the Antipodes, but which when brought to England lays at the same time of year—that is to say in our winter. But geese are strange animals, and are less susceptible to change than are most others whose life histories are equally well known.

After several more days of rest from the wearying iteration of daily marching, it became necessary for me to arrange for the further journey of 176 miles to Nagpur, where I could take the train for Calcutta. Two courses were open to me; one was to make use of a *tonga*, a car drawn by trotting-bullocks, relays of which are by a most admirable arrangement obtainable every six miles, and by means of which the distance can be accomplished in about three or four days with ease and comfort. The alternative, marching by stages, which would occupy about a fortnight, would involve much discomfort, but would give me more leisure to examine the rocks near the road, which, for the most part, had never been seen by eyes geological, and about which it was desirable to obtain as much information as was possible. Since, moreover, I should gain no time by pushing on to Nagpur ahead of my people and goods, where I should have to await their arrival, I elected the latter. At Raipur I engaged carts to carry the loads of two of the elephants which I sent eastwards to Sambalpur, where they were to remain for the rainy season till again wanted for the field. I also lightened very considerably the loads of the elephants which accompanied me to Nagpur both for their sake and on account of the men, as the daily loading and unloading was thereby much simplified. The marches were from ten to twenty miles long, and I endeavoured to arrange that the long and short ones should alternate, but in this respect I had to conform to the distances which separated the very excellent bungalows with which the road was provided. Owing to the great heat it was necessary that the men and elephants should march at night; but as it would have defeated my object—that of seeing the rocks—to have done so myself, and I should have lost a night's rest, I used, where the march was a double one, to stop during the middle of the day at an intermediate bungalow, thus employing the morning and evening hours only for the journey and examination of the geology. I left Raipur on the 4th of May, and four marches brought me to Chichola, sixty-five miles distant, where I met an Engineer of the Public Works Department, who was engaged in the construction of the road. He confirmed a report which I had previously heard as to the granitic hills of this neighbourhood being inhabited by bears. Several of the nearer hills had been beaten a short time previously, but there was one a few miles further off which had been left undisturbed for some years, and we agreed to try what a beat would produce. The preparations were on a moderate scale, scarcely more than fifty men having been assembled. The man who placed us said that the first passage from the hill which we saw would not be taken by the animals; but it looked so likely a place that I left the elephant Mowlah facing it, and instructed the mahout and a chuprasi, who were seated on the pad, in the event of any animal coming that way to simply clap their hands. I took up a position in a small tree a little further on, and a very uncomfortable and insecure position it was, as both my feet had to rest cramping one another in the fork of a tree about three feet from the ground; how I was to fire and hold on at the same time without any support for my back I did not know; but the event proved I was able to do so somehow. The Engineer climbed another tree fifty yards beyond me, and the beaters commenced their work. They had not reached the crest of the hill ere I heard the chuprasi clapping, and in another moment a bear broke, and I allowed it to come within a few feet of me before I fired a shot from the Express which would have killed it, but I gave it a second shot to terminate its agony. I had hardly reloaded when I again heard the clapping, and a hyæna rushed past me giving me a difficult shot from my constrained position; him also I laid low with a shot, when, for a third time, I heard the clapping, and another bear appeared and received exactly the same treatment as the first, so that I had the carcases of two bears and a hyæna lying at the foot of my tree. Some shots on the hill gave notice that something was going on there too, and we soon heard that one of the Engineer's men had shot another bear. Such a long time was expended in getting it out of the cleft in the rocks into which it had fallen, and in bringing it down the hill that we had no time for another beat; but we had every reason to be satisfied with the bag, save that my friend had not had a chance of a shot himself. It raised the number of large animals which I had shot during the trip to nine, viz.: one tiger, one leopard, one hyæna, two bears, two buffaloes, and two sambar, all of which, except the buffaloes, had been killed by single shots from the .450

Express rifle, so that I had good reason to be satisfied with the weapon.

May 9th.—Chichola to Baghnadi.—About two and a half miles beyond Chichola I examined, while marching to the next halting-place, a lode containing galena and copper-ores; the outcrop of the lode had been much cut into by men employed in preparing road metal, one of whom told me that all the visible fragments of ore had been removed. Certainly, save some stains of copper carbonates, I could detect no trace; but the locality had previously been visited, and had been reported on by one of my colleagues. As being one of the few *bonâ fide* lodes of these ores which are known to exist in India it is of some interest—its economic value is, however, quite unknown, and will remain so probably for some time. Otherwise, too, the locality is of interest as being, I believe, the only one where fluor spar is known to exist in India; it is strange that a mineral, which is so common in Europe, should be so rare in India.

May 10th.—Baghnadi to Dungargaon.—The hundreds of carts which were on the road laden with grain for Nagpur, and the number of empties returning for another load before the regular rains should set in, bore a testimony to the extraordinary development in the export trade from this country which had just been accomplished. It is but a few years since the people in parts of Chatisgurh were unable to pay their land revenue in consequence of the *abundance* of their harvests—grain was so cheap that it was impossible to carry enough of it to realise the amount of silver required. This state of things is never likely to occur again, and the corn of the Central Provinces has now found a place in the English markets which was vacated for it in the Russo-Turkish war. A proposed line of railway into the centre of Chatisgurh from Nagpur will serve very materially to develop this trade, and should the line be continued to Calcutta, the port at that city will, no doubt, obtain a share of the trade which must otherwise be confined to Bombay.

To-day, for the first time during my journey, I heard grey partridges calling. The bird, to the best of my belief, does not occur in any of the Districts or States which I had traversed. I also heard painted partridges, the common and plaintive cuckoos, and the yellow-breasted ground-thrush.

In Chatisgurh I first learnt what trotting-bullocks can accomplish, and was truly astonished at the activity of some very heavy-looking animals—a good pair can, I was told, trot their six miles an hour with ease. One sort of conveyance in use, which would make the inhabitants of Bengal stare, consists simply of a stout pole which connects the axle-tree with the bullock's yoke; on this the driver and one or more passengers sit straddle-wise with their legs dangling down. A more rudimentary wheeled equipage it is difficult to conceive of, yet some of them are made of choice wood, are highly ornamented, and are drawn by sleek and well-fed cattle. For officials travelling in their districts the tongas have many points to commend them. They will carry yourself, your luggage, and a servant, and in the villages near the main roads a pair of trotting bullocks can be hired to draw you from stage to stage. In Bengal such a convenient method of travelling is unknown, and, indeed, the cattle are, perhaps, hardly suited for such a purpose; but in the Madras Presidency the use of bullocks in this way is practised to a large extent.

May 12th.—Sakoli to Lukni.—I fonnd the people here singularly ignorant of the values of the ordinary Indian coinage—thus a punkah-puller, who was given two two-anna pieces, asked for a third as he said his pay was three annas. I was told that the men employed on the road always change their wages, which are paid in silver and copper, into cowries, in which form they prefer to accumulate their savings. It is by means of these exchanges that many Mahratta money-lenders commence their operations, and they rapidly increase their wealth by various nefarious practices. A man once in their clutches rarely escapes. They become thoroughly well versed in the sections of the law which affect their profession, and they evade the statute of limitations by getting new bonds from their victims, whom they often compel to take broken down buffaloes or cattle at fabulous prices, which are entered in the accounts as value received.

On the following day I reached Bandara, a well-kept town, I believe, but I did not visit it, preferring to avail myself of the rest afforded in a very excellent Dâk bungalow, and keep quiet for the day. Bandara is the chief town of a district which bears the same name. Three more marches brought me, on the 16th of May, to Nagpur, the goal of my long journey of about 1,000 miles. Having sent off my men by train to their homes, I remained for a few days at Nagpur where the heat was excessive by day, and it was necessary to sleep in the open *sub jove* by night. On the 21st I started for the Warora coal-mines which I had never previously had an opportunity of visiting. As they are the principal mines at present worked in the Central Provinces, I was particularly anxious to see them, and the methods of working in practice, in order that I might contrast them with the old-established customs in Bengal. I shall not, however, pause here to describe these mines, upon which a vast amount of money has been expended by the Government, to whom they at present belong.

Leaving Warora, a three days' journey by train brought me to Calcutta, which I reached on the morning of the 26th. The heat in the saloon carriage sometimes rose to 100° Fah.; but as I had it to myself for about 1,200 miles, I did not experience so much discomfort as I might have done had it been crowded with passengers. It proved, indeed, to be a very agreeable change from the sort of travelling I had just experienced. It was a humiliating fact to contemplate that in three days I travelled a greater distance by this means than I had been able to accomplish in six and a-half months' constant marching.

As I have in the course of the preceding pages alluded to the chief points of economic or general interest connected with the geology of the area traversed, I do not give any *resumé* of the geology here, the more particularly as an account and map of the tract have already been published, in which the results of my explorations are described.*

* "Records Geological Survey of India." Vol. x., p. 167.

CHAPTER XIV

LOHARDUGGA AND PALAMOW.

1877–78.

INSTRUCTIONS FOR SEASON—DEVELOPMENT OF THE PALAMOW COAL-FIELDS—COAL-MINES AT KURHURBALI—PARISNATH—COPPER, LEAD, AND ZINC LODE—TEA PLANTATION—CELTS—HAZARIBAGH—KOL MENHIRS—MAN-EATING TIGERS—GALENA AND ANTIMONY—I AM CRIPPLED BY AN ACCIDENT—BALUMATH—DISCOVER LIMESTONE—VALLEY OF THE AURUNGA—PALAMOW LIQUOR-SHOPS—PROFESSIONAL VISIT BY A NATIVE SURGEON—THE RAJA OF VETNAGHERI—JUGGULDUGGA HILLS—GENERAL ACCOUNT OF THE URAONS—STARLINGS—DEFICIENT CROPS AND SCARCITY OF FOOD—HOT SPRING—HOAR-FROST—LATIAHAR—THEFT IN CAMP—THE POLICE—BINDI—DESTITUTION—FOREST CONSERVANCY—PALAMOW FORT—DALTONGUNJ—CASTE AND THE PETTY NATIVE OFFICIALS—DALTONGUNJ COAL-FIELD—BEAT FOR TIGER—FOUR-HORNED ANTELOPES—KOEL RIVER—GIANT SILK-COTTON TREE—NATIVE IRON-TRADE—RATS—A TIGER'S DWELLING—MAN INJURED BY A TIGER—NIGHT ALARM OF THIEVES—PARIAH KITES—ANOTHER MAN INJURED BY A TIGER—ORNITHOLOGICAL COLLECTION—HUTAR COAL-FIELD—SUPPLIES—MEET THREE LEOPARDS—NILGAI—SUPAHI RIVER—A COOL RETREAT—GAZELLES—BIJKA HILL—STILBITE—SIT UP FOR A BEAR—INDIAN BEARS—THE GUL-GUL PÂT—THE KOREWAHS—WANT OF CARRIAGE IN PALAMOW—THE TATAPANI COAL-FIELD—HOT SPRINGS—PITCHED BATTLE BETWEEN ANTS—WHITE ANTS—RESUMÉ ON THE COAL-FIELDS—THE AURUNGA FIELD—THE HUTAR FIELD—IRON-ORES OF PALAMOW—AGURIAHS, OR NATIVE IRON-WORKERS—NETURHAT PLATEAU—TEA PLANTATIONS—LABOUR OF CHRISTIAN CONVERTS—DAMAGE TO MHOWA CROP—IRON ORE—CONCLUSION OF JUNGLE LIFE—CONCLUDING REMARKS.

It had long been known that a tract occupied by coal-measure rocks existed in a part of the district of Lohardugga, within the limits of the purgunas of Toree and Palamow. My instructions for the season were to explore and map these rocks, and ascertain the amount of coal they contained. To the extent and value of the iron deposits of various ages throughout the district my particular attention was also to be directed, since the establishment of iron-works, as well as the opening out of new coal-mines, formed portions of a scheme in connection with the Sone canals which was under the consideration of the Government. Before any decision as to outlay could be arrived at, reliable information regarding the mineral resources was required; and it was my duty to supply this want, as far as possible, within the limits of a single season.

November 7th.—Early this morning I reached the station of Giridi by train from Calcutta. This station is the terminus of a branch line from the East Indian Railway, and is in proximity to the mines of the Kurhurbali coal-field, the development of which has been unprecedented in India. The principal mines belong to the Railway Company, and are worked with considerable skill and judgment, and the weekly out-turn steadily increases, all the steam-coal being used by the railway. Other mines in this area belong to the Bengal and Equitable Coal Companies. This was my first visit to this coal-field. It was the only one of any size and importance throughout the Bengal province which I had not previously examined. Though of small size, the area being only eleven square miles, there are many points both of geological and economic interest about it; but these I shall not here pause to describe.

November 9th.—*Giridi to Kutwara.*—Two marches from Giridi to Kutwara and Hurladi brought me so close into the vicinity of Parisnath again that I was once more, for the fourth time, tempted to ascend it, the more particularly as a tea-garden had been opened out on its northern slope, which I was anxious to see. I also thought that the walk to the foot of the hills and thence up by a road about six miles long, with a descent of equal length to Nimia Ghât on the Trunk-road, where I sent a horse to await my coming, would afford an opportunity of getting myself into training after the relaxing effects of the Calcutta climate.

At Borogondo, not far from Hurladi, there is a mineral lode in which copper, lead, and zinc ores all occur. Unfortunately I did not know the exact position when passing, or I should have tarried to examine it. Some of the specimens of ore which I have seen from it are the most promising I have yet met with from any part of Bengal; and I would not be surprised if this deposit, when opened up, should prove to be of considerable value.

Passing through Madhubun, in which there are several large serais or rest-houses for Jain pilgrims to Parisnath, I commenced the ascent, which first traverses an outer ridge and then dips into a sort of sheltered valley, bounded on the south by the slopes of the main mass of the hill. In this valley the forest has been cleared and the already-mentioned tea-plantation laid out. The plants were, I believe, only about a year old, and as, when passing through, I had not the advantage of the guidance of the manager, who was not at home, I was unable to learn much of their condition and history. But it appeared to me that there was an abundant and rich soil; and the gentle slopes augured well for its preservation from being washed away by rain. A curious fact in connection with the clearance of forest for this garden was the discovery of two remarkably fine polished celts, one of which is precisely similar to a common form met with in Europe. Both of them are figured in Appendix B, plate II., figs. 9 and 10. The latter part of the climb up, where there were no trees and where I was exposed to the full force of the morning sun, was rather severe; but after a rest I reached the bungalow at the summit, where I found a caretaker in charge. Having breakfasted and visited several of the small votive temples close by, I set out on the descent, which, owing to jungle and long grass having asserted possession of the now-unused road, was not accomplished without some difficulty. At Nimia Ghât I found my horse awaiting me, and from thence cantered along the Grand Trunk road, which had a very deserted appearance as compared with what it had when I first saw it fourteen years previously, as described in the first chapter.

From Dumri, where I remained for the night, I made four marches to Hazaribagh. At the last halting-place, before reaching the station, I met the Commissioner of the Division, who had only been appointed a short time previously, and who was about to make a tour into the native states of Sirguja and Jushpur, &c. A few months later he died from fever contracted on this journey.

I remained in Hazaribagh for four days, making some final arrangements, and on the 20th marched westwards to Sultana and thence to Silla. Near the latter place there are some very ancient-looking Kol memorial stones or menhirs, which were ranged in broken lines bearing nearly due north and south. The stones were all of the gneiss rock, which occurs in the neighbourhood. I met with the tracks of a fine tiger in the bed of the Mohani, almost in the same spot as I had seen some previously in 1870, when examining the Chopé coal-field. Apparently the locality, though within seven miles of the station, was a regular haunt for tigers. For some months previously a family of man-eating tigers had been causing great loss of life in the country to the south of Hazaribagh. They had evaded all attempts which had been made to shoot them. On one occasion a colossal expedition, in which some British soldiers were employed, was sent out against them, and a wide tract of country was surrounded and beaten, but without success. As an example of their cunning and daring, it was said that an officer, when travelling by palki through their beat at night, employed a double set of torch-bearers, and had also with him some extra men to keep up a tattoo on drums, yet at one spot a tiger rushed out and carried off the last man of the party. On my return to Hazaribagh I saw one of these tigers, which had been captured in a pit-fall; it was subsequently sent to the Calcutta Zoological gardens. I think another of the family, too, was afterwards captured in the same way; the credit of ridding the country of these scourges, which had so completely foiled the sportsmen, being due to a native gentleman.

My next march was to Lepu, from whence I paid a visit to a place called Hisatu, where galena and antimony were said to have been found formerly. The grubbing at the outcrop had completely removed all trace of the ore, so it was difficult for me to form an opinion as to the nature of the deposit; and I had neither time nor suitable means for opening up the surface.

November 27th.—Goonia to Balumath.—To-day an accident happened, which seriously affected my comfort for the rest of the season, and writing now eighteen months after the event, I am not quite sure that I am free from its consequences. About four miles from Balumath I was met by the Sub-Inspector of Police, who had come out to escort me into the town. As I was riding along I heard a loud shouting and noise behind me, and, looking back, saw that my second horse, a rather spirited animal, had broken away from the sayce, and was in hot pursuit of the Inspector's pony, the Inspector having been dislodged from the saddle. As the natives were giving the animals a wide berth I dismounted, and was just about to capture the runaway, having my hand actually laid upon him, when my right foot turned under me, and I was flung backwards, and found myself dead lame. With some difficulty I got back to my horse, and rode after the fighting pair, and at last managed to capture them, after they had charged through and scattered a drove of pack bullocks, whose loads were sent flying in all directions. As there was a bungalow at Balumath I occupied it, though it was in a tumble-down condition, and remained there for five days, trying to cure the most severely-sprained ankle I have ever had.

December 2nd.—Balumath to Balunuggur.—Becoming tired of the inactivity, I started to-day to commence operations on the coal-field, intending to spare my foot as much as possible; but, as usual, I soon found that much riding was impracticable, that rocky beds of rivers had to be examined and hills ascended, and as I could not bring myself to leave the scene of action and march away to either of the district stations, I hobbled along for more than two months, often suffering much anguish, but having the satisfaction of accomplishing my work; and so, at the end of the season, having a full tale to show before taking leave of India on furlough.

On the road to Balunuggur I made a discovery of great importance in connection with the proposition to establish iron-works; this was a vast and inexhaustible deposit of nearly pure crystalline limestone, admirably suited for a flux in the smelting of the ores of iron which I subsequently found. To reach Balunuggur from Balumath one descends into the valley of the Aurunga, by a ghât or pass nearly 300 feet high. The panorama of the country in which my future work lay, as seen from the top of this pass, was a very beautiful one. Particularly striking were the effects produced by the patches of many-tinted cultivation scattered about through the more uniformly-coloured jungle, which surrounds two ranges of sandstone hills, occupying the centre of the valley. There were scarcely any bare spots to be seen, and though the previous rainfall had been lamentably insufficient for some of the crops, but little evidence of the drought was apparent in the verdure and brightness of the vegetation at this season.

At Balunuggur, I made my first acquaintance in Palamow with what is called the *bati* system, by which the Abkari, or revenue on the sale of intoxicating spirits, is worked by the Government. The whole area is divided up into circles, in each of which there is a *bati*, or shop, where the spirit from the mhowa flower is distilled and retailed; and the permission to hold these *batis* is sold to the highest bidders, the value varying with the position and the drinking capabilities of the neighbouring population. How the Abkari system works in other districts of Bengal I am not sufficiently acquainted with the subject to say, but I nowhere else have experienced such an amount of annoyance and discomfort as I did from these liquor-shops of Palamow. Generally speaking, near the large villages, they were situated close to the groves where I encamped, and, as they attracted all the bad characters of the neighbourhood, were scenes of squabbling and disorder, which were often prolonged late into the night. Though among my servants there were only a few who ever drank, there was one who from time to time used to get mad from drink, and place the whole camp in an uproar. All my efforts to obtain a substitute for this man, who occupied the position of sweeper, were unavailing; and I had to put up with his misconduct, which he continued to the very end of the trip, in spite of the infliction of the severest punishment I have ever given to a servant.

December 6th.—Balunuggur to Murup.—The work of examination of the coal-measures, upon which I was now fairly launched, proved very intricate, and necessitated my moving from camp to camp at a very much slower rate than was usual with me, and my days being spent in measuring river sections of the rocks, few incidents occurred suitable for reproduction here.

December 16th.—Masiatu.—My foot had become so bad again that I had to rest it for a couple of days here, and the Brahmin Zemindar of the place, hearing of my accident, proposed that his surgeon-in-ordinary, a Rajput, should make a professional visit. To this I agreed, and the man came into the tent for the purpose, a circle of admirers having assembled outside to see his treatment. His method amused me not a little, and his evident anxiety to appear quite equal to the occasion, in the sight of his patron, was intensely ludicrous. His first operation was to compress the prominent arteries and veins on my foot, and to make some learned remarks about them. He then minutely felt the extensor tendons of my toes, and proceeded to endeavour to make the said toes crepitate at the joints, using the end of his cloth to give him a good grip. This soon became exquisite torture, as my toes had not been accustomed to such manipulation, and I had to cry for mercy. At length he commenced the examination of the ankle, but to his method of doing so I was also compelled to object, as it threatened to more than neutralize the benefit I had derived from my two days' rest, for he gave my foot such sudden bends and jerks that I could stand his mode of treatment no longer. In the evening he came again, and was greatly gratified when I told him that the foot was less painful. He then applied some opium liniment, which had been prepared by my doctor; but he did not rub it into the ankle, as it might be expected that he would have done, but into the *sole* of the foot; before doing so he snuffed up the savour of the lotion with many indications of approval. As a fee for his consummate charlatanism I gave him a rupee, in spite of the protest of the Brahmin, who did not wish that he should be rewarded.

Though not in any way connected with the narrative, I cannot refrain from quoting here an extract from a newspaper, which I copied into my diary at this time. It is evident that the writer was not one of those who act on the principle that the use of language is to conceal thought. It was stated that the Raja of Vetnagheri had sent a subscription of 10,000 rupees to the Madras Famine Fund, "*in obedience to the orders of Government and the Collector, and to secure more honours*"—so much for voluntary charity.

December 25th.—Jugguldugga.—For the fortnight preceding this I had been occupied, in spite of my crippled condition, in mapping the coal-field, on which, after the principal river which traverses it, I bestowed the name of Aurunga. The village of Jugguldugga is at the foot of a small group of hills formed of sandstones younger than the coal-measures, and resting upon them. The weathering of these sandstones had produced grotesque outlines similar to those which I have already described in the Hingir field. Christmas Day, as spent by me, was only enlivened by a dance, which was performed by some Uraons. For some reason the Uraons of Palamow appear to be in a less prosperous condition than their neighbours in Lohardugga proper. The attractions offered by Assam and Cachar tea-planters and coolie-agents from Demerara and the Mauritius, are causing great numbers of them to emigrate, and large tracts of country are in consequence falling out of cultivation, and becoming depopulated.

As I have not given any general account of the Uraons in previous pages, I shall avail myself of this, the last, opportunity for doing so. The Uraons, or as they are generally called when away from their own country, the Dhangas, are hard-working cultivators, being in this respect vastly superior to any of the races I have previously described. Their houses are small, and badly made, and, the accommodation being scanty, the young men are all sent to sleep in a bachelor's hall, which occupies a central position in each village. There they are watched by a custodian, who is responsible for their good behaviour, and has power to fine absentees. The younger boys act as fags.

There is something very pleasing about the appearance of the Uraons, both men and women; and many of the latter are decidedly good-looking. Their colour varies much, from black to light mahogany; but the cast of their features is so constant that one can readily distinguish a Uraon from people of all other races. Their method of arranging their hair—the women with one-sided chignons, often decorated with flowers, and the men with a huge back-knot, in which a small wooden comb is carried, and the abundance of bead necklaces and brass ear-rings and ornaments in the lobes of the ear which are worn by both sexes, serve also to distinguish them wherever they are met with. The women wear the ordinary sari, with the end thrown over the right shoulder; but when at work in the fields the upper folds of the garment are often regarded as superfluous, and a very moderate skirt arrangement of the cloth is considered sufficient. Tattooing on the arms, back, brows, and temples is practised by the women.

The dancing places, called *Akhara*, which I have described on a previous page as being attached to the villages, afford opportunities for the youths and maidens to become acquainted with one another; and long attachments and real love matches are probably more common with the Uraons than any other people in India. With Hindus such a thing is never known, and with Mahomedans in that country it rarely occurs, also, that bride and bridegroom have any knowledge of each other before they are joined in wedlock.

Uraons will eat almost anything. Tigers, bears, snakes, frogs, &c., are all lawful food to them. Field-mice are esteemed as the very choicest food; and when, according to General Dalton, a young Uraon presents to a maiden a dish of grilled field-mice, his self-denial in doing so indicates that he entertains for her a serious affection compared with which all the attentions he may have paid to others at the *Akhara* count for nothing. According to the Rev. Mr. Batsch, the Uraon language is a poor one. It includes no original religious terms; those which are in use have been borrowed. There are no words to express abstract ideas, and none for actions of the mind or thoughts.

While in this neighbourhood I found the common starling (*Sturnus vulgaris*) to occur in abundance. The bird had never, so far as I could ascertain, been seen by anyone before in Chutia Nagpur, and its occurrence at this season was, I believe, to be attributed to the drought, and consequent scarcity of food in north-western India, which had driven it beyond its normal range.

December 28th.—Subano.—The prospects for the people of Palamow for the coming year were not very cheerful at this season. Owing to the short and late rainfall the rubbi crop promised very badly, and the bulk of the population would be dependent on the crop of mhowa flowers. People who in ordinary years would have had nine or ten maunds of grain stored for consumption, had only on an average about a third of that amount in their granaries. It was becoming clear to me that I should experience the very greatest difficulty in getting supplies of grain in the thinly-inhabited and poverty-stricken country I was about to enter.

January 1st.—Toobed to Pochra.—To-day I visited a hot spring at a place called Jarum. It was situated in the middle of the bed of a river, and there was consequently no vegetation about it. The maximum temperature was 132° F., and the water was kept in a bubbling condition by a flow of sulphureted hydrogen. Like the hot springs which I subsequently met with in the two other coal-fields which I examined, this one was on a line of fault or fracture. About this date the ground was generally covered with hoar-frost, and on the 3rd the temperature in the early morning stood at 35° F.

January 7th.—Latiahar to Zalim.—Latiahar, though the largest village in this tract of country, is of no great size or importance. While encamped here the native doctor had, for reasons best known to himself, pitched his tent at some distance away from the rest of the encampment. Early in the morning, just as I was about to get up, a piteous cry from him announced the fact that he had been robbed during the night. I found that the thieves had managed to remove from the tent, while the two occupants were asleep, the heavy medicine-chest and the doctor's clothes-box. From the latter about thirty rupees and a watch and chain had been extracted, and from the former the brass scruple and dram weights of the scales. These the thieves had no doubt mistaken for gold. I hoped that they might prove the means of ultimate detection. The medicine-bottles were all scattered about the adjoining field. The police were about as useful as usual under similar circumstances. The only suggestion that could be made was that a party of strolling dancers, who had been about the camp on the previous day, but who had already marched, might perhaps be connected with the theft. A constable was accordingly sent after them; but subsequent enquiries served to clear them completely of the possibility of their being implicated in any way. The only further information I received on the subject from the police was that a constable, about a month afterwards, brought to the camp an empty gin-bottle, which had been found in the house of a Dome, a tribe which furnishes the majority of the thieves in Palamow as elsewhere in India. It is the custom of the police to harry these people and ransack their houses after a theft has taken place. The result in this case was the discovery of the gin-bottle, which had, however, not been among the articles stolen from my camp.

January 11th.—Nowagurh to Bindi.—At Bindi, which is situated at the foot of a group of hills included in a tract of forest-reserve, I found that the people were in great destitution, and that the village was nearly deserted. Both here and elsewhere the people living on the edges of these forest-reserves complained to me of the great hardship caused to them by being shut out of the forest, which had previously afforded them a means of livelihood, or at least of collecting certain jungle products, the sale of which had enabled them to supplement their other means of subsistence. They said that if their cattle by any chance strayed across the boundary, the chuprasi in charge of the forest was down upon them at once, and they had either to bribe him, or accompany him to the magistrates' court, forty miles off, to answer the charge. This, and much more of the same kind, seemed very hard; but, as Government designed to pay compensation to people who could make a good case, and the reservation of forest tracts is a matter of imperial importance, it was better that the few should suffer, and, if necessary, migrate to other countries, rather than that the wholesale destruction of timber should be allowed to go on any longer.

January 20th.—Kunki to Bari and Daltongunj.—I had now completed the examination of the Aurunga field, which I found to occupy a distinct and isolated area; and so much being accomplished, I determined to give my foot some much-needed rest, before commencing examination of the next field on the west. On the road to Bari I visited the ruined Palamow forts, which are picturesquely situated on the banks of the Aurunga, where the bed of the river is much broken up by masses of gneiss rock. The old fort consists of particularly solid and lofty masonry walls and a number of temples, all of which are now deserted. I did not observe any tablets or inscriptions; but I was informed that the new fort, which crowns a neighbouring hill, contained one. With the history of these forts, and of the Rajas who occupied them, I shall not weary the reader.

In the afternoon I rode into Daltongunj, the sudder station of Palamow, where I found the Deputy-Commissioner, who was an old friend of mine, encamped, and made the acquaintance of the Assistant-Commissioner, who offered to put me up in his house while I remained invalided in the station. This station is not a lively one, there being seldom more than three English officials resident there. During my stay there the Mahomedan butcher one morning came to make complaint to the Assistant-Commissioner that the Hindu petty officials at the pound had refused, on religious grounds, to accept his bid for a bullock, which was ultimately sold for two-and-sixpence. It was pointed out to them that a more suitable way of asserting their religious views would have been to have got some one to out-bid the butcher. A case which was before the Assistant-Commissioner at this time was that of a Gosain or strolling priest, who was convicted of theft. The same gentry begged hard that he should be acquitted, on the ground that, as he was journeying to Jugernath, their religion would be disgraced if he were detained in prison. In spite of all this religion, they were a very bad lot, if the accounts of their nefarious practices which I heard were true, though perhaps they were not worse than those who occupy similar positions elsewhere in Bengal. The native subordinate service in Bengal, of all branches, is often, I believe, as corrupt and oppressive to their fellow-countrymen as any Turkish service can be. The way in which the peasantry are deceived and swindled by these men is something dreadful to contemplate. But they generally execute their depredations with the utmost cunning, taking good care to ingratiate themselves with, and render themselves invaluable to, the European officials over them.

Before leaving Daltongunj again for regular work I paid a visit to the Daltongunj coal-field, which lies a few miles to the north of the station, and encamped at Rajherra, near which the principal mines had been in operation. The demand for coal having ceased, there was nothing going on, and the open quarries were full of water. The coal is of excellent quality, and may yet be worked systematically, on a large scale, in connection with the irrigation works and canals at Dehri-on-the-Sone, for the supply of fuel to stations on the East Indian Railway beyond Arrah.

February 4th.—Daltongunj to Chando.—On leaving the station to resume regular work I was accompanied to the first halting-place by the Assistant-Commissioner and the Superintendent of Vaccination, in order that we might have a beat for a tiger which was known to live in the neighbourhood of Chando; two tigers were said to have been seen by some of the beaters, but they must have broken through the line, as they did not come our way. Some of the native matchlock-men shot a pair of the pretty little four-horned antelopes (*Tetraceros quadricornis*, Blainv.), which I subsequently found were not uncommon in these jungles.

February 6th.—Chando to Seraidih.—To the west of Seraidih the Koel river has in places a very rocky bed, and the nature of the rapids fully satisfied me that the river could not be relied on as a means of carriage for the coal, though some writers had maintained that it might be so employed.

At Seraidih there is a silk-cotton tree (*Bombax malabaricum*), which I believe to be the largest tree I have ever seen; unfortunately I do not retain the measurements of this vegetable monster. I did not realize its enormous dimensions until I saw the pack-cattle and elephants stalled between the huge flange-like buttresses which project from the main stem. I think I estimated by shadow-measurement the height to be 140 feet, but I cannot now refer to the note which I made. At Seraidih a considerable business is done in iron, which is smelted in the country further south. I reserve notices of this industry for the conclusion of this chapter. I found that many of the people, having empty granaries, in order to supply present wants were already hypothecating to the money-lenders their crops of wheat at a ruinous rate of interest of several hundreds per cent. per annum. Thus they were receiving four seers, or eight pounds of kodo—a very poor sort of grain—for five seers, or ten pounds of wheat, to be paid in a month. Now the relative values of wheat and kodo being as two to three, then five seers of wheat would be equal to seven and a-half seers of kodo, so that as four only were received, eighty-seven and a-half per cent. per month was being charged for the accommodation.

I employed the natives in this neighbourhood to search for rats and mice, which I wanted for a friend who was engaged in working out the smaller species of Indian mammals. A great number belonging to several species were brought, the most notable being a jerboa rat (*Gerbillus Indicus*), with very short fore-paws, and long and powerful hind ones, and a large coarse bandicoot, with black bristly hairs like a pig's.

I find I have not given any description in the previous pages of the custom of poisoning fish, which is very commonly practised by the inhabitants of these jungles. The fruits of some species of jungle-trees, and the bark or roots of others, furnish a variety of poisons which answer for this purpose. A pool in the bed of a river, or a rock basin, which is known to contain fish, having been selected, and cut off from the inflow of fresh water, the substances mentioned are thrown into it, and the fish becoming stupefied rise to the surface, when they are easily captured. No evil results appear to follow from the eating of these poisoned fish.

February 11th.—Bamundih.—A tiger having been reported as doing mischief in this neighbourhood, I had had a young buffalo tied up as bait, but found him untouched when I visited him this morning. Having assembled a few men, I beat two small valleys, which were said to be inhabited by the tiger and family. The place looked likely enough, and there were two caves, one a remarkable cylindrical hole in the sandstone, which widened out inside, and the second, a ledge under a waterfall, leading down a wooded valley to the Koel river. The tiger, however, was not at home, and I accordingly proceeded on my day's tramp.

February 12th.—Bamundih to Chipadohar.—Owing to rain we did not strike the tents till nearly mid-day. On arriving at Chipadohar, at about 4 p.m., I was told that at a spot about two miles off a tiger had, in the morning, killed a cow, and had wounded one of a party of five men who went to look for the carcase. It had rushed at them while they were still some little distance off, and had struck the man and wounded him in the face, one claw only entering his eye, his sight having been in all probability destroyed for ever; his elbow and hip on one side had also been torn. As soon as the elephants were unloaded I mounted Anarkalli, and, having reached the scene, quartered the grass jungle which was pointed out by the men. For some little time I failed to find any trace either of the tiger or the carcase, but at length the elephant shied at something, which proved on examination to be the foot of the cow. Further search revealed the carcase, or half of it, carefully concealed in a narrow ravine. This explained the absence of vultures, which caused me at first to doubt the existence of a carcase at all. Were vultures guided by scent to their food, as has been maintained by some, there can be no doubt that such concealment would not have availed to keep them off. I have often found, however, that a few leafy branches spread over a carcase are quite sufficient to protect it from the attack of vultures, who, even if they have already arrived at the spot, soon take their departure again. The tiger, I have no doubt, was close by, but the grass and bushy undergrowth afforded abundant cover, and we saw nothing of him, and as there was no tree in which I could remain on guard over the carcase, and the sun had set, I was compelled to give up the search for him, and return to camp, and a deficiency of beaters prevented me from trying for him on the following day.

February 15th.—Chipadohar to Saidope.—Early this morning, before dawn, I was awakened by a great uproar, the elephants trumpeting in concert with the shouts of the men. As I jumped out of bed, the man on guard screamed to me that someone had been carried off by a tiger. Rifle in hand I rushed out, and found that what had really happened was, that a thief had again visited the doctor's tent. He and his brother had been roused, and had gone a short distance in pursuit, when the thief dropped a bundle of clothes, but carried off a brass hookah. The doctor's piteous lamentations were to be heard all over the place, and he came up to my tent bewailing the sad condition of his feet from thorns encountered in the jungle. To follow up the thief in the darkness was, of course, impossible. It was not pleasant to feel that the camp was in all probability being followed up by thieves, who were doubtless on the look out for booty. In selecting the doctor's tent, they shewed that they had acquired a complete knowledge of our arrangements beforehand. The doctor seemed to think that I was somehow responsible for what had taken place, and recalled the fact of another doctor having been robbed, when with me, as I have related on page 275. I however scolded him for his want of care, and told him he might be held responsible for the loss of Government property in the first robbery. The servants, who are so fond of hitting one another when down, amused me by remarking that the doctor, though already well supplied with wrappings for the cold nights, had purchased a shawl recently from a Kabuli merchant, and that when swathed in all these coverings he was like a corpse, unconscious of what might go on close to him. "I, on the other hand," remarked Saidon, "purposely keep myself uncomfortable at night, lest I should sleep too soundly, and injury should be caused thereby to your honour's property."

February 16th.—Saidope.—I had often supposed that the scavenger or pariah kites (*Milvus govinda*), which, though generally to be seen about the tents, are not common in the jungles, must follow the camp for long distances, and to-day I had evidence that such was the case, from the fact that at a place some twelve miles distant, and separated from Saidope by hills and forests, some of the servants having captured a kite in a trap, had cruelly pulled out its tail feathers, thus marking it in a way that could not be mistaken, and to-day it was here in company with others picking up what it could from the cooking tent.

Another man had, I found, been wounded by a tiger near this about a week previously. With two others he had gone to the carcase of a cow which had been killed, in order to remove the hide. While they were squatted down, about to commence operations, the tiger rushed in from behind, and caught the man by the shoulder in its mouth. When he was brought to camp for treatment, the shoulder had swollen to an enormous size, owing to the wounds having been plugged with some native mess. His friends would not leave him with us for treatment, and I subsequently heard that he had died.

During this season I kept a man regularly employed in shooting small birds, and thus obtained many interesting species, some of which were previously unknown to occur in Chutia Nagpur. Shooting small birds, though necessary at times if one wants to thoroughly study the ornithology of a tract of country, is not a pleasant amusement, and I prefer having it done by deputy. A second man did the taxidermy, and as neither of them had any other duties to perform, they had an easy time of it; but it is rare to get one man who will be efficient in both capacities.

Most of the large birds I shot myself, and amongst them were several interesting eagles, spur-fowl, mergansers, &c.

February 19th.—Morwaie to Purro.—The exploration of the coal-field to which the name Hutar has been given, and which I had been engaged on since leaving Daltongunj, proved a very arduous undertaking, owing to the wildness of the country, and the density of the pathless undergrowth through which I had to force my way—a small thorny acacia which grew in the long grass being an especial cause of annoyance. The villages being small, supplies had to be sent from a long distance by the Zemindars who live in the more open country to the west of Daltongunj; but this service they performed, under the orders of the local officials, very satisfactorily, pack-bullocks bringing the grain as it was required.

February 22nd.—Purro.—Shortly after leaving camp this morning, on my way to work, I suddenly saw a leopard about 400 yards ahead of me in the bush-scattered plain. He was crouching and crawling about in such a peculiar way that I immediately thought that he must be stalking some game. Accordingly taking my rifle I proceeded to stalk him, but without observing much care, and making straight for him, as he appeared to be so engrossed that I did not think he would notice me. While approaching him I came in view of a second leopard which, seeing me while still 300 yards away, made off and was joined not only by the first but by a third also which appeared to be a female, the other two being probably males which were, perhaps, about to contend for the possession of her. The males went off with a crouching gait, but at a good pace, their bellies close down to the ground, while the other bounded off skittishly with heels and tail in the air. As I followed them up, I came into tolerably close proximity with a bull nilgai which stood gazing intently at the spot where the leopards had been. I might have shot him with ease, but preferred to follow up the leopards, which, however, I failed to see again. It occurred to me as another way of accounting for the gambols of the leopards that they were only playing a little game to attract the attention of the nilgai* while one of them should circumvent it. Nilgai were very abundant in this tract, and I frequently saw herds of females and young, or males which occurred either singly or in pairs.

To the north of Purro there is a deep gorge cut by the Supahi river, through a plateau formed of horizontal beds of the upper sandstones. The path which traverses this gorge runs high above the water, which occupies a very defined channel, in the sides of which the flat beds of reddish sandstones and clays are seen in section; several streams from the plateau, and one in particular, form picturesque cascades, which have eroded the sandstones into large basins or pot-holes, over the edges of which the limpid waters flow in regular pulses. The vegetation in this cool and sheltered retreat, and more particularly in the smaller valleys branching from it, is very fresh-looking and green; and within the spray of the waterfalls, ferns and the sundew, or *Drosera*, were flourishing. Tiger's tracks on the sandy portion of the bed of the river were not absent, as might be expected from the character of the place.

March 3rd.—*Hutar.*—Hutar is a small village which has furnished a name for the coal-field, since the fact of there being coal in its vicinity was first known, and recorded about 100 years ago by some European visitor. While encamped there I had a visit from the Assistant-Commissioner, who joined me for the purpose of having a beat in the neighbouring hills. One young sambar stag was brought to bag, but as usual the tigers managed to evade us. In this neighbourhood I saw a pair of gazelles, commonly called ravine deer (*Gazella Bennettii*). There are also a few in the neighbourhood of Daltongunj; but the most eastern point of their extension, according to my observation, was at Latiahar in Longitude 84° 35′, and beyond this they are not known to extend eastwards in Peninsular India. These

* More correctly this word in the singular should be written Nilgau, from *Nil*, or *Lil*, blue, and *gau*, a cow.

animals belong to the African element in the Indian fauna,* as has been pointed out by Mr. W. T. Blanford and other writers on the subject

March 9th.—Bijka.—The village of Bijka is situated near the western extremity of a *cul-de-sac*, bounded on the south by a scarp of sandstones which forms the already-mentioned plateau, rising at one point to form a steep sugar-loaf peak, called the Bijka hill, the summit of which is about 1,300 feet above the village. The ascent, by a very steep path on a warm morning, proved not a little severe to me in my lame condition. On the north the Bijka valley is bounded by irregular hills of metamorphic rocks, the coal-measures having been lowered against their bases along a particularly well-marked line of fracture, another, nearly parallel, fault having acted similarly on the south; while a cross fault on the west has permitted these younger rocks to be let down, as it were, into a socket of gneiss and granite. Between Bijka and a village to the north-west I found the granitic gneiss was traversed by veins of a salmon-coloured mineral called stilbite, which, though generally occurring in rocks of volcanic origin, has also occasionally been found in other countries with rocks which are of metamorphic character.

March 14th.—Bairce to Nowka.—The mhowa flowers were now nearly ready to fall; but from one tree only had any actually fallen, and this tree, I was told, had been visited by a bear which would very probably return to-night. Accordingly I had a machan erected close by the tree. It proved, when I ascended it in the afternoon, to be a rather crank and rickety affair; fortunately I had with me a light iron-chair upon which I could sit, but only in a very constrained position. After waiting for two hours very patiently I was just about to shout out for my men to come up to take the guns, when, in the moonlight I saw a very fine bear steadily plodding across the field towards me on my left, and in such a position that without

* "Ann. and Mag. of Nat. Hist.," October, 1876.

standing up and turning I could not possibly bring my rifle into position to cover him. I thought it best to remain quiet, as he appeared intent upon coming to my front; but, catching sight of me, he sheered off, and I let the chance slip hoping for a better one which never came, as he backed out of sight, and was soon lost to view, and did not return. On the next night, hoping to profit by my experience, I again went to the same place, but the bear did not visit the tree, though I saw him, like a ghostly apparition in the pale light, stalking along under the shelter of some rocks. On my return to camp I noticed that the people were very sensibly cutting their corn by moonlight, thus saving themselves from work in the mid-day sun.

The Indian, or, as it is sometimes called, the sloth bear (*Procheilus* (*Ursus*) *labiatus*, Blainv.), to which frequent allusion has already been made, deserves to be somewhat more fully described than has yet been done in these pages. Its distribution is strictly limited to the peninsula south of the Himalayas, and Ceylon. In Himalayan regions two other quite distinct species are found, viz.:—*Ursus isabellinus*, Horsf., and *U. Tibetanus*, F. Cuv. In Burmah and the Malayan countries to the east of India, there is another, *U. Malayanus*, which, though closely allied to the last, is undoubtedly distinct, while in Biluchistan, to the west of India, there is yet another species, *Ursus Gedrosianus*, Blanf., which has only been recently discovered and named.

By naturalists generally it is considered that the Indian bear cannot be regarded as belonging strictly to the genus *Ursus*. The fact that it has only four incisors in the upper jaw, its large and powerful claws, its long and mobile snout, and some of its habits, serve to separate it from the true bears, and accordingly it is classified in a genus or sub-genus by itself. With its general appearance most of my readers are probably familiar, as it is a common animal in zoological gardens and menageries in Europe. It is covered all over with long black and shaggy hair, except on the muzzle, which is dirty white, and on the chest, where there is a white V-shaped mark. It is an awkward, bow-legged looking animal, but is a splendid tree-climber, and can, when pressed, cover the ground at a great speed. It is found chiefly in the vicinity of rocks, and lives for the greater part of the year either in natural caves, or in holes which it scrapes for itself among the roots of trees on the banks of rivers. Occasionally, as to the west of Midnapur, it occurs in alluvial tracts which are intersected by numerous ravines, and covered with scrub jungle. Its food is somewhat varied, and it cannot be said to be a strictly vegetable feeder, for although it eats the fruits of several species of fig, the wild plum, or jujube (*Zizyphus jujuba*), the flowers of the mhowa, sugar-cane, &c., it also is fond of termites or white ants, the larvæ of several insects, and honey. If bears exist in any tract of country, the evidences of their presence are numerous and not to be mistaken. Where there have been white ants' nests you often find large holes scooped to the depth of three or four feet, sometimes too in very hard soil in the centre of roads, thus testifying to the great strength of the bears' fore-paws and claws. Such holes may readily be distinguished from those made by any other agency, by the marks of the claws, which they retain for many months. I have known of bears being shot when busily engaged in these holes, sucking up the termites from the deeply-seated galleries below. Again, the trunks of the banyan (*Ficus Indica*, Linn.), gular (*F. glomerata*, Roxb.), and the pakur (*F. infectoria*, Wild.), will be found, at the seasons when these species of figs are in fruit, to be deeply scored by the claws of the bears which have ascended them. The bushes of the jujube, in spite of their thorns, will also be seen to be trodden down and flattened by the bears as they have scrambled over them to pluck the fruit. The female bear, when pursued, carries her cubs on her back, they clinging on by their claws and being half-covered with the shaggy hair. I have already related several instances where this has come under my own observation. The curious thing about it is that the bear should be able to make the cub mount, before it runs off, when disturbed from its lair. These bears have from early infancy a peculiar habit of sucking and mumbling over their paws, the noise they make while doing so being audible from long distances.

March 17th.—Burkol.—To-day I ascended the Gul-gul pât or plateau. At first sight the ascent does not appear to be a very formidable undertaking, but there is a good deal of up and down work, and the route is somewhat circuitous before the top—which is at an elevation of 3,800 feet above the sea—is reached. The main mass of the hill or ridge is formed of vertical beds of granitic gneiss; these are capped by about 250 feet of a pisolitic laterite, which forms the level surface of the plateau. The summit is on a vast block of this rock, from which huge masses have been split off and lie tumbled confusedly on the flanks, with figs, wild mangoes, *Kydia*, and other trees growing between and upon them. A commanding view, more particularly of the Kunhur river and the neighbouring tracts of Sirguja, was obtained from the summit. At about 160 feet below this there is a perennial spring where I slung my hammock and rested for several hours. Taking another route on the descent, I passed through some clearances made on the slopes by the Korewahs, who seem to have been very industrious in cutting down forest. I have mentioned these people in a previous chapter, and shall therefore here give a short account of them. They belong to the Munda family of the aborigines, a fact which is fully testified by their language. In appearance they are perhaps the wildest race in the country; they are particularly notable for the unkempt condition of their matted locks of hair, in which they commonly hitch the shafts of their arrows. They themselves, according to General Dalton, account for their wild and uncouth appearance by saying that the first human beings who settled in Sirguja, being much troubled by the depredations of wild beasts in their crops, put up as scarecrows in their fields figures made of bamboos which were the most hideous caricatures of humanity that they could devise, in order to frighten the animals. When the Great Spirit saw the scarecrows, he hit on an expedient to save his votaries the trouble of reconstructing them. He animated the dangling figures, thus bringing into existence creatures ugly enough to frighten all the birds and beasts in creation, and they were the ancestors of the wild Korewahs. Despite their savage nature, the Korewahs are truthful to an extraordinary degree. General Dalton says of them, "when several are implicated in one offence I have found them most anxious that to each should be ascribed his fair share of it and no more—the oldest of the party invariably taking on himself the chief responsibility as leader or instigator, and doing his utmost to exculpate, as unaccountable agents, the young members of the gang."

A few months previous to my visit to this part of the country a party of Korewahs had made a raid from the highlands of Sirguja into British territory. When marching to the scene of their exploit —the house of a well-to-do landowner—their axes and bows and arrows were tied in bundles, and their appearance excited no particular notice. After news of the robbery had been received a party of police were sent off to capture the Korewahs, who however, shewed an intention of offering an armed resistance, and no little excitement prevailed, as it was thought that the whole of the tribe might rise in open rebellion. However, on a stronger force being sent in command of the Assistant-Superintendent of Police, and the aid of the Sirguja Raja having been obtained, the ringleaders were captured, and the whole country had quieted down ere the time when I reached it.

In the neighbourhood of Burkol I saw the only indigenous wheeled vehicles which I came across in the whole of Palamow; they were of a very rude construction and were only used for drawing timber. With the exception of the Uraons, the people of the sub-division do not use and cannot be induced to carry banghys, so that the only means of carriage is afforded by pack-bullocks. The proprietors belong to various castes, and are often Mahomedans. They penetrate the area and bear off the grain to the markets of the Ganges valley.

March 19th.—Gurria to Tatapani.—Having completed my examination of the Hutar coal-field, I crossed the British frontier, which is here coincident with the Kunhur river, and entered Sirguja in order to give a few days to the examination of another coal-field to which the name of Tatapani has been applied, that being the name of the purguna in which it occurs. This name is derived from two words signifying boiling water, and the village of Tatapani is situated in the vicinity of a number of hot springs, which present a very remarkable appearance. They all, with one exception, occur along a line of fracture and disturbance which has defined the limits of the coal-measures close by. It is not easy to say how many distinct active springs there may be, but there were certainly not less than a score; besides these, there are indications of many others whose action has either been temporarily or wholly suspended. As a rule the water rises in small basins, with a bottom formed of large-grained quartz sand. Round the edges of these basins there is frequently an encrustation of siliceous sinter. A strong odour of sulphureted hydrogen pervades the atmosphere all round. Proceeding from east to west the Fahrenheit temperatures, taken by a Negretti and Zambra's boiling point thermometer, were in the successive basins as follows:—185°, 174°, 162°, 130°, 170°, 168°, 166°, 154°, 184°, 180°. These were all taken in the forenoon of a day near the end of March, when the sun was hot and there was no perceptible condensation of the vapour. Early on the following morning the position of each spring was distinctly marked by a column of condensed steam. On this occasion the temperatures were somewhat different from what they had been the previous evening. The highest was in a basin off the general line of the others and north of a small temple; in it the thermometer registered 196°. I think it probable that this spring is situated on a small branching line of fault or fracture, of the existence of which the neighbouring rocks afford some evidence. The temple alluded to was originally built over what was considered to be the hottest spring; but that particular outlet being now closed, the temple has been allowed to fall into ruins. I was told that the locality is not regarded as being one of particular sanctity. In any more civilized part of India it would assuredly be a place of annual resort and the site of a festival.

While encamped here, I noticed on the roof of my tent a brownish substance, which, on examination, proved to consist of the bodies and dismembered limbs of the red ant (*Formica smaragdina*), the appearance and habits of which I have described in a former chapter. The slaughtered ants must have numbered many thousands, and what had happened appeared to have been that two columns had ascended the roof of the tent from different trees, and had met at the top of the pole, where they had engaged in mortal combat. The contending parties belonged to the same species, and it is marvellous that they should have been able to distinguish foes from friends. Among the pile of bodies, when swept together, there were to be seen heads detached from bodies, but still alive, the jaws clutching fragments of the bodies of their opponents.

Termites, or white ants, of which there are, I believe, several species in India, have attained a considerable notoriety on account of their destructive propensities, since few persons in India can have escaped suffering loss from them. Several particular kinds of timber and substances of mineral origin are alone capable of resisting their attacks. One species builds up hills of clay, with fluted spires culminating in a central minaret. It commences its operations on an old stump of timber or a clump of bamboos as a nucleus, which it gradually surrounds and envelopes, and the hill may ultimately rise to a height of six or eight feet above the surface. If you break down a portion of this hill you find that it is traversed in every direction by anastomosing galleries and passages, which are continued downwards beneath the surface to considerable depths. Great as are these structures compared to the size of the animal which constructs them, they are erected under the disadvantageous circumstance that the termite is obliged to work under cover of a tunnel of clay to protect its tender body from the many insects and birds which are ever ready to seize and devour it. In Calcutta termites are very destructive, and nowhere more so than in the new museum which has been built there within the last few years. Shortly after it was finished, each morning would disclose a number of new clay passages leading from the joints in the stone pavement of the ground-floor rooms to the show specimen-cases, and in a single night the white paper linings would be riddled and half-devoured by the hungry legions. The cases and chests of drawers were of teak timber, which is itself not touched by the termites; but they would pass through chinks and flaws produced by warping. Their extraordinary instinct in discovering the position of these can perhaps be best illustrated by the following: On one occasion I had arranged a number of mineral specimens, with their paper labels under them, in a drawer, one of a series at a height of about three feet from the ground. Two days later my attention was called to a clay tunnel on the outside of the drawers, near the lowest of the series, and on opening the one which contained the specimens I found that the labels had been almost completely eaten, only a few shreds of the paper remaining. I then found that the termites had entered by a flaw in the wood near the centre of the bottom of the drawer, which had been cunningly filled up with putty by the cabinet-maker. The drawer was otherwise quite sound, and fitted well. On inverting it I found that there was a covered tunnel running from the corner of the drawer to the flaw. The termites, who do not scamper about foraging as ants do, must then, by some instinct or sense, have not only known that this particular drawer in this particular cabinet contained paper, but that there was but one means possible to them of obtaining access to it, which means they accordingly adopted.

March 26th.—Nowadih to Daltongunj.—This day I reached Daltongunj, and as the examination of the coal-fields had been completed, save as regards the settling of some few points, which remained till I could revisit the ground on the return route, I shall here give a brief sketch of what I had ascertained regarding these fields, but for a full account of them must refer to my official report,* which, however, the general English reader, in all probability, will never see, nor can I venture to suppose that the subject would have very much interest for him should he see it, though it is needless, perhaps, to observe that India's future

* "Memoirs of the Geological Survey of India." Vol. XV. pt. i., pp. 1–127.

prosperity depends in no small degree on the development of her own resources in coal and iron. While remaining dependent upon Europe for a supply of these minerals, so essential to a country's prosperity, she must continue to import many articles which there is no reason she should not manufacture for herself, and must continue to send large sums of money out of the country, and so defer the much-to-be-desired equalization of the exchange.

The Aurunga coal-field occupies an area of about ninety-seven square miles, and includes representatives of four distinct groups of the Damuda and one of the Mahadeva series of sedimentary rocks. In the oldest but one of these groups, the Barakar, are found the principal coal-seams and iron-ores, and the area over which the rocks of this group are exposed is 58.5 square miles. The coal-seams are of great size; but the quality, as ascertained from examination on the spot and by assay,* is decidedly inferior to that of the coal in the Hutar and Daltongunj fields. Of coal of this inferior character I estimate that about 20,000,000 tons would be available; but, as it would probably prove unfit for smelting the very excellent iron-ores which occur in the field, and as it would not be equal to the coal of the other fields for locomotives, I do not think there is much prospect of its ever being worked to any great extent.

The Hutar field, which lies further west, and is cut in two by the Koel river, has an area of 78.6 square miles. In it the groups of the Damuda series are reduced to two; but the area of coal-measures is nearly equal to that in the Aurunga field, being fifty-seven square miles. There can be little doubt that the two fields were once continuous, though they are now separated by a distinct interval. The data for calculating the amount of coal available are imperfect, and I make no actual estimate. In quality† it com-

* The average composition is—Moisture, 6.7; Volatile, 29.2; Carbon, 36.5; Ash, 27.5.

† The average composition of eight specimens was—Moisture, 5.95; Volatile, 28.; Carbon, 55.35; Ash, 10.7.

pares very favourably with most Indian coals, but, from a deficiency of fixed carbon, has less heating power than the coal of the Daltongunj field. Unfortunately, neither the Hutar nor Daltongunj fields contain any rich deposits of iron, so that it would be necessary to carry the ores of the Aurunga field, and the limestones which are found close by, a distance of about fifty miles to the coal of Daltongunj, in order to manufacture the iron. This long carriage, which would necessitate the construction of a special branch line or tramway, will very possibly prevent the proposed iron-works from ever being established, or, if established, from ever proving a profitable undertaking. This difficulty of long carriage is constantly turning up in India with reference to the development of the resources. As an example I may mention that coal, which at the pit's mouth in Ranigunj may be purchased for five shillings, costs five pounds by the time it has reached Lahore; and between Calcutta and Bombay there is on the railway a point where English coal landed at the latter port meets the longer rail-borne coal of Bengal at equal prices.

The iron-ores to which my attention was particularly directed in Palamow admit of a triple classification, founded both on their geological relations and age, and on their chemical composition. In the first class there are magnetites or magnetic ores which occur in the crystalline and metamorphic rocks. In the second class there are siderites and hæmatites which are found in the coal-measures. And in the third class there are hæmatites which are found in the laterite. The magnetite is of great purity and excellent quality; but its abundance in any one spot in suitable form for extraction is very doubtful. The hæmatites of the laterite, being situated on the tops of lofty plateaus upwards of 3,000 feet high, are practically inaccessible, though the quality of the richer varieties leaves nothing to be desired. It is to the ores of the coal-measures, therefore, the siderites or iron carbonates, and hæmatites or iron oxides that I have been compelled to shew the preference, as being most likely to afford an inexhaustible and easily-worked supply of fairly good ore. Further details on this subject are not likely to prove of general interest, so I shall pass on to describe the method employed by the native Aguriahs or iron-smelters to produce malleable iron, and in doing so I must refer to the accompanying plate, taken from a photograph, which will, I trust, make the description intelligible. The Aguriahs, it is considered by the best authorities, belong to the Munda family of aborigines; but another tribe, the Kol-lohars, are, it is supposed, Uraons. Hindus are perhaps seldom met with as smelters; but the Lohars proper or ironsmiths may, I believe, be regarded as of Aryan origin. Whether or not the aborigines possessed a knowledge of iron manufacture, before they were conquered by the Hindus, is not known with any degree of certainty; but if, as some suppose, the art was introduced by Aryans, it is singular that we should find that the non-Aryans furnish the artizans of the present day.

The furnaces of the Aguriahs are generally erected under some old tamarind or other shady tree, on the outskirts of a village, or under sheds in a hamlet where Aguriahs alone dwell, and which is situated in convenient proximity to the ore, or to the jungle where the charcoal* is prepared. The furnaces are built of mud, and are about three feet high, tapering from below upwards, from a diameter of rather more than two feet at base to eighteen inches at top, with an internal diameter of about six inches, the hearth being somewhat wider. Supposing the Aguriah and his family to have collected the charcoal and ore, the latter has to be prepared before being placed in the furnace. The magnetic ores are first broken into small fragments by pounding, and are then reduced to a fine powder between a pair of millstones. The hæmatite ores are not usually subjected to any other preliminary treatment besides pounding. A bed of charcoal having been placed on the hearth, the furnace is filled with charcoal, and then fired. The blast is produced by a pair of kettledrum-like bellows, which consists of wooden

---

* The Sal (*Shorea robusta*) tree generally affords the timber for the charcoal; but in some tracts, as in Sambalpur, the Bija Sal (*Pterocarpus marsupium*) is preferred.

Plate X.]

AGURIAH IRON-SMELTERS, PALAMOW.

(From a Photograph by T. F. Peppé, Esq.)

basins loosely covered with leather, in the centre of which is a valve. Referring to the illustration it will be seen that strings attached to these leather covers are connected with a rude form of springs, which are made by simply planting bamboos or young trees into the ground in a slanting direction. The weight of the operator, or pair of operators, is alternately thrown from one drum to the other, the heels acting at each depression as stoppers to the valves. The blast is conveyed to the furnace by a pair of hollow bamboos, and has to be kept up steadily without intermission, for from six to eight hours. From time to time ore and füel are sprinkled on the top of the fire, and as the fusion proceeds the slag is tapped off by a hole pierced a few inches from the top of the hearth. For ten minutes before the conclusion of the process, the bellows are worked with extra vigour, and the supply of ore and fuel from above is stopped. The clay luting of the hearth is then broken down, and the ball, or *giri*, consisting of semi-molten iron, slag and charcoal, is taken out and immediately hammered, by which a considerable proportion of the included slag, which is still in a state of fusion, is squeezed out. In some cases the Aguriahs continue the further process, until after various reheatings in open furnaces and hammerings, they produce clean iron fit for the market, or even at times they work it up themselves into agricultural tools, &c. Not unfrequently, however, the Aguriahs' work ceases with the production of the *giri*, which passes into the hands of the Lohars. Four annas, or sixpence, is the price paid for an ordinary-sized *giri*, and as but two of these can be made in a very hard day's work of fifteen hours duration, and a considerable time has also to be expended on the preparation of charcoal and ore, the profits are very small. The fact is, that although the actual price which the iron fetches in the market is high, the profits made by the mahajans, or native merchants, and the immense disproportion between the time and labour expended and the out-turn, both combine to leave the unfortunate Aguriah in a miserable state of poverty.

March 29th.—Daltongunj to Kewatbar.—To-day I left Daltongunj, on the return march eastwards, and for the succeeding week was principally engaged in the examination of various deposits of iron-ore, which occur in the region extending up to the foot of the Neturhat plateau at Kotam, from whence, on the 6th of April, I ascended, in order to examine the hill, and visit some tea plantations which have been started on the summit. As the plateau is 3,600 feet above the sea, or 1,800 above Kotam, its ascent by a steep path was at this season a somewhat arduous undertaking. For the first 1,280 feet the only rock seen was granitic gneiss, resting upon which was a cap 420 feet thick, which consisted of trap and laterite, the exact line of demarcation between the two being concealed by fallen masses of the highest layers of the laterite. In places this laterite is very rich in iron, containing as much as 45.5 *per cent.* of the metal.

The open, saucer-like, surface of the plateau presents a curious appearance, with the slopes on the north and west under cultivation. There are two gardens here, one new one belonging to a small private company, while the other, which had been started about three years previously by the manager and a part proprietor of the former, appeared to be in a flourishing condition: plucking and manufacture was expected to commence in another year. The rate of pay given to the coolies here seemed to be absurdly high, being nearly double that which is paid in the vicinity of the stations of Ranchi and Hazaribagh. I was informed that at one time the experiment had been tried by the manager of importing fifty families of Christian Kols. Before they came he constantly told the local labourers that the Christians would show them what real work was. On their arrival they proved to be lazy and inefficient. They would not commence work till ten or eleven o'clock, and then had to be personally hunted out of their houses. Their awkward way of working made them the laughing-stock of the country side. In the end the manager had to give up the costly experiment, and they were sent back to their homes. The missionary patrons of the Kols charged the manager with having abused their *protégés*, and this he did not deny, as he said the men exasperated him beyond measure. It is possible that there may be another side to this story, but I fear the main fact, that Christian converts are in the habit of considering themselves too good to engage in mere manual work, is indisputable; and experience in Africa and elsewhere tends to show that other black races of people sometimes adopt similar views.

April 14th.—Balunuggur to Chiru.—I had been glad to observe during the early days of this month that there was a large crop of mhowa flowers, that the people were everywhere busily engaged in saving it, and that it promised to afford material aid towards enabling them to tide over the scarcity and want resulting from their poor harvests; but about this time heavy rains set in which served to destroy a great portion of the partially-dried crop—thus was the last hope of these poor people destroyed; how they managed to pull through the summer rains I never heard, but it must have been a hard time for them, though an absolute famine was not announced as existing in that part of the country.

At Chiru and in its neighbourhood I found the most important deposit of iron-ore which I had met with, and should the manufacture of iron ever be started in Palamow, from thence it will be that the material must be obtained. From Chiru I marched through the Karanpura Valley, for the purpose of making a comparison between some of the rocks seen there and those of the fields I had just explored.

On the 22nd I reached Hazaribagh, from whence I proceeded in a carriage drawn by coolies to the railway station at Giridi, and as soon as my camp arrived, some days later, I dismissed my followers, and took the train for Calcutta, thus bringing my jungle life in India to a conclusion for a season; for after two months spent in the preparation of the results of my explorations for publication, I found myself by the end of June free to set forth from India to enjoy two years' furlough at home. It has not altogether proved a period of rest, for the preparation of this volume, together with some other writings, have involved an amount of hard work which I little anticipated when I set about writing them. If I have succeeded in conducting the reader without weariness to this stage in the history of my life, and if I have interested, and perchance at times amused him by the record of it which I have here presented to him, I shall feel that my labour has not been altogether in vain. Should the work prove successful, it may be that hereafter I may have an opportunity of writing a sequel; but in regard to such a life as that which I have described, the proverb of the pitcher and the well cannot fail to suggest itself to the mind. Experience has shewn how manifold are the risks to be encountered, while the term of service at present required, before a full pension can be earned, affords but a faintly-seen vision in the far-distant future of a home at home for one who has adopted the career of a geologist under the Government of India.

APPENDIX A

Geological Formations.

The following table, which is extracted from the recently-published "Manual of the Geology of India,"* is given here for purposes of reference, as many of the formations are alluded to in this volume, and it may be of interest to some readers to know the position which these occupy in the general scale of sequence.

List of Geological Formations in Peninsular India.

Era	Formation	Deposits	Thickness
	Recent and Post-tertiary.	Blown sand. Soils including *regur,* Modern alluvial deposits of rivers, estuaries, and the sea-coast. *Khadur* of Indo-Gangetic plain, &c. Raised shell-beds of coast. Low-level laterite. Older alluvial deposits of Ganges, Narbada, Godavari, &c. Cave deposits.	Unknown. 100 feet deepest boring.
CÆNOZOIC.	*Tertiary.*	Miliolite of Katiawar, Pliocene, Miocene, and Eocene (nummulitic) beds of Cutch and Guzerat. Sandstones, clays, and lignites of the west coast, Travancore, and Ratnagiri, Cuddalore sandstones, High-level laterite.	2,700
MESOZOIC.	*Dekan trap Series.*	Upper traps and intertrappeans of Bombay. Middle traps. Lower traps and intertrappeans of Central India, Rajamahendri, &c. Lameta or infratrappean group. Infratrappeans of Rajamahendri.	6,000
	Marine Cretaceous Rocks.	Arialur, Trichinopoly, and Utatur groups. Bagh beds. Neocomian of Cutch.	3,000
	Marine Jurassic Rocks.	Umia, Katrol, Chari and Pacham groups of Cutch, Jessalmir limestones, Tripetty and Ragavapuram beds of east coast.	6,000

* By H. B. Medlicott, Esq., M.A., F.R.S., and W. T. Blanford, Esq., F.R.S.

Geological Formations—continued.

Era	System	Division	Formations	Thickness (feet)
MESOZOIC. / PALÆOZOIC(?)	*Gondwana System.*	*Upper*	Cutch and Jabalpur. Rajmahal and Mahadeva.	11,000
		Lower	Panchet. Damuda, Ranigunj or Kamthi, ironstone shales, and Barakar. Karharbari and Talchir.	13,000
AZOIC.	*Vindhyan Series.*	*Upper*	Bhanrer (Bundair). Rewah. Kaimur (Kymore).	12,000
		Lower	...Karnul, Bhima, Son, Semri.	2,000 (?)
	Transition or sub-metamorphic rocks.	*Upper*	Gwalior, Kadapah, and Kaladgi.	20,000
		Lower	Bijawars, Champanir beds, Arvali, Malani beds, transition beds of Behar, Bengal and Shillong (the last extra-peninsular).	(?)
	Metamorphic or Gneissic.		Gneiss, granitoid and schistose rocks.	(?)

APPENDIX B.

On the forms and Geographical Distribution of Stone Implements in India

IN a paper on the above subject, which was recently published in the Proceedings of the Royal Irish Academy,* I have given an abstract of all that is known regarding the distribution of ancient stone implements in India, and I am indebted to the Council of the Academy for permission to reproduce the accompanying plates. With two exceptions the figures in these plates are from specimens which have been found in Western Bengal; the two exceptions are of implements obtained in adjoining tracts in the Central Provinces. Notwithstanding the limited area in which the collection has been made, it is fairly representative of the principal types of form which have been found throughout the peninsula. I shall not here quote the details from a consideration of which I have arrived at the conclusions which are given below; nor is the map which illustrates these conclusions reproduced with this abbreviated account; those who are specially interested in the subject will doubtless refer to the original paper.

METHODS EMPLOYED IN THE MANUFACTURE OF THE IMPLEMENTS.

The stone implements of India admit of a triple classification, founded both on their forms and the materials of which they are made.

First. There are the chipped implements which are generally of quartzite or vein quartz.

Second. Flakes of agate, chert, hornstone, &c., with the cores from which they were struck off.

Third. The polished celts which are susceptible of sub-division into several distinct classes. With these I include, for convenience, the ring-stones.

The chipped implements may always be distinguished from apparently similar naturally-fractured stones, by the evidence which

* Second Series, Vol. I. (Pol. Lit. and Antiq.) Dublin, 1879.

they afford of a laboriously worked out design, which was, in most instances, to produce a central plane with a cutting edge all round, and this result was arrived at by making a succession of fractures, as is well represented in *figs.* 1, 2, and 3, of Plate 1; but with the agate and chert flakes it is by no means so easy to account for the process employed. The beautiful symmetry of the cores, especially those from Sind, indicate an amount of careful and skilled manipulation which the quartzite chippers rarely if ever possessed. In the Andaman Islands I was told that heat was an agent employed in facilitating fracture, but I could get no full account of the process. I doubt, too, if the Andamanese ever produced cores like those from Sind. Pressure has been rather vaguely suggested as the means by which these flakes were made; but no one, so far as I know, has by any application of it produced satisfactory results.

The polished celts, particularly those of hard materials, in all probability represent a great amount of work. Some of them, particularly those of the shouldered type, may have been sawn into shape. It is well known that fibres and thin laths, in conjunction with sand, have been used successfully to cut through iron fetters. A similar process, with suitable varieties of sand, may have been employed by the ancient manufacturers of celts.

Uses to which the Stone Implements were put.

Although it has been a common practice with many writers to speak of these chipped stone implements as axes, hatchets, &c., I do not think that any one can really be prepared to maintain that they could ever have been employed as such in the manner in which modern axes or hatchets are used. More unsuitable tools for actually cutting wood can hardly be conceived of, though as wedges for splitting wood, many, both of the chipped and polished kinds, would be fairly efficient instruments. Some may possibly have been used for scooping out canoes and wooden vessels, the operation being facilitated by a preliminary charring by fire. It is known that some have been used in Assam and adjoining countries on the North-east frontier as hoes in rude agriculture, and that for this purpose iron has, in certain remote tracts, only of late become available.

Although certain forms of the chipped quartzites may have been carried in cleft sticks as battle-axes or weapons of offence or defence against wild animals, I believe that the bulk of them were used for grubbing wild roots out of the ground. Some years ago I paid a good deal of attention to the subject of the jungle products, which afford a means of support to many of the aboriginal races.* Besides fruits,

---

* *Vide* Appendix E.

leaves, and stems, I ascertained that the roots, particularly of several species of *Dioscorea*, &c., furnished a substantial food for several months of every year. At the present day people belonging to such tribes may often be seen laboriously digging up these roots, either with a simply pointed stick, or a stick provided with an iron spike. I have a very vivid recollection of the appearance presented by a woman whom I saw thus engaged last year. Her countenance was of the lowest type I have ever seen ; to what race or tribe she belonged I did not ascertain, but as I saw her, with hunger in her eyes and an infant strapped on her back, while she crouched over the precious root which she was digging out, I could not but regard her as being in all probability a lineal descendant of the manufacturers and users of stone implements similar to those which are figured.

There is one class of stone implements unsuited to any of the above-mentioned purposes, but which, being provided with sharp edges, it seems very probable were used as skin scrapers. In connection with this I may mention, that on one occasion, as mentioned in Chapter X., in the Satpura Hills, in the Central Provinces, having shot a bear, I gave the carcase, with some knives, to the people who had brought it to camp, in order that they might take off the skin. These people belonged to a tribe who always carry a very small well-sharpened iron axe of a form I have not seen elsewhere. After working for a short time with the knives, they discarded them for the axes, which they removed from their wooden handles, and then placing their thumbs in the holes, grasped them firmly with their fingers and continued the flaying with astonishing rapidity. In a similar way I believe that the scrapers of stone may have been used for the preparation of skins which, when rudely dressed, afforded the only clothing of these early inhabitants. The various forms of traps and snares which are now commonly met with in the jungles may be survivals of the ancient methods which were employed to capture the wild animals.

Opinions differ much as to the probable uses of the ring-stones, of which examples of various sizes have been obtained in Madras, Jabalpur, and Mopani, in the Central Provinces, and Karakpur in Bengal, and in Burmah. They have been supposed to be weights for spindles, net sinkers, and in the case of the specimens from Karakpur, portions of querns or hand-mills. These last, indeed, appear to be of no great antiquity, and the suggestion is probably correct. I possess a specimen of perforated schist of very modern origin, of which I was able to ascertain the history. I picked it up one day at Almorah, in the Himalayas, and seeing it was modern, I thought it possible that I might be able to get a clue to the uses of the ancient forms, to which it had some resemblance. On enquiry I found it was simply a toy mill-stone which had been manufactured by or for the children of the village, and one small boy laughed outright when he saw me carrying it off.

The example (Plate II, Fig. 13) is, however, ancient beyond a doubt. I have already suggested in my original account of it that I am inclined to believe, from the facility with which it can be grasped, that it may have been used as a sort of "knuckle-duster" in encounters between men and wild animals. As a spindle whorl or net-sinker, it appears to me that it is unnecessarily heavy, and for either of these purposes a softer, more easily worked, stone than basalt would answer equally well.

The chief point of interest about it is its very close resemblance to forms which have not uncommonly been met with in Europe and likewise in Virginia, Pennsylvania, and other parts of North America.* To those who believe in an Asiatic origin for the North American Indians this fact may be of interest. These implements are commonly called hammer-stones; but I do not think it probable that they were employed in the manufacture of flakes, as has been suggested by some authorities.†

The flakes of chert, agate, &c., which were struck from the cores, were undoubtedly used as lancets, knives, arrow-heads, &c. I have, in Chapter V., Section 2, described how, in the Andaman Islands at the present day, in the vicinity of the settlements, flakes of bottle-glass are used as lancets and razors, they being found to be more efficient than the flakes of chert, &c., which were formerly used there. It is most probable that in some parts of the islands chert or hornstone flakes are still manufactured, and used for these purposes.

I cannot leave this part of the subject without making a suggestion as to a possible use of some of the forms whose efficiency as implements appear to be doubtful. In Burmah, Assam, &c., these objects are regarded either as being of supernatural origin, or as thunderbolts, as I have stated above. In Bandelkhand and the Central Provinces they have sometimes been found placed in the vicinity of Sivoid altars, or the well-known *lingum*. It seems, therefore, possible that some forms may have been specially prepared as votive offerings, and possessed a symbolical significance in a now forgotten cult. Possibly, however, the custom among certain of the

---

* *Vide* "American Naturalist," for March, 1873.

† I have recently seen a very interesting collection of stone implements from the Solomon Islands. The "celts" are mounted in cleft sticks, apparently for agricultural purposes. There are also two ring-stones fixed on sticks, making very formidable maces, or life-preservers. They are less bevelled than the specimen which is figured, but are otherwise very similar.

aboriginal tribes to make offerings of pottery-images, &c., to the evil spirits which they believe infest their forests and hills, and whom it is considered to be much more important to propitiate than it is to invoke the protection of the good spirits, may be a relic of that ancient time.

Miniature stone models of agricultural implements might very possibly have been offered on the altars of those deities or spirits who were supposed to preside over agriculture, and upon whose favour prosperity was believed to depend. We need not seek far in other religions for analogous offerings of types for actual things. There is an iron adze-shaped tool in use in Burmah at the present day very similar to the shouldered celts found in that province, which fact throws a doubt on the great antiquity claimed for the latter, since it is simply idle to suppose that these stone adzes can have been used for shaping wood.

General and Concluding Remarks on the Geographical Distribution.

Reviewing the facts given under the several geographical headings, and the further details in the Table appended to the already mentioned paper, it becomes apparent that it is possible, in the present state of our knowledge, to sub-divide India with the adjoining countries on the east and west into three great regions, each characterised by containing a certain class of stone implements. On the map which accompanies my original paper I have attempted to distinguish the limits of these regions respectively. It will be observed that there are patches detached from each, to which the geological term *outlier* may conveniently be applied.

Throughout this account I have not made use of the terms *neolithic* and *palæolithic*, convenient as they doubtless are, since they are calculated to convey what, in the case of India at least, I consider to be an erroneous idea of progression. The different forms of implements seem to be rather indices of race than of time. This opinion may appear to be unorthodox, and the picture of the rude manufacturer of the chipped quartzite being the progenitor of the artist who, in the progress of time, evolves the art of making highly-polished celts out of the hardest materials, though no doubt an attractive one, does not seem to fit in with the facts at our disposal. Of course in certain localities such an advance in art may have taken place; but the wide extent of country we are dealing with, and the magnitude of the data, render it possible to ignore such local cases, supposing them to exist, without vitiating the main results and conclusions.

It would be improper to omit all reference to the influence which the geological structure of the three great regions respectively may have had in determining the form and characters of the implements. It is clear that where chert, agate, or some similar forms of quartz do not occur naturally, we are not likely to find flakes and cores in abundance; and, therefore, a certain limit has been placed by external causes on the manufacturing capabilities of the people. At the same time each of the regions is so vast and the mineralogical resources are so varied, that the specialized characters of the implements appear to be all the more remarkable, since the materials for greater diversity are not wanting. In Burmah, however, according to Mr. Theobald, the implements are often of schist or basalt, which are quite unlike anything to be found in the areas where the implements occur.

We find that implements belonging to the first class (the chipped quartzites) occur throughout a vast area of India which extends in a north and south direction from Saugor to Madras, and east and west from Ranigunj in Bengal to Nimuch in Rajputana. This area overlaps the others to some extent, or it may be otherwise stated has outliers within their limits, as in Chutia Nagpur, and the Central Provinces, and Rajputana. In far distant Java implements of somewhat similar character appear to have been met with. This is a fact of considerable interest, pointing to a pre-historic connection.

The distribution of the flakes and cores, which constitute the second class, is limited to the area which extends north and south from Kerowlie in Rajputana to Peyton on the Godavari in Bombay, and east and west from Singhbhum in Western Bengal to Sukkur on the Indus, in Sind, and still further even to Gwadar in Biluchistan. The principal known outliers from this area are at Rajamahendri on the lower Godavari, and in the Andaman Islands.

The polished celts, &c., whose varieties make up the sub-divisions of the third class, occupy an area which extends from Upper Assam in the north-east to Singhbhum in Bengal, and from the Irawadi Valley in Burmah to Jabalpur in the Central Provinces. The doubtful case of a polished celt from Coorg (or Kurg) and a series of polished celts from the Shevaroy Hills, which are preserved in the British Museum, so far as I know, are the only examples of any being found outside these boundaries.

Such being the rough limits of the three areas of distribution, it is obvious that in Western Bengal and the Central Provinces—*i.e.*, in the most central parts of the peninsula—there is considerable mutual overlap. It now only remains to make an attempt to offer some rational explanation of this fact. Two theories have suggested themselves to me. According to the first, we may regard these central tracts as including a radiating point, from whence successive waves of emigration may, at different stages in the civilization and progression of the people, have spread, as the rising peninsula enlarged the area accessible. We cannot say with any degree of certainty whether the flake-makers or the quartz-chippers were the most ancient. The former, however, on this supposition, spread in directions to the west and north-west, while the latter found their way southwards to Madras, and even to Java in the south-east, where they met with the manufacturers of polished celts. These last, according to the same theory, spread eastwards from the central point of departure, till, through Burmah and the Malayan countries, they reached the confines of China. This theory is one that may commend itself to the notice of progressionists; but, for my own part, I am rather inclined to adopt the following as the more probable explanation. According to this second theory, our central area must be regarded as including a point of convergence rather than of divergence, of immigration rather than of emigration. As we recede from the central area, in the several directions above indicated, we find that the farther off we get, the respective forms become more abundant, and shew higher degrees of skill, being nearer the original seats of the races who manufactured. Thus none of the cores and flakes of the Central Provinces can compare with those of Sind for beauty of workmanship. The chipped quartzites of Madras, if not better formed, are certainly in greater variety and abundance than those of the Central Provinces, while, as regards the polished celts, the superiority of the workmanship of those from the Burmese and adjoining countries cannot well be disputed.

Having again recourse to the idea of the rising peninsula or island, which is, however, a by no means essential feature of this theory, we may suppose that as the central parts of the country became accessible, wanderers from the north-east and north-west, bringing with them a knowledge of their respective arts, came in contact with one another, and became the parents of some of the widely-distinct races who inhabit India at the present day. With the introduction of a knowledge of the art of making iron by the rude process which is still employed, the manufacture of stone implements gradually died out, though, as has been pointed out, it still lingers on the north-east frontier and in the Andaman Islands. At what time iron began to replace the stone we cannot say; but it is most probable, in spite of the fact of copper weapons having been discovered in certain places, that in India there has been no intervening bronze period.

It may be useful to add here Dr. Caldwell's views on the subject of the successive waves of immigration which have served to constitute the four separate strata into which the Indian population is at present sub-divided.*

---

* I quote from Colonel Dalton's "Ethnology of Bengal," p. 244. Colonel Dalton, in a foot-note, demurs to the correctness of the inclusion of the Bhils with the Kols, considering them to be rather Dravidian. *See* also on this subject Proc. Asiatic Soc. Bengal, 1873, pp. 130-133.

First and earliest. The forest tribes, such as Kols, Sontals, Bhils, &c., who may have entered India from the north-east.

Second. The Dravidians, who entered India from the north-west, and either advanced voluntarily towards their ultimate seats in the south of the peninsula, or were driven by the pressure of subsequent hordes following them in the same direction.

Third. We have the race of Scythian or non-Aryan immigrants from the north-west, whose language afterwards united with the Sanskrit to form the Prakrit dialect of Northern India.

Fourth. The Aryan invaders.

The resemblance between the above, and the conclusions which I have arrived at independently, more particularly as regards the source of the Kolarian manufacturers of the polished celts, is sufficiently obvious.

With regard to the Dravidians, who came from the north-west, it may be that they were the people who manufactured the flakes, and afterwards—when they had pushed off the Dekan basalt, further south, took to making the chipped quartzite axes from a material which then became more accessible to them.

In conclusion I would say that the suggestions I have put forward are, to the best of my belief, wholly new, though they first occurred to me many years ago. The progress of discovery has encouraged me to believe that they contain a strong element of probability. It is in the hope that the subject may attract the notice of ethnologists, philologists, and antiquarians, with all of whose special departments it is intimately connected, that I have at length ventured to give them publicity.

ANCIENT STONE IMPLEMENTS FROM

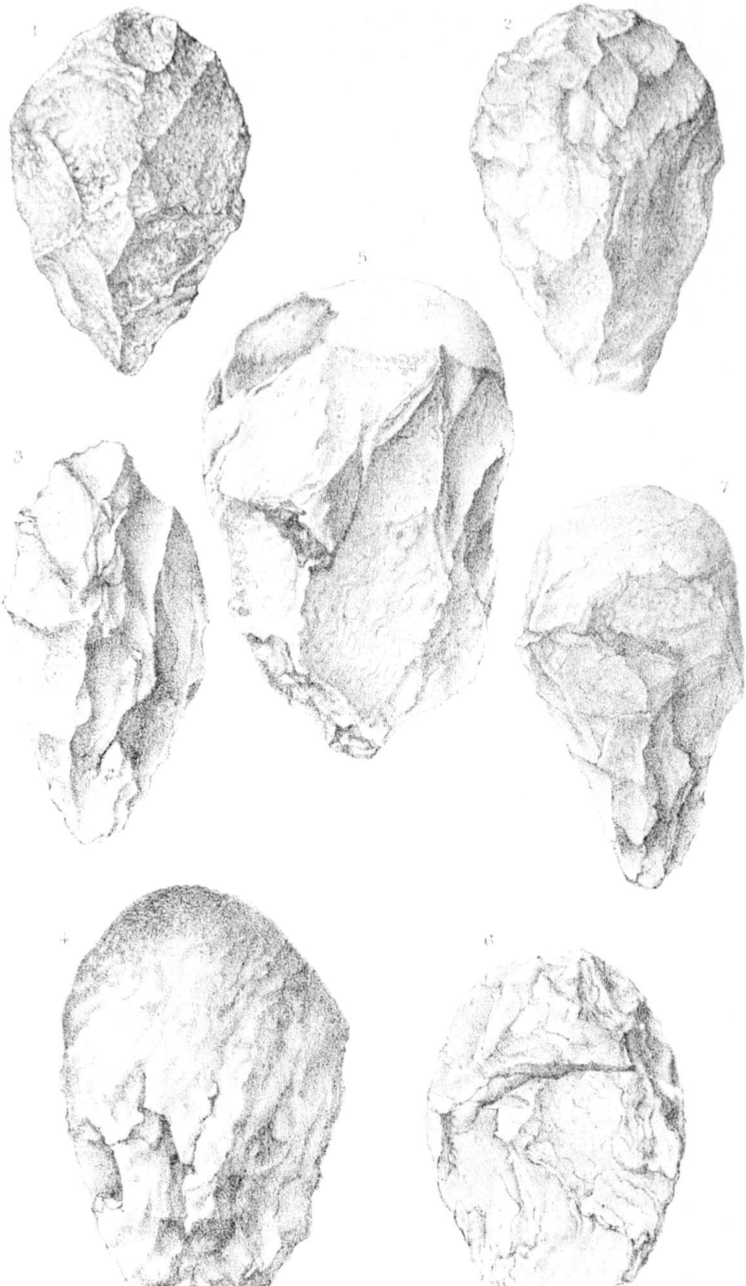

SCALE HALF NATURAL SIZE.

BENGAL & THE CENTRAL PROVINCES.

SCALE HALF NATURAL SIZE.

EXPLANATION OF PLATES.

Plate I.	1.	Chipped quartzite, Jeriah Coal-field, Western Bengal.
,,	2.	,, ,, S.S.W. of Beherinath Hill, Western Bengal.
,,	3.	,, ,, Ranigunj Coal-field, Western Bengal.
,,	4.	,, vein-quartz, Talchir, Orissa.
,,	5.	,, quartzite, Denkenal, Orissa.
,,	6.	,, ,, Ungul, Orissa.
,,	7.	,, ,, Sambalpur, Central Provinces.
Plate II.	8.	Polished argillaceous slate, Buradih, Chutia Nagpur, Western Bengal.
,,	9.	,, trap, Parisnath Hill, Western Bengal, with section.
,,	10.	,, argillaceous slate, Parisnath Hill, Western Bengal.
,,	11.	,, quartzite } Singhbhum. These are of the shouldered Burmese type.
,,	12.	,, trap }
,,	13.	Ring-stone, basalt, Mopani Coal-mines, Central Provinces, with section.
,,	14.	Core of horn-stone, Singhbhum.
,,	15.	Do. Do.

Scale.—Half natural size.

APPENDIX C.

On the Mammals and Birds occurring in the area which extends from the Ganges to the Godavari rivers.

LIST OF MAMMALS.

MONKEYS.

Presbytis entellus, Dufres.—The Langur is very local in its distribution; it is uncertain whether a distinct species does not come in towards the south.

Inuus rhesus, Desm.—The Bengal Monkey is not very common, being generally restricted to heavy forest, near the larger rivers.

BATS.*

Pteropus medius, Temm. (The flying-fox.)
Cynonycteris amplexicaudata, Geoff.
Megaderma lyra, Geoff.
Rhinolophus mitratus, Blyth.
Nyctinomus tragatus, Dobson.
Taphozous longimanus, Hardw.
Taphozous melanopogon, Temm.
Scotophilus temminckii, Horsf.
Vesperus Tickelli, Blyth.
Vesperugo abramus, Temm.
Kerivoula lanosa, Smith.

SHREWS.

Sorex cærulescens, Shaw.† The common, so-called, musk rat.

Tupaia Elliotti, Wat.—The Madras Tree-Shrew probably occurs throughout; but is more abundant in the Valley of the Mahanadi, and thence southwards.

---

* This list is extracted from Dobson's "Catalogue of Asiatic Cheiroptera."

† Other species of shrews occur, it is believed, but their names are not yet known.

BEAR.

Procheilus labiatus, Blainv.—The Indian Black Bear is found at intervals throughout, but is absent from some wide tracts for no apparent reason. Its habits have been described on p. 659.

RATEL-BADGER.

Mellivora Indica, Shaw.—The Indian Badger or Grave-digger occurs in rocky tracts throughout; but owing to its nocturnal habits its distribution is not very well known.

OTTER.

Lutra nair, F. Cuv. (?).—An otter, belonging I believe to this species, is found in most of the larger rivers in this area.

CATS.

Felis tigris, Linn.—The tiger is found throughout; but is rare in the open tracts and the heaviest forest.

Felis pardus, Linn.—The leopard is found throughout. The black variety is sometimes met with.

Felis chaus, Guld.—The jungle-cat, though not commonly met with, has been seen by me in most of the districts. Other species of cats very probably occur too, but I have not shot them. The occurrence of the Lynx is doubtful.

Felis jubata, Schreb.—The hunting-leopard appears to have been obtained in Sambalpur.

HYÆNA.

Hyæna striata, Zimm.—The hyæna is common throughout.

CIVET.

Viverra zibetha, Linn.—The large civet-cat is probably common in many parts of the region, but is not often seen. The lesser civet-cat (*Viverra malaccensis*) also in all probability occurs, but has not been seen nor obtained by me.

TREE-CAT.

Paradoxurus musanga, Marsden.—The common tree-cat has been seen by me on rare occasions in Manbhum and Western Chutia Nagpur.

ICHNEUMON OR MONGOOSE.

Herpestes Sp. (?).—I believe that there are two species of Mongoose or Ichneumon within the area; but they have not yet been properly identified. One specimen obtained by me had the characters of *H. monticolus*, W. Elliott.

WOLF, &c.

Canis pallipes, Sykes.—The Indian wolf has been seen by me in the valleys of the Damuda and Koel rivers, but not further south.

Canis aureus, Linn.—The Jackal occurs throughout, but is rare in heavy forest.

Cuon rutilans, Temm.—The Wild Dog occurs in packs, and is probably very migratory; but it is not often seen.

Vulpes Bengalensis, Shaw.—The Indian Fox is principally found in open cultivated tracts.

SQUIRRELS.

Sciurus maximus, Schreb (according to Jerdon).—The Central Indian Red Squirrel, is very local in its distribution. I have seen it on Parisnath, the banks of the Mahanadi, in Orissa, where it is common, and in Gangpur.

Sciurus palmarum, Gmel.—The common striped squirrel occurs in mango-groves, in some places in great abundance. It is said to be replaced by another nearly allied species, *S. tristriatus*, towards the south.

Pteromys oral, Tickell.—The brown flying-squirrel has only been seen by me in Raipur; it has, however, been obtained in Chutia Nagpur and Bustar.

RATS AND MICE.

Materials for an account of the *Muridæ* are very insufficient, and I shall not attempt to give a list of the species. Among those which I have obtained are the Indian Jerboa rat, *Gerbillus indicus*, Hardw., the Bandicoot, *Mus bandicota*, Bech., and the bush rat, *Golunda Elliotti*, Gray.

PORCUPINE.

Hystrix leucura, Sykes.—The Indian porcupine is the species which occurs throughout the area, where it lives in burrows in rocky hills, and is by no means rare.

HARE.

Lepus ruficaudatus, Geoff.—The common Indian hare occurs throughout.

ELEPHANT.

Elephas indicus, Cuv.—The elephant occurs in the hill ranges of Manbhum and Singhbum, in the Rajmahal Hills,* in Western Chutia Nagpur, and in the states of Mohurbunj, Hindole, Keonjur and Denkenal, in Orissa. South of the Mahanadi I do not know of its occurrence.

PIG.

Sus indicus, Schinz.—The wild pig occurs locally throughout.

---

* In 1870, there were two there, the sole survivors of former herds.

DEER.

Rucervus Duvaucellii, Cuvier.—The swamp deer is found in Western Chutia Nagpur ; but appears to be more common south of the Mahanadi.

Rusa Aristotelis, Cuv.—The sambar occurs pretty generally where there is heavy forest throughout the region.

Axis maculatus, Gray.—The spotted deer has a local distribution throughout.

Axis porcinus, Zimm.—The hog-deer has only been seen by me in Jaipur, and I have not heard of its occurrence elsewhere.

Cervulus aureus, Ham. Smith.—The barking-deer occurs throughout, and is very common in certain tracts.

Memimna indica, Gray.—The mouse-deer occurs in Manbhum and Orissa ; from its small size it often, probably, escapes observation.

ANTELOPES.

Portax pictus, Pallas.—The Nilgai occurs in open jungle in the more thinly inhabited tracts.

Tetraceros quadricornis, Blainv.—The four-horned antelope does not appear to be very common. I have only shot it in Palamow.

Antilope cervicapra, Pallas.—The antelope, or black-buck, occurs very locally in grassy plains in Western Chutia Nagpur, Sambalpur, and Jaipur.

GAZELLE.

Gazella, Bennettii, Sykes.—The Indian gazelle occurs in Sirguja and Palamow. I have seen it at Latiahar, Long. 84° 35′ which is its most eastern point of extension in the peninsula.

BOVINÆ.

Gavæus gaurus, Ham. Smith.—The gaur, or Indian bison, is found on most of the lofty plateaus throughout the region.

Bubalus arni, Kerr and Shaw.—The buffalo occurs in the south and extreme west of Chutia Nagpur ; in Sambalpur, Jaipur, Raipur, and Bustar.

ANT-EATER.

Manis pentadactyla, Linn.—The Indian scaly ant-eater is found inhabiting rocky hills in Chutia Nagpur and Sambalpur, but its distribution is not very well known at present.

BIRDS.

In a paper recently published in the Indian Ornithological Journal, called "Stray Feathers,"* I have given an account of the distribution of birds, so far as it is at present known, throughout the hilly region which extends from the Ganges, near the Rajmahal Hills, to the Godavari Valley.

It was my original intention to have reproduced the list of species in this appendix, but I have been compelled by the great size to which this volume has grown to curtail very considerably both this and the other appendices. The region included between the above-indicated limits corresponds, very nearly, with the Bengal sub-province of geographical distribution, as it has been defined by Mr. W. T. Blanford, F.R.S., in an important paper by him on the "African element in the Fauna of India."†

In preparing the list I have only included species and localities of which there is an absolute record in either printed or manuscript lists to which I have had access. The total number of species enumerated in the list is 418. Short lists which I give at the end of my paper serve to illustrate the value of the sub-province as a natural area of distribution. In these latter, species will be found which never appear to cross a sharply defined boundary line; on the other hand there are lists of species which, though crossing the boundary-line, do so but rarely, and occur within the sub-province merely as stragglers.

Those who have not paid much attention to the curious facts in connection with the geographical distribution of animals, which have been collected and discussed by Mr. A. Wallace and others, will be perhaps little prepared to hear that birds conform in a very remarkable degree to the distribution of other animals, which are not endowed with similar means of locomotion. In some cases the character of the vegetation has, no doubt, a great influence on the type of fauna to be found within a given area; but it is certain that so apparent a cause will not always serve to explain the facts which come under the notice of the field naturalist.

To a former arrangement of land surfaces the main features of the existing distribution of animals is generally traced; but some of the minor features appear to be connected with occult causes, which have still to be discovered and explained.

---

* "From the Ganges to the Godavari." "Stray Feathers." Vol. VII., p. 191.

† *Vide* "Ann. and Mag. of Nat. Hist." October, 1876.

APPENDIX D.

On the Mammals and Birds of the Andaman and Nicobar Islands.

MAMMALS.

Although it is probable that further research may result in the discovery of some few additions to the meagre list of mammals given below, it may still be taken as a tolerably well-established fact that the mammal fauna of these islands is a very poor one.

ANDAMAN, PREPARIS, AND COCO ISLANDS.

MONKEY.

Macacus Sp. (?)—I saw monkeys on Preparis; but, as I failed to obtain a specimen, I cannot say to what species they belonged. They may have been *M. carbonarius*, F. Cuv., as some of them were very dark, or nearly black; but it is possible that the species is *M. cynamologos*, Linn., which appears to be the one found in the Great Nicobar.

No well-authenticated case of a monkey having been obtained in the Andamans has yet been recorded; *M. Andamanensis* is known to be a spurious species. The reported occurrence of a species of *Loris* in Preparis needs confirmation.

BATS.

Pteropus Nicobaricus, Fitz and Zelebor.
Cynopterus brachyotus, Müller.
Rhinolophus Andamanensis, Dobson.
Vesperus Tickelli, Blyth.
Vesperus pachypus, Temm.

TREE-SHREW.

Tupaia peguana (?).—We obtained one specimen of tree-shrew on Preparis which appeared to be referable to this species.

TREE-CAT.

Paradoxurus Tytleri, Blyth.—This species is known only from the middle and southern Andamans, where specimens have from time to time been obtained.

SQUIRREL.

Sciurus Assamensis, McClell.—Two specimens obtained on Preparis appeared to belong to this species.

RATS AND MICE.

Mus Andamanensis, Blyth.—Whether this is really a distinct species seems open to doubt. Blyth himself, according to Jerdon ("Mammals of India," p. 194), identified it with *M. setifer* of Cantor. Jerdon suggests its identity with *M. rattoides*, Hodgson. By whatever name it is to be called, it seems probable that it is identical with the Nicobar animal *M. Novaræ*.

What other, if any, species of rats and mice occur in the Andamans is at present unknown.

PIG.

Sus Andamanensis, Blyth.—This is a small race of pig said to be a hybrid between two species from neighbouring countries; but its true history and origin can only be a matter of conjecture. A pig is found on the Cocos and also, I believe, on Preparis.

NICOBAR ISLANDS.

MONKEY.

Macacus cynomologos, Linn. This is the species which, according to Blyth, occurs in the Nicobars. Zelebor gives *M. carbonarius*, F. Cuv., from the Great Nicobar; but the former identification is more likely to be correct.

BATS.

Pteropus Nicobaricus, Fitz. and Zelebor.
Cynopteris Scherzei, Fitz. and Zelebor.
Phyllorhina Nicobariensis, Dobson.
Miniopteris pusillus, Dobson.

TREE-SHREW.

Cladobates Nicobaricus, Zelebor. — This interesting little mammal was obtained on the Great Nicobar by the "Novara" expedition, and afterwards by myself on the same island.

RATS.

Mus palmarum, Fitz., and *Mus Novaræ*, Fitz.—According to the "Saügethere" of the Reise Novara two species of rats were obtained on the Nicobars. But it is thought that there may perhaps be really only one, and that that is identical with *M. Andamanensis*.

PIG.

Sus Sp. (?)—The pig of the Nicobar Islands is said to have been introduced, and to have come from a Chinese stock.

BUFFALO.

Bubalus arni (?).—Buffaloes in a wild condition are found on the island of Kamorta. There is no doubt that they were originally introduced by the Danes. It has also been stated that there are herds of wild cattle; but this needs confirmation.

BIRDS.

The total number of species of birds known to occur in the islands which intervene between Arakan and Sumatra—namely, Preparis, the Cocos, Narkondam, Barren Island, the Andamans, and the Nicobars, and which have been observed at sea in the vicinity of these islands, amounts to but 188. If the waders and swimmers are omitted, to only 132. As among the waders two, at least, are locally-specialized forms, and in both orders species occur which belong properly to far-distant countries outside the geographical regions into which India and the adjoining countries are sub-divided, it is necessary for the purpose of making a complete analysis of the bird fauna that these orders should not be excluded from consideration.

In my earliest papers which I published on the subject of the ornithology of these islands I was inclined to separate the fauna of the Nicobars from that of the Andamans, in consequence of the latter being, I then thought, more nearly affined to the Indian or Indo-Burmese. Subsequent discoveries have shewn that the faunas of the two groups are linked together in such a way that they cannot be conveniently separated. There are, indeed, but four local species in the Nicobars, which are unrepresented by close allies in the Andamans (*vide* 6th sub-division, *infra*). In the Andamans, it is true, there are twenty-four local species not represented by near allies in the Nicobars ; but this fact is of less importance, since the Nicobars have not yet been thoroughly explored, and further research will probably diminish the number.

In the examination of the fauna of such groups of islands the specialised forms—the species which have been modified by local conditions from ultra-insular or continental types—claim a large share of attention, though it is mainly from the old well-known species that the greatest aid in the determination of the affinities is to be obtained. It would require more space than is here available for the purpose to go fully into this question. Mr. Hume's conclusion* from an analysis is, that the birds of these islands present a stronger affinity, owing to the greater number of identical genera, with those of India than with the Indo-Burmese or Indo-Malayan

* "Stray Feathers." Vol. II., p. 134.

countries. On the other hand, he points out that many common Indian genera are totally unrepresented in these islands, though they ought to be present were the affinity really very close. My own impression is that when full weight is given to all these factors, and when the birds have been more completely collected, the balance of evidence will favour the view that the closest affinity is with the bird fauna of Burmah. The occurrence of fresh-water fish in the Andamans identical with species found in Burmah, and the few mammals belonging also to allied or identical species from Burmah, certainly point in the direction of a land connection having formerly existed between the islands and Burmah; and the physical features, and I believe also the *flora*, afford evidence of similar character.* The question being connected with a very large subject as to the former distribution of land in the Indian Ocean, cannot be now discussed here, so that I shall pass to the enumeration of the local species.

The specialized forms† found in these islands only amount to fifty-nine. These may conveniently be grouped as follows :—

First. Species which occur in both the principal groups of islands without any local modification. Of these there are ten, viz. :—

Ninox affinis, Tytler.
N. Obscurus, Hume.
Alcedo Bengalensis, Gmel. *var.*
Zosterops Nicobariensis, Blyth.
Calornis Tytleri, Hume.
Eulabes Javanensis, Osbeck (var. *Andamanensis*, Tytler).
Janthænas palumboides, Hume.
Macropygia rufipennis, Blyth.
Megapodius Nicobariensis,‡ Blyth (?).
Turnix albiventris, Hume.

Second. Species which shew local variation not considered to amount to specific distinction. Of this there are but three examples. The racket-tailed drongo (*Dissemurus affinis*, Tytler), the ground-thrush (*Geocichla albogularis*, Blyth), and the green pigeon

---

* Mr. S. Kurz calls the flora a Malayo-Burmese one, *vide* "Vegetation of the Andamans," p. 15.

† Inclusive of five *varieties* of ultra-insular forms which do not bear distinctive names.

‡ The occurrence of *Megapodius* in the Andamans has not yet been ascertained; but, as a species is known to occur in the Cocos, it is not improbable that it may hereafter be found there.

(*Osmotreron chloroptera*, Blyth). In both of which the Nicobar examples are distinguished from the Andaman by certain small but constant characteristics.

Third. Species with allied representatives in the two groups respectively. Of these paired species there are six recognised.

ANDAMANS.	NICOBARS.
Spilornis Elgini, Tytler.	*S. minimus*, Hume.
Ephialtes Balli, Hume.	*E. Nicobaricus*, Hume.
Palæornis Tytleri, Hume.	*P. erythrogenys*, Blyth.
Oriolus Andamanensis, Tytler.	*O. macrourus*, Blyth.
Temenuchus Andamanensis, Blyth.	*T. erythropygius*, Blyth.
Munia fumigata, Wald.	*M. semistriata*, Hume.

Fourth. Species which are represented in one group by a specialized form ; in the other, by an ultra-insular ally.

ANDAMANS.	NICOBARS.
Pelargopsis Burmanica, Sharpe.	*P. intermedia*, Hume.
Halcyon chloris, Bodd.	*H. occipitalis*, Blyth.
Arachnecthra Andamanica, Hume.	*A. pectoralis*, Horsf.
Myiagra Tytleri, Beavan.	*M. azurea*, Bodd. var.
Carpophaga ænea, Linn.	*C. insularis*, Blyth.

Fifth. Species occurring in the Andamans without representatives in the Nicobars. Of these there are twenty-four, viz. :—

Spizaetus Andamanensis, Tytler.
Spilornis Davisoni, Hume.
Ephialtes modestus, Wald.
Strix De Roepstorffi, Hume.
Collocalia innominata, Hume.
Caprimulgus Andamanicus, Hume.
Halcyon saturatior, Hume.
Alcedo Beavani, Wald.
Palæornis magnirostris,* Ball.
Picus Andamanensis, Blyth.
Thriponax Hodgii, Blyth.
Centropus Andamanensis, Tytler.
Dicæum virescens, Hume.
Graucalus Dobsoni, Ball.

* These two last species should perhaps not strictly be included here, as, since their discrimination, they have been found to occur in ultra-insular regions.

Pericrocotus Andamanensis, Tytler.
Dissemuroides Andamanensis, Tytler.
Oreocinchla inframarginata, Blyth.
Brachypodius fuscoflavescens, Hume.
Oriolus melanocephalus, var.
Copsychus saularis, var.
Kittacinchla albiventris, Blyth.
Dendrocitta Baylei, Tytler.
Euryzona Canningi, Tytler.
Hypotænidia obscuriora, Hume.

Further research in the Nicobar islands will probably result in the discovery of species which will necessitate the transfer of some of the above under one of the other headings.

Sixth. Species occurring in the Nicobars without representatives in the Andamans:—

Palæornis caniceps, Blyth.
Æthopyga Nicobarica, Hume.
Hypsipetes Nicobariensis, Blyth.

Seventh. Species found in outlying islands not included in the two principal groups:—

Rhyticeros Narcondami, Hume, Narkondam.
Dissemuroides dicruriformis, Hume, Cocos.

These two species are of very great interest. The first, a hornbill, is a well marked form which is only known to occur on the outlying volcanic island of Narkondam; and the second, a king-crow, though closely allied to a species in the Andamans, is restricted in range to the Cocos.

Pressure of space prevents me from entering more fully into an account of the birds of these islands; but the subject is one of high interest, and the reader is referred to the papers by the late Marquis of Tweeddale in the "Ibis," and to those by Mr. Hume in "Stray Feathers," for further information.

APPENDIX E.

On Jungle Products used as articles of Food in Chutia Nagpur.

What I have said in various parts of this work, more particularly on pages 63, 65, and 71, regarding the food of the lower races of the population inhabiting the jungle tracts, renders it unnecessary to enlarge further on the subject here. Although from the time of my first acquaintance with these people I was struck with the important part played by various jungle products, as affording a means of subsistence, it was not till the Orissa famine in 1866-67, that I fully realised the extent to which they were employed and their number and variety. The result of my enquiries I embodied in a paper which was published in the "Journal of the Asiatic Society of Bengal,"* from which I extract the following table with sundry small alterations and corrections. Although it is not quite complete as, since its publication, I have met with several food-yielding plants which are not enumerated in it, still as it includes all the principal and the bulk of the minor products, it will serve the present purpose sufficiently well. Upwards of seventy species will be found in the table, and I have endeavoured as far as possible to arrange them in the order of their relative importance under the headings of seeds, fruits, leaves, stems, and roots. At the top of the lists are the species which may be regarded as staple articles of food, which are made use of in all years whether the harvest be abundant or not. These are followed by species less commonly used, and these last by others, which, though edible, are injurious to health if used in quantity.

The reservation of forest tracts, which prohibits the inhabitants from taking a blade of grass from within the boundaries, has resulted, as I have pointed out, in the people being cut off from these food sources throughout wide areas, and many have been forced to migrate in consequence to other regions, not yet included in reserves, where they can continue to supplement their scanty cultivation with the productions afforded to them by nature.

---

* Vol. XXXVI., p. 37.

List of Jungle Products used as articles of Food in Chutia Nagpur.

SEEDS.

NAMES.	VERNACULAR NAMES.	REMARKS.
Shorea robusta, *Roxb.*	Sal	Much used by the Sontals; occasionally roasted and eaten alone, but more frequently boiled up with the dried flowers of *mhowa*.
Bauhinia Vahlii, *W. & A.*	Chehúr	Sometimes stored, but more frequently roasted and eaten close to the spot where found.
Mucuna imbricata, *D. C.*	Kusee	
——— prurita, *Hook.*	Alkússa or Kiwách	
——— nivea, *Buch.*	Khamach ?	Sometimes cultivated.
Terminalia bellerica, *Roxb.*	Bhæra or Bora	Kernels if eaten in quantity are said to produce intoxication.
——— catappa, *Linn.*	Bádám	Seeds used as a substitute for almonds.
Fuirena ciliaris, *R. Br.*	Band-kobi	Seeds used as a sort of meal, and are sometimes ground into flour before use.
Cassia fistula, *Linn.*	Bunderlati or Amultás	Placentæ between the seeds used to make sherbet.
Nelumbium speciosum, *Willd.*	Moolum Puddoo or Bansera	
Ventilago calyculata, *Tulasne.*	?	Seeds eaten in the same way as those of Sal.

FRUITS.

NAMES.	VERNACULAR NAMES.	REMARKS.
Bassia latifolia, *Roxb.*	Moul or Mhowa	The fruit is dried in the sun and eaten in times of scarcity, and the seeds yield an oil which is used as a substitute for *ghi*. (See flowers.)
Buchanania latifolia, *Roxb.*	Piál or Piár	Fruit collected and sold in bazaars.
Mangifera Indica, *Linn.*	Am	Tree occasionally found wild in the jungle; use of fruit well known; seeds softened by steam and eaten in times of famine.
Spondias mangifera, *Pers.*	Amará	Fruit eaten raw when ripe; pickled when unripe.

Zizyphus jujuba, *Lam.*	Bier	Is dried and stored. A cultivated variety yields a much larger fruit.
Zizyphus œnoplia, *Mill.*	Siá-Kol or Makoi	A small black fruit having a slightly acid taste.
——— rugosa, *Lam.*	?	
Ficus Indica, *Roxb.*	Bur	Are much eaten in time of scarcity by the very poorest Sontals and Kols.
—— religiosa, *Linn.*	Pipul	
—— glomerata, *Roxb.*	Doomur	
Carissa carandas, *Linn.*	Benchi or Karroná	Is capable of much improvement by cultivation.
Trapa bispinosa, *Roxb.*	Páni-phul or Singhárá	Are procurable in large quantities in some of the tanks. They furnish a very wholesome food.
—— quadrispinosa, *Roxb.*		
Eugenia jambolana, *Lam.*	Jamún	Fruit is collected and sold in the bazaars.
Diospyros melanoxylon, *Roxb.*	Keond or Kaned	Ditto.
——— exsculpta, *Ham.*	?	
——— embryopteris, *Roxb.*	Makúr-kendi	
Olax scandens, *Roxb.*	Koko-aroo	
Ægle marmelos, *Corr.*	Bael	Chiefly used for making sherbet, but are also prepared in other ways.
Feronia elephantum, *Linn.*	Kuthbel	
Tamarindus Indica, *Linn.*	Tetul or Emle	Dried and exported in large quantities.
Alangium decapetalum, *Lam.*	Bágh-ankúra	Fruit somewhat astringent.
Flacourtia sapida, *Roxb.*	Katái	
——— cataphracta, *Roxb.*	Páni-zali	
Phyllanthus emblica, *Linn.*	Ourá	Used for making pickles.
Bauhinia variegata, *Linn*	Catchuá	
Mimusops elengi, *Linn.*	Bohl or Moulsere	
Semicarpus anacardium, *Linn.*	Bellá	Acrid, except when perfectly ripe.
Erycibe paniculata, *Roxb.*	?	
Schleichera trijuga, *Willd.*	Khusm	
Boswellia serrata, *Colebr.*	Sálgà	
Karivia umbellata, *Arn.*	Rakhalsusa	Both ripe and unripe fruit are eaten.
Coccinia grandis, *W. & A.*	Tela-kúcha	

FLOWERS.

NAMES.	VERNACULAR NAMES.	REMARKS.
Bassia latifolia, *Roxb.*	Moul or Mhowa	Extensively used throughout the district. Is generally cooked with *Sal* seeds. Price varies from 10 seers up to 8 maunds for one rupee.
Bauhinia variegata, *Linn.*	Catchná	Used in *tarkaris*, or vegetable curries.
Butea frondosa, *Roxb.*	Pulás	Stamens and young pods occasionally eaten.

LEAVES *(Ság)*.

NAMES.	VERNACULAR NAMES.	REMARKS.
Antidesma diandrum, *Tul.*	Muttá	Trees or shrubs.
——— ghœsembilla, *Gærtn.*	Umtoá	Trees or shrubs.
Flacourtia sapida, *Roxb.*	Benchi or Katái	Trees or shrubs.
Tamarindus Indica, *Linn.*	Tetul or Emle	Trees or shrubs.
Bauhinia purpurea, *Linn.?*	Koinár or Purenposi	Trees or shrubs.
Olax scandens, *Roxb.?*	Bhadwilá or Koko-aroo	Trees or shrubs.
Cassia Sp.?	Chakúra	Trees or shrubs.
Oxalis corniculata, *Linn.*	Amrool or Umtha	Herbs.
Marsilea quadrifoliata, *Linn.*	Susné	Herbs.
Amaranthus viridis, *Linn.*	Batwá	Herbs.
——— spinosus, *Linn.*	Kántá	Herbs.
Alternanthera sessilis, *R. Br.*	Sáronchi	Herbs.
Trichodesma Indicum, *R. Br.*	Hetmurria or Chota Kulpa	Herbs.
——— Zeylanicum, *R. Br.*	Burra Kulpa	Herbs.
Mollugo spergula, *Linn.*	Ghíma	Herbs.
Spermacoce hispida, *Linn.*	Burdmutta	Herbs.
Polygonum plebejum, *A. Br.*	Myá or Kaet	Herbs.

Colocasia antiquorum, *Schott.*	Kachú or Ulwa	Herbs.
Cissampelos, Sp.?	Poe	
Marsdenia tenacissima, *W. & A.*	Herina	
Jussieua repens, *Linn.*	Dhabnee	
Leucas Sp.?	Dhurup	
Polycarpon depressum, *Kurz.*	Cheera	

STEMS.

Bambusa stricta, *Roxb.*	Karáil or Kopar	Base of stem and young shoots are eaten. The native names given are those of the stem, not of the plant itself.
Phœnix acaulis, *Buch.*	Jungly-kájúr	Interior of stem (sago).
Nymphæa lotus, *Linn.*	Saluk or Sirke	Leaf stalks and underground stems.
Vitis quadrangularis, *Wall.*	Hurjora	Young shoots.

ROOTS.

Discorea, Sps.?	Bengo-aloe	These roots furnish considerable nutriment, and are extensively used throughout the country.
	Dola-aloe	
	Dudha-aloe	
	Kondre	
	Genti	
Nelumbium speciosum, *Willd.*	Moolum Puddoo or Bansera	
Scirpus kysoor, *Roxb.*	Kesúr	The bulbs are capable of being ground up into a useful flour.
Cyperus rotundus?		
Curcuma leucorrhiza, *Roxb.*	Tikur	Wild arrowroot. Other species also occur I believe.

FUNGI.

Geaster, Sp.?	Kukúri Chatú	
Agaricus, Sp.?	Kanchutak	

APPENDIX F.

Classified Table of Non-Aryan Races and Tribes mentioned in this Volume.

Andamanese	Negritto.
Aguriah	Kolarian or Munda Family.
Bhumiz	
Behur, or Birhor	
Gudaba, or Gudwa	
Ho, or Lurka-Kol	
Juang	
Keriah	
Korewah	
Mal-Paharia (?)	
Munda	
Mun of Burmah	
Paharia of Chutia Nagpur	
Saontar, or Munjwar	
Sontal	
Chero, Karwar — Hinduized	
Bendkar	Dravidian Family.
Gond, Gour, or Gore (= Maria of Bustar ?)	
Jhoria, or Jhara	
Khond, or Khunjwa	
Kol-Lohar	
Malé, Rajmahali, or Usul Paharia	
Meriah	
Nicobarese (?)	
Sowra, or Savara	
Uraon	
Uraon-Keriah	
Bhuiya, Bui — Hinduized	
Baiga	Tribes of uncertain position; some have adopted Hinduism, while others have, perhaps, fallen away from it by miscegenation.
Baori	
Karen	
Kaur (perhaps = Karwars)	
Pab	
Panka	
Rajwar	
Raj-gond	

Nath	Have adopted a form of Mahomedanism.
Brinjara, or Bunjara	Gipsies.
Bhatra Purji (= Pardis, or bird-catchers) (?)	Position unascertained.

APPENDIX G.

List of papers published by the Author on subjects referred to in this volume.

GEOLOGY.

In the "Memoirs of the Geological Survey of India."

1.—The Ramgurh Coal-field. Vol. VI., p. 109.
2.—The Chopé Coal-field. Vol. VIII., p. 347.
3.—Geology of the Rajmahal Hills. Vol. XIII., pt. ii.
4.—The Aurunga and Hutar Coal-fields, and the iron-ores of Palamow. Vol. XV., pt. i.

In the "Records of the Geological Survey of India."

5.—On the occurrence of Gold in the District of Singhbhum. Vol. II., p. 11.
6.—On the occurrence of Argentiferous Galena and Copper in Manbhum. Vol. III., p. 74.
7.—On the Copper deposits of Dhalbhum and Singhbhum. Vol. III., p. 94.
8.—The Raigurh and Hingir Coal-field (1st notice). Vol. IV., p. 101.
9.—The Bisrampur Coal-field. Vol. VI., p. 25.
10.—Barren Island and Narkondam.* Vol. VI., p. 81.
11.—On the discovery of a new locality for Copper in the Narbada Valley. Vol. VII., p. 62.
12.—On the building and ornamental stones of India. Vol. VII., p. 98.
13.—Geological notes made on a visit to the coal recently discovered in the country of the Luni Pathans, South-east corner of Afghanistan. Vol. VII., p. 145.
14.—The Raigurh and Hingir Coal-field (2nd notice). Vol. VIII., p. 102.

* Republished in the "Geological Magazine." Decade II. Vol. VI., 1879.

15.—On the Athgurh Sandstones, near Cuttack. Vol. x., p. 63.

16.—On the Geology of the Mahanadi basin and its vicinity. Vol. x., p. 167.

17.—On the Diamonds, Gold, and Lead-Ores of the Sambalpur District. Vol. x., p. 186.

18.—On the origin of the Kumaun Lakes. Vol. XI., p. 174.

In a Special Report.

19.—On the Coal-fields of Orissa. 1877.

In the "Journal of the Asiatic Society of Bengal."

20.—Brief notes on the Geology and on the fauna in the neighbourhood of Nankowri Harbour, Nicobar Islands. Vol. XXXIX., pt. ii., p. 25.

21.—Notes on the Geology of the vicinity of Port Blair—Andaman Islands. Vol. XXXIX., pt. ii., p. 231.

In the "British Association Reports."

22.—On the New Geological Map of India (abstract). Dublin, 1878.

MAMMALS.

In the "Proceedings of the Asiatic Society of Bengal."

23.—Elephants. 1868, p. 129.

24.—On the occurrence of Tupaia Elliotti in the Satpura Hills. 1874, p. 95.

25.—Notes on certain Mammals occurring in the Basin of Mahanadi. 1877, p. 168.

BIRDS.

In the "Journal of the Asiatic Society of Bengal."

26.—On the birds of the Nicobar Islands. Vol. XXXIX., p. 29.

27.—On birds observed in the neighbourhood of Port Blair, Andaman Islands. Vol. XXXIX., p. ii., pt. 240.

28.—On a collection of birds made in the Andaman Islands by Asst.-Surgeon G. E. Dobson, M.B. Vol. XLI., p. 273.

In "Stray Feathers."

29.—List of birds known to occur in the Andaman and Nicobar Islands. Vol. I., p. 52.

30.—On the Avifauna of Chutia Nagpur. Vol. II., p. 353.

31.—Avifauna of Chutia Nagpur. *Addenda et Corrigenda.* Vol. III., p. 288.

32.—Notes on some birds observed in the Suliman Hills—west of Dera Ghazi Khan. Vol. III., p. 204.

33.—Notes on some birds collected in Sambalpur and Orissa. Vol. IV., p. 231.

34.—Notes on birds observed in the region between the Mahanadi and Godavari rivers. Vol. V., p. 410.

35.—From the Ganges to the Godavari (on the distribution of birds, so far as it is at present known throughout the hilly region which extends from the Rajmahal Hills to the Godavari valley. Vol. VII., p. 191.

BOTANY.

In the "Journal of the Asiatic Society of Bengal."

36.– On Jungle products used as articles of food. Vol. XXXVI., p. 73.

37.—On the Flora of Manbhum. Vol. XXXVIII., pt. ii. p. 112.

In the "Journal of the Agri-Horticultural Society of India."

38.—Remarks on a kind of farina from the fruit of a Pandanus in the Nicobar Islands. 1870.

ETHNOLOGY. ANTIQUITIES. LANGUAGE.

In the "Proceedings of the Asiatic Society of Bengal."

39.—Ancient Stone Implements. Manbhum. 1867, p. 143.

40.—Ancient Stone Implements. India and Islands. 1867, p. 147.

41.—Ancient Stone Implements. Singhbhum. 1868, p. 177.

42.—Notes on the Keriahs, an aboriginal race living in the hill-tracts of Manbhum. 1868, p. 177.

43.—Copper Miners of Singhbhum. 1869, p. 170.

44.—Notes on a trip to the Nicobar Islands (abstract).* 1869, p. 251.

45.—Notes on a trio to the Andaman Islands (abstract). 1870. p. 177.

46.—Notes on children found living with wolves. 1873, p. 128.

47.—Ancient perforated stone found in the Satpura Hills. 1874, p. 96.

48.—Stone Implements of the Burmese type found in Singhbhum. 1875, p. 118.

---

* Printed *in extenso* in "Land and Water."

49.—Indian Boomerangs, or throwing-sticks. 1875, p. 136.
50.—Stone Implements found in the Tributary States of Orissa. 1876, p. 122.
51.—On an ancient Kitchen-midden at Chaudwar, in Cuttack. 1876, p. 120.
52.—Khond weapons and musical instruments. 1876, p. 114.
53.—Stone Implements from Parisnath. 1878, p. 125.

In the "Journal of the Asiatic Society of Bengal."

54.—Names of birds in four of the Aboriginal languages of Western Bengal. 1871, pt. i., p. 103.

In the "Indian Antiquary."

55.—Stone monuments in the District of Singbhum. 1872, p. 291.
56.—On the antiquities of the Ramgurh Hill. 1873, p. 243.
57.—On Nicobarese Hieroglyphics. Vol. IV., p. 341.

In the "Records of the Government of India."

58.—Note on the Nicobarese language. No. LXXVII.

In the "Proceedings of the Royal Irish Academy."

59.—On a visit to the Andamanese Home at Port Blair, Andaman Islands.* Ser. II., Vol. I.
60.—On the forms and Geographical Distribution of Ancient Stone implements in India. Ser. II., Vol. I., p. 387.

In the "Calcutta Review."

61.—The Nicobar Islands (Review).

Published separately.

62.—On the Physical Features, Geology, Fauna, Flora, Ancient Temples and Inhabitants of Mahendragiri District of Ganjam.

---

* Republished in the "Indian Antiquary."

GENERAL INDEX.

LATIN INDEX.*

* This does not include references to the names given in the Lists of Species in the Appendices.